JAMES F. ENGEL   Wheaton College, Graduate School

DAVID T. KOLLAT   Vice President and Director of Research
Management Horizons, Inc.
Columbus, Ohio

ROGER D. BLACKWELL   The Ohio State University

CONSUMER BEHAVIOR

2nd Edition

DRYDEN PRESS
HINSDALE, ILLINOIS

Editors' Foreword

The Advisory Editors of the Holt, Rinehart and Winston Marketing Series are proud to introduce the second edition of *Consumer Behavior* by Professors Engel, Kollat, and Blackwell. The first edition in 1968 was the first textbook to be published on consumer behavior. It was immediately and widely adopted and became established as the major work on consumer behavior. The book provided both a model for analyzing consumer behavior and a wealth of well-organized theory and empirical findings bearing on various aspects of consumer behavior. Since then, other books have appeared, but most are simpler copies of the framework established by the authors.

The second edition is in every sense a forward thrust from the first edition. Of most significance, the authors have revised their model after some years of experimentation and application to real consumer situations and the improvement has been positive. In addition, the authors have searched the new literature and revised and expanded each chapter to take the new work into account. The book is the richest synthesis of empirical findings on consumer behavior to be found in the literature. Furthermore, the second edition presents excellent new chapters on consumerism and on mathematical approaches to consumer behavior to reflect the new thinking in the area.

Altogether, we are confident that the second edition of this book will further secure its place as a classic in its field.

Paul E. Green
Philip Kotler

Preface

One of the most remarkable developments of the last decade is the dynamic emphasis on the consumer as the focal point of the economic system. Today's emphasis on consumerism is just one manifestation of the changes which have taken place. At one time, for example, the subject of consumer behavior received only incidental emphasis in marketing courses in schools of business. Today, however, it has come into its own as a distinct area for scholarly investigation as is attested by a burgeoning increase in published literature.

In part the awakened interest in the consumer is the result of a dramatic shift in demand-supply relationships, a change that has, in effect, placed the consumer in the fortunate position of being free to choose from many options. Thus business firms now are compelled to design and sell products that conform to the consumer's desires. "Consumer orientation" by the business firm, in turn, requires a solid basis of fact. It is not surprising, then, that analysis of the consumer has assumed a new importance.

Consumer welfare also has become a topic of great political significance because of growing signs that the economic system does not always function to serve the consumers' interests to a desirable extent. Hence, new legislation and regulatory activity have been proposed and implemented, but all too frequently these steps have been taken without a full understanding of the implications from the consumers' point of view.

A parallel development is a widespread recognition that consumer education is both necessary and desirable. As Toffler points out in *Future Shock*, the range of choice alternatives is beyond the grasp of any individual, and the rate of environmental change can have real pathological implications.[1] Therefore, con-

---

[1] Alvin Toffler, *Future Shock* (New York: Random House, 1970).

sumer education programs play an increasingly vital role, and these programs, in turn, must be based on a sophisticated understanding of consumer behavior from a variety of perspectives.

Finally, it is noteworthy that scholars from many fields are focusing attention on the consumer. It is recognized that this can be a useful testing ground for theories and methods of various types, and there is less current disdain in the social and behavior sciences for research in the "real world."

This book is written to meet the needs of practitioners from all perspectives, as well as those who have a more theoretical interest in the subject. More specifically, its objectives are: (1) to explore and evaluate an extensive body of both published and unpublished research evidence; (2) to advance generalizations or propositions from this evidence; (3) to assess the practical implications of the various processes and facets of consumer motivation and behavior; and (4) to pinpoint areas where research is lacking. Because of the backgrounds and interests of the authors, the perspective is that of the field of marketing. This fact also is true of the great majority of published literature, by the way, but those with differing interests will find much of value here in that we have attempted to assume a broader perspective wherever possible.

The reader who is looking for mere description should turn elsewhere. While no particular background in the behavioral sciences is assumed, the authors share the philosophy that more harm than good often is done by ignoring questions of methodology and theoretical substance. As a result, findings are critically assessed in an attempt to determine the extent to which valid generalizations and propositions can be advanced. Therefore, we have not avoided some of these more difficult issues.

This edition also differs somewhat from the first edition in that we have placed greater emphasis on problems of measurement and application of generalizations to practical problems. As a result, the book has a distinctly pragmatic focus. We are of the opinion that, while the study of consumer behavior is valuable in its own right as an academic discipline, it is of far greater importance to center on the problems faced by those who must make decisions based on an understanding of the consumer. This explains why there is little overt focus on the problems of developing formal theory.

The basic method of exposition is a conceptual model of consumer motivation that has been revised in some important respects since the first edition. The revised model specifies with greater clarity the relevant variables that shape consumer action and the ways in which each fits into a larger scheme. We have benefited substantially from other published models as is discussed in Chapter 3, and we feel that the revisions introduced over the first edition will prove helpful in basic understanding, measurement, and application.

The number of relevant published research findings since the first edition is almost astronomical. Therefore, we have had to be selective in those which are cited. While our objective has been to be comprehensive in each subject area, there undoubtedly are gaps in coverage due to the enormity of the literature.

Finally, every effort has been made to make the writing style as lucid as possible. We have tried to avoid introducing unnecessary complexity in large part because we feel that some contemporary writing in this subject area is guilty of the charge leveled by an eminent theologian against certain colleagues in his field: "Part of the shame of the theology of the recent past is that sometimes it has been made deliberately foggy, under the fatuous assumption that what cannot be understood is somehow more profound."[2]

We gratefully acknowledge the many comments and suggestions provided by users of the first edition. Wherever possible we have incorporated these contributions into our revisions. In addition, it is a pleasure to acknowledge inputs provided by our former doctoral candidates and respected colleagues, Professor B. Venkatesh of the University of Wisconsin at Madison and Professor Brian Sternthal of Northwestern University. Both contributed portions of several chapters, as noted in the text. Finally, other doctoral candidates at The Ohio State University over the years have advanced many ideas which have found their way into our thinking.

The editors of this book, Professor Philip Kotler of Northwestern University and Professor Paul Green of the University of Pennsylvania, critically evaluated the manuscript and contributed much to its final form. But, as has been true in all of our collaborative writing efforts, our wives and families deserve the greatest vote of thanks. Once again we dedicate this book to these unsung heroes.

Wheaton, Illinois   James F. Engel

Columbus, Ohio   David T. Kollat

Columbus, Ohio   Roger D. Blackwell

January, 1973

---

2   D. Elton Trueblood, *A Place to Stand* (New York: Harper & Row Publishers, 1969), p. 8.

Contents

Introduction and Overview

What is consumer behavior all about? Is it a legitimate subject of inquiry? Why should it receive emphasis as a separate area of study within the general field of marketing? These and many other questions are considered in this introduction, which serves as a framework of concepts around which subsequent parts of the text are built.

In Chapter 1 the role of consumer research and analysis in marketing management is defined and assessed. The discussion is broadened in Chapter 2 to encompass the various perspectives and viewpoints that are potentially applicable in approaching this subject. Using as a starting point the traditional approaches employed in the marketing literature, the text evaluates the various schools of thought in related behavioral sciences in terms of the usefulness of each. No one point of view is complete in its own right, and the approach used in this book borrows freely from many sources.

Of particular significance is Chapter 3, which presents a diagrammatic model of consumer motivation and behavior. A model of this type is indispensable for showing how various elements fit together to shape behavior. It begins with inputs of various types from the environment and ends with the consequences of a terminal act such as a purchase. All intervening steps and processes are clearly designated so that the relation of each to the whole becomes apparent. It is important that the chapter be given considerable critical emphasis, since the model presented here is followed step by step in subsequent chapters of the book.

CHAPTER 1

THE ROLE OF THE CONSUMER IN MARKETING

Imagine, if you will, an automobile showroom. There is a mirror on one side of the room, in reality a one-way glass. Behind the glass is a group of observers consisting of two psychologists, a sociologist, an anthropologist, an economist, a young law student, and a marketing director.

Into the showroom walks a man who has visited the dealer earlier in the week. This time the wife and teenage son accompany the man. While the potential customer talks with the salesman, the wife looks at the interiors of several models. The teenage son asks many questions of the salesman, mostly about performance and about accessory options. The father glances in the direction of other customers in the showroom, noting their appearance and the items in which they seem to be interested. Behind the glass, the observers are making careful notes of the situation against the low whirring background of a video-tape machine which is also recording the process.

After several minutes of interchange, the salesman ushers the customer to a desk and, despite a worried expression, the man signs a contract to purchase a new car. The salesman reassures the wife that her interior and color choices are good ones and continues to attempt to gain the friendship and answer questions from the teenage son. The customer asks several questions about the car even after he signs the contract. After the transaction, the observers compare notes and begin a discussion about why the customer bought the car.

The economist expresses himself first. He explains that the situation is not difficult to understand. The consumer stated that he expects regular employment during the next year and that his present car needs replacing. Furthermore, equilibrium was reached when the salesman offered a $100 reduction in price and the consumer responded with a purchase. "The situation presents no unusual problems," the economist states. "Under stable income conditions, a price reduction will stimulate additional sales."

One of the psychologists objects to the incompleteness of this explanation and asks why the customer bought this particular car and not one of another style or color. He refers to statements by the customer that indicate a favorable *attitude* to the brand he bought and to that style and color. He describes personality traits manifested by the customer. "And did you notice," queries the psychologist, "the request for more information about the warranty program after the sale had been completed? Cognitive dissonance may be occurring in this case."

The other psychologist, who has a reputation for methodological rigor in his laboratory experiments, expresses little interest in the whole affair. He protests the practice of making generalizations from a situation in which so many variables are free to vary. "To make predictions about behavior based upon observations such as this," he maintains, "can hardly be called behavioral *science*." Guardedly, he forms a few hypotheses about the effect of repeated exposures on learned response patterns and the need for controlled measurement of the effects of differential stimuli. While mumbling something about using pupillometers to measure the amount of information processing, he gathers some papers and explains that he must get back to the lab.

Some controversy develops between the sociologist and the anthropologist about which one should study specific parts of the situation. The sociologist speaks first stating that the consumer indicated he had driven a new car owned by his neighbor and that it was after this that he had become aware of how costly his old car was to repair. "Did you notice," the sociologist asks, "that the customer mentioned that he believes most people in his social class feel comfortable with this kind of car?" The anthropologist quickly interjects, "Yes, but did you also notice his reaction to the black customer who was looking at another car in the showroom?" Both observers then begin a discussion of the influence of the liberated views of his wife and the youthful values of his son.

At the mention of the youth subculture the law student—who works part-time for a group investigating consumer problems—changes the subject of the discussion to whether the consumer was adequately informed about the interest rate on his contract or the pollution qualities of the automobile he just bought. The student adds, "I question the relevancy of research which seems to be designed to answer the question of *how* to sell automobiles to people. The more meaningful issue is whether automobiles *should* be sold to people in view of our society's ecological corruption."

The marketing director finally speaks, although he is a little nervous in the presence of the experts. Nevertheless, he adjusts his cuff links and then speaks confidently. "Gentlemen, your opinions are very interesting. However, our company has much experience in these kinds of situations and I believe I can say that the customer chose our brand of car because of the extensive research and development that has gone into making it what he wants. Did you notice the feeling of pleasure the customer displayed sitting in those bucket seats, listening to the stereo music system? This car is designed for today's life styles. And as far as pollution is concerned, our company is as concerned as anyone. The new models have special antipolluting engine systems that reduce combustion materials by 17 percent, and in addition we have even more changes that within five years will reduce pollutants by over 48 percent." The marketing director adds, "Did you notice how our salesman skillfully answered all the questions of the customer and suggested additional information about equipment that would make the car more suitable for pulling the customer's camping trailer? That, gentlemen, is what our firm calls consumer orientation, and it sells cars."

This abbreviated scenario illustrates the subject matter of this book. The purpose of this text is to develop the ability to understand *why* individuals purchase what they do and how purchasing behavior influences and is influenced by various members of a society. To understand the automobile purchase described above requires much more information than is provided. Many influences on the customer were unobserved and perhaps incapable of being observed since they occurred prior to the investigation. A major goal of this book is to provide a framework for gathering the relevant information needed in the analysis of consumer behavior.

THE FIELD OF CONSUMER BEHAVIOR

Every human community develops a system by which it produces and distributes goods and services. In industrially advanced societies such as those of North America, Japan, Australia, and much of Europe, the system is complex and the available range of economic goods is wide. To understand consumption decisions fully would require the study of a person's entire lifetime experiences. Broadly considered, consumer behavior and human behavior would be nearly synonymous fields of study since the consumption of economic goods pervades almost every activity in which humans are involved. For practical reasons, the field must be limited to include only a portion of human activity.

Consumer Behavior Defined

Consumer behavior is defined as the *acts of individuals directly involved in obtaining and using economic goods and services, including the decision processes that precede and determine these acts.* Social scientists sometimes use the word "behavior" to include only overt or observable actions, but it is increasingly recognized that the overt act is only *one* portion of the decision process. A realistic analysis of consumer behavior must necessarily include less observable processes that accompany consumption. Consumer behavior involves the study not only of *what* people consume but *where, how often,* and *under what conditions* goods and services are consumed.

Buyer Behavior

The term "buyer behavior" is frequently used in the study of consumer behavior and it can have two different connotations. When applied to consumer behavior, buyer behavior refers to the acts of individuals directly involved in the exchange of money (or a money substitute) for economic goods and services and the decision processes that determine these acts. This will be clarified further in the next section.

Buyer behavior (or customer behavior) is often used as a *more* inclusive term than consumer behavior. In the more inclusive application, buyer behavior includes purchasing by institutional and industrial organizations and various levels of resellers. At a general level, models of human behavior which describe buying by ultimate consumers also describe buying by organizations and can be interpreted for both situations.[1] As variables in models of behavior become more specific, however, the importance varies between elements in a behavioral model describing industrial or consumer buying behavior. In this book, the focus is upon the buying by *ultimate consumers,* although the information at a general level has much applicability to other types of buyers.[2]

Purchasing and Consuming

The difference between buying and consuming is further clarified by Alderson, who correctly recognized that much of what is called the study of consumer behavior is in reality not the study of *consumption* but of consumer *buying.*[3] The difference between the buyer and the consumer is described by Alderson:

> The new approach draws a clear distinction between the consumer purchasing agent. It is the motivation of the purchasing agent which is most directly relevant in marketing. The prospective consumer of a given purchase and the person making the purchase are often two different people. In many cases the purchase is made for a household, and the purchasing agent is only one of those who will share in its use.[4]

---

[1] Such an approach is used in John A. Howard and Jagdish N. Sheth, *The Theory of Buyer Behavior* (New York: Wiley, 1969), esp. p. 17; Thomas S. Robertson, *Consumer Behavior* (Glenview, Ill.: Scott, Foresman, 1970), pp. 7–8.

[2] For more detailed models of organizational buying, see Patrick J. Robinson, Charles W. Faris, and Yoram Wind, *Industrial Buying and Creative Marketing* (Boston: Allyn and Bacon, 1967); Frederick E. Webster, Jr., "Modeling the Industrial Buying Process," *Journal of Marketing Research,* vol. 2, pp. 370–377 (Nov. 1965).

[3] Wroe Alderson, *Dynamic Marketing Behavior* (Homewood, Ill.: Irwin, 1965), p. 144; also Francesco M. Nicosia, *Consumer Decision Processes* (Englewood Cliffs, N.J.: Prentice-Hall, 1966), pp. 28–30.

[4] Wroe Alderson, *Marketing Behavior and Executive Action* (Homewood, Ill.: Irwin, 1957), pp. 165–166. Reprinted by permission of the publisher.

Purchasing is only one point in the decision process. It is inextricably linked to consumption of the product, both by the buyer and by other members of the group for which the buyer serves as purchasing agent. Even though consumer research usually focuses on the buyer, a careful analysis of consumer behavior must include the influences of the total family (or other group) on the behavior of the purchasing agent.

THE DECISION-PROCESS APPROACH

The auto-purchase illustration at the beginning of this book might stimulate the question, "Which of the observers was correct in explaining why the customer bought the car?" The answer is that all are partially correct, yet none is wholly correct. Each observer is approaching this situation with a particular perspective. Each is implying that a particular type of variable is the cause of behavior. Consumer analysts find that while most perspectives may be useful, by itself none is totally adequate.

Buying as a Process

The *decision-process approach* to analyzing consumer behavior has emerged in recent years and is the approach taken in this book (described in detail later). With this conceptualization, a purchase is *one stage* in a particular course of action undertaken by a consumer. In order to understand that one stage (the act of purchasing), it is necessary to examine the events that precede and follow the purchase.

A variety of influences are the cause of any actions undertaken by a consumer. Internal goal orientations provide receptivity to external variables originating in the social environment. What the consumer does with these social stimuli involves basic psychological processes that are specific to him. The combination of the external inputs and internal influences may evolve into a decision by a consumer to make a purchase. Even when the decision has been made, however, no purchase may result. Among other reasons, this outcome occurs when the marketing system does not provide adequate resources to stimulate execution of the transaction. Thus the study of consumer behavior, if it is to be realistic, must be based upon an understanding of social, individual, and institutional variables as they influence and constrain consumer decisions.

An Interdisciplinary Approach

The decision-process approach is an interdisciplinary approach. Major concepts for analyzing behavior are drawn from *general psychology*, the study of individual behavior. But consumers do not operate in isolation. Thus much of the empirical as well as theoretical work of *social psychology*, the study of interpersonal behavior, is more helpful than general psychology. The study of consumer behavior also relies heavily upon *sociology*, the study of groups and human interactions, and *cultural* or *social anthropology*. Sometimes it uses information from the field of *economic geography*, *linguistics*, and *political science*. *Philosophy*, to the degree that it represents reality, also provides a framework for analyzing *why* people behave as they do and has potential in the quest for understanding of consumer decisions.[5] Finally, consumer behavior is only understandable within a realistic framework of *economics*, the study of how men and society choose to employ scarce resources.

An Applied Discipline

Consumer behavior is an applied discipline, in many ways analogous to medicine, engineering, or law. An engineer, for example, uses the basic disciplines such as surveying, drafting, and materials analysis. Similarly, analysis of consumer behavior borrows and applies findings from many disciplines in an attempt to solve practical marketing problems. Occasionally those who study consumer behavior make direct contributions to the basic disciplines, although this is usually not necessarily a primary goal of work in this area.

Consumer analysts, like engineers, apply their skills toward a variety of ends. An engineer may help build a government building on one occasion and at another time assist with a building for General Motors. Similarly, some persons trained in consumer analysis may work for a Madison Avenue advertising agency designing consumer advertising, and other persons with the same training may work for the Federal Trade Commission to discover what constitutes deceptive advertising. Furthermore, the skills of consumer researchers are required in a socialist country to interpret consumer demand just as they are needed in a capitalist country.

Analytical Framework

The decision process used in this book provides an analytical framework rather than a description of specific reasons why consumers behave as they do. Essentially, the framework (1) defines the *structural variables* involved in consumer behavior and (2) indicates *relations among variables* in so far as those relationships can be determined. A variable is a *factor* or *influence* that enters into the measurement or prediction of consumer behavior.

Symbolic representation of the framework is essential for mathematical treatment of the decision process. For example, the variables might be symbolized in the following form:

$$y = f(x_1, x_2, \ldots, x_n)$$

where

y = some aspect of consumer behavior
x_i = various stimuli and/or processes
f = a rule that pairs each possible value of x with at most one value of y.

---

[5] Ron J. Markin, *The Psychology of Consumer Behavior* (Englewood Cliffs, N.J.: Prentice-Hall, 1969), esp. pp. 45–65.

This notation does nothing more than assert that a functional relationship exists. It does not specify the function rule. The consumer analyst is simply stating, "Give me the function rule and the values of x_i and I will give the value of y."

The specific nature of consumer behavior is constantly changing. Thus mere description is only of temporary value. Definition of the variables and relationships involved in determining behavior is of value for a very long time, however. A model of consumer behavior, such as the one in this book, provides an approach for solving a broad range of marketing problems.

CONSUMER BEHAVIOR AND SOCIETY

Why should consumer behavior be singled out as a topic for intensive study? One answer might simply be to understand more about an important category of human society. Social scientists study teenagers, families, students, social classes, and ethnic groups and such specialized segments as swinging couples and communes. The study of a group as large as consumers is certainly as justified as these.

More direct reasons exist for studying consumers, however. The applied discipline of consumer behavior is useful in the development of more efficient use of marketing resources and in more effective solutions to marketing management problems.

One motive for studying consumer behavior is to understand *macromarketing problems* better, or how a society meets the needs of its people. Those who have this interest as their primary motive for studying consumer behavior include many types of government officials, urban planners, economists, administrators of social agencies, and others with direct responsibility for the social welfare of a nation.

Other persons are concerned with *micromarketing problems*, or the administering of specific elements of an economy. These individuals include businessmen responsible for the marketing effort of a firm or an organization.

There is no clear-cut dichotomy between macro and micro interests in studying the consumer behavior present in a marketing-oriented society. In fact, it is difficult to consider one area without the other, and this conclusion becomes increasingly inescapable. The relationship between macro and micro problems is of such importance that an entire chapter is given over to a consideration of the consumer in society later in the book. A few key reasons for societal orientation in consumer behavior, however, are presented at this point.

Essential Input for Public Policy

The principle of individual choice permeates the economic theories and practices of many societies in the world. No disciplined determination of public policy can exist, therefore, without assumptions—correct or incorrect—about how consumers as individuals will choose to spend their money, time, energy, and votes. To design public policy that will be accepted by consumers and will be efficient as a solution to societal problems requires thorough understanding of the needs, desires, and aversions of the consumers for whom the policies are developed.

Kotler and Zaltman have commented that products with obvious value to a society, such as free medical care, pollution control, or public transportation, must be presented with understanding of consumer behavior and sophistication in marketing programs if the products are to be accepted by the society's consumers.[6] A good example of the need for consumer analysis as an input in public policy might be in the area of urban transportation. It is apparent from the failures of many United States urban transportation systems that there is an enormous need to design urban transit systems to appeal to individual consumers' tastes if high usage is to be attained. In an industrialized society, the practical alternative to designing public policy without analysis of consumer behavior is forceful coercion to gain acceptance.

In the communal society that is becoming common worldwide, more and more *individual* consumption decisions impact other individuals, especially in the tightly interwoven fabric of consumption.[7] The individual choices of consumers concerning automobiles, for example, affect immensely the air breathed by all other consumers. The choices of consumers about detergents, in another example, affect the water quality for many other consumers. When public policy is enacted without adequate understanding of why and how consumers are going to make their individual decisions, chaos in public policy may ensue to the detriment of those whom policy makers had hoped to help. It is increasingly difficult to consider consumer decisions "private" because of their impact on many "public" areas. This interlocking of interests is described by Laurence Feldman:

> . . . there are signs that the marketing system's ability to promote consumption and to provide consumers with a growing range of choice is increasingly inconsistent with the needs of the larger society. One reason for this is that marketing decisions have been made which expanded the range of consumer product choice but disregarded their environmental impact. There has been a failure to recognize that these products, which are marketing outputs designed for individual satisfaction, are simultaneously inputs to a larger environmental system and as such the well-being of society.[8]

Societal Definition of Marketing

Marketing has been defined in various ways, but it is used in this book as *the process in a society by which the demand structure for economic goods and services is anticipated or enlarged and satisfied through the conception, promotion, exchange, and physical distribution of such goods and services.* The

---

[6] Philip Kotler and Gerald Zaltman, "Social Marketing: An Approach to Planned Social Change," *J. Marketing*, vol. 35, pp. 3–12 (July 1971).

[7] Daniel Bell, "The Post-Industrial Society: A Speculative View," in Edward and Elizabeth Hutchings (eds.), *Scientific Progress and Human Values*, (New York: Elsevier, 1967), pp. 154–170.

[8] Laurence P. Feldman, "Societal Adaptation: A New Challenge for Marketing," *J. Marketing*, vol. 35, pp. 54–60 (July 1971). Reprinted by permission of the publisher.

demand structure referred to in this definition cannot realistically be regarded as static, because the needs and desires of a society are constantly changing. The marketing system must also be dynamic if it is to serve a society. A crucial element in understanding the marketing process and its components, therefore, is the understanding of consumer behavior. This includes understanding *what consumer needs are, how they were formed,* and *how they are influenced* by marketing activity.

It is difficult to consider the needs and best interests of consumers without at the same time considering the role of marketing. It is also difficult to consider how the marketing process functions without initially focusing attention on the behavior of consumers.

Marketing's Role in Complex Social Decisions

Marketing in a developed economy is a group behavior process in which millions of individuals are linked together with countless institutions. These interrelations must be analyzed if an evaluation is to be made that might increase the overall efficiency of marketing's role in helping to solve complex societal decision problems.

The complexity of social decisions concerning consumption and marketing can be illustrated by thinking of one relatively simple product—bread—and the marketing system required to satisfy consumer demand for the product. In an emerging society, predicting consumer behavior might be simple. Simply supply more basic bread and more will be quickly demanded. In postindustrial society, however, the process is immensely more complex.

Executives for each of the supplying firms must predict the total amount of bread needed by each city within their supply area. They must also predict what share of the market will be produced by their firm and what the most efficient way may be to match consumption with the various supply mills that the firm may have. Furthermore, each executive must decide how much rye, whole wheat, raisin, cinnamon, and other breads will be desired by consumers, as well as whether consumers may also choose hamburger buns, breakfast pastries, or other preference items. The planners must also consider that some consumers prefer to buy the products frozen in order to spread use over a longer time period (and avoid frequent trips to the grocery store).

After it has been determined how much of each bakery product is to be produced for an entire city, the really difficult decisions must be made. How many of each variety should be placed each day in each of the hundreds of grocery stores located at the consumers' convenience throughout the city? Planners must decide, for example, whether to put seven or eight loaves of rye bread in a specific neighborhood store. If they place too few in a store, consumers are unhappy when they do not get what they want. If too many loaves of a particular kind are placed in a store, the bread will not sell or will sell only at a reduced price after it has become partially stale. With dozens of bread categories, hundreds of possible outlets, and a multiplicity of consumer tastes, it is amazing that these decisions are made with few mistakes. With low profit margins on bread, there is little tolerance for error, however.

Bread is a simple product, perhaps, but consider the magnitude of decisions that must be made for automobiles, homes, clothing, and university educations to be matched at least roughly consonant with consumer preferences. The absurdity of trying to make these decisions without a great deal of understanding of how and why consumer preferences are formed is apparent.

It takes only a little contemplation of the existing society to understand that consumer decisions are, at least partially, subject to some order. Behavior is not totally random or beyond understanding. Tastes change, and sometimes rapidly, but there are principles which explain those changes. Consumers make decisions with a structure that permits partial prediction of outcomes. The *raison d'être* for this textbook and the study of consumer behavior is to improve predictions concerning what products consumers will buy and under what conditions they will buy them. Such predictions enable businessmen, economists, and governmental administrators to plan the resource and structural arrangements of a society to satisfy better the needs of the society. The more accurate the predictions of consumer response, the greater the potential for efficiency in the production and distribution of economic goods.

CONSUMER BEHAVIOR AND MANAGEMENT

Individuals responsible for managing business enterprises and other organizations need to understand consumer behavior in order to adapt the products and distributive resources of the organization to the demands of consumers. A few of the ways consumer research and analysis assist in attaining organizational objectives are described below.

Evaluating New Market Opportunities

An important reason for studying consumer behavior is evaluation of consumer groups with unsatisfied needs or desires. Success requirements for any organization include not only the ability to *recognize unmet needs,* but also to understand whether those needs will be expressed as *economically feasible markets,* and what *organizational response is required for success in selling to those needs.*[9] Firms which organize their resources capably and flexibly toward unmet needs are sometimes described as consumer oriented or operating under the "marketing concept."[10]

---

[9] Theodore Levitt, "The New Markets—Think before You Leap," *Harvard Business Rev.,* pp. 53–67 (May-June 1969).

[10] Much has been written about the marketing concept. A classic statement is Robert L. King, "An Interpretation of the Marketing Concept," paper presented at the 31st Annual Conf. of the Southern Economic Association, Memphis, Tenn. (Nov. 10, 1961); reprinted in Steven J. Shaw and C. McFerron Gittlinger (eds.), *Marketing in Business Management* (New York: Crowell-Collier-Macmillan, 1963), pp. 35–39; also Theodore N. Beckman, William R. Davidson, and James F. Engel, *Marketing,* 8th ed. (New York: Ronald, 1967), pp. 40–44.

Evaluation of new markets varies in difficulty according to the affluence and sophistication of a country's economy. In the case of an emerging nation, evaluating new markets may be simply a process of determining how much economic power can be generated and how quantities of basic needs—food, housing, medical care, and so on—can be supplied. When most of the citizens do not have enough basic food to eat, it is not difficult to locate new market opportunities. The best market opportunity is simply more food, probably of the same types already being consumed. Until a society reaches a point where a significant number of its members are above a subsistence level, the determination of new market opportunities is fairly obvious.

In an affluent, industrialized society new market opportunities do not arise by simply providing more of what is already being consumed (except, perhaps, for disadvantaged minorities within the society). New market opportunities arise because of other reasons, and these reasons make prediction of consumer response somewhat more difficult.

Geographic mobility is one reason why new market opportunities arise. People live where they did not live before and thus create new markets. They abandon old purchase loyalties and perhaps old product preferences. They seek consumption information from new sources. Aggressive business enterprises recognize the new markets created by geographic mobility and build new supermarkets, new discount houses, and new shopping centers. They use new media and new campaign themes to exploit the new market opportunities of suburbia and interurbia.

Social mobility provides another source of new market opportunities. As people become more educated and acquire a more sophisticated social milieu, their interests change and they participate in increased social interaction. They become aware of new types of leisure, requiring new types of products. With increased socialization, awareness of innovations such as health spas, stereo multiplexing systems, gourmet foods, and day-care centers is diffused rapidly. Thus mass markets for such items become feasible. Social positions change for *groups of individuals* as well as for *individuals within groups*, opening up markets previously confined to other consumer groups.

Psychic mobility in an affluent society results in new market opportunities for discerning firms. Along with physical and social mobility, people frequently express themselves more fully or change their conception of themselves and their environment. In this new conception, a man's inner self is no longer fixed and immutable. Personality is free to deviate from rigidly prescribed social norms, and people can express their desires (perhaps previously dormant) in many new ways. Apparel becomes not just a covering but an expression of one's feelings about himself and perhaps a badge of his approval of others. Home furnishings express a family's new ability to deviate from rigid prescriptions. The same is true for many other products. This occurs mostly, of course, in an economy where substantial portions of the population have discretionary income to purchase more than just more of the same. Understanding this phenomenon is a key to success for firms seeking growth by expansion in new market opportunities.

Choosing Market Segments

No two people are exactly alike. That statement is readily accepted when thinking of the physical aspects of a human being. It is also true, however, in other aspects of human behavior which eventually are manifested in individual preferences for consumption. Traditional economic and marketing thought contained the implicit assumption that people demanded products alike. On the contrary, however, personal preferences for many products are no more all alike than are fingerprints!

The challenge of market segmentation is to determine groups of people whose preferences are sufficiently similar to each other, yet different from other groups, to justify modification of a product to the preferences of that specific group. Concurrently, a challenge exists for marketing organizations to develop the product and distribution offered in such a way as to make differences from competitors discernible to consumers. Wroe Alderson has termed this the *search for differential advantage*.[11] The implications of this search for market segmentation and product differentiation will be analyzed in later chapters.

Increasing Efficiency of Strategy and Tactics

Competition in a marketing economy is a precarious activity, always subject to encroachment or outright assault by competitors. Effectiveness requires continual improvement in the efficiency of the strategy and tactics employed by firms that are successful marketers. Reliable analysis of consumer behavior is an essential input to the development of effective marketing strategy.[12]

Consumer analysis focuses on the *causes* rather than the results of effective marketing strategy. Analysis of sales trends, for example, would be an analysis of results. Consumer analysis seeks to determine the underlying conditions that are true about consumers, and which cause an obvious purpose of increasing the efficiency of existing strategies and tactics.

An approach to consumer analysis for designing strategy is provided by Table 1.1. This table presents the results as row headings and states of consumer satisfaction as column headings. Understanding the size and nature of each cell permits the improvement of strategy and tactics.

Numerous inputs for strategy are obtained from Table 1.1. Cell 1, for example, represents a situation where change is perhaps unneeded. It represents an "ideal" state of consumer response to a firm's strategy and a situation where consumers are likely to be highly resistant to the strategies of a competing firm. Cell 3, however, represents a result that would not be revealed by sales data alone. The consumers in that group are unsatisfied even though they are cus-

---

[11] Alderson, *op. cit.,*[3] pp. 184–210.

[12] For background material on marketing strategy, see David T. Kollat, Roger D. Blackwell, and James Robeson, *Strategic Marketing* (New York: Holt, Rinehart and Winston, 1972).

Table 1.1   MATRIX OF CONSUMER SATISFACTION AND PURCHASE PATTERN

	Completely Satisfied	*Partially Satisfied*	*Completely Unsatisfied*
Always Use	High loyalty, no search for alternative brands 1	2	Disloyal users, receptive to information about competitive brands 3
Sometimes Use	4	Unstable purchase behavior 5	6
Never Use	Nonproduct reasons for nonpurchase (price, channel facilities, and so on) 7	8	9

tomers, a situation highly vulnerable to competitive encroachment. Some might wonder why customers would be in the "always use" category if they are completely unsatisfied. Many reasons are possible. Perhaps there are no satisfactory alternative products; thus the consumer has no choice if he wishes the basic attributes of that product. Perhaps he shops at a retail outlet that carries only this brand and the product category is not of sufficient importance to cause switching of outlets. Perhaps he is simply unaware of other products that would be preferred. It may readily be seen that consumer analysis should be employed to determine the cell location *and* the reason for position in that cell of the matrix.

The most effective marketing strategy will be influenced by the position of market targets within various cells of the matrix of satisfaction and purchase. The strategy for reaching consumers in cell 7 might be improvement of distribution, lowering of price, or improvement of advertising, whereas the way to improve strategy in cells 2, 5, or 8 might be relatively minor product modification. Many other possibilities for analysis exist. Also, it should be realized that only three levels of measurement are shown in this example. In reality, the scale for consumer satisfaction is continuous rather than discrete, however, and the number of cells could be greatly expanded.

Realistic improvement of marketing strategy requires the analysis of consumer behavior for competitors using a similar matrix. It may be very useful to construct such a matrix for each competing brand in order to determine the market groups that are most likely to switch as a result of improvement in the aggressor's marketing strategy.

Questions for Analysis

Many questions about marketing strategy and tactics involving the analysis of consumer behavior need to be answered. It would be impossible to prepare a complete list of such questions, but some idea of the comprehensiveness of topics in marketing that can be improved by consumer analysis is suggested in the following list of questions considered in this book.

(1) Do consumers pass through a hierarchy of response stages in evaluating products?

(2) How are models of consumer behavior useful in the development of marketing strategy?

(3) What is the significance of motives in arousal of buying behavior?

(4) How is sensation translated into meaning about brands or products?

(5) What types of advertising appeals are the most effective in different product categories?

(6) How can the "boredom barrier" of advertising be broken?

(7) Is "subliminal" advertising effective?

(8) How do buyers learn about new brands and products?

(9) How do buyers form likes and dislikes toward salesmen and stores?

(10) How do new residents learn about stores and brands?

(11) How persuasible are prospective buyers?

(12) Do personality differences correlate highly with brand choice?

(13) Does advertising really bring about much attitude change?

(14) Does the development of favorable attitudes toward a brand lead automatically to more sales?

(15) What is a persuasive communication?

(16) How many times should an ad run?

(17) How important is the "youth culture" in the development of marketing strategy?

(18) Is it better to have one brand that appeals to all social classes or several brands designed for specific social classes?

(19) Do black consumers respond to marketing strategies differently than nonblack consumers?

(20) To what degree can marketing strategy that is effective in the United States also be effective in other countries?

(21) Can marketing efforts effectively increase informal conversations about a particular product enough to result in additional sales?

(22) What life styles will create markets for new products in the future?

(23) To what member of the family should promotion be directed?

(24) Can buyers be stimulated to buy products for which they do not recognize a need?

(25) How and when do buyers seek information about a product?

(26) What are the most influential information sources about a product?

(27) How does the importance of information source vary among market segments?

(28) To what extent can consumers be influenced while they are in retail stores?

(29) How do buyers evaluate alternative brands and suppliers?

(30) Which product attributes are evaluated by consumers?

(31) How do consumers choose retail stores?

(32) How important is the image of a firm?

(33) How do buyers react when preferred brands are unavailable?

(34) What types of consumers are "deal prone?"

(35) Should salesmen be recruited to have personalities similar to those of their customers or personalities different from customers?

(36) How effectively can "impulse" purchasing be stimulated?

(37) Under what circumstances does a marketing program have follow-up or "sleeper" effects?

(38) What is the optimum number and type of retail outlets?

(39) Are some customers more "loyal" to a brand than others? How does this influence marketing strategy?

(40) Do some persons consistently buy new products before other segments of the population?

Improving Retail Performance

A revolution in retailing institutions and performances appears to be underway in North America, much of Europe, Japan, Scandinavia, and certain other areas.[13] Consumer analysis is an essential input to the understanding of the cause of this revolution and in predicting the future changes that will be required to improve the efficiency of retailing performance.

Retailing is the final link in the process of moving goods from producer to consumer. It is for this reason that retailing places such heavy reliance on correct analysis of consumer behavior and is emphasized as a reason for consumer analysis. Regardless of how much value the manufacturer has built into his product, how well he has communicated this value to the consumer, and how smoothly his production and physical distribution system may be functioning, it is the retailer who either consummates or obstructs the sale.

There has been much progress in recent years in improvement of what might be called the cost-revenue approach to improved retailing performance, but there were limited advances in what might be called the demand-analysis approach. Significant advances have been made in accounting control, computerized inventory systems, merchandise planning, location selection, physical layout,

---

[13] A succinct synthesis of the major changes in distribution is provided by William R. Davidson, "Changes in Distributive Institutions," *J. Marketing*, vol. 34, pp. 7–10 (Jan. 1970).

warehousing, and other operational aspects of retailing management.[14] These technologies have been diffused so widely, however, that their potential for differentiating one retailing firm from another is approaching diminishing returns. The alternative is to increase the ability to understand, predict, and stimulate consumer response to a retailing firm's offering. Improved strategies to produce a more appealing offering provide an increasing potential as a basis for differentiating one retailing firm from another in profitability and consumer satisfaction.

Retailing performance is of critical concern in consumer behavior for another reason. The additional reason is the essential role retailing institutions play in total urban planning. The type of retailing institutions that will exist in cities of the next decade influence the kind of transportation cities will need, the kind of communication system (that is, the rise of telecommunications systems for transactions), the location and form of leisure activities, and the kind of integration with other time-consuming activities required for "new towns" and revitalization of existing cities. Thus the strategies of many types of business firms will be affected profoundly by the *form* and *place* of retailing transactions.

SUMMARY

Consumer behavior is defined as the acts of individuals directly involved in obtaining and using economic goods and services, including the decision processes that precede and determine these acts. Many of the principles that explain consumer behavior overlap with industrial behavior, although it is only the former that is emphasized in this text.

A useful method of analysis of consumer behavior is the decision-process approach which examines the events that precede and follow a purchase. Consumer behavior as a field of study is an interdisciplinary and applied approach based upon an analytical framework rather than merely a description of behavior.

The rationale for studying consumer behavior involves two primary emphases. One emphasis is upon macromarketing problems, or how a society meets the economic needs of its people. The other emphasis is upon micromarketing problems, or the administration of specific elements of an economy. Analysis of consumer behavior is increasingly an essential input in formulating public policies, in understanding the role of marketing in society, and in understanding the nature of planning in a society which permits individual choices. From a managerial perspective, consumer analysis is essential for evaluating new market opportunities, choosing market segments, increasing efficiency of marketing strategy and tactics, and improving retailing performance. This book emphasizes the relationships between decisions of both types with an awareness of the increasing impact individual consumer decisions have upon the well-being of the economic system.

---

[14] William R. Davidson and Alton F. Doody, *Retailing Management* (New York: Ronald, 1966); Ronald R. Gist, *Retailing: Concepts and Decisions* (New York: Wiley, 1968).

REVIEW AND DISCUSSION QUESTIONS

1. Which of the following decisions should be considered legitimate topics of concern in the study of consumer behavior? (a) selection of a college by a student, (b) purchase of a life insurance policy, (c) smoking a cigarette, (d) selecting a church to join, (e) selecting a dentist, (f) visiting an auto showroom to see new models being introduced, (g) purchasing a college textbook.

2. What are some instances in which the buying decisions of a purchasing agent (using Wroe Alderson's terminology) might not be closely related to the preferences of those who will consume the product?

3. In the beginning of this chapter an imaginary description was given of representatives from several disciplines. What differences in perspective on consumer behavior would you expect to find among the following types of researchers? (a) experimental psychologist, (b) social psychologist, (c) clinical psychologist, (d) anthropologist, (e) sociologist (differences between sociologists?), (f) economist, (g) others you may think of.

4. Which disciplines in the behavioral and social sciences appear to have the most to contribute to the study of consumer behavior?

5. The system for deciding what bread is to be produced and distributed is partially described in this chapter. Can you develop a system that would be more efficient than the one used in the United States today?

6. It is obvious that new markets have been created in the last few decades by such trends as the exodus to the suburbs. What new markets appear to be likely in the next few decades due to *geographic mobility?*

7. Describe some products that in recent years appear to have arisen because of *psychic mobility.*

8. What contributions does the analysis of consumer behavior make to the field of finance? of production? of real estate? of insurance? of top-management administration?

9. Refer to Table 1.1. What type of advertising strategy should a firm use for each cell, assuming that it is possible to reach each group of consumers?

10. Think of a specific firm that might be using Table 1.1. What are the reasons why consumers in the middle row sometimes buy this firm's brand and sometimes buy a competitive brand?

11. Suppose Table 1.1 represents the brand position of a competitor. In planning marketing strategy for your firm, in what order would you attack each of the competitor's cells?

12. Which areas of a firm's marketing strategy depend most upon an accurate understanding of consumer behavior?

CHAPTER 2

THE CONSUMER:
PERSPECTIVES AND VIEWPOINTS

The reasons for studying and analyzing consumer behavior and motivation were considered in Chapter 1. The motivation of human behavior, not surprisingly, is exceedingly complex and is the result of a myriad of influences and relationships. It is necessary, therefore, to present a model or representation of relationships among the factors underlying behavior. Such a model must of necessity be built from theories and hypotheses borrowed from many sources. It is the purpose of this chapter to discuss and evaluate many of the perspectives and viewpoints about the consumer that have emerged in marketing, economics, and in the related behavioral sciences. Chapter 3 then builds on these elements and presents a conceptual model of consumer behavior which serves as the organizational framework for the book.

THE STUDY OF HUMAN BEHAVIOR

The study of human beings presents real methodological difficulties which, in turn, have led to the variety of conceptual and empirical schemes confronting the analyst of consumer behavior. The major types of influences on the consumer and their interaction are discussed in the first part of this section, followed by a review of the resulting empirical procedures and problems.

The Psychological Field

Man is influenced by many forces, the sum total of which is represented in Figure 2.1 and is designated as the *psychological field.*

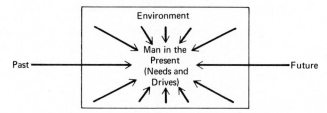

Figure 2.1   PSYCHOLOGICAL FIELD

As the figure indicates, man is motivated by basic needs that exist largely apart from the environment in which he lives and that are activated in the present time, without particular influence from the past or anticipation of the future. In this sense, man does not differ greatly from animals. The human being, however, is not time bound, in that he is fully capable of recalling and being influenced by the past as well as of being able to anticipate the future consequences of his behavior. The past may function through learned patterns of behavior and ways of thinking, many of which are largely unconscious. In addition, man is more profoundly influenced than are animals by the environment in which he lives and is especially affected by the social role of others. All of these factors are significant, and any realistic theory of buyer behavior must comprehend each major element in a consistent and realistic manner.

The role of the social environment requires further clarification. In one sense, other people serve a supportive function both in the goods they make and share and in the opportunity offered to share love and affection. Another role, however, is a constraining one, for man is seldom free to act as he would if his urges were permitted free expression. Social mores and guides become established which effectively limit his freedom of action. Many of these constraints obviously are necessary for the maintenance of order and become codified as laws. Others are necessary for the effective functioning of groups and emerge as *norms,* or accepted patterns of behavior in social settings.

By taking the perspective that man is subject to compound and sometimes conflicting motivational determinants, it is possible to understand the overwhelming complexity of the forces underlying behavior. Each individual must adapt to his unique psychological field, and, to him, this field is reality. He will establish patterns of behavior that permit a workable and meaningful pattern of adaptation.

Explaining Human Behavior

The complexity of the psychological field is not the only difficulty faced by the analyst of human action because mental processes cannot be observed directly. The result is that explanations of what transpires can be only an inference as to what must have taken place to cause the individual to act as he did. Figure 2.2 clarifies the nature of this dilemma.

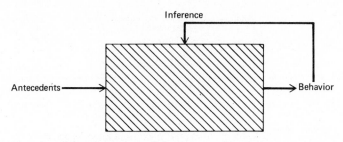

Figure 2.2 BASIC MODEL FOR STUDY OF HUMAN BEHAVIOR

Antecedents are the inputs or stimuli that trigger action, and behavior is the output or result. The individual's mental processes stand between inputs and outputs and are forever hidden from view. For this reason they are sometimes described as being located within an inpenetrable *black box*. Any explanation of what took place within the black box as a result of the input can be only an inference made by the analyst.

To take an example, assume that a person reacts negatively and perhaps violently when he answers his telephone and hears a voice say, "Good evening; we are pleased to tell you that you are one of the very few in this city who will be permitted to purchase *Blab* magazine at half price." He may slam the receiver in the salesman's ear. A relationship is thereby established between the antecedent (the call) and the behavior (slamming the receiver). This relationship is affected by something within the black box, but this "something," whatever it might be, cannot be observed directly from this sequence. Perhaps the analyst will conclude that the person has a strong attitude against telephone solicitation. Yet what is an attitude? It is only an inference that is made concerning some variable which intervened between the stimulus and the response.

The concept of *intervening variable* is an important one and is defined by one authority as follows:

> The qualifying adjective "intervening" is used to convey the notion that postulated states, conditions, or processes intervene between the behavior and its observable correlates or antecedents. Since these variables cannot be observed directly, their meanings are provided by explicit definitions and by their functional relations within the context of general theories of behavior.[1]

---

[1] Judson S. Brown, *The Motivation of Behavior* (New York: McGraw-Hill, 1961), p. 28. Reprinted by permission of the publisher.

The black-box model is made operational in the behavioral sciences mainly through analysis of the three possible relationships illustrated in Figure 2.3.

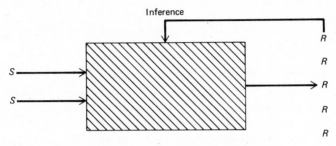

Figure 2.3   BLACK-BOX MODEL

The antecedents now are labeled S (stimulus), behavior is designed R (response), and the inference made regarding the influences on behavior is shown by an arrow. The most common empirical relationships, (1) S–R and (2) R–R, are illustrated in the figure.

S–R Relationships   This type of analysis involves the manipulation of a physical or an environmental stimulus that serves to trigger behavior and leads to a response. An inference is then made from the resulting behavior regarding the likely intervening variable or variables. The telephone salesman situation discussed above is an example.

R–R Relationships   Isolation of dependable S–R relations frequently presents methodological difficulties because of the problem of isolating the behavioral consequences of a given stimulus and ascertaining that findings are not contaminated by other influences. Behavior is sometimes analyzed over time, therefore, through examination of response patterns. Explanatory variables within the black box are then inferred from responses without direct reference to antecedents. Analysis of consumption of bread by a family over a one-month period is an example of an R–R study. No doubt a fairly regular pattern of behavior would emerge and thereby provide a basis for prediction of future bread consumption and purchasing patterns.

Level of Aggregation   The above discussion, of course, pertains primarily to situations in which the individual is used as the unit of analysis. In certain situations, however, groups of varying sizes may be a more useful unit. For example, the purchase of a major appliance is generally a family decision, and much is lost if each individual is studied without reference to the influence of others. Once again, however, an S–R model can be utilized since the family can respond to a stimulus. Similarly, one individual can serve as a stimulus to others. The R–R model can also be quite useful in this setting, and the resultant method of research is referred to as longitudinal analysis, in which individuals or families are studied frequently over an extended period of time.[2]

In other situations, entire market segments may be the most useful unit of analysis. The buying response of urban high-school girls to an advertisement for miniskirts in *Seventeen* magazine is an example. Clearly the decision regarding level of aggregation will differ from one marketing problem to the next.

The Inference Problem   It should be apparent from this brief discussion that many of the terms commonly used to explain human behavior (need and attitude are examples) are nothing more than inferred intervening variables. For this reason, many schools of thought have arisen, *each of which views the same phenomenon and postulates different intervening variables.* In part, these differences arise because analysts have different purposes and hence focus on different variables. The result, of course, is that there can be real disagreement on the meaning of such terms as "need," "motive," and "attitude." Indeed, it is difficult to find definitions that are acceptable to all; therefore, it is necessary to specify meanings of intervening variables with as much precision as possible.

The remainder of this chapter is largely devoted to discussing variations in perspectives used to explain consumer behavior, and it should now be clear why these variations exist. While some explanations may be preferable for certain purposes, seldom is one viewpoint totally in error. The utility of a theory is best judged in terms of the purposes of the analyst.

The most useful criterion used in testing the applicability of an explanation of a psychological phenomenon is the *law of parsimony,* which requires an "explanation of a phenomenon of human behavior with a minimum of assumptions and a maximum of conceptual precision."[3] First, a host of unrealistic assumptions can clearly limit the usefulness of a theory. As will be discussed in detail, this is the difficulty one faces when utilizing the microeconomic conception of consumer motivation. Moreover, precise definition of terms and conditions is required if the theory is to lend itself to empirical verification. Finally, theory must be consistent with reality.

Throughout this book the tests of the law of parsimony are applied, and every attempt is made to specify variables and relationships with sufficient precision. For this reason, some perspectives are adopted and utilized while others are rejected. Once again, however, recognition is given to the fact that others with different purposes might have made other decisions.

---

[2] Donald H. Granbois and James F. Engel, "Longitudinal Analysis of Marketing Behavior," in Peter D. Bennett (ed.), *Marketing and Economic Development* (Chicago: Amer. Marketing Assoc., 1965), pp. 205–275.

[3] James F. Engel, "Psychology and the Business Sciences," *Quart. J. Economics and Business*, vol. 1, p. 78 (1961).

THE CONSUMER IN ECONOMIC THEORY

The role of the consumer differs in microeconomics and macroeconomics; it is necessary, therefore, to look at each area of theory separately.

Microeconomic Theory

The so-called classical economist of the nineteenth century postulated a view of consumer motivation and behavior that is still sometimes present in contemporary theory, although it has been substantially modified. The basic assumptions are that an individual has complete knowledge of his wants and of all available means to satisfy these wants. In addition, preferences are assumed to be independent of the environment at the time in which choice is made, unlimited and nonsatiable, and consistent. The decision, then, is one of careful allocation of resources to maximize utility within the constraint imposed by a financial budget. The consumer presumably evaluates each alternative and thereby behaves rationally. Maximization of utility thus is hypothesized to be the *only* motive for behavior, and the result is a precise and elegant theory which lends itself to manipulation using tools of the calculus.

It appears as though the classical economist was guided by a desire to view man as behaving in a mechanistic manner, with largely the same reactions to a given situation. In reality, of course, behavior is seldom predictable to this extent. Furthermore, little or no attention was devoted to questioning the empirical reality of assumptions. A prime example of this deductive approach is the long-standing assumption that expenditures vary directly with income, increasing or decreasing as income increases or decreases.

The assumed income–consumption relationship has been challenged by reliable survey evidence, and this is one example of how microeconomic theory has undergone revision to make it more consonant with reality. The Survey Research Center at The University of Michigan has demonstrated that willingness to purchase consumer goods does not bear an invariably direct relation to income; in fact, purchases of durable goods can decline in a period of high and rising incomes.[4] It is recognized that buyers can anticipate the future and that attitudes such as optimism or pessimism concerning one's financial condition in the future can profoundly affect the decision to buy.

Perhaps the early economist cannot be blamed for arriving at such notions regarding consumer behavior. Theories were formulated in the nineteenth century that by no means approached the "affluent society" of today. For example, little income was available for expenditure on items other than the necessities of life. The hypothesized relation between income and spending, then, probably was not unrealistic for that time, since purchases for additional goods no doubt did tend to increase with income. Furthermore, when larger incomes finally did

---

[4] George Katona, *The Powerful Consumer* (New York: McGraw-Hill, 1960).

become more widespread, careful purchasing behavior approximating the assumptions of rationality may have been common because of the great variety of as yet unmet desires. Finally, the prevailing psychological theory of the times was primitive, and the economist was proceeding in much the same deductive mold of inquiry as other behavioral and social scientists.

The real criticism of the classical economist, perhaps, does not lie in assumed rationality, because maximization of utility is a reasonable *initial approximation* to the motivation underlying purchasing behavior. The reasons for this viewpoint are clarified later. The weakness of the classical view for our purposes is the tendency of some to embrace economics as a moralistic science which alleges how a sensible consumer *ought* to behave. It is not unusual, even today, to encounter statements that purchase on the basis of impulse or emotion is unwise and therefore irrational. Although this can be only a personal judgment, psychologists sometimes are inclined to take a similar point of view, as one authority points out:

> No assumption has spread more widely in modern psychology than that men are ruled by their emotions and that these are irrational. Although there is much to support this view, it has nevertheless been responsible for a systematic depreciation of the possibilities of intelligence and thinking in human affairs. Technically this formulation finds expression in the proposition that there is a cleavage between emotional and intellectual processes. It is held to be an axiom not only that emotions and thinking are different psychological operations, but that they are antithetical as well.[5]

Once again, however, it should be noted that many contemporary economists are modifying their assumptions.

Macroeconomic Theory

As a rule, the economist generally is not directly concerned with the buying choices of individuals, but rather focuses on choice patterns over time by large groups. His interest lies in patterns of behavior pertaining to major decisions such as allocation of income to savings or investment in consumer durable goods. The argument is frequently advanced that individual differences average out when many people are studied and thereby assume relatively little importance.

For purposes of marketing, it can legitimately be argued that much is lost through the process of aggregation, that important insights into buyer behavior are lost, and that marketing planning is thereby hampered. Yet the purpose of the macroeconomist is quite different; his goal is to isolate dependable statistical relations between purchase and certain underlying variables such as income and age. It is not necessary for him to understand the process of household

---

[5]   Solomon E. Asch, *Social Psychology* (Englewood Cliffs, N.J.: Prentice-Hall, 1952), p. 21. Reprinted by permission of the publisher.

decision making. Even granting these differences in purposes, however, the yield of data from macroanalysis has contributed much to marketing thought by clarifying relations between purchase and the underlying variables that have been analyzed.

THE CONSUMER IN THE MARKETING LITERATURE

Marketing thought has undergone dramatic changes through the post-World War II infusion of behavioral science concepts, and many of the traditional views of buyer behavior have given way. As a result, contemporary thought is a blend of the old and the new. But for purposes of clarity, it is necessary to discuss both the traditional viewpoint because of its prominence in some quarters and the more recent modifications coming from psychology and sociology.

The Traditional View of Buyer Motivation and Behavior

In approaching the subject of why consumers do what they do, it has become common to explain the causative variables in the black box through use of the term "motive."[6] In other words, motive assumes the entire burden of explanation. Classifications of motives quickly became extensive, and many marketing writers, following the trends in psychological thought in the 1930s, advanced lengthy lists. One leading psychologist, for example, listed approximately 30 motives that were presumably common to all individuals.[7] Examples are hunger, variety, sex, love, and curiosity. Other more general classifications also emerged, and the following appear most frequently in the marketing literature: (1) primary and selective; (2) rational and emotional; (3) patronage; and (4) conscious and dormant.

Primary buying motives are generally defined to be those that lead to the purchase or use of a class of article or service. A new rug may be purchased, for example, as opposed to other types of floor coverings. The reasons that influence the selection of a particular type of rug from among several possibilities, on the other hand, are referred to as *selective buying motives*. In this situation a desire for the warmth and sound-deadening capabilities of carpet might be regarded as primary motives, whereas the density of fiber, reputation for quality, and color might be selective motives underlying purchase of a given brand.

Rational and *emotional* motives are somewhat more difficult to define and distinguish. In general, the classifications seem to be based on the extent to which

---

6   This use of the term "motive" has its genesis in an influential book by Melvin T. Copeland, *Marketing Problems* (New York: A. W. Shaw Co., 1920).

7   H. A. Murray, *Explorations in Personality* (New York: Oxford University Press, 1938).

external and measurable product features are the reasons for purchase, as opposed to personal feelings or opinions. Rational motives generally are defined to include economy, efficiency, dependability, durability, convenience of use, enhancement of earnings, and many others. Emotional motives, however, typically include emulation, conformity, individuality, desire for comfort, desire for pleasure, ambition, and pride.

Motives that determine the source from which a purchase will be made are commonly known as *patronage motives*. Examples are convenience of location, breadth of assortments, and supporting services such as package wrapping and check cashing.

Finally, motives can be classified, according to some marketing writers, as either *conscious* or *dormant*. According to this point of view, conscious motives are felt and experienced and, as a result, need not be aroused or activated through advertising or other forms of marketing strategy. On the other hand, some motives may be dormant in that they are unrecognized and need to be brought to the buyer's attention in some manner.

The concept of motive as traditionally used in the marketing literature has proved to be inadequate for several reasons: (1) the weakness of "armchair" analysis; (2) the danger of obscuring other variables; and (3) the erroneous thinking propagated by the rational–emotional dichotomy.

The Weakness of "Armchair" Analysis   It is not an overstatement to say that the classifications of motives discussed above seldom if ever has been based on empirical evidence. Rather, they tend to represent personal opinion. It is doubtful that the lists would be very accurate or useful, since, as one authority points out:

> The mere listing of goals [motives] is of little value. Scientific progress is achieved only if the conditions are specified under which certain motives—or patterns of motives—are prevalent and if, in addition, it can be demonstrated that they produce different behavioral effects.[8]

Moreover, there is a very real danger of circular reasoning in that a motive is assigned as an explanation of the behavior from which it is inferred. It is somewhat trivial, for example, to observe a man studying radiology in the library and postulate that he has a need or motive for self-advancement. In other words, no real attempt is made to investigate the actual underlying reasons, and erroneous impressions can result.

Obscuring Other Variables   As traditionally utilized in marketing, the concept of motive is assigned a weight of explanation that it is seldom accorded in the behavioral sciences. Most people agree that motives are only one of the forces underlying behavior which functions to initiate action and to direct it toward a type of goal that, in the past, has proved to be satisfactory. But the final outcome is also affected by attitudes, personality traits, the influence of others, and many other factors. *In other words, the use of motive as the sole variable intervening*

---

[8]   Katona, *op. cit.*,[4] p. 116.

between stimulus and response is a gross oversimplification. Moreover, it does not permit the precision of understanding, necessary if marketing efforts are to be meaningfully adapted to buyer demand.

Fallacies of the Rational–Emotional Dichotomy   The distinction between rational and emotional motives is still popular in the literature today. The concept of rationality, it will be recalled, is central in classical economic theory, and it is assumed that the consumer behaves rationally by weighing alternatives and choosing those that maximize utility. As the term came to be used in marketing, however, it refers to the selection and evaluation of goods using *objective criteria* —that is, factors such as size, weight, and price, which can be evaluated by standards other than one's personal opinion. These factors, then, are what is meant by rational motives, whereas emotional motives comprehend purely personal considerations (beauty, desire for emulation, and so on) or *subjective criteria.*

If one distinguishes emotional considerations from so-called rational motives in this fashion, does this mean that a purchase for purely subjective reasons cannot be rational and hence purposeful? If the answer is yes, then this implies that utility can be maximized only if subjective factors are prevented from influencing the purchase, a somewhat ludicrous conclusion. The purposeful buyer approaches decisions to arrive at an act that most nearly satisfies his goals, whatever they may be. It is a fallacy to imply, for example, that the payment of a premium price for an automobile to stand out among others in one's neighborhood is nonrational and hence nonpurposeful. Indeed, subjective criteria frequently must dominate the so-called rational motives of economy and performance.

In all fairness, most marketing writers did not intend emotional motives to be regarded as nonpurposeful; but, if this were not the purpose, the term "rational" should never have been used as it has been. In effect, some writers have strayed far from the terms used in the parent field of economics.

It is preferable to avoid the concept of rationality altogether because of these unfortunate connotations. In doing so, thinking is brought more clearly into the focus now common in psychology, as stated by Snygg and Combs:

> Laying aside, for the moment, the objective facts about behavior that some of us have learned, let each of us look at his own behavior as we actually see it while we are behaving. We find lawfulness and determinism at once. From the point of view of the behaver himself, behavior is caused. It is purposeful. It always has a reason. . . . When we look at other people from an external, objective point of view their behavior may seem irrational because we do not experience the [psychological] field as they do. . . . But at the instant of behaving the actions of each person seem to him to be the best and most effective acts he can perform under the circumstances. If, at that instant, he knew how to behave more effectively, he would do so.[9]

---

[9]   Donald Snygg and Arthur W. Combs, *Individual Behavior* (New York: Harper & Row, 1949), p. 12.

The Need for a More Balanced Perspective   It is necessary to restore the term motive to its rightful place as only one influence on consumer behavior. Evaluative labels such as rational and emotional must be avoided. Consistent with contemporary psychological thought, therefore, this concept is not assigned the weight of explanation it has traditionally been given in marketing.

Interdisciplinary Contributions to Marketing Thought

Not surprisingly, the all-encompassing importance of adapting marketing efforts to buyer desires, especially significant since World War II, has prompted a search for new concepts and methods for this purpose. The result has been extensive interdisciplinary borrowing. While some people have considered the infusion of new perspectives into marketing to be nothing more than a fad, it cannot be denied that many of the contributions have been genuine and lasting. To some extent, however, concepts and methods have been borrowed by some who have either an inadequate knowledge of the related discipline and/or an incomplete grasp of the marketing problem to which the application is made. The result has been some unfortunate errors, which understandably has led certain marketing scholars to conclude that the behavioral sciences have little to offer. Therefore, it is important to clarify and assess the significance of recent interdisciplinary contributions.

Learning Theory   This important body of psychological thought has been mainly an outgrowth of the study of animal behavior in laboratories. Four central concepts are postulated: (1) drive; (2) cue; (3) response; and (4) reinforcement. In Figure 2.1 the contributions from psychology focus primarily on the individual organism existing in the present time period, and other aspects of the psychological field are either disregarded or held constant.

Drive is considered to be an internal stimulus activated by a need or motive, thereby energizing behavior and prompting action. Cues, on the other hand, are external or internal stimuli which serve to direct an appropriate response to satisfy the aroused drive. Response, of course, is the individual's reaction, and reinforcement occurs if the behavior proves to be rewarding. This means that the same action will probably be repeated again under similar circumstances if reinforcement is positive or avoided if reinforcement is negative. (All of these concepts will be discussed in detail in Chapter 9.)

The empirical method most used in learning theory is the S–R model, with few, if any, intervening variables given consideration. The tendency to avoid the inference into the black box has prompted many people to refer to this approach as *behaviorism*. The marketing significance of this theory was first observed when one of its leading proponents, John B. Watson, entered the advertising field.[10] He popularized a view that man enters this world with nothing other than a capacity to learn. His philosophy of advertising was that constant

---

[10]   John B. Watson, *Behaviorism* (New York: The People's Institute Publ. Co., 1925).

repetition would reinforce a response and lead to firm purchasing habits. Today's emphasis on repetitive advertising rests on this foundation as does advertising research devoted to discovering those appeals that stimulate the best short-run response.

Many current advertising campaigns represent a behaviorist philosophy. The Coca Cola campaign features the familiar shape and appearance of the coke bottle, and this theme has been repeated for many years. Also, Marlboro advertisements have long featured a theme of masculinity and "Marlboro country."

Repetition can be effective for certain types of products (see Chapter 15), but a purely behaviorist philosophy would be unsatisfactory. Man exercises a capacity to exclude through selective perception certain appeals that go contrary to his predispositions. There is no place in behaviorism for such practice. In addition, today's consumer is bombarded with many more commercial messages than the consumer of Watson's days of the late 1920s. It is now evident that repetition alone is generally insufficient to produce promotional success. Nevertheless, the enormous volume of contributions to this field have done much to clarify the laws of motivation and learning and thereby explain an important element of the psychological field.

Clinical or Psychoanalytic Theory This area of inquiry overcomes a major limitation of the behavioristic S–R model by introducing intervening variables, especially certain aspects of the social environment. It is impossible to discuss the evolution of psychoanalytic theory without placing Sigmund Freud, the founder, in a prominent position. He pioneered the analysis of personality complexities through rigorous observation, a revolutionary procedure for his time, and thereby shed initial light on basic reasons for individual personality differences.

Freud started with the assumption that the child enters the world with instinctive needs which he cannot gratify apart from others and systematically introduced social influence through the constraints that society exerts on human tendencies.[11] Continual frustration of needs then serves as a stimulus for more subtle means of instinct gratification. Instinctive needs reside in the *id* and are governed in their manifestations by the *ego*, which serves as the intellectual executive mediating between unrestrained instincts and social constraints. The *superego*, which in turn embodies values, limits action on the basis of ethical and moral considerations.

Felt guilt toward some urges, especially those with a sexual basis, leads to a tendency to remove these urges from the consciousness and channel them in socially acceptable ways in entirely unconscious fashions. Freud seemed to maintain that sex or *libido* is the most important of all instincts and that apparent motives for an act often can be found in the sexual drive exerting itself in unconscious and devious fashion. The alleged finding that women bake cakes to satisfy an unconscious desire to give birth no doubt has its genesis in the libido.[12]

---

[11] For an excellent summary of Freudian psychology, see Calvin Hall, *A Primer of Freudian Psychology* (New York: Mentor, 1954).

[12] Vance Packard, *The Hidden Persuaders* (New York: McKay, 1957), p. 77.

Later advocates of the psychoanalytic view added other repressed desires to those mentioned by Freud. Adler, for example, emphasized the urge for power and its manifestations.[13] This powerful motivation is reported to underlie the purchase of life insurance.[14] It has supposedly been discovered that the obvious surface motivations for this act are superseded by the fact that purchase of life insurance represents an emancipation from childhood and thereby marks a man's entrance into the adult world. In addition, it is alleged that life insurance represents a symbol of adult love which circumvents the self-centeredness of youth and even extends beyond death. Moreover, large amounts of life insurance may enhance feelings of potency and power in much the same manner as boasting of sexual achievements. Finally, life insurance purchased during one's years of striving is a positive achievement, a symbol of power and success, so to speak, representing that one's family will be provided for adequately.

While psychoanalytic theories have been depreciated in many quarters, it cannot be denied that theories of individual development, personality structure, and demonstration of the complexities of motivation have shaped contemporary psychological thought. Translation of these concepts from the clinic into a study of entire market segments of many individuals, however, is quite another matter. Some of the marketing advocates of this school of thought have borrowed techniques and concepts in somewhat gross fashion, and the result all too often has been a distortion of reality and overlooking of other important elements in the typical buyer's psychological field.

Quasi-Freudian notions found their way into marketing in the 1950s after the onset of so-called motivation research. This type of inquiry can represent a useful broadening of research methodology, but the wide publicity initially given to "Freudian motivation" substantially impeded for a period the development of other new approaches to the study of buyer motivation and behavior. Packard propagated the mistaken notion that appeals to the unconscious gave the marketer a new and hitherto uncapitalized-upon opportunity to manipulate the consumer.[15]

Assume that an advertiser is told by a motivation researcher that people buy electric blankets because of an unconscious desire to return to the security of the womb. Imagine the problem faced by a copywriter who is told that he must design a message around this finding. It seems reasonable to expect that such factors as weight of the blanket, constant heat, and ease of use are equally important influences that would thereby be overlooked. While unconscious desires can be important, they are virtually impossible to uncover empirically outside of months of psychoanalysis, and, when uncovered, they can be ugly and not lend themselves to effective selling appeals. To those who have maintained the contrary, a challenge is issued to publish findings in detail and permit them to be subjected to public scrutiny.

---

[13] Alfred Adler, *The Science of Living* (New York: Greenberg, 1929).

[14] Ernest Dichter, *The Strategy of Desire* (New York: Doubleday, 1960), pp. 215–220.

[15] Packard, *op. cit.*[12]

The Gestalt Model   This field of psychology originally placed primary emphasis on physical perception of stimuli (for example, why a book is still seen as a book even when viewed from an angle). The term "gestalt" means form or configuration, and gestalt theory was built around carefully designed experiments that proved rather conclusively that individual stimuli are perceived and interpreted in relation to the organization of one's experiences.[16]

Gestalt theory is perhaps most useful today in modified form as stated by Lewin in the 1930s.[17] Lewin postulated that man lives in a complex psychological field composed of many influences, all of which must be comprehended in a realistic theory of motivation. Behavior, according to this point of view, is motivated by the individual striving toward a stable organization of his psychological field through attempting to reduce tensions, reconcile conflicts, and make sense out of the world in which he lives. Man is thus assumed to be goal oriented.

The emphasis in this model is on man *and* his environment, with special attention paid to perception (that is, reception of stimuli through the five senses and attributing meaning to them). While the applications to marketing thus far have not been extensive, perception is of such central importance that it is given detailed treatment in Chapter 8.

Cognitive Theory   Basically an extension of the gestalt approach, contemporary social psychology has taken as a major focus the organization of values, attitudes, and information stored in an individual's memory.[18] Of special significance is the outcome of a state of imbalance in this structure. Imbalance can be introduced by contradictory information from the environment or by nonfitting relationships in the structure itself. A state of tension is thus generated which serves as a motivating force for change either within the structure or through some form of distortion of the external input.

Cognitive theory is discussed in detail later (Chapters 11, 14, and 15), but enough has been stated to indicate the nature of the contributions to the understanding of buyer behavior. Much advertising and selling is undertaken to achieve attitude change, and the literature on this subject from related behavioral sciences has become extensive. The application of many of these findings has perhaps been the most significant result thus far from the interdisciplinary approach.

Theories of Social Influence   None of the contributions discussed has taken as a primary focus the role of the social environment in an individual's psychological field. Much has been learned on this subject, however, and certain types of social influence on buyer behavior have been explored in depth.

---

[16] For a good exposition, see Wolfgang Köhler, *Gestalt Psychology* (New York: Liveright, 1947).

[17] Kurt Lewin, *Principles of Topological Psychology* (New York: McGraw-Hill, 1936).

[18] David Krech, Richard S. Crutchfield, and Egerton L. Ballachey, *Individual in Society* (New York: McGraw-Hill, 1962), chap. 2.

While there are, of course, many sources from which social influence can emanate, the greatest contributions have been in the areas of reference group theory, social class, and diffusion of innovations. Later chapters explore these concepts in depth, so little detail need be included here. The central concept is that of the *reference group* or social entity with which an individual identifies and uses as a standard of behavior. Social class is a type of reference group, and there is now much evidence that there are distinct differences in buying behavior among members of the various classes. Similarly, reference group influence underlies the process by which innovations become diffused within social groupings. Contributions to this subject have mostly been made by rural sociologists, although diffusion processes are now receiving preliminary exploration in marketing. Finally, sociology of the family, which centers on family role structures and interaction processes, contributes much in the way of useful concepts and methods to aid in understanding the household decision-making process.

Recapitulation

Clearly marketing thought has moved a considerable distance from the traditional practice of utilizing the concept of motive as the primary variable to explain buyer behavior. It is increasingly recognized that a buyer's psychological field is complex and that one cannot analyze one aspect of it to the exclusion of others. This fact has served as the principal stimulus for interdisciplinary borrowing.

The brief review in this chapter, however, should not be construed as implying that the interdisciplinary frontiers in marketing have been completely explored. Indeed, this movement is only in its infancy, and little more than certain bits and pieces have been contributed thus far. There are many areas of buyer behavior that have received little or no empirical study. One of the tasks of this book, therefore, is to identify the degree of certainty with which propositions about consumer motivation and behavior may be stated and thereby to identify those areas where research is most needed.

MODELS OF BUYER BEHAVIOR

Surprisingly, the literature of the related behavioral sciences yields comparatively few comprehensive models of behavior and decision-making.[19] In addition, only a few comprehensive models of buyer behavior have appeared in the marketing literature thus far. These contributions, however, have proved to be influential and are worthy of discussion. But first it is necessary to clarify the nature of a model and the resulting significance in the study of human behavior.

---

[19] For a review of some of the models that have appeared, see Francesco M. Nicosia, *Consumer Decision Processes: Marketing and Advertising Implications* (Englewood Cliffs, N.J.: Prentice-Hall, 1966), chap. 4.

The Nature and Significance of Models

A model is a replica of the phenomena it is intended to designate, that is, it specifies the elements and represents the nature of the relationships among these elements. As such, it provides a testable "map" of reality, and its utility lies in the extent to which the model makes possible a successful prediction of resulting behavior or outcomes.

There are many types of models, and space does not permit detailed discussion of all of them here.[20] Of special significance for purposes of this book is the *systems model*.[21] It is not possible to dissect a human organism and study its parts; as a result, the psychologist frequently resorts to the black box mentioned earlier, whereby the human being is analyzed as a *system* with outputs (behavior) in response to inputs. The objective is to gain an understanding of the individual as a *system of action* through clarifying relationships among inputs, motivational determinants, and goal-oriented output. Obviously such models can gain considerable complexity, and frequently the results appear in graphic, symbolic, verbal, or mathematical forms. The final form is often dependent upon the precision of the theories, facts, and assumptions upon which the model is built.

The models of buyer behavior to be discussed in this chapter are relatively unsophisticated, in that they are merely elaborate flow charts of the behavioral process that is depicted. Relations among elements often are only hypothesized because of the absence of needed research. Even so, there are several significant advantages offered which make such models a virtual necessity if progress is to be made:

(1) *A frame of reference is provided for research.* Through description of elements and relationships, gaps in information and potential areas for fruitful inquiry are identified with a clarity not otherwise possible.

(2) *Research findings can be integrated into a meaningful whole.* When a model is available of the entire process of consumer behavior, it becomes feasible to utilize research findings from a variety of behavioral sciences with greater sophistication and precision. In other words, an understanding of underlying relations provides a perspective for assessing the significance of new research data.

(3) *Models become useful in theory construction.* Researchable hypotheses flow readily from a carefully designed model, and a basis is thus provided for extending knowledge.

(4) *Explanations are provided for performance of the system.* A mere description of the motivational determinants of buyer action is of little use; it is necessary, rather, to explain relations and thereby gain in ability to

---

[20]   Irwin D. J. Bross, *Design for Decision* (New York: Free Press, 1953), chap. 10; also Paul H. Rigby, *Conceptual Foundations of Business Research* (New York: Wiley, 1965), chap. 6.

[21]   William Lazer, "The Role of Models in Marketing," *J. Marketing*, vol. 26, pp. 9–14 (1962).

predict outcomes under varying sets of circumstances. This process is virtually impossible without a model of some type, no matter how crude.

The Nicosia Model

Francesco Nicosia, one of the leading scholars in the field of consumer motivation and behavior, published one of the earliest comprehensive models, and his contribution has had a noteworthy influence.[22] The basic components of this model are reproduced in Figure 2.4.

Field One: from the Source of a Message to the Consumer's Attitude

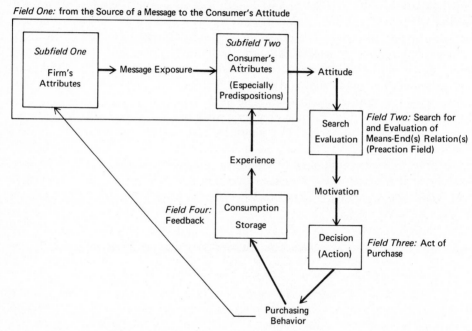

Figure 2.4   SUMMARY FLOW CHART OF THE NICOSIA MODEL OF BUYER BEHAVIOR.   Francesco M. Nicosia, *Consumer Decision Processes: Marketing and Advertising Implications* (Englewood Cliffs, N.J.: Prentice-Hall, 1966), p. 156. Reprinted by permission of the publisher.

Nicosia has used the technique of computer flow charting to designate elements and relationships, and it will be noticed that there are four basic *fields* in Figure 2.4. It is explicitly assumed that *field one* includes the output of an advertising message from a business firm and that the consumer recipient was previously in no way familiar with the advertised product. As the message (*subfield one*) reaches the consumer, it serves as an input into *subfield two*, referred to as the consumer's space, which is composed of his psychological attributes. As

---

[22]   Nicosia, *op. cit.,*[19] chap. 6–7.

this message is received and acted upon, the output hopefully is formation of an attitude toward the product, which then serves as the input for *field two. Field two* represents a search for and an evaluation of the advertised product and other available alternatives as well. The output from this field may or may not be a motivation to buy the advertised brand. If such a motivation emerges, it serves as the input for *field three*, the transformation of motivation into purchasing action. Finally, *field four* is storage or use of the purchased item, and the output is feedback of sales results to the business firm and retention of the consequences of the purchase in the buyer's memory.

This description truly cannot do full justice to the Nicosia model, because each field and subfield is spelled out in considerable detail. Nicosia has taken the important step of relating a wealth of research findings from many sources into his model and thus has made a needed contribution to the marketing literature. The variables underlying perceptual distortion, for example, and the conditions under which this tendency is engaged are discussed and clarified, albeit somewhat briefly.

One encounters certain difficulties in the practical application of this model, however. The brevity of published description emerges as an important handicap, especially in the sense that many of the qualifications and limitations in the evidence underlying the model are not spelled out. Thus, the reader is faced with difficulty in grasping areas where substantial knowledge exists and those in which further research is needed. In addition, the linkages between elements are fuzzy, although this results at least in part from the absence of necessary research into the buying process. In other words, it is not clear how this conceptual approach is applicable to the common kinds of problems faced daily by a marketing manager. Furthermore, those with a focus on more basic research are confronted with the same difficulties.

The Howard–Sheth Model

The first truly integrative model of buyer behavior was proposed by Howard in 1963.[23] Its basic contribution lies in a systematic and thorough utilization of learning theory. Howard introduced the useful distinction between true problem-solving behavior (similar to rational behavior postulated in microeconomic theory), limited problem solving, and automatic response behavior. This pioneering effort did much to solidify and enhance the interdisciplinary approach to analysis of buyer behavior. Elaboration was required, however, to strengthen the conceptual basis of the model and to clarify practical implications.

A meaningful step was taken toward provision of the necessary elaboration in the publication of *The Theory of Buyer Behavior* in 1969 by Howard and Sheth.[24] More variables were included, and the linkages between variables were

---

[23] John A. Howard, *Marketing Management Analysis and Planning*, rev. ed. (Homewood, Ill.: Irwin, 1963), chap. 3–4.

[24] John A. Howard and Jagdish N. Sheth, *The Theory of Buyer Behavior* (New York: Wiley, 1969).

stated with sufficient precision that this contribution stands as a notable advance toward the development of theory in this important area of marketing thought.

Description　A simplified diagram of the Howard–Sheth model appears in Figure 2.5. Notice that stimuli are designated as significative (that is, objective, discernible physical products), symbolic (linguistic or pictorial product representations), and social (information from the social environment regarding a purchase decision, especially word-of-mouth communication). The output consists of a five-phase process beginning with attention to a stimulus and ending with a purchase act. The black box is depicted as consisting of variables which affect perception and learning. These variables are labeled as "hypothetical" since they are not directly measurable at the present time. The output variables, on the other hand, stand as the measurable counterpart of certain of the hypothetical variables and are designated with a prime.

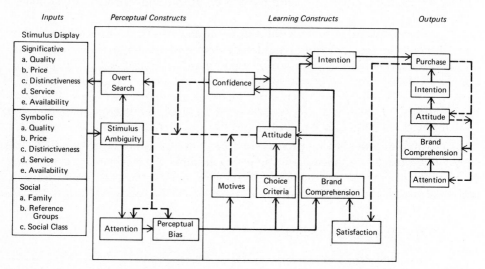

Figure 2.5　SIMPLIFIED DESCRIPTION OF THE HOWARD–SHETH MODEL OF BUYER BEHAVIOR. John A. Howard and Jagdish N. Sheth, *The Theory of Buyer Behavior* (New York: Wiley, 1969). Reprinted by permisssion of the publisher.

The variables are defined as follows:[25]

(1)　Output Variables

> *Attention':* A buyer's response indicating the magnitude of his information intake.
> *Brand comprehension':*　A verbal statement about brand knowledge in a product class.

---

[25]　Howard and Sheth, *op. cit.*[21] pp. 415–420.

Attitude':   A verbal evaluation of the potential of a brand to satisfy motives.

Intention':   A verbally stated expectation, made in cognizance of possible extenuating factors, that he will buy the most preferred brand the next time this action is necessary.

Purchase: The overt act of buying.

(2)   Learning Constructs

Motives: Buyer goals impinging upon a buying situation.

Brand comprehension: Knowledge of existence and characteristics of those brands which form the buyer's set of alternatives (called the "evoked set").

Choice criteria: An ordered set of motives relevant to the product class under consideration.

Attitude: Relative preferences of brands in the evoked-set based ratings along the choice criteria.

Intention: A forecast regarding when, where, and how the buyer will act toward a brand in view of external (exogenous) inhibiting factors such as high price, lack of availability, social influences, and so on.

Confidence: Degree of certainty perceived toward a brand.

Satisfaction: Degree of congruence between actual and expected purchase consequences.

(3)   Perceptual Constructs

Attention: Opening and closing of sensory receptors to control information intake.

Stimulus ambiguity: Perceived uncertainty and lack of meaningfulness of information received from the environment.

Perceptual bias: A distortion of information that is received.

Overt search: An active search for information.

Each of these variables and the probable linkages are described in depth in the Howard-Sheth book, and it is not possible to indicate in a few paragraphs the richness of resulting implications. The essence of the model can be described briefly, however.

A stimulus in one of the three specified categories strikes the five senses. The extent to which it succeeds in attracting attention is at least a partial function of stimulus ambiguity. Ambiguity, in turn, may trigger a search for further information. Once information is attended to, it then is subject to perceptual bias brought about by the intervention of such factors as attitudes and motives stored in memory (shown by dashed lines which represent a feedback relation).

The input of information can have the effect of changing the present status of motives and choice criteria (and hence attitude), brand comprehension, purchase intention, and actual purchase. Whether or not a person actually buys a given alternative, however, is a function of comprehension of brand attributes, strength of attitude toward the brand, confidence in the purchase, and intention (which is affected by perceived influence of the various exogenous constraints). Confidence, in turn, is strengthened by brand comprehension which becomes strengthened if the individual is satisfied with a buying action.

Contributions of the Theory The great strength of this theory lies in the fact that a multiplicity of variables are linked in a precise way. Indeed, the hypothesized relationships, at times, approach the rigor of formal theory. The authors' goal was to provide more than a simple description of the behavioral process, and they have succeeded to an admirable extent. Moreover, imaginative and meaningful use is made of contributions from the behavioral sciences at many points. The resulting influence on the field of marketing is indicated by the research this contribution has stimulated.[26]

Some Conceptual and Methodological Difficulties Those who have attempted to apply the Howard–Sheth model also have been confronted with certain difficulties. First, the distinction between hypothetical and measurable (intervening) variables is perplexing. While it is laudable to note that certain types of variables cannot be measured at present, their inclusion in a model may only serve to introduce unnecessary and confusing complexity. This is a violation of the law of parsimony discussed earlier. Obviously the hypothetical variables must be omitted in empirical research, and the resulting reduced form model is much sharper in the variables included and the relations between them.[27]

In addition, there are areas within the model that are inadequately explained at the present time. Perceptual bias, for example, is treated in a very general fashion without cognizance of experimental research recently undertaken with respect to attention and memory.[28]

Further light has been shed on necessary modifications and extensions through a research project undertaken for purposes of validation.[29] Data were collected from a panel of consumers over time with respect to purchase of a new product marketed in Argentina. The model was validated through the use of multiple regression equations in which a number of hypothesized relationships between variables were tested. For example, the theory predicts that perceptual bias is a function of stimulus ambiguity, attention, and motives. The former variable was treated as the dependent variable in the regression equation, whereas the latter were considered to be independent. The strength of the relationship then is shown by regression coefficients.

In general, the percentages of variation explained were quite low,

---

[26] J. U. Farley and L. W. Ring, "An Empirical Test of the Howard–Sheth Model of Buyer Behavior," *J. Marketing Research*, vol. 7, pp. 427–438 (1970).

[27] See, for example, D. R. Lehmann, T. V. O'Brien, J. U. Farley, and J. A. Howard, "Empirical Contributions to Buyer Behavior Theory," unpublished paper (New York: Columbia University, May 1971).

[28] N. Moray, *Selective Processes in Vision and Hearing* (London: Hutchinson Educational, 1969).

[29] Farley and Ring, *op. cit.*[26]; and Lehmann *et al.*, *op. cit.*[27]

although many were in the expected direction. It was found that some variables probably are not related as hypothesized and that others, not specified by the theory, appear to be correlated. This has led to some modifications in the structure of the theory on a tentative basis.[30] The following additional conclusions emerged:[31]

(1) The model is more recursive than was originally thought. This means that some variables which occur only at initial stages in the systems (such as attention) should be included in later relationships as well (intention is an example) rather than being assumed to feed through such intervening variables as attitudes.

(2) There is substantial measurement error which inhibits meaningful tests of the theory.

(3) The distinction between endogenous and exogenous variables is not sharp, and it may prove necessary to treat more variables as endogenous for more precise measurement and manipulation.

(4) Some variables are difficult to define operationally, and others are difficult to measure. In addition, there are some wide variations between the theoretical definition of a variable, such as perceptual bias and its operational specification. This can render the tests of the theory to date somewhat questionable.

Finally, acceptance of this model by those with a more pragmatic, application-centered emphasis may well have been impeded by some initially over-enthusiastic claims of its advocates. The state of the behavioral sciences in general and knowledge of consumer behavior in specific will not warrant a statement to the effect that giant breakthroughs have been made or soon will be made in understanding the consumer. While Howard and Sheth's contribution has been enormous, disappointment and even disillusionment can only accompany exaggerated claims.

Recapitulation   In summary, most scholars are unanimous in their assessment that the study of consumer motivation and behavior was advanced by publication of the Howard–Sheth model. Identification of certain weaknesses should be taken only as an indication that progress is yet to be made in many areas.

The Need for Clarification and Extension

It has not been possible to give full justice to the two models discussed in this chapter, and there are other contributions which also could have been mentioned.[32] The intent rather has been to review briefly two important pioneer-

---

[30]   These are clarified in Lehmann *et al.*, *op. cit.*[27]

[31]   Lehmann, *et al.*, *op. cit.*[27]

[32]   For another perspective, see Alan R. Andreasen, "Attitudes and Customer Behavior: A Decision Model," in Lee E. Preston (ed.), *New Research in Marketing* (Berkeley, Calif.: Institute of Business and Economic Research, 1965), pp. 1–16.

ing contributions which have justly received considerable praise. Nicosia and Howard and Sheth have made significant strides in the direction on assessing areas where a sound body of propositions emerges and others where knowledge is scanty. The road which they and others have traveled has opened the way for the necessary progress, because helpful insights have been provided into areas where the concepts and methods of the behavioral sciences can be utilized.

SUMMARY

The purpose of this chapter has been to suggest something of the complexities of the elements underlying consumer behavior and to provide some awareness of the variety of perspectives and viewpoints that have arisen. The concept of the psychological field was introduced to comprehend the sum total of *all* forces, including the past, present, and future. No explanation of human activity can be complete unless this perspective is assumed.

The process of analysis and explanation, however, is by no means easy. The analyst must, of necessity, study the human organism through responses to various stimuli or inputs. Any explanation of what took place thus can be only an inference made by the analyst. This explains why the same behavioral phenomena can be explained in so many different ways. Thus it is not surprising that the economist, marketing man, and psychologist would advance different explanations.

Theories of consumer behavior advanced by economists were then discussed, and it is clear that traditional explanations suffer from unrealistic assumptions. The same conclusion is also valid for the analyses appearing in the marketing literature prior to the recent influx of new perspectives from other disciplines. Some of the contributions from learning theory, clinical theory, gestalt psychology, cognitive theory, and theories of social influence were examined. Each was found to be of value, but the need still remains to be eclectic and to search for theories and explanations of consumer motivation and behavior from a variety of sources. No single perspective is complete in and of itself.

The black-box model was discussed in this chapter to indicate why different perspectives and viewpoints can arise concerning the same phenomena of individual behavior. One analyst may focus on individual needs, whereas another may direct his inquiry toward social influence. The point, of course, is that any individual's psychological field is complex, and behavior can be the result of many forces. Therefore it is dangerous to assume one theoretical perspective to the exclusion of others.

Each of the perspectives and viewpoints discussed here should be conceived as a building block, so to speak, to be used where appropriate in a more complex model which integrates elements and specifies relationships among them.

REVIEW AND DISCUSSION QUESTIONS

1. In what ways can the social environment act as a constraint on buyer behavior?

2. One authority says that an attitude is a "set to respond." Another says it is a

"tendency to evaluate people and things along a continuum of positive to negative." Still another says it is a "predisposition to think and act in a certain way." Why should there be such variation in usage of a common term?

3. Under what circumstances is the individual buyer the best unit of analysis? the family? a market segment?

4. Since the microeconomic conception of buyer violates the law of parsimony in several important ways, why is it still prevalent in economic theory?

5. A husband goes into a store with a shopping list which includes bread, milk, three cans of vegetable soup, and a box of whole cloves. He returns home, in addition, with cashews, pickled herring, shrimp, cocktail crackers, and two bottles of Burgundy wine. A $1.50 purchase grew to a total of $8.25. Would the concept of rational versus emotional motives help explain the buyer's purchasing behavior? What explanation can you give?

6. A research firm reports that "our findings based on 11 studies show that an advertisement can be repeated four times to the same audience before its impact begins to 'wear out.'" Would it be wise to include this as a rule of thumb in an advertising text? Why or why not?

7. In speaking of the dangers that can result from detailed psychological analysis of buyer motivation and behavior, Packard states, "Much of it seems to represent regress rather than progress for man in his struggle to become a rational and self-guiding being" (*Hidden Persuaders*, New York: McKay, 1957, p. 6). The main point is that persuaders now have new tools which enable them to manipulate the consumer and circumvent his processes of reasoning. Comment.

8. What arguments can be advanced to defend the widespread tendency for many people in marketing, especially those who have been trained since 1960, to specialize in one of the related behavioral or social sciences? What possible dangers might exist?

9. What is a model? What role does a model play in aiding understanding of buyer behavior?

10. What factors might account for the relative absence of models of decision-making behavior in the literature of both marketing and the related behavioral sciences?

11. Contrast the Howard–Sheth and Nicosia models, focusing on similarities and differences. It is suggested that the original sources of each be consulted for this purpose.

3

AN OVERVIEW OF CONSUMER DECISION-PROCESS BEHAVIOR

The nature and significance of the various elements of an individual's psychological field were discussed in the preceding chapter. It is the purpose of the present chapter to provide an overview of consumer decision-process behavior in order to lay the conceptual foundation for the remainder of the book. The discussion begins with a consideration of the nature of decision processes and the research strategies which are appropriate to understand these phenomena. Then a comprehensive model of consumer motivation and behavior is presented which builds upon the discussion in Chapter 2. Examples are provided to illustrate how this model proved useful in understanding the decision processes underlying the purchase of a small automobile (extended problem solving) versus a household laundry detergent (habitual or routine problem solving).

Most of the following chapters center on a limited component of this model. Therefore, it may prove useful to refer back to this chapter from time to time in order to retain a focus on the overall structure.

NATURE OF CONSUMER DECISION PROCESSES

This section presents various approaches to the study of behavior and demonstrates how the decision-process approach used in this text overcomes many of the problems that plague other approaches.

There are three basic ways to study consumer behavior empirically: (1) a *distributive* approach focusing on behavioral outcomes, (2) a *morphological* approach which describes the way a decision is made, and (3) an *analytical* approach which is similar to the morphological approach except for the fact that it assesses the impact of various influences on purchases (for example, advertisements or displays).[1] The latter two, of course, are highly similar and are more frequently referred to jointly as the *decision-process* approach.

The Distributive Approach

Until recently the majority of empirical studies of consumer behavior have utilized the distributive approach.[2] The strategy has been to attempt to predict the relations among various independent variables—economic, demographic, and social-psychological—and the outcomes of consumer decision making. In other words, behavior has been conceptualized and studied as an *act* rather than as a *process*.

Advantages There are certain advantages to this research strategy. Compared with the decision-process approach, research which utilizes the distributive strategy is relatively simple and probably less expensive. In cases where independent variables are highly correlated with the purchase of a brand, the approach is useful in estimating market potential and perhaps in selecting advertising media and vehicles. For example, if purchasers of a brand have a strong tendency to be in a certain income group, then the number of people in the group may be a sufficient approximation of market size, and, all other things being equal, media and vehicles having a high percentage of their circulation hitting this income group may be more appropriate than other media and vehicles. In these and other marketing management situations, the distributive approach is both attractive and relevant.[3]

---

[1] Robert A. Dahl, Mason Haire, and Paul F. Lazarsfeld, *Social Science Research on Business: Product and Potential* (New York: Columbia University Press, 1959), pp. 103–104.

[2] Robert Ferber, "Research on Household Behavior," *Amer. Economic Rev.*, vol. 52, pp. 19–63 (Mar. 1962).

[3] James M. Patterson, "Buying as a Process," *Business Horizons* p. 59, (Spring 1965).

Limitations There are several difficulties with this approach. Since World War II, economic and demographic variables have become increasingly less reliable as predictors of product and brand choice.[4] Similarly, personality variables have typically made minimal contributions to the understanding of consumer behavior, as is pointed out in Chapter 12. Consequently, in many instances, the distributive strategy is becoming less useful for many types of marketing management problems.

By its very nature, the distributive approach is of limited value in designing marketing strategies. Regardless of the degree of correlation between independent variables and brands purchased, the marketer does not know *why* this correlation exists. Lacking information about the sequence of events culminating in a purchase decision, a marketing manager is severely limited in his ability to influence or adapt to consumer behavior.

Finally, the distributive strategy "explains" consumer behavior at a very superficial level. A purchase decision is only a fraction of marketing-relevant consumption behavior. In most instances, purchase decisions are preceded by some configuration of decision making. Unless purchase decisions (outcomes) are related to these processes—and they seldom are—both the decision and the correlates of the decision may be misleading in the sense that they may be true only if certain mixtures of predecision processes take place. In order to understand, explain, and/or predict consumer behavior, frequently an approach is needed that is more complex than the distributive strategy.

The Decision–Process Approach

A decision-process strategy is concerned with the procedure an individual uses in reaching a decision. Almost 60 years ago Dewey itemized what he termed "steps in problem solving" to explain the process an individual goes through in solving a problem or making a decision.[5] Since that time, many conceptualizations of the steps or phases of problem solving have been advanced and used.[6] Until recently, however, consumer behavior has seldom been viewed from this perspective.

The decision-process formulation used in this text consists of five processes linked in a sequence: (1) problem recognition, (2) alternative evaluation —internal search, (3) alternative evaluation—external search, (4) purchase, and (5) outcomes. This is an attempt to describe the behavioral processes that intervene from the stage at which consumers recognize that some decision is necessary

---

[4] Nelson N. Foote, (ed.), *Household Decision Making* (New York: New York University Press, 1961), p. 2.

[5] John Dewey, *How We Think* (New York: Heath, 1910), p. 72.

[6] See, for example, Orville Brim, David C. Glass, David E. Lavin, and Norman Goodman, *Personality and Decision Processes* (Stanford, Calif.: Stanford University Press, 1962), p. 9; Robert M. Gagné, "Problem Solving and Thinking," in P. R. Farnsworth and Q. McNemar (eds.), *Annual Review of Psychology* (Palo Alto, Calif.: Annual Reviews, 1959), pp. 147–172.

to the point at which there is postpurchase evaluation of an alternative and its attributes.

Three qualifications need to be made. First, the consumer need not be, and, indeed, probably is not aware that he passes through these phases. Most people probably do not say, "I recognize a problem" or, "Now I am going to evaluate alternative brands." Second, this, like any other process conceptualization, has some time dimension. In some instances some consumers may pass through this process in a matter of seconds, while in other situations (the purchase of a home, for example) the process may occur over several months or even years. Finally, as is discussed in a later section of this chapter, all phases do not always occur.

A decision-process conceptualization has been used in the analysis of decisions ranging in scope from the solution of a mathematical or chess puzzle to the choice of a college or a spouse. As a prominent psychologist has noted, "it is this type of formal analysis of the basic phases of the process which permits one to see the similar nature of all decision problems."[7]

Advantages　There are two major advantages over the distributive approach. First, relative to the distributive approach, it is a more sophisticated and elaborate view of consumer behavior. It views behavior as a *process* rather than as a discrete act and is as concerned with *how a decision is reached as it is with the decision itself*. While the distributive approach is concerned only with the decision, the process approach involves the stages in the decision-making process that precede and follow the decision as well as the decision itself. Thus, the process approach is a more extended view of consumer behavior.

Equally—if not more—important is the fact that the decision-process approach provides more information for marketing decision making. Knowledge about such things as the process resulting in problem recognition, the relative importance of various information sources, the criteria used to evaluate alternative brands, and so on, is useful in designing product, pricing, channel, and, particularly, advertising and sales strategies. For example, a manufacturer of color television sets feels that consumers are unable technically to evaluate the performance of competing brands but yet desire a set that is technologically sophisticated. As a consequence, their advertising claims that parts used in their sets are also utilized in the space program as well as the fact that they are used during national disasters and other events where technological sophistication and dependability are important. Presumably the campaign creates enough confidence in the technological ability of the company that consumers can be confident about the technological performance of the television set, even though most people are not capable of making such an evaluation. Additional applications of a decision-process approach to consumer behavior will be explored in considerable detail later.

---

[7]　Brim *et al., op. cit.,*[6] p. 11.

Limitations   A truly behavioral approach to the analysis and study of consumer behavior is a rather recent phenomenon. This, coupled with the fact that most behavioral research has been of a distributive rather than a decision-making orientation,[8] means that there is substantially less empirical work in the decision-process area than many researchers would like to see.

Another problem stems from the fact that most studies typically find a great deal of variation among consumers in decision-process behavior. These variations appear to result from complex interactions of many independent variables. The validity of studies in which these variables are not accounted for may be subject to question.[9]

A further difficulty is that most decision-process studies have investigated only one or relatively few stages in the process. Little is therefore known about the relation between phases or the influence of one phase configuration on other phases. Among other things, this means that there is no empirical evidence of the exact processes involved in either limited or habitual decision-process behavior. Consequently, this text examines all stages in the decision-making process, even though some of them may not always occur.

Other problems result from the absence of what might be called a decision-process research tradition. Researchers commonly use different definitions of concepts and often construct their own summary indexes for various types of decision-making behavior. This situation obviously hampers comparisons of findings, syntheses, and the development of a growing body of knowledge having the desired degree of fidelity.

Finally, despite the fact that decision-process behavior occurs over time most studies of the process have not used longitudinal research designs.[10] This design is unique in its ability to measure changes in behavior from one period to the next. As a consequence, most process studies suffer from memory errors and biases resulting from respondent-interviewer interaction that could be minimized if longitudinal designs were employed.[11]

Evaluation

While there are problems involved in conceptualizing and studying consumer behavior from a decision-process perspective, it is increasingly recognized that the advantages offered outweigh the limitations. For this reason the comprehensive models discussed in the preceding chapter as well as the model to be presented in the next section all embody this approach. The reader should, how-

---

[8]   Ferber, *op. cit.*,[2] pp. 19–63.

[9]   Donald H. Granbois, "The Role of Communication in the Family Decision Making Process," in Stephen A. Greyser (ed.), *Toward Scientific Marketing* (Chicago: Amer. Marketing Assoc., 1963), pp. 44–57, at p. 48.

[10]   Francesco M. Nicosia, "Panel Designs and Analyses in Marketing," in Peter D. Bennett (ed.), *Marketing and Economic Development* (Chicago: Amer. Marketing Assoc. 1965), pp. 222–243, at p. 228.

[11]   Donald H. Granbois and James F. Engel, "The Longitudinal Approach to Studying Marketing Behavior," in Bennett, *op. cit.*,[10] pp. 205–221, at p. 216.

ever, retain an awareness of the problems discussed here, because of the fact that many of the findings and concepts discussed elsewhere in the book must be considered tentative until subjected to further research.

A MULTIMEDIATION MODEL OF CONSUMER BEHAVIOR

The model to be presented in this chapter, which provides the conceptual framework for the book, has emerged as the authors have worked together for a number of years in teaching, research, and writing. The earliest published version was presented in 1966,[12] and a more sophisticated version was utilized in the first edition of this text in 1968 as well as in other works published by the authors.[13] Since the first edition of this text appeared, the study of consumer behavior has advanced considerably. In addition, the experience of the authors as well as many others both in the United States and abroad has indicated certain areas where revisions were needed. Therefore, the earlier model was modified in a number of ways with the purposes of (1) providing a better description of the behavioral process and (2) clarifying relationships between variables so that more precise guidance is given for research and other applications. Wherever possible, functional relationships between variables are specified.

The term "multimediation" is applied to this model and refers to the fact that many processes intervene or mediate between exposure to a stimulus and final outcomes of behavior. As a result, many factors affect the outcome. This particular terminology has become common in the behavioral sciences.[14]

In this introductory chapter only anecdotal support is given for the model (that is, it is used to explain two distinctly different behavioral episodes). The more rigorous theoretical and empirical foundations are explored in later chapters. It should be noted, however, that a complex model of behavior never can be proven or validated in any final sense, as the discussion of the Howard–Sheth model in Chapter 2 indicated. [15] The only present criteria for accepting one over another are (1) does it make sense both in terms of intuition and existing knowledge, and (2) do predictions deduced from the model come true? A number of

---

[12]   James F. Engel and M. L. Light, "The Role of Psychological Commitment in Consumer Behavior: An Evaluation of the Theory of Cognitive Dissonance," in Frank M. Bass, Charles W. King, and Edgar A. Pessemier (eds.), *Application of the Sciences in Marketing Management* (New York: Wiley, 1968), pp. 39–68.

[13]   James F. Engel, Martin R. Warshaw, and Hugh G. Wales, *Promotional Strategy*, rev. ed. (Homewood, Ill.: Irwin, 1971); David T. Kollat, Roger D. Blackwell, and James F. Robeson, *Strategic Marketing* (New York: Holt, Rinehart and Winston, 1972).

[14]   See, for example, W. J. McGuire, "Personality and Susceptibility to Social Influence," in E. F. Borgatta and W. W. Lambert (eds.), *Handbook of Personality Theory and Research* (Chicago: Rand McNally, 1968).

[15]   D. R. Lehmann, T. V. O'Brien, F. U. Farley, and J. A. Howard, "Empirical Contributions to Buyer Behavior Theory," unpublished paper, (New York: Columbia University, May, 1971).

differing approaches could satisfy criteria, with the result that there probably never will be one *best* model.

The Individual's Psychological Makeup

The important components of the individual's "black box" or psychological makeup are presented in Figure 3.1.

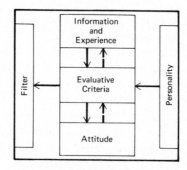

Figure 3.1   CENTRAL CONTROL UNIT

The *central control unit* (CCU) is the psychological command center, so to speak, for it includes both memory and the basic facilities for thinking and directing behavior. The primary components for purposes of understanding consumer behavior are information and experience, evaluative criteria, and attitudes, each of which, in turn, is affected by personality. These variables interact to form a filter through which incoming stimuli are processed. Each is an integral component with its own unique function as will become apparent shortly.

Stored Information and Experience   The consumer learns from experience and retains this information in either conscious or unconscious memory. Thus the individual learns to respond to stimuli of all types in consistent and predictable ways. These tendencies to classify and respond to stimuli correctly are sometimes referred to as *stimulus influences* in perception. Other information is retained in a less organized fashion, but it also is of importance in what the individual thinks and does.

The memory content of consumers in a target market segment is of relevance to marketing strategy. It is necessary to determine what consumers know with respect to available alternatives and their attributes, because this will directly affect buying action. A frequent advertising objective, for example, is to increase awareness of product features.

Evaluative Criteria   The term "evaluative criteria" refers to specifications used by a consumer to compare alternatives such as products and brands. Examples are price, performance, and durability. These criteria are concrete manifestations of his personality (traits and motives), stored information, and various social influences. Their purpose is to serve as standards or guide lines against which alternatives are compared and evaluated.

Management must be aware of criteria utilized by prospects in target market segments, because alternatives which fail to meet these specifications probably never will qualify in the decision-making process. In addition, they usually must be accepted as a "given," because they are a manifestation of deeper psychological processes and hence resist change. The resulting implications are explored in depth in Chapter 10.

Attitudes Toward Alternatives An attitude is defined as a mental and neural state of readiness to respond which is organized through experience and exerts a directive and/or dynamic influence on behavior.[16] More specifically, attitudes toward alternatives reflect an evaluation of a product, brand, or store along the evaluative criteria stored in the central control unit.[17] All things being equal, the alternatives with the highest rating summed across the evaluative criteria have the greatest probability of being purchased and consumed.

Reference to Figure 3.1 indicates that attitude is a function of information and experience and evaluative criteria. The direct relationship shown by the solid arrows occurs because the rating along evaluative criteria must be made on the basis of stored information and experience. Therefore, both evaluative criteria and stored information are legitimately conceived as components of attitude.

A dashed line also connects these variables indicating a feedback relationship. The feedback effect results from the fact that, once attitudes are formed, there tends to be a restriction on changes in evaluative criteria and stored information through filtering of incoming information to eliminate that which is contradictory.

Personality Each individual has certain ways of thinking, behaving, and responding that make him unique. The sum total of these factors is referred to here as personality.

Personality is depicted in Figure 3.1 as exerting a direct influence on evaluative criteria. As was discussed above, evaluative criteria are a product specific manifestation of underlying values, traits, and motives.

There are many ways in which knowledge of personality patterns among members of a target market segment are of use in marketing planning. For example, advertising copy can be much more effective if the artists and writers have a rich understanding of the total lifestyle of those to whom they are writing. Many other examples are given in Chapter 12.

---

[16] G. Allport, "Attitudes," in C. Murchison (ed.), *Handbook of Social Psychology* (Worcester, Mass.: Clark University Press, 1935), pp. 798–884.

[17] This conception is consistent with one which is now widely accepted in both psychology and marketing. See I. Ajzen and M. Fishbein, "Attitudinal and Normative Variables as Predictors of Specific Behavior: A Review of Research Generated by a Theoretical Model," paper presented at the Workshop on Attitude Research and Consumer Behavior, University of Illinois (Dec., 1970).

Filter All of the variables in the CCU interact to form a filter through which incoming stimuli are processed. Some stimuli will be discarded, whereas others will be attenuated. This occurs because the central nervous system cannot attend to all stimuli which are received and must, therefore, be selective.

It is increasingly evident that some type of filter exists for this purpose, but its exact nature and function are unclear. These issues are discussed in Chapter 8, but it is worth pointing out that initial filtration apparently is made on the basis of such stimulus properties as loudness and pitch.[18] Following the initial screening, further evaluation appears to be made in terms of stimulus *pertinence* or importance. It is at this point that the stored dispositions within the CCU act to regulate the flow of incoming information.[19] Authorities disagree on the exact details, but it is certain that the filter screens incoming stimuli and admits those that the individual wants to process and store in memory.

Information Processing

Incoming stimuli pass through the filter within the CCU and are processed in four distinct phases: (1) exposure, (2) attention, (3) comprehension, and (4) retention. These are shown in Figure 3.2 in sequential fashion as indicated by the solid arrows specifying linkages. Each stage, however, does not have an automatic relation with its immediately preceding stage. In other words, a stimulus is not necessarily comprehended, even though it captures attention. Other processes within the CCU act within the filter to shape the final outcome. The continuing influence of the CCU in this process is shown by arrows into the filter and back as feedback at each stage.

Exposure Everyone is continually bombarded with stimuli of all types which fall into two categories: (1) physical and (2) social. These most often are

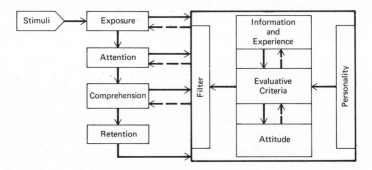

Figure 3.2 INFORMATION PROCESSING

---

[18] J. Deutsch and D. Deutsch, "Attention: Some Theoretical Considerations," *Psychological Rev.*, vol. 70, pp. 80–90 (1963).

[19] A. Treisman, "Selective Attention in Man," *Brit. Medical Bull.*, vol. 29, pp. 369–379 (1964).

received by the five senses (sensory receptors) in the form of a physical sensation (from the firing of a retinal cone or other physiological reaction).

One important stimulus input, of course, is the array of available purchase alternatives. Others include demands of family members, expected patterns of behavior in social settings (norms), and the behavior of friends. Still others are physical factors such as weather or the volume of traffic on a highway.

Attention   At this stage actual processing of the stimulus begins. Attention is defined as ". . . the taking possession by the mind, in clear and vivid form, of one out of what seems several simultaneously possible objects or trains of thought."[20] Attention is known to be highly selective, as was mentioned earlier, and much of the relevant evidence on this important subject is reviewed in Chapter 8.

If the individual is aroused by a state of bodily need, for example, it is logical to expect that he will be highly selective in what he sees, hears, touches, feels, and smells. In a sense, the aroused need activates an "on-off" switch to attention. He now is especially alert to those inputs which are relevant in satisfying the aroused drive. For example, assume that it is lunch time and the consumer has gone without breakfast. It is quite probable that attention will focus on those stimuli that are known from experience to be hunger satisfying. Thus, a picture of a juicy steak in a restaurant window or a big piece of chocolate cake in an advertisement are now likely to be noticed, whereas previously they were largely ignored.

Because selective attention is such a common phenomenon, it is of major importance in designing marketing programs. Stimuli must be developed so as to maximize the probability of being processed. It is becoming increasingly necessary to utilize measures of attention attraction before investment of funds in a marketing program. Recently several tools have proved to be especially promising for this purpose, all of which are discussed in Chapter 13. These include galvanic skin response (GSR) which appears to measure a state of general arousal and receptivity and pupil dilation response (PDR) which assesses load processing activity within the central control unit. Both offer a relatively direct way of measuring attention.[21]

Comprehension   Attention is a necessary but not sufficient precondition for comprehension. The CCU filter also serves to attenuate further and distort the stimulus input in such a manner that certain attributes are amplified whereas others are diminished or ignored. It is common for prospects to miss the point of a persuasive communication and attribute a meaning that never was intended. Often this distortion occurs to make the stimulus more consonant with the indi-

---

[20]   William James, *The Principles of Psychology,* vol. 1 (New York: Henry Holt, 1890), p. 403.

[21]   For an analysis of these measures, see J. S. Hensel, "Physiological Measures of Advertising Effectiveness: A Theoretical and Empirical Investigation," unpublished dissertation, (Columbus, Ohio: Ohio State University, 1970).

vidual's own beliefs and preferences. For example, the consumer with a preference for a particular brand of coffee brewed using traditional home methods may completely disregard taste test results documenting that freeze dried coffee tastes better than home brewed. This distortion can occur even though the consumer was exposed to, and attended, the freeze dried coffee message.

Retention   Information processing is selective in yet a third way. Those stimuli which finally become stored in conscious memory are a smaller set than the initial set. Not every comprehended message enters into working memory, because there is a known tendency to retain those stimuli which are consonant with CCU dispositions. The freeze dried coffee message probably would not be retained, for example, even if it were correctly comprehended. Retention is easily measured using question–answer methods following exposure.

The Decision Process

The decision process begins with problem recognition and proceeds through four other stages: (1) internal search and alternative evaluation, (2) external search and alternative evaluation, (3) purchasing processes, and (4) outcomes. Each stage is discussed in this section, although it should be emphasized once again that they are not present in every purchase decision. Those variations which occur are the subject of the concluding section of the chapter.

Problem Recognition   Problem recognition is depicted in Figure 3.3, and it occurs when the individual perceives a difference between an ideal and an actual state. Awareness of an external stimulus can be one initiating influence.[22]

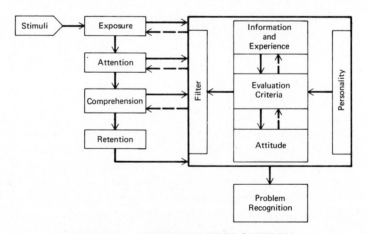

Figure 3.3   PROBLEM RECOGNITION

***

[22]   J. McV. Hunt, "Motivation Inherent in Information Processing and Action," in O. J. Harvey (ed.), *Motivation and Social Interaction* (New York: Ronald, 1963), pp. 35–95.

Assume that a consumer is thumbing through a magazine and sees an advertisement for a German chocolate cake mix. The picture of the cake, in itself, can serve to make him feel hungry and thereby initiate behavior. Such an outcome, however, will not occur in all situations, because the incoming stimulus can be screened out or distorted if it conflicts with his dispositions.

Problem recognition can occur through need activation which causes the individual to become alert, responsive, and vigilant because of the resulting feelings of discomfort.[23] The result is arousal of a state of *drive* which energizes need-satisfying action. The consumer, for example, becomes thirsty. In this situation a physiological need has aroused a state of drive, and the resulting feelings of discomfort initiate appropriate action. The ideal state, of course, is absence of thirst, and the aroused drive signifies that the actual state is short of the ideal.

Finally, problem recognition can be activated through a process of *autistic thinking*. Everyone has had the experience of thinking about a desirable consumption object and then being aroused to act.

Not every perceived discrepancy between actual and ideal, however, will result in problem recognition. There is a minimum level of perceived difference which must be surpassed before a problem is recognized. This threshold probably is learned and will vary with circumstances.

Action also can be constrained by the intervention of external influences as is represented in Figure 3.4. A family might recognize that a new automobile is needed and make purchase plans. A sudden change in income, however, can intervene to make this action an impossibility. A *hold* is thus introduced in the decision-making process; the recognized problem remains but action is postponed until the constraints are removed. A variety of factors can enter into the decision process as constraints, including cultural values, conflicting family

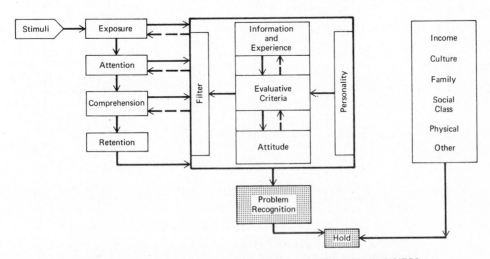

Figure 3.4 CONSTRAINTS ON THE DECISION PROCESS

---

23   D. O. Hebb, *The Organization of Behavior* (New York: Wiley, 1949).

desires, and so on. This also will affect all of the other stages in the process as will be shown later.

Alternative Evaluation   Once a problem is recognized and no constraints intervene to halt the decision process, the consumer must then assess the alternatives for action. The initial step will be a search of stored information and experience to determine whether or not alternatives are known and have been satisfactorily evaluated. If that does not prove to be sufficient, external search will be activated. These two phases of alternative evaluation are illustrated in Figure 3.5. Notice that the feedback of information from the two stages of search is depicted by the dashed lines. Also, the influence of environmental factors can introduce a hold in the process at either stage.

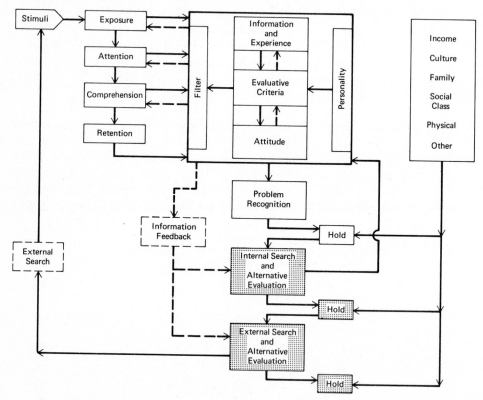

Figure 3.5 ALTERNATIVE EVALUATION: INTERNAL AND EXTERNAL SEARCH

(1) *Internal Search*   Internal search occurs instantaneously and largely unconsciously. If feedback shows that attitudes toward alternatives are formed and fully operative, it is probable, all other things being equal, that remaining stages in the decision process will be circumvented and the most preferred alternative purchased. If this is not the case, internal search will probe further to

inquire if evaluative criteria are formed and if there is a sufficient information base to permit alternative evaluation. In the event that further information is needed, external search is activated.

(2) *External Search*   In routine problem-solving behavior, external search generally will not be activated, because internal search has proved sufficient to identify the preferred alternative. Extended problem solving, however, can be quite different. A husband and wife, for instance, may make a decision to purchase a color television but have little or no awareness of the advantages and limitations of available brands. They may not, in addition, know the appropriate criteria to use in alternative evaluation. Hence, they will consult friends and relatives, read advertisements, consult product-rating agencies, or turn to other external information sources. Search will continue until information feedback signifies that enough is known to proceed.

There are individual differences in willingness to engage in external search. First, some people are known to be cautious and unwilling to act even when alternatives are known because of the perceived risk of a wrong decision. Hence additional justification is sought through further information. In other situations, however, an opposite result will be noted. This is when an awareness develops that the time and energy required for search outweigh any expected gains, even though the existing information base is insufficient.

The Purchase Process and Its Outcomes   The preceding steps lead to a decision to buy which then is acted upon through a purchase process. Decision making does not necessarily cease at this stage, however, because there still may be a necessity to select the appropriate outlet and to engage in negotiation before the purchase is made. These processes are discussed in Chapters 20 and 21. This stage is depicted in Figure 3.6 as well as two possible outcomes of purchase: (1) postpurchase evaluation and (2) further behavior.

(1) *Postpurchase Evaluation*   Once a family has purchased a television set they may doubt that the correct brand was selected. This is especially likely if the purchase is financially burdensome and several alternatives were rejected. The husband and wife now might be sensitive to information confirming their choice and thereby reducing this stage of postdecision dissonance. As Figure 3.6 designates, they may search for information to relieve doubts. This action, if it occurs at all, is seen only under extended problem-solving behavior, because it would be rare to have dissonance when there has been no prepurchase evaluation of other alternatives.

Dissonance, of course, is not the only outcome of purchase. It also is possible that problems with the product and its benefits can lead to a reconsideration of evaluation criteria. In this case the consumer learns from experience and will avoid mistakes of the same type in the future.

Obviously, the most common outcome is satisfaction with the purchase. This would serve to reinforce existing attitudes and the evaluative criteria on which they are based, in which case the probability of the same act in the future is strengthened.

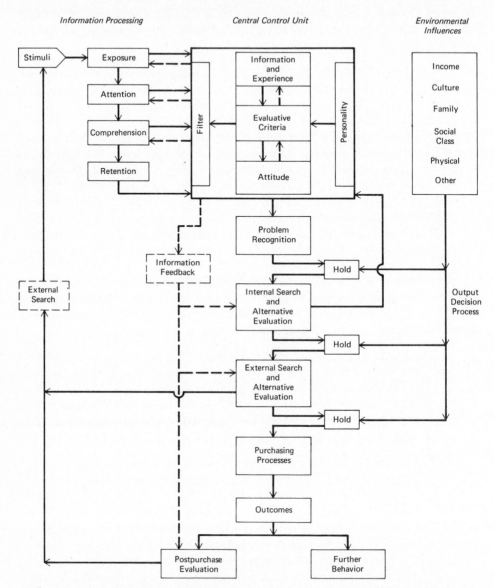

Figure 3.6   COMPLETE MODEL OF CONSUMER BEHAVIOR SHOWING PUR-
CHASING PROCESSES AND OUTCOMES

(2) *Further Behavior*   The outcome also can change circumstances and
thus trigger additional action. Assume that the purchase demands outlay of a
substantial sum of money to be procured through a loan. This means that a decision now must be made on the best type of financing. Behavior is sequential, and
one act rarely can be considered apart from its consequences.

Variation in Decision Processes

The model shown in Figure 3.6 is a complete representation of the most comprehensive type of decision-making, extended problem solving. It was previously noted, however, that most decisions are made on the basis of habit or routine. It is the purpose of this section to explore these variations and the underlying determinants.

Limited and Habitual Decision-Process Behavior   In a number of instances, internal search will not provide adequate information for evaluation of known alternatives. In other words, there is no need to procure information about the domain of feasible alternatives, but because not enough is known about each to permit a sound decision. This is referred to as *limited decision-process behavior*, and it also is represented by Figure 3.6.

The simplest and perhaps most common type of action is illustrated in Figure 3.7, *habitual decision-process behavior*. The sequence moves directly from internal search to the purchase. External constraints may be operative to halt the decision or delay its culmination, but their effect is likely to be much less under these circumstances. Postdecision evaluation usually will not occur because of the routine that is involved. In all other respects the process is identical to that discussed earlier. Thus the distinction between three types of decision making is more one of degree than of kind.

Determinants of the Type of Decision Process[24]   The consumer often will perceive some risk in the purchase and consumption of goods and services. Risk may be financial, physical, social, or some combination of the three.[25] Decision making, particularly external search, occurs in order to reduce perceived risk to tolerable levels.[26]

Specific ways in which decision making may reduce perceived risk flow from a consideration of the factors influencing both the degree of perceived risk and its importance to the consumer. Although fragmentary, and often lacking in fidelity, the evidence suggests that four types of variables affect the extent of decision making: (1) situational variables, (2) product characteristics, (3) consumer characteristics, and (4) environmental factors.

(1) *Situational Variables*   Consumers have a higher probability of engaging in extended decision-process behavior when:

---

[24]   This section is adapted from Donald H. Granbois, "Research Approaches to Decision Making in the Family," unpublished review article (Bloomington, Ind.: Indiana University Graduate School of Business, 1964), pp. 22–25.

[25]   Raymond A. Bauer, "Consumer Behavior as Risk Taking," in Robert S. Hancock (ed.), *Dynamic Marketing for a Changing World* (Chicago: Amer. Marketing Assoc., 1960), pp. 389–398, at p. 390.

[26]   Bauer, *op. cit.*[25]

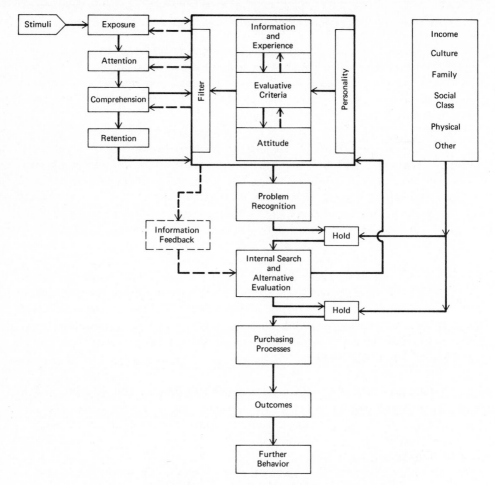

Figure 3.7 HABITUAL DECISION-PROCESS BEHAVIOR

(a) There has been little or no relevant experience because an individual has never purchased the product.

(b) There is no past experience because the product is new.

(c) Past experience is perceived as obsolete because the product is purchased infrequently.

(d) Past experience with the product has been unsatisfactory.[27]

(e) The purchase is considered to be discretionary rather than necessary.[28]

---

[27] These four situational variables have been investigated in George Katona, *The Mass Consumption Society* (New York: McGraw-Hill, 1964), pp. 289–290.

[28] George Katona and Eva Mueller, "A Study of Purchase Decisions," in Lincoln H. Clark (ed.), *Consumer Behavior: The Dynamics of Consumer Reaction* (New York: New York University Press, 1965), pp. 30–87, at p. 80.

(f)   The purchase is considered to be particularly important; for example, a gift.[29]

(g)   The purchase is socially "visible."[30]

(2) *Product Characteristics*   Extended decision-process behavior is more likely to occur when:

(a)   The consumer feels committed to the product for an extended period of time, so that future needs and/or product performance are difficult to forecast.[31]

(b)   The consumer perceives available alternatives as having both desirable and undesirable attributes.[32]

(c)   The product is high priced relative to the consumer's income.[33]

(3) *Consumer Characteristics*   Decision-process behavior is more likely to be extended rather than limited or habitual when:[34]

(a)   The consumer has a college education.

(b)   The consumer is in the middle-income category as opposed to high or low income. (Middle income is defined in this case as $5000–$7500.)

(c)   The consumer is under 35 years old.

(d)   The consumer's occupation falls in the white-collar class.

(e)   The consumer enjoys "shopping around."

(f)   The consumer perceives no urgent or immediate need for the product.

(4) *Environmental Factors*   Consumers have a higher probability of engaging in extended decision-process behavior when:

(a)   A difference is perceived between an individual's customary behavior and that of a group to which he belongs and/or an important reference group.[35]

(b)   There is disagreement among family members about requirements and/or the relative desirability of alternatives.[36]

(c)   Strong new stimuli or precipitating circumstances exist. These may consist of general news (threat of war, inflation, and so on) or of news regarding specific products that may be transmitted by advertisers.[37]

---

[29]   Katona, *op. cit.,*[27] pp. 289–290.

[30]   Dahl, *et al., op. cit.,*[1] pp. 134–135.

[31]   Donald Granbois, *op. cit.,*[24] p. 24.

[32]   James F. Engel, "Psychology and the Business Sciences," *Quart. Rev. Economics and Business,* vol. 1, pp. 75–83 (1961).

[33]   Katona, *op. cit.,*[27] pp. 289–290.

[34]   All consumer characteristics were obtained from the Katona and Mueller, *op. cit.,*[28] p. 80.

[35]   Katona, *op. cit.,*[27] pp. 289–290.

[36]   Granbois, *op. cit.,*[24] p. 24.

[37]   Katona, *op. cit.,*[27] pp. 289–290.

Many factors, then, are likely to evoke extended decision-process behavior. The extent of decision making varies greatly depending on the consumer and his social environment as well as certain product and situational characteristics.

USING THE MODEL TO EXPLAIN CONSUMER BEHAVIOR

The discussion of the model and its components has, by necessity, been brief, and it is useful to trace two distinctly different buying situations: (1) the purchase of a small automobile and (2) the purchase of a laundry detergent.

While the discussion thus far has largely centered on an individual consumer, it is clear that social influences are important. The outcomes from one person's actions can serve as inputs for others. The model, therefore, can easily be utilized to explain the buying process of a family as well as that of an individual.

The Purchase of a Small Automobile

For most consumers the purchase of a new domestic automobile manufactured to compete with foreign imports will require extended problem-solving behavior. Experience with the Vega, Pinto, or Gremlin is limited by their newness, the financial commitment is considerable, and the psychological stakes in selecting the right alternative are high.

A research study in the Columbus, Ohio, market shed considerable light on how people undertake this type of problem solving.[38] Two samples were interviewed by telephone: (1) all purchasers of Ford Pinto from the date of introduction through November 1, 1970, and (2) a comparable group of purchasers of the Volkswagen (VW) during the same period. The interview focused on differences in buyer characteristics as well as variations in buying behavior.

Demographic and Personality Differences   Pinto buyers tend to concentrate in the following demographic categories:

25–44 years of age (48 percent)
Incomes between $15,000 and $19,999 (29 percent) or $7500–$9999 (27 percent)
One or two family members (42 percent)
Home owners (61 percent)
Husband is prime user (50 percent), wife is prime user (30 percent)

The VW purchaser is different in several respects:

---

[38]   Undertaken as a graduate class project at The Ohio State University under a grant from the Ford Motor Company.

16–24 years of age (40 percent)
Income between $10,000 and $14,999 (38 percent)
Three or four family members (62 percent)
Home owners (62 percent)
Husband is prime user (58 percent), wife is prime user (20 percent)

Therefore, the Pinto buyer tends to be somewhat older and is concentrated in either a relatively low or relatively high income class, is either single or married with no children, and the wife is the prime user to a greater extent.

Not surprisingly, the great majority of Pinto buyers (76 percent) classed themselves as willing to try new brands, versus 53 percent of VW buyers. As such, they view themselves as innovators who are receptive to new product concepts.

Problem Recognition Problem recognition usually occurs from factors beyond the marketer's control. In the purchase of a new automobile, for example, a problem becomes recognized most frequently when the currently owned vehicle becomes unsatisfactory for a variety of reasons. This may be generated by mechanical wear.

Alternative Evaluation Figure 3.8 depicts in summary form the evaluative criteria which were felt to be important. Both groups rate mileage and purchase price as being dominant, but VW buyers seem to place greater importance on maintenance costs and handling, even though the rank order is the same. Safety ranks fifth, but after this point some major differences emerge. The Pinto buyer placed more emphasis on such factors as styling and comfort, whereas the VW owner was more concerned with the warranty.

(1) *Attitudes toward Alternatives* Respondents also were asked to rate Pinto, VW, and Vega along the various evaluative criteria in order to generate an attitude rating. There is a tendency to rate one's current alternative high in all respects, but there are some significant variations nonetheless. Figure 3.9 shows the percentages of those who considered an evaluative criterion to be important *and* also rated their make as being superior along that dimension.

Notice that Pinto owners rate their own make to be *lowest* on the two criteria which they previously indicated to be most important. VW owners, on the other hand, rate their car to be superior in these terms. Therefore, those who purchased Pinto deliberately sacrificed in mileage and price to gain what they perceived to be advantages in maintenance costs, safety, handling, styling, and comfort. These appear to be the product advantages which Pinto has over the VW in the buyers' eyes. These factors, in turn, should be emphasized in Ford advertising, whereas mileage and price should receive only secondary consideration at best.

The Pinto, of course, was designed to make significant inroads into the imported car market. From these data some interesting problems are highlighted.

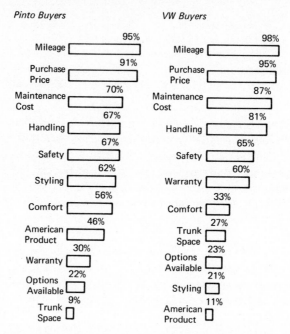

Figure 3.8 RESPONDENT RATINGS OF EVALUATIVE CRITERIA IN TERMS OF IMPORTANCE IN THE PURCHASE DECISION

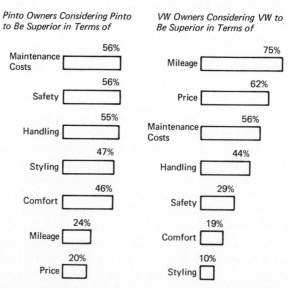

Figure 3.9 RESPONDENT RATINGS OF THE AUTOMOBILE THEY PURCHASED AS BEING SUPERIOR ALONG EVALUATIVE CRITERIA

Pinto really cannot compete in terms of mileage and price, the very features most desired by the VW buyer. Handling, styling, and comfort are only minor criteria, and these seem to be the factors on which Pinto excels. It would appear, therefore, on the basis of these data, that only a small percentage of VW buyers will switch to Pinto unless some changes are made in Ford's marketing program.

(2) *External Search for Information*   Not surprisingly, the primary source of information that attracted respondents to the make they purchased was magazines for Pinto buyers (26 percent) as opposed to word-of-mouth for VW buyers (58 percent). The long-standing success of the VW accounts for the heavy emphasis on personal communication, whereas the mass media play a greater role for a new product. Newspapers (16 percent) and television (15 percent) also were important media for the Pinto.

Most buyers of both makes (68 percent) did not seek further information before visiting a dealer. Of those purchasers of VW who did seek more information, most turned once again to friends and relatives, whereas buyers of Pinto made use of the mass media in roughly equal proportions.

(3) *Makes Considered*   Of those who purchased the VW, 38 percent considered only VW, but nearly 30 percent gave some consideration to purchasing a Pinto. Most apparently did not seriously pursue the Pinto option, however. On the other hand, only 17 percent of those who purchased Pinto confined their consideration to that one make. It is interesting to point out, however, that less than 25 percent contemplated an import, whereas the great majority considered only a domestic make. It thus appears that most buyers of the Pinto would not have purchased an import and that the potential inroads into the market for the imports may be less than was initially thought.

Purchase Process   The great majority of both groups shopped less than one week, and almost all confined their shopping period to one month or less. Similarly, most of those interviewed visited only one dealer before purchasing. Therefore, the prospective buyer of Pinto or VW has a high predisposition to act once he enters the dealership. It apparently is felt that there is little to be gained from price bargaining across multiple dealerships.

Once in the dealership the role of the salesman most often is considered to be only of minor importance. VW purchasers, however, are more likely to rate the salesman as being very important (35 percent versus 18 percent). On the other hand, 74 percent of the Pinto buyers indicated that the test drive was important in their decision, versus only 36 percent of VW buyers. This underscores the role the Pinto salesman plays in encouraging the prospect to get behind the wheel. Therefore, a major role still remains for salesmanship within the dealership.

Postpurchase Evaluation   A surprisingly high percentage of both groups (almost 100 percent) indicated satisfaction with their car once it was delivered. Economy is the feature most liked about both makes (mentioned by approximately two thirds of the respondents). Pinto buyers also mentioned such aesthetic qualities as style, whereas the VW owner was more likely to mention his satisfaction with performance and dependability.

Implications Many implications for marketing strategy emerge from this study. It would appear, for example, that the Pinto will not make major inroads into the foreign car market unless considerable emphasis is placed on performance features as opposed to style and comfort. On the other hand, there appears to be a prime segment for Pinto that desires these features and is less predisposed to consider a foreign make. The mass media play a significant role in stimulating awareness and interest, but the salesman in the showroom must be motivated to get the prospect to take a test drive before a sale will be consumated.

The VW, on the other hand, is well entrenched and benefits from substantial word-of-mouth communication. While the salesman in the showroom is still considered to be of significance, both advertising and selling are of less importance than the efforts of satisfied customers. This automobile is purchased on the basis of price and performance, and only a minority of those in this segment evidence a strong interest in the comfort and style features offered by the Pinto. Therefore, it would appear that the VW will continue to retain a substantial market share without major changes in the product or other marketing efforts.

The Purchase of a Laundry Detergent [39]

Laundry detergents generally are purchased on the basis of habit rather than extended problem solving. A problem is recognized when the housewife runs out of detergent, and her decision usually calls for purchase of a preferred brand on her next visit to the grocery store. There is no need to engage in conscious weighing of alternatives or external search for information. The situation changes, of course, when a significant new product comes on the market, but innovations of that magnitude are a rarity in this industry.

Survey results showed that women evaluate a detergent on the following bases: (1) cleaning ability (96 percent), (2) low suds (54 percent), (3) safety to colors (48 percent), (4) whitening and brightening ability (44 percent), (5) price (31 percent), and (6) fresh smell (20 percent). In addition to these evaluative criteria, 86 percent favored a powdered form, and 60 percent prefer to use warm water.

Several major brands were found to rate highest on these criteria, with Tide being the dominant favorite. These ratings of brand attitude closely paralleled market shares. The result is strong loyalty toward one or two preferred brands and only relatively small incidence of permanent brand switching. If the housewife does switch it tends to be a temporary action to take advantage of a price reduction.

Those who were interviewed, for the most part, evidenced satisfaction

---

[39] This section is based on a study undertaken at The Ohio State University for classroom purposes in cooperation with the Procter and Gamble Company.

with their present alternative. Postdecision evaluation, therefore, seldom takes place.

It becomes difficult under this type of decision making based on strong brand loyalty to induce a brand switch through marketing efforts. Thus, the objectives for the leading manufacturers usually call for maintenance of the present market share through continual product improvement to prevent competitive inroads and a high level of advertising to retain present levels of awareness and preference. Also it is important to feature price reductions through coupons and other means both to stimulate consumer purchase and to generate interest by retailers in stocking and displaying the product.

SUMMARY

This chapter has provided the conceptual framework for the remainder of the book. A conceptual model was presented which delineates the psychological variables which are of greatest significance in understanding consumer motivation and behavior (stored information, evaluative criteria, attitude toward alternatives, personality), the perceptual process (stimulus inputs into a filter, attention, comprehension, and retention), the decision process (problem recognition, internal search, external search, purchase, and outcomes), and the influence of external constraining forces (norms, family income, and so on). Each of these variables and processes is discussed at length elsewhere in the book. The chapter concluded with two examples of consumer studies where this model was utilized to gain insights into decision processes and necessary marketing strategies.

REVIEW AND DISCUSSION QUESTIONS

1. Distinguish among the distributive, morphological, and analytical approaches to the study of consumer behavior.

2. What are the major problems associated with a distributive approach to consumer behavior?

3. How might a large manufacturer of automatic washers and dryers use a decision-process approach to better understand how consumers purchase his product?

4. Mrs. Jones is ironing and watching her favorite afternoon soap opera, which is on the air from 2:30 to 3:00 P.M. There are seven commercials in 30 minutes, and she does not leave the room. Yet she cannot recall a single commercial after the show has ended, whereas she can recount the plot of the story in detail. What explanations can be given?

5. Much buying supposedly occurs on impulse, that is, a person sees a display or other stimulus and buys with little or no forethought. Can impulse behavior be accounted for in the model? How?

6. In analyzing the entire model, is it complete in the sense of encompassing all the major elements in the psychological field? What changes, if any, might be made?

7. Compare and contrast the decision processes that might be involved in the purchase of a sport coat if the purchase is represented as (a) extended decision-process behavior, (b) limited decision-process behavior, (c) habitual decision-process behavior. Which type of decision making would be most likely? Why?

8. Indicate which type of decision making would be most likely in each of the following situations (assume all other things are equal): (a) past experience with the product has been unsatisfactory, (b) the product is purchased each week, (c) a new home has been purchased, (d) the consumer earns less than $3000 per year, (e) the product is needed immediately.

9. What is meant by the lack of a decision-process research tradition? How can this lack be remedied?

10. What is meant by perceived risk? What is the relevance of this concept?

11. Discuss the relations that exist between (a) problem recognition and attitudes, (b) external search and perception, (c) alternative evaluation and attitudes, (d) postpurchase evaluation and the central control unit.

12. "Charles Terwilliger is a high school senior and faces the dilemma of choosing a college. He is a good student and has made all-state mention as defensive end in football. His father is a graduate of a well-known eastern school and would like to see Charles go there. Two schools in his home state have offered him football scholarships, and one has twice been national champion in the past five years. Charles's three best friends, however, are going to live at home and go to the local university, whereas the girl he has dated for three years will be attending a university on the West Coast, 2000 miles away. He has applied to all of these schools and has been accepted. He needs financial aid and plans to become a consulting engineer. Finally he accepts the football tender at the school in his state which has been national champion; in addition, this university has a good engineering curriculum. The problem, though, is that he has no friends there and has no real desire to join a fraternity, the apparent key to popularity." To test your grasp of the model presented in this chapter, explain what must have happened during and after this decision. Make any assumptions that are necessary.

Group Influences on Consumer Behavior

In the preceding chapters, the decision processes of consumers have been presented in brief outline form. Now the task is to begin to examine the determinants of behavior in much more detail.

The question can be asked: Where should one begin in the effort to understand why people do the things they do and make the choices they make? Although a variety of answers is available to that question, one logical beginning is with the cultural or group influences that shape and influence a person into what is thought of as "human" behavior. Some of these influences become operative with the first "cooing" and smiling of the human group that surrounds a newborn baby. The influences continue throughout a lifetime and include such direct participation of others in consumer processes as when a friend expresses his approval of a purchase or even accompanies the buyer to the store to offer opinions concerning the choice.

Four chapters analyze the group influences on consumer behavior. They present some of the most interesting and important—yet often neglected and misunderstood—aspects of the study of consumer behavior.

Chapter 4 analyzes one of the broadest categories of group behavior that can be observed—culture. Culture refers to the learned patterns of behavior and symbolism that are passed from one generation to another and represents the totality of values that characterize a society. This chapter contains a substantial description of methods for studying culture including the potential of a cross-cultural approach to understanding consumer behavior both on a national basis and for subcultures within a society.

American values are changing. Chapter 4 analyzes the fundamental forces affecting these changes, including institutional changes and early lifetime experiences within the American society. This chapter concludes with a discussion of emerging American values, especially the impact that attitudes associated with youthfulness appear to have upon the total culture.

Is social class becoming more or less important as a phenomenon in the American culture? Chapter 5 analyzes this issue and the entire process of stratification. Social classes have the important task of transmitting cultural behavior patterns to specific groups of families. This chapter describes the Warner six-class classification system and the distinctive consumption patterns that appear to characterize each class. In addition, this chapter reviews a substantial amount of empirical research relating to the decision process approach to understanding consumer behavior.

Chapter 6 describes reference group and subcultural influences on behavior. The role of reference groups as inputs to the learning of attitudes is discussed as well as the role of reference groups in society as conformity-enforcing devices. Reference groups are also important in evaluations of an individual's self-concept.

Black consumer behavior has emerged in the last few years in the white consciousness. Along with this new consciousness is an emerging literature dealing with the black subculture. The chapter concludes with a description of the empirical conclusions of this literature.

Chapter 7 concludes this section of the book with a discussion of family influences on consumer behavior. This chapter describes the basic terminology used in discussing family structure as well as findings concerning the ways families transmit culture to individuals and affect cultural patterns of family decision-making.

4

THE CULTURAL CONTEXT OF CONSUMER BEHAVIOR

Culture is the underlying determinant of human decision making. While psychology describes *how* human choices are made, anthropology and the study of culture explains *why* some choices are preferred over others. A realistic analysis of consumer choice, therefore, must include understanding of the cultural context which molds human desires and shapes human decision making. This chapter focuses upon the values of human groups and the interactions between individuals rather than the individuals themselves. Such a perspective is sometimes described as culturalogical rather than psychological in nature.[1]

Smaller groups within the larger society develop their own culture. Included in the culture are characteristic solutions to consumption problems as well as many other forms of behavior. When speaking of the culture of the smaller groups within the larger society, it is common to speak of these forms of behavior as a subculture. In the chapters that follow, a closer examination is provided of some social and racial subcultures.

---

[1] Amplification of this perspective is found in the many works of Leslie White. Especially see Leslie White, *The Evolution of Culture* (New York: McGraw-Hill, 1959). An opposing position to White's emphasis on cultural determinism is found in Herbert J. Muller, *Freedom in the Modern World* (New York: Harper & Row, 1966).

NATURE OF CULTURE

"Culture" is a term used in many varied ways. Two anthropologists once studied 164 definitions of culture and wrote a book about the varying definitions.[2] They concluded that it is not yet possible to find a completely satisfactory definition that applies to all usages.

Culture is used in this book to mean the *complex of values, ideas, attitudes, and other meaningful symbols created by man to shape human behavior and the artifacts of that behavior as they are transmitted from one generation to the next.*[3] Culture *does not* refer to the instinctive response tendencies of man nor does it include the inventive innovations occurring within an individual's lifetime that take place as one-time solutions to unique problem situations.

Culture includes both *abstract* and *material* elements. Abstract elements include values, attitudes, ideas, personality types, and summary constructs such as religion. These are referred to in Figure 4.1 as learned patterns of behavior, feeling, and reaction that are transmitted from one generation to succeeding ones. Material elements of the culture are multifarious. They include, for example, such diverse items as computers, drawings, tools, buildings, products of all types, advertisements, and many of the other items that are the *artifacts of a society.* Although material aspects of culture greatly affect (and are the product of) consumer choices, abstract elements and especially values are the topic of analysis here.

The process of a consumer absorbing or learning the culture in which he

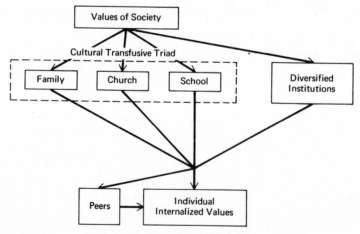

Figure 4.1 INTERGENERATIONAL VALUE TRANSMISSION

---

[2] Alfred L. Kroeber and Clyde Kluckhohn, "Culture: A Critical Review of Concepts and Definitions," *Papers of the Peabody Museum,* vol. 27 (1952).

[3] Alfred L. Kroeber and Talcott Parsons, "The Concepts of Culture and of Social System," *Amer. Sociological Rev.,* vol. 23, p. 583 (Oct. 1958).

is raised is called *socialization* or enculturation. Sometimes a person leaves one society to live in another and must learn the new culture. The process of learning a new culture or subculture other than the one in which he was raised is called *acculturation.*

Many groups of people contribute to the socialization or acculturation of an individual. The process of a culture's being transmitted to the point that it becomes part of an individual's central control unit is illustrated in Figure 4.1. The most basic influence upon an individual is the family. This is true for a number of reasons, including the fact that the family is the primary screening agent of culture during the formative childhood years when a high proportion of culture is assimilated. The influence of all other groups is "filtered" by members of the family in the early years of the typical individual.

Reference groups such as work groups for adults and friendship groups for all ages are important transmitters of culture. They may also "filter" the values of the broader culture and shape the broader values to conform with values of the reference group. Social classes, racial, and other ethnic groups are also important in defining and transmitting culture to the individual. This entire process can be termed "cultural mediation," as shown in Figure 4.1.

The significance of culture in determining human behavior is described in this articulate statement of the sociologist R. P. Cuzzort:

> The profundity of the concept (culture) comes from the extent to which it can be applied to innumerable realms of human conduct. To the extent we can do this, we are able to ascertain that man is not ruled so much by biological or physiological demands as he is by different ways of perceiving the world; these modes of viewing the world are shaped by his cultural background. For example, I recall once hearing a physiologist refer to love as simply deoxyribonucleic acid calling out to itself. A student of culture is aware, by contrast, that for culture-bound creatures like man, love is considerably more. Culture can prescribe whether or not man is more likely to fall in love with a fat girl or a thin girl. It can determine whether people will fall in love at all. It can determine whether husbands will respond jealously or happily to the attentions that other men give their wives. It can affect the extent to which men are aggressive or passive in making love. It can influence the extent to which people are aware or unaware of their sexual natures. In a word, a comprehension of the nature of culture extends our understanding of the degree to which man is more than chemistry or physiology or a set of biological drives or animal instincts.[4]

BASIC ASSUMPTIONS ABOUT CULTURE

The importance of culture as a determinant of behavior has caused many people to take a closer look in an attempt to discover more about the dynamics

---

[4]   R. P. Cuzzort, *Humanity and Modern Sociological Thought* (New York: Holt, Rinehart and Winston, 1969), p. 256.

of culture. The assumptions described below are generally accepted by anthropologists.[5]

Culture as Learned Responses

Most of what is considered "human" behavior represents learned phenomena. In contrast, the ant knows how to be an ant because its genes provide this behavior as part of the nervous system. A puppy or a kitten has many instinctive values but also learns from its environment. At the other end of the spectrum, humans have to learn almost everything about how to be human from experience.

Culture provides *transmitted solutions to recurring problems*. The cultural field presents a set of stimuli to an individual and also a set of responses appropriate to those stimuli. The individual either is directly rewarded for adopting those responses (or punished for not adopting them) or indirectly associates them with other stimulus situations that are rewarding. Through this process, the individual is *enculturated* or *socialized*, that is, the responses of a culture become his own set of response tendencies. Of course, an individual may not accept all of the responses defined by his culture. This occurs when he has no occasion to practice some aspect of culture or when he is not personally rewarded for doing so.

Cultural items learned early in life tend to resist change more strongly than those learned late in life. This fact has important implications for marketing strategy, since those cultural elements learned early in life are likely to be highly resistant to promotional effort. The appropriate strategy for deeply ingrained culturally defined behavior is to modify product or promotional offerings to conform with cultural values rather than attempt to change these culturally determined preferences. It is recognized also, however, that advertising and other marketing efforts play a role in value transmission and socialization as people develop throughout life.[6]

Culture as Inculcated Values

In addition to describing culture as a learned phenomenon, it has been observed that culture is inculcated, passed from one generation to another by specific groups and institutions. Primarily, culture is passed on from parents to their offspring, but other institutions have important roles. Ethnic, educational, and religious institutions are all instruments of inculcating the values of one generation in the succeeding generation. The role of institutions in transmitting values is amplified later in this chapter.

---

[5] This discussion is based upon G. P. Murdock, "Uniformities in Culture," *Amer. Sociological Rev.*, vol. 5, pp. 361–369 (1940); Omark K. Moore and Donald Lewis, "Learning Theory and Culture,'" *Psychological Rev.*, vol. 59, pp. 380–388 (1952).

[6] A particularly strong statement of this position is found in Jules Henry, *Culture Against Man* (New York: Random House, 1963); Jules Henry, *Pathways to Madness* (New York: Random House, 1971).

Culture as a Social Phenomenon

Cultural habits are *shared by aggregates of people* living in organized societies. A characteristic way of behaving or thinking that belongs to only one individual is not culture. Culture refers only to *group habits.* Group habits are developed and reinforced through social pressure upon those who are interacting with one another.

The social nature of culture is important to marketing analysts because marketing is concerned more with group behavior than the behavior of a specific individual. When the culutre of a group is studied, model ways of thinking and behaving are determined. Since marketing strategy must necessarily be built upon assumptions about large numbers of consumers or market segments, it is important to determine commonalities of behavior which result from culturally determined variables.

Culture as Gratifying Responses

Culture exists to meet the basic biological and secondary needs of a society. Elements within a culture become extinguished when they no longer are gratifying to members of the society. This is because of the role of reinforcement in learning.

One theory of social stratification, for example, contends that a society provides cultural rewards to its members who can satisfy the needs of the society in perpetuating itself. For example, physicians and scientists must engage in many years of difficult, relatively nonproductive labor before they are able to perform useful service for society. The society requires the services of these individuals for survival. To induce individuals to enter these strenuous positions, therefore, the culture of a society develops in such a way that material and social rewards are given to people to enter the essential occupations. In an era when national defense is a great need of society, it would be predicted that the culture would give esteem and other rewards to military strategists or defense-related scientists. As a society changes from strong national defense needs to need for solution to ecological problems, the culture of a society should evolve in such a way, for example, as to reward antipollution scientists rather than military leaders. This evolution is not regarded as the process of human decision making but rather of the "culture" itself.

For marketing strategists, the principle of culture as gratification yields insight into the type of products that will be retained in a society and the type of business practices that will be rewarded, tolerated, or punished. Only products and business practices that gratify the current needs of a society will be retained in the long run.[7]

---

[7] For amplification of this concept as an input into the evaluation of the social responsibility of corporate activities, see David T. Kollat, Roger D. Blackwell, and James F. Robeson, *Strategic Marketing* (New York: Holt, Rinehart and Winston, 1972).

Culture as an Adaptive Process

Culture is adaptive, either through a dialectical or evolutionary process. Culture responds to the physical and social environment in which it operates and has contact. Dialectical or sharply discontinuous cultural change, associated with Hegel and Marx, occurs when the value system of a culture becomes associated with the gratification of only one class or a group in the environment. In such instances, other classes of the society reject the logic of the value system and replace it (often suddenly, in a revolution) with a new value system. In an evolutionary process, change occurs but is a process of modification rather than revolution.[8]

The adaptive nature of culture is important in developing an understanding of consumer behavior. In the past, cultural change normally was slow and gradual. It appears, however, that the vastly accelerated technological change that characterizes contemporary societies is also reflected in the values and ideas of the society. The changing nature of American values will be analyzed in more depth later in this chapter. Before such an analysis, however, it will be helpful to describe some of the research methods that are used to study culture.

METHODS OF STUDYING CULTURE

Conventional methods of marketing and sociological research, as well as techniques specifically developed for the purpose, are used in the study of culture. Questionnaires, attitude scaling devices, projective techniques, clinical analysis, psychodrama, and many other methods are used in the study of values.[9] The analysis of data may involve many standard techniques, including analysis of variance and nonparametric tests of significance, regression and factor analysis, and many other measures of association or tests of relationship.

Consumer researchers should be careful not to use only the "rigorous" methodologies and thus omit methodologies that produce more useful insights

---

[8] A lucid discussion of the contrasting philosophies of dialectical and evolutionary change in the values of a society is provided by an economist who has influenced marketing thought considerably. See Kenneth Boulding, *A Primer on Social Dynamics* (New York: Free Press, 1970), esp. chap. 2, "Organizers of Social Evolution."

[9] Introductions to methodology for cultural research and descriptions of specific technique can be found in B. K. Stravianis, "Research Methods in Cultural Anthropology," *Psychological Rev.*, vol. 57, pp. 334–344 (1950); Gardner Lindzey, *Projective Techniques and Cross-Cultural Research* (New York: Appleton, 1961); Charles E. Osgood and Thomas A. Sebeck, "Psycholinguistics: A Survey of Theory and Research Problems," a Morton Prince Memorial Supplement to *J. Abnormal and Social Psychology*, vol. 49 (1954); Francis L. K. Hsu (ed.), *Psychological Anthropology: Approaches to Culture and Personality* (Homewood, Ill.: Dorsey Press, 1961); Bert Kaplan (ed.), *Studying Personality Cross-Culturally* (New York: Harper & Row, 1961); R. L. Carneiro and S. F. Tobias, "The Application of Scale Analysis to the Study of Cultural Evolution," *Transcript, New York Academy of Science*, ser. II, vol. 26, pp. 196–207 (1963).

into changing values. Becker analyzed sociological methodology and came to the conclusion that sophisticated quantitative methodology is not a necessary prerequisite to meaningful research; rather, major awards for outstanding contributions have often gone to studies centering on individual qualitative analysis. After studying the annual winners of major sociological awards between 1958 and 1968, Becker observed:

> Methodologists particularly slight three methods used by prize winners. They seldom write on participant observation, the method that produced Skolnick's *Justice Without Trial* and Goffman's *Asylums*. They seldom write on historical analysis, the method that produced Erickson's *Wayward Puritans* and Bendix's *Work and Authority in Industry*. And they seldom write on what few of us even perceive as a method—the knitting together of diverse kinds of research and publicly available materials which produced Frazier's *Black Bourgeoisie*. All three methods allow human judgment to operate, unhampered by algorithmic procedures, though they all allow the full presentation of the bases of those judgments that satisfy scientific requirements.[10]

It is particularly important to be aware of this philosophy when studying values and changes in value systems. An attempt is made in the following paragraphs to describe some methodologies as distinct approaches, but it should be kept in mind that studies and culture often are hybrid approaches and frequently utilize personal insight and logical synthesis. The methods described below include field studies using mass observations and participant observation, content analysis, cross-sectional studies, and longitudinal studies. Another method might be considered as a separate methodology or as a combination of some of the above. This approach, called crosscultural methodology, is presented in a separate section following this one.

Intensive Field Studies

Intensive field studies are common as a method of gathering cultural data. Field studies involve the placement of investigators into a culture for intensive collection of data through observation or the administration of tests. Two types of field studies are described below.

Mass Observations The technique of mass observation refers to the process of researchers mingling with the members of a culture, interacting with informants who appear to understand the culture of the group, listening to conversations, and attempting to synthesize these experiences into conclusions about the culture.

Numerous studies in marketing use the mass observation method. Studies of United States culture are often reported in general news magazines or trade journals rather than in scholarly journals. For cultures other than those of the United States, professional marketing journals sometimes carry studies using the mass observation method.

---

[10] Howard S. Becker, *Sociological Work* (Chicago: Aldine, 1970), pp. 6–7.

African culture and its effects on marketing have been reported frequently in the marketing literature. Deeply ingrained cultural values against free enterprise and trade are reported by Albaum and Rutman to exist in Tanganyika.[11] The Bantu markets of South Africa have such a low cultural definition of women's status that all purchases must be approved by men, according to Omana.[12] Fragmentation of markets is substantial in South Africa because of the existence of a variety of subcultures, reports Thorelli.[13] He finds that there are even greater differences between the consumption preferences of young and old and between urban and rural than in western cultures.

In Nigeria, mass observation studies reveal the importance of curiosity as a cultural value in the acceptance of new products. Other cultural values in Nigeria are reported by Baker:

> A deep seated impression of recent colonial rules is one that permeates widely. Status consideration is another, though appropriate symbols can vary. Personalities are important but dissimilar: the Yoruba of the western region is a very out-going and friendly individual, while the Hausa of the northern region is rather quiet and reserved. Religious preferences are primarily Christian and Moslem, and each demands a certain awareness of its respective precepts. Colors may be important; for the Yoruba, blue is widely favored. Even the direction of hands and eyes is sometimes significant.[14]

Other field studies have reported cultural influences on marketing in Spain,[15] Peru,[16] Chile,[17] and various Latin American countries.[18] Sometimes such field studies report only economic and technical aspects of the culture. The usefulness of such studies might be improved by the addition of information about the value systems underlying the markets.[19]

A major problem with mass-observation techniques is that they often rely upon the observer's ability to be objective and comprehensive and on his

---

[11] Gerald Albaum and Gilbert L. Rutman, "The Cooperative-Based Marketing System in Tanganyika," *J. Marketing*, vol. 31, pp. 54–58 (Oct. 1967).

[12] Charles J. Omana, "Marketing in Sub-Sahara Africa," in Peter D. Bennett (ed.), *Marketing and Economic Development* (Chicago: Amer. Marketing Assoc., 1965), pp. 128–139.

[13] Hans B. Thorelli, "South Africa: Its Multi-Cultural Marketing System," *J. Marketing*, vol. 32, pp. 40–48 (Apr. 1968).

[14] Raymond W. Baker, "Marketing in Nigeria," *J. Marketing*, vol. 29, pp. 40–48, at pp. 46–47 (July 1965). Reprinted by permission of the publisher.

[15] Edwin H. Lewis, "Marketing in Spain," *J. Marketing*, vol. 28, pp. 17–21 (Oct. 1964); Joseph R. Guerin, "Limitations of Supermarkets in Spain," *J. Marketing*, vol. 28, pp. 22–26 (Oct. 1964).

[16] Donald G. Halper, "The Environment for Marketing in Peru," *J. Marketing*, vol. 30, pp. 42–46 (July 1966).

[17] Peter D. Bennett, "Retailing Evolution or Revolution in Chile," *J. Marketing*, vol. 30, pp. 38–41 (July 1966).

[18] Charles C. Slater, "Marketing Processes in Developing Latin American Societies," *J. Marketing*, vol. 32, pp. 50–55 (July 1968).

[19] An example would be Berend H. Feddersen, "Markets behind the Iron Curtain," *J. Marketing*, vol. 31, pp. 1–5 (July 1967).

ability to select the proper sample. The user of the research must depend upon the observer's ability rather than methodological guarantees. Marketing analysts often sympathize with the objections to mass-observation techniques stated by Duijker and Frijda, ". . . there is no systematic sampling; the situations are not standardized; (and) much of the material gathered is irrelevant to the specific problem studied."[20]

Participant-Observer Studies   Field studies of a culture by an investigator or team of investigators living in intimate contact with a culture and making voluminous notes of what is observed are called participant-observer studies. The data collection may include records of what is observed, interviews with "key" informants, and very structured methods such as attitude scales, projective tests, and other forms.

The contemporary ethnographic researcher lives among the people he is observing and questioning, and is attempting to become an accepted part of the cultural unit under study. A classic study using such a method is Whiting's *Becoming a Kwoma*,[21] in which the investigator spent nearly a year developing relationships with residents of the tiny village of Rumbima in New Zealand in order to collect data on the most basic values of the society. One authority has described the approach of the anthropologist in this manner:

> He studies his fellow men not solely as a dispassionate observer but also as a participant observer. He tries to feel with them, to see things as they see them, to experience some portion of their life with them. On the other hand, he tries to balance his identifications with detached objectivity.[22]

The participant-observer study has been relatively unused in marketing studies as a formal technique, but it offers much potential. Informally, the technique is used all the time because the marketing researcher working with a common consumer product is already a "participant observer" in the culture absorbing the product the marketer sells. Eventually, however, consumer researchers may send observers into alien subcultures to conduct in-depth cultural studies. For example, a company might station an ethnographer in cultural subunits such as a black family, a retirement village, an apartment community of young non-college-educated couples, or an area of the city composed of a different social class from that of the marketing executives and researchers. The ethnographer is trained to make careful observations of every element of behavior relevant to purchasing of the product as well as background material in the form of general cultural values. In addition to his own observations, the

---

20   H. C. J. Duijker and N. H. Frijda, *National Character and National Stereotypes: Confluence*, vol. 1 (Amsterdam: North-Holland, 1960), p. 120.

21   John W. M. Whiting, *Becoming a Kwoma* (New Haven, Conn.: Yale University Press, 1941).

22   Clyde Kluckhohn, "Common Humanity and Diverse Cultures," in Daniel Lerner (ed.), *The Human Meaning of the Social Sciences* (Cleveland, Ohio: World Publ. Co., 1959), pp. 251–252.

ethnographer relies upon interaction with informants for explanations, clarifications, and amplifications of the activities he has observed.

Observer-participant studies have two major weaknesses: (1) they usually do not have a systematic sampling plan[23] and (2) the presence of the observer as a participant may introduce changes in the culture.[24] Thus the anthropological field study is sometimes criticized for its lack of objectivity and comprehensiveness. However, what the anthropologist sacrifices in methodological rigor in his participant-observer field he makes up for in an approach that is often richer in content, more ramified, and more pertinent to behavior in everyday life settings.

True field studies of the type described above appear not to have been conducted for the specific purpose of studying consumer purchasing decisions. Studies with purposes similar to the field studies but necessitating less intensive investigation have been conducted using surveys, panels, and in-depth interviews.[25] In some cases, the findings on social class presented in the next chapter were developed through anthropological field studies, so that there appears to be reason for considerable interest in such studies by marketing analysts. Ultimately, the true ethnographic field study may offer the most intensive approach possible to understanding the cultural traits and configurations that characterize consumer purchasing decisions.

Content Analysis

Content analysis is a technique for determining the values, themes, role prescriptions, norms of behavior, and other elements of a culture from the verbal materials produced by the people of a culture in the ordinary course of events.[26] The main advantages of content analysis are that (1) it can be used where personal contact is difficult or impossible, and (2) it is unobtrusive; a culture can be studied without individuals within the culture being aware of the investigation.

The breadth of topics that can be studied in a culture as well as sources for information are illustrated by some of the following studies. The achievement motivations that characterize a society were studied with content analysis of

---

[23] For a discussion of informant sampling problems in ethnographic research, see B. D. Paul, "Interview Techniques and Field Relationships," in A. L. Kroeber *et al.* (eds.), *Anthropology Today: An Encyclopedia* (Chicago: University of Chicago Press, 1953), pp. 430–451.

[24] Methods to prevent reactivity in a wide variety of research problems, including participant observation, are presented in Eugene J. Webb, Donald T. Campbell, Richard D. Schwartz, and Lee Sechrest, *Unobtrusive Measures: Nonreactive Research in the Social Sciences* (Chicago: Rand McNally, 1966).

[25] Studies of culture using standard marketing research techniques can be found in most marketing and advertising journals. The most complete description of cultural values surrounding consumer products and decision processes in America based primarily on depth interviews is in Ernest Dichter, *Handbook of Consumer Motivations* (New York: McGraw-Hill, 1964).

[26] For details of the method, see Bernard Berelson, *Content Analysis in Communication Research* (New York: Free Press, 1952). See also various readings in I. Pool (ed.), *Trends in Content Analysis* (Urbana, Ill.: University of Illinois Press, 1959); R. C. North, O. R. Holsti, M. G. Zaniovich, and Dina A. Zinnes, *Content Analysis: A Handbook with Applications for the Study of Internatonal Crisis* (Evanston, Ill.: Northwestern University Press, 1963).

children's stories by McClelland[27] and by DeCharms and Moeller.[28] Values in Hitler's Germany were compared with those of other countries by content analyses of plays,[29] songbooks,[30] handbooks for youth organizations,[31] speeches,[32] and newspapers.[33] More recently values of the elite classes in Russia and other topics have been studied with content analyses of newspapers and magazines by Lasswell,[34] Pool,[35] Wayne,[36] Angell,[37] and Singer.[38]

Marketing studies have used content analysis very little. Singh and Huang have examined advertising content in India and America with a crosscultural content analysis.[39] The classic study using content analysis in marketing is not strictly a consumer behavior study, however. Kassarjian, in a meticuously controlled study, analyzed the role of Negroes in advertising using content analysis and found substantial increase in Negro occupational roles over a two-decade period.[40] In spite of the objectivity of content analysis and its ability to provide information over a considerable time span more easily than other methods, it has found relatively little use in consumer behavior to date.

Cross-Sectional Studies

Cross-sectional studies of culture have been applied to marketing problems recently. They have the same goals as mass observations and participant-observer studies but are based upon more systematic sampling procedures in an

[27]   D. C. McClelland, *The Achieving Society* (Princeton, N.J.: Van Nostrand, 1961).

[28]   R. DeCharms and G. Moeller, "Values Expressed in American Children's Readers 1800–1950," *J. Abnormal and Social Psychology,* vol. 64, pp. 136–142 (1962).

[29]   D. W. McGranahan and I. Wayne, "German and American Traits Reflected on Popular Drama," *Human Relations,* vol. 1, pp. 429–455 (1948).

[30]   H. Sebald, "Studying National Character through Comparative Content Analysis," *Social Forces,* vol. 40, pp. 318–322 (1962).

[31]   H. S. Lewin, "Hitler, Youth and the Boy Scouts of America," *Human Relations,* vol. 1, pp. 206–227 (1947).

[32]   R. K. White, "Hitler, Roosevelt and the Nature of War Propaganda," *J. Abnormal and Social Psychology,* vol. 44, pp. 157–174 (1949).

[33]   H. D. Lassell, "The World Attention Survey," *Public Opinion Quart.,* vol. 6, pp. 456–462 (1941).

[34]   H. D. Lasswell, "The World Attention Survey," *Public Opinion Quart.,* vol. 3, pp. 456–462 (1941).

[35]   I. Pool, *The "Prestige Papers": A Survey of Their Editorials* (Palo Alto, Calif.: Stanford University Press, 1952).

[36]   I. Wayne, "American and Soviet Themes and Values: A Content Analysis of Pictures in Popular Magazines," *Public Opinion Quart.,* vol. 20, pp. 315–320 (1956).

[37]   R. C. Angell "Social Values of Soviet and American Elites: Content Analysis of Elite Media," *J. Conflict Resolution,* vol. 8, pp. 330–385 (1964).

[38]   J. D. Singer, "Soviet and American Foreign Policy Attitudes: Content Analysis of Elite Articulations," *J. Conflict Resolution,* vol. 8, pp. 424–485 (1964).

[39]   P. N. Singh and S. C. Huang, "Some Socio-Cultural and Psychological Dominants of Advertising in India: A Comparative Study," *J. Social Psychology,* vol. 57, pp. 113–121 (1962).

[40]   Harold H. Kassarjian, "The Negro and American Advertising, 1946–1965," *J. Marketing Research,* vol. 6, pp. 29–39 (Feb. 1969).

attempt to produce a representative cross section of the culture or subculture investigated. Questions are formulated which will reveal values or behavioral norms of a culture and are presented to a large sample, often using probability or quota selection procedures.

A number of cross-sectional studies have focused on the youth subculture in recent years. The methodology involved in these studies involves considerable sophistication in the study of values.[41] The nature of the questions asked to determine values can be best illustrated by presentation of results from the study (Table 4.1).

Table 4.1 CBS CROSS-SECTIONAL STUDY OF YOUTH AND PARENTS (SELECTED QUESTIONS AND RESPONSES)

(1) The following statements represent some traditional American values. Which of them do you *personally believe in* and which do you *not believe in?*

	Youth			Parents		
	Total Youth (%)	College (%)	Non-college (%)	Total Parents (%)	Parents College Youth (%)	Parents Non-college Youth (%)
(a) Hard work will always pay off						
Believe in	74	56	79	83	76	85
Do not believe in	26	43	21	17	24	15
(b) Everyone should save as much as he can regularly and not have to lean on family and friends the minute he runs into financial problems						
Believe in	86	76	88	96	90	98
Do not believe in	14	24	11	3	10	2
(c) Depending on how much strength and character a person has, he can pretty well control what happens to him						
Believe in	74	62	77	74	71	75
Do not believe in	26	38	23	24	28	23

[41] CBS News, *Generations Apart* (New York: Columbia Broadcasting System, 1969), pp. 2–3.

Table 4.1 CBS CROSS-SECTIONAL STUDY OF YOUTH AND PARENTS
(SELECTED QUESTIONS AND RESPONSES) (*Continued*)

	Youth			*Parents*		
	Total Youth (%)	*College (%)*	*Non-college (%)*	*Total Parents (%)*	*Parents College Youth (%)*	*Parents Non-college Youth (%)*
(d) Belonging to some organized religion is important in a person's life						
Believe in	66	42	71	89	81	91
Do not believe in	34	57	28	11	17	9

(2) Many people feel that we are undergoing a period of rapid social change in this country today, and that people's values are changing at the same time. Which of the following changes would you *welcome*, which would you *reject*, and which would *leave you indifferent*?

(a) Less emphasis on money						
Would welcome	57	72	54	Not asked of		
Would reject	13	11	13	parents		
Leave indifferent	30	17	33			
(b) Less emphasis on working hard						
Would welcome	30	24	32			
Would reject	46	48	45			
Leave indifferent	23	28	22			
(c) More emphasis on law and order						
Would welcome	76	57	81			
Would reject	10	23	7			
Leave indifferent	12	19	11			
(f) More sexual freedom						
Would welcome	27	43	22			
Would reject	39	24	43			
Leave indifferent	34	33	34			
(g) More vigorous protests by blacks and other minority groups						
Would welcome	12	23	9			
Would reject	73	56	77			
Leave indifferent	15	20	14			

Table 4.1   CBS CROSS-SECTIONAL STUDY OF YOUTH AND PARENTS
(SELECTED QUESTIONS AND RESPONSES) (*Continued*)

(18) Which of the following considerations will have a relatively strong influence on
your choice of career?

	Youth			Parents		
	Total Youth (%)	*College (%)*	*Non-college (%)*	*Total Parents (%)*	*Parents College Youth (%)*	*Parents Non-college Youth (%)*
Your family	35	31	36	Not asked of parents		
The money that you can earn	47	41	49			
The prestige or status of the job	21	23	20			
The security of the job	45	42	46			
The ability to express yourself	47	66	43			
The challenge of the job	52	71	47			
The opportunity to make a meaningful contribution	60	76	56			

(24) For each of the following, please tell me whether you feel it needs no substantial
change, needs moderate change, needs fundamental reform, or should be done
away with.

Big business						
No substantial change	20	10	23	Not asked of parents		
Moderate change	52	52	52			
Fundamental reform	24	34	21			
Done away with	3	3	3			
The military						
No substantial change	20	10	23			
Moderate change	43	29	46			
Fundamental reform	29	49	25			
Done away with	7	11	6			
The universities						
No substantial change	20	11	23			
Moderate change	50	56	49			
Fundamental reform	28	32	27			
Done away with	1	—	1			

NOTE: Question numbers and letters correspond to source.

SOURCE: From the CBS News, "Generations Apart" survey published in *Public Opinion:
Changing Attitudes on Contemporary Political and Social Issues* (New York: R. R.
Bowker, 1972).

Another method of obtaining a cross-sectional analysis of values is illustrated by the *National Review* study of campus values.[42] It is a useful example because it illustrates the principle that representative studies of diverse groups may yield more insight than the "averaging out" process of a national probability sample. The schools listed in Table 4.2 illustrate the diversity which is often hidden in "national samples."

Table 4.2 CROSS-SECTIONAL STUDY OF VALUES IN REPRESENTATIVE CAMPUSES (SELECTED QUESTIONS AND RESPONSES)

19-36. Indicate your views on the following twenty political proposals for the United States by writing in a number signifying the following:
(1) Definitely in favor
(2) Somewhat in favor
(3) Indifferent or no opinion
(4) Somewhat opposed
(5) Definitely opposed

19. Full socialization of all industries:

	SL %	Wms %	Yale %	Marq %	BU %	Ind %	SC %	Hwd %	Reed %	Dav %	Bran %	Stan %
(1)	11	2	8	2	9	4	—	10	11	4	7	3
(2)	34	13	17	9	29	14	8	26	27	11	30	17
(3)	9	7	11	11	11	9	11	18	16	8	8	7
(4)	21	28	25	21	20	20	18	16	14	25	26	23
(5)	24	49	40	56	29	51	61	25	29	51	23	48

20. Socialization of basic industries

	SL	Wms	Yale	Marq	BU	Ind	SC	Hwd	Reed	Dav	Bran	Stan
(1)	34	10	21	9	26	13	4	31	29	12	25	15
(2)	41	29	34	23	34	20	24	27	28	23	34	29
(3)	8	8	6	10	9	8	12	13	11	5	8	8
(4)	5	28	22	26	15	22	20	15	13	31	17	22
(5)	9	26	17	32	13	34	40	9	16	28	11	24

21. National Health Insurance

	SL	Wms	Yale	Marq	BU	Ind	SC	Hwd	Reed	Dav	Bran	Stan
(1)	63	39	54	28	56	30	31	54	58	27	61	32
(2)	18	35	28	35	27	28	34	25	18	46	22	38
(4)	14	14	13	15	11	20	15	14	10	11	9	15
(4)	3	6	3	13	3	10	12	3	8	9	1	7
(5)	—	5	2	8	1	8	7	—	3	5	2	4

30. Have you ever smoked marijuana?
(1) Yes   (2) No

---

[42] Philip P. Ardery, "Opinion on the Campus," *National Rev.*, vol. 23, pp. 635–6 (June 15, 1971).

Table 4.2 CROSS-SECTIONAL STUDY OF VALUES IN REPRESENTATIVE
CAMPUSES (SELECTED QUESTIONS AND RESPONSES) *(Continued)*

	SL %	Wms %	Yale %	Marq %	BU %	Ind %	SC %	Hwd %	Reed %	Dav %	Bran %	Stan %
(1)	82	75	65	33	74	42	34	40	76	33	65	66
(2)	18	24	34	67	25	58	65	56	22	66	33	33

48. All things considered, do you think more lenient college administrations
standards for black applicants should be adopted?
    (1) Yes   (2) No   (3) Unsure or no opinion

	SL %	Wms %	Yale %	Marq %	BU %	Ind %	SC %	Hwd %	Reed %	Dav %	Bran %	Stan %
(1)	59	61	55	36	42	38	24	63	50	54	62	63
(2)	26	24	25	48	38	45	65	24	22	35	22	20
(3)	11	11	17	15	15	12	9	9	23	9	13	17

91. Would you say that at the present time
    (1) I am in substantial agreement with the religious tradition in which I
    was raised?
    (2) I partially agree with the religious tradition in which I was raised but
    have important reservations?
    (3) I wholly reject the religious tradition in which I was raised?

	SL %	Wms %	Yale %	Marq %	BU %	Ind %	SC %	Hwd %	Reed %	Dav %	Bran %	Stan %
(1)	13	8	11	17	9	17	18	11	10	10	20	9
(2)	65	71	54	74	56	52	62	63	47	74	61	61
(3)	22	20	33	6	32	27	19	24	40	16	19	27

95. Below are several very brief, rough statements of various conceptions of the
Deity. Check the one that most nearly approximates your views.
    (1) There is an immensely wise, omnipotent, three-person God Who created
    the universe and Who maintains an active concern for human affairs.
    (2) There is a God precisely as described in (1) except that He is absolutely
    One and in no sense possesses trinitarian nature.
    (3) I believe in a God about Whom nothing definite can be affirmed except
    that I sometimes sense Him as a mighty "spiritual presence" permeating
    all mankind and nature.
    (4) There is a vast, impersonal principle of order or natural uniformity work-
    ing throughout the whole universe and which, though not conscious of
    mere human life, I choose to call "God."
    (5) Because of our ignorance in this matter, I see no adequate grounds for
    either affirming or denying the existence of God.
    (6) I reject all belief in anything that could reasonably be called "God" and
    regard every such notion as a fiction unworthy of worship.
    (7) Other

Table 4.2 CROSS-SECTIONAL STUDY OF VALUES IN REPRESENTATIVE
CAMPUSES (SELECTED QUESTIONS AND RESPONSES) (*Continued*)

	SL %	Wms %	Yale %	Marq %	BU %	Ind %	SC %	Hwd %	Reed %	Dav %	Bran %	Stan %
(1)	3	5	14	45	9	24	39	21	5	23	2	15
(2)	3	3	2	3	2	4	1	3	2	1	3	1
(3)	22	28	26	29	30	29	25	23	8	35	20	25
(4)	22	21	20	6	22	16	10	21	17	13	28	24
(5	22	18	16	4	18	13	11	16	29	11	23	15
(6)	9	4	8	2	6	4	3	4	16	6	8	9
(7)	11	17	7	8	6	6	5	6	16	8	9	7

NOTES: Question numbers correspond to source.
The schools included were Sarah Lawrence College (SL), a small, private, non-sectarian women's school; Williams College (Wms), a small, private nonsectarian men's liberal arts college in New England; Yale University (Yale), a large, private nonsectarian school in Connecticut; Marquette University (Marq), a large, Milwaukee-based coeducational Catholic school; Boston University (BU), a large, private coeducational school with many commuter students; Indiana University, (Ind), a giant Midwestern land-grant institution dominating the small city of Bloomington; the University of South Carolina (SC), a recently integrated state-supported school of the South; Howard University (Hwd), a private, nondenominational, predominantly black university in Washington, D.C.; Reed College (Reed), a small, private coeducational school in Portland, Ore., noted for educational and political progressivism; Davisons College (Dav), a small, private Presbyterian men's school in rural North Carolina; Brandeis University (Bran), a medium-sized school in Boston with a predominantly Jewish student body and a reputation for political liberalism; and Stanford University (Stan), a large, private California university traditionally catering to the upper middle and upper classes.

SOURCE: Philip P. Ardery, "Opinion on the Campus," *National Rev.*, 150 E. 35 St., N.Y., N.Y., vol. 23, pp. 635–650 (June 15, 1971).

Another type of cross-sectional study of values is illustrated in a study by the U.S. Department of Health, Education and Welfare. Mail responses were obtained from a panel of 251 randomly selected students in 53 urban and suburban schools. The panel members were designated as "correspondents" and asked to report the values of their school. The authors describe the advantages of this type of study over the usual poll or survey:

(1) The free and discursive answers to open-end questions furnish opinion clues beyond the scope of the usual poll.

(2) Since correspondents are asked to report the views that prevail among their friends and classmateş, rather than merely their own opinions, they are regarded as providing opinion "coverage" rather than a statistical opinion sample.

(3) Results are given in words rather than in numbers . . . analysis is qualitative as well as quantitative. The purpose is to present the main patterning of opinions rather than an exact count.

(4) Where mention of a point is volunteered rather than directly elicited, relatively small proportions may be significant and

salience must be judged in comparison with other points volunteered.[43]

Longitudinal Studies of Values

Longitudinal research involves studies of specified phenomena running over an extended period of time. Longitudinal studies have been used in other areas of consumer research, but only recently has this method of research been applied much to the study of values. Longitudinal research is essential, however, for accurate monitoring of changes in values and preparing a data base useful for the prediction of future value systems. Two basic types of longitudinal studies exist: continuous panels and repeated representative samples.

Continuous Panels   A continuous panel is a group of consumers who agree to respond to requests for information on a repeated basis over an extended period of time.[44] The panel is often selected to correspond with demographic characteristics of the population. Panel members are asked the same questions in repeated time periods to measure changes in their attitudes, values, or behavior.

The panel as a source of information has the following weaknesses:

> First, there is the question of whether persons who are willing to join a panel and to continue participating over a period of time are *ipso facto* "different" from other persons. There is some evidence to suggest that panel members *are* different. . .
>
> A second inherent problem in panels is that membership in a panel may, *in itself*, affect the behavior of the members, or at least affect what they *report*.[45]

It has generally not been practical in the past to measure values by interviewing the same consumers because of the long time periods between interviews needed for analysis of value shifts.

Repeated Samples   A more practical method of measuring value shifts is through repeated studies of representative samples of the culture under investigation. Generally, the selection of respondents should involve carefully designed probability samples to achieve projectability. Examples of the type of longitudinal studies of consumer values which will hopefully become more common are provided by Table 4.3, based upon data from the Opinion Research Corporation.

Other studies of cultural, economic, and social changes over time, using various methodologies, are comprehensively reviewed in the very useful Russell

---

[43]   Elizabeth Herzog, Cecelia E. Sudia, Barbara Rosengard, and Jane Harwood, "Teenagers Discuss the 'Generation Gap' "; Youth Reports no. 1 (Washington, D.C.: U.S. Department of Health, Education, and Welfare, 1970), p. i.

[44]   For a good introductory discussion of the characteristics of consumer panels, see Robert D. Buzzell, Donald F. Cox, and Rex V. Brown, *Marketing Research and Information Systems* (New York: McGraw-Hill, 1969), pp. 230–240; also Paul E. Green and Donald S. Tull, *Research for Marketing Decisions* (Englewood Cliffs, N.J.: Prentice-Hall, 1970), pp. 97–102.

[45]   Buzzell *et al., op. cit.,*[44] pp. 231–232.

Table 4.3   LONGITUDINAL STUDIES OF AMERICAN VALUES
(SELECTED SURVEYS)

	1958	1959	1961	1963	1965	1967	Latest*
Changing Values Toward Business			*Percent Who Agree*				
In many industries one or two companies have too much control	57	61	59	58	60		65
As they get bigger, companies get cold and impersonal	55	60	59	58	59		64
Too much power is concentrated in a few companies	53	57	54	52	54		61
Changing Values Toward Minorities	*Percent Who Would Vote for President if he were:*						
Catholic	68			84		89	88
Jew	62			77		82	86
Negro	38			47		54	67

NOTE: *Exact date of "latest" varies.
SOURCE: Joseph R. Goeke, "America's Future as Reflected in Public Opinion Trends," *The Futurist,* published by the World Future Society, P.O. Box 30369, Betheseda Branch, Wash., D.C. 20014, pp. 79–84 (Apr. 1971).

Sage Foundation report, *Indicators of Social Change.*[46] It should be emphasized that one of the most important reasons for monitoring changes in value systems and other environmental influences is to predict future trends with sufficient accuracy to aid in the development of more effective marketing strategy. Effective organizations of all types are increasingly oriented toward the future and cultural analysis is central to the methodolgy of futurology.[47]

CROSSCULTURAL ANALYSIS OF CONSUMER BEHAVIOR

Organizations of all types are increasingly global in nature. The research methodologies and analytical perspectives required to understand consumer behavior also need to be global in nature. One approach for accomplishing this

---

[46]   Eleanor B. Sheldon and Wilbert E. Moore (eds.), *Indicators of Social Change: Concepts and Measurements* (New York: Russell Sage Foundation, 1968).

[47]   For expansion of this perspective and a review of relevant research techniques, see David T. Kollat, "Environmental Forecasting and Strategic Planning: Perspectives on the Methodology of Futurology," paper presented at the American Marketing Association Fall Conf., Minneapolis, Minn. (Sept. 1, 1971).

is the set of methods and knowledge developed in the discipline of anthropology known as crosscultural analysis.

Crosscultural analysis is the systematic comparison of similarities and differences in the behavioral and material aspects of cultures. Crosscultural analysis is appropriate in the investigation of domestic marketing problems (such as youth and middle-aged market segments, black and white markets, geographic markets, or rural and urban markets) and for the investigation of foreign markets.

Crosscultural Analysis in Anthropology

Crosscultural methods of analysis were developed in anthropology and are founded upon an interest in cataloguing similarities and contrasts among peoples of various cultures.[48] Among societies so remotely located that they could not possibly have come into contact with each other, remarkable similarities are found in the methods with which they handle common problems. Some of the similarities between cultures, defined as items prohibited or compelled by the culture, are described in Table 4.4.

Table 4.4 BEHAVIORS PROHIBITED AND COMPELLED IN 25 PRIMITIVE CULTURES

---

(1) *Behavior Items Both Prohibited and Compelled in the 25 Cultures*

Eating, drinking, vocalizing, talking, defecating, urinating, playing, marrying, working, harming others, harming self.

(2) *Behavior Items Prohibited*

Sucking, cannibalism, biting, crying, . . . incest, adultery, . . . murdering, stealing, assuming another's prerogatives, harming food, hindering manufacturing, hindering course of war, inviting bad luck, . . . being angry, . . . deceiving others, angering others, committing suicide, destroying goods, committing treason, being jealous, being irresponsible, hating, playing, being lazy.

(3) *Behavior Items Compelled*

Wailing, weeping, sleeping, giving, entering, being formal, . . . mourning, naming others, respecting others, cleansing self, protecting others, obeying others, purifying self, being secluded, helping others, learning, avoiding retaliation, . . . avenging, being hospitable, concealing parts of body, . . . expressing grief, fighting outgroup, pacifying others, being friendly, thanking others, being fertile, participating in food quest, . . . being brave, avoiding bad luck, ensuring good luck, aiding food quest, being generous, being kind, manufacturing, being industrious.

SOURCE: C. S. Ford, "Society, Culture, and the Human Organism," *J. General Psychology,* vol. 20, pp. 135–179 (1939); reprinted in Frank W. Moore (ed.), *Readings in Cross-Cultural Methodology* (New Haven, Conn.: Human Relations Area Files Press, 1961), pp. 130–165, at p. 158.

---

[48] For a discussion of this premise, see Clyde Kluckhohn, "Universal Categories of Culture," in A. L. Kroeber (ed.), *Anthropology Today* (Chicago: University of Chicago Press, 1953), pp. 507–523.

Crosscultural Research Methodology

The methodology of crosscultural studies in anthropology and in consumer behavior involves all of the methodologies described earlier in this chapter, but adapted to the special requirements of making systematic comparisons across cultures. Cultural methods require special techniques to handle differences in language, structural characteristics of the societies, values of the investigator that differ from the culture he is studying. The details of these methods are beyond the scope of this book.[49] Scientific studies of crosscultural problem can usually be conceptualized, however, into the following stages:

(1) Statistical comparisons of societies involved in the study

(2) Broad typological comparisons

(3) Descriptive, functional analyses of one or more aspects of culture

(4) Descriptive and analytical comparisons of total cultures

(5) Restudies by the same investigator

(6) Restudies by different investigators.

Developing Crosscultural Marketing Strategies

The rising importance of global markets to marketing strategists[50] has caused increasing attention to be given to the importance of cultural analysis of consumer behavior. Two marketing educators have advocated the position that success requirements for international operations include executives who have developed "cultural competence." Among other things, the following elements are needed:

(1) Sensitivity to cultural differences

(2) Cultural empathy, or the ability to "understand the inner logic and coherence of other ways of life, plus the restraint not to judge them as bad because they are different from one's own ways"

(3) Ability to withstand the initial cultural shock, or "the sum of sudden jolts that awaits the unwary American abroad"

(4) Ability to cope with and to adapt to foreign environment without "going native."[51]

---

[49] An excellent volume of crosscultural methods is Frank W. Moore (ed.), *Readings in Cross-Cultural Methodology* (New Haven, Conn.: Human Relations Area Files Press, 1961); also Oscar Lewis, "Comparisons in Cultural Anthropology," in William L. Thomas, Jr. (ed.), *Current Anthropology: A Supplement to Anthropology Today* (Chicago: University of Chicago Press, 1956), pp. 259–292.

[50] Background data concerning global markets are presented in many sources. For example, see Kollat *et al., op. cit.,*[7] chap. 8.

[51] Y. Hugh Furuhashi and Harry F. Evarts, "Educating Men for International Marketing," *J. Marketing,* vol. 31, pp. 51–53 (Jan. 1967). The authors attribute some of these ideas to Harlan Cleveland, Gerald J. Mangone, and John Clark Adams, *The Overseas Americans* (New York: McGraw-Hill, 1960).

The perils of cultural incompetence are aptly illustrated by the following case example of a western-oriented tobacco company attempting to enter a new market:

> The managers of a joint-venture tobacco company in an Asian country were warned that their proposed new locally named (a token adaptation) and manufactured filtered cigarettes would fail. Filters had not yet been introduced there. Nevertheless, the resident Western managers, along with their local executives whose SRC (self-reference criterion) was dominantly Western because of their social class and education, puffed smugly on their own U.S. filtered cigarettes while the product flopped, leaving the company with idle equipment and uncovered setup and launch costs.
>
> The basic reason for the prediction of failure was a difference in fear of death—especially from cancer of the lungs. A life expectancy of 29 years in that Asian country does not place many people in the lung cancer age bracket. Moreover, for those in this age bracket, there is not the general cultural value of sanitation, the literacy rate, or a *Reader's Digest* type of magazine to motivate them to give up unfiltered cigarettes.[52]

The possibility of standardizing marketing strategy to a degree for markets throughout the world has developed great interest in recent years. Buzzell, in an article richly illustrated with many case examples, has delineated the many obstacles to standardization but discerns a trend toward management strategies that permit greater standardization.[53] The initiative to treat consumer behavior as subject to cultural universals is often attributed to Elinder[54] and to Fatt who states that "even different peoples are *basically* the same, and that an international advertising campaign with a truly universal appeal can be effective in any market."[55] Fatt illustrates his position:

> The desire to be beautiful is universal. Such appeals as "mother and child," "freedom from pain," "glow of health," know no boundaries.
>
> In a sense, the young women in Tokyo and the young women in Berlin are sisters not only "under the skin," but on their skin and on their lips and fingernails, and even in their hair styles. If they could, the girls of Moscow would follow suit; and some of them do.[56]

---

[52] James A. Lee, "Cultural Analysis in Overseas Operations," *Harvard Business Rev.*, vol. 44, pp. 106–114, at p. 107 (Mar.–Apr., 1966).

[53] Robert D. Buzzell, "Can You Standardize Multinational Marketing?" *Harvard Business Rev.*, vol. 46, pp. 102–113 (Nov.–Dec., 1968).

[54] Erik Elinder, "How International Can European Advertising Be?" *J. Marketing*, vol. 29, pp. 7–11 (Apr. 1965).

[55] Arthur C. Fatt, "The Danger of 'Local' International Advertising," *J. Marketing*, vol. 31, pp. 60–62 (Jan. 1967).

[56] Fatt, *op. cit.*,[55] p. 61; also Arthur C. Fatt, "A Multi-National Approach to International Advertising," *International Executive*, vol. 7, pp. 5–6 (Winter 1965).

There is a growing literature to indicate that marketing technology and theory are universal even though cultural differences do exist[57] and business examples can be provided to show that a marketing strategy can be developed that is applicable on a worldwide basis.[58] On the other hand, empirical research shows that nearly two thirds of international firms practice policies that emphasize a localized, decentralized policy.[59] The more emphasis managers put on cultural similarities rather than differences, the more likely their firms are to emphasize standardized, centralized marketing strategy rather than localized strategy.[60] The extent of centralization practiced is amplified, however, by a study of internationally oriented firms which shows that while advertising and pricing decisions are typically localized, product and to some extent distribution decisions are more centralized.[61] A realistic assessment of the standardization–localization controversy is that the firm must select from a variety of strategies ranging from a "one product, one message, worldwide" strategy to a strategy emphasizing new product inventions for localized markets, depending upon the product, markets, and costs.[62] The choice of strategies rests heavily, however, upon adequate understanding of the cultural underpinnings of the market.[63]

---

[57] Robert Bartels, "Are Domestic and International Marketing Dissimilar?" *J. Marketing*, vol. 32, pp. 56–61 (July 1968); Isaiah A. Litvak and Peter M. Banting, "A Conceptual Framework for International Business Arrangement," in Robert L. King (ed.), *Marketing and the New Science of Planning* (Chicago: Amer. Marketing Assoc., 1968), pp. 460-467. For empirical refutation of these theories, however, see Susan P. Douglas, "Patterns and Parallels of Marketing Structures in Several Countries," *MSU Business Topics*, vol. 19, pp. 38–47 (Spring 1971).

[58] Dean Peebles, "Goodyear's Worldwide Advertising," *The International Advertiser*, vol. 8, pp. 19–22 (Jan. 1967) (both good and weak examples are cited in this article); Walter P. Margulies, "Why Global Marketing Requires a Global Focus on Product Design," *Business Aboard* pp. 22–23; (Aug. 22, 1966); Norman Heller, "How Pepsi-Cola Does It in 110 Countries," in John S. Wright and Jac L. Goldstrucker (eds.), *New Ideas for Successful Marketing* (Chicago: Amer. Marketing Assoc. 1966), pp. 700–715.

[59] James H. Donnelly, Jr., and John K. Ryans, Jr., "The Role of Culture in Organizing Overseas Operations: The Advertising Experience," *University of Washington Business Rev.*, vol. 30, pp. 35–41 (Autumn 1969). For additional details, see John K. Ryans, Jr., and James H. Donnelly, Jr., "Selected Practices of United States 'International' Advertising Agencies," *University of Washington Business Rev.*, vol. 3, pp. 43–55 (Autumn 1970). This study is also briefly reported in John K. Ryans, Jr., and James H. Donnelly, Jr., "Standardized Global Advertising, a Call as Yet Unanswered," *J. Marketing*, vol. 33, pp. 57–59 (Apr. 1969).

[60] *Op. cit.*[59]

[61] R. J. Aylmer, "Who Makes Marketing Decisions in the Multinational Firm?" *J. Marketing*, vol. 34, pp. 25–30 (Oct. 1970).

[62] An excellent evaluation of strategic alternatives is provided by Warren J. Keegan, "Multinational Product Planning: Strategic Alternatives," *J. Marketing*, vol. 33, pp. 58–62 (Jan. 1969); also Warren J. Keegan, "Multi-national Marketing Strategy and Organization: An Overview," in Reed Moyer (ed.), *Changing Marketing Systems* (Chicago: Amer. Marketing Assoc. 1967), pp. 203–209.

[63] A useful analysis showing the relationship between culture and variations in strategy is found in Montrose Sommers and Jerome Kernan, "Why Products Flourish Here, Fizzle There," *Columbia J. World Business*, vol. 2, pp. 89–97 (Mar.–Apr. 1967).

Crosscultural Marketing Research

Marketing researchers have begun to conduct crosscultural studies in recent years, although the practice is still embryonic. The previous lack of cross-cultural studies is probably due to lack of familiarity with crosscultural methods, the expense of such studies for academic researchers, and the tendency for United States multinational business firms to spend only a minimum amount on marketing research when entering foreign markets compared to their expenditures on domestic markets.[64]

British marketing researchers appear to have a longer history of cross-cultural research than United States researchers, and recently their findings have been tested for applicability to United States markets. Ehrenberg and Goodhardt report that mathematical models of repeat-buying habits developed from data on British consumers yield useful results for United States purchasers.[65] This study is important because it lends credence to the belief that consumer models and theories are applicable on a worldwide basis. Other crosscultural studies have been conducted by Dunn[66] using the case method of comparison and Lorimor and Dunn using the semantic differential and other measures of advertising effectiveness.[67] The semantic differential has also been used successfully in a study of Japanese and United States ratings of products from various countries.[68] The problems of attitude scaling have been investigated in the context of French–English differences among consumers in Quebec, Canada.[69] The use of traditional economic comparisons for crosscultural analysis is illustrated by Goldman's study of Soviet and American consumers.[70]

A pioneering crosscultural study was recently published by Sethi and involved a cluster analysis of 86 countries on 12 environmental and societal factors. While this study did not involve values, it does provide provocative methodology that might be applied to additional dimensions. Using the BC TRY system of cluster analysis to group variables in such a way as to maximize within-group similarities and between-group differences, Sethi found clusters which he labeled: (1) production and transportation, (2) personal consumption, (3) trade,

---

[64] Support for this statement is provided in a study by Richard H. Holton, "Marketing Policies in Multinational Corporations," *Calif. Management Rev.*, vol. 13, pp. 57–67, at p. 62 (Summer 1971).

[65] A.S.C. Ehrenberg and G. J. Goodhardt, "A Comparison of American and British Repeat-Buying Habits," *J. Marketing Research*, vol. 5, pp. 29–33 (Feb. 1968).

[66] S. Watson Dunn, "The Case Study Approach in Cross-Cultural Research," *J. Marketing Research*, vol. 3, pp. 26–31 (Feb. 1966).

[67] E. S. Lorimor and S. Watson Dunn, "Four Measures of Cross-Cultural Advertising Effectiveness," *J. Advertising Research*, vol. 8, pp. 11–13 (1968).

[68] Akira Nagashima, "A Comparison of Japanese and U.S. Attitudes toward Foreign Products," *J. Marketing*, vol. 34, pp. 68–74 (Jan. 1970).

[69] Richard W. Crosby, "Attitude Measurement in a Bilingual Culture," *J. Marketing Research*, vol. 6, pp. 421–426 (Nov. 1969).

[70] Marshall I. Goldman, "A Cross-Cultural Comparison of the Soviet and American Consumer," in Moyer, *op. cit.*,[62] pp. 195–199.

and (4) health and education. After the variables were grouped, countries were classified into clusters according to their scores on the clustered variables. Seven clusters were formed from the 86 countries. For example, countries such as Nigeria, Sudan, Dahomey, Tanzania, and South Vietnam were part of one cluster while Syria, Thailand, United Arab Republic, and the Philippines were part of the countries in another cluster. The United States could not be grouped with any of the other countries.[71] While this study is embryonic and does not yield data corresponding to consumer decisions or marketing strategy, it does provide the basis for much additional development potentially valuable in understanding ways of grouping markets together for common marketing programs.

To conclude this section on crosscultural marketing research, Table 4.5 is presented. In some instances, marketing strategists are confronted with cultures quite similar and in others with cultures very different. In too many unfortunate cases, what has "worked" in the United States has been applied to a foreign market without understanding if the cultural conditions were the same or not. A marketing strategist can improve his prediction of success by a careful analysis of the cultural conditions in his existing market, followed by another careful analysis of the cultural conditions in the market he contemplates entering. Where differences are observed, adjustment in the strategy employed can be undertaken. An outline for systematically analyzing the cultural determinants of success in each market is provided in Table 4.5. This outline is designed to be used either with formal research methods (such as those described above) or, if research is not feasible, as an outline for critical thinking and analysis in the design of global strategy.

Table 4.5   OUTLINE OF CROSSCULTURAL ANALYSIS OF CONSUMER BEHAVIOR

---

(1)   *Determine relevant motivations in the culture:*

What needs are fulfilled with this product in the minds of members of the culture? How are these needs presently fulfilled? Do members of this culture readily recognize these needs?

(2)   *Determine characteristic behavior patterns:*

What patterns are characteristic of purchasing behavior? What forms of division of labor exist within the family structure? How frequently are products of this type purchased? What size packages are normally purchased? Do any of these characteristic behaviors conflict with behavior expected for this product? How strongly ingrained are the behavior patterns that conflict with those needed for distribution of this product?

(3)   *Determine what broad cultural values are relevant to this product:*

Are there strong values about work, morality, religion, family relations, and so on, that relate to this product? Does this product connote attributes that are in

---

[71]   S. Prakash Sethi, "Comparative Cluster Analysis for World Markets," *J. Marketing Research*, vol. 8, pp. 348–354 (August 1971).

Table 4.5   OUTLINE OF CROSSCULTURAL ANALYSIS OF CONSUMER
BEHAVIOR (*Continued*)

conflict with these cultural values? Can conflicts with values be avoided by changing the product? Are there positive values in this culture with which the product might be identified?

(4)   *Determine characteristic forms of decision making:*

Do members of the culture display a studied approach to decisions concerning innovations or an impulsive approach? What is the form of the decision process? Upon what information sources do members of the culture rely? Do members of the culture tend to be rigid or flexible in the acceptance of new ideas? What criteria do they use in evaluating alternatives?

(5)   *Evaluate promotion methods appropriate to the culture:*

What role does advertising occupy in the culture? What themes, words, or illustrations are taboo? What language problems exist in present markets that cannot be translated into this culture? What types of salesmen are accepted by members of the culture? Are such salesmen available?

(6)   *Determine appropriate institutions for this product in the minds of consumers:*

What types of retailers and intermediary institutions are available? What services do these institutions offer that are expected by the consumer? What alternatives are available for obtaining services needed for the product but not offered by existing institutions? How are various types of retailers regarded by consumers? Will changes in the distribution structure be readily accepted?

FUNDAMENTAL FORCES OF CHANGE IN AMERICAN VALUES

Change is the key word of contemporary American life. Values are no exception. Values once were thought of as relatively permanent and passed from one generation to another with little alteration. Values are still passed from one generation to another, but in forms sometimes barely recognizable by either generation. Many values are still relatively permanent and they may even constitute the majority. It is apparent, however, that significant changes in some values are occurring at an increasing pace. Furthermore, the values most in transition frequently have considerable effect on consumer purchasing decisions.

Two types of influences may be isolated that bear the responsibility for values "learned" by the members of a society. One source of influence is the set of institutions that transfuse values from one generation to another. The other influences on values are the critical events experienced in a lifetime, particularly those of the early, formative years.

Institutional Influences on Values

A triad of institutions occupy a central position in the transfusion of values to individuals. Figure 4.1 illustrates the process of value transmission through the family, church, and school, as well as diversified institutions such as government and the media. The individual may accept all or only a part of the values transmitted to him, and while the individual is the key variable, he is influenced by his peers and their values. As long as each of the institutions is stable, the values transmitted are likely to be stable. However, as these institutions change (sometimes rapidly), the nature of values shared by contemporary consumers can be expected to change also. The last section of this chapter describes some of the changes that have occurred since World War II which are influencing the strategic consumer markets of the Seventies. While the changes are described in the context of the United States, it appears that they may also apply to much of the rest of the world.

Changing Family Influences   In most cultures, the family is the dominant transfusive agent of values. Several trends indicate a decline in this influence with the effect that values are stimulated toward more flexibility and change. Preschools are one type of influence. In the past, children spent the formative years of zero to six with their parents. Since the Fifties, this parent–child interaction has decreased markedly, permitting values to be learned outside the family to an increasing extent.

A second trend is the increasing divorce rate. Rather than learning the stable values that accompany traditional parent roles, children increasingly learn values from the media and peers. The same effect is often created in families with weekend fathers. In an agrarian society and later in blue-collar economy, children spent time with their fathers. At the end of World War II, blue-collar workers were about 15 percent more numerous than white-collar workers. But by the end of the Sixties, there were 30 percent more persons involved in white-collar pursuits than in blue-collar jobs.[72] The elite of white-collar fathers frequently have extensive travel and longer, irregular working hours, leaving less opportunity to implant their values among children. Working wives also contribute to leaving the children open to value transmission by institutions other than the family. During the second half of the 1940s only about 20 percent of married women were employed, but the rate increased so rapidly that by 1969 nearly 40 percent of all married women were working.

Geographical separation also contributes to decline of family influences. Massive increases in the proportion of young people attending college has created a situation where a much higher percentage of families take career positions geographically distant from where the family grew up and from the influence of the extended family. It is considerably more difficult to communicate and instill

---

[72]   *The Consumer of the Seventies* (New York: Conference Board, 1969), p. 36.

values of the extended families by letter and telephone than it is through personal, face-to-face contact.

Collectively, these changes have resulted in considerably less parent–child involvement and hence, less opportunity for parents to communicate, explain, and justify their values to their children. This is a major reason why the values of consumers in the Seventies differ from those of their parents.

Declining Religious Influences   Churches and other religious institutions in America have historically played an important role in teaching people what is right and wrong and hence in transmitting basic values from one generation to another. Although church membership increased to 64 percent in 1960, it since has plateaued and experienced a slight decline since 1967.[73] Church membership is one thing; church attendance is another. Gallup polls indicate that the proportion of the nation's adults attending church during a typical week has declined from about 49 percent in 1958 to 42 percent in 1968, a decrease of 14 percent.[74] A Gallup survey in 1969 found that 70 percent of adults felt that religion was losing its influence on American life. In 1957, only 14 percent held this view.[75] Furthermore, there is considerable evidence that *young people* reject the values of institutionalized religion to a greater degree than the previous generation. (For example, see Table 4.1, question 1D and Table 4.2, question 91.) Also young people who reject religious values and institutions are much more likely to hold radical rather than conservative values about other topics.[76]

The net effect of declining religious institutions is to allow values of the new consumer of the Seventies to be established in more personal and presumably more diversified ways. While there are indications from the media of youth and in the emergence of new types of free-form religious groupings that new consumers do not necessarily reject religious relationships and personal interest in the Divine,[77] it is apparent that the traditionally rigid value transmission of religious institutions is in serious decline.

Rising Influence of Educational Institutions   A third major institutional influence on values is the educational system. When a vacuum in effective value transmission emerged among families and churches, a more aggressive role

---

[73]   *Yearbook of American Churches,* annual editions. (New York: National Councils of the Churches of Christ).

[74]   *Op. cit.*[73]

[75]   *Washington Post* (June 7, 1969).

[76]   John Jameson and Richard M. Hessler, "The Natives are Restless: The Ethos and Mythos of Student Power," *Human Organization,* vol. 29, pp. 81–94, Table 5, (Summer 1970); also CBS News, *op. cit.,* pp. 54, 82.

[77]   These movements are described in William S. Cannon, *The Jesus Revolution* (Nashville, Tenn.: Broadman, 1971); Walker L. Knight, *Jesus People Come Alive* (Wheaton, Ill.: Tyndale House Pub., 1971). A good overview is in the Religion section of *Time,* vol. 97, pp. 56–63 (June 21, 1971).

evolved for schools.[78] Schools gained more contact with young consumers through rising enrollments in preschools and in universities. Other factors, however, also played an important part in the role of schools in transmitting different values.

Prior to World War II, teachers and professors originated primarily from the upper middle class. Upper-class parents sent their children to college also, but not to become teachers. Conversely, most lower-class families did not have the opportunity to send their children to college at all. Thus, historically, most teachers had upper-middle-class backgrounds and reflected in their teaching what have come to be known as the traditional American values. During the 1950s a new breed of teachers emerged as college enrollments from all social classes soared. While the middle classes still dominated teaching, teachers and professors now came to some extent from the entire spectrum of society. Children in schools could reasonably expect to encounter learning from at least a few teachers with values quite different from their own—and in some cases radically different.

A second trend occurred involving the emergence and proliferation of new teaching techniques. Previously, teaching methods emphasized description and memorization. This approach to "learning" implicitly, if not explicitly, says, "This is the way things are; just learn it," with no latitude for questioning. During the past two decades, however, there has been a gradual but steady trend away from description and memorization in favor of analytical approaches emphasizing questioning of the old and the formulation of new approaches and solutions. In many instances this approach concludes that there is no one correct answer. The case method in business school is an example of this approach.

The result is a "spillover" of questioning and rejection of rigid definitions of "right and wrong" from the educational system into the basic values of life.[79] To paraphrase MacLeish, "The central reality of our time is that individuals, particularly younger people, are no longer willing to lead unexamined lives."[80] To an increasing extent, consumers' minds do not operate in black and white but rather in the more realistic and complicated nuances of full color.

Intergenerational Motivating Factors

"Every man is a product of his environment" is a familiar truism. A less familiar one is that "Men strive to achieve as adults what they feel they were deprived of in early stages of life." These generalizations suggest another set of reasons why values are changing—the lifetime experiences of the youth of the Fifties and Sixties are fundamentally and qualitatively different from those of previous generations. This gap has no parallels; it is probably unprecedented.

---

[78]   For an expansion of these ideas, see Harvey C. Burke, "The University in Transition," *Business Horizons*, vol. 12, pp. 5–17 (Aug. 1969).

[79]   Jameson and Hessler, *op. cit.,*[76] p. 81.

[80]   Statement attributed to Archibald MacLeish.

Pre-World War II Consumers By far the majority of contemporary American consumers were not yet born during the Great Depression of the 1930s and for most Americans, even World War II predates their personal history. Yet severity of these two events had a profound and indelible impact on the lives of consumers who experienced them. The fact that the effects of these events were so pervasive made their impact a national experience as well as a private one. Hence there is a marked tendency for consumers who experienced the Depression and World War II to hold values that emphasize job security, patriotism, and the acquisition of wealth and material goods. These were the things they were deprived of as children. What has come to be known as conventional values and life styles, reflected in older consumers, were a logical consequence of the experiences of the Depression and World War II.

Post-World War II Consumers Instead of the ravages of the Depression, the strategic consumer markets of the Seventies experienced during childhood the greatest period of prolonged economic expansion in the history of the United States. During the 1950s, the economy nearly doubled and repeated the growth again in the Sixties. Even though a substantial amount of this growth represented inflation, there remained a tremendous proliferation of affluence.

The critical lifetime experiences of contemporary consumers vary greatly, but among the prominent ones are the following: the nuclear age, the civil rights movement, pockets of poverty amidst mass affluence, questionable space exploration, the Vietnam War, concern about ecology, pervasive university experiences, and a revolution in communication technology.[81]

These influences are manifested in some consumer segments holding beliefs that the United States has inverted national priorities from what they should be, reactions against social and institutional rigidity, and reactions toward the hypocrisy perceived to exist throughout the society.[82] For many consumers, a new value has emerged as a reaction to countries fighting each other, races quarreling, social classes resenting each other, and parents bickering. This new emphasis is on "community," understanding, and, to oversimplify, on love.

Marketing organizations have recognized the new values with cosmetics bearing the name of love, soft-drink advertisements featuring a people orientation rather than product emphasis for "those with a lot to live," and advertisements featuring music, themes, and artwork stressing communication, humanity, and many forms of love. Even the design of apartment projects has been affected with the desire to build a "community" of persons with similar interests and activities rather than simply to sell square feet of shelter.

---

[81] These are adapted from several sources. Many are discussed in Margaret Mead, "The Generation Gap That Has No Parallels," *The Providence Sunday J.* p. N–43. (Oct. 4, 1970). For underlying data, see CBS News, *op. cit.;*[41] Ardery, *op. cit.;*[42] Herzog *et al., op. cit.,*[43] also "What They Believe," *Fortune,* pp. 70–71 ff (Jan. 1969).

[82] In addition to *op. cit.,*[82] see Daniel Bell, "Social Trends of the 70's", *Conference Board Record,* pp. 6–8 (June 1970).

EMERGING AMERICAN VALUES

A set of cultural traits are emerging which, as generalizations, can be described as the emerging American values. These values are built upon a relatively permanent cultural base inherited from past generations. They are being modified in important ways, however, for the reasons described in the preceding sections of this chapter. The modifications are occurring at varying rates, and much research is needed to determine the rapidity with which new values are replacing old ones and the pervasiveness of acceptance. Because marketing is a discipline oriented toward the changes that are likely to occur in the future as a basis for strategic planning, the emphasis in the following pages is upon the emerging trends rather than on the present or the past. The emerging values described below include youthfulness, changing religious conceptions, creative eroticism, and the leisure life.

Youthfulness

The young are changing the character of America. They are "greening" America according to the hypothesis of some.[83] Significantly, marketing organizations have successfully developed major programs and strategies to appeal to the value of "youthfulness" in the American society. The most successful of these appear to have targeted their communications to the *values of youth* rather than to market segments rigidly defined on the basis of age. In fact, *youth* probably should be defined not as an age group, but rather as a *set of attitudes correlated with age.* Key among these attitudes is *receptivity to change.*

Strategic Growth Markets   The significant population growth in the 1970s in the United States (and many other countries) is concentrated among consumers in the 25 to 34 age group. Between 1970 and 1980, the number of persons between 30 and 34 will increase by 53.2 percent and the number of persons aged 25 to 29 will increase by 40.3 percent.[84] By contrast, the *total* population is projected to increase only 13 or 14 percent during this same period —and for some of the middle-aged groups there will be *actual (not just relative) decreases.* The impact on values (through influences in society) can be understood even more clearly by analyzing the changes in spending power. In 1967, for example, families in the 25 to 34 age category possessed only 18.4 percent of the income in the United States, but by 1980 this same group is projected to com-

---

[83]   Charles A. Reich, *The Greening of America* (New York: Random House, 1970); Jean-Francois Revel, *Without Marx or Jesus* (New York: Doubleday, 1971).

[84]   Department of Commerce, *Current Population Reports,* P-25, and authors' calculations.

mand at least 26 percent of all income and will be the economy's most important age category in terms of purchasing power.[85]

Longevity–Learning Inversion A major reason for the influence of youth on the rest of American values may be called the *longevity–learning inversion*. In the past the family member who was best able to determine if the crops should be harvested before it rained or if a child was seriously ill was *typically* the grandfather, who had the most experience in judging threatening skies, or the grandmother, who had felt the most temperature-laden brows and who knew just the right remedy. Today, however, the experience of these members of the family has been replaced by education in the science of agriculure and education in the medical sciences. Thus, usefulness of longevity has been replaced by education.

With changes in technology and an accelerated culture, corporations are placing more emphasis on education and creativity to solve today's problems. They place an increasing value on the M.B.A. or the bright young designer rather than the senior executive who has limited education but lots of years of experience. Organizations may give lip service to the need for seniority and longevity, but the successful ones are putting more and more of their dollars and destinies into the hands of the well educated and the creative. Of course, neither education nor creativity is the exclusive domain of the young, but the young have more opportunities than their predecessors to acquire and develop both. Consequently, it is the young that increasingly are given the responsibilities for running corporations, government, and society in general.

Because society values and rewards youth (and youth—linked characteristics such as education, creativity, and sexual attractiveness), people who are not young in age want to be perceived as youthful. Marketing strategists have realized this and successfully promoted clothing, automobiles, home furnishings, personal grooming items, and many other products with a youthful approach, even though the average purchaser was middle aged. One automobile manufacturer successfully introduced a sporty, new small car with an image of racing, sexual attractiveness, and communication messages designed to attract youth. The car sold in large quantities, but the age of the typical buyer was 46. The *number* of youthful consumers in the American market is large; the *influence* that they have upon values and consumer purchases in other age groups is even more striking.[86]

---

[85] U.S. Department of Commerce, National Industrial Conference Board, and authors' calculations. For additional data, see Kollat *et al., op. cit.,*[7] chap. 6. The impact of young people is also described in "44 Million Young Adults—A New Wave of Buyers," *U.S. News and World Report*, pp. 16–19 (Jan. 17, 1972).

[86] The importance of youthfulness on marketing strategies surpasses the amount of discussion that is permitted here. See the following references: "Identity Crisis in the Consumer Markets," *Fortune*, vol. 83, pp. 92–95ff (Mar. 1971); Lee Adler, "Cashing-In on the Cop-Out," *Business Horizons*, vol. 13, pp. 19–30 (Feb. 1970); "Youth Market: Are They Mini-Adults or Maxi Mysteries?" *Marketing/Communications*, pp. 54–57 (Dec. 1970); Joseph S. Coyle, "A Big Bright Bid for the Young Consumer," *Progressive Grocer*, pp. 70–78 (June 1971); Irvin Penner, "The College Credit Market," *Stores*, pp. 14–16 (Sept. 1970); *A Study of Young People* (New York: Doyle Dane Bernback, 1966). For a discussion of adapting managerial strategies to youthful values, see Roger D. Blackwell and David T. Kollat, *Marketing to Youth in the Seventies* (Columbus, Ohio: Management Horizons, 1970).

Changing Religious Conceptions

America has a history of religiosity as a basic value. Under religiosity are subsumed many cultural values such as attitudes toward work, toward humanity, morality, and estimates of one's self-worth. The Jewish and Christian faiths, which dominate America's culture, emphasize the worth of an individual. This manifests itself in a belief that objects which are an extension of an individual's personality are important; thus consumption of products appealing to self-expression, to effective presentation of one's personal characteristics, and to fulfillment of reasonable physical needs is sanctioned in the culture. At the same time, however, American religious values have generally emphasized that the way to get these socially and individually desirable goal objects is through hard work, thrifty purchase behavior, and accumulation of wealth. These latter values, identified especially with the Puritan ethic, are increasingly challenged within the American culture.

The Puritan ethic is being replaced with a "theology of pleasure" which emphasizes a new type of individuality and release from prohibitions on sensate consumption decisions. The demand for play and pleasure is consistent with the economics of affluence but has been constrained until recently by the Puritan ethic. Bell amplifies:

> The Puritan ethic might be described most simply by the phrase "delayed gratification." It is, of course, the Malthusian injunction for prudence in a world of scarcity. But the claim of the American economic system was that it had introduced abundance, and the nature of abundance is to encourage prodigality rather than prudence. The "higher standard of living," not work as an end in itself, then becomes the engine of change. The glorification of plenty, rather than the bending to niggardly nature, becomes the justification of the system. But all of this was highly incongruent with the theological and sociological foundations of nineteenth century Protestantism, which was in turn the foundation of the American value system.[87]

Marketing strategists have found the changing conceptions of religious values to be important in facilitating new marketing tactics. Colors and designs can be bright and sensual; cosmetics and grooming aids can emphasize pleasure with the body; credit can be stimulated with appeals to enjoy products now and pay later; even banks can throw off their stodgy, conservative image with psychodelically designed checks.

The magnitude of change in religious conceptions is difficult to assess. After an exhaustive examination of religious studies, Demerath concluded that religious trends must be interpreted cautiously but that a liberalization of faith in America is occurring.[88] While it is difficult to find concensus about the continu-

---

87   Daniel Bell, "The Cultural Contradictions of Capitalism," *The Public Interest,* no. 21, pp. 16–43, at p. 38 (Fall 1970).

88   N. J. Demerath, III, "Trends and Anti-Trends in Religious Change," in Sheldon and Moore, *op. cit.,*[16] pp. 349–445. A massive compilation of current trends in religions is also available in Donald R. Cutler (ed.), *The Religious Situation: 1969* (Boston: Beacon, 1969).

ance and future direction of religious values, Cox, after assessing many viewpoints, concludes that in all religious groups the "Dionysiac" element marked by ectasy, joy, emotion, and movement will assert itself and that members of society will assemble their own "collage" or personal symbol system.[89] This would appear to facilitate individualized but luxuriant consumption.

Creative Eroticism

Creative eroticism has emerged as an American value of significant interest to marketers. The term refers to the playful, slightly disguised appeals to sexual motives as opposed to blatant sexuality or pornography. Creative eroticism describes the transition from rigid prohibitions on fun with sex to the present freedom in most situations although not to the extent of complete release of inhibitions. Forerunner college students overwhelmingly reject the value that one must be married before he can "live with" someone.[90] Of college youth in general 64 percent believe that premarital sexual relations are not a moral issue, but at the same time 77 percent believe that extramarital sexual relations are morally wrong. A much higher proportion thought their parents would feel either issue was morally wrong.[91] Studies at Harvard indicate that the proportion of senior males reporting sex during the previous year rose from 69.3 percent in the 1960s to 80.2 percent in 1970.[92]

The marketing implications of shifting values about sex have become apparent. Advertisements have dropped most inhibitions about what can be shown and have become "creative" in developing the themes. The Noxema girl suggesting that he "take it all off," the White Owl girl, and Miss Springmaid seductively displaying towels and sheets (in women's magazines) have become, in themselves, a part of the American culture.[93]

The Leisure Life

One of the changing values in America is the increasing emphasis upon leisure, replacing the values of hard work and long hours.[94] Mead expresses the change this way:

---

[89]   Harvey Cox, "The Future of Christianity and the Church," *The Futurist,* pp. 122–129; (Aug. 1970); also see other views on the future of religion in the same publication, pp. 129–138, and "Christianity's Conflicting Views of the Future," *The Futurist,* pp. 95–96 (Aug. 1969).

[90]   "What They Believe," *op. cit.,*[82] p. 180.

[91]   CBS News, *op. cit.,*[41] p. 17.

[92]   Rebecca S. Vreeland, "Dating Patterns of Harvard Men," *Psychology Today,* (January, 1972).

[93]   For a review of psychological studies concerning the effect of sexual material in communications and a defense of advertising, see William A. Yoell, *How Sexy is Advertising?* (Peekskill, N.Y.: Behavior Research Institute, 1971).

[94]   George Fisk, *Leisure Spending Behavior* (Philadelphia: University of Pennsylvania Press, 1963).

> As once it was wrong to play so hard that it might affect one's work,
> now it is wrong to work so hard that it may affect family life.[95]

The changing value toward leisure or recreation has been recognized by many business firms as the underlying factor for huge amounts of consumer goods.[96]

Analysis of consumer behavior is facilitated by viewing leisure expenditures as consisting of money and/or time. Thus, consumers may be analyzed in terms of their *money budget* and their *time budget*. Time, however, is the ultimate constraint whereas money budgets have no theoretical expansion limit. It can readily be seen that as discretionary income continues to increase in a society, markets for time-related goods or services become more important. The consumer implications are described by Garretson and Mauser:

> The affluent citizen . . . will be oriented *to buying time rather than product*. His chief concern will be to provide himself with free time in which he can conveniently use products that function to conserve time for leisure and pleasure. It is scarcity which creates value. Hence, as *scarcity of product disappears, the scarcity of time ascends the value scale*.[97]

The amount of time spent in search behavior is also a determinant of consumer choice as well as time spent in product consumption or time avoidance values.[98]

A definition of leisure useful for analysis of consumer behavior is provided by Voss:

> Leisure . . . may be defined as follows: *Leisure* is a period of time referred to as *discretionary time*. It is that period of time when an individual feels no sense of economic, legal, moral, or social compulsion or obligation, nor of physiological necessity. The choice of how to utilize this time period is solely his.[99]

The questions that marketing strategists must answer then, include: How many hours of each day are spent for work, nondiscretionary time, and discretionary time? What products are purchased for use in each type of time? How much will consumers pay for time-saving products in order to increase their discretionary time? How much additional work time will consumers accept in order to pay for time-saving or time-using (leisure) goods?

---

[95] "The Pattern of Leisure in Contemporary American Culture," *Annals of the American Academy of Political and Social Science*, vol. 313, p. 14 (1957).

[96] "83 Billion Dollars for Leisure—Now the Fastest-Growing Business in America," *U.S. News and World Report*, pp. 58–60 (Sept. 15, 1969); *Investment Opportunities in a $150-Billion Market* (New York: Merrill, Lynch, Pierce, Fenner and Smith, 1968). Note that the impreciseness of definitions of leisure is indicated by the titles of these articles.

[97] Robert C. Garretson and Ferdinand F. Mauser, "The Future Challenges Marketing," *Harvard Business Rev.*, vol. 41, pp. 168 ff (Nov.–Dec. 1963).

[98] Philip B. Schary, "Consumption and the Problem of Time," *J. Marketing*, vol. 35, pp. 50–55 (Apr. 1971).

[99] Justin Voss, "The Definition of Leisure," *J. Economic Issues*, vol. 1, pp. 91–106 (June 1967). For other conceptions of leisure, see Max Kaplan, "Leisure: Issues for American Business," paper presented to National Association of Business Economists, pp. 7–8 (Oct. 26, 1970).

Answers to the above questions are difficult. Ennis, in a comprehensive review of the methodological problems in measuring leisure, concludes that baseline studies of time usage are urgently needed.[100] One review of a number of time and leisure studies is provided by Riley and Foner.[101] This study, however, emphasizes the time consumption habits of older persons as compared to younger market segments.

A consumer choice that is increasingly apparent is the placement of greater value on blocks of time for discretionary purposes.[102] This emphasizes the need to focus analysis upon the *form* of discretionary time as well as the *amounts* of additional leisure. Longer vacations, earlier retirement, more holidays are increasingly demanded by consumers as "lumps of leisure." The emergence of the 4-day work week is another example of consumers choice of blocked time providing additional discretion.[103] The impact of the 4-day work week is as great in the analysis of consumption as in production. When Henry Ford lead the way in 1926 in converting from a 6-day week to a 5-day week, he is reported to have said, "It is the influence of leisure on consumption which makes the short day and the short week so necessary."[104]

Other Values

There are many other values that characterize the American culture and that are accepted by a broad spectrum of the population. It is not possible to describe the others here, but they include the changing roles of women, tendencies toward other direction, increasing influence of children, and the very major role of urbanization as an influence on values. A major study of American values, with emphasis on their influence on consumer behavior, has been conducted by Daniel Yankelovich, Inc. These trends are reported in Table 4.6.

This concludes the discussion of emerging values. Much more discussion is warranted because culture provides a major influence on consumer decisions. New and improved methodologies will undoubtedly also emerge in order to

---

[100] Phillip H. Ennis, "The Definition and Measurement of Leisure," in Sheldon and Moore, *op. cit.*,[46] pp. 525–572.

[101] Matilda W. Riley and Anne Foner, "Leisure Roles," in *Aging and Society* (New York: Russell Sage Foundation, 1968), chap. 22, pp. 511–535.

[102] A useful review is found in Geoffrey H. Moore and Janice N. Hedges, "Trends in Labor and Leisure," *Monthly Labor Rev.*, pp. 3–11 (Feb. 1971).

[103] Riva Poor (ed.), *4 Days, 40 Hours: Reporting a Revolution in Work and Leisure* (Cambridge, Mass.: Bursk and Poor Publ., 1970); also John Wittman, "The Compressed Workweek," *Manpower*, pp. 18–19 (July 1971); Wilbur Cross, "The Four-Day Work Week is Coming Sooner Than You Think," *Business Management*, pp. 14–15 ff (Apr. 1971); Janice N. Hedges, "A Look at the 4-Day Workweek," *Monthly Labor Rev.*, pp. 33–37 (Oct. 1971).

[104] In addition to previous footnotes, basic sources on changing values toward time and leisure include the following: Sebastian de Grazia, *Of Time, Work and Leisure* (New York: Twentieth Century Fund, 1962); Gary Becker, "A Theory of the Allocation of Time," *Economic J.*, pp. 494–517 (Sept. 1965); Steffan B. Linder, *The Harried Leisure Class* (New York: Columbia University Press, 1970); Bevars D. Mabry, "An Analysis of Work and Other Constraints on Choices of Activities," *Western Economics J.*, vol. 8, pp. 213–225 (Sept. 1970).

Table 4.6   THE 30 SOCIAL TRENDS THAT ALTER CONSUMPTION

(1)   *Psychology of Affluence*

Trend toward physical self-enhancement: Spending more time, effort, and money on improving one's physical appearance; the things people do to enhance their looks.

Trend toward personalization: Expressing one's individuality through products, possessions, and new life styles; the need to be "a little bit different" from other people.

Trend toward physical health and well-being: The level of concern with one's health, diet, and what people do to take better care of themselves.

Trend toward new forms of materialism: The new status symbols and the extent of deemphasis on money and material possessions.

Trend toward social and cultural self-expression: The "culture explosion" and what it means to various segments of the population.

Trend toward personal creativity: The growing conviction that being "creative" is not confined to the artist. Each man can be creative in his own way, as expressed through a wide variety of activities, hobbies, and new uses of leisure time.

Trend toward meaningful work: The spread of the demand for work that is challenging and meaningful over and above how well it pays.

(2)   *Antifunctional Trends*

Trend toward the "new romanticism": The desire to restore romance, mystery, and adventure to modern life.

Trend toward novelty and change: The search for constant change, novelty, new experience, reaction against sameness, and habit.

Trend toward adding beauty to one's daily surroundings: The stress on beauty in the home and the things people do and buy to achieve it.

Trend toward sensuousness: Placing greater emphasis on a total sensory experience—touching, feeling, smelling, and psychedelic phenomena; a moving away from the purely linear, logical, and visual.

Trend toward mysticism: The search for new modes of spiritual experience and beliefs, as typified by the growing interest in astrology.

Trend toward Introspection: An enhanced need for self-understanding and life experiences in contrast to automatic conformity to external pressures and expectations.

(3)   *Reaction against Complexity Trends*

Trend toward life simplification: The turning away from complicated products, services and ways of life.

Trend toward return to nature: Rejection of the artificial, the "chemical," the man-made improvements on nature; the adoption of more "natural" ways of dressing, eating, and living.

Trend toward increased ethnicity: Finding new satisfactions and identifications in foods, dress, customs, and life styles of various ethnic groups such as Black, Italian, Irish, Polish, Jewish, German.

Trend toward increased community involvement: Increasing affiliation with

Table 4.6 THE 30 SOCIAL TRENDS THAT ALTER CONSUMPTION
(*Continued*)

---

local, community, and neighborhood activities; greater involvement in local groups.

Trend toward greater reliance on technology versus tradition: Distrust of tradition and reputation that is based on age and experience, due to the swift tempo of change; greater confidence in science and technology.

Trend away from bigness: The departure from the belief that "big" necessarily means "good," beginning to manifest itself with respect to "big" brands, "big" stores.

(4) *Trends That Move Away from Puritan Values*

Trend toward pleasure for its own sake: Putting pleasure before duty; changing life styles and what that means for product usage and communication.

Trend toward blurring of the sexes: Moving away from traditional distinctions between men and women and the role each should play in marriage, work, and other walks of life.

Trend toward living in the present: Straying from traditional beliefs in planning, saving, and living for the future.

Trend toward more liberal sexual attitudes: The relaxation of sexual prohibitions and the devaluation of "virtue" in the traditional sense, among women.

Trend toward acceptance of stimulants and drugs: Greater acceptance of artificial agents (legal and illegal) for mood change, stimulation, and relaxation as opposed to the view that these should be accomplished by strength of character alone.

Trend toward relaxation of self-improvement standards: The inclination to stop working as hard at self-improvement, letting yourself be whatever you are.

Trend toward individual religions: Rejection of institutionalized religions and the substitution of more personalized forms of religious experience, characterized by the emergence of numerous small and more intimate religious sects and cults.

(5) *Trends Related to Child Centeredness*

Trend toward greater tolerance of chaos and disorder: Less need for schedules, routines, plans, regular shopping, and purchasing; tolerance of less order and cleanliness in the home, less regular eating and entertaining patterns.

Trend toward challenge to authority: Less automatic acceptance of the authority and "correctness" of public figures, institutions and established brands.

Trend toward rejection of hypocrisy: Less acceptance of sham, exaggeration, indirection, and misleading language.

Trends toward female careerism: Belief that homemaking is not sufficient as the sole source of fulfillment and that more challenging and productive work for the woman is needed.

Trend toward familism: Renewed faith in the belief that the essential life satisfactions stem from activities centering on the immediate family unit rather than on "outside" sources such as work and community affairs.

SOURCE: *Marketing News*, pp. 7–8 (Mid-May 1971).

measure these important constraints and stimulants to consumer behavior.[105] The forecasting of values and their impact upon society is almost certain to become an important part of the consumer researcher's skills.[106]

SUMMARY

Human decision making is molded and influenced in broad, decisive ways by the culture in which it operates. Culture includes both abstract and material elements. Material artifacts include products offered to consumers. But it is the abstract elements such as values and attitudes that influence what people accept and want. Consequently, marketing strategists need research-based information concerning values and other aspects of culture that influence consumption decisions.

Culture is represented as a learned set of responses and is inculcated in each succeeding generation. When culturally defined responses are dysfunctional (not gratifying) in a society, they are adapted and become new forms of response.

Four basic methods of studying culture are described in this chapter. These include intensive field studies, content analysis, cross-sectional studies, and longitudinal studies of values.

Crosscultural analysis is described in this chapter as a systematic comparison of the similarities and differences in the behavioral and material aspects of cultures. Crosscultural analysis provides an approach to understanding market segments based upon subcultural values. It has been more widely used by marketing strategists for examining global markets.

The final portion of this chapter describes the fundamental forces of change in American values. These are identified as institutional influences including the family, religious groups, and schools, and intergenerational motivating influences of the Great Depression and the era of the Fifties.

The chapter concludes with a discussion of emerging American values such as youthfulness, evolving religious conceptions, creative eroticism, leisure, and other value trends. The purpose of this discussion is to present major influences on the planning of marketing strategies involving consumer products and services.

REVIEW AND DISCUSSION QUESTIONS

1. What role is played by social and cultural influences on human decision making? Relate your answer to the model of consumer decision making presented in Chapter 3.

2. Many alternative definitions of culture are possible. What are the essential elements that should be included in a definition of culture?

---

[105] A discussion of new typologies for conducting research on values is found in Henry Clark, "The Changing Character of American Values," *The Futurist*, pp. 9–11 (Feb. 1970).

[106] Alvin Toffler, *Future Shock* (New York: Random House, 1970).

3. A cultural trait may be known to exist and be a strong influence in a given society, yet the marketing analyst may find that an individual within that society does not share that cultural trait at all. He may simply ignore the cultural trait or openly reject it. Why does this occur?

4. Four basic methodologies used in studying values are presented. Describe the nature of each.

5. Outline a research project using the participant-observer methodology in a way that would be useful in developing a marketing strategy.

6. What is meant by crosscultural analysis? Discuss its relevance in developing marketing strategy.

7. Select from the topics of family, religious groups, or schools and prepare a report on changes that are occurring in these institutions.

8. Describe what is meant by the longevity–learning inversion and discuss its relevance to marketing strategists.

9. In what way is the rise of urbanism related to the changing values described in this chapter.

10. Describe the impact on consumption that can be predicted with the rise of the 4-day work week.

CHAPTER **5**

SOCIAL STRATIFICATION

"Birds of a feather flock together," says an old adage. It is more than an idle folk saying, for in this truism lies the concept of stratification of society into groups that feel as if they "belong together." The people in each group recognize or feel that other persons rank above them, often without knowing on what basis the ranking occurs. In India, stratification is called the caste system. In medieval Europe, it was based upon the estate into which one was born. In the United States and much of the rest of the world, stratification of the social system is called the class system, or social class. This chapter describes the nature of stratification, measurement techniques and issues, social-class behavior patterns, and social-class influence on consumer decision making.

THE PROCESS OF STRATIFICATION

The process of stratification in a social system occurs in at least two forms. There is within-group stratification and between-group stratification. The first form reflects the esteem or deference a person is accorded by other members of his social group. (This form of stratification is discussed in the chapter following the present one.) Between-group stratification refers to ordering of groups (of individuals or families) within a community. That is, an individual is accorded a certain amount of esteem or deference within a community based upon the amount of esteem generally accorded to the *group* of which he is a member. Between-group stratification specifies behavior that is expected and perceived to characterize each group and is the basis of social class formation.

Students of behavior need to maintain an objective, detached viewpoint when studying social classes. To some, it may seem "un-American" to talk about social classes in a "land of the free" where every man is guaranteed equal rights; to those persons it might appear undemocratic to give recognition to the fact that classes exist and characterize organization of the society. To others, it may seem anti-Marxist to disclose that no known society exists or has existed in which social inequality is not present.[1] Even animal societies have stratification and exhibit class behavior.[2] A detached viewpoint may be difficult, but researchers must objectively explore the nature of class behavior if they are to understand realistically the nature of human decision making and behavior.

Social Class Defined

Social classes may be defined as *relatively permanent and homogeneous divisions in a society into which individuals or families sharing similar values, life styles, interests, and behavior can be categorized.* There is little agreement, however, concerning the nature of those divisions or the criteria for defining them.[3]

Homogeneous Behavior   Social classes are considered to be the largest homogeneous grouping within the society. All of the members *tend* to behave like one another. With life styles, values, personalities, and interests manifesting homogeneity, it is expected that consumer decision making should also display similarities within a social class. This assumption is of critical importance for the consumer analyst.

Social classes *restrict behavior between individuals of differing social classes,* especially in intimate relationships. People have their close social relation-

---

[1]   The fact that stratification is ubiquitous is recognized by nearly all sociologists, although there is considerable question whether stratification is "inevitable." The class article delineating why stratification has arisen in all societies is that by Kingsley Davis and Wilbert E. Moore, "Some Principles of Stratification," *Amer. Sociological Rev.*, vol. 5, pp. 242–249 (1945). For an opposing view, see Melvin M. Tumin, "Some Principles of Stratification: A Critical Analysis," *Amer. Sociological Rev.*, vol. 13, pp. 387–393 (1953).

[2]   This has been verified in studies of insects, deer, mice, wolves, birds, and other animals. One of the most fascinating studies was conducted by a Norwegian zoologist who observed social stratification in a society of hens and found that each hen tends to maintain a definite position in the peck order of the group. (Thus, the existence of what most kinds of workers have known to exist all along: the pecking order.) The researcher concludes, "There are no two hens within the same community who do not exactly know who is superordinate and who is subordinate." Se. T. Schjelderup-Ebbe, "Social Behavior of Birds," in C. Murchison (ed.), *A Handbook of Social Psychology* (Worcester, Mass.: Clark University Press, 1935).

[3]   An excellent discussion of the problems in defining social class, stratification, and status and of the theoretical perspectives that exist in status research is found in Thomas E. Lasswell, *Class and Stratum: An Introduction to Concepts and Research* (Boston: Houghton Mifflin Co., 1965), chaps. 1–4.

ships with people of similar classes, which tends to restrict interpersonal communications about products and stores to persons within a consumer's own social class.

Hierarchical Positions   An important reality of social classes is that they are hierarchical. When people are asked about other groups of people, they tend to compare themselves in superior or inferior positions. People may not know the basis of the ranking, but they do know that ranking exists in their own minds and in the minds of other people. Social class exists as a *position* without reference to a specific person. A person can be defined as a member of a social *class* even if that member violates the normal behavior of the class.

Multidimensional Measures   Social classes are considered unidimensionally but typically measured multidimensionally. When thinking of social classes, people usually think of a single underlying variable. Yet, that variable has never been identified. It may be some combination of power, privilege, prestige, influence, good manners, or something else. A single variable has not been identified and may not exist.

In the absence of knowledge about the true variable upon which groups within a society are stratified, it is necessary to use proxy variables such as wealth, power, prestige, or interactions. Usually, social class is treated as some combination of these. *No one of these proxy variables is equivalent to social class.* It is misleading, for example, to think of income as the same as social class even though they are correlated. Social class, or whatever true variable of social position is the underlying basis for stratifying the society, is a much richer concept than any of the proxy variables that typically are used as measures.

Continuous Measures   In theory, social classes are discrete divisions in society. In practice, this is rarely observed and social classes are treated as a continuous variable. Individuals in a class system (which is mobile in contrast to a caste system prohibiting movement between divisions in society) are constantly moving into higher classes or dropping into lower ones. The classes themselves experience change, at least on the fringes, as they become larger or smaller, adapt to new environmental conditions, or modify existing behavior norms.

It is useful to measure social classes as *loci of variables* rather than as unique attributes. The members of one social class may possess much more of a variable but other social classes will share some of that variable. The fact that social classes do not fit into neat, discrete groups possessing a unique culture causes conceptual ambiguity and methodological complexity but must be accepted as the true situation.

Social Class and Status

The *status* of an individual is not the same concept as social class. Status is defined as an individual's rank in the total social system (or subsystem) as perceived by other members of the system. The status of an individual is determined partially by the status of the *social group* (class) to which he belongs and partially by the *personal characteristics* of the individual. Personal characteristics that affect the status of an individual include (1) his rank within the social class and (2) special contributions to society.

Rank within Class Individuals vary in their rank within a class. A physician who earns $90,000 a year, for example, can be expected to have higher perceived rank within his social class than a physician earning only $20,000. Thus, the *status* of the first physician is higher than that of the second, even though they may be of equivalent social classes (if they possess other characteristics that are similar in addition to occupation).

Special Services to Society An individual's *status* is improved by performing special services that are approved by the society, especially when they are of an unusual nature. For example, a professor who makes an important scientific breakthrough enhances his status, a businessman who serves as an elected official enhances his status if the position is perceived as important, and a writer who has a best seller achieves higher status than a writer of unsuccessful material.

Status Characteristics It is common in consumer research to measure the *status characteristics* of an individual and to avoid the concept of social class. The theoretical difficulties with the concept of social class have been so perplexing that many sociologists simply compute a measure of "status characteristics" or of socioeconomic status and use this in the same way they might use social class.

Frequently the terms "social class" and "status" are used interchangeably, and sometimes the results are not altered by doing so. This is often true in marketing, because research is concerned chiefly with market *segments* rather than individuals. Since social classes are groups of individuals with roughly equivalent status, it may be possible to measure status characteristics and infer the behavioral norms of the social class.

Social Classes Transmit Culture

The totality of culture is made specific for a family and ultimately an individual through social classes. They define the expectations of society for groups of people and for families within the groups. The family then transmits these cultural expectations to the individual.

Social classes create different patternings of behavior specific to groups of people but drawn from a common and pervasive group of elements in the core culture. The variations among classes in cultural manifestations may be subtle or they may be obvious, and the marketer seeks to understand what these differences are.

The effects of social class influences pervade all of life. Variations in cultural patternings among social classes begin before birth and continue after death. A summary of some cultural patternings influenced by social class serves to illustrate this point.

(1) An individual's *probability of being born* is influenced by the fertility rates of his family's social class.

(2) The *probability of an individual living* beyond birth is influenced by the social class into which he is born.

(3) The type of *childhood training* an individual receives is heavily influenced by his social class environment.

(4) The amount and type of *education* an individual receives is influenced by his social class environment.

(5) The nature of his *personal interactions* and development of communicative skills is influenced by his social class environment.

(6) The *occupation* he enters will be heavily influenced by the social class of his father and the cumulative effects of social class and individual experiences as a child.

(7) The *religion* of an individual is influenced by his social class.

(8) The types of *activities* and patterns of behavior exhibited by an individual are influenced by his social class.

(9) The amount of *economic goods and the way an individual regards them* is influenced by his social class.

(10) The kind of *funeral* an individual receives is influenced by the social class of the survivors.

SOCIAL-CLASS DETERMINANTS

Sociological theory relating to social class has centered upon two topics. First, sociologists have attempted to answer the question of why social classes develop in a society. Second, they have asked the question, "Given the fact that social classes exist, what determines the social class of a specific individual?" It is the second question that is of most direct relevance to consumer analysts.[4] One

---

[4] The reader who is interested in the first question, that of the general sociological theory of stratification, has available a number of excellent sources. See, for example, Davis and Moore, *op. cit.*;[1] also Talcott Parsons, *The Social System* (New York: Free Press, 1955); Bernard Barber, *Social Stratification: A Comparative Analysis of Structure and Process* (New York: Harcourt, 1957); Robert K. Merton, *Social Theory and Social Structure* (New York: Free Press, 1949); Gerhard E. Lenski, *Power and Privilege: A Theory of Social Stratification* (New York: McGraw-Hill, 1966). See p. 439 of Lenski for an attempt to diagram a general theory of stratification. For useful bibliographies, see Donald G. MacRae, "Social Stratification: A Trend Report and Bibliography," *Current Sociology*, vol. 2, no. 1, entire issue (1953–1954); Harold W. Pfautz, "The Current Literature on Social Stratification: Critique and Bibliography," *Amer. J. Sociology*, vol. 58, pp. 391–418 (1953).

very useful schema for understanding the determinants of social class and status has been developed by Kahl. It is used here, with considerable modification, to describe the determinants of an individual's status.[5]

Occupation

Whenever strangers meet, a question soon asked is, "What kind of work do you do?" This question provides a good clue to the social class of the individual. It is used by consumer analysts in measuring social class and is often the most accurate single indicator available. Hewitt concludes:

> A feature of industrial society is that occupations are the social positions most important for differential evaluation, perhaps because the work that men do intimately affects their life chance and life styles. Even though prestige ideologies often stress the intrinsic worth of all men, occupational status is the single most important basis for according prestige, honor, and respect.[6]

It has been shown that individuals are able to rate abstract titles in terms of prestige, even if they do not know who fills them. These prestige ratings of occupation are central to determining the rank of a person in the social class system. The data in Table 5.1 show that these ratings are also relatively permanent. In the classic study that underlies Table 5.1, for example, it was found that the correlation coefficient between ratings in 1947 and in 1963 (Pearson product moment) was 0.99, indicating that the prestige of occupations had changed very little in this period.[7]

The stability in ratings of prestige associated with occupations exists also on a crossnational basis. Various studies have indicated that physicians rate very high in almost all societies, for example. The correlations for ranks of all occupations tend to exhibit very high correlations (usually above 0.9) among nations in a crosscultural sample.[8]

---

[5] Joseph A. Kahl, *The American Class Structure* (New York: Holt, Rinehart and Winston, 1957), pp. 8–10. For an interpretation of these six dimensions of social class in marketing similar to the interpretation presented in this volume, see Edgar Crane, *Marketing Communication* (New York: Wiley, 1966), pp. 326–329.

[6] John P. Hewitt, *Social Stratification and Deviant Behavior* (New York: Random House, 1970), p. 25.

[7] Robert W. Hodge, Paul M. Siegel, and Peter H. Rossi, "Occupational Prestige in the United States: 1925–1963," in Reinhard Bendix and Seymour M. Lipset (eds.), *Class, Status, and Power,* 2nd ed. (New York: Free Press, 1966), pp. 322–334, at p. 326.

[8] Alex Inkeles and Peter H. Rossi, "National Comparisons of Occupational Prestige," *Amer. J. Sociology,* vol. 61, pp. 329–339 (1956); Robert W. Hodge, Donald J. Treiman, and Peter H. Rossi, "A Comparative Study of Occupational Prestige," in Bendix and Lipset, *op. cit.,*[7] pp. 309–321.

Table 5.1 PRESTIGE RATINGS OF OCCUPATIONS IN THE UNITED STATES, 1947 AND 1963

Occupation	1947 Rank	1963 Rank
U.S. Supreme Court Justice	1	1
Physician	2.5	2
Nuclear physicist	18	3.5
Scientist	8	3.5
Government scientist	10.5	5.5
State governor	2.5	5.5
Cabinet member in the federal government	4.5	8
College professor	8	8
U.S. representative in Congress	8	8
Chemist	18	11
Lawyer	18	11
Diplomat in the U.S. foreign service	4.5	11
Dentist	18	14
Architect	18	14
County judge	13	14
Psychologist	22	17.5
Minister	13	17.5
Member of the board of directors of a large corporation	18	17.5
Mayor of a large city	6	17.5
Priest	6	21.5
Head of a department in a state government	13	21.5
Civil engineer	23	21.5
Airline pilot	24.5	21.5
Banker	10.5	24.5
Biologist	29	24.5
Sociologist	26.5	26
Instructor in public schools	34	27.5
Captain in the regular army	31.5	27.5
Accountant for a large business	29	29.5
Public school teacher	36	29.5
Owner of a factory that employs about 100 people	26.5	31.5
Building contractor	26.5	31.5
Artist who paints pictures that are exhibited in galleries	24.5	34.5
Musician in a symphony orchestra	29	34.5
Author of novels	29	34.5
Economist	34	34.5
Official of an international labor union	40.5	37
Railroad engineer	40.5	39
Electrician	45	39
County agricultural agent	37.5	39
Owner-operator of a printing shop	42.5	41.5
Trained machinist	45	41.5
Farm owner and operator	39	44

Table 5.1 PRESTIGE RATINGS OF OCCUPATIONS IN THE UNITED STATES
1947 AND 1963 (*Continued*)

Occupation	1947 Rank	1963 Rank
Undertaker	47	44
Welfare worker for a city government	45	44
Newspaper columnist	42.5	46
Policeman	55	47
Reporter on a daily newspaper	48	48
Radio announcer	40.5	49.5
Bookkeeper	51.5	49.5
Tenant farmer—one who owns livestock and machinery and manages the farm	51.5	51.5
Insurance agent	51.5	51.5
Carpenter	58	53
Manager of a small store in a city	49	54.5
Local official of a labor union	62	54.5
Mail carrier	57	57
Railroad conductor	55	57
Traveling salesman for a wholesale concern	51.5	57
Plumber	59.5	59
Automobile repairman	59.5	60
Playground director	55	62.5
Barber	66	62.5
Machine operator in a factory	64.5	62.5
Owner-operator of a lunch stand	62	62.5
Corporal in the regular army	64.5	65.5
Garage mechanic	62	65.5
Truck driver	71	67
Fisherman who owns his own boat	68	68
Clerk in a store	68	70
Milk route man	71	70
Streetcar motorman	68	70
Lumberjack	73	72.5
Restaurant cook	71	72.5
Singer in a nightclub	74.5	74
Filling-station attendant	74.5	75
Dock worker	81.5	77.5
Railroad section hand	79.5	77.5
Night watchman	81.5	77.5
Coal miner	77.5	77.5
Restaurant waiter	79.5	80.5
Taxi driver	77.5	80.5
Farm hand	76	83
Janitor	85.5	83
Bartender	85.5	83
Clothes presser in a laundry	83	85
Soda fountain clerk	84	86

Table 5.1   PRESTIGE RATINGS OF OCCUPATIONS IN THE UNITED STATES
1947 AND 1963 (*Continued*)

Occupation	1947 Rank	1963 Rank
Share-cropper—one who owns no livestock or equipment and does not manage farm	87	87
Garbage collector	88	88
Street sweeper	89	89
Shoe shiner	90	90

SOURCE: Robert W. Hodge, Paul M. Siegel, and Peter H. Rossi, "Occupational Prestige in the United States: 1925–1963," in Reinhard Bendix and Seymour Martin Lipset (eds), *Class, Status, and Power,* 2nd ed. (New York: Free Press, 1966), pp. 322–334, at pp. 324–325.

Personal Performance

A person's social class is determined partially by the degree to which he performs well within his occupational class. This includes the deference or attitude of respect given to an individual by other persons in the society. Frequently, deference refers directly to job performance. Statements such as, "He is the finest young lawyer in our city," "Frank is the only mechanic I know that I really trust my car to," or "That professor is making the most significant contributions to knowledge of anyone in his field" are examples of evaluations of personal performance. Operationally, job performance is sometimes measured by the amount of income variation *within* an occupation. Thus in one status-rating system, physicians making more than $45,000 a year are given a higher than normal rating, physicians making between $15,000 and $45,000 a year are given the normal rating for their occupation, and physicians earning less than $15,000 a year are lowered from their normal status rating.

Personal performance can relate to activities other than job performance. A person's status may be affected by the prestige or sentiment given him for acts that society approves. An individual who is unusually kind and considerate of others may receive the respect of his peers. A person who performs some beneficial service such as serving as chairman of a community fund or civic club may receive improved status, as was noted earlier. Even a reputation as "a good father and husband" may contribute to one's status.

Interactions

One group of sociologists is sometimes called the "who-invited-whom-to-dinner" school. They recognize that people feel most comfortable when they are "with their own kind," and place primary analysis on patterns of association. Having frequent and intimate association with other occupants of a particular social class is essential to the definition of one's own class. Meredith Wilson's unsinkable Molly Brown, for example, could not enter the elite social classes of

Denver without the proper friends, in spite of her wealth, luxurious residence, and European education.

Interactions may well be the most important key to understanding social classes in spite of the difficulty of measuring them. One commentator has observed, "the essence of social class is the way a man is treated by his fellows and, reciprocally, the way he treats them."[9] The importance of social intimacy as a determinant of social class has been further amplified by Barber:

> The assumption underlying the use of the interactional indicator of social class position is that social intimacy is expressive of social equality. The assumption rests on the fact that the kind of interchange of sentiments and ideas that goes on in intimate association is possible only among people who know each other well and who value each other equally. It is, in other words, possible only among social class equals, and therefore it is an indicator of social class equality.[10]

Limitations on social interaction are rigidly enforced in most social structures. In India, interaction among certain social castes is prohibited on religious grounds.[11] In the United States, restrictions are more subtle but nevertheless are present. The intensive studies of Hollingshead reveal that most marriages —83 percent—occur within the same or adjacent social classes.[12] Hollingshead's investigations of public school behavior reveal definite patterns of restricted association (which he labeled with names such as the elite, the good kids, and the grubby gang) and found that dating tended to be restricted among these classes by parents.[13] Perhaps the most obvious example of restricted interaction is the existence of the *Social Register* in twelve United States cities, which incorporates very rigid criteria for gaining admission to intimate interactions in the top social classes.[14]

Possessions

Possessions are symbols of class membership. They are necessary but not sufficient criteria for class membership. The importance of possessions relates not only to the amount of possessions that an individual has but also to the nature of

---

[9] T. H. Marshall, *Citizenship and Social Class and Other Essays* (Cambridge: Cambridge Univ. Press, 1950), p. 92.

[10] Barber, *op. cit.*,[4] p. 122.

[11] For examples of the prescriptions for the caste system, see Marc Galanter, "The Problem of Group Membership," in Bendix and Lipset, *op. cit.*,[7] pp. 628–640, reprinted from *J. Indian Law Institute*.

[12] A. B. Hollingshead, "Cultural Factors in the Selection of Marriage Mates," *Amer. Sociological Rev.*, vol. 15, pp. 619–627 (1950).

[13] A. B. Hollingshead, *Elmstown's Youth* (New York: Wiley, 1949), p. 483. Another study discovered similar restricted dating patterns and was able to trace them to definite parental influences tending to restrict interaction among classes. See Marvin B. Sussman, "Parental Participation in Mate Selection and Its Effect upon Family Continuity," *Social Forces*, vol. 32, pp. 76–81 (1953).

[14] For a description of the *Social Register* and an analysis of the criteria for gaining admission to it, see E. Digby Baltzell, "Who's Who in America and the Social Register," in Bendix and Lipset, *op. cit.*,[7] pp. 266–275.

his choices. Thus, whether he chooses wall-to-wall carpeting or an Oriental rug, both of equal price, may be an important determinant and symbol of social class. Probably the most important possession in terms of social-class determination is a family's residence, both location and type. Other important "possessions" include the college an individual attends (for upper classes), the type of vacation an individual chooses, the automobile (although its exact importance in the United States is questionable), clothing, furniture, and appliances that are chosen for the home, and the type of wealth possessed by a family.

The way an individual chooses and uses possessions is sometimes referred to as his "life style." Decisions about possessions and their relation to social class are questions of extreme importance to the consumer analyst. Accordingly, they will be discussed at length later in this chapter.

Value Orientations

Values, or beliefs about what an individual thinks is important, are determinants and manifestations of social class. When a group of people tend to share a common set of abstract convictions that organize and relate a large number of specific values, they are called value orientations, and certain value orientations are known to characterize specific social classes.

A crucial issue in analyzing consumer behavior is to determine what value orientations characterize market segments. These beliefs may refer to values about society such as beliefs in capitalism or other political ideals. They also refer to attitudes toward such subjects as child rearing, family structure, sexual behavior, work, and achievement. They may also refer to values about decision making. These value orientations are of central importance in marketing and will be discussed later in the chapter.

Class Consciousness

Another determinant and manifestation of social class is the class consciousness of groups within the society and of individuals within those groups. Individuals who are relatively unconscious of class differences in the society tend to perceive less discrepancy between their position and that of others. Thus they may be less motivated toward attaining goods as symbols of class.

In the United States, most people have some idea of social classes, but those ideas are often nebulous or not strongly held. Some studies have indicated sizable proportions of the population that believe there are no social classes or cannot define specific social classes. The higher an individual's social class, the more class conscious he is likely to be.

MEASUREMENT OF SOCIAL CLASSES

Many methods have been developed for measuring social class and describing the values and behavior of social class. In sociological research, these methods focus more on *what classes exist* and *why*. For marketing analysts, the more important question is *what behavior differences exist* between classes, usually with the assumption that these may aid in market segmentation strategies. There is little concensus concerning the relative value of the many measures of social class because each method tends to be adapted to the special requirements of a research purpose.[15] It is useful to remember that marketing strategists often should do the same. Four principal *types* of methods used for classifying the social class of an individual have been described: (1) reputational, (2) sociometric, (3) subjective, and (4) objective.[16]

Reputational Methods

Reputational methods of measuring social class involve asking people to rank the social position of other persons. Usually, respondents are asked to rank people they know in the particular community in which they live. Even people who say they are not class conscious almost always can divide the community into social groups and tell in which group the people they know belong. The class titles and the number of classes vary among respondents, but the class structure of the community can be determined by matching up quite a few interviews. The following is an example of a typical interview asking for a description of the social-class structure to which residents of the community belong. Researchers have found that the number of classes observed by informants increases in proportion to the social status of the informant and that informants generally overstate their own social class.

EXAMPLE OF AN EVALUATED PARTICIPATION INTERVIEW
USED IN ESTABLISHING SOCIAL CLASS BY THE
REPUTATIONAL METHOD

This interview is with Mr. George Green, long-time resident of the town and a member of the city government.

You'll find out there's a definite division between the men and the women in the upper stratum in this town. The men are common like us. They'll talk to you at any time. But the women draw the class line, and no one gets over or around it. I can see this just as clearly as I can see you.

We're in a unique position here because of my relation to a couple of families in this group. A cousin of mine married Jim Radcliffe. This relates us to several other people. We've been invited over to their house to parties a few times, and I'm disturbed at how these people look down at others in town. They have several cliques within the larger stratum. Below this stratum is the one composed of prominent business and professional families. Some of these who have money and family are rated in the top group. However, if they have only family and not much money, they rank in the upper-middle class.

---

15 A discussion of social class measures is found in Thomas E. Lasswell, "Social Stratification: 1964–1969," *Annals of the American Academy of Political and Social Science,* vol. 38, esp. pp. 109–112 (July 1969).

16 David Krech, Richard S. Crutchfield, and Egerton L. Ballachey, *Individual in Society* (New York: McGraw-Hill, 1962), pp. 313–319.

The small business men and the foremen out at the mill are in the lower but middle stratum. I mean a lower stratum than the one we have been talking about. I don't know much about their social life, but I know just about where they fit in here in town. The sub-foremen, machinists, several stationary operators, and people like that are in the lowest middle stratum. The ordinary workmen in the foundry and the mill are mostly ranked as lower class around here. But they're not as low as the older Poles, the canal renters, and the people back of the tannery.

The Poles and the poor Americans who work in the mill are on the bottom. These poor Americans and Poles may be working side by side on the same job and getting the same income, but socially they're miles apart. You might say they're each an exclusive group. The several social strata in town are segregated into definite areas, and in each you generally find a class distinction.

Now, that's about the way that the town is divided. That's the way it looks to me, and I am pretty sure that's the way it is.[17]

The reputational method was developed in the United States by Warner and is the basis of much of the most important empirical research on social classes in America. A comprehensive set of instructions for interpreting the interviews and for collaborating social-class ratings has been devised and is called the evaluative participation method of establishing the social class of a person.[18]

Sociometric Methods

Sociometric studies involve observing and asking people about their intimate associations with other people. The reports and observations can be analyzed with standard sociometric techniques to determine the cliques and social classes. The most famous study using techniques of this nature is that of Hollingshead.[19] Most of the studies using formal sociometric methods in connection with social class have been with children.[20] Sociometric methods are undoubtedly useful in theoretical social-class research, but as of the present are untested and probably overly expensive for most consumer research.

Subjective Methods

Subjective methods of determining social classes ask respondents to *rate themselves* on social class. Such methods have been used on occasion but are of limited use for consumer analysts for two reasons: (1) respondents tend to

---

[17] W. Lloyd Warner, Marchia Meeker, and Kenneth Eels, *Social Class in America: A Manual of Procedure for the Measurement of Social Status* (Chicago: Science Research Associates, 1949), pp. 56–57.

[18] Warner *et al.*, *op. cit.*,[17] pp. 47–120.

[19] Hollingshead, *op. cit.*[13]

[20] For an example of this type of research, see Celia Burns Stendler, *Children of Brasstown, University of Illinois Bull.*, vol. 46, no. 59 (Urbana, Ill.: Bureau of Research and Service of the College of Education, 1949).

overrate their own class position (often by one class rank) and (2) respondents avoid the connotative terms "upper" and "lower" classes and thus exaggerate the size of the middle classes.

The problems with a subjective method do not disqualify the method from social-class research. Important findings have been generated by Centers[21] and other investigators using the subjective method, especially with regard to the subject of class consciousness. The value of the method in marketing studies as yet appears to be minimal, however. What is needed is a self-administered rating scale to identify consumer social classes on a subjective basis without actually asking the respondent his social class. Such a scale would ask the consumer to choose statements relating indirectly to social class that he agrees with or that characterize him. If such a self-administered scale of social class could be developed, it would be useful in mail questionnaires and other types of consumer surveys. It is a topic that should receive research priority.

Objective Methods

Objective methods of determining social classes rely upon the assigning of classes (or status) on the basis of respondents possessing some value of a stratified variable. The most often used variables are occupation, income, education, size and type of residence, ownership of possessions, and organizational affiliations. Most consumer research uses the objective method for classifying respondents into a social class. Objective methods can be divided into those that involve single indexes and those that use multiple indexes.

Single-Item Indexes Occupation is generally accepted as the single best proxy indicator of social class. Occupational position and individual life styles have demonstrated high correlations for two reasons. People who share similarly ranked occupational levels often share roughly similar access to the means of achieving a particular life style. Leisure time, income independence, knowledge, and power are often common to specific or occupational categories. Second, people in similar occupations often develop common interests and are thus likely to interact with one another. Of particular interest to consumer analysts is the conclusion of social-class researchers Barth and Watson:

> The products of such occupational interaction are likely to be an increased concensus concerning the types of activities, interests, and

---

[21] Richard Centers, *The Psychology of Social Classes* (Princeton, N.J.: Princeton Univ. Press, 1949), esp. pp. 34–54. For other studies using the subjective method, see G. Gallup and S. F. Rae, *The Pulse of Democracy* (New York: Simon and Schuster, 1940); Hadley Cantril, "Identification with Social and Economic Class," *J. Abnormal and Social Psychology*, vol. 38, pp. 74–79 (Jan. 1943); Philip E. Converse, "The Shifting Role of Class in Political Attitudes and Behavior," in Eleanor E. Maccoby, Theodore M. Newcomb, and Eugene L. Hartley (eds.), *Readings in Social Psychology*, 3rd ed. (New York: Holt, Rinehart and Winston, 1958), pp. 388–399.

possessions that are important; some agreement as to how, in general, family resources should be allocated in order to implement the achievement of these goals; and the development of a shared set of norms of evaluation.[22]

An example of an occupational scale is the North–Hatt scale (also called the National Opinion Research Center scale) reprinted in Table 5.1. The scale values are sometimes used but present a problem because only 90 occupations are included.[23] A simple but widely used occupational method is the Edwards scale which has been adopted by the Bureau of the Census and the American Marketing Association.[24] An occupational measure that is useful for consumer research is the Duncan scale which gives considerable weight in its derivation to educational attainment.[25] The Duncan scale achieves its value because of its objectiveness, its specificity, its comprehensiveness (425 occupations are rated), and its relative recency (1960). In consumer research it has proved useful in studying random samples of consumers as well as special consumer groups (innovators).[26]

Occupational methods are not without faults. Researchers object to the arbitrary job hierarchy of some scales. Blue-collar workers are often placed below white-collar workers without empirical support.[27] Also in the often used Edwards scale specific jobs within each occupational category can vary greatly. The occupational title "managers, officials, and proprietors, except farm, not elsewhere classified" includes the president of General Motors and the manager of the GM basement coffee shop. The implication for marketing researchers is either to use more specific scales (such as Duncan) or to adapt standardized scales to the specialized requirements of consumer analysis.

In addition to occupation, some indexes have been constructed on the basis only of possessions. In one famous index, Chapin found that the furniture

[22] Ernest A. T. Barth and Walter B. Watson, "Social Stratification and the Family in Mass Society," *Social Forces*, vol. 45, p. 394 (Mar. 1967).

[23] C. C. North and Paul K. Hatt, "Jobs and Occupations: A Popular Evaluation," in L. Wilson and W. L. Kolb (eds.), *Sociological Analysis* (New York: Harcourt, 1949), pp. 464–474.

[24] Alba M. Edwards, *A Social Economic Grouping of the Gainful Workers of the United States* (Washington, D.C.: U.S. Government Printing Office, 1939); U.S. Bureau of the Census, *1960 Census of Population Classified Index of Occupations and Industries* (Washington, D.C.: U.S. Government Printing Office, 1960); American Marketing Association, "Occupation and Educational Scales," *J. Marketing*, vol. 15 (Apr. 1951). See comments about this scale in Theodore Caplow, *The Sociology of Work* (Minneapolis, Minn.: University of Minnesota Press, 1954), esp. pp. 42–48.

[25] Albert J. Reiss, Jr., Otis Dudley Duncan, Paul K. Hatt, and Cecil C. North, *Occupations and Social Status* (New York: Free Press, 1961).

[26] Robert J. Kegerreis, James F. Engel, and Roger D. Blackwell, "Innovativeness and Diffusiveness: A Marketing View of the Characteristics of Earliest Adopters," in David T. Kollat, Roger D. Blackwell, and James F. Engel (eds.), *Research in Consumer Behavior* (New York: Holt, Rinehart and Winston, 1970), pp. 671–689, esp. pp. 677–678.

[27] Milton M. Gordon, *Social Class in American Sociology* (Durham, N.C.: Duke University Press, 1958), pp. 223–227.

an interviewer could observe in the living room of respondents was an excellent indicator of more general measures of social class.[28] Chapin was able to measure social class on the basis of observations of the type of floor in the living room, the presence of draperies, the number of armchairs, the number of bookcases, the presence of a sewing machine, the number and type of periodicals displayed, and other items. A study by Lauman and House, cited later in this chapter, suggests that objective measures of possessions, adequately updated, may be useful to consumer researchers.

Single-item indices of social class should be regarded as useful only when more complex (and costly) methods are not possible. Occupation, the best single indicator of social class, does not exhaust the relevant dimensions of class. In addition, the occupational structure does not always parallel the social-class structure; nor does income, the amount or type of possessions, residence, or any single indicator. Consequently the desire for objective methods of measuring social class has brought about a search for *multiple-item indices.*

Multiple-Item Indices   Multiple-item indices combine several indicators of social class in an attempt to determine the best set of objective predictors of social class as validated by reputational or sociometric methods. Several methods exist.

Warner's ISC   A multiple-item index that has received much empirical investigation is Warner's *Index of Status Characteristics* (ISC). Several advantages accrue to its use:

(1)   It has been validated with reputational methods.[29]

(2)   It has been validated with scales of other investigators.[30]

---

[28]   F. Stuart Chapin, *Contemporary American Institutions* (New York: Harper & Row, 1935), chap. 19. Chapin's scale was originally a multiple-item index including income, cultural equipment, material possessions, and group activities. The scale for living-room equipment correlated so highly with the combined index that the other variates were dropped from the index. The index was modified for rural use in William H. Sewell, *The Construction and Standardization of a Scale for the Measurement of the Socio-Economic Status of Oklahoma Farm Families,* Tech. Bull. no. 9 (Stillwater, Okla.: Oklahoma A & M Agricultural Experiment Station, 1940). A more recent scale of similar nature has been developed in England and is described in Dennis Chapman, *The Home and Social Status* (London: Routledge, 1955).

[29]   The correlation between ISC and EP, for example, is greater than 0.97 in Warner's study of Jonesville. For other estimates of the validity of ISC as predictor of social class as measured by EP, see Warner *et al., op. cit.,*[17] pp. 163–175.

[30]   Hollingshead and Warner conducted independent investigations of social classes in Morris, Ill. The two methods were used to classify 134 families measured in both studies, and Hollingshead concluded, "the agreement between the two studies was so high that it should be clear that the two stratification techniques as used by independent investigators produced a valid and reliable index of stratification in the samples studied." *Hollingshead,* pp. 40–41.

(3) It has been used in a variety of communities, with modifications, and has been used on a national basis in both large and small cities.[31]

(4) It has received considerable theoretical support.[32]

The ISC measures four variables: occupation, source of income, house type, and dwelling area. Originally Warner included amount of income and education in the ISC. Later he concluded that the predictive power of a four-variable ISC was not significantly changed by the deletion of amount of income and education.

After obtaining ratings for each variable for a respondent, the respondent's rating is multiplied by a weight and each product is summated.[33] The weights for each variable, which were obtained by regression analysis, are as follows:[34]

Occupation   Rating × 4
Source of income Rating × 3
House type   Rating × 3
Dwelling area   Rating × 2

The social-class scores obtained through this method are not equivalent numerically among communities and must be adjusted if they are to be used on a national basis.

Other Multiple-Item Indexes A number of other multiple-item indexes exist, most of which are related to Warner's ISC. Some of these have received

---

[31] The occupation and source of income components of the ISC have been used in modified form for a national sample in Paul K. Hatt, "Occupation and Social Stratification," *Amer. J. Sociology,* vol. 55, pp. 533–543 (1950). Social Research, Inc., uses a modified form of the ISC in national samples of metropolitan areas with good results. See the description of methodology in Lee Rainwater, Richard P. Coleman, and Gerald Handel, *Workingman's Wife* (New York: Oceana, 1959), pp. 224–225. The problems of using the ISC in very backward rural areas, however, are described in M. C. Hill and A. N. Whiting "Some Theoretical and Methodological Problems in Community Studies," *Social Forces,* vol. 29, pp. 117–124 (1950).

[32] Perhaps the best theoretical validity support is provided by Kahl and Davis' factor analysis of 19 different indicators of social class, in which they found that occupation, quality of house, and residential area are central in the ISC. See Joseph A. Kahl and James A. Davis, "A Comparison of Indexes of Socio-Economic Status," *Amer. Sociological Rev.,* vol. 20, pp. 317–325. (1955). The hypothesis that ISC measures one underlying dimension of social class is tested with positive results in John L. Haer, "A Test of the Unidimensionality of the Index of Status Characteristics," *Social Forces,* vol. 34, pp. 56–58 (Oct. 1955).

[33] A methodological question that plagues Warner's research and many other social-class rating techniques is the assumption being made in the data scale. Warner, in his analysis, uses arithmetic averages and parametric tests of significance and measures of correlation such as the test and the Pearsonian product moment. The use of parametric ratings such as 6 and 7 is equal to the distance between 1 and 2, and so forth. It is doubtful, however, that the scale being used by Warner (and others) possesses any more than ordinal properties. Thus, nonparametric statistics are the appropriate form. It appears that Warner and his associates have assumed that the errors from using parametric statistics are not sufficient to warrant use of the less powerful forms of statistical analysis.

[34] Warner, *et al., op. cit.,*[17] p. 124.

considerable application in consumer research or appear to have the potential of being useful.

Richard Coleman's *Index of Urban Status* (IUS) is used in consumer studies conducted by the Social Research Institute. This index uses the same four variables, and in a similar manner as Warner's ISC. However, the IUS includes two additional variables, education and associational behavior.[35] Education of respondent families is rated for both the husband and the wife on a seven-point scale. Associational behavior is rated on the basis of formal club and religious memberships and informal friendships.

Carman has worked on an *index of cultural classes*, specifically for application to marketing problems.[36] He postulates that of the different variables with which class is stratified (power, status, culture), culture is of most relevance to marketing. Carman's research attempts to locate separate subcultures in the United States. These classes, Carman's research indicates, display distinct behavioral characteristics. The purpose of his research is to determine proxy variables that measure these classes. With a factor analysis of 9318 randomly selected households from the 1960 census of population, Carman isolates occupation, education of household, and expenditures for housing as useful proxy variables for behavioral differences in marketing patterns (home clothes dryer ownership).[37]

Hollingshead's *index of social position* (ISP) is similar to Warner's ISC except that it is a three-variable index with ratings for area of residence, occupation, and education.[38] The index can be reduced to a two-variable index with little loss (by eliminating area of residence) and is useful for making comparisons among communities. Another scale perhaps useful in conducting research on the consumption patterns of college students is the *index of class position*, developed by Ellis, Lane, and Olesen.[39] It is similar to the ISP except that college students are asked to report their *father's* occupation and also to subjectively evaluate their father's position in the class structure.

There are also measures of social class that rely only on demographic information ascertainable without directly involving the respondent. Shevky and his associates produced an index of social rank based only upon *census tract* data.[40] Social rank can be inferred from the ratio of (1) craftsmen, operatives,

[35]   Rainwater, *et al., op. cit.*[31]

[36]   James M. Carman, *The Application of Social Class in Market Segmentation* (Berkeley, Calif.: Institute of Business and Economic Research, University of California Graduate School of Business Administration, 1965).

[37]   Carman, *op. cit.*,[36] p. 63.

[38]   Jerome K. Myers and Bertram H. Roberts, *Family and Class Dynamics in Mental Illness* (New York: Wiley, 1959), pp. 24–25.

[39]   Robert A. Ellis, Clayton Lane, and Virginia Olesen, "The Index of Class Position: An Improved Intercommunity Measure of Stratification," *Amer. Sociological Rev.*, vol. 28, pp. 271–277 (Apr. 1963).

[40]   Eshref Shevky and Wendell Bell, *Social Area Analysis: Theory, Illustrative Application and Computational Procedures* (Stanford, Calif.: Stanford University Press, 1955).

and laborers in each tract, (2) education as measured by number of persons aged 25 years or more who had completed grade school, and (3) income. Very useful studies relating sales of a product to the social-class characteristics of a geographical area are possible using this index. Another scale to measure social class, based upon external ratings of housing, has been devised by Mack.[41]

Status Crystallization A central problem in the use of all multiple-item indices of social class is what to do about individuals who rate high on one variable but low on another. Status crystallization is defined as the consistency that exists among ratings of multiple variables. Lenski devised an index of status crystallization and studied respondents who have a low degree of status crystallization.[42] He concluded that such individuals are more liberal in their political views and more willing to support programs of social change. Individuals such as the black doctor, the successful businessman with little education, and the poorly paid white-collar worker are examples of persons with low status crystallization who are subject to certain pressures from the social order not felt by persons with more highly crystallized status. Research would seem to be appropriate to determine if the conditions that lead to political liberalism and acceptance of social change also contribute to early adoption of new products or unstable consumption patterns. Lenski's index of status crystallization should be useful in such research.

A Summary Paradigm

The theoretical and methodological considerations of measuring social class are summarized in a paradigm developed by Coleman.[43] This paradigm (presented in Table 5.2) outlines the assumptions and perspectives that underlie the various approaches to studying social strata. It should be apparent to a researcher that the appropriate method for measuring social class is a function of the problem being investigated, the resources available, and the scope of the investigation. Attempts to evaluate the efficiency of methods, however, have typically lead to emphasis on objective methods such as Warner's ISC and other composite weighted scales.[44]

---

[41] Raymond W. Mack, "Housing as an Index of Social Class," *Social Forces,* vol. 29, pp. 391–400 (1951).

[42] Gerhard E. Lenski, "Status Crystallization: A Non-Vertical Dimension of Social Status," *Amer. Sociological Rev.,* vol. 21, pp. 458–464 (Aug. 1956). A provocative extension of the problem of status incongruence, with some references of potential interest in marketing, can be found in Andrzej Malewski, "The Degree of Status Incongruence and Its Effects," *Polish Sociological Bull.* (1963), reprinted in Bendix and Lipset, *op. cit.,*[7] pp. 303–308.

[43] John A. Coleman, "A Paradigm for the Study of Social Strata," *Sociology and Social Research,* vol. 50, pp. 338–350 (Apr. 1966).

[44] John L. Haer, "Predicting Utility of Five Indices of Social Stratification," *Amer. Sociological Rev.,* vol. 22, pp. 541–546 (Oct. 1957).

Table 5.2 A PARADIGM FOR THE STUDY OF SOCIAL STRATA

Perspective	Type of Category Studied	Principal Research Device	Nomenclature	Unit of Analysis
(1) Prestige	Statistical category (reality is in the mind of the raters)	Use of raters	Prestige groups	Groups, real or statistical, ranked in a hierarchy of prestige
(2) Culture	People who share symbolic meanings, ways of doing, thinking	Questionnaires, interviews, participant observation of behavior differences	Strata (culture)	Populations with demonstrably different symbolic systems of norms
(3) Associational	Cliques, face-to-face groups	Sociometric techniques to measure interaction	Cliques	Real primary group in interaction
(4) Influence: power/authority	Real interest groups in conflict	Re-creation of decision-making processes	Social classes	Interest groups in conflict
(5) Demography	Statistical category (reality is in the mind of the sociologist)	Useful ordering of census data into discrete categories	Demographic categories	Whole populations divided into demographic categories
(6) Social psychology	Reference groups to which I think that I belong (reality is in the mind of the self-rater)	Self-rating	Strata (reference group)	Perceptions of samples of the population

SOURCE: John A. Coleman, "A Paradigm for the Study of Social Strata," *Sociology and Social Research*, vol. 50, pp. 338–350 (Apr. 1966).

SOCIAL CLASSES IN AMERICA

It is important for marketing strategists to understand and conduct research on each of the social classes in America. The need for research stems from the fact that most marketing strategy is directed toward social classes far below the executives and researchers who develop the strategy. College students and college-educated executives must remember that advertising, selling themes, television programs, and other aspects of the marketing programs are directed primarily toward social classes who have different values and behavior and generally are not college educated. (Barely over half of the adult population in the United States has graduated from high school.) Marketing decisions are made mostly by upper- middle- or lower-upper-class men to reach mostly middle- and lower-class consumers. Research is required to understand the differences in class behavior.

Before social class behavior can be described, however, consideration should be given to questions concerning the changing nature of social class.

Embourgoisement of America?

In recent years, some sociologists have questioned the validity of social classes. They maintain that the life styles of middle-class persons have become increasingly representative of the vast majority of Americans. This is referred to as the "embourgoisement" of society or the massification theory.

An active critic of social class is Nisbet who claims that political power in the United States has been spread among the voters and that economic power has been profoundly altered by the separation of property ownership and corporate control. Nisbet therefore concludes that social status has become "disengaged" from any clearly definable set of ranks:

> However useful social class may be as a concept in the study of the historical past, or of contemporary non-Western societies, particularly underdeveloped societies, it has become nearly valueless for the interpretation of American society. . . . That political power, wealth, life chances, and social status are unevenly distributed in American population is not of course in question. What is in question is whether a concept drawn historically from the structure of preindustrial predemocratic, prerationalized society can be of significant help in the classification of such a society as ours is today.[45]

The embourgoisement theory is advanced most strongly with the claim that past differences between manual and nonmanual workers are disappearing. Lenski comments:

---

[45] R. A. Nisbet, "The Decline and Fall of Social Class," in R. A. Nisbet (ed.), *Tradition and Revolt* (New York: Random House, 1968), p. 106.

> In the earlier years of industralization, a greater cultural chasm separated workers from the middle classes. This is now disappearing or at least being substantially reduced.[46]

Elsewhere Lenski states that the massification of manual workers is a result of mass media influences teaching them to think and act like the middle class, especially among the upper stratum of the working class, consisting of skilled and supervisory workers.[47] Mayer much earlier also believed that craftsmen, foremen, and skilled mechanics share a "white-collar" style of life partially because their salaries exceed many lower-middle-class white-collar employees and small business owners.[48]

Empirical Investigations   Speculations about declining cultural differences among occupational or social classes are not consistent with empirical research. Research by Berger and Hamilton indicated that a wide gap remains between manual and nonmanual workers, clearly illustrated by different concepts of values, tastes, social participation, and political orientation.[49]

A comprehensive study by Glenn examined the massification versus differentiation theories. Analyzing trends reflected in national surveys conducted at intervals of eight or more years, Glenn concluded that differences in attitudes and behavior *have not* diminished. Looking at other groups in addition to social class, Glenn found that differences in attitudes and behavior have been *increasing* among (1) people from the southern United States and those from other parts of the country, (2) people of lower education levels and those with greater education, (3) people from manual jobs versus people with nonmanual occupations, (4) white individuals versus nonwhites, and (5) Protestants as compared to Catholics.[50]

In another study of responses to 113 questions from twenty Gallup polls and three National Opinion Research Center surveys, it was concluded that the attitudes of skilled manual workers are appropriately considered part of the working class. Skilled and manual workers (and also farmers and farm managers) indicated in this study different response to drinking alcohol, watching television, or listening to the radio than did professional and semiprofessional workers on the same topics.[51]

Inequality in America   The argument that America is becoming classless has further been taken to task by Mills and his followers. They maintain that the

---

[46]   Gerhard Lenski, *Power and Privilege* (New York: McGraw-Hill, 1966), p. 381.

[47]   Gerhard Lenski, *The Religious Factor* (New York: Doubleday, 1961), p. 44.

[48]   Kurt B. Mayer, *Class and Society* (New York: Random House, 1955), pp. 41–42.

[49]   Bennett Berger, *Working-Class Suburb* (Berkeley: University of California Press, 1960); Richard F. Hamilton, "The Behavior and Values of Skilled Workers," in Arthur B. Shostak and William Gomberg (eds.), *Blue-Collar World* (Englewood Cliffs, N.J.: Prentice-Hall, 1964), pp. 42–57.

[50]   Norval D. Glenn, "Massification Versus Differentiation: Some Trend Data from National Surveys," *Social Forces*, vol. 46, p. 172 (Dec. 1967).

[51]   Norval D. Glenn and Jon P. Alstop, "Cultural Distances Among Occupation Categories," *Amer. Sociological Rev.*, vol. 33, p. 370 (June 1968).

institutions of industrially advanced societies have produced a marked concentration of power which has created an elite class. Reiterating Mills, Domhoff notes:

> A "governing" class is a social upper class which owns a disproportionate amount of a country's yearly income, and contributes a disproportionate number of its members to the controlling institutions and key decision-making groups of the country.[52]

In separate research efforts, the findings of Lampman, Kolko, Miller, and Lundberg have served to dispel the theory purporting America to be an "egalitarian" society.[53] Each of the researchers has, by diverse methods, found United States society to be typified, not by massification or homogeneity, but by differentiation and heterogeneity.

Children's Perceptions   Perhaps one of the best demonstrations of the reality of stratification in America is provided by Simmons and Rosenberg.[54] As part of a larger study, the researchers examined the perception of the stratification system of children. A sample of 1917 black and white children of varying social backgrounds from grades 3 to 12 were interviewed. Parents of the children were also interviewed on the same questions for comparison with responses of their children.

The children perceived occupation prestige and inequality of opportunity with dramatic awareness. As early as the elementary school stage, children rated 15 occupations in a prestige order almost identical to that of their parents and of the older high-school pupils. Using a Spearman rho rank-order correlation, the rank orders of elementary school children and adults correlated 0.93, well beyond the 0.01 level of significance. The Pearson product moment correlation of absolute scores showed a correlation of 0.96. The high correlations held for all categories of children, whether white or black, middle or working class, and regardless of age.[55] It was also found that both younger and older children reject the doctrine of equality of opportunity in obtaining "the good things in life."[56]

Social-Class Overlays   The changing nature of social class is perhaps best characterized as new patterns "overlaying" old patterns. Social-class behavior and attitudes may become more subtle and more complicated but are not disappearing. Old norms are not discarded; rather new ones are added to the old ones to

---

[52]   G. W. Domhoff, *Who Rules America?* (New York: Spectrum Books, 1967), p. 5.

[53]   Robert J. Lampman, *The Share of Top Wealth-Holders in National Wealth, 1922–1955* (Princeton, N.J.: Princeton University Press, 1962); Herman Miller, *Rich Man, Poor Man* (New York: Signet, 1965), p. 151; Gabriel Kolko, *Wealth and Power in America* (New York: Praeger, 1962), p. 34; Ferdinand Lundberg, *The Rich and the Super Rich* (New York: Lyle Stuart, 1968).

[54]   Robert G. Simmons and Morris Rosenberg, "Functions of Childrens' Perceptions of the Stratification System," *Amer. Sociological Rev.,* vol. 36, pp. 235–249 (Apr. 1971).

[55]   Simmons and Rosenberg, *op. cit.,*[54] p. 237.

[56]   Simmons and Rosenberg, *op. cit.,*[54] pp. 239–240.

make an even more complicated pattern to confront the sociological or consumer researcher.

Bensman and Vidich, noted for their earlier research on social classes of a small town, recently reported on their research in the larger urban setting and provide support for the contention of social-class overlays:

> . . . classes do not simply disappear. . . . New life styles may replace older ones even while the economic basis of both styles remains the same. More likely, however, new life styles will not completely replace old ones, but will simply become accretions on them. Any innovations in life styles thus increase the complexity of the class system because older classes and styles cannot coexist with the new ones.[57]

Class Distribution

The lower middle and upper lower classes are the largest groups of consumers in America. This is the "middle majority"—to which most marketing organizations must sell.

The exact distribution of individuals into separate class categories depends upon the definitions used for each class. The mainstream of social research has commonly used a six-class system. One organization that has dealt with social class extensively is Social Research, Inc., of Chicago. Based upon their continuing studies, they have prepared estimates of class distribution in America. These estimates, which have been used extensively by marketing strategists, are presented in Figure 5.1.

Somewhat similar results have been reported in Carman's study of cultural classes, except that he reports a smaller percentage in the lower lower class. He found 0.38 percent in upper, 10.82 percent in upper middle, 30.82 percent in lower middle, 49.96 percent in upper lower, and 8.02 percent in lower lower class.[58] Numerous studies have been conducted establishing the proportion of individuals in each class, although the categories are generally not directly comparable with each other.[59] An inspection of the studies over time leads to the conclusion, however, that the proportion in middle and upper classes is fairly stable, but that the proportion in lower lower class has been declining substantially with corresponding increases in the upper lower class.

The six-class categorization of Warner is used in the following pages to describe social-class behavior norms. The discussion that follows is only a skeleton outline of the most important identifying characteristics of each social class,

---

[57] Joseph Bensman and Arthur J. Vidich, *The New American Society* (Chicago: Quandrangle Books, 1971), p. 139.

[58] Carman, *op. cit.*,[36] p. 53.

[59] W. L. Warner, J. O. Low, P. S. Lunt, and L. Srole, *Yankee City* (New Haven, Conn.: Yale University Press, 1963), p. 43; Richard Centers, *op. cit.*,[21] p. 77; August B. Hollingshead and Frederick C. Redich, "Social Stratification and Psychiatric Disorders," *Amer. Sociological Rev.*, vol. 18, pp. 163–167 (1953); Arthur J. Vidich and Joseph Bensman, *Small Town in Mass Society* (Princeton, N.J.: Princeton University Press, 1958, Anchor edition, 1960), p. 52.

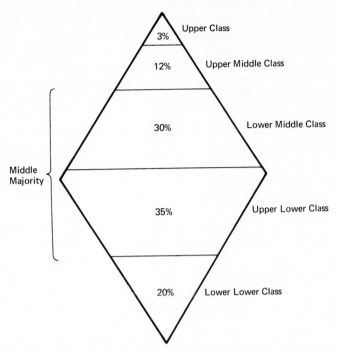

Figure 5.1 SOCIAL CLASSES IN THE UNITED STATES. Charles B. McCann, *Women and Department Store Newspaper Advertising* (Chicago: Social Research, 1957), p. 94

especially as they relate to marketing strategies. The details presented here are obtained from many empirical studies, so that full documentation is not possible. Primarily, however, these generalizations are developed from the studies of Warner, Coleman, Davis, the Gardners, and Levy.

Upper Upper

Upper uppers are the social elite of society.[60] Inherited wealth from socially prominent families is the key to admission. They run the debutante balls, give large sums to philanthropic causes, and belong to the top clubs. Frequently they maintain more than one home—an apartment in the "gold coast" area of the city and a large home in a fashionable suburb. Children must attend private preparatory schools and graduate from the best colleges.

---

[60] In addition to the studies by Warner, Hollingshead, and others, which investigate all social classes, there are good studies that primarily deal with the elite social classes: E. Digby Baltzell, *op. cit.*,[14] pp. 266–275; C. Wright Mills, *The Power Elite* (New York: Oxford University Press, 1956); Harold Kaufman, *Prestige Classes in a New York Rural Community*, memo 260 (Ithaca, N.Y.: Cornell University Agricultural Experiment Station, 1944).

Consumers in this group spend money as if it were unimportant, not niggardly but not with display either, for that would imply that money is important. Originally, this class looked to the British aristocracy as a reference group.[61] Thus, English Tudor homes, spacious lawns, elegant social gatherings, and conservative clothing styles have come to characterize consumption decisions. The social position of individuals within this group is so secure, however, that they can deviate substantially from class norms if they choose to without losing status.

The upper class is of limited interest in the planning of marketing strategy for mass-market products, except if it serves as a reference group for lower classes. There is no agreement, however, about how strongly this class influences the consumption decisions of lower social classes. For some products a "trickle-down" influence appears to exist, but for others no influence or a "trickle-up" pattern may exist.[62]

The upper uppers normally exist as a separate class only in large metropolitan areas. Because they frequently maintain residences in several areas of the country and because they serve as officers and directors of national corporations, there is a tendency for upper uppers to be recognized as such wherever they travel. They are probably the nearest to a truly "national" class that exists in the United States.

Lower Upper

Lower upper individuals often earn more money than upper uppers. Lower uppers include the very-high-income professional people, the presidents of major corporations who have "earned" their position rather than inherited it, and entrepreneurs who have made large amounts of money in real estate, stocks, or business.

They are often socially mobile, having parents in the middle classes. They are the true *nouveaux riches*. They are college educated but not from a prestige college, unless they attended on a scholarship. They are in many clubs and accept positions of leadership in civic and religious affairs. They are *active people* who have attained the material symbols of the upper classes but are still seeking the security of personal esteem and interactions. These people

---

[61] "The higher a person climbs in the social structure of America, the more Anglophile he becomes. Upper-class universities, such as Harvard, Yale, and Princeton, bear a striking resemblance to Oxford and Cambridge, Ivy League style clothing shows British influence, and British sports such as sailing, polo, and riding are upper-class American favorites." See Margaret C. Pirie, "Marketing and Social Classes: An Anthropologist's View," *Management Rev.*, vol. 49, pp. 45–48, at p. 46 (Sept. 1960).

[62] The question of influence trickling down has been studied from a number of research perspectives. For the classic study from a *social-class perspective*, see Bernard Barber and Lyle S. Lobel, "Fashion in Women's Clothes and the American Social System," *Social Forces*, vol. 31, pp. 124–131 (1952); also Lloyd A. Fallers, "A Note on the 'Trickle Effect'," *Public Opinion Quart.*, vol. 5, pp. 314–321 (1954), reprinted in Perry Bliss, *Marketing and the Behavioral Sciences* (Boston: Allyn and Bacon, 1963), pp. 208–216.

will not join the true elite, the upper uppers, but their children probably will if they are sent to the right schools and choose the right marriage partners.

Conspicuousness in consumption decisions is the pattern for lower uppers. They use products as symbols or badges of their wealth. They buy the largest homes in the best suburbs, the most expensive automobiles, swimming pools, yachts, and other symbols that are perceived by others as obvious indicators of wealth. The women are dressed in the most expensive fashions—usually more innovatively than the upper uppers.

The lower uppers guard their status very carefully. This prevents them from being confused with those below them and helps to obtain interactions with the upper uppers. The children are given many possessions; the children themselves are symbols of the family's wealth and position.

The upper upper and lower upper classes are usually lumped together in the development of marketing plans. For mass markets these two groups have little importance because of their small size. However, they may be important markets for many specialized luxury goods.

Upper Middle

The key word in understanding upper middles is "career." They are successful professionals and businessmen with earnings usually in the $15,000 to $30,000 range. Consumption behavior, their sense of accomplishment, and a whole way of life are centered upon the husband's career. If he should lose his ability to keep that career or if he does not perform well, the family falls from its position.

Education is an important value in the upper middle families. As a class, they are the most educated group in society. Many have professional or graduate degrees, since lawyers, physicians, scientists, and college professors are typical occupations of upper middle-class men. Almost every male in this class has a college degree, although it is probably from a state university rather than a prestige school. The education usually is for a specific profession or the skill of business administration. Upper middle families as a rule are demanding of their children. They know that unless the children develop professional or administrative skills and upper middle values, their chance of remaining in this class is small. The fear is well grounded, for the upper middle class has a higher proportion than any other class of children dropping to a lower stratum.

The *quality market* for many products is the upper middle class. Purchases by upper middle families are conspicuous but careful. It is considered important to them to appear fashionable, to have an attractive home in a good area, and to have well-dressed, attractive children. The wife is judged on how well she achieves these goals. She, in turn, acts as chauffeur (getting the kids to dancing school, the tutor, and the dramatic club), as interior decorator, and as fashion coordinator.

Gracious living is the pattern of life that the family seeks. The home is where the physician, lawyer, or businessman entertains potential clients and friends who may recommend him. The wife who can maintain a home that presents a picture of gracious living at the frequent social gatherings of these people is therefore a valuable supplement to the husband's career. The home, the automobile, and even the wife are symbols of the husband's success and personal competence.

Lower Middle

The lower middle class is probably what most people are thinking of when they describe a "typical" American, for lower middle families exemplify the core of respectability, conscientious work habits, and adherence to culturally defined norms and standards.[63] Lower-middle-class families go to church regularly. They obey the law. They are very upset when their children use marijuana or are busted for drugs. They are not innovators. They conform to current patterns of taste and behavior.

The *home* is very important to the lower middle family; the majority own rather than rent. They want the home to be neat, well painted, and in a respectable area of town. As such, they are an excellent market for do-it-yourself products. The mothers fear that their children will be ashamed of their home (possibly because many of the mothers rose from a lower class and remember similar feelings). Thus, the women work very hard at having the interior neat, up to date, and respectable. They have little confidence in their own tastes, however, and usually adopt "standardized" home furnishings. This is in contrast to the upper middle housewife, who feels freer to experiment with new styles and new arrangements, and the upper lower housewife, who is not very concerned about the overall plan for furnishing the home. The lower middle housewife rarely is inside an upper-middle- or upper-class home and therefore must rely on magazines or literature from retailers to tell her how to plan her furnishings. She reads and follows the advice of the medium-level shelter and service magazines, tries to make her house "pretty."

Lower-middle-class women "work" more at their shopping than other classes. They acquire clothing and furniture one item at a time rather than as a coordinated unit. Most of their nonfood purchase decisions are demanding and tedious. This attitude is expressed in an interview with a typical lower middle housewife:

> I'm always buying clothing for the family. I look around and buy the best I can for as little as I can. With supermarkets, I watch for ads on Thursdays. For example, I just bought a blanket and I went to three

---

[63] For a description of these attitudes and behaviors, see C. Wright Mills, *White Collar: The American Middle Classes* (New York: Oxford University Press, 1951). For a description of middle-majority consumption decision processes, see Albert Shepard, "Familiar Affluence's Changing Buying Drives of Middle Majority," *Advertising Age*, vol. 32, pp. 46, 48 (Jan. 2, 1961). For a description of the British middle class, see John Raynor, *The Middle Class* (London: Longmans, 1969).

stores to look. As it happened, we bought at Lits; they had the nicest blanket for the best price.[64]

It appears that the lower-middle-class housewife displays the highest degree of price sensitivity of any class, although this hypothesis needs additional research to confirm and/or qualify it.

Lower Middle Subclasses   The lower middle class can be divided into various subclasses in order to get a clearer picture of the characteristics displayed by its members. Coleman describes the group as follows:

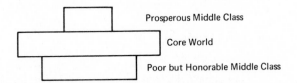

Prosperous Middle Class

Core World

Poor but Honorable Middle Class

(1)   *The Prosperous Middle Class:*   Includes small businessmen who are prosperous, less successful professionals, above-average salesmen, and certain types of white-collar workers who are well paid, such as computer technicians. Some of these may be making as much as $18,000 a year and many are in the $10,000 to $14,000 range. They may have the income to rise higher in the class structure but prefer the good life of color TV sets, nice cars, boats, and a savings account rather than spending money for the residence and activities they would need to compete with upper middles. These groups are often excellent markets for expensive products used inside the home and for leisure goods.

(2)   *The Core World of Lower Middle Class:*   Includes store keepers, bank tellers, technicians, chain store managers, and average salesmen. They typically earn $8000–$12,000. Their small, well-kept homes line the streets of the still respectable areas of a city and the middle-class suburbs, but are noticeably absent in the better suburbs.

(3)   *Poor but Honorables:*   Includes ministers (of some denominations), social workers, public school teachers, and other professionals who are poorly paid relative to their education and responsibility. They must dress reasonably well, eat in restaurants fairly often, and purchase books and journals. Consequently, they have even less money than other lower middles left for purchase of household items and durable goods. They must seek purchasing strategies which help mitigate this dilemma and are receptive to marketing offers which assist in this.[65]

---

[64]   An interview quoted from research conducted by Social Research, Inc., Sidney Levy, "Social Class and Consumer Behavior," in Joseph W. Newman (ed.), *On Knowing the Consumer* (New York: Wiley, 1966), pp. 146–160.

[65]   These categories are based upon various papers and seminars conducted by Richard Coleman, based upon studies at Social Research, Inc.

The lower middle class is usually considered to be "white collar." Some groups exhibit such similar values that they are grouped with lower middles or placed together under a different categorization system. These include the "gray collars"—firemen, policemen, mailmen, and similar types who are not laborers and have positions of responsibility in society. Another group is termed the "aristocrat blue collars." These are highly paid skilled workers such as printers, plumbers, and other tradesmen, and factory foremen. When they maintain well-kept homes in respectable areas, send their children to college (which many now do), and participate in church and civic activities, they can hardly be distinguished as a marketing group from white-collar workers.

Upper Lower

Upper lower social classes—the largest segment in the social system—exhibit a routine life.[66] It is characterized by a day-to-day existence of unchanging activities. They live in dull areas of the city, either in small houses or in apartments. The "hard hats" are included in this class. Males work at generally uncreative jobs requiring manual activity and only moderate skill or education. They would change to a better occupation if they could, but are reluctant to leave because of a belief that conditions in a new job are unlikely to be better.[67] Also, they fear technological obsolescence and wish to retain the security that accrues to seniority. Because of unions and seniority, many of the blue-collar workers may earn incomes that give them considerable affluence.

The housewife in upper lower households sees her life as crowded and busy but one of monotony. She is unaware of any other existence, however. Her primary reason for existence, as she sees it, is to be a mother of her children. Children are called the "most prized possession in the home" and she places their desires before those of the husband.[68] She buys the children little things she believes will make them happy rather than saving her money for larger purchases. She has relatively little insight into their motivation or behavior and is both puzzled and upset when they behave in an unexpected or unwanted manner.

The purchase decisions of the working-class wife are characterized as impulsive in the case of new decisions and brand loyalty in the case of previously

---

[66] The primary reference work on upper lower class for consumer analysis is Rainwater et al., op. cit.[31] Confirmation of the interactions part of this study is found in Floyd Dotson, "Patterns of Voluntary Association among Urban Working-Class Families," Amer. Sociological Rev., vol. 16, pp. 687–693 (Oct. 1961).

[67] For amplification, see Ely Chinoy, Automobile Workers and the American Dream (New York: Doubleday, 1955); also Robert H. Guest, "Work Careers and Aspirations of Automobile Workers," Amer. Sociological Rev., vol. 19, pp. 155–163 (1954); Robert Blauner, "Work Satisfaction and Industrial Trends in Modern Society," in Bendix and Lipset, op. cit.,[7] pp. 473–487; Herbert H. Hyman, "The Value Systems of Different Classes," in Bendix and Lipset, op. cit.,[7] pp. 488–499.

[68] The social roles of this and the other classes is gaining some flexibility, however. See Helena Z. Lopata, Occupation Housewife (New York: Oxford University Press, 1971).

purchased items. She likes "national" brands because purchasing them is one way to "prove" her knowledge as a buyer, a role in which she actually feels (probably correctly) that she has little skill.

The upper lower housewife has little social contact outside the home and family. She does not know how to organize her affairs or is prohibited financially from leaving the home to attend civic organizations or church activities. She does not enjoy such activities anyway, and her group activity is probably limited to a few school-related meetings in which she may become involved in order to enhance her status as a mother. Social interaction is limited to the close neighbors and to relatives. If she takes a vacation, it will probably be a visit to relatives in another city.

The typical upper-lower-class family is not a social climber. They do not expect to rise above their present status as many middle- and upper-class families do. Upper lower persons are concerned that they not be confused with the lower lowers, who are characterized as "slum dwellers."

Upper Lower "Stars"   In nearly every social class there are some persons who have the values, interactions, and symbols of that class but earn well above the average amount of income. From the marketer's perspective they are the "stars" of that class. They are "overprivileged," not in an absolute sense, but *relative to their social class.*[69]

The upper lower stars earn good incomes, often as much as $12,000 and sometimes more. Instead of spending their money to purchase a large home or live in a nice suburb, they remain in a low-status neighborhood and house and put the money *inside* the house. The husbands give their wives "white kitchens" rather than mink coats. The kitchens are often the best equipped in the city, with the most modern appliances and deluxe models. Similar purchase decisions are made for other consumer products as the upper lower family elects the good life (consumption of products that they enjoy) rather than status.

Ethnic Leaders   Another group of people in the lower social classes that have unusually high incomes (and perhaps influence) is composed of ethnic group leaders. These include insurance salesmen, funeral directors, dentists, and some physicians who are a member of the ethnic group they serve. They make a good income but are content to stay in their own world rather than live with other professional persons. They minimize the external symbols of class in their neighborhood, and this leaves them a considerable amount of discretionary income.

---

[69]   The concept of overprivileged and underprivileged social classes is important for the marketer attempting to use social classes as a basis for market segmentation. See Richard P. Coleman, "The Significance of Social Stratification in Selling," in Martin L. Bell (ed.), *Marketing: A Maturing Discipline, Proc. Amer. Assoc.* (Dec. 1960), pp. 171–184.

Lower Lower

The lower lower social class contains the "disreputable" people of the society.[70] The average American wishes the lower lower person—and the slum in which he lives—did not exist, but he still feels that the social position of the slum dweller is the individual's own fault. The individuals in this class may try to rise above it on some occasions, but upon meeting failure they become reconciled to their position and stop trying to change their status.

The lower lower often rejects the standards associated with middle-class morality and behavior. He "gets his kicks" whenever he can, and this includes buying impulsively. The lack of planning in his purchases often causes him to adopt inferior decision strategies. He pays too much for products, he buys on credit at a high interest rate, and he does not evaluate the quality of the product in the way that middle-class consumers usually do.

The lower lower is likely to be poorly educated and have a low IQ. Thus he obtains only limited amounts of information because of the restricted flow of communications addressed to him. He has limited power to think abstractly and thus is attracted to simple, concrete illustrations and symbols.

There is a tendency to neglect the lower lower in marketing planning because of the low purchasing power of the group and because of the lack of affinity which the rest of society has for this group. However, it is a large market for food products and some other types of products. Moreover, empirical studies consistently reveal relatively large numbers of television sets, automobiles, and other durable goods being sold to this class.[71] Food stamps, subsidized housing programs, and other government assistance has also increased the importance of these group selected marketing strategies.

Social Class and the Life Cycle

The influence of social class on consumer behavior varies at different stages of the life cycle. The culture of a society is specific in its social-class expectations, so that a member of a particular social class will engage in a different set of behaviors at one stage of the life cycle than at another. This concept is discussed in more detail in Chapter 7.

---

[70] There are a number of studies on the lower lower social class, or major components of it, and these should increase in number as poverty increases as a topic of social concern. For an insightful inquiry into this class, see David Matza, "The Disreputable Poor," in Bendix and Lipset, *op. cit.*,[7] pp. 289–302; also Genevieve Knupfer, "Portrait of the Underdog," *Public Opinion Quart.*, vol. 11, pp. 103–114 (1947).

[71] David Caplovitz, *The Poor Pay More* (New York: Free Press, 1963).

SOCIAL-CLASS INFLUENCES ON INDIVIDUAL PSYCHOLOGICAL MAKEUP

There is a great amount of research showing influence of social class on the psychological makeup of individuals. Some representative findings from this research are presented below to show how the central control unit of consumers can be expected to function in various social classes and to build a base of knowledge to describe consumption decisions in a later section.

Attitudes and Self-conception

Attitudes and values provide goals which aid alternative evaluation and provide motivation for search and evaluation. These are *transmitted differentially among social classes*. Some of the early research by Martineau determined basic differences in motives between the middle class and lower class (the classes of most interest to marketers). These are described below:[72]

	Middle Class	*Lower Class*
(1)	Pointed to the future	Pointed to the present and past
(2)	Viewpoint embraces a long expanse of time	Lives and thinks in a short expanse of time
(3)	More urban identification	More rural identification
(4)	Stresses rationality	Nonrational essentially
(5)	Has a well-structured sense of the universe	Vague and unclear structuring of the world
(6)	Horizons vastly extended or not limited	Horizons sharply defined and limited
(7)	Greater sense of choice making	Limited sense of choice making
(8)	Self-confident, willing to take risks	Very much concerned with security and insecurity
(9)	Immaterial and abstract in thinking	Concrete and perceptive in thinking
(10)	See himself tied to national happenings	World revolves around his family and his body

The concept of what the ideal man or the ideal woman should be like varied markedly among social classes. The differences are so great that market segmentation may be an absolute necessity for products such as hair preparations,

---

[72] Pierre Martineau, "Social Classes and Spending Behavior," *J. Marketing*, vol. 23, pp. 121–130 (Oct. 1958).

clothing, soaps, and other personal items.[73] The emphases on what a "real man" should be are examined in the following illustration.

Upper-middle-class men tolerate a much more "feminine" conception of a real man. They do not think that a real man has to be crudely tough to be effective. They think that being clean, fastidious, and well groomed is part of being a successful person and demonstrate the kind of narcissism one expects in a higher status person. They think of hygiene, grooming, and dress as especially related to one's career and how it is being lived up to. A higher status man may have distinctive specialized hobbies; some tendency to think of women as pals— and they think he should be a friend; and the idea that masculine know-how finds expression in knowing one's way about the world—in jet planes, restaurants, modern business.

Lower-middle-class people think a good man is particularly a good father, a responsible husband, a man who builds a solid home life. He is serious, earnest, somewhat depressed, eager for his children to do well in school so that they might become well established, and fearful that they might be trespassed against by lower-class people. He is the most conventional, generally, in dress, resistant to Ivy League and Continental influences, and hopeful that the double-breasted suit will come back to cover up his bulging middle.

Working-class people think that a real man is a sturdy guy who can make a decent living. Lower-class men like to have body know-how, physical adeptness, and manual skills, to understand how things work. They want to get along, to get some fun out of life. They expect to work fairly hard and to relax as hard as they can, because they feel life uses them up faster than it does higher status people.[74]

Personality

Personality varies among social classes as well as among individuals within a social class. The personality traits that are most prevalent in the higher social classes are, quite naturally, those that society prizes most. Various tests have indicated that high-status children are more likely than low-status children to possess the traits of honesty, self-confidence, mental health, linguistic skill, test intelligence, cooperative attitude, spontaneity, and politeness.[75] There is substantial evidence to indicate that lower-class individuals are more impulsive and uninhibited and put a premium on physical gratification, on free expression of

---

[73] Levy, *op. cit.*,[64] pp. 148–151. See also a much earlier study with similar findings in Centers, *op. cit.*,[21] esp. pp. 141–159.

[74] Centers, *op. cit.*,[21] pp. 151–152.

[75] Kaare Svalastoga, *Social Differentiation* (New York: McKay, 1965), p. 88. The relations between social class and personality have been investigated extensively. For representative studies, see Robert J. Havighurst, "Social Class and Basic Personality Structure," *Sociology and Social Research*, vol. 26, pp. 355–363 (1952); C. Kluckhohn, H. A. Murray and D. Schneider (eds.), *Personality in Nature, Society and Culture* (New York: Knopf, 1953).

aggression, and on spending and sharing.[76] Middle classes, compared to lower classes, are more self-sufficient and more dominant in their interpersonal relations.[77]

Learning and Intelligence

The higher an individual's class, the greater is the probability that he will have high intelligence and learn rapidly. This is a natural expectation because of the greater access to education, more encouraging home values, and better health that also correlate with social class. The IQ of children from the business and professional classes is on the average about 15 to 25 points higher than that of children from working-class families.[78] The higher the occupational level of the father, the higher the probability that the IQ of the father, the IQ of the mother, and the IQ of the child will also be high.[79] It has also been found that persons remaining in rural areas have lower IQs, on the average, than those who move from rural to urban areas.[80]

The impact of the intelligence findings for marketing is significant. When developing a product or promotional material for the mass markets, the information must be presented at a lower level than it would be for upper classes. (This is an axiom that is sometimes not considered by social critics who view advertising from their own social class and intelligence perspective rather than from that of the mass market.) Studies have indicated that the lower classes have significantly less ability to understand complexity and abstraction than the classes above them.[81] The social-class findings on learning, therefore, indicate very strongly the need to consider the social status of the intended market when developing advertising appeals and planning the number of repetitions for messages.

---

[76] J. A. Clausen, "Social and Psychological Factors in Narcotics Addiction," *Law and Contemporary Problems*, vol. 22, pp. 34–51 (1957); B. M Spinley, *The Deprived and the Privileged: Personality Development in English Society* (London: Routledge, 1953).

[77] Orville Brim, Bentley Glass, and David E. Lavin, *Personality and Decision Processes* (Palo Alto, Calif.: Stanford University Press, 1962), p. 123.

[78] Kenneth Eels, Allison Davis, Robert J. Havighurst, Virgil E. Herrick, and Ralph Tyler, *Intelligence and Cultural Differences: A Study of Cultural Learning and Problem-Solving* (Chicago: University of Chicago Press, 1951), p. 53; also Robert S. Lynd and Helen M. Lynd, *Middletown: A Study in American Culture* (New York: Harcourt, 1956), pp. 36–37; Hollingshead, *op. cit.*,[13] p. 175.

[79] The scores for all of these variables are highly correlated. The Ohio State University Intelligence Test was the measure of intelligence used in this study. See C. T. Pihlblad and C. L. Gregory, "Occupational Selection and Intelligence in Rural Communities and Small Towns in Missouri," *Amer. Sociological Rev.*, vol. 21, pp. 63–71 (Feb. 1956).

[80] C. T. Pihlblad and C. L. Gregory, "Selective Aspects of Migration among Missouri High School Graduates," *Amer. Sociological Rev.*, vol. 19, pp. 314–324 (June 1954).

[81] Brim *et al.*, *op. cit.*,[77] p. 123.

The Family

Differences in family structure and behavior patterns exist among social classes. An inverse relation exists between the socioeconomic status of a class and its fertility rate. Although this is true generally, the very lowest fertility rate occurs among the lower middle class. Apparently, these families realize that having large families inhibits them from enjoying many of the accouterments of higher classes and accordingly restrict family size.[82]

The role of familiar influences in buying behavior is described in detail in Chapter 7. Since social classes have a significant impact upon the family, some of the research findings relating to class behavior are presented at this point. It should be noted that while these findings are empirical and have general acceptance, they may need to be qualified when one is dealing with the analysis of consumer decisions for specific products.

(1) Husbands and wives usually come from homogeneous social-class backgrounds even though they usually are heterogenous in their basic psychological needs.[83] Thus, when compatibility within couples is desired, social class may be a better basis for market segmentation than psychological variables.

(2) The higher the social class of a family, the less likely is the chance that there will be a family instability or disorganization.[84]

(3) Middle- and upper-class husbands have greater authority over their wives and children than do lower-class husbands, although the ideology and values of middle- and upper-class husbands are more likely to be permissive and equalitarian.[85]

(4) There are wide variations among classes in values and behavior in raising children. Middle-class families have a more accepting and equalitarian relationship with their children than working-class families. Upper middles are concerned about their child being active and alert and want products that will add to their success, competence, and proficiency as mothers and fathers. Lower middle classes stress control and conformity. Lower middle and upper lower classes are both very concerned about the neatness and cleanliness of the child, eliminating dirty diapers at an earlier age, and getting children to obey adults.[86]

---

[82] For the evidence to support this hypothesis as well as an excellent review of the literature relating social class to fertility, see Dennis H. Wrong, "Trends in Class Fertility in Western Nations," *Can. J. Economics and Political Science,* vol. 5, pp. 216–229 (May 1958), reprinted in Bendix and Lipset, *op. cit.,*[7] pp. 353–361.

[83] Robert F. Winch, *Mate Selection* (New York: Harper & Row, 1958).

[84] William J. Goode, "Marital Satisfaction and Instability," *International Social Science J.,* vol. 14, pp. 507–526 (1962), reprinted in Bendix and Lipset, *op. cit.,*[7] pp. 377–387; also Levy, *op. cit.,*[64] p. 149.

[85] William J. Goode, "Family and Mobility," in Bendix and Lipset, *op. cit.,*[7] pp. 582–601; also Lopata, *op. cit.*[68]

[86] An excellent review of differences in child-raising among social classes is in Urie Bronfenbrenner, "Socialization and Social Class through Time and Space," in Maccoby, *et al., op. cit.,*[21] pp. 399–425; also Levy, *op. cit.,*[64] pp. 149–150; Rainwater, *et. al., op. cit.,*[31] chap. 5.

(5) Sexual behavior is very much influenced by social class for the male but is influenced to a lesser extent among females.[87] The patterns followed by families vary considerably among classes and are determinants of consumption for products that enter into the intimate relations of a family.

(6) The status of women relative to men is low and, contrary to popular impressions, continues to decline.[88] This is a sensitive issue but one that some marketing organizations have attempted to recognize and appeal to in their advertising slogans and in the understanding of women's status and rights which they attempt to communicate.

Social Language

The language patterns of an individual are closely correlated with that individual's social class. Ellis has reported a revealing set of experiments on this topic. In one experiment he measured social class of respondents and had them make a 40-second recording of the fable, "The Tortoise and the Hare." These short recordings were played to groups of 15 to 30 regionally diverse college students who served as judges. The average ratings of social class by these judges correlated 0.80 with the speakers' social classes.[89] When the studies were conducted in such a way that speakers were asked through role playing to "fake" their voices to make them sound upper class, the student judges' correlation with measured actual class was still 0.65.[90] All of the subjects used proper grammar, but their choice of vocabulary, sentence length, sentence structure, and fluency varied by social class. In still another approach, Ellis had the speakers count from one to twenty, and even in this situation, college students' rankings correlated 0.65 with social class of the speakers.

An additional study by Harms found that the credibility of speakers is also associated with status. High-status persons are perceived as being more credible than low-status persons.[91]

---

[87] Alfred C. Kinsey, Wardell B. Pomeroy, and Clyde E. Martin, *Sexual Behavior in the Human Male* (Philadelphia: Saunders, 1948); Alfred C. Kinsey, Wardell B. Pomeroy, Clyde E. Martin, and Paul H. Gebhard, *Sexual Behavior in the Human Female* (Philadelphia: Saunders, 1958). For applications, see Ralph Leezenbaum, "The New American Woman and Marketing," *Marketing/Communications*, pp. 22–28 (July 1970).

[88] Primary documentation is found in Dean D. Knudsen, "The Declining Status of Women: Popular Myths and the Failure of Functionalist Thought," *Social Forces*, vol. 48, pp. 183-193 (Dec. 1969); also Cynthia F. Epstein, "Encountering the Male Establishment: Sex-Status Limits on Women's Careers in the Professions," *Amer. J. of Sociology*, vol. 75, pp. 969–981 (May 1970). A thorough statistical review of these and related trends is found in the following articles: Elizabeth Duncan Koontz, "The Women's Bureau Looks to the Future," Elizabeth Waldman, "Changes in the Labor Force Activity of Women," Janice Neipert Hedges, "Women Workers and Manpower Demands in the 1970's," all in *Monthly Labor Rev.*, pp. 3–29 (June 1970).

[89] Dean S. Ellis, "Speech and Social Status in America," *Social Forces*, vol. 45, pp. 431–437 (Mar. 1967).

[90] Ellis, *op. cit.*[89]

[91] L. S. Harms, "Listener Judgments of Status Cues in Speech," *Quart. J. Speech*, vol. 47, pp. 164–168 (Apr. 1961).

Social-class differences may take many forms.[92] The use of slang and colorful but trite phrases characterizes the lower classes. They also use double negatives, use the past participle for the complete verb form, and tend to mispronounce words (such as "tahr" for "tire"). Upper classes are clearly marked by their pitch and tonality, their avoidance of euphemisms and popular phrases, economy of words (they use 20 percent fewer words for the same thought), neatness of enunciation, and pronunciation of words.[93] The meaning of words also varies among classes. For example, "lunch" to the upper-class person is "dinner" to the lower-class person and "supper" to the lower-class person is "dinner" to the upper-class person.

Religion

Religious affiliation is highly correlated with social class. Upper classes are most likely to belong to Episcopal or Unitarian churches. Middle classes usually belong to Methodist, Presbyterian, or Baptist churches. Lower classes typically belong to Baptist, Catholic, or the smaller Protestant groups. Upper-middle-class Jews are likely to belong to Reformed or Conservative congregations or, in the case of uppers, perhaps not to be members of synagogue congregations at all. Lower-class Jews are more likely to belong to Orthodox congregations.[94]

The preceding describes the social-class influence on an individual's psychological makeup in a general way. Marketing strategists desire more specific data concerning the influence of social class upon consumption decisions. Information from such studies is described in the concluding section of this chapter.

SOCIAL CLASS AND CONSUMPTION DECISIONS

Unlike many of the behavioral sciences, much social class research of recent years has been concerned specifically with consumption decisions. In addition, consumer analysts have made contributions to sociological research concerning social class as well as to the literature directly concerned with marketing strategy and programs. Consequently, there are a number of empirically based generalizations available concerning social class for marketing decisions and for understanding more fully the decision-making stages involved in typical consumption areas.

---

[92] Leonard Schatzman and Anselm Strauss, "Social Class and Modes of Communication," *Amer. J. Sociology,* vol. 60, pp. 329–338 (Jan. 1955); also H. L. Mencken, *The American Language: An Inquiry into the Development of English in the United States* (New York: Knopf, 1960). A classic study in the relationship between language and social class is G. B. Shaw's *Pygmalion,* or the musical version *My Fair Lady.*

[93] Clifton Fadiman, "Is There an Upper-Class American Language?" *Holiday,* pp. 66 ff (Oct. 1956).

[94] N. J. Demerath, III, "Social Class, Religious Affiliation, and Styles of Religious Involvement," in Bendix and Lipset, *op. cit.,*[7] pp. 388–394. For additional data see Norval D. Glenn and Ruth Hyland, "Religious Preference and Wordly Success: Some Evidence from National Surveys," *Amer. Sociological Rev.,* vol. 32 (Feb. 1967).

Social Class and Market Segmentation

Social class is useful as an approach to understanding market segments, although it has not been proven to be superior to other bases of market segmentation. It is clear that social class is a useful perspective for looking at some product categories and some marketing strategies,[95] although there is considerable skepticism about universal value in marketing strategy. Frank, Massy, and Wind, after assessing social-class studies, concluded that the *potential* is greater than realized values. They point out that lack of success in some marketing research may, among other reasons, be due to the inadequacy of a unidimensional measure in explaining the complexity of social class and the failure of researchers to apply Coleman's concept of variation in income *within* social classes ("overprivileged" and "underprivileged" members of each social class).[96]

Income Versus Social Class Controversy exists concerning the relative efficiency of income and social class as bases for market segmentation. Wasson has shown that expenditures for food, shelter, and education are related to occupational class.[97] His analysis of data presented in Table 5.3 shows that when occupational class is held constant, there is no clear relationship between expenditure allocations and income. A government survey indicates that middle-class white-collar workers value housing and quality of neighborhood more highly than do blue-collar workers in the same income class with corresponding expenditure levels.[98]

Unsatisfactory results were obtained when comparing social class to income for segmentation in a study by Myers, Stanton, and Haug. Their research compared social class and income as correlates of buying behavior for a variety of low-cost packaged goods in Los Angeles. Five income groups and five social-class groups were used. They found that both variables were significantly related to buying, but that the chi-square values for income were considerably larger than those for social class.[99] They do note that the results might be different for big-ticket items than for the low-priced products of their study.

A measure of relative occupational class income is proposed as a solution

[95] Richard P. Coleman and Bernice L. Newgarten, *Social Status in the City* (San Francisco: Jessey-Bess, 1971), Levy, *op. cit.*;[64] Coleman, *op. cit.*;[69] Martineau, *op. cit.*;[72] Philip Kotler, "Behavioral Model for Analyzing Buyers," *J. Marketing*, vol. 29, p. 43 (Oct. 1965); John A. Howard, *Marketing Management: Analysis and Planning* (Homewood, Ill.: Irwin, 1963), p. 114; John A. Howard and Jagdish N. Sheth, *The Theory of Buyer Behavior* (New York: Wiley, 1969), pp. 87–89.

[96] Ronald E. Frank, William F. Massy, and Yoram Wind, *Market Segmentation* (Englewood Cliffs, N.J.: Prentice-Hall, 1972), pp. 47–49.

[97] Chester R. Wasson, "Is It Time to Quit Thinking of Income Classes?" *J. Marketing*, vol. 33, pp. 54–56 (Apr. 1969).

[98] *Survey of Consumer Expenditures*, supplement 2, part A, BLS Report, (Washington, D.C.: U.S. Department of Labor, July 1964).

[99] James H. Myers, Roger R. Stanton, and Arne F. Haug, "Correlates of Buying Behavior: Social Class vs. Income," *J. Marketing*, vol. 35, pp. 8–15 (Oct. 1971).

Table 5.3 AVERAGE PERCENTAGE OF TOTAL EXPENDITURE ALLOCATED TO SELECTED CATEGORIES BY THE MAJOR OCCUPATIONAL CLASSES AT THE SAME INCOME LEVELS (URBAN EMPLOYED FAMILIES, UNITED STATES, 1960–1961)

Occupation of Head	Food Income Group				Shelter Income Group				Education and Reading Income Group			
	1	*2*	*3*	*4*	*1*	*2*	*3*	*4*	*1*	*2*	*3*	*4*
White Collar:												
Professionals	21	23	23	23	16	17	16	14	2.5	2.2	2.1	2.2
Clerical, and so on	24	24	24	24	16	15	14	13	1.7	1.7	1.8	2.0
Blue Collar:												
Skilled	25	26	24	25	14	13	12	11	1.3	1.4	1.5	2.0
Semiskilled	27	26	26	25	14	13	12	11	1.0	1.4	1.7	1.5
Unskilled	28	27	25	24	14	13	13	11	1.2	1.5	1.9	1.7

SOURCE: *Survey of Consumer Expenditures,* supplement 2, part A, U.S. Department of Labor, BLS Report 237-8 (July 1964).

NOTE: Income groups: 1 = $4000-$4900; 2 = $5000-5900; 3 = $6000-$7400; 4 = $7500-$9900.

by one researcher. Peters, using a concept closely related to Coleman's "over-privileged" group, analyzed families in terms of their relationship to the median income *within* their occupation. He found that the buying behavior of relatively well-off blue-collar workers is more like that of affluent white-collar and professional workers than that of less well-off blue-collar workers.[100] With respect to the superiority of relative occupational class income versus the use of occupation or income alone as variables with which to segment markets, Peters' evidence was mixed.

Pragmatic Acceptance A pragmatic approach to social class as a basis of market segmentation appears to be the most acceptable at the present time. It is clear that some product categories and some marketing problems yield to insights generated from a social-class approach. Others, at least with present methodology, are better approached with other perspectives. A consumer researcher should use social-class perspectives when they aid in the solution of a particular marketing problem but not expect them to apply to every situation.

The following paragraphs describe some of the more specific conclusions about usefulness of social class in analyzing consumption decisions.

---

[100] William H. Peters, "Relative Occupational Class Income: A Significant Variable in the Marketing of Automobiles," *J. Marketing,* vol. 34, pp. 74–77 (Apr. 1970).

Evaluative Criteria

Evaluative criteria refer to the specifications that a consumer utilizes to compare products and brands, as noted in Chapter 3. These criteria are a reflection of the individual's goals and basic desires with respect to a purchase. Since they are shaped by his basic attitudes, past experience, and interaction with family and social environment, it can be expected that they would frequently be related to social class.

Clothing The kind, quality, and style of clothing an individual wears appears to be linked to that individual's social class as a statistical generalization. Hoult found that clothing furnishes a quick, visual cue to the class culture of the wearer.[101] Ostermeier and Eicher investigated the social-class characteristics of adolescent girls and report that when asked to give the characteristics of the popular girls, "dressed well" was the response most frequently given.[102] More significantly they found a relationship between clothing, social class, and social acceptance. Earlier, Gordon also found that clothing and appearance become symbols of social differentiation because of their high visibility.[103] In another study, Rich and Jain found high interest in clothing fashions among all social classes, but their data seem to indicate greater attention to fashion information among upper social classes.[104]

Home Furnishings The criteria a family uses to furnish a home appear to be closely related to social class.[105] In a probability survey of 897 respondents, Laumann and House noted the contents and characteristics of the living room on a 53-item check-list inventory. They clustered the living room furniture using a technique called smallest space analysis (SSA). Figure 5.2 depicts how the 53 variables arranged themselves in a two-dimensional space. The clusters reflected style of decor: (1) high status—modern, (2) high status—traditional, (3) low status—traditional, and (4) low status—modern. When people (rather than furnishings) were mapped in a multidimensional scalogram analysis (MSA), interesting conclusions were obtained. Traditional respondents represented the established upper class (white, Anglo-Saxon, Protestants not recently upwardly mobile within

[101] Thomas Ford Hoult, "Experimental Measurement of Clothing as a Factor in Some Social Rating of Selected American Men," *Amer. Sociological Rev.*, vol. 19, pp. 324–325 (June 1954).

[102] Arlene Bjorngaard Ostermeier and Joanne Bubolz Eicher, "Clothing and Appearance as Related to Social Class and Social Acceptance of Adolescent Girls," *Michigan State University Quart. Bull.*, vol. 48, pp. 431–436 (Feb. 1966).

[103] C. Wayne Gordon, *The Social System of the High School* (New York: Free Press, 1957), p. 114.

[104] Stuart U. Rich and Subhash C. Jain, "Social Class and Life Cycle as Predictors of Shopping Behavior," *J. Marketing Research*, vol. 5, pp. 41–49 (Feb. 1968).

[105] Edward O. Laumann and James S. House, "Living Room Styles and Social Attributes: The Patterning of Material Artifacts in a Modern Urban Community," *Sociology and Social Research*, vol. 54, pp. 321–342 (Apr. 1970).

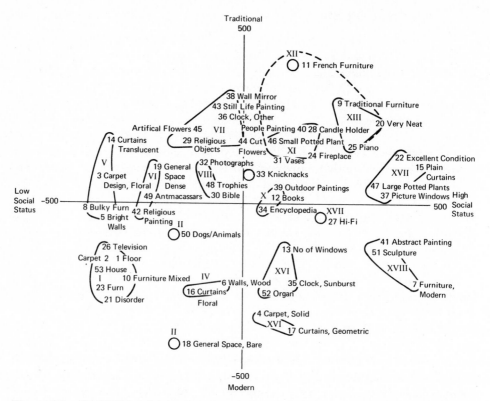

Figure 5.2 GRAPHIC PORTRAYAL OF THE BEST TWO-SPACE SOLUTION FOR LIVING-ROOM OBJECTS. Edward O. Laumann and James S. House, "Living Room Styles and Social Attributes: The Patterning of Material Artifacts in a Modern Urban Community," *Sociology and Social Research*, vol. 54, pp. 321–342, at p. 326 (Apr. 1970)

the present generation). The modern respondents were generally upwardly mobile within this generation and from non-Anglo-Saxon, Catholic origins. They were, according to Laumann and House, the *nouveaux riches*.[106]

Laumann and House propose the theory that the *nouveaux riches* have a strong need to validate their newly found status, yet have not been accepted socially by the traditional upper classes. They turn to conspicuous consumption but with "taste" if it is to validate their claim to high status in respects other than mere money. The researchers conclude that the criteria used by this class reflect the *chic* norms of tastemakers:

> Discovery of such norms is easy in a society that possesses a class of professional tastemakers (e.g., architects, interior decorators, fashion

designers) and taste-setting media (ranging from *Better Homes and Gardens* through the *New Yorker*). Normative consumption trends are evident in styles of decor adopted by business and government for their new offices and stores. In all cases, the norms today favor modern decor.[107]

Leisure The percentage of family income spent for leisure, independent of income, has not been found to vary much between social classes[108] but the evaluative criteria used in selecting type of recreation is heavily influenced by social class. Bridge is an upper-class game, while bingo is lower class. Tennis is an upper-class sport, boxing is predominantly lower class. Opera is upper class, roller derby is lower class.[109]

Leisure activities may be characterized within a prestige hierarchy associated with occupational status. In a random sample of males and females, Bishop and Ikeda examined leisure patterns and status (using the North–Hatt occupational scale and Warner's ISC).[110] A multiple discriminant analysis produced three discriminant functions accounting for 53.1 percent of variance. Social status accounted for the most variance in leisure patterns—27.9 percent. Table 5.4 presents the results of the discriminant analysis, displaying the leisure activities with positive or negative associations with status. Prestigeful activities such as ice skating, bicycling, swimming, basketball, and tennis involve fairly rapid movement with extreme use of arms and legs, possibly suggesting a compensatory form of leisure for the otherwise sedentary life of many prestige occupations. Bishop and Ikeda also claim that most of these pursuits do not necessarily require a lot of time to the degree that activities such as hunting, fishing, or boating would. Thus, the authors suggest, time may be a critical element in the prestige classes' uses of leisure.[111]

Choice of leisure activities is also affected by social class–family interaction. There is a linear association between occupational stratum and couple participation in commercial leisure pursuits, with the exception that couples of the very highest occupational stratum reflect a slight decrease in recreation interaction compared to the upper middle class.[112] Rainwater, Coleman, and Handel have characterized the working class wife as not sharing in her husband's recreational activities because she is absorbed in domestic activities and because her husband has no desire for her to participate.[113] Other investigators, however,

[107]   Laumann and House, *op. cit.*,[105] p. 337.

[108]   Carman, *op. cit.*,[36] p. 31.

[109]   Bert N. Adams and James E. Butler, "Occupation Status and Husband–Wife Social Participation," *Social Forces*, vol. 45, pp. 501–507, at p. 506 (June 1967).

[110]   Doyle W. Bishop and Masaru Ikeda, "Status and Role Factors in the Leisure Behavior of Different Occupations," *Sociology and Social Research*, vol. 54, pp. 190–208 (Jan. 1970).

[111]   Bishop and Ikeda, *op. cit.*,[110] pp. 200–201.

[112]   Adams and Butler, *op. cit.*,[109] p. 504.

[113]   Rainwater *et. al.*, *op. cit.*,[31] p. 76.

Table 5.4 LEISURE PATTERNS AND
OCCUPATIONAL PRESTIGE RESULTS
OF DISCRIMINANT ANALYSIS

Activity	Discriminant 1
Watch television	0.44
Attend clubs/organizations	
Visit friends	
Read books	.39
Play cards, table games	
Arts and crafts, hobbies	0.44
Participate in drama activities	
Listen to records	
Work on house, garden	0.79
Attend adult classes	0.60
Attend sports events	
Attend movies	
Attend play, concerts, art shows	1.00
Go bowling	0.39
Go dancing	0.63
Go swimming indoors	0.63
Play basketball	0.60
Go picnicking	0.45
Play tennis	0.57
Play golf	0.42
Play softball	0.94
Go bicycling	0.69
Go camping	
Walk for pleasure	
Go hunting	0.57
Go fishing	0.80
Go boating	
Drive for pleasure	
Go swimming outdoors	0.49
Go skiing	0.50
Go sledding, tobogganing	
Go ice skating	0.83
Percent of variance	27.9

SOURCE: Doyle W. Bishop and Masaru Ikeda, "Status and Role Factors in the Leisure Behavior of Different Occupations," *Sociology and Social Research*, vol. 54, pp. 190–
208 (Jan. 1970).

report an increasing importance of commercial recreation in the lives of lower-status persons.[114]

The heaviest users of both commercial leisure facilities and public facilities (such as parks, museums, and swimming pools) are the middle classes since upper classes frequently have their own facilities and the lower classes frequently cannot afford them or do not have the propensity to participate in them.[115]

Credit Cards Credit-card acceptance and usage appears to be related to some extent to social class. Mathews and Slocum concluded that the lower classes preferred to use bank credit cards for durable and necessity goods (appliances, furniture, clothing) in contrast to the upper class desire to charge luxury items (gasoline, luggage, restaurants).[116] They also found more favorable attitudes toward credit usage among higher social classes. In a later study by the same investigators, however, they concluded that income was equally valuable as a basis for segmentation.[117]

In a major study by Plummer, it was found that charge cards were surprisingly widespread and cut across many demographic segments of the population. The most frequent users, however, were of higher income, better education, middle age, and professional occupation.[118] By investigating life styles, Plummer also concluded that users of commercial bank charge cards, in contrast to nonusers, exhibited a "contemporary state of mind" which helped explain usage along with social class and income data.[119]

Other products Evaluative criteria for other products have been found to be related to social class. For automobiles, Peters found his measure of relative occupational class income useful. He found that the "average" income group within each social class bought many more foreign economy, intermediate-sized, and compact cars than would have been expected. The "overprivileged" group within each social class owned more medium-sized and large cars and fewer foreign economy cars.[120] In another study using Q methodology, Sommers found that lower-class housewives felt appliances represented their "self-concept" in contrast to upper-class housewives who chose clothing as products most symbolic of themselves.[121]

---

[114] Alfred C. Clarke, "The Use of Leisure and Its Relation to Levels of Occupational Prestige," *Amer. Sociological Rev.*, vol. 21, p. 304 (June 1956).

[115] Lasswell, *op. cit.*,[3] pp. 258–264.

[116] H. Lee Mathews and John W. Slocum, Jr., "Social Class and Commercial Bank Credit Card Usage," *J. Marketing*, vol. 33, pp. 71–78 (Jan. 1969).

[117] John W. Slocum and H. Lee Mathews, "Social Class and Income as Indicators of Consumer Credit Behavior," *J. Marketing*, vol. 34, pp. 69–74 (Apr. 1970).

[118] Joseph T. Plummer, "Life Style Patterns and Commercial Bank Credit Card Usage," *J. Marketing*, vol. 35, pp. 35–41 (Apr. 1971).

[119] Plummer, *op. cit.*,[118] p. 41.

[120] Peters, *op. cit.*,[100] p. 77.

[121] Montrose S. Sommers, "The Use of Product Symbolism to Differentiate Social Strata," *University of Houston Business Rev.*, vol. 11, pp. 1–102 (Fall 1964).

Search Processes

The amount and type of search undertaken by an individual varies by social class as well as by product and situation category. Unfortunately, the lowest social classes have limited information sources and are therefore at a disadvantage at filtering out misinformation and fraud in a complex, urbanized society.[122] To compensate, working-class women often rely on relatives or close friends for information about consumption decisions.[123] Middle-class women put more reliance upon media-acquired information and actively engage in external search from the media.[124] Upper-class individuals have far more access to media information than do lower-class individuals.[125]

Individuals also appear to be more responsive to information sources that they perceive to be compatible with their own social class, and there are good examples of marketers who have customized a basic promotional strategy to the requirements of specific classes.[126] It is clear that sharp differences exist in the class connotations of standard media sources such as newspapers and television, even though all classes have some exposure to them. One study in 15 major cities found, for example, that upper-middle-class people consistently preferred the NBC channel, while lower middles preferred CBS, in keeping with the class images of the networks at that time.[127]

Interpersonal communications vary in other ways. In one study of blue-collar families, the researchers found significant differences between urban and suburban residents. Suburbanites indicated greater neighbor familiarity and displayed a greater sensitivity for their neighbor's work and church activities than did urban counterparts. Conversely, a higher proportion of city dwellers claimed virtually no knowledge of their neighbor's activities, income, or education.[128] The hypothesis generated from such a study would be that personal communications would be more important concerning consumption decisions than media for suburban consumers compared to city dwellers.

Purchasing Processes

Social status appears to have a great deal of influence on where and how people feel they should shop. Evidence indicates that lower-status people prefer local, face-to-face places where they get friendly service and easy credit.[129]

---

[122]   Caplovitz, *op. cit.,*[71]

[123]   Rainwater *et. al., op. cit.,*[31] p. 166.

[124]   Rainwater *et al., op. cit.*[31]

[125]   Haer, *op. cit.*[44]

[126]   Mozell C. Hill, "Ice Cream in Contemporary Society," *New Sociology,* vol. 2, pp. 23–24 (1963).

[127]   Ira O. Glick and Sidney J. Levy, *Living With Television* (Chicago: Aldine, 1962).

[128]   Irving Tallman and Romona Morgner, "Life-Style Differences Among Urban and Suburban Blue-Collar Families," *Social Forces,* vol. 48, pp. 334–348 (Mar. 1970); also Rita J. Simon, Gail Crotts, and Linda Mahan, "An Empirical Note About Married Women and their Friends," *Social Forces,* vol. 48, pp. 520–525 (June 1970).

[129]   Levy, *op. cit.,*[61] p. 153.

Upper middle housewives feel much more confident in their shopping ability and will venture to new places to shop or will range throughout a department store to find what they want. The discount store especially appeals to the middle classes because they are most careful and economy minded in their buying.[130] The lower classes may not have found what they wanted in the discount stores in early years because of the initial failure of these stores to carry national brands. It has been found that lower-class women rely on national brands whenever possible to make sure they "are getting a good buy."[131] It has also been found that working-class women are reluctant to try a new store. They limit their shopping to a few stores.[132]

Consumers have an image of what social class a store appeals to, even if a consumer has no shopping experience in that store. Figure 5.3 illustrates this situation. Women were asked to evaluate a department store on various factors that would establish the status group the store served. An interesting feature of this study is that women were able to accurately rate a store they had never seen merely by seeing its advertisements.[133]

Women report that they enjoy shopping regardless of social class, but women in different social classes have varying reasons for their enjoyment. Rich and Jain found that women in upper classes more frequently specify a pleasant store atmosphere and displays with excitement as an enjoyable feature, but lower classes emphasize acquiring household things or clothing as enjoyable.[134] Upper classes shop more frequently than middle or lower classes.[135]

Shopping by husband and wife together is most likely to occur among lower-middle-class families. Adams and Butler found the greatest propensity to shop together among lower white-collar, skilled, and semiskilled classes.[136] Shopping, especially for the middle-class family, has taken on the characteristics of a form of recreation for many.

SUMMARY

Social classes are relatively permanent and homogeneous divisions in a society in which groups of people are compared with one another. These groups are recognized as having inferior or superior positions by the individuals who comprise the society, although the basis of superiority is not established.

Social classes are discrete groups in theory, but in practice they are

[130]   Pierre Martineau, "The Pattern of the Social Classes," in Richard Clewett (ed.), *Marketing's Role in Scientific Marketing* (Chicago: Amer. Marketing Assoc., 1957), pp. 233–249, at p. 248.

[131]   M. Ross, "Uptown and Downtown," *Amer. Sociological Rev.*, vol. 30, pp. 255–259 (1965).

[132]   Ross, *op. cit.*[131]

[133]   Charles B. McCann, *Women and Department Store Newspaper Advertising* (Chicago: Social Research, 1957), pp. 15–55.

[134]   Rich and Jain, *op. cit.*[104]

[135]   Rich and Jain, *op. cit.*[104]

[136]   Adams and Butler, *op. cit.*,[109] p. 506.

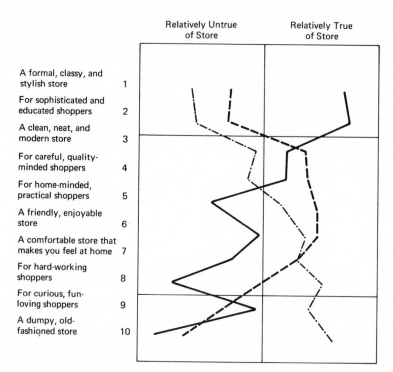

	Relatively Untrue of Store	Relatively True of Store

A formal, classy, and stylish store 1

For sophisticated and educated shoppers 2

A clean, neat, and modern store 3

For careful, quality-minded shoppers 4

For home-minded, practical shoppers 5

A friendly, enjoyable store 6

A comfortable store that makes you feel at home 7

For hard-working shoppers 8

For curious, fun-loving shoppers 9

A dumpy, old-fashioned store 10

Figure 5.3 HOUSEWIFE PERCEPTIONS OF DEPARTMENT-STORE STATUS. SOLID LINE—TWO HIGHEST STATUS STORES; DASHED LINE— TWO MIDDLE-STATUS STORES; DOT-AND-DASH LINE—TWO LOW-EST STATUS STORES. Charles B. McCann, *Women and Department Store Newspaper Advertising* (Chicago: Social Research, 1957), pp. 15–55. Reprinted by permission of the publisher.

treated as continuous. Some people, therefore, exhibit behavior that is partially aligned with one social class and partially aligned with another. One reason for this phenomenon is multidimensionality, which exists when people rank in different positions on the specific determinants of social class.

Occupation is the most important *single* measure of an individual's social class. Other important variables are the personal performance of an individual within his occupational group, the interactions he has with other individuals, his possessions, the value orientations of his group, and his class consciousness. Measurement of social class may involve any or all of these determinants.

Social classes in America are frequently divided into six groups: upper upper, lower upper, upper middle, lower middle, upper lower, and lower lower. Each of these groups displays characteristic values and behaviors that are useful in analyzing consumer decisions.

REVIEW AND DISCUSSION QUESTIONS

1. What variables determine an individual's social class? In what order of importance should they be ranked?
2. In what way does income relate to social class? Why is it used so little as an indicator of social class? What should be its proper value as an indicator of social class?
3. Prepare an outline of the major problems involved in the measurement of social classes.
4. Some observers of contemporary America believe that social classes have declined in importance and presence but others disagree. Outline your analysis of what has happened in recent years to social classes in America.
5. A marketing researcher is speculating on the influence of the upper classes on the consumption decisions of the lower classes for the following products: automobiles, food, clothing, baby care products. What conclusions would you expect for each of those products? Describe a research project that could be used to determine the answer to this question.
6. The leisure products group of a large conglomerate is constantly seeking additional products for expanding markets and additional penetration for existing products. What conclusions that would be helpful in the design of marketing strategy might be reached concerning social class and leisure?
7. The operator of a large discount chain is contemplating a new store in an area of upper lower families. He asks for a consulting report defining the precautions he should take to insure patronage among this group. What would you place in such a report? Assume that the area was mostly lower-lower families. Would you recommend he enter this market?
8. Prepare a research report comparing the search processes of the major social classes of consumers in America.

CHAPTER 6

REFERENCE GROUP AND
SUBCULTURE INFLUENCES

The role of group influence in providing individual behavior is illustrated in the following quotation by Slotkin. The dialogue occurs with a person taken to a mental hospital during a hot summer spell, whose responses appeared normal until the following dialogue:

Q. How did you happen to come here?
A. I don't know. I was just minding my own business.
Q. Who brought you here?
A. The police.
Q. What had you been doing?
A. Nothing. Just minding my own business.
Q. What were you doing at the time?
A. Just walking along the street.
Q. What Street?
A. (He gave the name of one of the busiest streets in the city.)
Q. What had you done just before that?
A. It was hot, so I took my clothes off.
Q. All your clothes?
A. No. Not my shoes and stockings.

Q. Why not those too?

A. The sidewalk was too hot.[1]

This man probably viewed his behavior as acceptable to himself but judged by the group norms of his society, his behavior was unacceptable and must therefore be modified. While this individual *deviated from the norms*, it is quite obvious that most individuals in contemporary society modify their behavior (even if personal comfort might be achieved through deviance) to *conform to group norms.*

This chapter describes some theories which explain group conformity and deviance and the influences and constraints these provide on an individual's central control unit and decision making. The chapter also describes subcultural influence, especially racial groups, as an additional influence to culture and social class described in previous chapters and to family described in the following chapter.

THE NATURE OF REFERENCE GROUPS

A reference group is any interacting aggregation of people *that influences an individual's attitudes or behavior.* The use of the term *group* may be misleading because another individual (such as popular recording star, film personality, or social leader) may perform the same function as a group.[2] (See Chapter 17.) However, it has become accepted to consider reference influences in groups (two or more interacting individuals), and the conventional approach is followed in this chapter. The unique aspect is that the group influences the self-conception, attitude, or behavior of an individual by serving as a *reference point* for that individual.

Many types of reference groups exist. *Primary groups* are aggregates of individuals small enough and intimate enough that all the members can communicate with each other face to face.[3] These include the family, groups of playmates among children, close friendship groups in the neighborhood or on the job, and other intimate groupings. *Secondary groups* are social organizations such as professional associations, religious organizations, trade unions, and similar groups which may include within them numerous sets of primary groups. Markin describes why primary groups are thought to be of such interest to marketing strategists:

> What we like and buy, where we shop and how often, what we spend and what we save, will to a considerable extent be affected by the almost constant indoctrination of our primary group memberships.[4]

---

[1]   James S. Slotkin, *Social Anthropology* (New York: Macmillan, 1950), pp. 70–71.

[2]   Herbert Hyman, "Reflections on Reference Groups," *Public Opinion Quart.*, vol. 24, pp. 383–396 (Fall, 1960).

[3]   George Homans, *The Human Group* (London: Routledge, 1961), p. 1.

[4]   Ron J. Markin, *The Psychology of Consumer Behavior* (Englewood Cliffs, N.J.: Prentice-Hall, 1969), p. 209.

Reference groups include both *formal groups* (defined structure and usually specified membership requirements) and *informal groups* which occur on the basis of proximity, interests, or other bases with less specified structure or membership. The former are easier to study, but the latter may be of more influence on consumption decisions.

Other categories of groups may be defined. *Membership groups* are those aggregates of people to which a person is recognized by others as belonging. An *aspirational group* is one to which an individual wishes or *aspires* to belong. A *dissociative group* is one with whose values or behavior an individual does not want to be associated. In all definitions of a group is implied the existence of functional interdependence rather than a mere statistical summation of individuals.[5]

FUNCTIONS OF REFERENCE GROUPS

Reference groups function in three ways of major interest to consumer analysts. First, reference groups serve important inputs to an individual's learning of his attitudes and awareness of alternative behaviors and life styles. This is described below as adult and childhood socialization. Second, reference groups serve the society as conformity enforcing devices. Third, reference groups are important in evaluations of an individual's self-concept.

Adult and Childhood Socialization

The awareness and learning of behavior alternatives is accomplished efficiently through the influence of reference groups. A company manual explains to the new employee, for example, when coffee breaks are to be taken, but informal work groups teach him when they are actually taken as well as where and how and perhaps whether donuts are normally consumed along with coffee. In contemporary societies, individuals are constantly moving between schools, communities, and jobs, and the process of socialization and acculturation permits an individual to know what behavior is likely to result in stability both for the individual and for the group.

The process of socialization has been described by Schein as "the process by which a new member learns the value system, the norms, and the required behavior patterns of the society, organizations, or group which he is entering."[6]

---

[5] This is in harmony with a general definition of a social group by Greer, "A social group is an aggregate of individuals who exist in a state of functional interdependence, from which evolves a flow of communication, and a consequent ordering of behavior;" Scott A. Greer, *Social Organization* (New York: Doubleday, 1955), p. 18. For amplification of the concept of a group, see James W. Vander Zanden, *Sociology: A Systematic Approach* (New York: Ronald, 1970), pp. 174–195.

[6] Edgar H. Schein, "Organization Socialization and the Profession of Management," in David A. Kolb, Irwin M. Rubin, and James M. McIntyre (eds.), *Organizational Psychology* (Englewood Cliffs, N.J.: Prentice-Hall, 1971), pp. 1–14, at p. 3.

Schein is especially concerned with formal organizations, but he notes that the norms, values, and behavior patterns usually included in socialization are:

(1) The basic *goals* of the organization.
(2) The preferred *means* by which those goals should be attained.
(3) The basic responsibilities of the member in the role which is being granted to him by the organization.
(4) The *behavior patterns* which are required for effective performance in the role.
(5) A set of rules or principles which pertain to the *maintenance of the identity and integrity* of the organization.[7]

As children, socialization occurs through the influence of playmates in the neighborhood and especially through institutional groups such as schools. At one time it was thought that the childhood socialization experiences were the only really important ones, and that adult socialization influences were trivial. In recent years it has become recognized, however, that although childhood experiences are extremely important in determining attitudes, values, and other components of consumer decision making, adult socialization can also occur and markedly influence evaluative criteria or other aspects of decision making.[8] The acceptance of a product not previously used by an individual may be influenced in much the same way as the changes brought about by reference groups in an individual's acceptance of marijuana:

> Throughout the history of any individual's experience with such drugs, society will confront him with situations that produce appreciable changes in the self. His initial willingness to experiment with drugs that are legally and morally forbidden comes about, typically, after he has begun to participate in circles where drugs are regarded as morally appropriate, as much less dangerous than popularly believed, and as productive of desirable kinds of experience.
>
> When the person first takes any drug, the subjective experience he has will itself be a consequence of the anticipated responses he has learned to expect as a result of his interaction with more experienced users, responses he has incorporated into his self. For example, the novice marijuana user usually experiences nothing at all when he first uses the drug. It is only when other users have pointed out to him subtle variations in how he feels, in how things look and sound to him, that he is willing to credit the drug with having had any effect on him at all.
>
> . . . this example serves simply as an instance of the utility of regarding all of society as a socializing mechanism which operates throughout a person's life, creating changes in his self and his behavior. We can just as well view families, occupations, work places, and neighborhoods in this fashion as we can deviant groups and legal authorities.

---

[7] Schein, *op. cit.*[6]

[8] Orville G. Brim and Stanton Wheeler, *Socialization After Childhood* (New York: Wiley, 1966).

All studies of social organizations of any kind are thus simultaneously studies of adult socialization.[9]

Social Basis of Attitude Formation

The socialization function of groups is an important basis for understanding the nature of attitude formation and change. (See Chapters 13 and 14.) The classic study illustrating the role of reference groups in the formation and change of attitudes is the Bennington study by Newcomb in which he measured the attitude change toward political ideologies by females as they attended college and assimilated the attitudes of their fellow students. In this study, Newcomb concluded, "Attitudes are not acquired in a social vacuum. Their acquisition is a function of relating oneself to some group or groups, either positively or negatively."[10]

The degree and type of influence exerted by a reference group upon an individual's evaluative criteria are difficult to predict and research on this topic is limited. To be more precise, the marketing studies to date have generally been of the type which establishes the existence of a relationship between an individual's attitudes and those of a group but fails to establish the nature or strength of that relationship. The subject is complicated by the fact that consumers are members of many groups and will differentially accept influences of each group. Wilensky and Ladinsky found in studies of professors, lawyers, and engineers, for example, that there is conflict between an individual's assimilation of influence by his occupational group and his religious group, especially for minority religious men in majority settings.[11] A review of numerous studies (especially concerning poor people) reveals that individuals of minority groups generally assimilate the values of majority groups if they are to produce success in dealing with majority groups. These same studies reveal that minority individuals who achieve influence among majority groups do so at the expense of losing their influence among their own minority group.[12]

Differential response to reference group models is also generated by the nature of individual predispositions. This is illustrated by the Bryan and Walbek studies in which children won money which they could give to the March of

---

[9] Edward Norbeck, Douglas Price-Williams, and William McCord, "The Self and Adult Socialization," in Howard S. Becker (ed.), *Sociological Work* (Chicago: Aldine, 1970), pp. 297–299.

[10] Theodore M. Newcomb, "Attitude Development as a Function of Reference Groups: The Bennington Study," in Eleanor E. Maccoby, Theodore M. Newcomb, and Eugene L. Hartley (eds.), *Readings in Social Psychology*, 3rd ed. (New York: Holt, Rinehart and Winston, 1958), pp. 265–275.

[11] Harold L. Wilensky and Jack Ladinsky, "From Religious Community to Occupational Group: Structural Assimilation Among Professors, Lawyers, and Engineers," *Amer. Sociological Rev.*, vol. 32, pp. 541–561 (Aug. 1967).

[12] Bradley S. Greenberg and Brenda Dervin, *Use of the Mass Media by the Urban Poor* (New York: Praeger, 1970), p. 99.

Dimes or keep for themselves. They were exposed to role models (older children) under a variety of conditions in which the role models preached charity or greed and also behaved with charity or greed. As would be expected, the children also talked about charity and actually gave more when the role model talked about charity and carried through in his behavior by giving. The interesting aspect of this experiment, however, is that when the role model preached greed, the followers actually increased their own response toward charity and rated the role model unfavorably. This bit of evidence may indicate that group values and behavior are effective as a positive reference when the group behavior agrees with the individual's preexisting values.[13]

The influence of reference groups on attitudes, perception, and other aspects of behavior is discussed at numerous other points in this text.[14]

Compliance to Group Norms

The functions of reference groups are sometimes termed "normative" in that they cause people to behave in similar patterns as well as "evaluative" in providing a reference point by an individual of his own behavior.[15] The normative function of reference groups is of great interest to marketing strategists because it is a determinant of whether or not a product will be accepted by large enough groups to make it successful. Thus, some attention to the theory of normative pressure on important concepts is needed.

Norms Defined Norms are quantitative statements or beliefs by the majority of group members defining what the activities of group members should be. Norms may be said to exist when members agree or appear to agree that they will act with regularity concerning the subject of the norm. When a new member joins or wishes to join a group, he receives pressure to conform to the norms of that group. Although he may deviate from some norms while accepting others, he will find that conforming is often rewarded by the rest of the group while nonconformity to that particular group's norms brings lack of reward from the members. Thus norms become stable expectations held by a concensus of the group concerning the behavior rules for individual members.[16]

The Equation of Human Exchange Sociologist George Homans has provided a theory to explain why people conform to group norms. Homans' equation of human exchange is built upon the premise that interpersonal activities and

---

[13] J. H. Bryan and N. H. Walbek, "Preaching and Practicing Self-Sacrifice: Children's Actions and Reactions," *Child Development*, vol. 41, pp. 329–353 (1970).

[14] For a review of additional studies on this topic, see Marvin Karlins and Herbert I. Abelson, *Persuasion* (New York: Springer, 1970), pp. 41–67.

[15] Harold H. Kelley, "Two Functions of Reference Groups," in G. E. Swanson, T. M. Newcomb, and E. L. Hartley (eds.), *Readings in Social Psychology*, rev. ed., (New York: Holt, Rinehart and Winston, 1952).

[16] For amplification, see John W. Thibaut and Harold H. Kelley, *The Social Psychology of Groups* (New York: Wiley, 1957), chap. 8.

sentiments (defined as symbols of approval or esteem for another person) emitted by one individual responding to another are more or less *reinforcing* or *punishing* to the behavior of the other individual. That is, they are more or less *valuable* to him.[17] If someone is asked to join another person for a cup of coffee, for example, there will be *rewards* (companionship, coffee, esteem indicated by the invitation, etc.) but there may also be *costs* (time lost, perhaps association with a person of lower status, giving up association with other possibly more valuable persons, and other costs). The nature of interactions will be determined by an individual's perception of the *profit of the interaction.* Homans defines this in familiar economic terms:

$$\text{profit} = \text{rewards} - \text{costs}.$$

Individuals arrange their social relations in such a way as to maximize total profit. The groups a person chooses to belong to and the degree to which the individual adheres to the norms of that group are based upon the *net* profit figure, not rewards or costs alone. Rewards and costs are difficult to measure when such values as altruism, pride, or aggression are involved. While this inhibits research, it does not alter the theory as an explanation of social interaction.

Homans derives propositions that tend to explain when interactions between two persons will occur:

(1) If in the past the occurrence of a particular stimulus situation has been the occasion on which a man's activity has been rewarded, then the more similar the present stimulus situation is to the past one, the more likely he is to omit the activity, or some similar activity, now.

(2) The more often within a given period of time a man's activity rewards the activity of another, the more often the other will emit the activity.

(3) The more valuable to a man a unit of the activity another gives him, the more often he will emit activity rewarded by the activity of the other.

(4) The more often a man has in the recent past received a rewarding activity from another, the less valuable any further unit of that activity becomes to him (and therefore from proposition (3), the less often he will emit the activity that gets him that reward).[18]

With this set of propositions, the consumer analyst has a set of tools to understand the formation of informal reference groups and the types of influence that result. Through a process analogous to marginal analysis in economics, persons of equal status will be drawn together in stable interaction patterns. The only time they will interact with persons of higher status than themselves is when they are prepared to bestow some significant expression such as material goods

---

[17] George Homans, *Social Behavior: Its Elementary Forms* (New York: Harcourt, 1961). See chap. 3 and 4 for an outline of Homans' theory.

[18] Homans, *op. cit.,*[17] pp. 53–55.

(a fee), a help (he performs some special service that the high-status person is not qualified to perform), an expression of sentiment (thanks, a plaque, praise related to other persons who are in a position to reward the high-status persons, and so on), or a subjective reward (such as a feeling of altruism or pride on the part of the high-status person). The only time this person is willing to interact with people of lower status is when they are willing to grant a similar reward to him. This theory explains the development of informal groups such as acquaintances and close friends and formal groups such as the family and work groups (where negative rewards in the form of loss of job, disinheritance, and so on, are possible).

Norms and Group Leadership   Homans' theory also explains the norms of the group. Norms represent what the majority of the group members find rewarding. They will find rewarding, with respect to at least one important variable, the behavior of a high-status member. Thus, his opinion on the variable on which he achieves his status is likely to become the norm of the group. This does not mean, however, that every behavior emitted by the high-status member will be accepted by the group. The high-status member frequently, in fact, has opinions that differ substantially from other members within the reference group. The group members permit such deviations, however, because of the idiosyncrasy credit he has built up from his other interactions with group members.[19]

Wiggins, Dill, and Schwartz clarified leadership influence in their experiments which indicate that persons reward the behavior of a high-status individual in a group even if he violates norms somewhat, until he so seriously violates norms as to threaten harm to the rest of the group. Then they stop rewarding his behavior.[20] In general, however, it can be said that group leaders usually exhibit behavior and characteristics that provide rewards for the rest of the group and thus permit leadership within the group. Bavelas found that group leaders are more active within and on behalf of the group, show superior judgment, are more intelligent, and are personally better adjusted than other members of the group.[21] Other characteristics that appear to be most correlated with voluntary group leadership are height and weight, physical appearance and dress, self-confidence and self-assurance, sociability and friendliness, determination and energy.[22]

Creating Conformity   Group pressure causes individuals to conform to group norms. (This does not prevent the existence of great heterogeneity within

[19]   E. P. Hollander, "Conformity, Status, and Idiosyncrasy Credit," *Psychological Rev.*, vol. 65, pp. 117–127 (1958).

[20]   J. A. Wiggins, F. Dill, and R. D. Schwartz, "On 'Status-Liability'," *Sociometry*, vol. 28, pp. 197–209 (June 1965).

[21]   A. Bavelas, "Leadership: Man and Function," *Administrative Science Quart.*, vol. 4, pp. 491–498 (Dec. 1960).

[22]   Bernard Berelson and Gary A. Steiner, *Human Behavior: An Inventory of Scientific Findings* (New York: Harcourt, 1964), pp. 341–342. A useful synthesis of research on formal group leadership is provided by Joseph E. McGrath and Irwin Altman, *Small Group Research* (New York: Holt, Rinehart and Winston, 1966).

the total society because diverse groups with disparate behavioral norms simultaneously exist in a society.) One of the classic studies in this area was performed by Asch and demonstrated conforming tendencies of individuals as a function of individual and situational characteristics. Asch confronted individuals with two straight lines of equal length. Under normal conditions, the test is easy enough that virtually no mistakes in individual judgment of length occur among respondents. In the experimental situation, however, three confederates were asked to give their answer first. Under this pressure to conform, 37 percent of the naive respondents chose the wrong answer.[23]

The amount of conformity exhibited by an individual is a function of several variables. Asch found that the pressure for conformity increased for an individual as the number of persons agreeing (on the incorrect answer) increased.[24] The more stable and cohesive a group is, the more likely it is to exercise conformity power on deviant members.[25] On the other hand, when few definite or rigid standards can be used to evaluate the norms of the group, nonconformity is likely to increase.[26] Many individual differences are helpful in explaining conformity[27] including the conclusion that other-directed persons (using the terminology of David Riesman) are more *conforming* than innerdirected persons.[28]

Group Pressure in Everyday Life Pressure to conform to group norms is omnipresent in all aspects of life. Of particular interest to marketing strategists is the influence of group norms on conformity in a wide range of household products and everyday behavior patterns. This is dramatically illustrated in an intensive study by Gans of the new town, Levittown:

> The culture of the block jelled quite rapidly too. Standards of lawn care were agreed upon as soon as it was time to do something about the lawn, and by unspoken agreement, the front lawn would be cared for conscientiously, but the backyard was of less importance. Those who deviated from this norm—either neglecting their lawn or working on it too industrially—were brought into line through wise cracks. When I, in a burst of compulsive concern, worked very hard on my

[23] S. E. Asch, "Effects of Group Pressure upon the Modification and Distortion of Judgment," in Harold Guetzkow (ed.), *Groups, Leadership, and Men* (Pittsburgh, Pa.: Carnegie Press, 1951).

[24] Asch, *op. cit.*[23]

[25] Leon Festinger, "Informal Social Communication," *Psychological Rev.*, vol. 57, pp. 271–292 (1950).

[26] F. Stuart Chapin, "Social Institutions and Voluntary Associations," in Joseph B. Gittler (ed.), *Review of Sociology: Analysis of a Decade* (New York: Wiley, 1957), pp. 259–288, at p. 269.

[27] For a comprehensive description of variations in conformity see David Krech, Richard S. Crutchfield and Egerton L. Ballachey, *Individual in Society* (New York: McGraw-Hill, 1962), pp. 486–530.

[28] Richard Centers and Mirian Horowitz, "Social Character and Conformity: A Differential in Susceptibility to Social Influence," *J. Social Psychology*, vol. 68, pp. 60, 343–349 (1963).

lawn at the start, one of my neighbors laughed and said he would have to move out if I was going to have "that fancy a lawn." Since I was not interested in a "fancy lawn," I found it easy to take the hint, but those who wanted a perfect lawn stayed away from the talkfests that usually developed evenings and on Saturday mornings when the men were ostensibly working on the lawns, so as not to be joked about and chastised as ratebusters.[29]

The conformity pressures in social activities are understood further by this description:

> Perhaps the best illustration of the rapid definition of block norms came at a party around Christmas time. A former New York suburbanite invited everyone to a stand-up cocktail party, but within an hour it had turned into an informal gathering, climaxed by a slightly drunken group sing. The almost immediate transformation from an upper middle class party to a lower middle class get-together took place for several reasons. Most of the guests were unfamiliar with cocktail parties and were not willing to stand up in the prescribed fashion. The hostess was dressed up in a bright Capri pants, but one of the neighbors, of working-class background, had never seen such pants, and thinking they were pajamas, concluded the party had been called off. Only when guests started arriving did she realize her error and later everyone, she included, laughed about it. The hostess' husband had objected to what he called a "Westchester County party" from the start, and the hostess went along with the dramatic metamorphosis too. She had not been putting on airs, but had thought her neighbors were like those in New York. From then on, social life on the block followed the norms of lower middle class entertaining.[30]

Anomie and Deviance   Behavior of group members is sometimes understood more completely with the concept of *anomie*. The term was originally translated from Durkheim as "normlessness."[31] Actually, the concept as used by sociologists does not mean that norms do not exist but rather a weakened respect for norms in a group or society. It is an ambivalence that causes people to conform grudgingly or to nonconform but with misgivings.[32] (Psychologists also use the term to mean a state of mind characterized by a sense of rootlessness.) One type of anomie is the situation which exists where two norms exist, one for public purposes but another for commonly accepted noncompliance to the public norms. This is called the patterned evasion of norms. Zanden describes examples as:

---

[29]   Herbert J. Gans, "The Levittowners: Ways of Life and Politics in a New Suburban Community," in Frank L. Sweetser (ed.), *Studies in American Urban Society* (New York: Crowell, 1970), pp. 185–220, at p. 185.

[30]   Gans, *op. cit.*,[29] p. 186.

[31]   Emile Durkheim, *Suicide*, trans. by George Simpson (New York: Free Press, 1951).

[32]   Harry M. Johnson, *Sociology: A Systematic Introduction* (New York: Harcourt, 1960), pp. 557–558.

. . . prohibition versus bootlegging; sexual chastity versus clande-
stine affairs and prostitution; classroom honesty versus established
patterns of exam cribbing; impersonal, disinterested, honest government versus political graft, "fixing," and the like; professional codes
versus fee splitting among doctors, ambulance chasing among lawyers,
and so on; an income tax system versus cheating on tax returns; and
concepts of truth versus fraudulent advertising.[33]

Self-Concept Evaluation

Sociology and psychology are blended together with a concept called
the *self*. Sometimes psychology appears to be the study of completely autonomous
individuals or the distinctive characteristics of each human. Sociology, conversely,
is sometimes thought to view human behavior only in terms of automatons abso-
lutely molded by society. Neither view is correct, of course, and the concept of
the *self* provides a bridge between the disciplines. A group of theorists in sociology and social psychology who emphasize the inner aspects of behavior in a
social context are known as "social interactionists" built upon original contributions of Cooley and Mead.[34]

The self is defined by Hewitt as having five components:

> The first component is an organized set of motivations. . . . The
> second component of the self is a series of social roles to which the
> person is committed, along with a knowledge of how to play them.
> Social roles are clusters of norms that are related to particular positions
> that a person occupies. . . . The third component of the self is a more
> general set of commitments to social norms and their underlying values.
> . . . The fourth component of the self is a set of cognitive abilities,
> including the ability to create and understand symbols, which guide
> response to the intended meanings of others in social interaction and
> provide a "map" of the physical and social setting in which the person
> finds himself. . . . The fifth and final component of the self is a set of
> ideas about one's qualities, capabilities, commitments, and motives—
> a self-image—that is developed by the individual in the course of his
> socialization.[35]

A person's self-concept causes the individual to see himself through the
eyes of other persons and in doing so, he takes into account their behavior,
feelings, and attitudes, the approval or disapproval of others. A person's con-

---

[33] Vander Zanden, *op. cit.*,[5] p. 116. For an excellent discussion of the societal implications of anomie, see pp. 115–131 of this source. Also, see Kenneth R. Schneider, *Destiny of
Change* (New York: Holt, Rinehart and Winston, 1968), pp. 81–104.

[34] Charles Horton Cooley, *Human Nature and the Social Order* (New York:
Scribner, 1902); George Herbert Mead, *Mind, Self, and Society* (Chicago: University of
Chicago Press, 1934). For discussion of this topic from a variety of perspectives, see Jerome
G. Manis and Bernard N. Meltzer (eds.), *Symbolic Interaction: A Reader in Social Psychology*
(Boston: Allyn and Bacon, 1967).

[35] John P. Hewitt, *Social Stratification and Deviant Behavior* (New York: Random
House, 1970), pp. 32–33.

ception of himself has been shown by Quarantelli and Cooper to be closely related to his perceptions of how other people approve or disapprove and think of him.[36]

The importance of the self-concept for marketing strategists lies in the proposition that the symbols that people manage as a function of their self include the goods and services they use and the way they use them. The style of life adopted by an individual includes the consumption of goods in the proper way to reflect his or her perceived status among others.[37] In making evaluations of his own and other status levels, the consumer may be determining what presentation of his self is being perceived by other people, hoping to present an image of self to others compatible with his idealized self.[38] An individual's reference group is the checkpoint or standard with which to make judgments.[39]

A marketing example of products as symbols enhancing the self-concept is provided in Figure 6.1 from Grubb and Grathwohl.[40] Assume that an individual A perceives himself as being thrifty, economical, and practical. He may purchase a Volkswagen as a symbol of these qualities thereby achieving internal self-enhancement. The audience B may include peers, parents, and significant others. The double-headed arrows b and c in Figure 6.1 indicate that the Volkswagen is attributed meaning by A and that the audience B is also attributing meaning to it. If the Volkswagen X has a commonly understood meaning between A and the reference group B, communication of self has occurred and the reaction of B will provide self-enhancement to individual A. Empirical support for this process in automobiles is provided by Grubb and Hupp[41] and Birdwell[42] and for beer, soap, cigarettes, and toothpaste by Dolich,[43] and in some other brand/store selection situations.[44] Most of these studies focus on the psychological approach to self-

---

[36] E. L. Quarantelli and Joseph Cooper, "Self-Conceptions and Others: A Further Test of Median Hypotheses," *Sociological Quart.*, vol. 7, pp. 281–297 (Summer 1966).

[37] See commentary on Max Weber in Hugh Dalziel Duncan, *Symbols and Social Theory* (New York: Oxford University Press, 1969), pp. 39–42.

[38] Erving Goffman, *The Presentation of Self in Everyday Life* (New York: Doubleday, 1959).

[39] Tamtosu Shibutani, "Reference Groups as Perspectives," *Amer. J. Sociology*, vol. 6, pp. 562–569 (May 1955).

[40] Edward L. Grubb and Harrison L. Grathwohl, "Consumer Self-Concept, Symbolism and Market Behavior: A Theoretical Approach," *J. Marketing*, vol. 31, pp. 22–27 (Oct. 1967).

[41] Edward L. Grubb and Gregg Hupp, "Perception of Self, Generalized Stereotypes, and Brand Selection," *J. Marketing Research*, vol. 5, pp. 58–63 (Feb. 1968).

[42] Al E. Birdwell, "A Study of the Influence of Image Congruence on Consumer Choice," unpublished Ph.D. dissertation (Austin, Tex.: University of Texas, 1964).

[43] Ira J. Dolich, "Congruence Relationships between Self Images and Product Brands," *J. Marketing Research*, vol. 6, pp. 80–84 (Feb. 1969).

[44] The importance of self-concepts in retail store evaluation is presented in Joseph Barry Mason and Morris L. Mayer, "The Problem of the Self-Concept in Store Image Studies," *J. Marketing*, vol. 34, pp. 67–69 (Apr. 1970). Significant methodological flaws in this study have been suggested, however, by Ira J. Dolich and Ned Shilling, "A Critical Evaluation of 'The Problem of Self-Concept in Store Image Studies'," *J. Marketing*, vol. 35, pp. 71–73 (Jan. 1971).

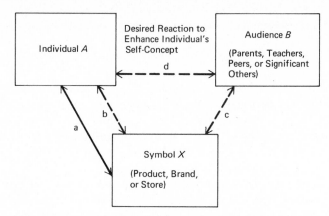

Figure 6.1 RELATIONSHIP OF THE CONSUMPTION OF GOODS AS SYMBOLS TO SELF-CONCEPT. Edward L. Grubb and Harrison L. Grathwohl, "Consumer Self-Concept, Symbolism and Market Behavior: A Theoretical Approach," *J. Marketing*, vol. 31, p. 25 (Oct. 1967). Reprinted with permission of the authors and the publisher.

concepts more than the formative or reference group influences on the self, except for Dolich. These studies as a group do suggest the congruence of self-concept and brand choice and the need for additional research to understand the development of marketing strategies involving the creation of reference group influence on brands as symbols of the self.

MARKETING ANALYSIS OF REFERENCE-GROUP INFLUENCE

Marketing researchers have given limited empirical attention to reference-group influences. Various marketing analysts have described the importance of group influences upon consumer behavior,[45] but the reports of comprehensive, conclusive research are few. Most of the studies that have been reported by marketing researchers may be categorized in two groups: (1) studies to determine the reality of reference-group influences on consumption decisions and (2) studies to determine the consumption situations most likely to be affected by group influences.

---

[45] Numerous examples of how reference-group theory appears to influence marketing decisions are found in James H. Myers and William H. Reynolds, *Consumer Behavior and Marketing Management* (Boston: Houghton Mifflin, 1967), pp. 169–194; also Thomas S. Robertson, *Consumer Behavior* (Glenview, Ill.: Scott, Foresman, 1970), pp. 69–80; Perry Bliss, *Marketing Management and the Behavioral Environment* (Englewood Cliffs, N.J.: Prentice-Hall, 1970), pp. 30–42.

Reality of Reference-Group Influence

The reality of reference-group influence on consumption decisions has been demonstrated in an experiment involving the purchasing of bread. Stafford, in a carefully designed experiment, introduced various "brands" of bread to groups of housewives.[46] The "brands" of bread were all identical and had plain wrappers with no symbols except identifying consonants chosen from the middle of the alphabet. The subjects in the experiment were randomly selected from preexisting reference groups and were unaware that the breads were identical or that the experiment was studying interpersonal influences. The result of the study indicated that preferences formed for each "brand" (letter of alphabet) which could be attributed to the influence of the group upon individual choice. From this study, Stafford concluded that informal groups have a definite influence on their members toward conformity behavior with respect to brands of bread preferred.[47]

An experimental study by Venkatesan also demonstrated the influence of group pressures on consumption decisions.[48] Venkatesan presented business students with three suits (*A,B,C*) of identical style, color and size and asked them to choose the *best* suit. *Control groups*, in which the choices of other members were unknown, were compared to *conformity groups* in which a naive subject was grouped with confederates who unanimously chose the same suit. In the absence of any group influence, each suit was equally likely to be selected, but in the conformity condition, individuals significantly yielded to the group conformity, choosing the majority preference.[49]

The significance of both the Stafford and the Venkatesan experiments lies in the diversity of product types represented by bread and suits. In terms of *amount* of group influences, the results were not impressive. In another experiment, Hansen found very little imitative or group influence.[50]

Consumption Situations Affected by Reference Groups

The amount and nature of group influence on individual consumption decisions appears to be affected by the product category involved, the characteristics of the group, and the communications process. These situations are described briefly.

---

[46] James E. Stafford, "Effects of Group Influence on Consumer Brand Preferences," *J. Marketing Research*, vol. 3, pp. 68–75 (Feb. 1966).

[47] Stafford, *op. cit.*[46]

[48] M. Venkatesan, "Experimental Study of Consumer Behavior Conformity and Independence," *J. Marketing Research*, vol. 3, pp. 384–387 (Nov. 1966).

[49] Venkatesan, *op. cit.*[48]

[50] Flemming Hansen, "Primary Group Influence and Consumer Conformity," in Philip R. McDonald (ed.), *Marketing Involvement in Society and the Economy* (Chicago: Amer. Marketing Assoc., 1969), pp. 300–305.

Product Categories   Most studies show that the amount of reference-group influence upon consumption is affected by the product category involved. An early study by Bourne identified products subject to strong reference-group influences as those about which there exist norms specifying behaviors relating to products.[51] Table 6.1 presents the Bourne analysis, showing that some products have significant specifications among American friendship reference groups. These are called product-plus brand-plus category. People talk about and have norms concerning the purchase of automobiles, cigarettes, beer, and drugs and have norms about specific brands of these products. In the product-minus brand-minus category, conversely, are found products such as soap, canned peaches, and radios.

Table 6.1   REFERENCE-GROUP INFLUENCE ON PRODUCT DECISIONS

	Weak−	*Strong+*		
Strong +	Clothing Furniture Magazines Refrigerator (type) Toilet soap	Cars Cigarettes Beer (prem. vs. reg.) Drugs	+	
				Brand *or*
Weak −	Soap Canned peaches Laundry soap Refrigerator (brand) Radios	Air conditioners Instant coffee TV (black and white)	−	*Type*
	−	*Product*	+	

SOURCE: Foundation for Research on Human Behavior, *Group Influence in Marketing and Public Relations* (Ann Arbor, Mich.: The Foundation, 1956), p. 8.

The Bourne research indicates that product conspicuousness is the most important of the various determinants of whether or not products will be strongly influenced by reference groups. The authors conclude:

> The conspicuousness of a product is perhaps the most general attribute bearing on its susceptibility to reference-group influence. There are two aspects to conspicuousness in this particular context that help to determine reference-group influence. First, the article must be conspicuous in the most obvious sense that it can be seen and identified by others. Secondly, it must be conspicuous in the sense of standing out and being noticed. In other words, no matter how visible a product

---

[51] Foundation for Research on Human Behavior, *Group Influence in Marketing and Public Relations* (Ann Arbor, Mich.: The Foundation, 1956).

is, if virtually everyone owns it, it is not conspicuous in this second sense of the word.[52]

A well-known study of early usage of room air conditioners was undertaken in a suburb of Philadelphia. In this study by White, wide variations were observed in adoption among blocks of the row houses and were attributed to interpersonal communication and imitation. White concluded, however, that the product was influenced by group interactions, but that specific brands and store choices were not so influenced.[53]

Other studies of beer, deodorant, after-shave lotion, and cigarettes show considerable variation in susceptibility to group influence among product categories.[54] Witt concludes that there is need for additional research that might yield a product taxonomy of susceptibility of purchase decisions to referent influence.[55]

Group Characteristics   The amount of reference-group influence is determined partially by characteristics of the group. Specifically, some studies demonstrate that the more cohesive the group is, the greater the group influence is likely to be on individual choices.[55] Stafford found that cohesiveness appears to have its most important function in providing an agreeable environment in which informal leaders can effectively operate. More importantly, Stafford concluded that the higher the degree of brand loyalty exhibited by a group leader, the more likely the other members are to prefer the same brand and the more likely they are to become brand loyal.[56]

It appears likely that further research will discover additional group characteristics of importance in determining the nature of group influence.

Communications Process   The nature of the communication process is also a determinant of the amount of reference-group influence. Venkatesan found that when strong conformity pressure was used to induce subjects to respond with the same product choice as the group, a *reactance* condition existed. People resisted attempts to restrict independent choice.[57] Lewin found that attitudes strongly influenced by reference groups could be most effectively changed by *group discussions* rather than strong communications from salesmen or mass media.[58] An experimental study by Cook attempted to test several related

[52]   Foundation for Research on Human Behavior, *op. cit.*,[51] pp. 7–8.

[53]   Robert E. Witt and Grady D. Bruce, "Purchase Decisions and Group Influence," *J. Marketing Research*, vol. 7, pp. 533–555 (Nov. 1970); Robert E. Witt, "Group Influence on Consumer Brand Choice," in McDonald, *op. cit.*,[50] pp. 306–309.

[54]   Witt and Bruce, *op. cit.*[53]

[55]   Robert E. Witt, "Informal Social Group Influence on Consumer Brand Choice," *J. Marketing Research*, vol. 6, pp. 473–476 (Nov. 1969). Lack of evidence for the cohesive hypothesis was reported, however, in Hansen, *op. cit.*[50]

[56]   Stafford, *op. cit.*[46]

[57]   Venkatesan, *op. cit.*[48]

[58]   Kurt Lewin, "Group Decision and Social Change," in Maccoby *et al.*, *op. cit.*,[10] pp. 197–211. See chap. 13 for additional information concerning persuasive communications.

hypotheses concerning reference groups and communication with lack of striking results.[59] Cook did find that groups with similar social characteristics produced more attitude change than heterogeneous groups, as underlying theory would predict. Unfortunately, however, in Cook's experiment the attitude change toward the product (Volkswagen) was negative rather than positive.[60]

An assessment of the marketing literature concerning reference groups leads to the conclusion that the potential is as yet not achieved. The concept of reference groups is of obvious theoretical significance in understanding human behavior. Attempts to apply it to marketing problems on other than a theoretical or descriptive basis have been unproductive. There is no evidence that reference groups are viable market segments. The importance of the concept for marketing strategists lies in the understanding of *why behavior develops* as it does rather than in the ability to influence behavior. Accurate knowledge of relevant reference groups for categories of consumers should, however, become one of the inputs that a marketing strategist needs to develop marketing programs.

SUBCULTURAL INFLUENCES ON CONSUMPTION

It is difficult to separate influences on an individual's consumption attributable to reference groups versus those attributable to various subcultures in which the individual is included. Actually, the distinction between reference-group influence and subculture influence is somewhat fuzzy. In many cases, the same individuals are included in reference groups important for another individual and also part of the subculture influencing the individual. Subcultural influences on consumption, therefore, are described in the following pages rather than in Chapter 5 where the term was introduced and defined. Subcultural influences usually are more comprehensive in influence and more enduring than reference groups. Often, however, the reference groups to which an individual belongs are drawn almost entirely from the subculture to which he also belongs.

Four types of subcultures are described below. They are nationality groups, religious groups, geographic areas, and racial groups. The last type, because of its importance in contemporary American culture, is given a more extended analysis.

Nationality Groups

Nearly every large community contains relatively homogeneous groups within the city composed of nationality groups. Examples include Puerto Ricans, Scandinavians, Germans, Italians, Polish, and Irish. Some of these become

[59] Victor J. Cook, "Group Decision, Social Comparison, and Persuasion in Changing Attitudes," *J. Advertising Research*, vol. 7, pp. 31–37 (Mar. 1967).

[60] Cook, *op. cit.*[59]

acculturated to their surrounding environment and lose their identity as a nationality group. In other situations, members retain their native language, live and move about only in a restricted area of the city, interact primarily with other members of the nationality, and search for products similar to those in "the old country."

Areas of the city become known as Little Poland, Andersonville, or Chinatown—because they sell the products of these groups and provide a center for cultural maintenance and perhaps housing. Frequently newspapers and radio stations (and occasional television programs) are beamed to these markets. A dealer organization strong in ethnic markets may be essential in large cities. It is probably impossible to be successful on a large scale basis in New York City, for example, without thorough knowledge, understanding of, and adaptation of strategies to ethnic markets. General Motors is reported to be more successful than its competitors in New York City because of its strong penetration into ethnic markets through a dealer organization built upon subcultural realities. As immigration continues to decrease, it can be expected that European subcultures will decline in importance in the United States, although there appears to be emergence of Puerto Rican, Mexican, and African subcultural influences. In other parts of North America, French-speaking Canadians maintain a distinct subculture which influences consumer decision making.

Religious Groups

Religious groups may provide important subcultures among those groups in which members conform closely to group norms. Mormons, for example, may refrain from purchasing tobacco, liquor, and certain stimulants; Christian Scientists restrict their search for information about and use of medicines; Seventh Day Adventists limit their purchase of meat; Jewish consumers may purchase kosher or other traditional foods; Christians from fundamental denominations avoid ostentatious displays of wealth and consumption, the Amish avoid mechanized life styles and individualized personal appearance. Some groups identified with the Jesus Movement are creating a new subculture based upon emulation of first century Christianity, in contrast to contemporary conspicuous consumption.

As religious groups lose adherents and as mobility causes adherents to become spatially separated, the completeness of the subculture declines as a constraint on behavior, but basic values of the subculture may continue to influence some aspects of decision making.

Geographic Areas

Geographic areas in a nation develop their own culture. In the United States, the Southwest appears to have a characteristic style of life that emphasizes the casual form of dress, outdoor entertaining, and unique forms of recreation. Decision making in the Southwest is presumably less rigid and perhaps more innovative than the conservative, inhibited attitudes toward new products that are supposedly characteristic of the Midwest. A fair assessment would seem to be that even though these geographic differences are still important, mobility is contributing to their decline.

BLACK CULTURAL INFLUENCES ON CONSUMPTION

Racial influences provide another subculture affecting consumption. In the United States, the black subculture predominates among nonwhite groups, although Oriental groups are sometimes important in some mainland communities and in Hawaii.

Black culture does not mean the same as black skin color. The black culture arises out of a common heritage of slavery conditioned by income deprivation, a shared history of discrimination and suffering, confined housing opportunities, and denial of participation in many aspects of the majority culture. Some persons with black skin grew up with mostly white neighbors and friends, were relatively affluent, and were not exposed to the black culture (because it has not generally been presented in white communications media or educational institutions). These individuals may not share black life styles, may have difficulty communicating in the black idiom and may prefer the music of Carole King to Aretha Franklin. Conversely, in contemporary society there are some white individuals who have chosen to assimilate black culture even though they retain white skin.

It should be understood that the "black market" must be considered as consisting of a core of values and economic realities with recognition of substantial variation just as there is among white markets. Within the black market, segmentation strategies are possible just as is true in dealing with white markets. The smaller size of black markets limits the feasibility of segmentation strategies, however. Also, greater homogeneity in black markets than in white markets seems to be an accurate generalization. In addition, black consumers are adopting many of the consumption patterns of middle-class white majority society. The dilemma of black consumers, Bauer *et al.* report, is whether to accept consumption values of the white culture or whether to reject them. It appears that, in general, black consumers implicitly accept middle-class white values toward consumption but are at a disadvantage in obtaining them.[61]

Structural Influences on Black Culture

Structural influences shape black subculture and simultaneously inhibit its manifestations. Four primary structural influences include poverty, inadequate educational institutions, differential family characteristics, and discrimination. These are briefly described.

---

[61] Raymond A. Bauer, Scott M. Cunningham, and Lawrence H. Wortzel, "The Marketing Dilemma of Negroes," *J. Marketing*, vol. 29, pp. 1–6 (July 1965). An updated version is in Raymond A. Bauer and Scott M. Cunningham, "The Negro Market," *J. Advertising Research*, vol. 10, pp. 3–13 (Apr. 1970).

Income Deprivation   The black culture is frequently confused with the low-income culture. There is good reason why this confusion exists. Black consumers average much less income than do white consumers. Even Spanish Americans (the "brown" subculture) earn more on the average than do black consumers, even though blacks have higher rates of education than browns.[62] Figure 6.2 shows the average incomes for the year 1970. More dramatic perhaps is the proportion of black consumers who live below the poverty level as defined by the U.S. Department of Commerce. Table 6.2 shows that 31 percent of blacks were below the poverty level in 1969 compared to 10 percent of whites. A discouraging factor that enters the culture is that the gap of relative deprivation increases continuously. Between 1960 and 1968, nonwhite income in the United States increased at a faster *rate* than white—4.9 percent compared to 3.4 percent. In the same period, however, the *actual gap* between white and nonwhite median income *widened* from $3063 in 1960 to $3347 in 1968 because of the larger base of white families.[63]

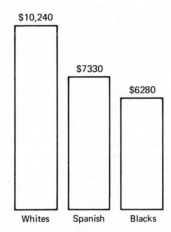

Figure 6.2   MEDIAN-FAMILY 1970 INCOME.   Census Bureau, "Selected Characteristics of Persons and Families of Spanish Origin," ser. P-20, no. 224

The structural realities of income deprivation have two effects on studies of the black subculture. First, there is the direct effect on the culture—on the thinking of poor consumers which becomes a part of the value system passed on to the other members of the culture who may not be poor. The second effect is one of *methodological complexity* in research on black consumption. The question in many marketing studies becomes one of separating out the effects on consumption due to lack of income versus the effects of being a part of the black

---

[62]   "Brown is Richer than Black," *Sales Management*, p. 2 (Dec. 31, 1971).

[63]   Bureau of Labor Statistics, *The Social and Economic Status of Negroes in The United States* (Washington, D.C.: U.S. Government Printing Office, 1970).

Table 6.2 PERSONS BELOW THE POVERTY LEVEL PER YEAR
(United States 1960–1969, Selected Years)

	1960		1965		1969	
Race	Number below Poverty Level (millions)	Percent below Poverty Level	Number below Poverty Level (millions)	Percent below Poverty Level	Number below Poverty Level (millions)	Percent below Poverty Level
White	28.3	18	22.5	13	16.7	10
Negro and Other Races	11.5	56	10.7	47	7.6	31
Total	39.9	22	33.2	17	24.3	12

SOURCE: U.S. Department of Commerce, *Current Population Reports*, ser. P-20.

NOTE: The poverty threshold for a nonfarm family of four was $2973 in 1959 and $3743 in 1969.

subculture. Some of the studies reported later attempt to correct for this situation, but frequently marketing studies do not focus on this distinction.

It is important to note that although a predominant cultural fact is income deprivation, it is still possible to have significant numbers of black consumers who are middle or upper income. Also, Figure 6.3 shows that there is a considerable overlap in the earnings distributions of whites and blacks.[64] It is in this overlap area that marketing analysts particularly need to know about consumption differences truly attributable to subcultural influences.

Educational Deprivation The inadequacy of educational institutions to equip black consumers to compete in the marketplace is a significant structural characteristic of the subculture. In spite of rising numbers of blacks enrolled in schools, the evidence is clear that the institutions are ineffective at educating students to be interested in learning, or successful in societal participation.[65] The

---

[64] Arnold Strasser, "Differentials and Overlaps in Annual Earnings of Blacks and Whites," *Monthly Labor Rev.* pp. 16–26 (Dec. 1971).

[65] Thomas F. Pettigrew, "Racial Segregation and Negro Education," in Daniel P. Moynihan (ed.), *Toward a National Urban Policy* (New York: Basic Books, 1970), pp. 167–177; also Howard M. Bahr and Jack P. Gibbs, "Racial Differentiation in American Metropolitan Areas," *Social Forces*, vol. 45, pp. 521–532, esp. pp. 522–523 (June 1967). Differences in education and other structural variables are analyzed in Charles B. Nam and Mary G. Powers, "Variations in Socioeconomic Structure by Race, Residence, and the Life Cycle," *Amer. Sociological Rev.*, vol. 30, pp. 97–103 (Feb. 1965); Cavin F. Schmid and Charles E. Nobbe, "Socioeconomic Differentials among Nonwhite Races," *Amer. Sociological Rev.*, vol. 30, pp. 909–922 (Dec. 1965). For a discussion of integration and education, see Laurence T. Cagle, "Social Characteristics and Educational Aspirations of Northern, Lower-Class, Predominantly Negro Parents Who Accepted and Declined a School Integration Opportunity," *J. Negro Education*, vol. 37, pp. 406–417 (Fall 1968).

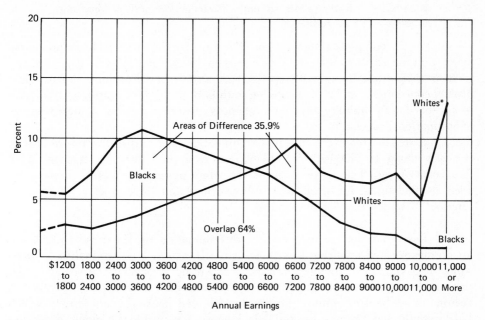

Figure 6.3 PERCENT DISTRIBUTION OF WHITE AND BLACK MEN WITH FOUR QUARTERS OF EARNINGS, BY PRIVATE TOTAL NONAGRICULTURAL SECTOR EARNINGS, 1956. *INCLUDES WORKERS OF ALL RACES OTHER THAN NEGRO. Arnold Strasser, "Differentials and Overlaps in Annual Earnings of Blacks and Whites," *Monthly Labor Rev.*, pp. 16–26, at p. 23 (Dec. 1971)

inadequacy of educational institutions may create inability of consumers to form evaluative criteria about products as efficiently as members of other subcultures and may restrict search processes to personal or friendship sources rather than more informative media.

Differential Family Characteristics The differential family characteristics of the black subculture are important influences on the black consumers. Alleged instability of black families influences other values. The high proportion of black families headed by females also accounts for some of the poverty of black families. A study by the U.S. Department of Labor concluded:

> At the heart of the deterioration of the fabric of Negro society is the deterioration of the Negro family . . .
> There is probably no single fact of Negro American life so little understood by whites. . . . It is more difficult, however, for whites to perceive the effect that three centuries of exploitation have had on the fabric of Negro society itself. Here the consequences of the historic injustices done to Negro Americans are silent and hidden from view. But here is where the true injury has occurred; unless this damage

is repaired, all the effort to end discrimination and poverty and injustice will come to little.[66]

A very complete review of the literature by Farley and Hermalin shows major differences in family stability between blacks and whites using criteria such as proportion living with spouse, proportion of illegitimate births, pre-marital conceptions, and children living with both parents.[67] Duncan and Duncan found that family stability affects life chances on such variables as improvement in occupational success.[68]

A striking feature of the black population now and in the future is that it is very young. In 1966 half of all black persons in the United States were under 21.4 years of age. The median age of the white population was 28.7 years. By 1985 the median age for blacks will be between 19 and 25 years as compared to a range of 27 to 30 years for the whites.

Discrimination The effects of discrimination on the black subculture are so massive and enduring that they cannot be ignored in the analysis of consumer behavior, even though analysis of the topic is beyond the scope of the present discussion.[69] No analysis of expenditure patterns by black families is reasonable without examining the effects of forced housing conditions to which black families have been subjected. Black consumers wishing to move to middle- and upper-class areas of the city have often been prohibited from doing so. Even if some houses were available on an open basis, the black consumer's choices may have been limited by the unavailability of normal financing and social pressure from the potential neighbors.[70] The pressures may be so great that the black family is discouraged from moving into housing in which it can take pride in ownership. One possible alternative is to purchase status products other than housing.[71]

Evaluative criteria of black consumers may be considerably different

---

[66] Office of Policy Planning and Research of U.S. Department of Labor, *The Negro Family: The Case for National Action* (Washington, D.C.: U.S. Government Printing Office, 1965), p. 5. This reference includes many statistical data on black families.

[67] Reynolds Farley and Albert I. Hermalin, "Family Stability: A Comparison of Trends Between Blacks and Whites," *Amer. Sociological Rev.*, vol. 36, pp. 1–17 (Feb. 1971). An interesting study comparing *fertility* among blacks and other minority groups shows that the higher fertility rates of blacks are associated with education and urbanization. When those two variables are controlled, blacks have *lower* fertility rates than whites. See Calvin Gold-scheider and Peter R. Uhlenberg, "Minority Group Status and Fertility," *Amer. J. Sociology*, vol. 74, pp. 361–372 (Jan. 1969).

[68] Beverly Duncan and Otis D. Duncan, "Family Stability and Occupational Success," *Social Problems*, vol. 16, pp. 286–301 (Winter 1969).

[69] For an introduction to this topic, see *Report of the National Advisory Commission on Civil Disorders* (New York: Bantam, 1968); Michael Harrington, *The Other America* (New York: Macmillan, 1962); William H. Grier and Price M. Cobbs, *Black Rage* (New York: Basic Books, 1968); Stokeley Carmichael and Charles Hamilton, *Black Power: The Politics of Liberation* (New York: Random House, 1967).

[70] James F. Engel and Roger D. Blackwell, "Attitudes of Affluent Suburbia toward the Negro Neighbor," *MSU Business Topics*, pp. 42–49 (Autumn 1969).

[71] Bauer and Cunningham, *op. cit.*[62]

when the effects are considered of being eliminated from sources of power in the businesses that provide their goods, the government that is supposed to protect their interests as consumers,[72] or even the unions that are supposed to obtain jobs with which to buy goods.[73] One study concluded through a Markov model analysis that racial differences in occupation would decline sharply after only one generation in which discrimination was absent.[74] It seems reasonable to assume that the black subculture would provide feelings of skepticism toward claims of white-owned businesses that have contributed to keeping them locked in segregated residential patterns, limited employment opportunities, and supported invisibility in the media.[75] It is not surprising that advertisers should worry about the effect of their advertising upon black consumers when attitudes are held such as those of a seventeen-year old black male involved in the Newark riots of 1967:

> I'm not out to get Whitey . . . I'm just out to get out . . . They talk about getting out . . . They carried signs about getting out . . . Now looks like you got to burn the place down and shoot your way out. . .[76]

Black Consumption Patterns

The black subculture provides consumption patterns of significance to marketing analysts. Since most marketing and behavioral research is conducted on nonblack markets, it is useful to compare patterns in black markets with non-black markets. The similarities between black and white markets are much greater than the differences, but there are differences.[77] A black Vice President for Special Markets at Pepsi-Cola states that most of the so-called racial behavior of blacks involves their reactions to the interracial situation.[78]

Developing strategy to satisfy black consumption patterns requires careful attention and understanding of many factors in addition to statistical differences between black and nonblack consumers.[79] An example is provided by

---

[72] Richard F. America, Jr., "What Do You People Want?" *Harvard Business Rev.*, vol. 47, pp. 103–112 (Mar.–Apr. 1969). America's solution to this problem is to transfer ownership of 10 percent of business to minority groups.

[73] Richard L. Rowan, "Discrimination and Apprentice Regulation in the Building Trades," *J. Business*, (Oct. 1967); Leonard A. Rapping, "Union-Induced Racial Entry Barriers," *J. Human Resources*, vol. 4, pp. 447–474 (1971).

[74] Stanley Lieberson and Glenn V. Fuguitt, "Negro–White Occupational Differences in the Absence of Discrimination," *Amer. J. Sociology*, vol. 73, pp. 188–200 (Sept. 1967).

[75] The effects of segregation are clearly shown in Bonnie Bullough, "Alienation in the Ghetto," *Amer. J. Sociology*, vol. 72, pp. 469–478 (Mar. 1967).

[76] David Gottlieb, "Poor Youth: A Study in Forced Alienation," *J. Social Issues*, vol. 25, pp. 91–119 (1969).

[77] The debate on this subject is discussed in Raymond O. Oladipupo, *How Distinct is the Negro Market?* (New York: Ogilvy and Mather, 1970).

[78] H. Naylor Fitzhugh, in "The Negro Market—Two Viewpoints," *Media Scope*, pp. 70–78, at p. 72 (Nov. 1967).

[79] D. Parke Gibson, *The $30 Billion Negro* (New York: Macmillan, 1969).

a fast-food chain that completed market research on blacks and found they averaged significantly less purchases of the chain's product than whites. However, the chain's stores located in black inner-city areas had some of the highest volumes of any stores. At first, executives were bewildered by the findings which appeared to contradict their experience. The answer, of course, involved the population density ratios of the areas surrounding each store.

Studies identifying black cultural influences on consumption have been reviewed thoroughly by Bauer and Cunningham;[80] thus only a few major examples are provided below:

(1) Blacks save more out of a given income than do whites with the same incomes.[81] Blacks use fewer savings and insurance services, however, and end up with less total financial resources than white families of equivalent income and tend to use the less advantageous types of financial services with the end result that the savings approach of blacks tends to widen the gap of well-being between black and white households.[82]

(2) Blacks spend more for clothing and nonautomobile transportation, less for food, housing, medical care, and automobile transportation, and equivalent amounts for recreation and leisure, home furnishings, and equipment than comparable levels of whites.[83]

(3) Blacks tend to own more higher price-class automobiles (Cadillacs), higher priced models regardless of make, and automobiles with more cylinders than comparable-income white families. In this study, race was more closely related to automobile characteristics than income, education, sex, age, family size, or miles driven per week.[84]

(4) Blacks appear to be more brand loyal than equivalent whites.[85]

(5) Black families purchase more milk and soft drinks, less tea and coffee, and more liquor than white families. In 1962 blacks accounted for almost one half of all rum consumption in the United States, 41 percent of all gin, over 50 percent of all Scotch whiskies, and over 77 percent of the Canadian whiskies.[86]

---

[80]   Raymond A. Bauer and Scott M. Cunningham, *Studies in the Negro Market* (Cambridge, Mass.: Marketing Science Institute, 1970).

[81]   Marcus Alexis, "Some Negro–White Differences in Consumption," *Amer. J. Economics and Sociology*, vol. 21 (Jan. 1962).

[82]   S. Roxanne Hiltz, "Black and White in the Consumer Financial System," *Amer. J. Sociology*, vol. 76, pp. 987–999 (1971). For changes, see Charles Van Jassel, "The Negro as a Consumer—What We Know and What We Ought to Know," in M. S. Moyer and R. E. Vosburgh (eds.), *Marketing for Tomorrow . . . Today* (Chicago: Amer. Marketing Assoc. 1967), pp. 166–168.

[83]   Alexis, *op. cit.*;[82] also James Stafford, Keith Cox, and James Higginbottom, "Some Consumption Pattern Differences Between Urban Whites and Negroes," *Social Science Quart.*, pp. 619–630 (Dec. 1968).

[84]   Fred C. Akers, "Negro and White Automobile-Buying Behavior: New Evidence," *J. Marketing Research*, vol. 5, pp. 283–290 (August, 1968).

[85]   Frank G. Davis, "Differential Factors in the Negro Market," (Chicago: National Association of Market Developers, 1959), p. 6; privately published report based upon data collected by *Ebony* magazine.

[86]   Data from Bernard Howard and Co., Inc., and *Ebony*, reported in Oladipupo, *op. cit.*,[78] pp. 30–34.

(6)   Blacks spend more time in commuting to work, travel longer distances, and have lower per capita consumption of automobiles than whites.[87]

Search Processes and Interpersonal Communications

Considerable research on communications in black communities and search processes of black consumers has occurred in recent years. Major findings are reported below with attention first given to mass-media influences and then to interpersonal communications.

(1)   Black consumers appear to be reached more effectively by general media for advertisers appearing in both black and white and by black-oriented media for products specifically directed to black consumers.[88]

(2)   The use of black models in advertising has not increased in the period of 1946 to 1965 but the social status of blacks in ads has increased.[89]

(3)   Black consumers react more favorably to advertisements with all black models or to integrated models than to advertisements with all white models.[90] Whites in these same studies appear to react to black models as favorably or more so than white models, although this varies by product category[91] and by amount of prejudice.[92] Black consumers *under the age of 30* appear to react unfavorably to advertisements with integrated settings.[93]

(4)   Black consumers appear to respond (in recall and attitude shift) more positively to advertisements than do white consumers.[94]

---

[87]   James O. Wheeler, "Transportation Problems in Negro Ghettos," *Sociology and Social Research*, vol. 53, pp. 171–179 (Jan. 1969).

[88]   John V. Petrof, "Reaching the Negro Market: A Segregated vs. a General Newspaper," *J. Advertising Research*, vol. 8, pp. 40–43 (Apr. 1968).

[89]   Harold H. Kassarjian, "The Negro and American Advertising, 1946–1965," *J. Marketing Research*, vol. 6, pp. 29–39 (Feb. 1969); also William H. Boyenton, "The Negro Turns to Advertising," *Journalism Quart.*, vol. 42, pp. 227–235 (Spring 1965). Motivations of advertisers for using black models are reported in Taylor W. Meloan, "Afro-American Advertising Policy and Strategy," in Bernard A. Morin (ed.), *Marketing in a Changing World* (Chicago: Amer. Marketing Assoc. 1969), pp. 20–23.

[90]   Arnold M. Barban, "The Dilemma of 'Integrated' Advertising," *J. Business*, vol. 42, pp. 477–496 (Oct. 1969); B. Stuart Tolley and John J. Goett, "Reactions to Blacks in Newspapers," *J. Advertising Research*, vol. 11, pp. 11–17 (Apr. 1971); John W. Gould, Normal B. Sigband, and Cyril E. Zoerner, Jr., "Black Consumer Reactions to 'Integrated' Advertising: An Exploratory Study," *J. Marketing*, vol. 34, pp. 20–26 (July 1970).

[91]   William V. Muse, "Product-Related Response to Use of Black Models in Advertising," *J. Marketing Research*, vol. 8, pp. 107–109 (Feb. 1971); James E. Stafford and Al E. Birdwell, "Verbal versus Non-Verbal Measures of Attitudes: The Pupilometer," paper presented at the Consumer Behavior Workshop, American Marketing Association, Columbus, Ohio (August 1969).

[92]   James W. Cagley and Richard N. Cardozo, "Racial Prejudice and Integrated Advertising: An Experimental Study," in McDonald, *op. cit.*,[50] pp. 52–56.

[93]   Gould *et al.*, *op. cit.*,[91] p. 25.

[94]   Tolley and Goett, *op. cit.*,[91] pp. 13–14; Petrof, *op. cit.*,[89] p. 42.

(5) Black television viewers dislike programs emphasizing white-oriented subjects such as families, organizations, and similar topics and watch more on the weekend in contrast to whites' higher viewing through the week.[95]

(6) Participation by blacks in social organizations is higher than by whites of comparable socioeconomic characteristics, especially in the lowest income groups. Blacks are more likely than whites to belong to church and political groups and equally likely to belong to civic groups.[96]

(7) Black opinion leadership and community control appears currently to be in a period of conflict between "old line" upper-class black leaders who were acceptable to white power holders, and upwardly mobile, usually young, aggressive blacks willing to tap latent aggressions toward "uppity niggers," "Jew merchants," and "crackers."[97]

Purchasing Processes

Purchasing patterns of blacks and whites do not show dramatic differences, although some black characteristics are found in studies of this subject. Basically, the black housewife is a practical and economical shopper first and foremost and a "black" second.[98] Some distinctives of the black culture are reported, however, in the following studies.

(1) Black consumers appear to have more awareness of both private and national brands than white consumers and to be better informed about prices than white counterparts.[99]

(2) Black consumers appear to respond as well to package designs (for beer) designed for white consumers as for packages designed specifically for black consumers.[100]

---

[95] James W. Carey, "Variations in Negro–White Television Preference," *J. Broadcasting*, vol. 10, pp. 199–211 (1966).

[96] These findings are in contrast with previously held beliefs about black social interaction, but the evidence is reasonably convincing for the more recent conclusions. See Anthony M. Orum, "A Reappraisal of the Social and Political Participation of Negroes," *Amer. J. Sociology*, vol. 72, pp. 32–46 (July 1966); Marvin E. Olsen, "Social and Political Participation of Blacks," *Amer. Sociological Rev.*, vol. 35, pp. 682–696 (1970).

[97] These terms and research are from Seymour Leventman, "Class and Ethnic Tensions: Minority Group Leadership in Transition," *Sociology and Social Research*, vol. 50, pp. 371–376 (Apr. 1966); also Frank A. Petroni, "Uncle Toms: White Stereotypes in the Black Movement," *Human Organization*, vol. 29, pp. 260–266 (Winter 1970).

[98] W. Leonard Evans, Jr., "Ghetto Marketing: What Now?" in Robert L. King (ed.), *Marketing and the New Science of Planning* (Chicago: Amer. Marketing Assoc., 1968), pp. 528–531.

[99] Robert L. King and Earl Robert DeManche, "Comparative Acceptance of Selected Private-Branded Food Products by Low-Income Negro and White Families," in McDonald, *op. cit.,*[50] pp. 63–69. The sample size in this study is very small, however. Feldman and Starr[102] also found that black consumers were more concerned with price than white consumers who were more concerned with value.

[100] Herbert E. Krugman, "White and Negro Responses to Package Designs," *J. Marketing Research*, vol. 3, pp. 199–200 (May 1966).

(3)   Black consumers tend not to shop by phone or mail order as much as white consumers.[101]

(4)   Black grocery consumers tend to make frequent trips to neighborhood stores. This may be due to inadequate refrigeration and storage and lack of transportation that would allow them to carry large amounts of groceries.[102]

(5)   Black consumers tend to shop at discount stores compared to department stores more than do comparable white consumers.[103]

(6)   Black consumers tend to be unhappier with supermarket facilities and functions than do white consumers (with complaints including poor prices, poor cleanliness, crowded conditions, poor displays, and unfriendly employees).[104]

This section on purchasing process can be concluded with a discussion of whether the "poor" (including both blacks and whites) pay more than do affluent people. The assertion was made by Caplovitz that the poor do pay more.[105] There is an extensive literature on this question and some of the studies are contradictory.[106] The conclusion that seems to be emerging is that retailers generally do not *discriminate* between buyers on the basis of income or ethnic characteristics. Thus, it has been shown that chain supermarkets do not charge higher prices in the ghetto but in fact may charge *lower* prices about as often as higher.[107] In a study of appliance buying, discrimination was not found,[108] and among automobile salesmen a pattern was found of charging higher prices to *higher* income persons.[109] However, ethnic groups and the poor may still pay more because of less supermarkets available to them, differences in quality and service,

---

[101]   Laurence P. Feldman and Alvin D. Star, "Racial Factors in Shopping Behavior," in Keith Cox and Ben Enis (eds.), *A New Measure of Responsibility for Marketing* (Chicago: Amer. Marketing Assoc. 1968), pp. 216–226.

[102]   Donald F. Dixon and Daniel J. McLaughlin, Jr., "Shopping Behavior, Expenditure Patterns, and Inner City Food Prices," *J. Marketing Research,* vol. 8, pp. 960–999 (Feb. 1971); Feldman and Star present data to show that blacks do not shop more frequently than whites, however.

[103]   Feldman and Star, *op. cit.*[102]

[104]   John V. Petrof, "Attitudes of the Urban Poor Toward Their Neighborhood Supermarkets," *J. Retailing,* vol. 47, pp. 3–17 (Spring 1971).

[105]   David Caplovitz, *The Poor Pay More* (New York: Free Press, 1963).

[106]   This literature is reviewed in Robert G. Mogull, "Where Do We Stand on Inner City Prices?" *The Southern Journal of Business* VI pp. 32–40 (July 1971); Donald E. Sexton, Jr., "Do Blacks Pay More?" *J. Marketing Research,* vol. 8, pp. 420–426 (Nov. 1971).

[107]   U.S. Bureau of Labor Statistics, *A Study of Prices in Food Stores Located in Low and Higher Income Areas of Six Large Cities* (Washington, D.C.: U.S. Government Printing Office, 1966); B. W. Marion, L. A. Simonds, and D. E. Moore, "Food Marketing in Low-Income Areas: A Case Study of Columbus, Ohio," *Bull. Business Research,* vol. 45, pp. 1–8 (August 1970).

[108]   Norman Kangun, "Race and Price Discrimination in the Marketplace: A Further Study," *Mississippi Valley J. of Economics and Business,* vol. 5, pp. 66–75 (Spring 1970). This study includes Indian families as well as black families.

[109]   Gordon L. Wise, "Automobile Salesmen's Perceptions of New Car Prospects," *Bull. Business Research,* vol. 46, pp. 2–6 (Feb. 1971).

differences in credit costs, and a pattern of purchasing in smaller quantities and package sizes.[110]

Minority Subcultures and Marketing

The previous discussion of subcultural influences on consumer behavior is important in understanding a variety of marketing problems. First, this form of analysis should aid analysts seeking to discover and define minority marketing problems. Groups that have their own subculture have often been the object of discrimination and other problems. Analysis and understanding is a necessary prerequisite for either internal or external action to correct problem areas. Increasingly it appears that a concern of consumer analysts will be how to teach individuals and groups to be "buying strategists" as well as to teach businesses how to be marketing strategists.

Second, the analysis of subcultural influences assists in efforts to develop and make minority marketing more effective. In the case of black markets, the emerging trend appears to be to assist black business firms in their efforts to service members of the black subculture as well as to assist white dominated firms in their efforts to tap a growing market.

SUMMARY

This chapter has described the influence of two social forces: reference groups and subcultures. Reference groups are defined as any interaction aggregation of people that influences an individual's attitudes or behavior. This includes small face-to-face (primary) groups and organizations (secondary) groups. A group to which one aspires but does not belong may also be relevant as an influence on a consumer's behavior.

Reference groups accomplish adult and childhood socialization and perform normative as well as evaluative functions. A group develops and specifies norms to which individuals desiring membership must adhere. The Homans equation of human exchange describes the interaction process as one involving a net profit based upon rewards (such as esteem) less costs of interaction.

Group influences provide an environment for attitude formation, for determination of individual deviation from norms, and for development and evaluation of the self-concept. Marketing research has established the presence of reference group influence in many types of products but to date has given limited empirical insight into the determination of group influence.

Subcultural influences are usually more comprehensive and enduring than reference groups. Four types of subcultures are described in this chapter: nationality groups, religious groups, geographic areas, and racial groups. The contemporary black culture in the United States has been influenced by a variety of factors such as income deprivation, inadequate educational institutions, differ-

110   Sexton, *op. cit.*;[107] Marion *et al.*, *op. cit.*;[108] Mogull, *op. cit.*;[107] Richard Teach, "Supermarket Pricing Practices in Various Areas of a Large City," in McDonald, *op. cit.*,[50] pp. 57–62.

ential family characteristics, and discrimination. There is no "black market" any more than a "white market." Rather there is market segmentation within the black population. A group of characteristics, influenced by the structural realities described above, do emerge as "core" values and patterns which have become associated with black consumption, search processes and communication, and purchasing processes.

REVIEW AND DISCUSSION QUESTIONS

1. Define the following terms and assess their importance in consumer analysis: (a) reference group, (b) membership group, (c) aspirational group, (d) dissociative group, and (e) primary group.

2. In what ways are reference groups associated with adult socialization? Describe some examples of this that might affect consumer decisions.

3. Why is the concept of "group norms" of relevance to marketing strategists?

4. Explain the Homans equation of human exchange and critically assess its importance in understanding the formation of reference groups.

5. Assume that a large manufacturer of living room furniture has asked for an analysis of the term "self-concept" as it relates to his marketing problems. Outline your analysis of the relevance of the term.

6. Design an experiment that would serve to clarify the concept of reference groups as a variable in marketing analysis.

7. Analyze the similarities and differences between the Puerto Rican subculture and the black subculture. Present a logical analysis for the existence of differences that may exist.

8. Assume that a major marketer of soft drinks in the United States receives a marketing research study which indicates low penetration in the rapidly expanding black market. Prepare a marketing strategy to expand his market position.

7

FAMILY INFLUENCES
ON CONSUMER BEHAVIOR

How important are other family members in influencing what a consumer purchases? What is the relative influence of the wife, husband, and children in selecting the make of a car, the body style, and other features? Should a furniture manufacturer direct marketing efforts to all family members or just the wife? Should a cereal manufacturer advertise to the mother or the child?

Answers to these types of questions are useful in designing marketing strategies and programs. This chapter discusses those unique aspects of the family that are relevant for an understanding of consumer behavior, demonstrates how family influences affect an individual's personality characteristics, attitudes, and evaluative criteria, and discusses, in an introductory way, the role and influence of family members in purchasing decisions. Additional dimensions of role structures will be discussed in Part V.

INTRODUCTION

Family Terminology

The term "family" is used in a wide variety of ways. Definitions are relative to purposes, that is, they are means or tools rather than ends. For purposes of this book, the following terminology is adequate. *Nuclear* family means the immediate group of father, mother, and child(ren) living together. The *extended* family refers to the nuclear family and other relatives, including grandparents, uncles and aunts, cousins, and in-laws. The family one is born into is called the *family of orientation,* while the one established by marriage is the *family of procreation.*[1] The discussion here is concerned primarily with the influence of the nuclear family, although occasional reference is made to the extended family and the family of orientation.

Unique Aspects of the Family

Wherever man is, regardless of the circumstances of his life, the family is present. Although family forms and functions vary from culture to culture, the family as an institution is universal.[2] From an individual consumer's point of view, the family differs in a number of respects from larger social systems, and these unique aspects are important in understanding the role of the family in influencing individual behavior.

In contrast to larger social systems, the nuclear family is a *primary* group. As such it is characterized by intimate face-to-face association and cooperation. Indeed, the family is perhaps the ultimate in face-to-face intimacy and meaningfulness.[3] This intimacy and association means, among other things, that the family is often uniquely important in its influence on individual personality, attitudes, and motives.[4] More is said about this in the next section.

The family differs from other reference groups in that it is both an earning and a consuming unit. The consumption needs of each individual as well as family needs, such as a car and home, must be satisfied from a common pool of financial resources. This means that individual needs must sometimes be subordinated to those of other family members or to the needs of the family as a whole.

Because the family is a primary group that both earns and consumes, it differs from larger social systems in the sense that it performs what might be termed a *mediating* function. The norms of larger social systems—culture, subculture, reference groups, social class, and so on—are filtered through and interpreted by individuals in a family setting. This process of mediation may substantially alter the influences of larger social systems on individual consumption behavior.

There are, then, many ways in which the family differs from larger reference groups. While there are other unique aspects of the family, the above are most relevant for our purposes.[5]

---

[1] These definitions are widely accepted. See, for example, Bernard Berelson and Gary A. Steiner, *Human Behavior* (New York: Harcourt, 1964), p. 297.

[2] William F. Kenkel, *The Family in Perspective* (New York: Appleton, 1966), p. 3.

[3] Clifford Kirkpatrick, *The Family as Process and Institution* (New York: Ronald, 1963), p. 4; Kenkel, *op. cit.,*[2] pp. 391–392.

[4] See, for example, Gardner Murphy, "New Knowledge about Family Dynamics," *Pastoral Psychology,* vol. 2, pp. 39–47 (1960); William A. Westley and Nathan B. Erstein, "Family Structure and Emotional Health: A Case Study Approach," *Marriage and Family Living,* vol. 22, pp. 25-27 (1960).

[5] For other unique aspects of the family, see Kirkpatrick, *op. cit.,*[3] pp. 4–6.

FAMILY INFLUENCES ON INDIVIDUAL PERSONALITY CHARACTERISTICS, ATTITUDES, AND EVALUATIVE CRITERIA

Family influences are important in two major ways: (1) they influence individual personality characteristics, attitudes, and evaluative criteria, and (2) they affect the decision-making process that is involved in the purchase of goods and services. This and the following section are concerned with the first type of influence, while the second type is explored in the last two major sections.

Figure 7.1 illustrates the relations among larger social systems, the family, and the individual. As indicated, the nuclear family plays two important roles. First, other family members have certain personality characteristics, evaluative criteria, and attitudes, and the family as a whole has certain needs. Second, the nuclear family often performs a mediating function as described above. These two functions are stimuli into the individual's central control unit subject to the complex processes of exposure, attention, comprehension, and retention. As such, they have varying degrees of influence on an individual's psychological makeup.

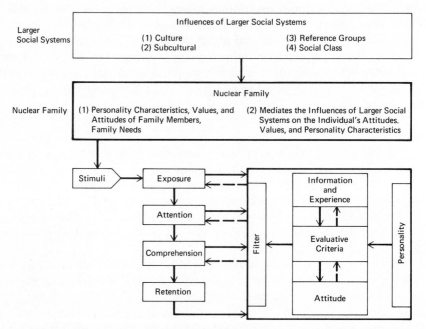

Figure 7.1 FAMILY INFLUENCES ON INDIVIDUAL PERSONALITY CHARAC-TERISTICS, ATTITUDES, AND EVALUATIVE CRITERIA

Assimilation Processes

As an individual interacts with other family members, he simultaneously both influences the personality characteristics, evaluative criteria, and attitudes of others and in turn is influenced by others. Since a family is a primary group and because it shares a finite amount of financial resources and has many common consumption needs, the personality characteristics, evaluative criteria and attitudes of family members tend to converge and are typically more homogeneous than would be the case if they were not in the same family.[6]

Conflict Resolution Processes

Although the generalization that family influences tend to cause family members' psychological characteristics to converge is true in most instances, it leaves many issues unresolved. For example, what is the relative influence of various family members in these processes? Do husbands exert more influence than wives? What is the role of children? What happens when the motives, attitudes, and/or evaluative criteria of family members conflict? How are these conflicts resolved and what is the nature of the conflict resolution process? What happens when they are not resolved?

Many researchers have advanced propositions, hypotheses, and theories concerning the relative importance of family members in influencing these phenomena[7] and the anatomy of the conflict resolution process.[8] Unfortunately, research at this *level* has little value to marketers at the present time because the role and influence of family members varies widely from one phenomenon to another, and so it is hazardous to assume that general patterns apply to the processes involved in purchasing specific products and services.[9] For this reason, the practitioner should focus on the role and influence of family members in the context of his specific product or service.

FAMILY LIFE CYCLE

Over time most consumers pass through a series of stages in their lives known as the family life cycle. A common typology of stages is:

(1) Bachelor stage; young single people not living at home.

(2) Newly married couples; young, no children.

(3) Full nest I; young married couples with youngest child under six.

---

[6] See, for example, Robert Bales and Talcott Parsons, *Family Socialization and Interaction Processes* (New York: Free Press, 1955).

[7] For illustrative investigations, see James N. Morgan, "Household Decision Making," in Nelson Foote (ed.), *Household Decision Making* (New York: New York University Press, 1961), p. 91; Robert F. Kelley and Michael B. Egan, "Husband and Wife Interaction in a Consumer Decision Process," in Robert L. King (ed.), *Marketing and the New Science of Planning* (Chicago: Amer. Marketing Assoc., 1969), pp. 250–258.

[8] See, for example, Richard W. Pollay, "A Model of Family Decision Making," *Brit. J. Marketing*, vol. 2, pp. 206–216 (1968).

[9] See, for example, Donald M. Wolfe, "Power and Authority in the Family," in D. Cartwright (ed.), *Studies in Social Power* (Ann Arbor, Mich.: Research Center for Group Dynamics, 1958), pp. 98–116; D. Byrne and B. Blaylock, "Similarity of Attitudes between Husbands and Wives," *J. Abnormal and Social Psychology*, vol. 67, pp. 636–640 (1963).

(4) Full nest II; young married couples with youngest child six or over.

(5) Full nest III; older married couples with dependent children.

(6) Empty nest I; older married couples, no children living with them, household head in labor force.

(7) Empty nest II; older married couples, no children living at home, household head retired.

(8) Solitary survivor in labor force.

(9) Solitary survivor, retired.

The life-cycle concept is useful because several studies indicate that family needs, income, assets and debts, and expenditures vary at different life-cycle stages. Because the life-cycle concept combines trends in earning power with demands placed on income, it is one of the most powerful ways of classifying and segmenting individuals and families. A brief summary of the major dimensions of each stage in the life cycle follows.[10]

Bachelor Stage

Although earnings are relatively low, they are subject to few rigid demands, so consumers in this stage typically have substantial discretionary income. Part of this income is used to purchase a car and basic equipment and furnishings for their first residence away from home—usually an apartment. They tend to be more fashion and recreation oriented, spending a substantial proportion of their income on clothing, alcoholic beverages, food away from home, vacations, leisure time pursuits, and other products and services involved in the mating game.

Newly Married Couples

Newly married couples without children are usually better off financially than they have been in the past and will be in the near future because the wife is usually employed. Families at this stage also spend a substantial amount of their income on cars, clothing, vacations, and other leisure time activities. They also have the highest purchase rate and highest average purchase of durable goods, particularly furniture and appliances.

Full Nest I

With the arrival of the first child, most wives stop working outside the home, and consequently family income declines. Simultaneously, the young child creates new problems which change the way the family spends its income. The

---

10 The summary of life cycle stages is adapted from William D. Wells and George Gubar, "The Life Cycle Concept in Marketing Research," *J. Marketing Research*, vol. 3, pp. 355–363 (Nov. 1966); S. G. Barton, "The Life Cycle and Buying Patterns," in Lincoln H. Clark, (ed.), *Consumer Behavior*, vol. 2 (New York: New York University Press, 1955), pp. 53–57; John B. Lansing and Leslie Kish, "Family Life Cycle as an Independent Variable," *Amer. Sociological Rev.*, pp. 512–519 (Oct. 1957); John B. Lansing and James N. Morgan, "Consumer Finances over the Life Cycle," in Clark, pp. 36–51; David Riesman and Howard Roseborough, "Careers and Consumer Behavior," in Clark, pp. 1–18.

couple is likely to move into their first home, purchase furniture and furnishings for the child, buy a washer, dryer, and home maintenance items, and purchase such products as baby food, chest rubs, cough medicine, vitamins, toys, wagons, sleds, and skates. These requirements reduce family savings and the husband and wife are often dissatisfied with their financial position.

Full Nest II

At this stage the youngest child is six or over, the husband's income has improved, and the wife often returns to work outside the home. Consequently, the family's financial position usually improves. Consumption patterns continue to be heavily influenced by the children as the family tends to buy food and cleaning supplies in larger sized packages, bicycles, pianos, and music lessons.

Full Nest III

As the family grows older their financial position usually continues to improve because the husband's income rises, the wife returns to work or enjoys a higher salary, and the children earn money from occasional employment. The family typically replaces several pieces of furniture, purchases another automobile, buys several luxury appliances, and spends a considerable amount of money on dental services and education for the children.

Empty Nest I

At this stage the family is most satisfied with their financial position and the amount of money saved because income has continued to increase, and the children have left home and are no longer financially dependent on their parents. The couple often make home improvements, buy luxury items, and spend a greater proportion of their income on vacations, travel, and recreation.

Empty Nest II

By this time the household head has retired and so the couple usually suffers a noticeable reduction in income. Expenditures become more health oriented, centering on such items as medical appliances, medical care, products which aid health, sleep, and digestion, and perhaps a smaller home, apartment, or condominium in a more agreeable climate.

The Solitary Survivor

If still in the labor force, solitary survivors still enjoy good income. They may sell their home and usually spend more money on vacations, recreation, and the types of health-oriented products and services mentioned above.

The retired solitary survivor follows the same general consumption pattern except on a lower scale because of the reduction in income. In addition, these individuals have special needs for attention, affection, and security.

Marketing Implications

Although the above discussion of stages in the family life cycle is simplistic and incomplete, it provides an adequate background for identifying the major uses of the variable. Specifically, the life-cycle concept can be used to:

(1) *Segment Markets* Studies of consumer expenditures reveal that the consumption of many products and services varies significantly by stage in family life cycle. Moreover, the qualitative level at which families satisfy basic consumption needs varies from one stage to another. Therefore, life cycle is often a useful tool for identifying heavy buyers of a product category.[11]

(2) *Forecast Demand* The Census Bureau publishes estimates of the future size and age structure of the family population.[12] In addition, it is possible to obtain consumption rates of products and services broken out by life cycle, age, and other demographic data.[13] By identifying the heavy consumption patterns of those age and life cycle segments that are predicted to expand significantly, it is possible to identify products and services that are likely to enjoy above average growth rates in the future. This type of information is useful in estimating future market potential for the firm's current product line and in making product-line-extension decisions.

FAMILY ROLE STRUCTURES

In the two previous sections it was shown how various characteristics of family members and families influence an individual's personality characteristics, evaluative criteria, and attitudes as well as purchasing patterns. This section is concerned with the role and influence of family members in the decision-making process.

Family role[14] structure[15] means the behavior of nuclear family members at

---

[11] For specific examples see the sources identified in footnote 10.

[12] U.S. Department of Commerce, *Current Population Reports*, ser. P-25.

[13] See, for example, National Industrial Conference Board, *Expenditure Patterns of the American Family* (New York: *Life*, 1965).

[14] This is consistent with, although not nearly as elaborate as, the usual definition of role. See, for example, D. Kretch, R. Crutchfield, and E. Ballachey, *Individual in Society* (New York: McGraw-Hill, 1962), pp. 310–311.

[15] Role structure is actually considerably more complex than this, since it results from the interaction of a status structure, a communication structure, an attraction structure, and many other structures. See, for example, T. M. Newcomb, R. H. Turner, and P. E. Converse, *Social Psychology* (New York: Holt, Rinehart and Winston, 1965), p. 346. We are concerned with those dimensions of the status and communication structures that influence consumption decisions.

each stage in the decision-making process. Role structures are of fundamental importance to the marketing executive for they often influence the design and packaging of products, the types of retail outlets handling the product, media strategies, creative strategies, and many other types of decisions.[16]

Types of Decision-Process Role Structures

While the role of family members in decision making is usually conceptualized as a continuum of influence, practical problems of research make it convenient to utilize role-structure categories. Although considerable variation exists in the categories that are used, one of the more complex is (1) *autonomic,* or when an equal number of decisions is made by each spouse, (2) *husband dominant,* (3) *wife dominant,* and (4) *syncratic,* or when most decisions are made by both husband and wife.[17] With few exceptions,[18] marketers usually use simpler categories, for example, husband more than wife, wife more than husband, both husband and wife,[19] or simply, husband only, wife only, or children only.[20] Thus there are various category systems used, and, as is discussed in the next section, this presents several problems.

Determinants of Decision-Process Role Structures

Most studies find major variation among families in the role of family members in decision-making behavior. While many of these studies have methodological problems, enough of them have been conducted to justify the specification of several tentative bases, or determinants, of decision-making role structures. These include cultural, subcultural, and reference group influences, several characteristics of the nuclear family, the type of product, and the stage in the decision-making process.

Cultural Influences   For a variety of reasons, all societies have somewhat different role specifications for men and women. These role specifications are learned early in life through a process of social conditioning. As is true in other small groups, the nuclear family is generally characterized by an *instrumental*

---

[16]   See, for example, R. S. Alexander, "Some Aspects of Sex Differences in Relation to Marketing," *J. Marketing,* vol. 12, pp. 158–172 (Oct. 1947).

[17]   See, for example, P. G. Herbst, "Conceptual Framework for Studying the Family," in O. A. Oeser and S. B. Hammond (eds.), *Social Structure and Personality in a City* (London: Routledge, 1954).

[18]   Elizabeth H. Wolgast, "Do Husbands or Wives Make Purchasing Decisions?" *J. Marketing,* vol. 23, pp. 151–158 (Oct. 1958); Paul D. Converse and Merle Crawford, "Family Buying: Who Does It? Who Influences It?" *Current Economic Comment,* vol. 2, pp. 38–50 (Nov. 1949).

[19]   See, for example, Harry Sharp and Paul Mott, "Consumer Decisions in the Metropolitan Family," *J. Marketing,* vol. 21, pp. 149–156 (Oct. 1956); Carl R. Gisler, "Is the Buying Influence of Men Underestimated?" *Printer's Ink,* p. 38 ff (Sept. 24, 1948).

[20]   "Customer Traffic Patterns: Key to Selling Efficiency," *Progressive Grocer,* pp. k-75–k-106 (Jan. 1967).

leader and an *expressive*[21] leader.[22] The many cultural prescriptions of our society usually operate in such a way as to train the male for the instrumental role and the female for the expressive role.[23]

Cultural prescriptions and norms, however, are often rather general, so that there is a usually considerable latitude for individual interpretation. As a consequence, other factors are needed to account for differences between families.

Subcultural Influences Since role specifications for men and women often vary from country to country, family role structures might be expected to vary by ethnic group. While this is probably true to some extent, the degree of variation should not be exaggerated. For example, husband-dominant role structures are not necessarily more prevalent among certain foreign-born families and Catholics than they are among other families.[24] Albeit ethnic group differences exist, there seems to be a tendency over time for these groups to divest themselves of the family role structures characteristic of their native country.[25]

Reference Group Influences Cultural and subcultural influences on role structure are interpreted by the members of the family of orientation. There is considerable evidence that many characteristics of the family of orientation affect role structure in the nuclear family. Such factors as conflict with the mother and reaction to home discipline influence whether the general decision-making role structure is wife dominant, husband dominant, or some other structure.[26] There is also some evidence that the authority structure existing in the family of orientation is often projected to the nuclear family.[27]

Friends, acquaintances, and members of other peer groups also influence the decision-process role structure in a nuclear family. In some instances peer group influences are even more important than the family of orientation in shaping nuclear family role structures, that is, the way in which one's friends divide decision-making tasks sometimes exerts more influence on a couple than the role structures used by their respective parents.[28]

Characteristics of the Nuclear Family In addition to cultural, subcultural, and reference group influences, several characteristics of the individual's

---

[21] "Instrumental" refers to the need for leadership and task fulfillment, while "expressive" refers to the need for morale and cohesion. See Berelson and Steiner, *op. cit.*,[1] p. 314.

[22] William F. Kenkel, "Family Interaction in Decision Making on Spending," in Foote, *op cit.*,[7] pp. 145–147.

[23] Mirra Komarovsky, "Cultural Contradictions and Sex Roles," *Amer. J. Sociology*, vol. 52, pp. 184–189 (Nov. 1946).

[24] Robert O. Blood, Jr., and Donald M. Wolfe, *Husbands and Wives: The Dynamics of Married Living* (New York: Free Press, 1960).

[25] Sister Frances J. Woods, *Cultural Values of American Ethnic Groups* (New York: Harper & Row, 1956), chaps. 11–12.

[26] Yi-Chuang Lu, "Predicting Roles in Marriage," *Amer. J. Sociology*, vol. 58, pp. 51–55 (July 1952).

[27] Hazel L. Ingersoll, "Transmission of Authority Patterns in the Family," *Marriage and Family Living*, vol. 10, p. 36 (Spring 1948).

[28] Lionel J. Neiman, "The Influence of Peer Groups upon Attitudes toward the Female Role," *Social Problems*, vol. 2, pp. 104–111 (Oct. 1954).

nuclear family influence the role of other family members in the buying process.

(1) *Stage in Life Cycle* Several studies have shown that the role of family members in decision making changes throughout the life of the family. Generally, the first few years of marriage are characterized by an unusually large amount of joint husband–wife decision making and shopping. However, as the length of the marriage increases, each spouse becomes both more familiar with the needs and attitudes of family members and more competent in decision making. Consequently, the degree of joint decision making typically declines over a family's life cycle.[29]

(2) *Social Class* A curvilinear relationship usually exists between a family's social class (as measured by income and occupation) and the degree of joint decision making. Joint decision making is *least* common in lower and upper social classes and *most* common among the middle social classes. Whereas women tend to be more dominant in the lower classes, men have a greater tendency to dominate in upper-social-class families.[30]

(3) *Employment Status of Wife* The employment status of the wife affects her role in decision making. Generally, but not always, the relative influence of the wife is greater if she works outside the home.[31] The wife's influence increases because she increases her financial and intellectual resources and hence becomes less dependent on her husband for the satisfaction of her needs.[32]

(4) *Location* There is some evidence that joint decision making is more common among families living in rural areas. Housewives in rural areas, however, are typically less influential in decision making than their urban counterparts.[33]

(5) *Personality Characteristics* The personality characteristics of the individuals involved in decision making may also have an influence on the roles they play. For example, wives who have a strong need for love and affection will generally have less influence in purchasing decisions.[34]

(6) *Social Networks* Certain characteristics of an individual's social relationships influence the type of role structure that is used in decision making. Although based on a small sample, there is some evidence that the degree of joint decision making varies inversely with the "connectedness" of a nuclear

---

[29] See, for example, Wolgast, *op. cit.*,[18] p. 154; Blood and Wolfe, *op. cit.*,[24] pp. 41–44; Mirra Komarovsky "Class Differences in Family Decision Making on Expenditures," in Foote, *op. cit.*,[7] p. 261; Donald H. Granbois, "A Study of the Family Decision Making Process in the Purchase of Major Household Goods," unpublished doctoral dissertation, (Bloomington, Ind.: Indiana University Graduate School of Business, 1962), pp. 98.

[30] The curvilinear hypothesis was advanced in Komarovsky, *op. cit.*,[29] pp. 259–264. This hypothesis is supported by Converse and Crawford, *op. cit.*,[18] p. 45; Blood and Wolfe, *op. cit.*,[24] pp. 37–37; Eugene A. Wilkening, "Joint Decision Making in Farm Families," *Amer. Sociological Rev.*, vol. 23, pp. 187–192 (Apr. 1958); Sharp and Mott, *op. cit.*,[19] p. 152; and several other studies.

[31] See Blood and Wolfe, *op. cit.*,[24] pp. 40–41; R. O. Blood and R. L. Hamblin, "The Effects of the Wife's Employment on the Family Power Structure," *Social Forces*, vol. 36, pp. 347–352 (1958); David M. Heer, "Dominance and the Working Wife," *Social Forces*, vol. 36, pp. 341–347 (1958).

[32] Wolfe, *op. cit.*,[9] p. 109.

[33] Wolgast, *op. cit.*,[18] p. 154.

[34] Wolfe, *op. cit.*,[9] p. 111.

family's social network. "Connectedness" means the degree to which husband and wife have friends in common. A closely knit group of friends for *each* spouse has a tendency to act as a norm formulating and enforcing reference group. When neither husband nor wife belongs to a connected social network they have a greater tendency to engage in joint decision making.[35]

(7) **Summary Hypotheses** Two somewhat similar hypotheses have been advanced in an attempt to explain why the above-mentioned characteristics of the nuclear family influence family role structures. The *relative contributions* hypothesis explains role structures in terms of the relative resources (income, decision-making ability) contributed by individuals comprising the nuclear family. The greater the relative contribution of an individual, the greater the influence in decision making. For example, husbands having high income, high occupational prestige, and high social status generally have more decision making authority than husbands whose wives work. Husbands in these situations have more influence because these characteristics enable them to contribute more to the complicated task of decision making, not because successful men are expected to be more powerful at home.[36]

The *least-interested-partner* hypothesis focuses not on the value to each spouse of the resources contributed by the other, but on the value placed on these resources outside the marriage. The greater the difference between the value to the wife of the resources contributed by her husband and the value to the wife of the resources she might earn outside the existing marriage, the greater the influence of the husband in decision making.[37]

Of the two, the least-interested-partner hypothesis seems to be the most powerful. It explains as much variation in family role structures as the relative-contributions hypothesis, and, in addition, it can accommodate the changing patterns of family-member interaction that occur over the life cycle. However, both hypotheses are limited explanations in the sense that they do not explain differences in role structures attributable to cultural and reference group influences, geographic location, or social networks. Nevertheless, the least-interested-partner hypothesis is a convenient way of summarizing much of what is known about the basis of family role structures.

Type of Product The degree of joint decision making varies considerably from product to product. The extent of joint decision making tends to increase as the price of the product increases. In the purchase of lower priced products, there is generally a tendency for purchase decisions to be delegated to the husband and wife according to their respective skills and knowledge.[38]

---

[35]   Elizabeth Bott, *Family and Social Network* (London: Tavistock Pub., 1957), pp. 59–60. For a more sophisticated view, see Barbara E. Harrell-Bond, "Conjugal Role Behavior," *Human Relations*, vol. 22, pp. 77–91 (1969).

[36]   Blood and Wolfe, *op. cit.,*[24] pp. 12–13, 30–33.

[37]   David M. Heer, "The Measurement and Bases of Family Power: An Overview," *Marriage and Family Living*, vol. 25, pp. 133–139 (1965).

[38]   See, for example, Wolgast, *op. cit.,*[18] pp. 151–158; Sharp and Mott, *op. cit.,*[19] pp. 149–156; "Customer Traffic Patterns . . . ," *op. cit.*[20]

These skills and knowledge may be actual in the sense that they really exist, or perceived in the sense that cultural and reference group norms prescribe that they should exist. For example, as a result of certain cultural prescriptions, a husband is "supposed" to know more about mechanical things and generally plays a more important role in the purchase of products having complex, mechanical attributes. On the other hand, cultural and reference group norms, as well as many other factors, operate in such a way that a man is not "supposed" to know much about ironing or irons. Thus, he is likely to be less influential in the purchase of these types of products.

Stage in the Decision Process There is considerable evidence that the roles of members of the nuclear family vary by stage in the decision process.[39] For example, the husband may recognize the problem while the wife engages in external search, with both the husband and the wife evaluating alternatives and the wife actually purchasing a specific brand. This is obviously a more sophisticated view of family-member interaction, and little is presently known about why the roles of family members vary by stage in the decision-making process.

MEASURING FAMILY ROLE STRUCTURE

While the determinants discussed above are useful in understanding basic role-structure patterns, at the present time they are too general for the marketing executive. It is necessary to be more specific.

The first step is to determine whether the role and influence of more than one family member should be considered at *any* stage in the decision-making process for a specific product or service. A "no" decision should be made only if the analyst has research data for his specific product. If so, the next step is to identify the relevant family member and proceed to measure his behavior at each stage in the decision process using the techniques discussed in Part V of this volume.

Without specific research evidence, it should be assumed that the role and influence of family members should be measured at each stage in the process. The remainder of this section presents guidelines for conducting this research.

Choice of Product

Role-structure categories can be used to describe the general pattern of influence in a family, the general pattern of decision making, or the profile of decision making for specific products and brands. As indicated above, studies

---

[39] G. H. Brown, "The Automobile Buying Decision within the Family," in Foote, *op. cit.,*[7] pp. 193–199; Harry L. Davis, "Dimensions of Marital Roles in Consumer Decision-Making," *J. Marketing Research*, vol. 7, pp. 168–177 (May 1970); Richard A. Scott, "Husband-Wife Interaction in a Household Purchase Decision," *Southern J. Business*, vol. 5, pp. 218–225 (July 1970); "A Pilot Study of the Roles of Husbands and Wives in Purchasing Decisions," *Life*, parts I–X (1965).

indicate that the influence of family members often varies widely from product to product.[40] Hence it is dangerous to generalize from studies that construct role structures for general decision-making behavior, or even studies of closely related products or services. Rather, at the present time it is necessary to measure the role and influence of family members for the marketer's specific product or service.

Decision-Process Framework

Most role-structure studies have viewed purchasing as an act rather than a process. Role structures have been constructed on the basis of answers to such questions as, "Who usually makes the decision to purchase?" or "Who influences the decision?"

Yet as was pointed out above, there is considerable evidence that the role and influence of family members varies by stage in the decision process.[41] Consequently, meaningless answers are likely to result from the types of questions itemized in the preceding paragraph. What appear to be contradictory results may be caused by respondents' answering in terms of different stages in the decision process.[42] Therefore, role structure studies should measure the influence of family members at each stage in the decision-making process rather than simply the purchase.

Research Designs and Questioning Techniques

Several methods have been used to identify the roles of family members in making purchase decisions. The most common approaches are as follows:

(1) General questions about influence.

(2) Direct questions about specific decisions and activities.[43]

(3) Questions concerning how conflicts are resolved in the family.[44]

(4) Where there is disagreement among family members, a comparison of the brand purchased and the brand preferred by family members.[45]

(5) Given a fixed imaginary income, the proportion of purchases suggested by each family member and the amounts of money other family members agree to spend on the items suggested by that individual.[46]

---

[40] "A Pilot Study . . . ," *op. cit.*;[39] Davis, *op. cit.*,[39] pp. 168–177.

[41] See sources listed in footnote 39.

[42] Mirra Komarovsky, "Discussion," in Foote, *op. cit.*,[7] p. 181.

[43] Examples include Sharp and Mott, *op. cit.*,[19] pp. 149–156; Wolgast, *op. cit.*,[18] pp. 151–158.

[44] Wolgast, *op. cit.*,[18] pp. 151–158; Martin Gold and Carol Slater, "Office, Factory, Store and Family," *Amer. Sociological Rev.*, vol. 23, pp. 64–74 (Feb. 1958).

[45] "Family Participation and Influence in Shopping and Brand Selection," *Life*, parts I and II (1964).

[46] William F. Kenkel and Dean K. Hoffman, "Real and Conceived Roles in Family Decision Making," *Marriage and Family Living*, vol. 28, pp. 311–316 (Nov. 1956).

Research to date indicates that these different measures of the same phenomenon are not closely related. Several studies have found little relationship between interaction measures (techniques 3 and 5) and self reports (techniques 1 and 2).[47] Answers to direct questions are subject to many biases,[48] while direct observation of imaginary decisions sometimes produce biases because of the hypothetical nature of the decisions.[49] It has also been shown that families interacting in a laboratory setting sometimes differ from those observed at home.[50]

At the present time there does not appear to be any research design that can overcome the problems involved in identifying roles. The best interim approach seems to be to use direct questions about specific decisions and activities at each stage in the decision-making process for the marketer's product or service. This questioning should probably be conducted in the respondent's home rather than some other setting.

Role-Structure Categories

The relevant role-structure categories depend on the specific product or service under consideration. In many product categories only the husband and wife are involved. In this case a defensible approach is to measure the *relative* influence for each specific decision at each stage in the decision process on a five-point Likert scale where husband decides = 1; husband has more influence than wife = 2; equal influence = 3; wife has more influence than husband = 4; and wife decides = 5.

Children are involved in many types of purchase situations, and the nature of their influence is not always obvious.[51] For example, while it is well known that children influence cereal and soft-drink purchases, other areas of influence are not so well recognized, dog food being an example. In other instances children exert a passive influence in the sense that one of the spouses continues to buy brands until she finds one that the children will consume.[52] Many role-structure studies probably grossly underestimate the influence of children,

---

[47] James G. March, "Influence Measurement in Experimental and Semi-Experimental Groups," *Sociometry,* vol. 19, pp. 260–271 (Dec. 1956); David H. Olson, "The Measurement of Family Power by Self-Report and Behavior Methods," *J. Marriage and the Family,* vol. 31, pp. 545–550 (Aug. 1969).

[48] Gold and Slater, *op. cit.,*[44] pp. 64–74; William F. Kenkel, "Influence Differentiation in Family Decision Making," *Sociology and Social Research,* vol. 42, pp. 18–25 (Sept.–Oct. 1957).

[49] Heer, *op. cit.;*[37] Morgan, *op. cit.,*[7] p. 94.

[50] John F. O'Rourke, "Field and Laboratory: The Decision Making Behavior of Family Groups in Two Experimental Conditions," *Sociometry,* vol. 27, pp. 422–435 (Dec. 1963).

[51] See, for example, Lewis A. Berey and Richard W. Pollay, "The Influencing Role of the Child in Family Decision Making," *J. Marketing Research,* vol. 5, pp. 70–72 (Feb. 1968).

[52] William D. Wells, "Children as Consumers," in Joseph Newman (ed.), *On Knowing the Consumer* (New York: Wiley, 1966), pp. 138–139.

and research approaches sufficiently comprehensive to account for their influence have not appeared in the public literature and therefore need to be designed and tested.

Respondent Selection

In measuring role structures it is necessary to decide which member(s) of the nuclear family should be asked about the influence of family members in purchasing decisions. The respondent selection decision is important since the reported influence of family members often varies considerably depending on which family members are interviewed.

The most common approach is to interview wives, yet there is disagreement concerning the extent to which they can accurately report purchase influence. Some researchers have found a substantial or acceptable similarity between husbands' and wives' responses.[53] But others have found that the percentage of couples whose responses agree averages only slightly more than 50 percent.[54]

Weighing the evidence, it seems that the responses of husbands and wives are very similar on an aggregate basis but dissimilar on a within-family basis. In other words, within-family differences tend to cancel out at an aggregate level.

This suggests that the questioning of one spouse is sufficient for those who want data only about aggregate purchase influence. ("What percentage of husbands decide about what make of car to buy?")[55] Pretesting is recommended to make certain that the single spouse accurately reports for the family.[56]

On the other hand, if the researcher uses purchase influence as a segmenting variable or as a prelude to further research, then questioning one spouse is not sufficient since differences within the family become important.[57] In this case it is necessary to interview both spouses independently and concurrently.

The appropriate procedure for resolving husband–wife differences has still not been determined. One researcher suggests that the role structure should be the unweighted mean of each spouse's replies.[58]

[53] Blood and Wolfe, *op. cit.,*[21] p. 273; Wolgast, *op. cit.,*[18] p. 153; David M. Heer, "Husband and Wife Perceptions of Family Power Structure," *Marriage and Family Living*, vol. 36, pp. 65–67 (Feb. 1962).

[54] Robert Ferber, "On the Reliability of Purchase Influence Studies," *J. Marketing*, vol. 19, pp. 225–232 (Jan. 1955); John Scanzoni, "A Note on the Sufficiency of Wife Responses in Family Research," *Pacific Sociological Rev.*, vol. 8, pp. 109–115 (Fall 1965).

[55] Harry L. Davis, "Measurement of Husband–Wife Influence in Consumer Purchase Decisions," *J. Marketing Research*, vol. 8, pp. 305–312 (Aug. 1971).

[56] Donald H. Granbois and Ronald P. Willett, "Equivalence of Family Role Measures Based on Husband and Wife Data," *J. Marriage and the Family*, vol. 32, pp. 68–72 (1970).

[57] Davis, *op. cit.*[55]

[58] Shirley A. Starr, "Obtaining Household Opinions from a Single Respondent," "*Public Opinion Quart.*, vol. 27, p. 391 (Fall 1953).

Interviewing

It has been demonstrated that the sex of the interviewer or observer influences the roles husbands and wives say they play in a purchase situation.[59] To overcome this bias, either self-administered questionnaires should be used or the sex of the observer should be randomly assigned to respondents.

SUMMARY

As a primary group, the family is perhaps the ultimate in face-to-face inter-action, and from the individual consumer's point of view it differs from larger reference groups in that these family members must satisfy their unique and joint consumption needs from a common and relatively fixed amount of financial resources. As a consequence of these and other factors, family influences affect individual personality characteristics, attitudes, evaluative criteria, and consumption patterns, and these influences change as the individual proceeds through the family life cycle.

Family role structures—or the behavior of nuclear family members at each stage in the decision-making process—are of fundamental importance to marketers. Types of role structures, determinants of role structures, and methods of measuring role structures were analyzed, thereby laying the foundation for the discussion of the influence of role structures on consumer decision processes as presented in Part V.

REVIEW AND DISCUSSION QUESTIONS

1. What is meant by the term "family?" What type of family is most relevant in the study of consumer behavior?

2. From an individual's point of view, how does the family differ from larger reference groups?

3. According to the text, a family is a *mediating* social system. What does this mean and of what importance is it?

4. Many students of consumer behavior maintain that the family rather than the individuals should be the unit of analysis. What are the advantages and disadvantages of using the family as the unit of analysis?

5. In a given purchase situation, assuming that the motives of other family members are operative, how would marketing strategy differ depending on whether the motives of other family members are compatible with an individual's motives? Using an actual product of your own choice, compare and contrast the types of marketing strategies that could be used when motive compatibility prevails as opposed to when it does not.

---

[59] William F. Kenkel, "Sex of Observer and Spousal Roles in Decision-Making," *Marriage and Family Living*, vol. 23, pp. 185–186 (May 1951).

6. A major manufacturer of household carpeting observes that in the purchase of carpeting the attitudes of several family members are often operative but incompatible. What type(s) of marketing strategy should be followed?

7. What is meant by a family role structure?

8. What influence does family role structure have on marketing strategy?

9. Family role structures can be used to describe the general pattern of household decision making or the pattern of decision making for a specific product. Which type should a marketer be interested in? Why?

10. The text stated that sophisticated role-structure studies need to focus on the influence of family members at each stage in the decision-making process rather than simply on the purchase. Why? Give examples of how purchase role structures may be misleading to a marketer.

The Nature and Influence of Individual Predispositions

The model of motivation and behavior discussed in Chapter 3 is now followed systematically in the remainder of the book. This part has as its purpose the discussion of the components of the central control unit. These predispositions interact to perform two vitally important functions: (1) filtration of stimulus inputs in information processing and (2) control and direction of behavior. These functions are discussed at length in Chapter 8. A considerable body of evidence is reviewed to show that the consumer, by and large, sees and hears what he wants to see and hear. The resulting implications for marketing planning are enormous, as will become apparent in later chapters.

Chapter 9 is addressed to learning processes. Clearly no one chapter can do justice to this vast topic, but the reader is introduced to a number of theories and concepts which are elaborated in succeeding chapters. Moreover, learning is of such importance in the study of general psychology that an awareness of the main variables and research generalizations is valuable in understanding human behavior in any area of activity.

The formation and function of attitudes is the subject of Chapters 10 and 11. Attitudes consist of ratings of alternatives along important attributes or dimensions called evaluative criteria. Hence the role and measurement of evaluative criteria is considered first in Chapter 10. Chapter 11 continues the discussion with a focus on attitude theory and measurement. The all-encompassing question of whether or not attitude change is a valid marketing goal is evaluated at length. Later chapters (14 and 15) review methods of attitude change.

This part ends with an analysis of personality influences on consumer behavior in Chapter 12. Personality has been the subject of considerable research in marketing for many years, most of which has not met the expectation of those involved. It now appears, however, that certain types of measures can provide highly useful information for marketing strategy. Hence this chapter provides some strategic insights which at one time were not thought to be possible.

CHAPTER 8

THE CENTRAL CONTROL UNIT: ITS NATURE AND FUNCTION

The central control unit (CCU) represented in Figure 8.1 is the basis of man's rational processes. It functions to shape individual behavior in two crucial ways: (1) by control and interpretation of the information received through the senses from the outside world and (2) by direction of consumer actions. As a result it is necessary to understand these two functions before examining the role of individual dispositions in more depth. This chapter lays the basis for much of the later discussion, especially that in Part IV.

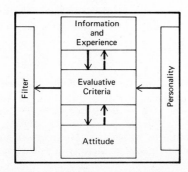

Figure 8.1   CENTRAL CONTROL UNIT

INFORMATION PROCESSING

Information processing is one of man's most significant activities. His senses are constantly besieged with stimuli, and complex mechanisms exist to interpret sensory information and extract content. It is the purpose of this section to describe the process by which man "makes sense" of his world.

Cognitive Processes

Information processing usually is referred to by the more encompassing term "cognition" which means ". . . all the processes by which the sensory input is transformed, reduced, elaborated, stored, recovered and used."[1] As the expanded model in Figure 8.2 depicts, the stages in this activity include (1) exposure, (2) attention, (3) comprehension, and (4) retention.[2] Of central importance is the filtering process within the CCU, because it serves to regulate those stimuli which receive intensive analysis and storage within long-term or permanent memory.

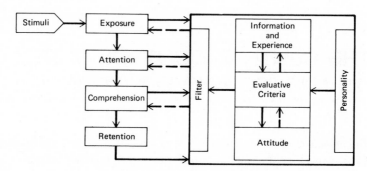

Figure 8.2. INFORMATION PROCESSING WITHIN CENTRAL CONTROL UNIT

The filter is now thought to contain a short-term memory unit in which incoming information is stored while it receives preliminary interpretation.[3] Neisser refers to short-term storage as *iconic* and *echoic memory.*[4] Iconic memory is the persistence of visual impressions for at most one second after the stimulus itself has terminated. The similar process with auditory stimuli is echoic memory.

---

[1] U. Neisser, *Cognitive Psychology* (New York: Appleton, 1966), p. 4.

[2] This conception is similar to that proposed by W. J. McGuire, "Personality and Susceptibility to Social Influence," in E. F. Borgatta and W. W. Lambert (eds.), *Handbook of Personality Theory and Research* (Chicago: Rand McNally, 1968).

[3] Neisser, *op. cit.;*[1] also D. A. Norman, *Memory and Attention* (New York: Wiley, 1969); D. A. Norman, "Toward a Theory of Memory and Attention," *Psychological Rev.,* vol. 75, pp. 522–536 (1968).

[4] Neisser, *op. cit.,*[1] esp. chap. 2.

Far more stimuli receive this preattentive processing than actually enter into memory. The consumer's attention might be attracted, for example, by a newspaper advertisement simply because it is the only four color stimulus in an otherwise all black and white medium. What he does with it, however, is entirely dependent upon further processing within the filter, at which time the input is analyzed for the extent of its pertinence to him.

All of the dispositions within the CCU interact within the filter during the second-stage analysis for pertinence. Those inputs which pass this critical screening are the subject of the individual's attention.[5] In other words, attention (or the focalization of consciousness[6]) is the first stage of filter output. It was previously thought that the central nervous system filter acted to prevent entry of unwanted stimuli to the senses,[7] but this view is no longer widely held.[8]

The filter also works at all stages of the information-processing effort as the diagram in Figure 8.2 indicates. Therefore, attention does not guarantee comprehension, and comprehension does not guarantee retention.

The implications of this process will be discussed at length later, but it is worth noting that the marketer's greatest problem generally is not in getting exposure to his message. That requires careful media selection. The real difficulty lies in designing messages in such a way that the filter is not activated to prevent further processing or distort the input. Generally this will require that the message content be compatible with the individual's dispositions. For example, a message trying to make a smoker out of a confirmed nonsmoker probably is destined to failure. It would not be especially difficult to select media to expose many people, but the individual's antismoking sentiments probably would activate the CCU filter and prevent effective entry of the message.

Exposure

Exposure occurs when an individual is confronted with a stimulus in such a way that one or more of his senses will be activated. Each of the senses transforms resulting stimulus energy so that it is received by the brain in the form of nerve impulses which generate the sensations of sight, hearing, smell, touch, and taste.[9]

One of the difficulties which must be faced when using the mass media is the large amount of evidence documenting that people selectively expose them-

---

[5] Norman, "Toward a Theory of Memory and Attention," *op. cit.*,[3] pp. 526–527.

[6] W. James, *The Principles of Psychology*, vol. 1 (New York: Henry Holt, 1890), pp. 403–404.

[7] D. F. Broadbent, *Perception and Communication* (New York: Pergamon, 1958).

[8] See, for example, A. Treisman, "Verbal Cues, Language and Meaning in Attention," *Amer. J. Psychology*, vol. 77, pp. 206–241 (1964); J. Deutsch and D. Deutsch, "Attention: Some Theoretical Considerations," *Psychological Rev.*, vol. 70, pp. 80–90 (1963); Neisser, *op. cit.*;[1] Norman, *op. cit.*;[3] N. Moray, *Selective Processes in Vision and Hearing* (London: Hutchinson, 1969), chap. 10.

[9] For a useful but technical source on sensation, see S. S. Stevens (ed.), *Handbook of Experimental Psychology* (New York: Wiley, 1951), chap. 3–11.

selves to stimuli. This phenomenon seems to be especially pronounced in the case of persuasive communication. Some of the earlier evidence came from the 1940 presidential campaign in which it was found that "exposure to political communications during the presidential campaign is concentrated in the same group of people not spread among the people at large."[10] Interest in the election apparently was the motivation for exposure to some campaign propaganda and avoidance of others. Another representative finding is that a largely Republican audience watched a 20-hour telethon intended for non-Republicans.[11]

Selective exposure also has been discovered outside of the field of politics. In one study, for example, there was a distinct bias in the audience for articles alleging a relationship between smoking and cancer. Data showed that 67 percent of the nonsmokers claimed high readership of the articles, versus only 44 percent of smokers.[12]

From these data it is reasonable to expect exposure of only a subset of all possible prospects any time an attempt is made to influence the consumer. Will the consumer then simply avoid any advertisements or other messages which he considers to be irrelevant? If so, why? There are many authorities who would argue affirmatively that the individual censors his stimulus input to avoid disturbance of existing beliefs and dispositions. This censoring is now referred to as "maintenance of cognitive consistency."[13] For example, Katz argues as follows:

> ... (a) that an individual self-censors his intake of communications so as to shield his beliefs and practices from attack; (b) that an individual seeks out communications which support his beliefs and practices; and (c) that the latter is particularly true when the beliefs or practices in question have undergone attack or the individual has otherwise been made less confident of them.[14]

Not all authorities agree, however, that selective exposure is a motivated act. Sears argues that the evidence only serves to document that there is an attitudinal bias in the composition of the audiences studied. They present the alternative point of view that other factors shape audience composition such as

[10] P. F. Lazarsfeld, B. B. Berelson, and H. Gaudet, "Radio and the Printed Page as Factors in Political Opinion and Voting," in W. Schramm (ed.), *Mass Communications* (Urbana, Ill.: University of Illinois Press, 1949), p. 484.

[11] W. Schramm and R. F. Carter, "Effectiveness of a Political Telethon," *Public Opinion Quart.*, vol. 23, pp. 121–126 (1960).

[12] C. Cannell and J. C. MacDonald, "The Impact of Health News on Attitudes and Behavior," *Journalism Quart.*, vol. 33, pp. 315–323 (1956).

[13] See, for example, J. Mills, "Interest in Supporting and Discrepant Information," in R. P. Abelson, E. Aronson, W. J. McGuire, T. M. Newcomb, M. J. Rosenberg, and P. H. Tannenbaum (eds.), *Theories of Cognitive Consistency: A Sourcebook* (Chicago: Rand McNally, 1968), pp. 771–776; J. E. Singer, "Consistency as a Stimulus Processing Mechanism," in Abelson *et al., op. cit.*,[13] pp. 337–342.

[14] E. Katz, "On Reopening the Question of Selectivity in Exposure to Mass Communications," in Abelson *et al., op. cit.*,[13] p. 789.

education and background.[15] In other words, a predominance of Chevrolet owners in the audience of a Chevrolet commercial on the Bonanza show may not represent attitudinal bias at all but may be a function of other considerations. Sears would not deny that people process information selectively, but he feels that this occurs *after* exposure, *not before*.

Here, then, is the heart of the issue; some maintain that there is motivated avoidance of persuasion, others claim that there are other explanations for selectivity. Probably both points of view are right in that no one explanation can account for all instances. In any event, selective exposure is a problem that any communicator must contend with, because the actual audience almost always is less than the desired audience.

Attention

Once exposure has occurred, stimuli enter temporary storage within the CCU filter in the form of iconic or echoic memory. Then there is preattentive processing followed by analysis for pertinence.

Preattentive Processing The first step in preattentive processing is triggering of the orientation reaction—the response of an individual when presented with a new stimulus.[16] It may take the form of a turning in direction, a growing sense of alertness, and so on. Its function is to prepare the organism to contend with novel stimuli. Activities which were previously underway are stopped, and the system is mobilized for action. It has some specific additional physical manifestations:[17]

(1) An increase in the sensitivity of the sensory organs. This occurs as pupil dilation and photomechanical changes which lead to lowered reaction times for stimuli.

(2) Changes in skeletal muscles which direct the sense organs. Turning the head is an example.

(3) Changes in general skeletal musculature in the form of increased muscle tone and greater readiness for activity.

(4) Generation of a state of arousal as indicated by electroencephalogram scores.

(5) Elevation in galvanic skin response accompanied by a reduction in heart rate.

At this stage stimuli receive a preliminary analysis for meaning based largely on such physical properties as loudness, pitch, and so on. The span of

---

[15] D. O. Sears, "The Paradox of De Facto Selective Exposure Without Preferences for Supportive Information," in Abelson *et al., op. cit.,*[13] pp. 777–787.

[16] R. Lynn, *Attention Arousal and the Orientation Reaction* (Oxford: Pergamon, 1966).

[17] Lynn, *op. cit.*[16]

apprehension appears to be limited to that which can be synthesized and stored while iconic or echoic memory lasts—usually one second or less. Hence there is no real resolution at this point of such subtle aspects as emotional content or fine structure.

This preliminary analysis is assisted by learned tendencies to organize and categorize stimuli based on physical properties. The human being, for example, exhibits a tendency to perceive an object against its background; the resulting interaction between object (figure) and background (ground) lends a predictable element which helps in making a correct judgment.

For one illustration of stimulus influences examine Figure 8.3. Does it contain rows of dots or columns of dots? Most people will report seeing rows, for the reason that they are closer together in the horizontal direction. As a result, they are identified as being in greater *proximity*. It is natural, of course, to assume that objects in proximity somehow belong together, and this type of stimulus organization induces a pervasive response pattern.[18]

Figure 8.3   AN ILLUSTRATION OF PROXIMITY

An understanding of stimulus influences can be of great use to an artist or designer. Through skillful use of these principles he can be nearly certain of producing a desired esthetic effect when the stimulus is received.

Analysis for Pertinence   The further processing of the stimulus to determine pertinence for the individual is referred to by Neisser as *focal attention*.[19] Whereas preattentive processes are almost automatic, focal attention requires an internally directed scan. Those stimuli which are passed on through the filter are those which are seen to be of importance as the following discussion indicates.

(1) **The Influence of Need States**   It is well documented that both physical and psychological need will affect stimulus processing through the CCU filter. For example, hungry people are more likely to give food-related responses when

---

[18]   For more examples, see W. N. Dember, *The Psychology of Perception* (New York: Holt, Rinehart and Winston, 1961).

[19]   Neisser, *op. cit.*,[1] pp. 102–104.

ambiguous stimuli are seen or heard.[20] In another experiment those with a strong affiliation motive identified a greater number of pictures of persons as standing out most clearly in a larger grouping of pictures than did those with a weaker affiliation drive.[21] This could mean that the hungry consumer will more readily notice food advertisements than his counterpart. Similarly, an appeal to social acceptance through avoidance of body odor will most likely be of greatest effectiveness with those who fear social rejection.

(2) **Perceptual Defense and Vigilance** It has been found rather consistently that values influence the speed of recognition for value-related words. For example, words that connote important values often are perceived more readily, and this form of selective attention has come to be called *perceptual vigilance.*[22] Although this area of research has been plagued with methodological difficulties, it is generally accepted that vigilance does occur.[23] It would seem reasonable, as a result, to hypothesize that preferred brand names will be recognized more quickly than nonpreferred brands. This was confirmed in two studies, and this finding may shed some light on why certain advertisements are noticed more readily than others.[24] The key may lie in the extent to which the brand name is featured.

The opposite of perceptual vigilance is *perceptual defense,* whereby recognition of threatening or low-valued stimuli is delayed or even avoided altogether.[25] Presumably the pertinence for the individual is negative, and there is evidence that barriers can be raised to prevent or inhibit attention to the stimulus.[26] It is possible that consumers avoid promotion for nonpreferred brands in this manner, although there is no direct evidence on this point.

(3) **Maintenance of Cognitive Consistency** The elements within the CCU interact to provide an individual's "map of his world." Attitudes are especially important in this context. As was mentioned earlier, there is a demonstrated human tendency to resist changes in this map which is referred to as maintenance of cognitive consistency. It is known, for example, that attitudes resist change to

---

[20] J. W. Atkinson and D. C. McClelland, "The Projective Expression of Needs: II. The Effect of Different Intensities of the Hunger Drive on Thematic Apperception," *J. Experimental Psychology,* vol. 38, pp. 643-658 (1948).

[21] J. W. Atkinson and E. L. Walker, "The Affiliation Motive and Perceptual Sensitivity to Faces," *J. Abnormal and Social Psychology,* vol. 53, pp. 38–41 (1956).

[22] L. Postman and B. Schneider, "Personal Values, Visual Recognition, and Recall," *Psychological Rev.,* vol. 58, pp. 271–284 (1951).

[23] D. E. Broadbent, "Word-Frequency Effect and Response Bias," *Psychological Rev.,* vol. 74, pp. 1–15 (1967).

[24] Homer E. Spence and James F. Engel, "The Impact of Brand Preference on the Perception of Brand Names: A Laboratory Analysis," in P. R. McDonald (ed.), *Marketing Involvement in Society and the Economy* (Chicago: Amer. Marketing Assoc., 1970), pp. 267-271.

[25] D. P. Spence, "Subliminal Perception and Perceptual Defense: Two Sides of a Single Problem," *Behavioral Science,* vol. 12, pp. 183–193 (1967).

[26] This literature is thoroughly reviewed in Spence, *op. cit.*[25]

the extent that they are strongly held. This cognitive structure, therefore, functions to enable the individual to cope with his environment, and it is not surprising that we strive to maintain this organization.[27]

For purposes of illustration, assume that a person has arrived at the conclusion that the addition of fluoride to water can be harmful. He then is exposed to a radio commercial while driving to work which urges him to vote for fluoridation at the next election. He is fully capable of screening this stimulus out once it has received preattentive processing. It would be rejected on the grounds of pertinence, for the reason that it could introduce a state of inconsistency which is psychologically uncomfortable.[28]

Selective Attention to Marketing Stimuli Is the impact of marketing stimuli, especially advertisements and other attempts to persuade, affected by selective attention? The answer is overwhelmingly affirmative. Bogart notes that "Advertising research data accurately reflect the fact that many messages register negative impressions or no impressions at all on many of the people who are exposed to the sight or sound of them."[29] The consumer, for example, can observe an advertisement with the corner of his eye, engage in preattentive processing, and then redirect attention accordingly.[30]

There are many reasons why selective attention takes place. The most probable explanation lies in the fact that consumers daily are bombarded with more commercial stimuli than they can process. Estimates of the number of commercial messages confronting the average individual each day range from 250 to 3000. It is quite possible that a given message will not capture attention simply because it is "lost in the noise."

Also it cannot be denied that most commercial stimuli are of low interest and relevance to the consumer. He might not go beyond preattentive processing because of the existence of a *boredom barrier*. Bogart's analysis of this issue is highly relevant:

> . . . a cornerstone of communications research has long been the notion of selective perception, the idea that people tend to pay attention to messages that support their predispositions and to block out incongruent messages. . . . The problem must be posed quite differently in the case of messages that arouse no contradictory prior judgments, simply because they arouse no reactions at all. Perhaps the main contribution that advertising research can make to this study of communications is in the domain of inattention to low-key stimuli, as exemplified by the ever increasing flow of unsolicited and unwanted mes-

---

[27] For a cogent analysis, see E. E. Jones and H. D. Gerard, *Foundations of Social Psychology* (New York: Wiley, 1967), chap. 7.

[28] M. J. Rosenberg, "Inconsistency Arousal and Reduction in Attitude Change," in I. D. Steiner and M. Fishbein (eds.), *Current Studies in Social Psychology* (New York: Holt, Rinehart and Winston, 1965), pp. 123–124.

[29] Leo Bogart, "Where Does Advertising Research Go From Here?" Reprinted from the *J. Advertising Research,* vol. 9, p. 6 (1969), by the Advertising Research Foundation Inc.

[30] Leo Bogart, *Strategy in Advertising* (New York: Harcourt, 1967), chap. 5.

sages to which people are subjected in our overcommunicative civilization.[31]

Finally, maintenance of cognitive consistency is another possible cause of selective attention. The consumer may be committed to a brand or store and hence resist a challenge to his preference. This is most likely when a large outlay of funds has accompanied the purchase or when the consumer's ego is somehow involved with this action and preference. Admittedly, however, this tends to be the exception rather than the rule.

Comprehension

The fact that a stimulus has received focal attention and analysis for pertinence does not guarantee that it will be comprehended correctly. The filter within the CCU also can function to categorize the meaning of the stimulus in a way which deviates from objective reality. There are many ways in which this takes place, but two have received special prominence in the literature of the behavioral sciences: (1) distortion of physical stimulus properties and (2) miscomprehension of communication message content.

Distortion of Physical Stimulus Properties   A study was undertaken in 1947 which has proved to be a landmark because of its influence on later research.[32] It was discovered that children from the lowest economic classes overestimate the size of coins. The assumption is that economic deprivation affects the process of perception. There is contradictory evidence on this subject, but most authorities now accept that need and other personal characteristics can affect the outcome of cognitive processes.[33]

Many relevant studies have also been undertaken using a distorted room so designed that it appears normal in its proportions when viewed from a certain perspective.[34] One interesting finding is that people standing in the room are seen as distorted rather than the room itself, apparently because the effects of past experience lead the individual to the conclusion that a room cannot be distorted in this manner. This tendency to see people as being distorted, however, is completely absent when a married person views his or her spouse. The emotional relationship between partners thus affects cognitive processing.

This type of distortion frequently occurs in consumer decision making. A soft-drink company, for example, introduced a new product which fell far short

---

[31]   Bogart, *op. cit.*,[29] p. 6.

[32]   J. S. Bruner and Cecile C. Goodman, "Value and Need as Organizing Factors in Perception," *J. Abnormal and Social Psychology*, vol. 42, pp. 33–44 (1947).

[33]   Noel Jenkin, "Affective Processes in Perception," *Psychological Bull.*, vol. 54, pp. 100–127 (1957).

[34]   W. J. Wittreich, "Visual Perception and Personality," *Scientific American*, vol. 200, pp. 56–60 (1959).

of its sales potential.[35] A taste test was conducted in which samples of this brand and competitive brands were compared with and without labels. The findings disclosed that the brand under analysis received excellent ratings in comparison with others when it was unlabeled. The ratings were completely reversed, however, when labels were in place. It thus appears that the product image, name, or some other consideration affected taste ratings. As a result the promotional program was totally revamped while product formulation was left unchanged.

Miscomprehension of Communication Message Content   The findings on this topic are extensive, and evidence is examined under the following headings: (1) basic evidence and (2) the mechanisms of miscomprehension.

(1) **Basic Evidence**   Two early studies provided clues that the CCU can function to bring about miscomprehension,[36] but even up until the time of World War II this possibility was largely overlooked. Hovland, Lumsdaine, and Sheffield, for example, pointed out that the Army assumed that exposing soldiers to information about the war and its background would produce a greater desire to fight.[37] They report data showing that there was widespread misunderstanding of the content of these messages.

One possible explanation is that everyone has certain expectations about the content of the stimuli confronting him, and it is known that the reaction often reflects the expectation rather than the stimulus itself.[38] For example, a liquid cold remedy was introduced in test market in the attempt to make inroads into the market share of Vick's Nyquil. The advertisements used were highly similar to those employed by Nyquil, and there was considerable evidence that consumers thought they were viewing Nyquil ads. They were familiar with Nyquil and hence miscomprehended the competitor's promotional efforts.

It is also likely that miscomprehension occurs to prevent disturbance of existing preferences and dispositions. There was a widely publicized series of television debates between Kennedy and Nixon in 1960, and the results are intriguing. It appears that voting intentions were not changed to any significant extent.[39] Although Kennedy's image apparently was improved somewhat, the primary effect was adjustment of the images of the candidates to suit the political preferences of viewers.

(2) **Mechanisms of Miscomprehension**   Some of the mechanisms used for this purpose were documented by Berelson, Lazarsfeld, and McPhee:

---

[35]   "Twink: Perception of Taste," in R. D. Blackwell, J. F. Engel, and D. T. Kollat, *Cases in Consumer Behavior* (New York: Holt, Rinehart and Winston, 1969), pp. 38–43.

[36]   See, for example, A. L. Edwards, "Political Frames of Reference as a Factor Influencing Recognition," *J. Abnormal and Social Psychology*, vol. 36, pp. 34–50 (1941).

[37]   C. I. Hovland, A. A. Lumsdaine, and F. D. Sheffield, *Experiments on Mass Communication*, vol. 3 (Princeton, N.J.: Princeton University Press, 1949).

[38]   Norman, *op. cit.*[3]

[39]   K. Lang and Gladys E. Lang, "Ordeal by Debate: Viewer Reactions," *Public Opinion Quart.*, vol. 25, pp. 277–288 (1961).

> In the course of the campaign . . . strength of party support influ-
> ences the perception of political issues. The more intensely one holds
> a vote position, the more likely he is to see the political environment
> as favorable to himself, as confirming his own beliefs. He is less likely
> to perceive uncongenial and contradictory events or points of view and
> hence presumably less likely to revise his own original position. In this
> manner perception can play a major role in the spiraling effect of
> political reinforcement.[40]

In this study it was discovered that strong party members consistently comprehended the stand of a preferred candidate on issues as being in harmony with
their own viewpoints, regardless of reality. Conversely, those less interested in
partisan politics showed a reduced tendency to misinterpret a candidate's stand.

Some of the most clear-cut examples of mechanisms used for miscomprehension are reported by Cooper and Jahoda.[41] They analyzed reactions to a
persuasive cartoon featuring "Mr. Biggot." The purpose of this cartoon was to
induce prejudice recipients to reject their prejudices by avoiding identification
with Mr. Biggot. Yet many persons missed the point by ridiculing him, transform-
ing him into a foreigner, making him appear inferior, and otherwise sidetracking
the issue to avoid threat to their own prejudice. Others admitted the principle
of the message but claimed that it did not depict the situation correctly or claimed
that one is entitled to his own prejudices. Moreover, others interpreted the
message in various ways which were satisfactory to them. Finally, others claimed
that they "didn't get the point," presumably because the message was too difficult.

Another common means of avoiding the implications of a message is to
reject both the source and content as being biased. This subject is discussed in
more detail in a later chapter, but an example will help to clarify the ways in
which avoidance takes place. In one landmark study, it was hypothesized that
favorable reactions to a communication will increase as the distance decreases
between the viewpoint of the recipient and that advocated in the message.[42]
Opinions were measured toward the controversial issue of repeal of prohibition
in Oklahoma, and subsequent communications were administered that differed
from subjects' own positions on the topic in varying degrees. When the discrepancy was large (that is, the message was outside of the individual's latitude of
acceptable positions), the message was perceived as less fair, less informed, less
grammatical, less logical, and so on. Similar tendencies of this type have been
reported by others.[43]

---

[40] B. R. Berelson, P. F. Lazarsfeld, and W. N. McPhee, *Voting* (Chicago: University
of Chicago Press, 1954), p. 223.

[41] Eunice Cooper and Marie Jahoda, "The Evasion of Propaganda: How Prejudiced
People Respond to Anti-Prejudice Propaganda," *J. Psychology*, vol. 23, pp. 15–25 (1947).

[42] C. I. Hovland, O. J. Harvey, and M. Sherif, "Assimilation and Contrast Effects in
Reactions to Communication and Attitude Change," *J. Abnormal and Social Psychology*, vol.
55, pp. 244–252 (1957).

[43] See, for example, M. Manis, "The Interpretation of Opinion Statements as a
Function of Recipient Attitude," *J. Abnormal and Social Psychology*, vol. 60, pp. 340–344
(1960).

Although the persuasive intent of a communication may be interfered with, the communication of facts often is unaffected. Baur, for example, reported that an intensive propaganda campaign by a watershed association changed knowledge and awareness without affecting opinions.[44] Similarly, it was concluded that the major result of orientation film intended to influence willingness of soldiers to fight during World War II was a noticeable gain in specific information.[45] To cite one example, soldiers recalled much about how Britons were able to withstand Nazi bombings, but opinions of the British as allies were largely unchanged.

Retention

Not everything that is attended to and comprehended will be retained in long-term memory, because memory is known to be highly selective. Bartlett reports the interesting story of the Paramount Chief of the Swazi people in Africa who visited Great Britain for the first time.[46] The only thing he could remember clearly from his trip was the uplifted hand of the policemen signaling traffic to stop. This gesture was interpreted by him as the traditional sign of friendship of his people. Similarly, it is reported that a Swazi herdsman could describe in exact detail the cattle purchased by his Scottish employer one year before. In both cases Bartlett concluded that these details were remembered because of their importance to the tribesmen involved. In other words, memory as well as attention and comprehension are directly affected by the *pertinence* of stimuli to the individual.

Stimulus content will fade from short-term memory unless it undergoes *rehearsal*.[47] Rehearsal, while not well understood, appears to be a type of inner speech, and memory capacity, in part, is a function of the difficulty of rehearsing many items at once.[48] It is quite probable that the only material which receives rehearsal is that which is judged during information processing as having the greatest pertinence to the individual's needs and existing dispositions. As a result, material which is felt to be threatening to cognitive consistency can easily be kept from permanent memory.

Selective Retention of Communication Messages The evidence on retention of communication content is contradictory. Some maintain that there is

---

[44] E. J. Baur, "Opinion Change in a Public Controversy," *Public Opinion Quart.,* vol. 24, pp. 212–226 (1962).

[45] Hovland *et al., op. cit.*[37]

[46] F. C. Bartlett, "Social Factors in Recall," in Eleanor E. Maccoby, T. M. Newcomb, and E. L. Hartley (eds.), *Readings in Social Psychology*, 3rd ed. (New York: Holt, Rinehart and Winston, 1958), pp. 47–53.

[47] George Sperling, "Successive Approximations to a Model for Short-Term Memory," in A. F. Sanders (ed.), *Attention and Performance* (Amsterdam: North-Holland, 1967), pp. 286–292.

[48] Nancy C. Waugh and D. A. Norman, "Primary Memory," *Psychological Rev.,* vol. 62, pp. 92–93 (1965).

selective forgetting of material which contradicts existing attitudes. One experimenter found a consistent tendency toward forgetting aspects of the New Deal of the 1930s which conflicted with a person's political leanings.[49] Similarly, recall of a statement appears to be a function of a judgment with respect to its truth—the more it is seen as being true, the greater the probability of recall. Finally, Levine and Murphy reported results that showed recall to be more accurate when the learned material was consistent with the individual's initial bias toward the subject under consideration.[50] Others have been unable to replicate these findings, however.[51] The most defensible conclusion at this point is that a probable attitude–memory relationship does exist but functions only under certain conditions which are not well understood.[52]

Selective Retention of Marketing Stimuli There is no question that marketing stimuli are rapidly forgotten after initial exposure. For example, only 24 percent could name at least one advertised product on a television show, fewer than one third could identify a commercial appearing within less than two minutes prior to an interview, and residual recall of commercial content after a longer period levels off at 12 percent or less.[53] The data in Table 8.1 reveal even more the extent of forgetting in five product categories.

The boredom barrier mentioned earlier is the most probable explanation of these findings. Advertising stimuli, by and large, have only marginal pertinence for the consumer in most viewing or listening situations. Thus they will not receive the rehearsal which is necessary for entrance into long-term memory. Those advertisements which have shown the greatest promotional effectiveness, however, produce significantly higher recall.[54]

It is also possible that existing brand or product preferences are protected through failure to recall contradictory stimuli. Thus prevention of cognitive inconsistency could be another explanation, but it is likely to function in only a minority of situations.

---

[49] A. L. Edwards, "Political Frames of Reference as a Factor Influencing Recognition," *J. Abnormal and Social Psychology*, vol. 51, pp. 34–50 (1955).

[50] J. M. Levine and G. Murphy, "The Learning and Forgetting of Controversial Material," in T. M. Newcomb and E. L. Hartley (eds.), *Readings in Social Psychology* (New York: Henry Holt, 1947), pp. 108–115.

[51] A. G. Greenwald and J. S. Sakumura, "Attitude in Selective Learning: Where are the Phenomena of Yesteryear?" *J. Personality and Social Psychology*, vol. 7, pp. 387–397 (1967); Patricia Waly and S. W. Cook, "Attitude as a Determinant of Learning and Memory: A Failure to Confirm," *J. Personality and Social Psychology*, vol. 4, pp. 280–288 (1966).

[52] J. C. Brigham and S. W. Cook, "The Influence of Attitude on the Recall of Controversial Material: A Failure to Confirm," *J. Experimental Social Psychology*, vol. 5, pp. 240–243 (1969).

[53] Bogart, *op. cit.*,[30] chap. 5.

[54] V. Appel, "On Advertising Wear-Out," *J. Advertising Research*, vol. 11, pp. 11–13 (1971).

Table 8.1 REGISTRATION OF FEATURED IDEA; RECALL AFTER 24 HOURS

	Magazines		Television	
		Recall		Recall
	Number	Range	Number	Range
	of Ads	%	of Ads	(%)
Tires				
	13	0- 3.9	13	0- 3.9
	21	4- 7.9	5	4- 7.9
	11	8-11.9	5	8-11.9
	2	12-15.9	4	12-15.9
	3	16-19.9		
	2	24-27.9		
	2	28-31.9		
Automobiles				
	20	0- 1.9	49	0- 1.9
	33	2- 3.9	29	2- 3.9
	47	4- 5.9	19	4- 5.9
	27	6- 7.9	6	6- 7.9
	12	8- 9.9	4	8- 9.9
	7	10-11.9	2	10-11.9
	7	12-13.9	2	12-13.9
	1	14-15.9	4	14-15.9
	1	16-17.9	1	16
	1	18-19.9		
	3	20-21.9		
	3	22-23.9		
	1	24		
Life insurance				
	24	0- 1.9	8	0- 1.9
	23	2- 3.9	13	2- 3.9
	10	4- 5.9	7	4- 5.9
	2	6- 7.9	5	6- 7.9
	1	8- 9.9	3	8- 9.9
			1	10-11.9
			1	14-15.9
			1	18-19.9
			1	20-21.9
TV sets				
	5	0- 1.9	6	0- 1.9
	6	2- 3.9	9	2- 3.9
	4	4- 5.9	4	4- 5.9
	4	6- 7.9	3	6- 7.9
	3	8- 9.9	1	8- 9.9

Table 8.1 REGISTRATION OF
FEATURED IDEA; RECALL
AFTER 24 HOURS (*Continued*)

Magazines		Television	
	Recall		Recall
Number	Range	Number	Range
of Ads	(%)	of Ads	(%)
1	10-11.9	3	10-11.9
2	12-13.9	2	12-13.9
1	14-15.9	1	14-15.9
1	18-19.9	3	16-17.9
Aftershaves, colognes			
2	0- 3.9	7	0- 3.9
10	4- 7.9	4	4- 7.9
3	8-11.9	3	8-11.9
1	12-15.9	2	12-15.9
1	16-19.9	1	16-19.9
1	20-23.9	3	24-27

SOURCE: *Advertising Age,* p. 52 (Apr. 12,
1971). (Reprinted with permission
from the April 12, 1971 issue of
Advertising Age. Copyright 1971 by
Crain Communications, Inc.)

Subliminal Information Processing

Before concluding this section it is necessary to comment briefly on
whether or not people can be influenced to act in a certain way without their
awareness. The more technical term for this is *subliminal perception,* and it is
said to occur when stimuli are correctly processed when presented at a speed
which is below threshold (that is, faster than the point at which correct stimulus
identification occurs 50 percent of the time).[55]

A controversy arose many years ago when the words DRINK COKE
and EAT POPCORN were presumably flashed on a movie screen at speeds below
the thresholds of audience members.[56] The sales of Coca Cola allegedly increased
57.7 percent while sales of popcorn increased 18.1 percent. In reality, these findings have unanimously been dismissed as being invalid, and all attempts at
replication have failed. Nonetheless, the popular press sounded the alarm that it
is possible to influence the consumer without his awareness. If so, a serious
ethical issue is presented.

---

[55] Dember, *op. cit.,*[18] chap. 2.

[56] J. J. Bachrach, "The Ethics of Tachistoscopy," *Bull. Atomic Scientists,* vol. 15,
pp. 212–215 (1959).

Fortunately the critics' fears are without foundation. It is known that the processing of stimuli is largely unaffected when stimuli are presented at subliminal levels. One study showed that GSR scores (electroconductivity of the skin) respond before individuals can give verbal responses when they are presented with such taboo stimuli as swearwords.[57] Therefore, perceptual defense can function at subthreshold levels. Other studies have found the same effect, and one of the most conclusive demonstrates that GSR does not register at all when speed of exposure is so high that no perception is possible.[58] As a result, the individual apparently retains the ability to filter out unwanted stimuli right up to that point at which sensation itself is impossible.

Given these findings, it seems obvious that subliminal advertising cannot circumvent a person's natural defenses. Then there would appear to be no merit in using fragmentary stimuli and thereby increasing the probability that the message will not be seen or heard.

INFLUENCE OF BEHAVIOR

The second major function of the CCU is to direct and shape the individual's behavior. In this sense it is said that the dispositions within the CCU individually and collectively provide a *set to respond*.

To provide just one illustration, a strongly held brand preference can be a set to respond. The consumer who has found that a particular brand of coffee satisfies her husband's desires is not likely to purchase another brand when the need arises. Unless conditions somehow change (perhaps an entirely new product concept comes on the market), this preference will be maintained.

Much of the effort of a firm's marketing program is directed toward influencing or changing existing dispositions. The object might be to provide new information so that existing preferences and beliefs are seen as being inadequate. The vital question, of course, pertains to the extent to which these changes can be brought about.

The dispositions within the CCU fall into two main categories: (1) personality and (2) attitudinal. Personality, of course, is depicted in Figure 8.1 as an underlying variable. The remaining dispositions (information, evaluative criteria, and attitude) all are related in that an attitude is a rating along an evaluative criterion which, in turn, is based on information. There are real differences in the extent to which these dispositions can be changed as the following discussion indicates.

---

[57] E. McGinnies, "Emotionality and Perceptual Defense," *Psychological Rev.*, vol. 56, pp. 244–251 (1949).

[58] J. H. Voor, "Subliminal Perception and Subception," *J. Psychology*, vol. 41, pp. 437–458 (1956).

Personality

For marketing purposes, personality usually is measured by what has come to be known as AIO (attitude, interest, and opinion) measures. This type of scale effectively isolates some of the mainsprings of behavior, that is, basic motives, traits, and values. Such factors, of course, are resistant to change even through use of psychotherapy. Obviously this will not be a goal of the marketer.

Personality data, however, find growing use in marketing planning as discussion in Chapter 12 indicates. The advertiser, for example, is very interested in the types of people in media audiences, since clues are provided for design of messages. It is worthwhile to know that *Newsweek* readers differ from readers of *Time* in that they look more for security, worry about government and union power, read the Bible more, agree that hippies should be drafted, claim that they have old-fashioned tastes and habits, are concerned about health, and have a negative attitude toward advertising.[59] Obviously the *Newsweek* reader is likely to be more receptive to messages that are conservative in design and layout and that avoid "way out" colors and contemporary appeals.

Attitude

The AIO score measures general motives, values, and attitudes—those dispositions which affect a broad range of behavior. Attitude as it is used here, on the other hand, refers to the consumer's assessment of the utility of an alternative to satisfying his purchasing and consumption requirements as expressed in evaluative criteria.

Attitude change is a complex issue discussed at length in Chapters 11, 14, and 15, but two generalizations should be stated at this point. First, and most important, attitudes *can* be changed to the extent that they are not strongly held. When the opposite situation prevails there is a corresponding increase in the probability that the CCU filter will be activated to prevent disturbance of attitude structure. Second, all things being equal, a change in attitude will be reflected by a change in purchasing behavior. Attitudes are positively correlated with intentions, which, in turn, are positively correlated with behavior. Thus it may be concluded that attitude change is a valid marketing goal.

SUMMARY

The purpose of this chapter has been to clarify the two basic functions of the CCU: (1) information processing and (2) direction of behavior. The first function was discussed in detail to provide a grasp of the four phases in information processing: (1) exposure, (2) attention, (3) comprehension, and (4) retention.

---

[59] D. Tigert, "A Psychographic Profile of Magazine Audiences: An Investigation of Media's Climate," paper presented at the Consumer Research Workshop, Ohio State University (Aug. 1969).

It was pointed out that, following exposure, stimuli first receive a preattentive analysis followed by further processing to determine the pertinence of the stimulus for the individual in terms of his needs and dispositions. If this screening is positive, the stimulus can be said to have captured attention. Not all stimuli which capture attention are correctly comprehended, however, because of the further working of the CCU filter, and even fewer are retained in long-term memory. Thus each stage may be considered as a necessary but not sufficient condition for the following stage. It is apparent that the individual is highly selective in his information processing.

The CCU also functions to provide a directive influence on behavior. Certain of the stored dispositions such as personality must be accepted as given and adapted to accordingly. Others such as attitude can be changed, and there is a corresponding change in behavior. These issues were not discussed in depth since they provide the subject matter for the next four chapters.

REVIEW AND DISCUSSION QUESTIONS

1. Define the term "cognitive processes." What is the relevance for the study of consumer behavior?

2. Would a detailed knowledge of the neural pathways of the brain for optic sensations be of use to an advertising artist? to a researcher specializing in response to advertising? Discuss fully.

3. A reader's attention is attracted by a center-fold advertisement in a news magazine. The advertisement is in four colors and features the new model of a popular compact automobile. What does it mean to say that attention is attracted? What are the stages in this process? How might they have taken place? Is there anything the artists and writers can do to influence preattentive processing? Analysis for pertinence?

4. Assume that a housewife cannot recall seeing advertisements for any brand of hair spray other than her preferred brand, even though she had the opportunity in a given day to see 20 or more competing ads. What explanations can be given?

5. What is meant by the "boredom barrier?" What influence does it have on response to marketing stimuli?

6. A leading critic of advertising contends that advertising has the power to influence people to buy unwisely—to act in a way which they would not otherwise do. In other words, advertising is a tool for manipulation of the consumer. What would your response be to this criticism?

7. Under what conditions is it possible for perceptual defense to affect the perception of brand names?

8. Assume that you have been given the assignment to investigate the possibility of subliminal presentation of advertisements on television for canned soup. What problems would occur? What would happen if a similar attempt were to be made with advertisements designed to appear in women's magazines?

CHAPTER 9

LEARNING PROCESSES

The *dynamic* nature of a multimediation model of consumer decision making is its fundamental characteristic. Analysts of consumer behavior are not so much interested in a description of consumer decisions at a single point of time as they are interested in the process by which those decisions change and are influenced to change. The process of change is the essential reality of the model and is the focus of attention in this chapter.

THE NATURE OF LEARNING

The process of consumer buying is a learned process, as is nearly everything else that is a part of a consumer's life. The human species, unlike other animals, possesses an extremely high proportion of unused mental capacity at birth. He has very few instincts or innate response tendencies relative to lower animals. While this may be detrimental to man in the sense that he is helpless for a long period in his early years, it is favorable in that he has greater capacity for adaptation in response to changed survival conditions. More important to the understanding of consumer behavior, the great unused capacity at birth provides for the potential of much greater interpersonal variation in choice behavior than would be possible if man were born with a high proportion of his behavior innately determined.

Learning and the CCU

Much of everything stored in the central control unit (CCU) is learned (Figure 9.1). Everyday response tasks such as walking and talking are examples of learned behavior, as every parent can readily testify. Man also learns who— even what—is his mother and what he should expect from her. Man also learns what other people expect of him—his role. Similarly, the evaluative criteria stored in the CCU are learned, as are portions of his personality, the filtering process, and his attitudes. Attitudes, in particular, have in recent years increasingly become the subject of analysis from a learning theory perspective.[1] Nothing is quite so important in predicting what choice will be made by a consumer as knowledge of past experience in similar situations. This fundamental role of learning in economic behavior is described by Katona:

> Learning, in the broadest sense of the term, is a basic feature of any organism. The human organism acquires forms of behavior, it acquires forms of action, of knowledge, of emotions. What has been done does not necessarily belong only to the past and is not necessarily lost. It may or may not exert influence on present behavior. Under what

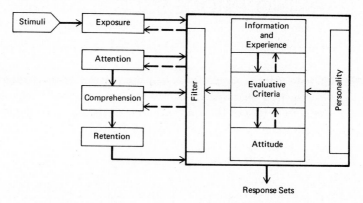

Figure 9.1 LEARNING PROCESS AND THE CENTRAL CONTROL UNIT

---

[1] Many examples could be cited, including the following: B. R. Bugelski and M. Hersen, "Conditioning Acceptance or Rejection of Information," *J. Experimental Psychology,* vol. 71, pp. 619–623 (1966); D. Byrne, R. K. Young, and W. Griffitt, "The Reinforcement Properties of Attitude Statements," *J. Experimental Research in Personality,* vol. 1, pp. 266–276 (1966); J. N. Carriero, "The Conditioning of Negative Attitudes to Unfamiliar Items of Information," *J. Verbal Learning and Verbal Behavior,* vol. 6, pp. 128–135 (1967); L. Krasner, J. B. Knowles, and L. P. Ullmann, "Effect of Verbal Conditioning of Attitudes on Subsequent Motor Performance," *J. Personality and Social Psychology,* vol. 1, pp. 407–412 (1965); A. W. Staats, "An Outline of an Integrated Learning Theory and of Attitude Formation and Function," in M. Fishbein (ed.), *Readings in Attitude Theory and Measurement* (New York: Wiley, 1960).

conditions and in what ways past experience affects later behavior is one of the most important problems of psychology.[2]

Definition of Learning

Learning may be defined in a variety of ways but is defined here as *changes in response tendencies due to the effects of experience*.[3] More traditionally, learning is defined as *changes in behavior*. That terminology is acceptable if it is not meant to include only overt behavior. Learned behavior must include attitudes, emotions, evaluative criteria, personality, and many other constructs which may not be expressed in overt form.

Exclusions   There are several changes in response tendencies that occur over time that should not be considered learning. These include species response tendencies (usually called instincts or reflexes), changes due to maturation (neuromuscular–glandular growth), and changes due to temporary states of the organism such as fatigue, drugs, or hunger. These states may affect the learning and may be difficult to isolate from learning in certain cases of interest to the marketing analyst but must be considered fundamentally different from learning.

The Study of Learning

No other field in psychology has generated the volume or quality of empirical research as has the study of learning. At one time, the experimental methods in psychology and learning theory were almost synonymous. Even today, learning experiments provide the classic methodological contributions.

With thousands of sophisticated research projects from which to draw and with a considerable amount of conceptual development, one might expect that learning would be one topic in which solid, indisputable generalizations would be possible. On the contrary, few topics are more disputed and tentative. Experimental results provide many contradictory findings and even more contradictory interpretations. Thus it is impossible to speak meaningfully of the theory of learning; it is possible only to speak of learning theories. Good research supports leading proponents of these theories. This led Hilgard and Bower to comment on the dilemma one can fall into:

> The student of learning, conscientiously trying to understand learning phenomena and the laws regulating them, is likely to despair of finding a secure position if opposing points of view are presented as equally plausible, so that the choice between them is made arbi-

---

[2]   George Katona, *Psychological Analysis of Economic Behavior* (New York: McGraw-Hill, 1951), p. 30. Reprinted by permission of the publisher.

[3]   For a description of other definitions of learning, see John F. Hall, *The Psychology of Learning* (Philadelphia: Lippincott, 1966), pp. 3–6. This book also serves as an excellent introduction to learning research.

trary. He may fall into a vapid eclecticism, with the general formula, "There's much to be said on all sides."[4]

Two Types of Learning

Two types of learning have been identified which appear to involve fundamentally different types of learning and consumer behavior. In *classical conditioning*, one stimulus that is known to elicit a response (such as an electrical shock) is paired with a neutral or unconditioned stimulus (such as light or buzzer). As the response (such as a reflex) occurs to the original stimulus, an increase will occur in the tendency for the second stimulus to elicit a similar response. The Pavlovian dog experiments serve as a model for classical conditioning.[5]

Instrumental conditioning, also referred to as operant conditioning, is learning that increases the *frequency* or *probability* of a particular response being emitted. The Skinner box illustrates instrumental learning.[6] A Skinner box has a bar that can be depressed by a rat within the box. By giving the rat a piece of grain (reward) or an electrical shock from the floor (punishment), the rate of pressing the bar can be changed; this is operant conditioning.

Marketing Implications　The characteristics of classical conditioning and instrumental learning are suggested in Table 9.1. A consumer analyst might interpret these characteristics to give helpful insight to the role of learning theories in marketing problems.

Classical conditioning probably explains much of advertising effect, the effect of observing friends using a product, marketing facilities, and actual product usage. For example, a television advertisement depicting an attractive, pleasurable situation is sensed by a consumer. That stimulus, to which the consumer already has a pleasant response, is known as the unconditioned stimulus and his emotion or feeling (or perhaps attitude) is known as an unconditioned response. After several presentations or even one very effective presentation, the specific brand being advertised termed the (to-be) conditioned stimulus, may evoke the same pleasant emotion and is then called the conditioned response. This process is shown in Figure 9.2 with the output of the conditioning process being transferred into the content of the CCU. There it becomes part of the filter which controls attention to future stimuli.

Instrumental learning is concerned with situations where the consumer must make choices or decisions about which action to take. This implies a "problem" or goal toward which responses are directed with the prediction that

---

　　　[4] Ernest R. Hilgard and George H. Bower, *Theories of Learning,* 3rd ed. (New York: Appleton, 1966). Copyright 1966 by Meredith Publishing Co., Des Moines, Iowa. Reprinted by permission of Appleton-Century-Crofts.

　　　[5] Ivan P. Pavlov, *Conditioned Reflexes,* transl. by G. V. Anrep (London: Oxford University Press, 1927).

　　　[6] B. F. Skinner, *Behavior of Organisms: An Experimental Analysis* (New York: Appleton, 1966).

Table 9.1 SUGGESTED DISTINCTIONS BETWEEN TWO KINDS OF LEARNING

	Classical Conditioning	*Instrumental Learning*
(1)	Outcome independent of what the learner does	Outcome depends on what the learner does
(2)	A strong and reliable stimulus–response relationship already present	Variable responding prior to learning
(3)	Change is mainly in the effectiveness of a stimulus	Change is mainly in the frequency of a response
(4)	Typically involves behavior controlled by the autonomic nervous system	Typically involves behavior controlled by the somatic nervous system
(5)	Involves involuntary responses	Involves voluntary responses
(6)	Involves feelings or expectancies	Involves overt acts or directed thoughts
(7)	Produces changes in opinions, tastes, and goals	Produces changes in goal-directed actions

SOURCE: Winfred F. Hill, *Psychology: Principles and Problems* (Philadelphia: Lippincott, 1970), p. 62. Reprinted by permission of the publisher.

the consumer will modify his behavior with experience toward those purchases, search strategies, or other activities which will yield the highest (perceived) satisfaction or reinforcement. This does not imply that any single action will be rewarding and in fact, trial and error may create many "poor" responses.

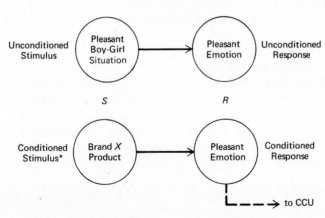

Figure 9.2 CLASSICAL CONDITIONING OF BRAND PREFERENCE

It should be apparent that the decision-process model presented in this book assumes a close relationship between conditioning and instrumental learning. Consumers choose decision strategies which are goal directed and maximize satisfaction in terms of the evaluative criteria of those consumers. Those evaluative criteria, however, are a direct result of the attitudes, personality, and other influences acquired through a lifetime of conditioning. One might tentatively postulate, therefore, that the principles of conditioning offer the most insight to the "upper" portion of the decision model and that instrumental learning offers the most insight to the "lower" portion of the model. It might also be tentatively postulated that habitual decision-process behavior is more akin to instrumental behavior as a response is repeatedly made which is reinforced, and extended problem-solving behavior relies more on conditioning principles because of the feelings and expectancies built up through the conditioning of emotional and perceptual responses.

COMPONENTS OF THE LEARNING PROCESS

The CCU of the consumer is constantly emitting signals for action, called responses or response sets. Coincidently, the CCU is receiving a variety of stimulus inputs. When specific stimuli become associated with specific responses in a sufficiently permanent manner that the occurrence of the stimulus elicits or tends to elicit a particular response, learning has occurred. To understand this process it is necessary to clarify the role of drive, cue stimuli, responses, reinforcement, and retention.[7]

Drive

Learning frequently occurs in the presence of *drive*—any strong stimulus that impels action. Drive arouses an individual and keeps him ready to respond; thus it is the basis of motivation. A motive differs from drive mainly in that it is purposeful, or directed toward a specific goal, whereas drive refers to an increased probability of activity without specifying the nature of the activity.

Drive is illustrated by the folk expression, "A good salesman is a hungry salesman." The meaning of this statement is that a stimulus-deprived individual will exhibit a higher level of activity and that he will tend to repeat those responses he was emitting when something occurred (such as sales) that tended to satisfy his drive. Within a specified range of drive intensity he may learn effective methods more aggressively than a relatively satisfied salesman. Thus drive is an important condition for accelerating the emission of responses that lead to learning.

Two types of drives are believed to exist. *Primary drives* are based upon innate physiological needs such as thirst, hunger, pain avoidance, and sex. *Secondary drives* are *learned* rather than innate and are derived from the primary drives. Examples of secondary drives include the desire for money, fear, pride, and rivalry.

---

[7] The concepts used in this section are mainly from Neal E. Miller and John Dollard, *Social Learning and Imitation* (London: Kegan, Trench and Co., 1945); also J. C. Dollard and N. E. Miller, *Personality and Psychotherapy* (New York: McGraw-Hill, 1950).

Considering the drive state of an organism is often helpful in explaining the way brand preferences are formed. For example, if on a very hot summer afternoon a very thirsty consumer is presented with the stimulus of a cold beer he may find this stimulus very rewarding, or drive reducing. The learning theorist might predict that this single event would be much more important in forming brand loyalty for that brand of beer than repeated applications of a competing beer in a lower drive stage. Many other illustrations could be given to show why isolated events in the life of a consumer are important in forming preferences and response tendencies.

Individuals operate under many drives at the same time. To predict behavior, it is necessary to establish which drives are stimulating the *most* energizing behavior. Vivid examples can be cited to illustrate how secondary drives may become more important than primary drives. Gandhi's hunger strike is an example of a situation where the secondary drive for freedom or for leadership was dominant over the primary drive of hunger. In war, soldiers fall on grenades to protect comrades at the certain destruction of their own life. The explanation is that secondary drives toward patriotism, altruism, or some other goal have been learned and are dominant over more basic drives. Self-preservation is not always highest in the hierarchy of drives.

Less dramatically, the consumer researcher needs to analyze the hierarchy of drives that refer to a product if he is to predict situations under which learning is likely to occur.

Before advancing to the next topic, perhaps it should be emphasized that learning to like a product or acquiring a drive that can be satisfied by a specific product may be remote from actually purchasing the product. Many people have a secondary drive that can be satisfied by owning a Rolls Royce, for example. They have a positive response set toward purchasing and driving one. Yet not many consumers ever purchase a Rolls Royce. Many other variables are involved in a purchase decision.

Cue Stimuli

Cue stimuli are any objects existing in the environment as perceived by the individual. The goal of the marketer is to discover or create cue stimuli of sufficient importance that they become drive stimuli or elicit other responses appropriate to his objects. It is common to speak of cue stimuli simply as "stimuli" or to use the terms "cue" and "stimulus" interchangeably. The goal here is to discover the conditions under which a stimulus will increase the probability of eliciting a specified response.

Generalization Generalization is a process inferred when a response elicited by a stimulus is also elicited by a different but similar stimulus. If two stimuli are exactly alike, of course, they will have the same probability of evoking a specified response, but it is known that the more dissimilar the stimuli become, the lower will be the probability of evoking the same response.[8] This is called the *gradient of generalization.*

Hovland's classic studies illustrate the process of generalization. In his experiments, subjects were conditioned to react to a tone of either 1967 cycles per second or 153 cycles per second. When presented with tones of other frequencies, the number of responses were found to be in proportion to the closeness of the tone to the conditioned stimuli.[9] Other experiments with auditory stimuli have clarified the nature of generalization gradients,[10] and experiments have verified generalization with other types of stimuli such as different hues of color,[11] different light intensities,[12] sizes of stimuli,[13] temporal variation,[14] and language or verbal stimuli.[15]

Generalization makes possible stability in man's actions across time. If it were necessary to learn a new response every time one was confronted with a new stimulus, man's activity would be chaotic. Individuals see the similarities between stimulus situations, however, and emit responses that are both appropriate and stable. When one judges another person or situation on the basis of stereotype, he is using the process of generalization.

Important research questions are generated for consumer research by the topic of generalization, because it underlies *image formation.* Consumers generalize what the products, prices, and quality levels will be in a store based upon limited knowledge or "cues" about that store.[16] Even consumers who have never visited a store are able to estimate what prices would be in that store for specific products. At a practical level of consumer analysis, it is important for a marketer to understand the kind of generalization that is occurring about his store or brand.

---

[8]   Benton J. Underwood, *Experimental Psychology* (New York: Appleton, 1949), p. 252.

[9]   Carl I. Hovland, "The Generalization of Conditioned Responses: I. The Sensory Generalization of Conditioned Responses with Varying Frequencies of Tone," *J. General Psychology*, vol. 17, pp. 125–148 (1937).

[10]   H. R. Blackwell and H. Schlosberg, "Octave Generalization, Pitch Discrimination, and Loudness Thresholds in the White Rat," *J. Experimental Psychology*, vol. 38, pp. 407–419 (1943); W. C. Miller and J. E. Greene, "Generalization of an Avoidance Response to Various Intensities of Tone," *J. Comparative Physiological Psychology*, vol. 47, pp. 136–139 (1954).

[11]   S. H. White, "Generalization of an Instrumental Response With Variations in Two Attributes of the CS," *J. Experimental Psychology*, vol. 56, pp. 339–343 (1958).

[12]   W. E. Vandament and I. E. Price, "Primary Stimulus Generalization under Different Percentages of Reinforcement in Eyelid Conditioning," *J. Experimental Psychology*, vol. 67, pp. 162–167 (1964).

[13]   G. R. Grice and E. Saltz, "The Generalization of an Instrumental Response to Stimuli Varying in the Size Dimension," *J. Experimental Psychology*, vol. 40, pp. 702–708 (1950).

[14]   G. Rosenbaum, "Temporal Gradients of Response Strength with Two Levels of Motivation," *J. Experimental Psychology*, vol. 41, pp. 261–267 (1951).

[15]   P. J. Lang, J. Geer, and M. Hnatiow, "Semantic Generalization of Conditioned Autonomic Responses," *J. Experimental Psychology*, vol. 65, pp. 552–558 (1963).

[16]   R. D. Blackwell, "Evaluating a Store's Image," *Bull. Business Research* (Ohio State University), vol. 41, pp. 4–6 (May 1966).

At a more basic level, research is needed to determine the basis for generalization about stores and brands.

Discrimination   This is a process whereby an organism learns to emit a response to a stimulus but avoids making the same response to a similar but somewhat different stimulus. Examples include a rat learning to respond to the color white but not to black, a pigeon learning to peck a green bar in order to obtain a reward but not a red bar, a child learning to call one tall male "Daddy" but not all tall males, or a consumer learning to prefer Burger King as a place to eat but not other fast food chains.

Significant contributions to the understanding of discrimination have been made by Hull and his student Spence. They found that stimuli had excitatory potential (the ability to energize behavior) based upon the number of previous positively reinforced trials and inhibitory power based upon previous nonreinforced trials. Their analysis of discrimination is summarized as follows:

(1)   Every reinforced trial leads to an increment in excitatory strength for a given stimulus and its reinforced response,

(2)   every nonreinforced trial results in an inhibitory increment to a given stimulus and its nonreinforced response,

(3)   both excitatory and inhibitory tendencies generalize to stimuli along a stimulus continuum,

(4)   there is the algebraic summation of excitatory and inhibitory increments which results in

(5)   a discriminatory response based upon these algebraic summations.[17]

Applications   Studies on generalization and discrimination aid in understanding the adoption of new products and establishing believability of new claims for products. When a marketer wants to introduce a new product to customers of a currently accepted product with the hope they will buy both new and old, stimuli presented to the consumer should be similar to those surrounding the first product in order to facilitate generalization. This often accounts for the marketing strategy of "family" or "blanket" brands. Also, an advertiser may use the same theme, the same personnel, or the same format to introduce a new claim in addition to that which is already accepted.

A marketing goal is often to stimulate consumers to switch to a new brand, to try an improved product, or to perceive a product to have a new quality. The stimuli presented should be dissimilar to facilitate discrimination. An advertiser may find that consumers are not presently buying his product because the taste is not acceptable. The new claim must be sufficiently dissimilar to the old claim to stimulate the consumer to respond in a new way. A variety of tests could be devised to determine if this will be accomplished.

---

[17]   Clark L. Hull, *Essentials of Behavior* (New Haven, Conn.: Yale University Press, 1951).

When individuals have difficulty discriminating between stimulus situations, behavior becomes random. This was shown by Pavlov in his early experiments[18] and has been repeated in many other experiments. Pavlov used meat powder to condition a dog to salivate whenever presented with a luminous circle on a screen in front of it. After the dog had learned to salivate when presented with the circle, he began presenting a luminous ellipse *not* accompanied by meat powder. The dog gradually learned to salivate when presented with the circle and *not* to salivate when presented with the ellipse; it had learned to discriminate. Pavlov then began to make the ellipse more and more like the circle and alternated its presentation with the circle. The dog continued to make correct responses until the ellipse became very close to the shape of the circle (although still slightly different). After several weeks of having difficulty discriminating, the dog had a nervous breakdown, which Pavlov termed "experimental neurosis." This and related experiments all point to the conclusion that when stimulus situations are quite similar and yet the individual must emit dichotomous responses, behavior becomes random. If this finding can be generalized to consumer behavior, one would expect that brand loyalty, for example, would be most unstable among products that are difficult to differentiate from one another. Buying decisions would either be subject to random switching or be decided on something other than learned preferences such as price cuts, deals, or special promotions.

Stimulus Sampling   The learning model of Estes places emphasis on the stimulus situation in explaining learning[19] and has influenced marketing thought to a considerable degree through the learning theory contribution of Kuehn.[20]

Estes describes the probability of a response not as a function of one stimulus but of a stimulus situation made up of many small stimulus elements. Whenever a response occurs, all the stimulus elements *sampled* on that trial become conditioned to that response. If the same sample of stimuli were to occur again, the result would be the same response that was conditioned to the original, identical set of stimuli. Since it is unlikely that an identical set of stimuli will be sampled again, the probability of any act occurring as a response to a stimulus situation is a function of the number of stimulus elements in the common set. With additional trials, it can be predicted that additional stimulus elements will become conditioned to the response act. Since something less than 100 percent of stimulus elements will be sampled, the probability of a response will be a probability less than one, not certainty. Thus behavior is a stochastic process. Two other psychologists have developed a parallel approach to predicting behavior[21]

[18]   Ivan P. Pavlov, *op. cit.*[5]

[19]   William K. Estes, "Toward a Statistical Theory of Learning," *Psychological Rev.,* vol. 57, pp. 94–107 (1950).

[20]   Alfred A. Kuehn, "Consumer Brand Choice—A Learning Process?" in Ronald E. Frank, Alfred A. Kuehn, and William F. Massy (eds.), *Quantitative Techniques in Marketing Analysis* (Homewood, Ill.: Irwin, 1962), pp. 390–403.

[21]   R. R. Bush and F. Mosteller, *Stochastic Models for Learning* (New York: Wiley, 1951).

as a function of learning, and it is the combined work of these men from which Kuehn's learning model[22] of brand loyalty evolved.[23]

Responses

Responses can be as simple as jerking one's leg when struck with a rubber mallet or as complex as trying to rub one's stomach in a circular motion with one's left hand while patting one's head with one's right. Responses also include attitudes, familiarity, perception, and other complex phenomena. Usually, however, learning psychologists attempt measurement of learning in behavioral terms. That is, responses must be operationally defined and preferably physically observable.

Psychological studies involve a variety of measures of learning. Experiments measure the *frequency* of response (time elapsed between stimulus and response), and *amplitude* of response (such as loudness in decibels, strength of pull by rats in a harness, amount of pressure on a pedal). In consumer research the frequency of responses can be measured with eye cameras,[24] operant behavior equipment,[25] and binocular rivalry techniques.[26] The speed of responses can be

---

[22] Because Kuehn's model represents a primary theoretical contribution to learning theory *in marketing,* it is useful to describe its genealogy. Kuehn's model is an S-R (stimulus-response) or contiguity model. It is based upon the work of Bush and Mosteller and Estes, which in turn evolved from the theories of Edwin R. Guthrie, who postulated that whenever a stimulus and a response occur together, learning occurs. This, in turn, reflects the basic behavioralism of John B. Watson. It is correct to say, then, that Kuehn's model is derived basically from a stimulus–response model of learning.

[23] The statistical models of Estes, Bush, and Mosteller have generated a rich literature, spawned in the cooperative minds of psychologists and mathematicians. One of the questions that has received a great deal of attention is whether individuals *learn* the probabilities of reinforced responses and match their own actions with those learned probabilities. The evidence has been conflicting on this point. One study demonstrated that individuals do not match responses correctly but tend to base their responses primarily on the most recent experiences. See Ward Edwards, "Probability Learning in 1000 Trials," *J. Experimental Psychology,* vol. 62, pp. 385–394 (1961); also Gordon M. Becker, "Sequential Decision Making: Wald's Model and Estimates of Parameters," *J. Experimental Psychology,* vol. 55, pp. 628–636 (1958); R. Allen Gardner, "Multiple-Choice Decision-Behavior," *Amer. J. Psychology,* vol. 71, pp. 710–717 (1950). Evidence that supports the models is found in Paul M. Fitts, James R. Peterson, and Gerson Wolpe, "Cognitive Aspects of Information Processing: II. Adjustments to Stimulus Redundancy," *J. Experimental Psychology,* vol. 65, pp. 423–432 (1963). For theoretical discussions of statistical models in learning decision-making behavior, see Merrill M. Flood, "Stochastic Learning Theory Applied to Choice Experiments with Rats, Dogs, and Men," *Behavioral Science,* vol. 7, pp. 289–314 (1962); S. S. Komorita, "Probability Learning under Equivalent Data Collection Methods," *J. Experimental Psychology,* vol. 55, pp. 115–120 (1958); John E. Overall, "A Cognitive Probability Model for Learning," *Psychometrika,* vol. 25, pp. 159–172 (1960). For a general description of research in this area, see John Cohen, *Chance, Skill and Luck: The Psychology of Guessing and Gambling* (Baltimore: Penguin, 1960).

[24] J. S. Karslake, "The Purdue Eye Camera: A Practical Apparatus for Studying the Attention Value of Advertisements," *J. Applied Psychology,* vol. 24, pp. 417–440 (1940).

[25] Ogden R. Lindsley, "A Behavioral Measure of Television Viewing," *J. Advertising Research,* pp. 2–12 (Sept. 1962); also James C. Becknell, Jr., "Utilizing Pre-Testing Devices to Reduce Variance in Advertising Experiments," in *Proc. 11th Annual Conf.* (New York: Advertising Research Foundation, Oct. 5, 1965), p. 35.

[26] Harry W. Daniels, "A Visual Perception Laboratory in Commercial Research," *Perceptual and Motor Skills,* vol. 8, pp. 331–338 (1958).

measured with tachistoscopes and various recording devices,[27] and amplitude of responses can be measured with galvanic skin response equipment,[28] pupil dilation equipment,[29] and other devices.[30] Many other techniques for measuring consumer responses in learning experiments are possible, of course, using only ordinary paper-and-pencil or verbal reporting techniques.

Reinforcement

Reinforcement (or reward—a synonymous term) is defined variously. Miller originally defined reinforcement as reduction in drive and Hull similarly defined it as reduction in stimulus. However, the application of some objects has been shown to be reinforcing without involving drive reduction or stimulus reduction. Thus, some learning psychologists define reinforcement merely as "environmental events exhibiting the property of increasing the probability of occurrence of responses they accompany."

When animals are used in learning experiments, the rewards usually reduce some primary drive. Thus rats, cats, and dogs learn tasks and receive as a reward food, water, a receptive female, or the removal of aversive stimuli.

Secondary rewards (objects or situations that have taken on reward properties because they have been conditioned to other rewards) are of more relevance to consumer analysts.

Schedules of Reinforcement Different *schedules of reinforcement* result in different and characteristic patterns of behavior. Learning will occur most rapidly when each correct response is rewarded (100-percent reinforcement). However, learning is more lasting when reinforcement is partial. This is demonstrated in Figure 9.3. The figure indicates that many more nonreinforced responses are necessary to achieve extinction of a habit learned under interval reinforcement than to a response learned under continuous reinforcement. The explanation for this appears to be that *discrimination* between conditions necessary for reinforcement and conditions irrelevant to reinforcement is difficult with partial reinforcement.

Is Reward Necessary for Learning? Some learning theorists consider rewards essential in any explanation of learning, yet experiments have been designed to show that learning need not involve rewards. Consumer analysts are interested in such types of learning experiments because they may yield information about the question of whether advertising is effective by sheer repetition.

---

[27] *Tachistoscope Tests and Recall and Recognition Techniques in the Study of Memory* (New York: Advertising Research Foundation, 1957).

[28] J. D. Montagu and E. M. Coles, "Mechanism and Measurement of the Galvanic Skin Response," *"Psychological Bull.,"* vol. 66, pp. 261–279 (1966).

[29] Herbert E. Krugman, "Some Applications of Pupil Measurement," *J. Marketing Research,* vol. 1, pp. 16–19 (Nov. 1964).

[30] R. D. Blackwell, J. Hensel, M. Phillips, and B. Sternthal, *Laboratory Equipment for Marketing Research* (Dubuque, Iowa: Kendall-Hunt Publ. Co., 1970).

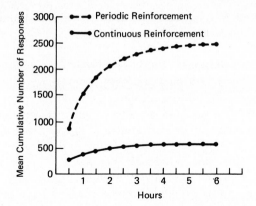

Figure 9.3   EFFECTS OF 100-PERCENT REINFORCEMENT AND PARTIAL RE-
INFORCEMENT ON THE NUMBER OF TRIALS TO EXTINCTION.   W.
O. Jenkins, H. McFann, and F. L. Clayton, "A Methodological Study of Extinc-
tion Following Aperiodis and Continuous Reinforcement," *J. Comparative
Physiological Psychology*, vol. 43, pp. 155–167, at p. 158 (1950). Reprinted
by permission of the Amer. Psychological Assoc.

Brogden carefully executed a study in which 11 kittens formed an
experimental group and 12 more kittens formed a control group.[31] Both groups
were placed in a cage that could be rotated by the kittens. The kittens were
observed carefully, and when any kitten in the experimental group engaged in
cage-turning activity, a 1000-cycle tone of moderate intensity was presented,
until each of the kittens in the experimental group had been presented with the
pairing of tone and response 30 times. Each of the control group kittens was also
observed engaging in cage-turning activity 30 times.

When pairing of *contiguous* stimulus and response had been accomplished, Brogden then presented the tone to each kitten in both groups. The
kittens in the experimental group emitted the conditioned response five times as
frequently as the control group. This result is interpreted to indicate that learning
can occur without the presence of reinforcement or drive. Mednick commented
on the experiment as follows:

> Apparently all that is necessary for an association to develop
> between a stimulus and a response is that they occur together fre-
> quently. Reward does not seem to be necessary. When reward is used,
> however, conditioning proceeds far more rapidly and with greater
> vigor.[32]

Many theorists are unwilling to accept the position that reinforcement is
not involved in some way. Regardless of the theoretical position one adopts to

---

[31]   This experiment, conducted by W. J. Brogden, is described in Sarnoff A. Mednick,
Learning (Englewood Cliffs, N.J.: Prentice-Hall, 1964), pp. 25–26.

[32]   Mednick, *op. cit.*,[31] p. 26.

explain the phenomenon, it appears that merely seeing a stimulus repeatedly can result in learning. This is discussed more thoroughly in Chapter 15.

Reinforcement-Response Behavior Responses sometimes are learned because they occur *with* reinforcing stimuli, not because they are *elicited by* stimuli.[33] Much behavior is purposeful, but this is not necessarily every response emitted by man. When desirable events occur (rewards), man (and other animals) tends to repeat the response he was emitting at the time of the reward. This increases the probability of that response being emitted when rewards are presented again. Over time, an individual may learn to associate the (originally random) behavior with the reward. The report of a very famous study of pigeons illustrates how this principle results in seemingly "irrational" behavior:

> Suppose we give a pigeon a small amount of food every fifteen seconds regardless of what it is doing. When the food is first given, the pigeon will be behaving in some way—if only standing still—and conditioning will take place. It is then more probable that the same behavior will be in progress when the food is given again. If this proves to be the case, the "operant" will be further strengthened. If not, some other behavior will be strengthened. Eventually, a given bit of behavior reaches a frequency at which it is often reinforced. It then becomes a permanent part of the repertoire of the bird, even though the food has been given by a clock which is unrelated to the bird's behavior. Conspicuous responses which have been established in this way include turning sharply to one side, hopping from one foot to the other and back, bowing and scraping, turning around, strutting, and raising the head.[34]

It is believed that operant conditioning of this sort describes superstitious behavior and other forms of difficult-to-understand performance. For example, a student learns to use a "lucky" pen on exams or believes he "does better" wearing a certain type of clothing. "Sure cures" for colds and other illnesses are learned by primitive peoples. A housewife visits a supermarket much like all other supermarkets but receives a special bargain. This increases her probability of returning to that store. Thus she is more likely to receive other bargains at that store. Gradually, she may learn to prefer that store and emit the response of regularly shopping there.

Superstitious or "irrational" habits are particularly difficult to extinguish. Consumers can endure many nonreinforced trials with only an occasional reinforcement because of the reinforcement schedule under which such responses are generally learned. Usually, reinforcement in such situations has been infrequent and sporadic; this is the most difficult kind of learning to extinguish.

---

[33] This view is primarily associated with Skinner. He believes that stimulus-response learning (called type S learning) may also occur but that it is far less important than operant conditioning (called type R learning). See B. F. Skinner, *The Behavior of Organisms: An Experimental Analysis* (New York: Appleton, 1966); B. F. Skinner, *Science and Human Behavior* (New York: Macmillan, 1953).

[34] Skinner, *Science and Human Behavior, op. cit.,*[33] p. 85.

Amount and Timing of Reward Learning increases as a function of the number of reinforced trials. This is a well-accepted finding. There is some evidence to indicate that the amount of reward applied on each trial does not affect learning,[35] although there is equally good evidence to indicate that the larger the reward, the more rapid the learning.[36] Most evidence indicates that learning also occurs more rapidly when there is little or no interval between response and reward.[37] There are many qualifications attached to any statement concerning the amount and timing of reinforcement,[38] and to date there has been little attempt empirically to study the role of reinforcement in consumer learning.

Retention and Forgetting

The stability of learned material over time is defined as retention and the converse is forgetting. The preceding pages referred to learning in the abstract; that is, the point at which the material was considered "learned" with no regard to the duration of that learning. This is a major concern in advertising and other types of marketing strategy, however.

Considerable theoretical dispute exists about the nature of the forgetting process. One school of thought advocates the *"interference" theory*.[39] This position holds that the reason people "forget" a learned message is that other learning of similar messages interferes. This interference may be of two types, and considerable debate exists about the importance or strength of each. Suppose that a consumer watched a television program and "learned" a message for detergent *A*. Soon afterward and before she had an opportunity to "remember" detergent *A* in the supermarket, she may have seen an advertisement for detergent *B*. Since the *B* advertisement has an inhibitory effect on the retention of the earlier learned *A* advertisement, this type of forgetting (of *A*) is termed *retroactive inhibition* (RI). On the other hand, if the consumer "learned" the *A* advertisement and then viewed the *B* advertisement a different type of interference would occur. If she tried to recall the *B* advertisement, the *A* advertisement would interfere with her remembering of the *B* advertisement. This latter type of interference is termed *proactive inhibition* (PI).

---

[35] L. B. Miller and B. W. Estes, "Monetary Reward and Motivation in Discrimination Learning," *J. Experimental Psychology*, vol. 61, pp. 501–504 (1961); B. W. Estes, L. B. Miller, and M. E. Curtin, "Supplementary Report: Monetary Incentive and Motivation in Discrimination Learning—Sex Differences," *J. Experimental Psychology*, vol. 63, p. 320 (1962).

[36] Sidney Siegel and J. M. Andrews, "Magnitude of Reinforcement and Choice Behavior in Children," *J. Experimental Psychology*, vol. 63, pp. 337–341 (1962). After examining approximately 35 studies investigating the effects of variation in reward, Hall concludes: "When performance during acquisition trials is measured by either rate, amplitude, or probability of response, the majority of studies using animals reveal that performance during acquisition trials is related to the amount of reinforcement that is provided." Hall, *op. cit.*,[3] p. 181.

[37] Hall, *op. cit.*,[3] pp. 208–280.

[38] For a complete review of the role of rewards in strengthening stimulus responses, see Hull, *op. cit.*,[17] pp. 177–230.

[39] For a concise description of interference, see Winfred F. Hill, *Psychology: Principles and Problems* (Philadelphia: Lippincott, 1970), pp. 312–321.

Interference theory has been criticized because it failed to explain the large loss of retention in short time spans that could not be accounted for by interference. For example, a person might memorize a telephone number but forget it very quickly. An alternative explanation is known as *decay* or *trace theory*. Trace theories postulate that each stimulus received by an individual leaves a neural trace which decays quickly unless repetition or rehearsal occur. These postulates are derived from theories which emphasize physiological or neuropsychological models of learning.[40]

The resolution of these theories of forgetting has not been achieved. It appears that the most logical (and most useful) explanation is that *all* three types (RI, PI, and decay) occur and account for the forgetting of material. One of the results of this controversy has been to stimulate interest in looking both at long-term memory (LTM) and short-term memory (STM) as considerations in retention.[41] A hypothetical model of the retention process has been developed by Jung and is presented in Figure 9.4. It shows the presentation of thirteen "trigrams" passing through immediate memory with some immediately forgotten as a result of decay. Selective processes operate allowing eight of the trigrams to be encoded, organized, and rehearsed. These trigrams enter into "primary" memory, but due to RI and PI, not all will be retained and some ("cow") will intrude from some earlier learning experience.[42]

Extinction Extinction of a well-learned response is usually difficult to achieve. Under repeated conditions of nonreinforcement, however, there is a tendency for the conditioned response to decrease or disappear. One experiment illustrates the difficulty in achieving extinction. In this type of experiment dogs are conditioned to jump over a shoulder-high barrier in order to avoid a severe electrical shock. The dogs learn the response of jumping to the "safe" side of the box in a few trials. Ten seconds after jumping into the "safe" side of the box, the dog must jump again to the other side of the box, over the barrier. If the dog does not jump every 10 seconds, he receives another shock. Solomon[43] found, however, that after as few reinforcements as 20, the electricity can be discon-

---

[40] D. O. Hebb, *The Organization of Behavior* (New York: Wiley, 1949); also D. O. Hebb, "A Neuropsychological Theory," in S. Koch (ed.), *Psychology: A Study of a Science*, vol. 1 (New York: McGraw-Hill, 1959), pp. 622–643. Hebb explains the learning process by describing changes in the *neurons* of an organism's brain. When repetition of a neural pattern occurs, he believes that a microscopic growth or chemical change will decrease "synaptic resistance" and allow one neuron to activate another, thus producing response patterns. This *cell assembly* corresponds to a particular event sensed from the environment. Each item in the stream of thought going through an individual's brain is a *phase sequence* which, when assembled together, results in thinking or problem-solving ability.

[41] For example, see A. W. Melton, "Implications of Short-Term Memory for a General Theory of Memory," *J. Verbal Learning and Verbal Behavior*, vol. 2, pp. 1–21 (1963); L. Postman, "Short-Term Memory and Incidental Learning," in A. W. Melton (ed.), *Categories of Human Learning* (New York: Academic Press), 1964.

[42] John Jung, *Verbal Learning* (New York: Holt, Rinehart and Winston, 1968), pp. 142–143.

[43] R. L. Solomon and L. C. Wynne, *Psychological Monographs*, vol. 67, no. 354 (1953).

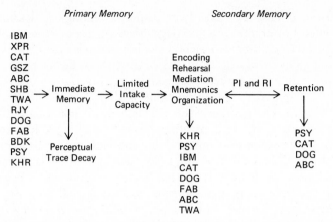

Primary Memory   *Secondary Memory*

Figure 9.4 HYPOTHETICAL EXAMPLE OF THE PROCESS INVOLVED IN MEM-
ORY OF A SINGLE LIST AS MEASURED BY THE METHOD OF RECALL.
John Jung, *Verbal Learning* (New York: Holt, Rinehart and Winston, 1968),
p. 142

tinued and the dogs will continue to jump, sometimes for hundreds of times.[44]
Extinction is virtually impossible to attain, unless the dogs are physically
restrained by putting a ceiling on the box that prevents jumping.

Once something is learned, it appears that it is never truly *unlearned*.
Thus, to say that a response tendency is extinguished merely means that the
response in question has been *repressed* (through nonreinforcement) or it may
be *replaced* by learning of an incompatible response. The return of response
strength after extinction, without intervening reinforcement, is called *spontaneous
recovery*. In experimental situations, animals that have had a particular response
extinguished will often begin emitting the conditioned response after a period of
rest. Spontaneous recovery is not unusual among people when they are confused,
under stress, or in other unusual states. In such situations, they sometimes will
recover response tendencies that have been extinguished for many years.

The original response strength of an extinguished habit can also be
recovered instantly when a previously extinguished response is rewarded in an
isolated instance. It is believed that undesirable habits are much more difficult
to extinguish, therefore, by "cutting down" than by quitting entirely. These
principles of extinction may serve to explain consumer preferences for a product,
even in the face of numerous instances of using a competitive product.

Most research indicates that *it is easier to replace a conditioned response
with an incompatible response than to extinguish the original response*. This
would indicate that it should be easier to develop consumer preference for a new
product than merely to develop consumer discontent with an existing product.

---

[44] Extinction is more difficult in this experiment than many examples, however,
because secondary reinforcement appears to occur. If the dog does not jump within 10 seconds,
it experiences strong fear. Fear itself thus serves as a reinforcer.

Distributed Practice The least disputed findings in learning research concern the effects of practice on learning. Practice refers to the number of trials or opportunities for emitting a specified response that occur in achieving learning.

It takes fewer trials to learn something if there are rest periods between trials.[45] This is called distributed practice. It occasionally occurs that even the amount of *time* required to learn something is shorter with distributed practice than massed practice (no rest periods), although this is not usually the case. The greater efficiency of distributed practice versus massed practice was originally determined in the learning of complex skills, although it now has been shown to be true for nearly all kinds of learning tasks. The bulk of research on the effects of practice is now conducted in verbal-learning situations.[46] Because of the similarity of verbal-learning experimental situations and the presentation of advertising messages, this area of learning research appears to have much direct relevance to the analysis of consumer behavior.

LEARNING THEORY AND MARKETING RESEARCH

Marketing research has a peculiar relationship to learning theory. Marketing typically deals with large-scale complex learning situations. The theory described in this chapter, however, is typically developed from small-scale tightly controlled experiments in which only a few factors are allowed to vary. The dilemma of the marketing analyst is in evaluating the applicability of research which has been artifically simplified to the extent that generalizability may be seriously questioned.

The best answer that can be offered is that learning theory provides a beginning, a foundation for understanding the dynamics of consumer preferences. The best that can be done is to work out relationships rigorously in the laboratory and then to test the limits of generalizability by applying them to increasingly more complicated situations. There is considerable face validity in direct applications of learning theory to the content and media scheduling of advertising materials, of course, but there appears to be reasonable hope for the broader generalizations as well.

---

[45] For a description of theories of distributed practice, see Hilgard and Bower, *op. cit.*,[4] pp. 317–338.

[46] Probably the most important contribution to the understanding of distributed practice in verbal learning is provided in the studies of Benton J. Underwood. At least 30 studies by Underwood appeared in the 1950s and early 1960s, mostly in the *J. Experimental Psychology*, and many are of interest to the advertising practitioner. For typical studies, see "Studies of Distributed Practice: II. Learning and Retention of Paired-Adjective Lists with Two Levels of Intralist Similarity," *J. Experimental Psychology*, vol. 42, pp. 153–161 (1951); "Studies in Distributed Practice: XI. An Attempt to Resolve Conflicting Facts on Retention of Serial Nonsense Lists," *J. Experimental Psychology*, vol. 45, pp. 355–359 (1953); B. J. Underwood and R. W. Schulz, "Studies of Distributed Practice: XXI. Effect of Interference from Language Habits," *J. Experimental Psychology*, vol. 62, pp. 571–575 (1961).

The role of learning theory can perhaps be amplified by careful reflection on an observation, written in 1885, about the nature of buying behavior:

> The first time a man looks at an advertisement, he does not see it.
> The second time he does not notice it.
> The third time he is conscious of its existence.
> The fourth time he faintly remembers having seen it before.
> The fifth time he reads it.
> The sixth time he turns up his nose at it.
> The seventh time he reads it through and says, "Oh brother!"
> The eighth time he says, "Here's that confounded thing again!"
> The ninth time he wonders if it amounts to anything.
> The tenth time he thinks he will ask his neighbor if he has tried it.
> The eleventh time he wonders how the advertiser makes it pay.
> The twelfth time he thinks perhaps it may be worth something.
> The thirteenth time he thinks it must be a good thing.
> The fourteenth time he remembers that he has wanted such a thing for a long time.
> The fifteenth time he is tantalized because he cannot afford to buy it.
> The sixteenth time he thinks he will buy it some day.
> The seventeenth time he makes a memorandum of it.
> The eighteenth time he swears at his poverty.
> The nineteenth time he counts his money carefully.
> The twentieth time he sees it, he buys the article, or instructs his wife to do so.[47]

SUMMARY

The characteristic that produces a *dynamic* model of consumer behavior is learning. Learning is the process by which consumer preferences are constantly modified and updated. More specifically learning is defined as changes in response tendencies due to the effects of experience. Nearly everything man does and feels is a result of learned responses.

The study of learning has a thorough and rigorous foundation. There are many ways of categorizing learning, but two of the most fundamental varieties are *classical conditioning* and *instrumental learning*. The principles underlying classical conditioning are useful in understanding how brands, products, and other symbols take on meaning for consumers; how stimuli that are neutral or uncondi- tioned take on the meaning of other stimuli. The principles of instrumental learning help to explain problem-solving activities of consumers and deal with the ways specified response patterns are increased in their frequency of occurrence from among the variety of responses that might be chosen by a consumer.

This chapter describes in some detail five components of the learning process that receive considerable attention and research by psychologists. *Drive* is any impelling stimulus that energizes behavior. *Cues* and *stimuli* are any environ-

---

[47] Thomas Smith, *Hints to Intending Advertisers* (London, 1885); quoted in Her- bert E. Krugman, "An Application of Learning Theory to TV Copy Testing," *Public Opinion Quart.*, vol. 26, pp. 626–634 (1962).

mental objects sensed by an organism. *Reinforcement* tends to strengthen the association between stimuli and responses. *Retention* refers to the stability of learned material over time. Research indicates that materials learned well are difficult to extinguish and are more likely to be replaced with new material rather than unlearned.

REVIEW AND DISCUSSION QUESTIONS

1. "Learning is the most fundamental of all human psychological processes." Defend or criticize this statement.

2. How should learning be defined? What problems exist in the definition you use?

3. Analyze the relative importance of learning theory to the understanding of human behavior compared to other forms of animal life.

4. Explain the nature of the central control unit and its relationship to learning.

5. Distinguish between classical conditioning and instrumental learning and assess the relative importance of each in an analysis of consumer behavior.

6. Are primary or secondary drives of most importance to marketing analysts? Defend your answer and give examples.

7. "The consumer can be taught to prefer any product a marketing firm chooses to offer." Analyze this statement fully. Do you agree?

8. Assess the importance of generalization and discrimination in consumer behavior.

9. How important is the concept of reinforcement in the learning of consumer preferences? Do rewards exist when a consumer watches a television commercial?

10. To what degree is the "experimental neurosis" finding with Pavlov's dog relevant to understanding brand choice with popular consumer goods?

11. What findings from learning psychology appear to have the most promise as stimulants to research in consumer behavior?

CHAPTER 10

EVALUATIVE CRITERIA

This chapter continues discussion of the functions of the central control unit (CCU) and is the first of three that focus on the elements within the CCU. As Figure 10.1 indicates, the subject here is evaluative criteria—*those specifications used by the consumer to compare and evaluate products and brands.* In other words, these are the dimensions used by the consumer in alternative evaluation.

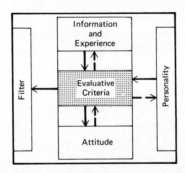

Figure 10.1 EVALUATIVE CRITERIA

It is important to understand the criteria consumers use, because a purchase usually will not be made unless these specifications are manifested in the entire marketing mix of a firm—the physical product, price, distribution, advertising copy, and so on. In addition, from a research point of view, evaluative criteria provide the dimensions for measurement of attitude as the following chapter makes clear. Hence, this chapter provides important insights into attitude measurements which are further elaborated in Chapters 11, 14, and 15.

NATURE OF EVALUATIVE CRITERIA

Evaluative criteria specify those dimensions which the consumer deems to be important in his choice of alternatives. They can either be *objective* (specific physical features such as price or durability) or *subjective* (symbolic values or benefits such as the perceived "youthfulness" of the product[1]). It is not uncommon for virtually identical products to receive widely varying evaluations because of perceived subjective differences. One airline may be preferred over another, for example, because it is evaluated as being more exciting and energetic than its more conservative, affluent counterpart.

Psychological Foundations

The model in Figure 10.1 indicates that evaluative criteria are shaped by personality and by stored information and experience. It is obvious that the consumer must have some knowledge of the class of alternatives before specifying those dimensions which are important in his decision making. Of even greater importance is the fact that evaluative criteria are a concrete manifestation of personality—those characteristics that determine general behavior, especially those which make the individual unique in comparison with others.[2] Because of this personality anchoring, evaluative criteria frequently are highly resistant to change. This, of course, has some important marketing implications as later discussion will indicate.

Personality is generally viewed as encompassing two related variables—motives and response traits. A motive is "a state of the organism in which bodily energy is mobilized and directed in a selected fashion toward states of affairs, often though not necessarily in the external environment, called goals."[3] A response trait, on the other hand, is a characteristic mode of reacting and behaving; some examples are dominance, social poise, and dependence.[4] These patterns

---

[1] I. S. White, "New Product Differentiation: 'Physical and Symbolic Dimensions'," in B. A. Morin (ed.), *Marketing in a Changing World* (Chicago: Amer. Marketing Assoc., 1969), p. 100.

[2] D. O. Hebb, *A Textbook of Psychology* (Philadelphia: Saunders, 1966).

[3] T. M. Newcomb, R. H. Turner, and P. E. Converse, *Social Psychology* (New York: Holt, Rinehart and Winston, 1965), p. 22.

[4] D. Krech, R. S. Crutchfield, and E. L. Ballachey, *Individual in Society* (New York: McGraw-Hill, 1962), chap. 4.

of values, goals, and behavior interact and are manifested in a variety of ways in behavior.

Consider, for example, the studies of achievement motivation by McClelland and his colleagues. Some of the major findings of more than 20 years of research are as follows:

(1) American males with a high achievement need most often come from middle class, have a good memory for incompleted tasks, and are active in college and community affairs.[5]

(2) Those high in achievement are more likely to take risks in situations where achievement is possible through individual efforts.[6] Furthermore, they stay at a task longer than the average person if they perceive a chance for success.[7]

(3) A need for achievement is reflected in development of internal standards; there is little desire to conform to social pressure in situations where internal and external standards conflict.[8]

These findings, in themselves, are of little value in explaining or predicting consumer behavior for reasons elaborated in Chapter 12. Consider, however, the ways in which achievement motivation might be reflected in the criteria utilized to evaluate types and brands of cameras: "allows me to take the best pictures," "allows me to make my own settings and adjustments without automatic gadgets," "gives pictures I can be proud of." The nonachievement-oriented consumer, on the other hand, might place far greater importance on automatic features which would guarantee an acceptable picture with fewer risks. Here are two distinct market segments with widely variant product specifications, and such data cannot be ignored in marketing planning. It is unlikely that either could be induced to switch the evaluative criteria used without changes first taking place in the underlying motive pattern.

Social Determinants

Reference groups may be important factors in the evaluative criteria a consumer utilizes. In clothing purchases, for example, friends and relatives can have a strong influence on the specific style which is selected, and the same would appear to hold true for the use of price, brand, and fabric. The same is true in

---

[5] D. C. McClelland, *The Achieving Society* (Princeton, N.J.: Van Nostrand, 1961), pp. 43–46.

[6] McClelland, *op. cit.*,[5] pp. 43–46.

[7] N. T. Feather, "The Relationship of Persistence at a Task to Expectation of Success and Achievement-Related Motives," *J. Abnormal and Social Psychology*, vol. 63, pp. 552–561 (1961).

[8] R. M. deCharms, H. W. Morrison, W. Reitman, and D. C. McClelland, "Behavioral Correlates of Directly and Indirectly Measured Achievement Motivation," in D. C. McClelland (ed.), *Studies in Motivation* (New York: Appleton, 1955), pp. 414–423.

many other purchase situations such as carpeting, homes, furniture, and automobiles, to mention only a few examples.[9]

Family members also have a significant role in formation of evaluative criteria. It is known that husbands and wives differ in the criteria used to evaluate automobiles, and the same is probably true in many other purchasing situations.[10]

Characteristics of Evaluative Criteria

Important characteristics include strength, the number used in reaching a decision, and relative importance.

Strength   Consumers who utilize the same criterion such as price can vary widely in the strength with which the criterion is held in a specific purchasing situation. It might for one person be the determining factor. With another it may be held in only a weak, unstructured sense.

Number Used   While firm generalizations are not possible, it is obvious that there are distinct limitations on the number of criteria that an individual can weigh simultaneously. Most studies show that six or less are generally used as is illustrated by the following examples:

(1)   Nylon stockings are selected on the basis of high quality and potential for long wear.[11]

(2)   Detergent manufacturers have found that housewives tend to judge the cleaning power of a detergent on the basis of suds level and smell. Similarly, the color of the detergent and its package is a cue often used to judge mildness.

Relative Importance   Frequently one or two criteria stand out above others as being critical in that they must be satisfied before a purchase will be made, even though all other criteria are satisfied. This has been found to be true in dress buying behavior and in other situations discussed later in the chapter.[12]

TYPES OF EVALUATIVE CRITERIA

Some of the more common types of evaluative criteria are price, label, image, appearance, performance, material, color, and durability. Several deserve special comment because of the attention afforded them in published research.

---

[9]   F. S. Bourne, *Group Influence in Marketing and Public Relations* (Ann Arbor, Mich.: Foundation for Research on Human Behavior, 1956).

[10]   G. H. Brown, "The Automobile Buying Decision within the Family," in N. Foote (ed.), *Household Decision Making* (New York: New York University Press, 1961), pp. 193–199.

[11]   D. H. Cox, "The Measurement of Information Values: A Study in Consumer Decision Making," in W. S. Decker (ed.), *Emerging Concepts in Marketing* (Chicago: Amer. Marketing Assoc., 1962), pp. 414–415.

[12]   J. E. Jacobi and F. G. Walters, "Dress Buying of Consumers," *J. Marketing*, vol. 23, pp. 168–172 (1958).

Reputation of Brand

Brand reputation frequently emerges as a dominant criterion as it did in a recent study of toothpaste, dress shirts, and suits[13] and in an earlier study of over-the-counter drug items.[14] Brand appears to be a common surrogate indicator of product quality, and its importance seems to vary with the ease by which quality can be judged objectively. If ease of evaluation is low, the consumer often will perceive a high level of risk in the purchase.[15] Reliance on a well-known brand name with a reputation of long-standing quality can be an effective strategy to reduce risk.

In the case of headache and cold remedies, there is no way in which the average consumer can judge purity and quality. Brand thus becomes especially crucial as a surrogate indicator. It is such a dominant factor with many consumers, for example, that they will pay many times more for a branded item even though they are aware that government regulations require that all aspirin products contain the same chemical formulation.

Price

There has been considerable interest in the role and significance of price, perhaps because of the relation of marketing to its parent field of economics. A number of recent studies have focused on the price–quality relationship, and there is additional evidence on the ways in which price is used as an evaluative criterion.

The Price–Quality Relationship One premise of economic theory is that price can be used as a surrogate indicator of product quality, in which case the demand curve will show a backward slope. In one of the first experimental studies on this relationship, Leavitt found that shoppers tend to choose a higher–priced item when the only difference between brands is price, presumably because of perceived higher quality.[16] A follow-up study by Tull and his colleagues found the same relationship[17] as have others,[18] but the exact form is unclear. As

[13] D. M. Gardner, "Is There a Generalized Price–Quality Relationship?" *J. Marketing Research*, vol. 8, pp. 241–243 (1971).

[14] J. F. Engel, D. A. Knapp, and D. E. Knapp, "Sources of Influence in the Acceptance of New Products for Self-Medication: Preliminary Findings," in R. M. Haas (ed.), *Science, Technology and Marketing* (Chicago: Amer. Marketing Assoc., 1966), pp. 776–782.

[15] R. A. Bauer, "Consumer Behavior as Risk Taking," in *Dynamic Marketing for a Changing World* (Chicago: Amer. Marketing Assoc., 1960), pp. 389–398.

[16] H. J. Leavitt, "A Note on Some Experimental Findings about the Meanings of Price," *J. Business*, vol. 27, pp. 205–210 (1954).

[17] D. S. Tull, R. A. Boring, and M. H. Gonsior, "A Note on the Relationship of Price and Imputed Quality," *J. Business*, vol. 37, p. 186 (1964).

[18] J. E. Stafford and B. M. Enis, "The Price–Quality Relationship: An Extension," *J. Marketing Research*, vol. 6, pp. 456–458 (1969); I. R. Andrews and E. R. Valenzi, "The Relationship Between Price and Blind-Rated Quality for Margarines and Butters," *J. Marketing Research*, vol. 7, pp. 393–395 (1970); M. E. Massey, "Consumer Reactions to Price–Quality Relations: An Exploratory Study," *Business Rev.*, pp. 25–48 (1963); B. P. Shapiro, "The Psychology of Pricing," *Harvard Business Rev.* pp. 14–25, 160 (1968).

McConnell[19] and Peterson[20] report, it may be nonlinear, in that demand will increase as price increases and vice versa without a corresponding proportional change in price and demand. It appears that price is an indicant of quality within certain upper and lower limits.[21] Above these bounds price is perceived to be too high, and below the limits the product is evaluated as being of insufficient quality.

Most of the above studies have looked at price in isolation as the sole criterion of quality judgments. That this has overstated the effects on quality perceptions has become apparent in later experiments.[22] Stafford and Enis report, for example, that quality judgments are affected by an interaction of price and store image.[23] In other situations, price has no influence on perceived quality, especially when other relevant information cues are available such as the merchandise itself, product ratings, and the brand.[24]

It appears that a positive price–quality relationship is most probable under these conditions:

(1)   When the consumer has confidence in price as a predictor of quality.[25]

(2)   When there are perceived quality variations between brands.[26]

(3)   When quality is difficult to judge in other ways, especially when there are no other quality-connoting criteria such as brand name or store location.[27] This factor is commonly assumed to be of central importance,[28] although it had only a minor role at best in the only study which has specifically manipulated this variable.[29]

Other Factors Affecting Price   Apart from the price–quality question, the use of price as a criterion varies from product to product.[30] One study found,

---

[19]   J. D. McConnell, "The Price–Quality Relationship in an Experimental Setting," *J. Marketing Research*, vol. 5, pp. 300–303 (1968).

[20]   R. A. Peterson, "The Price-Perceived Quality Relationship: Experimental Evidence," *J. Marketing Research*, vol. 7, pp. 525–528 (1970).

[21]   A. Gabor and C. W. J. Granger, "Price Sensitivity of the Consumer," *J. Advertising Research*, vol. 4, pp. 40–44 (1964); A. Gabor and C. W. J. Granger, "Price as an Indicator of Quality: Report on an Enquiry," *Economica*, vol. 33, pp. 43–70 (1966).

[22]   Peterson, *op. cit.*[20]

[23]   Stafford and Enis, *op. cit.*[18]

[24]   Gardner, *op. cit.*;[13] J. Jacoby, J. C. Olson, and R. A. Haddock, "Price, Brand Name, and Product Composition Characteristics as Determinants of Perceived Quality," *J. Applied Psychology*, vol. 55, pp. 570–580 (1971); V. R. Rao, "Salience of Price in the Perception of Product Quality: A Multidimensional Measurement Approach," paper presented at the American Marketing Association (Aug. 1971).

[25]   Z. V. Lambert, "Product Perception: An Important Variable in Price Strategy," *J. Marketing*, vol. 34, pp. 68–76 (1970).

[26]   Lambert, *op. cit.*[25]

[27]   B. P. Shapiro, "The Effect of Price on Purchase Behavior" in D. L. Sparks (ed.), *Broadening the Concept of Marketing* (Chicago: Amer. Marketing Assoc., 1970), p. 43.

[28]   Peterson, *op. cit.*;[20] Stafford and Enis, *op. cit.*;[18] McConnell, *op. cit.*[19]

[29]   Lambert, *op. cit.*[25]

[30]   Gabor and Granger, *op. cit.*[21]

for example, that concern with price was high for detergents but low for cereal.[31] In some cases, price is of greater significance when the product is perceived to be socially visible.[32]

Second, the role of price often is overrated. Consumers are not always looking for the lowest possible price or even the best price–quality ratio; other factors often assume greater importance.[33] In addition, consumers often are unaware of the price level when decisions are made.[34] In one study, for example, 25 percent of those interviewed did not know the relative price of the brand of toothpaste they had purchased.[35]

In addition, there are indications that price is a more complex criterion than many authorities seem to feel. Since consumers often are unaware of the exact prices for many products, it may be as Gabor and Granger suggest that there is a range of acceptable prices.[36] As long as price falls within this zone it may not be much of a factor, but it can become quite significant when the ranges are exceeded. This zone of acceptable prices may be the result of the consumer's perception of prices asked or paid in the past, his attitude about what the fair price should be, and the price that will allow the seller to cover his costs and earn a reasonable profit.[37]

Finally, there is some indication that the role of price is affected by the number of alternatives. The greater the number of options for satisfaction of need, the less important price tends to become.[38]

Other Criteria

The literature on other criteria used is quite meager, undoubtedly for the reason that there are substantial variations between products and between consumers.[39] It is worth emphasizing again that consumers do not always use

[31] W. D. Wells and L. A. LoSciuto, "Direct Observation of Purchasing Behavior," *J. Marketing Research*, vol. 3, pp. 227–233 (1966).

[32] Lambert, *op. cit.*[25]

[33] E. Katz and P. F. Lazarsfeld, *Personal Influence* (New York: Free Press, 1955); I. S. White, "The Perception of Value in Products," in J. Newman (ed.), *On Knowing the Consumer* (New York: Wiley, 1966), pp. 90–106, esp. pp. 92–93; Wells and LoSciuto, *op. cit.*[31]

[34] F. E. Brown, "Price Image Versus Price Reality," *J. Marketing Research*, vol. 6, pp. 185–191 (1969); C. S. Craig, J. F. Engel, and W. W. Talarzyk, "Consumer Decision-Making: On the Importance of Price," in D. M. Gardner (ed.), *Proc. 2nd Annual Conf. of the Association for Consumer Research* (College Park, Md.: College of Business and Public Administration, University of Maryland, 1971), pp. 243–255.

[35] G. Haines, "A Study of Why People Purchase New Products," in Haas, *op. cit.*,[14] pp. 665–685, at p. 683.

[36] Gabor and Granger, *op. cit.*[21]

[37] A. O. Oxenfeldt, *Establishing a New Product Program: Guides for Effective Planning and Organization* (New York: Amer. Management Assoc., 1958), pp. 17–18.

[38] L. K. Anderson, J. R. Taylor, and R. J. Holloway, "The Consumer and His Alternatives: An Experimental Approach," *J. Marketing Research*, vol. 3, p. 64 (1966).

[39] For some additional evidence see S. A. Smith, "How Do Consumers Choose Between Brands of Durable Goods?" *J. Retailing*, pp. 18–26, 87 (Summer, 1970).

physical or objective criteria to evaluate alternatives.[40] Subjective factors can become dominant as the following example illustrates:

> Company *A* designed a calculator for office use. Company *B* was well established in the field. Company *A* conducted an experiment utilizing three testing conditions: (1) *appropriate brand labeling*; both machines were placed in each office with their correct company and brand names; (2) *reverse brand labeling*; both machines were placed in each office with the company and brand names reversed; and (3) *blind labeling*; both machines were unidentified except for neutral letters *X* and *Y*. The results of the test indicated that under *appropriate brand labeling*, Company *A*'s machine was rated somewhat inferior to Company *B*'s but when labels were reversed, Company *A*'s machine rated far superior to Company *B*'s. In the *blind-labeling* situation, Company *A* was also rated superior, but the margin was not as great.[41]

MEASURING EVALUATIVE CRITERIA

Because of the growing recognition of the importance of understanding the evaluative criteria that consumers use,[42] considerable attention must be paid to problems of measurement. There are four distinct measurement problems: (1) determining awareness of the product category, (2) assessing the categories of evaluative criteria, (3) reducing redundancy in data, and (4) measuring the importance of each category.

Awareness

It is not uncommon for a durable-goods purchase to be made with no specific product or brand feature in mind.[43] Under such circumstances a questionnaire focusing on salient evaluative criteria is likely to produce meaningless results. Therefore, the first step is to determine the consumer's experience with the product category.

Assessing Categories of Criteria

To isolate the criteria that are used, there are several research approaches which might be utilized: (1) direct questioning, (2) depth questioning, (3) dual questioning, (4) projective questioning, and (5) nonmetric multidimensional scaling.

---

[40]   I. S. White, *op. cit.*[33]

[41]   White, *op. cit.*,[33] pp. 101–102.

[42]   John A. Howard and Jagdish N. Sheth, *The Theory of Buyer Behavior* (New York: Wiley, 1969), esp. pp. 118–126.

[43]   Eva Mueller, "A Study of Purchase Decisions. Part 2. The Sample Survey," in L. H. Clark (ed.), *Consumer Behavior, vol. 1: The Dynamics of Consumer Reaction* (New York: New York University Press, 1955), p. 49.

Direct Questioning   In this approach the individual is requested to state the reasons for his buying action on the assumption that he is aware of salient criteria and will state them when asked. Those which receive the most frequent mention or highest ranking then are considered to be the dominant or determinant factors. While offering simplicity and ease of analysis, this approach is fraught with dangers that other procedures are designed to remedy.

Depth Questioning   The attribute labels mentioned in direct questioning often are highly ambiguous.[44] For example, assume that a consumer says price is important in the purchase of an electric iron. She might be saying one or more of several things: (1) "I would not purchase an iron costing more than $20," (2) "I will not pay $8–$10 more for the built-in sprinkling mechanism," (3) "I will seriously consider a brand only if it is within the $8–$14 range," or (4) "I know there are price differences between stores, so I will shop around." Obviously the questioning procedure should go into sufficient depth to probe the meaning of attribute labels. This can be done through a free-form guided interview (depth interview) in which respondents, either individually or collectively in a group, expand on their answers.

Dual Questioning   Another difficulty with the direct questioning approach is that a criterion such as style may not be mentioned for the reason that all available alternatives are essentially similar.[45] Under different circumstances it might well emerge as being of significance. This can be overcome by dual questioning which calls for a two-phase rating: (1) importance of attribute and (2) the extent of perceived differences between alternatives along the dimension in question.[46] These two ratings then are combined into one score.

Projective Questioning   It is frequently objected that the consumer will not verbalize the reasons for his decision in a direct interview.[47] One proposed remedy is the projective approach which usually attempts to elicit a response in third person. An example would be, "What product features do most of the people around here consider to be important in buying a dishwasher?" Presumably biases will be overcome through a feeling by the respondent that he or she is not revealing personal opinions. The underlying premise of the projective approach has not been verified experimentally,[48] so it is seldom used.

---

[44]   T. T. Semon, "On the Perception of Appliance Attributes," *J. Marketing Research,* vol. 6, p. 101 (1969).

[45]   Semon, *op. cit.*[44]

[46]   M. I. Alpert, "Identification of Determinant Attributes: A Comparison of Methods," *J. Marketing Research,* vol. 8, pp. 184–191 (1971).

[47]   See, for example, E. Dichter, *The Strategy of Desire* (New York: Doubleday, 1960).

[48]   J. F. Engel and H. G. Wales, "Spoken Versus Pictured Questions on Taboo Topics," *J. Advertising Research,* vol. 2, pp. 11–17 (1962).

Nonmetric Multidimensional Scaling It is an undeniable fact that many find great difficulty in spelling out the reasons for the actions. Therefore, a research aproach which can avoid asking this type of question has great intuitive appeal. This is one of several advantages offered by nonmetric multidimensional scaling (MDS) which has found growing use in recent years.[49]

Respondents are asked to rate similarities between alternatives, two at a time, usually on a 10–12-point scale ranging from similar to dissimilar. Alternatives then are rank ordered in terms of perceived similarities (or dissimilarities), and a computer algorithm generates a Euclidean-space configuration of two or more dimensions which best reproduces the original rank order of the input data.[50] The dimensions of the computer output can then be interpreted as the evaluative criteria used in the ratings of similarity–dissimilarity.

An example will clarify the nature of MDS. Company X opened 10 outlets in two midwest cities in the quick-service franchised restaurant field. An attempt was made to gain competitive advantage through a higher priced, higher quality menu. After one year of operation, it was felt that a survey was needed to evaluate success to date. Part of the study focused on ratings of the 10 leading competitors, including Company X.

Each of the 10 competitors was rated in terms of perceived similarities to others along a ten-point scale. The MDS computer output generated a configuration of these competitors in two dimensions. This configuration closely reproduced the original rank-order-data matrix as is indicated by a Kruskal Stress score of .046 (the lower the better). It appeared that the axes of the resulting solution were *service* and *quality/price*. These descriptive labels were suggested by other data from the original questionnaire. The price/quality dimension was most important in the perceived similarity ratings (it explained 63 percent of the variance). The data from the MDS solution appear in Figure 10.2.

Notice that respondents never were asked to specify evaluative criteria. These are inferred from the output configuration. This, of course, can offer an advantage. It also should be apparent, however, that the labeling of the axes is extremely subjective. Another disadvantage is that categories of evaluative criteria cannot be determined until alternatives are rated, thus placing greater demands on data collection. Finally, there are some troublesome methodological issues, but space limitations will not permit elaboration.[51]

Which Method Is Best? Some light was shed on the comparative usefulness of several of the above approaches in one study which analyzed direct,

---

[49] For a good introduction to this subject, see P. E. Green and D. S. Tull, *Research for Marketing Decisions* (Englewood Cliffs, N.J.: Prentice-Hall, 1970), chap. 7.

[50] F. W. Young and W. S. Torgerson, "TORSCA, a Fortran IV Program for Shepard–Kruskal Multidimensional Scaling Analysis," *Behavioral Science*, vol. 12, pp. 498–499 (1967).

[51] P. E. Green and F. J. Carmone, *Multidimensional Scaling and Related Techniques in Marketing Analysis* (Boston: Allyn and Bacon, 1970); Howard and Sheth, *op. cit.*,[42] chap. 6.

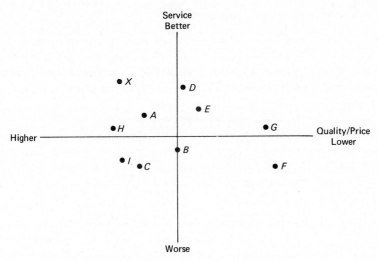

Figure 10.2 TWO-DIMENSIONAL MDS CONFIGURATION OF TEN QUICK-SERVICE RESTAURANTS. Axis I—quality/price: 63 percent; axis II—service: 18 percent. Kruskal stress: 0.046

projective, and dual questioning.[52] It was found that dual questioning is the superior approach to use in isolating attributes in preference ratings, followed by direct and projective questioning in that order.

Dual questioning, of course, offers the distinct advantages of isolating attributes and determining the presence or absence of perceived differences between alternatives on these dimensions. Hence, it is the recommended approach when it is felt that respondents can and will verbalize the rationale for their choice. If barriers seem to exist which inhibit accurate response, MDS may be the preferred approach.

Reduction of Redundancy in the Data

It is not uncommon to require respondents to utilize categories of evaluative criteria in the questioning process which, in reality, are tapping the same dimension. Thus, it may be possible to condense 10 or 15 to a smaller subset. A variety of statistical techniques is available for this purpose, referred to by the generic label "factor analysis."[53] Each method summarizes linear relationships among a set of variables and thereby discloses the underlying correlations which may exist.

[52] Alpert, *op. cit.*[46]

[53] For a good introduction to this subject, see H. H. Harmon, *Modern Factor Analysis,* 2nd ed. (Chicago: University of Chicago Press, 1960).

Measuring Attribute Importance

Once appropriate categories of evaluative criteria have been isolated, the next step is to assess the importance of each. There are three possible approaches: (1) a rating prior to evaluation of alternatives; (2) multiple-regression analysis after alternatives have been evaluated, and (3) conjoint analysis.

Rating Scales   The most common procedure is to ask respondents to assess the importance of each criterion prior to evaluation of the alternatives. In the restaurant example given earlier it was known from a previous study that consumers use nine basic factors when making decisions. They were asked as part of the larger study to rate the importance of each on a nine-point scale as follows:

	Important					*Unimportant*			
Good products	1	2	3	4	5	6	7	8	9
Good service	1	2	3	4	5	6	7	8	9
Low prices	1	2	3	4	5	6	7	8	9
Clean facilities	1	2	3	4	5	6	7	8	9
Open 24 hours	1	2	3	4	5	6	7	8	9
Well-known company	1	2	3	4	5	6	7	8	9
Wide range of choices	1	2	3	4	5	6	7	8	9
Convenient location	1	2	3	4	5	6	7	8	9
Many outlets	1	2	3	4	5	6	7	8	9

An alternative is to employ paired adjectives such as "nutritious" and "not nutritious" using a similar numerical rating scale.[54] Also, some prefer to ask respondents to allocate 100 points across the categories to reflect their ranking of importance.

There always is the question of proper phrasing for the scale intervals. Only one study has specifically focused on methods for assigning weights to evaluative criteria, and the following results are reported:[55]

(1)   Rank orders of attribute importance appear to be quite stable across versions; simple "yes–no" or "1–6" judgments work as well as a more difficult task such as assigning points to attributes ranging from 0 to 100.

(2)   The use of a "1–6" gradient scale seems to generate finer distinctions

---

[54]   For useful insights into the wording of these adjectives, see J. H. Myers and W. G. Warner, "Semantic Properties of Selected Evaluation Adjectives," *J. Marketing Research*, vol. 5, pp. 409–412 (1968).

[55]   D. E. Schendel, W. L. Wilkie, and J. M. McCann, "An Experimental Investigation of 'Attribute Importance'," in Gardner, *op. cit.*,[34] pp. 404–416.

when used alone than an arbitrary dichotomy for importance such as "yes–no."

(3) There are some differences between these versions, which raises the question of the wisdom of using a single measuring device.

Further research obviously is needed. Not only must it be determined how relative rankings of attribute importance change from one method to another, but further inquiries also must employ some type of external criterion of importance against which each approach can be assessed. In the absence of this type of evidence, it is recommended that a nondichotomous rating scale be used, and the number of scale positions is apparently a matter of the researcher's personal preference.

Multiple Regression At times it is difficult for the respondent to rate each criterion, especially when the list is long. It is feasible to omit this step and go directly to the rating of alternatives along each attribute, thus generating an attitude score. It then is possible to compute a multiple regression between ratings of alternatives and stated preference for the same alternatives. The relative importance of contribution of each evaluative criterion to the rating emerges as a standardized regression coefficient (beta weight). The beta weight specifies the percentage of the variation in preference ratings accounted for by each criterion.

This approach has been used successfully by some authorities. In an analysis of preferences for instant breakfast products, for example, taste was found to be the criterion which explained more variance than all other criteria combined.[56]

Conjoint Analysis Both of the above procedures require a respondent to rate each attribute one at a time. The possibility of interaction effects between criteria thus is overlooked. A mouthwash that provides both taste and germ-killing power, for example, may be rated more positively than it would be on either criterion considered singly. A new development in mathematical psychology called conjoint measurement permits measurement of "bundles of benefits" as well as part-worth contributions of each benefit to an overall rating of preference.[57] The only input data required are rank-ordered ratings of various benefit groupings, and the computational algorithm (usually the Kruskal Monanova program[58]) transforms these ordinal rankings into an interval scale and computes values reflecting the contributory importance of each benefit or evaluative criterion.[59]

---

[56] J. N. Sheth, "An Investigation of Relationships among Evaluative Beliefs, Affect, Behavioral Intention, and Behavior," unpublished paper (Urbana, Ill.: University of Illinois, 1970).

[57] P. E. Green and V. R. Rao, "Conjoint Measurement for Quantifying Judgmental Data," *J. Marketing Research*, vol. 8, pp. 355–363 (1971).

[58] J. B. Kruskal, "Analysis of Factorial Experiments by Estimating Monotone Transformations of the Data," *J. Royal Statistical Society*, ser. B, vol. 27, pp. 251–263 (Mar. 1965).

[59] The methodological details are thoroughly discussed in Green and Rao, *op. cit.*[57]

This methodology was used to determine the nature of market segments for aerosol hard-surface floor cleaners based on differences in product benefits evaluation.[60] Preliminary research established the following benefits as being of major interest: (1) makes the floor covering seem fresh and new, (2) does not take out color or fade the floor covering, (3) restores the floor covering to like-new brightness, (4) cleans away deep-down ground-in soil, and (5) protects the floor covering against resoiling. Cards were made up for all pairs of benefits (10), all quadruples of benefits (5) and one quintuple of benefits, a total of 16 cards. Respondents were asked to rank these 16 combinations in terms of what they would most like to see in this type of product. The Monanova analysis disclosed a cluster of two highly valued benefits, "cleans away deep-down, ground-in soil" and "protects the floor covering against resoiling." The other benefits were valued about equally and well below the above two.

This approach offers two distinct benefits: (1) it considers clusters or groups of criteria, and (2) the input data are ordinal rankings. It is only experimental as of this writing, but it appears to have promise.

Concluding Comments

For most applications, the following procedure would appear to be most satisfactory: (1) assess awareness of the product class and eliminate further study of those individuals with low scores, (2) isolate categories of evaluative criteria through dual questioning augmented by probing to clarify the meaning of evaluative labels, (3) factor analyze the data matrix to reduce redundancies and to disclose intercorrelations in the data, and (4) establish an importance rating for each criterion directly through a rating scale. If respondents seem to be unable to specify salient dimensions, MDS might be advisable. Similarly, statistical estimating procedures can be utilized to determine importance weightings if direct ratings are, for some reason, to be avoided.

CAN EVALUATIVE CRITERIA BE CHANGED?

It was pointed out earlier that evaluative criteria have their roots in stored information and experience, personality, and reference-group influence. As a result, they often resist change, thus raising a dilemma for marketing. In the final analysis this question becomes one of consumer education.

The Marketer's Dilemma

A market research study was undertaken and results indicated that the following criteria are used by a large segment of people to evaluate headache

---

[60] P. E. Green, Y. Wind, and A. K. Jain, "Benefit Bundles Analysis and Market Segmentation," unpublished paper (Philadelphia: University of Pennsylvania, Oct. 1971).

remedies (on a scale of 1–6, where 1 represents very important and 6 represents very unimportant):

Speed of relief	1.5
Reputation of brand	1.7
Quality of ingredients	2.3
Price	4.3
No side effects	4.8
Used by friends	5.6

Brand *A* was found to rate relatively well on most criteria, especially on price, but it rates poorly on reputation of brand. The brand has a six-percent share of market and sells at a price roughly 40 percent below that of the three leading competitors.

Management now is faced with a dilemma, since its price advantage is of comparative unimportance to most buyers, and reputation of the brand is weak. This later factor is especially critical because, as was discussed earlier, reputation of brand often is a surrogate indicator of product quality.

One alternative for remedial action is to convince buyers that all brands are identical; hence, the "rational" consumer should buy on the basis of price. From a strictly objective point of view, this could be in the best interest of consumers since government ratings (USP) do guarantee that all products sold contain the same chemical formulation. An advertising message with this theme, however, probably would prove ineffective with most of the members of this market segment. Reputation of brand is a strongly held evaluative criterion, and, similarly, there are strong negative views regarding the importance of price. The message probably will be screened out in the information-processing stage through selective attention. Even if the consumer is aware of the advertisement, he will probably distort the content and retain his views unchallenged. The reasons for this selective screening were discussed earlier, and it can be a major inhibitor to promotional success.

Others have tried this first option with minimal success. Aluminum manufacturers tried for many years to convince consumers that a light-weight cooking utensil could be as high in quality as the more traditional heavier product. It was found that this belief was exceedingly difficult to change. Similarly, a manufacturer of ceiling tile found to his dismay that it was impossible to sell a tile without holes. The reason was a deepseated conviction that sound absorption capability was in proportion to the number of holes per square foot. Many other examples could be given. It should not be concluded that evaluative criteria *never* change; rather, change is most likely when the underlying determinants of the criterion change.

The discussion thus far has assumed that the manufacturer will use only the mass media in an attempt to change beliefs about price, and the difficulties are obvious. Another approach, however, is to employ personal selling. At times, consumers are quite receptive to help from a sales person, especially when they have had little relevant past experience, when something has happened to change previous beliefs, or when there is high perceived risk surrounding the purchase. Training of sales people to suggest more appropriate evaluative criteria has proved highly successful for the EMBA Mink Company, the Royal Worcester Porcelain Company, and many others.[61] Unfortunately, personal selling seems to be a lost art in the case of over-the-counter drugs. Greatest emphasis now lies on self-service, and, furthermore, unpublished results from the Ohio State University self-medication studies show that pharmacists tend to be ineffective information sources.

Given the difficulties in changing evaluative criteria, the manufacturer should turn to other options: (1) settle for the present market, (2) introduce appropriate changes in the marketing mix to adapt more accurately to consumers' criteria, or (3) attack a different segment which uses price as a criterion. If the current share is profitable, it may be most appropriate to introduce no changes. If this is not the situation, serious consideration should be given to raising the price and making real efforts to solidify brand image and reputation through intensified advertising and point-of-sale promotion. The final option is to redirect efforts to a segment which is more willing to buy a low-priced item without demanding a well-known brand.

Benefit Segmentation

As a general rule it can be stated that the best strategy usually is to accept *strongly held evaluative criteria* as given and make modifications in the marketing mix where necessary to match company offerings with consumer specifications.[62] The only exception would arise when (1) evaluative criteria are fluid and consumers appear to be receptive to new information, or (2) the criteria are not strongly held and hence some likelihood of change is shown through marketing influence.

Often good marketing opportunities are discovered by analysis of consumer attribute preferences; it is not unusual to uncover one or more segments which are not being adequately served by existing alternatives. This is referred to as "benefit segmentation."[63]

Table 10.1 shows the results of a hypothetical benefit segmentation of the under $50.00 camera market. Notice that three segments emerge: (1) "do it yourselfers," (2) "black-box users," and (3) "timid photographers." Do it yourselfers take pride in their pictures and prefer a camera which allows them to make all necessary settings and adjustments. The black-box user, on the other hand, prefers an instrument which he can aim and shoot with no difficulty. Finally, the timid

---

[61] J. F. Engel, W. W. Talarzyk, and C. M. Larson, *Cases in Promotional Strategy* (Homewood, Ill.: Irwin, 1971), pp. 361–366, 373–380.

[62] F. Hansen, "Consumer Choice Behavior: An Experimental Approach," *J. Marketing Research,* vol. 6, pp. 436–443 (1969).

[63] R. I. Haley, "Benefit Segmentation: A Decision-Oriented Research Tool," *J. Marketing,* vol. 32, pp. 30–35 (1968); R. I. Haley, "Beyond Benefit Segmentation," *J. Advertising Research,* vol. 11, pp. 3–8 (1971).

Table 10.1   A BENEFIT SEGMENTATION OF THE UNDER $50.00 CAMERA MARKET

"Do it Yourselfer" (25 percent)
    Great pride in good pictures
    Gratification from making settings and adjustments
    Pride in a complex camera
    Sees a good picture as resulting from his expertise

"Black Box User" (40 percent)
    Taking pictures seen only as a necessary evil
    Little pride expressed if the picture is good
    Desire for camera to be as simple as possible

"Timid Photographer" (35 percent)
    Great pride in good pictures
    High perceived risk that the picture will not be good
    No confidence in ability to manipulate camera and settings
    Desires camera to guarantee a good picture without his effort

SOURCE: James F. Engel, Henry Fiorillo, and Murray A. Cayley (eds.), *Market Segmentation: Concepts and Strategy* (New York: Holt, Rinehart and Winston, 1972), p. 18. Reprinted by permission of the publisher.

photographer shares the do it yourselfer's concern over high picture quality but lacks confidence in his ability to manipulate settings and gadgets. He wants a high-quality completely automatic camera which almost guarantees a perfect picture.

At the present time the do-it-yourself market for under $50.00 cameras is not being adequately supplied as is illustrated by the continued sale of used Kodak Pony cameras which, until fairly recently, featured full settings and adjustments. Thus a market opportunity appears to exist for an enterprising firm. Other segments are being satisfied by a wide variety of alternatives.

Notice how these data can be utilized in promotional strategy. Product benefits can be highlighted and amplified in the message so that maximum appeal is made to stated preferences. The timid photographer could be appealed to, for instance, by demonstrating that the only requirement is to "aim and shoot."

Consumer Education

There are a number of instances where the consumer probably does not get maximum value from his outlays. The headache remedy case is a good example where a lower personal expenditure will provide comparable therapeutic effects. Unfortunately many consumers tend to be ignorant of such facts, especially those with minimal educational backgrounds. Therefore, there is a real need for consumer education, especially in the area of substituting objective criteria, where possible, for subjective considerations.

Consumers' Union has been in the vanguard of the consumer education movement for many years, and the circulation of *Consumers' Reports* now approaches two million. This magazine publishes product tests that compare alternatives on many dimensions which are impossible for the consumer without extensive testing equipment. He thus is able to make a decision on a more objective basis. The purchaser of a high-fidelity speaker, for instance, can make his selection on the basis of performance curves, compatibility with various types of inputs, and other objective considerations in addition to the way in which it "sounds" to him.

There is increasing emphasis on the consumer in the schools. It seems especially appropriate to offer this subject so that the young consumer can learn how to be a wise buyer before he actually enters the market in a major way.

It is not the purpose to discuss consumer education fully at this point, since it is considered in one of the concluding chapters. Rather, the intent is to point out that evaluative criteria can be changed through education. In a world in which the pace of change is almost overwhelming,[64] the role of this type of education will increase.

SUMMARY

This chapter has examined one of the major components of the CCU —evaluative criteria. Evaluative criteria are those specifications, either subjective or objective, used by consumers to compare and evaluate alternatives. They are a product-specific manifestation of stored knowledge surrounding the product class as well as such personality determinants as motives and response traits. In addition, there can be distinct reference group and family influences on the criteria which are employed. Because of these roots in such basic dispositions, evaluative criteria are difficult to change through marketing influences and usually must be accepted as given and adapted to accordingly. Considerable emphasis was placed on measurement, and the following phases were discussed: (1) assessment of product-class awareness, (2) isolation of categories of criteria, (3) determination of the importance of each criterion, and (4) measurement of inter-correlations and redundancies in the data. Many of the practical implications emerge more sharply in the next chapter, since evaluative criteria provide the foundation for attitude measurement.

REVIEW AND DISCUSSION QUESTIONS

1. What are evaluative criteria? What criteria did you use when you purchased your last pair of shoes? How did these differ, if at all, from those used by others in your family?

2. It is frequently alleged that the consumer is irrational and fails to buy wisely

---

[64] For a pertinent analysis of the effects of change, see A. Toffler, *Future Shock* (New York: Random House, 1970).

if he does not make maximum use of objective criteria in his purchasing decisions. Evaluate.

3. One of the major criteria mentioned by many college girls in the purchase of an underarm deodorant is that "it makes me feel more confident in the presence of others." From your understanding of psychological and social influences on behavior, assess the probable underlying determinants of this evaluative criterion.

4. How important is reputation of brand as an alternative criterion in each of these product classes? Hand soap, toilet paper, panty hose, men's shirts, china and glassware, and gasoline. What are the reasons for your answers?

5. Summarize the evidence on the price–quality relationship. Would you expect this relationship in each of the types of products mentioned in question 4? Why or why not?

6. What is the "fair price" theory? How would it function in the purchase of gasoline?

7. Before World War II, the Customer Research Department of the General Motors Corporation regularly asked people to appraise the relative importance of certain product attributes using direct questions. It usually was found that highest marks were given to dependability and safety; styling was rated lower, and price was somewhere in between. What uses, if any, can be made of these data in marketing planning?

8. What arguments can you advance in favor of using MDS to isolate salient evaluative criteria? What are the weaknesses of this approach?

9. What are surrogate indicators? Why are they used?

10. Using a product of your own choice, prepare a research proposal indicating how you would determine the evaluative criteria which are being used in the purchase process.

11. Today considerable importance is being placed on consumer education. What are the causes of the so-called "consumer movement?" What is the role of the business firm in educating consumers on how to buy wisely?

CHAPTER 11

ATTITUDES

This chapter continues the discussion of the dispositions within the central control unit that affect both information processing and behavior. The focus is on attitudes—a person's basic orientations for or against various alternatives for purchasing and consumption. Attitudes form a coherent system of evaluative orientations, and it is not an overstatement to say that they comprise the most important component of one's "map of one's world."

This chapter raises the introductory issues of (1) the nature and function of attitudes, (2) attitude measurement, and (3) fundamental considerations in attitude change. Chapter 14 will continue the discussion, with the emphasis lying on the use of persuasive communications to bring about attitude change.

THE NATURE AND FUNCTION OF ATTITUDES

It is necessary to be very precise in defining this variable, because the variety of published definitions and descriptions is almost endless.[1] This question is explored first, followed by a consideration of attitude organization and function.

---

[1] W. J. McGuire, "The Nature of Attitudes and Attitude Change," in G. Lindsey

The section concludes with the important issue of whether or not attitude change is a valid marketing goal.

The Nature of Attitudes

According to one widely accepted definition, attitude is a mental and neural state of readiness to respond which is organized through experience and exerts a directive and/or dynamic influence on behavior.[2] This definition is too global for marketing purposes, however, since attitude in this basic sense is more appropriately considered as a component of personality which will be discussed in the next chapter.

In a more narrow context, attitude is used here to refer to a consumer's assessment of the ability of an alternative to satisfy his purchasing and consumption requirements as expressed in evaluative criteria. These ratings, in turn, utilize stored information, with the result that attitude becomes the focal variable of the central control unit as Figure 11.1 depicts.

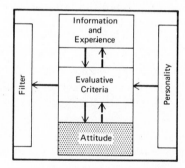

Figure 11.1   ATTITUDE

It is traditionally accepted that there are three underlying attitude components: (1) *cognitive*—the manner in which the attitude object is perceived, (2) *affective*—feelings of like or dislike, and (3) *behavioral*—action tendencies toward the attitude object. The definition used here provides a measure of the affective dimension through ratings of alternatives along the cognitive dimension. The behavioral dimension is not specifically comprehended in the definition, because it is best conceived as corresponding to *behavioral intentions*. Intentions,

and E. Aronson (eds.), *Handbook of Social Psychology* (Reading, Mass.: Addison-Wesley, 1968), pp. 136–141; T. M. Ostrom, "The Emergence of Attitude Theory: 1939–1950," in H. E. Greenwald, T. C. Brock, and T. M. Ostrom (eds.), *Psychological Foundations of Attitude* (New York: Academic Press, 1968), pp. 1–32; C. A. Kiesler, B. E. Collins, and N. Miller, *Attitude Change—A Critical Analysis of Theoretical Approaches* (New York: Wiley, 1969), chap. 1; P. Zimbardo and E. B. Ebbesen, *Influencing Attitudes and Changing Behavior* (Reading, Mass.: Addison-Wesley, 1969).

    [2] G. Allport, "Attitudes," in C. Murchison (ed.), *Handbook of Social Psychology* (Worcester, Mass.: Clark University Press, 1935), pp. 798–884.

in turn, do not become significant until a problem is recognized and problem-solving behavior commences. It is shown later in the chapter that attitude closely correlates with intentions.

Attitude Organization

Attitudes do not exist in isolation; indeed, a complex structure results which appears to have at its heart a consistent tendency to maintain balance and resist change from influences of various types. Moreover, the internal components (that is, the affective, cognitive, and behavioral dimensions) also exist in balance. Human beings appear to have a basic motivation to maintain consistency and possess a set of abilities to screen reality for this purpose.[3] It is necessary to grasp why attitude change is sometimes resisted and the nature of the mechanisms which can be used for that purpose.

Internal Consistency　In his pioneering treatise on the internal organization of an attitude, Rosenberg asserted that most individuals cannot long tolerate an inconsistency or imbalance between the affective and cognitive components.[4] When affective and cognitive consistency is attained, the attitude is said to be in a stable state which persists over time. There is a tolerance limit for inconsistency, and the attitude will become unstable and undergo reorganization when this threshold is exceeded. Perhaps new information is received which challenges previously held beliefs regarding a preferred brand. Reorganization will now take place until balance is once again restored through (1) rejection of the stimulus input which introduced the inconsistency, (2) a fragmentation or splitting of the attitude so as to isolate each mutually inconsistent affective or cognitive component, or (3) some sort of accommodation so that a new attitude emerges with internal stability.

Interattitude Structure　Each person maintains basic values and social relationships which are seen to have high personal goal relevance. Each of these can serve as a significant *anchor* for attitudes in that dispositions are formed and retained which reflect a positive orientation toward the person's conception of himself.

Attitudes that are closely related to the self concept and basic values are said to have *centrality*. Attitudes with central anchoring points, in turn, tend to become organized so that a change in one affects the others. Therefore, the person strives to attain balance in his attitudinal structure, and attitude change may be difficult:

> Insofar as a person's attitude toward something is imbedded in a larger latticework of attitudes—and such things as the amount of stored

---

[3]　M. J. Rosenberg, "Inconsistency Arousal and Reduction in Attitude Change," in I. D. Steiner and M. Fishbein (eds.), *Current Studies in Social Psychology* (New York: Holt, Rinehart and Winston, 1965), pp. 123–124.

[4]　Rosenberg, *op. cit.*[3]

information about the object, its personal goal relevance and psychological centrality are all indicators of such imbedding—any attempt to change the attitude must come to grips with the fact that *this attitude is anchored by the other attitudes in the system*. Such an attitude does not exist in a vacuum; if *it* changes, then other compensatory changes must follow to restore balance.[5]

A striving toward maintenance of balance and resistance to change, on the other hand, is greatly reduced when attitudes are peripheral to the self-concept, basic values, and other significant focal objects.

Do attitudes toward marketing alternatives ever attain such a degree of centrality that change is resisted? This can happen on occasion, although it must be admitted that product or brand attitudes generally reflect far less personal commitment. Attitudes toward brands of coffee, however, often attain high centrality. Many housewives are of the belief that their competence as a cook and even as a wife is determined in part by the quality of the coffee they serve. When one brand is perceived as producing satisfactory results, the resulting attitude is likely to be so imbedded that change is unlikely.

Determinants of Attitude Strength The probability of change varies inversely with attitude strength. In addition to centrality, the other basic determinant of strength is the amount of stored information and past experience which underlies the rating of the alternative. In other words, "Attitudes about an object are more subject to change through contradictory incoming information *when the existing mass of stored information about the object is smaller*."[6] When centrality and/or stored information both are high, on the other hand, attempts to bring about change may well result in selective attention, comprehension, and retention.

Attitude Functions

Attitudes have traditionally been viewed as serving four functions: (1) adjustment, (2) ego defensive, (3) value expressive, and (4) knowledge.[7]

Adjustment Attitudes serve as a means to reach a desired goal or to avoid an undesired one. For example, a neighborhood gas station is perceived as offering friendly high-quality service. The surprised and pleased consumer forms a favorable attitude toward this station and centers his patronage there. His attitude thus serves to provide guidance as he attempts to maximize satisfaction.

---

[5] T. M. Newcomb, R. H. Turner, and P. E. Converse, *Social Psychology* (New York: Holt, Rinehart and Winston, 1965), p. 136.

[6] Newcomb, *et al., op. cit.*,[5] p. 91.

[7] D. Katz, "The Functional Approach to the Study of Attitudes," *Public Opinion Quart.*, vol. 24, pp. 163–204 (1960).

Ego Defensive In other situations, the attitude may have centrality as was discussed above. In those circumstances, attitudes are formed to protect and enhance the ego.

Value Expressive Attitudes also are formed to give concrete expression to basic values. Heavy users of a widely known condiment were found to have strong preference for this product. The product, in turn, connoted tradition and was seen as embodying fundamental American values. For those whose own values were compatible there tended to be strong loyalty.

Knowledge Finally, attitudes help provide a frame of reference for understanding and adapting to the world. Individuals rarely can engage in conscious problem solving every time the need arises. Preferences thus can be instrumental in formation of routines for thought and analysis.

Is Attitude Change a Valid Marketing Goal?

Attitudes affect both information processing and behavior. Given this fact, it would appear to be a valid conclusion that a change in attitude will be accompanied by a change in behavior. The evidence is far from conclusive on this point, however, and there are many issues to be considered.

Negative Evidence As early as 1934 it was shown that behavior was not predicted from written statements which presumably reflected attitudes toward minority groups.[8] Festinger, in fact, was unable to find any consistent published evidence that attitudes and behavior are related, although it must be pointed out that his review neglected vast areas of relevant findings.[9] Others agree with Festinger's negative conclusions,[10] and Deutscher stated that "disparities between thought and action are the central methodological problem of the social sciences.[11] Fishbein concludes that:

> After more than 70–75 years of attitude research, there is still little, if any, consistent evidence supporting the hypothesis that knowledge of an individual's attitude toward some object will allow one to predict the way he will behave with respect to that object. Indeed, what little evidence there is to support any relationship

---

[8] R. T. LaPiere, "Attitudes vs. Actions," *Social Forces*, vol. 13, pp. 230–237 (1934).

[9] L. Festinger, "Behavioral Support for Opinion Change," *Public Opinion Quart.*, vol. 28, pp. 404–417 (1964).

[10] A. G. Greenwald, "Effects of a Prior Commitment on Behavior Change After a Persuasive Communication," *Public Opinion Quart.*, vol. 29, pp. 595–601 (1965–1966); L. S. Linn, "Verbal Attitudes and Overt Behavior: A Study of Racial Discrimination," *Social Forces*, vol. 43, pp. 353–363 (1965); S. Bellin and L. Kriesberg, "Relationship Between Attitudes, Circumstances, and Behavior: The Case of Applying for Public Housing," *Sociology and Social Research*, vol. 51, pp. 453–469 (1967).

[11] L. Deutscher, "Words and Deeds: Social Science and Social Policy," *Social Problems*, vol. 3, p. 235 (1966).

between attitude and behavior comes from studies that a person tends to bring his attitude into line with his behavior rather than from studies demonstrating that behavior is a function of attitude.[12]

Positive Evidence　There also is a considerable body of evidence which demonstrates that attitudes and behavior are related, with the result that attitude change results in behavioral change. It has been reported, for example, that good commercials affect both attitude and behavior;[13] attitudes will predict behavior when proper attention is paid to measurement;[14] attitudes toward trading stamps are reflected in trading stamp usage;[15] first brand awareness (one type of attitude scale) predicts short-term purchase behavior;[16] and the use of price as an evaluative criterion in convenience goods purchases can be predicted by an attitude battery.[17]

Several marketing researchers feel that attitude change should be a primary goal of promotional strategy. DuBois, for example, reported that the better the level of attitude, the more users you hold and the more nonusers you attract.[18] In addition, studies at Grey Advertising, Inc. have led to this conclusion:

> More and more psychologists are coming to the conclusion that to result in a sale an advertisement must bring about a positive change in the *attitude* of the reader or viewer. . . . That there is a definite relationship between *change of attitude* toward a brand and buying action is not only a logical conclusion but is supported by a preponderance of *evidence*.[19]

The Problem　Why is there such a divergence of viewpoint on this vitally important subject? There are several possible explanations: (1) the fault lies in measurement instruments, (2) attitude is improperly conceived and defined, and (3) insufficient attention is paid to other considerations which intervene to affect behavior.

---

[12]　M. Fishbein, "Attitude and the Prediction of Behavior," in M. Fishbein (ed.), *Attitude Theory and Measurement* (New York: Wiley, 1967), p. 477.

[13]　J. K. Lair, "Splitsville: A Split-Half Study of Television Commercial Pretesting," *Dissertation Abstracts*, vol. 27, pp. 2894–2895 (1965).

[14]　J. M. Fendrich, "A Study of the Association Among Verbal Attitudes, Commitment, and Overt Behavior in Different Experimental Conditions," *Social Forces*, vol. 45, pp. 347–355 (1967).

[15]　Jon G. Udel, "Can Attitude Measurement Predict Consumer Behavior?" *J. Marketing*, vol. 29, pp. 46–50 (1965).

[16]　J. N. Axelrod, "Attitude Measurements that Predict Purchases," *J. Advertising Research*, vol. 8, p. 3 (Mar. 1968).

[17]　S. Craig, "Consumer Reactions to Price Changes: An Experimental Investigation," unpublished doctoral dissertation, (Columbus, Ohio: Ohio State University, 1971).

[18]　C. DuBois, "Twelve Brands on a Seesaw," in *Proc. 13th Annual Conf.* (New York: Advertising Research Foundation, 1968).

[19]　*Grey Matter*, vol. 39, p. 1 (Nov. 1968).

(1) **Measurement Instruments** It may be surprising to read that there is only fragmentary evidence documenting that current research tools are valid, that is, that they measure what they purport to measure. In one study, for example, great differences were found in the predictive validity of various attitude-scaling procedures.[20] Ehrlich found that minor wording changes can make a great difference.[21] Similarly, Little and Hill indicate that the relationship between attitude and behavior is a function of the measuring instrument, the extent to which the behavior predicted is within the range of common experience, and the extent to which the behavior is repetitive in nature.[22] Much of the published evidence, therefore, may have serious methodological flaws.

Another authority examined 33 studies, most of which showed only a minimal relationship between behavior and attitude.[23] He concluded that four conditions must be met before prediction is possible: (1) the unit of observation must be an individual rather than a group, (2) there must be at least one attitude and behavior measure for each person, (3) attitude and behavior must be measured on separate occasions, and (4) the behavioral response must not be the individual's own retrospective report of his own behavior. Most of the published studies violate at least one of these criteria.

(2) **Improper Conception and Definition** Often the attitude measure centers on dispositions toward a group of objects rather than a specified individual object. This error was found in most of the studies evaluated by Wicker.[24] A housewife's purchase of a detergent brand obviously will be predicted more accurately by attitude toward the brand as compared with attitude toward the product class.

(3) **Failure to Consider Other Behavioral Influences** Frequently outside factors intervene to induce a person to act in a manner which is not predicted by his attitudes; in such circumstances attitude cannot predict behavior with great accuracy. Thus special consideration also must be given to the moderating effect of social norms,[25] economic circumstances and expectations,[26] attitude toward the situation in which the behavior takes place,[27] and a variety of other factors such

---

[20] Axelrod, *op. cit.*[16]

[21] H. J. Ehrlich, "Instrument Error and the Study of Prejudice," *Social Forces*, vol. 43, pp. 197–206 (1964).

[22] C. R. Little and R. J. Hill, "Attitude Conditions and Measurement Techniques," *Sociometry*, vol. 39, p. 203 (1967).

[23] A. W. Wicker, "Attitudes vs. Actions: The Relationship of Verbal and Overt Behavioral Responses to Attitude Objects," *J. Social Issues*, vol. 25, pp. 41–78 (1969).

[24] Wicker, *op. cit.*[23]

[25] I. Ajzen and M. Fishbein, "Attitudinal and Normative Variables as Predictors of Specific Behaviors: A Review of Research Generated by a Theoretical Model," paper presented at the Workshop on Attitude Research and Consumer Behavior, University of Illinois (Dec. 1970).

[26] George Katona, *The Powerful Consumer* (New York: McGraw-Hill, 1960).

[27] M. Rokeach, "Attitude Change and Behavioral Change," *Public Opinion Quart.*, vol. 30, pp. 529–550 (1966–1967); R. Sandel, "Effects of Attitudinal and Situational Factors on Reported Choice Behavior," *J. Marketing Research*, vol. 5, pp. 405–408 (1968).

as exposure to new information, opportunity to make brand choice, the influence of competing brands, the effect of store environment, price and financial constraints, and family decision processes.[28] Day, for example, added this latter group of factors to attitude in a set of equations and found a high correlation with behavior.[29]

Is There a Middle Ground? Much of the controversy can be removed, of course, through proper attention to measurement. As is shown in the next section, methodological difficulties need not remain as a hinderance. It also is necessary, however, to give explicit consideration to the various moderating factors when attempts are made to predict behavior from attitude. It is now known that *behavioral intentions* can be predicted from attitude plus other considerations which might enter in a specific situation.[30] Action, in turn, can be predicted from intentions, all other things equal. It thus appears to be necessary to use intention as an intervening variable between attitude and behavior. This is especially appropriate when it is recalled that the behavioral component of attitude becomes relevant in a behavioral sense only when a problem is recognized and problem-solving activity has commenced. This component now becomes activated in the form of a behavioral intention.

The relationship between attitude, intention, and behavior is illustrated in Figure 11.2 which is based, in part, on research by Sheth.[31] Sheth has presented data which document that attitude can be estimated accurately from ratings along evaluative criteria. Brand intentions then can be predicted from attitude if explicit measurement also is made of relatively enduring environmental factors such as social norms. Finally, behavior can be predicted from intentions only if consideration is given unexpected, temporary environmental influences.[32] Sheth was unable to predict behavior accurately from attitude itself.

Further evidence on the usefulness of measures of intentions comes from a study by Douglas and Wind who presented the following conclusions:[33]

(1) Purchase intentions are a good predictor of fashion behavior, and a five-point scale was found to have the highest predictive ability.

(2) Purchase intentions for novel fashion items proved to be more accurate than stated intentions to purchase more common items.

---

[28] G. Day, *Buyer Attitudes and Brand Choice Behavior* (New York: Free Press, 1970).

[29] Day, *op. cit.*[28]

[30] Ajzen and Fishbein, *op. cit.*;[25] D. E. Dulany, "Awareness, Rules, and Propositional Control: A Confrontation with S–R Behavior Theory," in T. R. Dixon and D. L. Horton (eds.), *Verbal Behavior and General Behavior Theory* (Englewood Cliffs, N.J.: Prentice-Hall, 1968), pp. 340–387.

[31] J. N. Sheth, "An Investigation of Relationships Among Evaluative Beliefs, Affect, Behavioral Intention, and Behavior," unpublished paper (Urbana, Ill.: University of Illinois, 1970).

[32] Sheth, *op. cit.*[31]

[33] S. P. Douglas and Y. Wind, "Intentions to Buy as Predictors of Buying Behavior," paper presented at the 2nd Annual Conf. of the Association for Consumer Research (Sept. 1971).

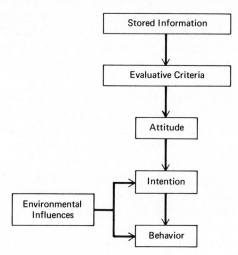

Figure 11.2 RELATIONSHIP BETWEEN ATTITUDE, INTENTION, AND BE-HAVIOR

(3) Measures of specific intentions were less accurate than measures of general intentions as predictors of behavior over a long period of time, but they proved more accurate than general measures as predictors of immediately subsequent behavior.

From the discussion in this section it thus may be concluded that attitude usually will not predict behavior accurately unless intention is utilized as an intervening variable. Intentions, in turn, predict behavior to the extent that outside moderating influences are absent or at a minimum. When these environmental constraints are operative, their influence also must be accounted for if behavior is to be predicted. Therefore, *attitude change is a valid marketing goal,* because a change in attitude is reflected by a change in behavior as expressed through changed intentions.

ATTITUDE MEASUREMENT

There are many methods of attitude measurement, and it is not the purpose of this section to provide a general methodological review.[34] This is because attitude has been defined in a highly specific manner as being a measure of the perceived value of alternatives for purchase or consumption along appropriate evaluative criteria. Therefore, the emphasis here is on two methods which are finding widespread contemporary use for this purpose: (1) a rating of alter-

---

[34] For an introduction to attitude measurement, the following sources are recommended: P. E. Green and D. S. Tull, *Research for Marketing Decisions,* 2nd ed. (Englewood Cliffs, N.J.: Prentice-Hall, 1970), chap. 6; J. H. Myers and M. I. Alpert, "Determining Buying Attitudes: Meaning and Measurement," *J. Marketing,* vol. 32, pp. 13–20 (1968).

natives and (2) nonmetric multidimensional scaling. A procedure then is discussed for assessment of the determinants of attitude strength, and the section concludes with the measurement of attitude over time.

Rating of Alternatives

In recent years growing use has been made of measurements which compute attitude as a rating of the subject matter in question along a number of criteria. Two of the most popular measures have been proposed by Rosenberg[35] and by Fishbein.[36] These approaches are very similar, and the following formula shows the manner in which they have been adapted for purposes of consumer research:[37]

$$A_b = \sum_{i=1}^{n} W_i B_{ib}$$

where

A_b = attitude toward a particular alternative b
W_i = weight or importance of evaluative criterion i
B_{ib} = evaluative aspect or belief with respect to utility of alternative b to satisfy evaluative criterion i
n = number of evaluative criteria important in selection of an alternative in category under consideration.

In this formula W_i is the weight or importance of the evaluative criterion, and B_{ib} is the evaluation of the alternative along that criterion. This rating is performed for each evaluative criterion, and the summed score is attitude toward the alternative.

The determination of evaluative criteria was discussed in the preceding chapter. It will be recalled that the usual procedure is to isolate the appropriate dimensions and then to assess the importance of each W_i through some type of

		Very *Satisfactory*					*Very* *Unsatisfactory*
Decay	Brand *A*	1	2	3	4	5	6
Prevention	Brand *B*	1	2	3	4	5	6
Taste	Brand *A*	1	2	3	4	5	6
	Brand *B*	1	2	3	4	5	6

---

[35] M. J. Rosenberg, "Cognitive Structure and Attitudinal Affect," *J. Abnormal and Social Psychology*, vol. 53, pp. 367–372 (1956).

[36] M. Fishbein, "The Relationships Between Beliefs, Attitudes and Behavior," in S. Feldman (ed.), *Cognitive Consistency* (New York: Academic Press, 1966), pp. 199–223.

[37] W. W. Talarzyk and R. Moinpour, "Comparison of an Attitude Model and Coombsian Unfolding Analysis for the Prediction of Individual Brand Preference," paper presented at the Workshop on Attitude Research and Consumer Behavior, University of Illinois (Dec. 1970).

scale. The next step is to measure beliefs about the utility of individual brands through use of a scaling technique such as that shown on page 275.[38] The score for each individual consists of the sum of his rating for each brand on each criterion B_{ib} times the importance of that criterion W_i.

Data from one study utilizing this formula appear in Table 11.1. Five brands of mouthwash were rated along five criteria, of which germ-killing power and effectiveness were perceived as being of greatest importance. No summary score of A_b is provided, but the detailed ratings often are of greater use in marketing planning. From these data, for example, it is apparent that Listerine holds first place in preference, and, correspondingly, it has the highest ratings on the two most important evaluative criteria. Cepacol, on the other hand, is least preferred and has consistently the lowest ratings across all criteria. Additional data from this study showed that Cepacol is most preferred by those with a masters or doctor degree but, unfortunately, mouthwash consumption is lowest in this seg-

Table 11.1 AN EXAMPLE OF BRAND ATTITUDES COMPUTED AS A RATING ALONG EVALUATIVE CRITERIA

(a) *Frequency of Attribute-Importance Ranking*

	Ranking (in percent)				
Attribute	*1st*	*2nd*	*3rd*	*4th*	*5th*
Kills germs	49.3	31.9	11.9	5.9	1.0
Taste/flavor	15.1	22.6	43.0	18.5	0.7
Price	4.7	12.2	22.9	52.8	7.4
Color	0.2	0.3	1.1	9.3	89.1
Effectiveness	30.9	33.1	21.0	13.4	1.6

(b) *Average Consumer Ratings of Mouthwash Brands on Relevant Attributes*

	Average Score on				
Brands	*Kills Germs*	*Taste/ Flavor*	*Price*	*Color*	*Effective- ness*
Micrin	2.22	2.46	2.60	1.85	2.21
Cepacol	2.40	2.92	2.70	2.29	2.36
Listerine	1.63	2.86	2.29	2.27	1.64
Lavoris	2.31	2.38	2.50	1.81	2.27
Colgate 100	2.35	2.52	2.68	1.87	2.32

SOURCE: "General Consumer Products," in J. F. Engel, W. W. Talarzyk, and C. M. Larson (eds.), *Cases in Promotional Strategy* (Homewood, Ill.: Irwin, 1971), pp. 90–91. Reprinted by permission of the publisher.

---

[38] F. M. Bass and W. W. Talarzyk, "Relative Contribution of Perceived Instrumentality and Value Importance in Determining Attitudes toward Brands," paper presented at American Marketing Association (Aug. 1970).

ment.[39] Management now must determine what must be done to improve these ratings. If the product, in fact, is competitive in terms of germ killing and the other attributes, the solution may be to advertise this fact. In any event, useful information has been provided for marketing planning.

Use of the W_i Component   There is disagreement about the necessity of utilizing the W_i component in computing an attitude score. In one study it was found that overall brand preference was predicted accurately through use only of the ratings B_{ib}; in fact, inclusion of the W_i score tended to repress the accuracy of predictions.[40] Others have found essentially the same results,[41] but some have arrived at a different conclusion. Hansen, for example, reports that choice is predicted with greater accuracy when both the B_{ib} and W_i components are included.[42] While there is no final consensus at this point, Scott and Bennett caution that W_i scores should be used when there are probable differences between segments of respondents in the weights placed on criteria.[43] The B_{ib} component may be used in isolation only when there is reason to expect that respondents do not differ greatly in importance weights.

Computing the Attitude Score   The summated weighting used in the above formula has been found to be a useful measure of the affective component of attitude by many researchers.[44] There is some concern, however, that predictions of preference and brand choice tend to be quite low. One possible reason may be the use of regression analysis based upon a summated rating of both components. Cohen and Ahtola used a disaggregative approach whereby choice was predicted through use of W_i and B_{ib} scores for each criterion in a multiple-discriminant analysis.[45] In other words, scores were not summed across criteria

[39]   "General Consumer Products," in J. F. Engel, W. W. Talarzyk, and C. M. Larson, *Cases in Promotional Strategy* (Homewood, Ill.: Irwin, 1971), p. 91.

[40]   J. N. Sheth and W. W. Talarzyk, "Relative Contribution of Perceived Instrumentality and Value Importance in Determining Attitudes Toward Brands, paper presented at American Marketing Association (Aug. 1970).

[41]   R. Moinpour and D. L. MacLachlan, "The Relations Among Attribute and Importance Components of Rosenberg–Fishbein Type Attitude Models: An Empirical Investigation," paper presented at the Association for Consumer Research, (Sept. 1971); J. E. Scott and P. D. Bennett, "Cognitive Models of Attitude Structure: 'Value Importance' is Important," paper presented at the American Marketing Association (Sept. 1971).

[42]   F. Hansen, "Consumer Choice Behavior: An Experimental Approach," *J. Marketing Research,* vol. 11, pp. 436–443 (1969).

[43]   Scott and Bennett, *op. cit.*[41]

[44]   F. M. Bass, E. A. Pessemier, and D. R. Lehmann, "An Experimental Study of Relationships Between Attitudes, Brand Preference and Choice," paper no. 307 (Lafayette, Ind.: Herman C. Krannert Graduate School of Industrial Administration, Purdue University, Apr. 1971); Sheth, *op. cit.*;[31] Bass and Talarzyk, *op. cit.*;[38] S. W. Bither and S. J. Miller, "A Cognitive Theory View of Brand Preference," in P. R. McDonald (ed.), *Marketing Involvement in Society and the Economy* (Chicago: Amer. Marketing Assoc., 1970), pp. 280–286; S. W. Bither and T. P. Copley, "Cognitive Information Processing and Brand Attitude" paper presented at the American Marketing Assoc. (Aug. 1970).

[45]   J. B. Cohen and O. T. Ahtola, "An Expectancy X Value Analysis of the Relationship Between Consumer Attitudes and Behavior," paper presented at the Association for Consumer Research (Sept. 1971).

but were used so that each score entered into the prediction equation. With this procedure they were able to classify or predict over 86 percent of brand choices.

From Cohen and Ahtola's results, there would appear to be a real predictive advantage in using the nonaggregative multiple-discriminant-analysis approach. Also, multiple-discriminant analysis assumes that the independent variable brand choice is dichotomous (buy or not buy) and hence is a more appropriate method for this purpose than multiple regression.[46]

Nonmetric Multidimensional Scaling

An alternate procedure is to begin with perceived similarities between alternatives. It will be recalled from the preceding chapter that the computer algorithms of multidimensional scaling (MDS) then generate a configuration of perceived similarities as points in a Euclidean space of two or more dimensions. The data themselves reveal the attributes on which consumers are evaluating the alternatives. Preference ratings also may be mapped into this space utilizing Coombsian unfolding analysis (MDU).[47] The unfolding model assumes that individuals and stimuli are mapped into points in a common space and that an individual's preference ordering between any two stimuli reflects the stimulus point which is nearer his ideal point.

An illustration of ratings generated by this procedure appears in Figure 11.3. As the first step in Coombsian analysis, the dissimilarities as perceived between brands were rank ordered after averaging over all subjects and submitted to a computer algorithm TORSCA-9.[48] A configuration of the nine brands as points in a Euclidean space of two dimensions was obtained. This solution indicates the perception of similarities between the nine brands by the average respondent (shown in circles). Points clustered together were considered to be more similar than points further apart. Also the preference mapping for the average subject was computed by the Carroll and Chang unfolding algorithm,[49] and the average ideal point and the ideal points for some of the individual subjects appear as Xs. The apparent evaluative criteria utilized in these ratings were "buffer" and "strength."

The attitude for an individual brand is estimated by the square of the distance of that brand from the ideal point, and a rank ordering of these distances discloses how one alternative rates to others. From the map in Figure 11.3 it is apparent that none of the brands are especially close to the average ideal point. This may indicate that there are unmet needs and an opportunity for new product development.

There has been one study which specifically compared the predictions

---

[46] Green and Tull, *op. cit.*,[34] pp. 369–398.

[47] C. H. Coombs, *A Theory of Data* (New York: Wiley, 1964).

[48] F. W. Young, "TORSCA-O: A Fortran 4 Program for Nonmetric Multidimensional Scaling," *Behavioral Science*, vol. 13, pp. 343–344 (1968).

[49] J. D. Carroll and J. Chang, "Relating Preference Data to Multidimensional Scaling Solutions via a Generalization of Coombs' Unfolding Model," mimeograph, Bell Telephone Laboratories (1967).

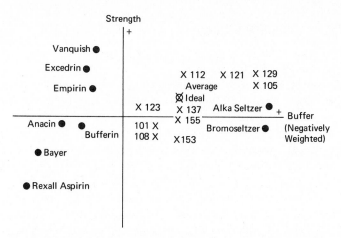

Figure 11.3 TWO-DIMENSIONAL MAP SHOWING PREFERENCES AND PER-CEPTIONS OF SIMILARITIES BETWEEN BRANDS USING NONMETRIC SCALING × SUBJECT'S IDEAL POINT. W. W. Talarzyk and M. Moinpour, "Comparison of an Attitude Model and Coombsian Unfolding Analysis for the Prediction of Individual Brand Preference," paper presented at the Workshop on Attitude Research and Consumer Behavior, University of Illinois (Dec. 1970)

of the summated rating approach with that generated by the combination of MDS–MDU discussed in this section.[50] It was found that the summated rating following the Fishbein–Rosenberg procedure more accurately predicted brand preferences, but the differences were not especially large. Thus the choice of one approach over the other may largely be a matter of individual preference, but there are some advantages to nonmetric scaling:

(1) It utilizes nonmetric rank-order data and hence is methodologically less demanding than its counterpart in data collection.
(2) Evaluative criteria do not need to be specified in advance. The respondent is told to make brand comparisons on any bases that he chooses, and the dimensions used should emerge from the resulting perceptual map.

The major disadvantage of MDS–MDU is the difficulty to label the axes of the perceptual space. This requires careful judgment, and the resulting labels may not be the actual evaluative criteria underlying the ratings.

The summated rating, on the other hand, offers the advantage of generating clearcut ratings along individual criteria. The diagnostic advantages in marketing planning were discussed earlier. This may be the determining consideration in many applications.

---

[50]   Talarzyk and Moinpour, *op. cit.*[37]

Assessing Attitude Strength

Two major determinants of attitude strength were mentioned earlier: (1) centrality and (2) the information basis. A strong positive rating on a scale of affect (that is, A_b) may not adequately reflect attitude strength, so a further analysis frequently is warranted before attempts are made to bring about attitude change.

Analysis of Centrality Is a prospect's attitude toward an alternative anchored in his conception of his self-worth? In other words, does the attitude have centrality? If so, he is likely to resist any changes in this disposition, and centrality is not necessarily indicated by a conventional attitude rating. Two consumers, for example, may be equally favorable toward one brand of automobile; yet one will consider no other brand, while the other person is quite open minded. The probability of attitude change differs greatly between these two people.

Sherif and his colleagues in an extensive series of studies have discovered that centrality (or ego involvement) is indicated by the number of alternatives the individual will consider to be acceptable versus those that are unacceptable.[51] The former category is termed the *latitude of acceptance*, whereas the *latitude of rejection* embraces the alternatives which are considered to be unacceptable. The more involved and personally committed the individual is with respect to an alternative, the greater is the latitude of rejection in relation to the latitude of acceptance. The *latitude of noncommitment* (those alternatives which are neither acceptable nor nonacceptable) will approach zero.

This approach is made operational by giving the subject a list of alternatives and asking him for his most preferred selection. He then is asked to evaluate others against this anchor. Other acceptable alternatives comprise the latitude of acceptance, and a similar procedure is followed for the remaining latitudes. There is preliminary evidence that loyalty or commitment to a brand is reflected by the number of brands in the respective latitudes. Specifically, loyalty becomes stronger as the proportion of brands in the rejection region increases while the proportion in the acceptance region decreases.[52]

Given the initial measure of attitude A_b and a measure of centrality, it is possible to relate the two and gain additional insights as is indicated in Figure 11.4. Those in cell I are highly loyal users whose favorable attitude is based on

---

[51] C. W. Sherif, M. Sherif, and R. E. Nebergall, *Attitude and Attitude Change* (New Haven, Conn.: Yale University Press, 1961). For an alternate approach, see N. T. Hupfer and D. M. Gardner, "Differential Involvement with Products and Issues: An Exploratory Study" paper presented at the Association for Consumer Research (Sept. 1971).

[52] H. E. Brown, "The Role of Personality and Perceived Risk in the Purchase of Branded Headache and Pain and Cold Remedies," unpublished doctoral dissertation (Columbus, Ohio: Ohio State University, 1969); J. Jacoby and J. C. Olson, "An Attitudinal Model of Brand Loyalty: Conceptual Underpinnings and Instrumentation Research," paper presented at the Workshop on Attitude Research and Consumer Behavior, University of Illinois (Dec. 1970).

centrality. Their region of acceptance would contain only the preferred brand, and the region of rejection would contain most of the other alternatives. They are not likely to switch preferences as a result of competitive efforts. Current customers in cell III, on the other hand, are more vulnerable, because their favorable attitude is not based on high ego involvement with the product. The brand purchased probably is of only minor concern, and brand switching could readily occur.

Centrality

Attitude A_b	High		Medium		Low	
	User	Nonuser	User	Nonuser	User	Nonuser
Favorable	I				III	
Neutral						IV
Unfavorable		II				

Figure 11.4 THE RELATIONSHIP OF ATTITUDE (A_b) TO CENTRALITY

The nonuser analysis also is revealing. The nonusers in cell II probably are "off limits" for the company. They are strongly negative, and this rating is based on high centrality. The nonusers in cell IV, however, are essentially indifferent, and the product is of little personal importance. Hence they probably could be induced to try the brand, although it is not likely that they ever would become loyal customers.

Analysis of the Information Basis It is known that a classification of people in terms of the extent of stored information utilized in making attitudinal judgments will result in better prediction of behavior.[53] A general method of analysis is presented in Figure 11.5.

Assume once again that there are three categories of attitude and three categories of knowledge ranging from high to low. Cell I shows nonusers with an unfavorable attitude based on extensive knowledge. Their rating, in other words, probably has been carefully considered and is not likely to be changed. Cell III, however, contains promising prospects, because a neutral rating is based on little information. It is likely that attitude will change if they are provided with relevant information.

Cell II presents some interesting considerations. The customers have a favorable attitude, but it is not anchored in much knowledge. Perhaps attitude can be strengthened by suggesting new ways in which the product can be used.

---

[53] R. S. Halpern, "Some Observations About Attitudes, Attitude Measurement and Behavior," in L. Adler and I. Crespi (eds.), *Attitude Research on the Rocks* (Chicago: Amer. Marketing Assoc., 1968), p. 41.

Knowledge

Attitude A_b	High		Medium		Low	
	User	Nonuser	User	Nonuser	User	Nonuser
Favorable					II	
Neutral						III
Unfavorable	I					

Figure 11.5 THE RELATIONSHIP OF ATTITUDE (A_b) TO KNOWLEDGE

A Composite Analysis Analyses of the types discussed here should disclose some segments where attitude change is more probable than others. The best prospects are those with no worse than a mildly negative attitude based on low knowledge and low centrality. The analysis also should center on attitudes of current users. The firm's greatest asset is loyal customers whose favorable dispositions are based on high information and high centrality. Others may be wavering in their loyalty, however, with the result that remedial efforts are needed in the form of suggested new uses, product modifications, and so on. Through this approach it is possible to array segments so that the most responsive targets are isolated as well as the least responsive, and valuable clues are provided for marketing strategy.

Attitude Analysis over Time

Attitudes should be monitored to assess changes. It might be found, for example, that loyalty among consumers in the most profitable segment is eroding. If so, remedial efforts should be undertaken. Similar analyses of competitors' customers also make it possible to detect areas of possible inroads.

Analysis over time, of course, requires reinterviews of people from one period to the next. This is referred to as *longitudinal analysis,*[54] and the basic means of analysis is the *turnover table.* An illustration appears in Figure 11.6.

The vertical axis represents attitudes at time 1; 23 percent were favorable, 72 percent neutral, and 5 percent unfavorable. Attitudes were measured again at time 2, and totals are given in the last row: 28 percent were favorable, 64 percent neutral, and 8 percent negative.

On the surface, these changes in totals are not great, but the underlying dynamic of change is not obvious from the totals. This is evident only from the entries in the cells. If no changes had taken place between the two periods, there would only be three entries in the table, and all would be on the diagonal. The

---

[54] "Longitudinal Analysis," a symposium appearing in P. D. Bennett (ed.), *Marketing and Economic Development* (Chicago: Amer. Marketing Assoc., 1966).

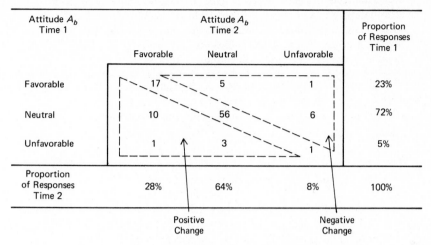

Figure 11.6 ATTITUDE CHANGE OVER TIME

favorable–favorable cell, for example, would contain 23 percent, and so on; but there were many shifts off the diagonal. Notice that 5 percent who were favorable at time 1 now are neutral, and another one percent have become negative (determined by reading the first row and analyzing percentages of movement off the diagonal). The negative change was more than offset, however, by shifts in the positive direction. Figures in the second row show that 10 percent who were neutral at time 1 now are positive, and 6 percent have become negative. In total, 26 percent of those interviewed have shifted position in one direction or another —14 percent in the favorable direction and 12 percent in the unfavorable direction.

Considerable diagnostic information is provided for marketing planning. Assume, for example, that a sampling campaign was directed toward changing the preferences of those who were neutral at time 1. There was a net positive attitude shift of 4 percent (10 percent minus 6 percent), and it may be that the sampling effort paid off. This type of information can only be gained by reinterviews of the same people.

Longitudinal analysis can be both expensive and methodologically demanding.[55] Many large firms have established consumer panels for this purpose, however, and find that the gains outweigh the costs.

ATTITUDE CHANGE

Given that attitudes can be measured and that attitude change is a valid marketing goal, what should the business firm do to change preferences? This is a difficult question to answer definitely without consideration of the details of strategy discussed in later chapters, but, as a generalization:

---

[55]   Bennet, *op. cit.*[54]

. . . the type of message that is likely to be most effective in inducing attitude change is one well tailored to fit the particular attitude structure, being relevant to the motivational bases of the attitude, yet involving arguments that are sufficiently novel that it is likely the individual is already fortified with counter information.[56]

It is known that a change in one of the dimensions of attitude (cognitive, affective, or behavioral) will often lead to a change in others because of the pervasive tendency to resolve and overcome the resulting cognitive inconsistency.[57] Therefore, any of the following strategies are valid:

(1) New information can be provided to augment stored information and hence lead to change ratings along evaluative criteria. A consumer, for instance, may be unaware of the change in package design of a previously disliked brand of shoe polish so that it now is possible to make application without dirtying the hands. This fact could generate product trial. This is one of the most common procedures in attitude change, and its effectiveness has been demonstrated in a variety of situations.[58]

(2) Evaluative criteria can be changed. At one time the size of high-fidelity speakers was felt to be an important indicator of quality—the larger the better. Attitudes toward the first smaller speakers utilizing a different principle of construction thus were negative, and it was necessary to change the underlying evaluative criterion. Once this was done, the small speaker became standard.

(3) Attempts can be made to demonstrate that the alternative does meet important evaluative criteria.[59] This can be done through advertising or personal selling, but a better approach is to provide a free sample or otherwise induce trial.

(4) A change can be made in the behavioral component by inducing the person to engage in attitude-discrepant behavior. In the high-fidelity speaker example mentioned above, attitudes often changed once the consumer listened to the smaller unit. Dissonance was generated between beliefs and this new information, and attitude change often resulted.

The specific strategy to use in advertising and persuasive communication of all types is the subject matter of Chapter 14.

SUMMARY

This chapter has examined the nature, significance, and measurement of attitudes. Following contemporary psychological theory, attitude was defined as a rating of the utility of an alternative for purchase or consumption along pertinent evaluative criteria. Since attitudes play an important role in determining both

---

[56] Newcomb, *et al., op. cit.*,[5] p. 98.

[57] Rosenberg, *op. cit.*[3]

[58] For a good summary of the evidence, see Newcomb, *et al., op. cit.*,[5] chap. 4.

[59] Bither and Copley, *op. cit.*[44]

information processing and behavior, attitude change is a valid marketing goal. It was shown that attitudes are related to behavioral intentions, and intentions are related to behavior. Hence a change in attitude will, all things being equal, change both intentions and behavior. The discussion then shifted to the problems of measurement, and two basic approaches were discussed: (1) a summated rating following the tradition of Fishbein and Rosenberg and (2) nonmetric scaling using unfolding analysis and multidimensional scaling. Additional procedures were suggested to shed light on attitude strength through consideration of the degree of stored information underlying the attitudinal rating and the extent of ego involvement (centrality). The chapter concluded with an overview of the basic approaches to attitude change.

REVIEW AND DISCUSSION QUESTIONS

1. Consult five basic textbooks in introductory or social psychology and list the definitions of attitude. What differences can you detect? Why do different authorities offer varying definitions of such a familiar concept?

2. Consumers form attitudes toward product types, brands, and stores. What functions do these attitudes perform?

3. Is a consumer's attitude toward a brand of laundry detergent likely to have centrality? Would a different answer be given if the question concerned a brand of lawn fertilizer? If the answer is yes to one or both of these situations, what is the significance for marketing planning?

4. What explanations can you give for the contradictory evidence regarding the relationship of a change in attitude to a change in behavior? Is attitude change a valid marketing goal? What is the relationship between attitude and intention?

5. A marketing research study undertaken for a major appliance manufacturer disclosed that 30 percent plan on purchasing a trash compactor in the next three months and 15 percent plan on purchasing a new iron. How much confidence should be placed in the predictive accuracy of these intention measurements? Are there differences in predictive accuracy between products? Why or why not?

6. Contrast the summated rating approach to attitude measurement with nonmetric scaling. In which circumstances is one preferable to another?

7. How could the perceptual map appearing in Figure 11.3 be used in new product planning?

8. One housewife indicated a strong preference for her brand of hair spray but also indicated that two other brands were about equally acceptable. Another indicated an equally strong preference but would not be willing to consider another alternative. Are there likely to be differences in brand loyalty? Why?

9. What is meant by a turnover table? How can it be used in marketing planning?

10. One leading New York advertising agency refuses to use attitude change as a criterion of advertising success. Another agency uses *only* attitude change for this purpose. What reasons could be given for such a major difference?

CHAPTER **12**

PERSONALITY

The subject of this chapter is the influence of personality on consumer behavior. Personality is depicted in Figure 12.1 as affecting evaluative criteria and is an integral component of the central control unit.

The chapter begins with a discussion of personality theories that have been utilized in marketing and consumer behavior research. These theories provide the structure for a review of a large body of evidence, all of which has implications for the analysis of buyer behavior.

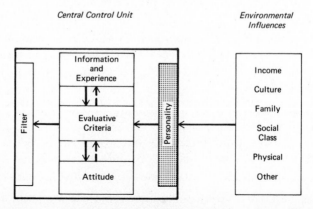

Figure 12.1 PERSONALITY IN THE CENTRAL CONTROL UNIT

Throughout the discussion, the objective is to assess the manner in which the experimental evidence on personality can be applied in marketing. Special attention is devoted to areas that appear to have the greatest future research implications. Of necessity, much that is known about personality in the sense of clinical treatment of individual behavior disorders is not reviewed here because of its limited relevance. A complete discussion of personality theory and research for that purpose is available elsewhere.[1]

PERSONALITY THEORIES UTILIZED IN MARKETING

No consensus exists about the components of personality and the manner in which these components become organized into a meaningful whole. Therefore, for purposes of background, it is necessary to examine several differing points of view.

Most definitions of personality are quite general, and the term is frequently used in different ways. These definitions, however, obtain a degree of commonality with the suggestion that personality is linked to the concept of consistent responses to environmental stimuli.[2] This concept has been embodied in most personality theories utilized in contemporary marketing research. Three of these theories—psychoanalytic, social-psychological, and trait-factor—are discussed in more detail below.

Psychoanalytic Theory

The psychoanalytic theory[3] posits that the human personality system consists of the id, ego, and superego. The id is the source of psychic energy and seeks immediate gratification for biological or instinctual needs. The superego represents societal or personal norms and serves as an ethical constraint on behavior. The ego mediates the hedonistic demands of the id and the moralistic prohibitions of the superego. The dynamic interaction of these elements results in unconscious motivations that are manifested in observed human behavior.

The psychoanalytic theory served as the conceptual basis for the motivation research movement. According to the philosophy of this movement, consumer behavior was the result of unconscious consumer motives. These unconscious motives could be determined only through indirect assessment methods that

---

[1]   See, for example, J. P. Guilford, *Personality* (New York: McGraw-Hill, 1959); C. S. Hall and G. Lindzey, *Theories of Personality*, 2nd ed. (New York: Wiley, 1970).

[2]   H. H. Kassarjian, "Personality and Consumer Behavior: A Review," *J. Marketing Research*, vol. 8, pp. 409–418, at p. 409 (Chicago: Amer. Marketing Assoc., Nov. 1971).

[3]   For a marketing level view of psychoanalytic theory, see W. D. Wells and A. D. Beard, "Personality and Consumer Behavior," in Scott Ward and T. S. Robertson (eds.), *Consumer Behavior: Theoretical Sources*, in press; Hall and Lindzey, *op. cit.*;[1] R. J. Markin, *The Psychology of Consumer Behavior* (Englewood Cliffs, N.J.: Prentice-Hall, 1969); Kassarjian, *op. cit.*[2]

included a wide assortment of projective and related psychological techniques.[4]

The motivation research movement produced some extraordinary findings. Kotler reports the following hypotheses as typical psychoanalytic explanations of consumer purchase motivations:

(1)   A man buys a convertible as a substitute "mistress."

(2)   A woman is very serious when she bakes a cake because unconsciously she is going through the symbolic act of birth.

(3)   Men want their cigars to be odiferous in order to prove that they (the men) are masculine.[5]

These subjective interpretations of consumer motivations highlight the danger of using an inappropriate personality model to explain consumer behavior. Psychoanalytic theory was developed to distinguish between normal and abnormal personalities in a clinical setting. Emphasis is decidedly on the individual. Yet, marketers must be primarily concerned about groups, or segments, of consumers. Even if accurate individual information could be obtained, it probably could not be used.[6] In addition to this major criticism, small sample sizes and subjective interpretation of responses militated against wide applicability of these results.

Psychoanalytic theory, operationalized in motivation research experiments, did serve as the initial impetus to the systematic study of personality in consumer behavior. From a conceptual standpoint, personality was explicitly considered as a separate variable for organized study within a consumer decision framework.[7] From a pragmatic standpoint, a significant amount of practical personality research was undertaken, reviewed later in this chapter.

Social-Psychological Theory

Social-psychological theory[8] differs from psychoanalytic theory in two important respects. First, social variables,[9] not biological instincts, are considered to be the most important determinant in shaping personality. Second, behavioral

---

[4]   For an extended discussion of these methods, see Robert Ferber and H. G. Wales, *Motivation and Market Behavior* (Homewood, Ill.: Irwin, 1958), pp. 76–223.

[5]   Philip Kotler, *Marketing Management* (Englewood Cliffs, N.J.: Prentice-Hall, 1967), p. 88.

[6]   Wells and Beard, *op. cit.,*[3] p. 54.

[7]   This trend was not unique to the study of personality. Robertson observed that MR encouraged marketers to abandon traditional demographic analysis and move toward a richer conceptualization of psychological variables that had import beyond personality research. See Thomas Robertson, *Consumer Behavior* (Glenview, Ill.: Scott, Foresman, 1970), pp. 38–39.

[8]   Social-psychological personality theory specifically recognizes the interdependence of the individual and society. The individual strives to meet the needs of society, while society helps the individual to attain his goals. The theory is, therefore, not exclusively sociological or psychological, but rather a combination of the two (review Chapter 6). This theoretical orientation is most widely associated with Adler, Horney, Fromm, and Sullivan. For a more complete explanation of this approach, see Hall and Lindzey, *op. cit.,*[1] chap. 4, pp. 117–159.

[9]   There was no general agreement among the social theorists as to the relative importance of social variables. Fromm emphasized the importance of social context, while Sullivan and Horney stressed interpersonal behavior, and Adler eclectically employed many different variables (Hall and Lindzey, *op. cit.,*[1] pp. 154–155).

motivation is conscious. Man knows his needs and wants, and his behavior is directed to meet these needs.[10]

The Horney paradigm is a representative example of social-psychological personality theory. This model suggests that human behavior results from three predominant, interpersonal orientations—compliant, aggressive, and detached.[11]

Cohen has developed a research methodology utilizing the Horney paradigm to explain consumer behavior. The CAD scale[12] is used to measure predominate interpersonal orientation in the sample of consumers. Some consumer behavior response measure is then taken (that is, product usage), and interpersonal orientation is used as the criterion variable.

This technique has been utilized in studies of social influence[13] and product usage and media preferences.[14] Although significant differences were found along interpersonal dimensions, the results are not unequivocal. More research is needed to determine the marketing relevance of this technique.[15]

Trait-Factor Theory

Trait-factor theory represents a quantitative approach to the study of personality. This theory postulates that an individual's personality is composed of definite predispositional attributes called traits. A trait is more specifically defined as "any distinguishable, relatively enduring way in which one individual differs from another."[16] Traits, therefore, can alternatively be considered individual difference variables.

Three assumptions delineate this theory. It is assumed that traits are common to many individuals[17] and vary in absolute amounts between individuals.[18] It is further assumed that these traits are relatively stable, and exert fairly universal effects on behavior regardless of the environmental situation.[19] It follows directly from this assumption that a consistent functioning of personality

---

[10]   Hall and Lindzey, *op. cit.*,[1] pp. 155–156.

[11]   Compliant people are dependent on other people for love and affection, and are said to move *toward* others. Aggressive people are motivated by the need for power, and move *against* others. Detached people are self-sufficient and independent, and move away from others. For a marketing-level explanation of the Horney paradigm, see J. B. Cohn, "An Interpersonal Orientation to the Study of Consumer Behavior," *J. Marketing Research*, vol. 4, pp. 270–278 (Aug. 1967); J. B. Cohen, "Toward an Interpersonal Theory of Consumer Behavior," *California Management Rev.*, vol. 10, pp. 73–80 (1968).

[12]   The CAD scale is a 35-item Likert scale developed by Cohen. The scale and scoring procedure appear in Cohen (1967); *op. cit.*,[11] pp. 277–278.

[13]   J. B. Cohen, and E. Golden, "Informational Social Influence and Product Evaluation," unpublished Working Paper (Urbana, Ill.: College of Commerce and Business Administration, University of Illinois, 1971).

[14]   Same references as in footnote 11.

[15]   Kassarjian, *op. cit.*,[2] p. 410.

[16]   Guilford, *op. cit.*,[1] p. 6.

[17]   Guilford, *op. cit.*, pp. 73–74.

[18]   W. Mischel, *Personality and Assessment* (New York: Wiley, 1968), p. 6.

[19]   N. Sanford, *Issues in Personality Theory* (San Francisco: Jossey-Bass, 1970), pp. 8–9. The issue of pervasiveness, or consistent functioning of personality across social situations, is an important consideration in personality research. Many social scientists have indicated the importance of situational characteristics on behavior. This issue is discussed in more detail in the chapter.

variables is predictive of a wide variety of behavior. The final assumption asserts that traits can be inferred from the measurement of behavioral indicators.[20] The most commonly used measurement technique is the standard psychological inventory. Factor analysis also plays an important part in determining relevant traits in a particular situation.[21]

Trait-factor theory has been used almost exclusively as the conceptual basis of marketing personality research. In this research, the typical study attempts to find a relationship between a set of personality variables and assorted consumer behaviors.[22] Personality variables, measured by a standard inventory, are multiple independent variables, and the dependent variable (that is, purchase behavior) is measured as the situation demands. Multiple correlation and regression are then utilized to determine a measure of the degree of relationship between the variables, and a regression equation is employed to predict the dependent variable.[23]

A considerable body of data has been generated using this methodology. These data are reviewed in the following section. Trait-factor theory is then assessed in the light of this evidence.

USING PERSONALITY MEASURES TO PREDICT BUYER BEHAVIOR

A number of research studies have appeared in the marketing literature which have a common objective of predicting consumer behavior through the use of various types of personality measures. These studies fall into two general classifications: (1) susceptibility to social influence and (2) product and brand choice. In the discussion that follows these studies are evaluated critically, because, as will become apparent, results frequently have fallen short of expectations. This section concludes with a discussion of implications of this research for market segmentation strategies.

Susceptibility to Social Influence

Susceptibility to social influence, or influenceability, is an important contemporary marketing topic. McGuire defines influenceability as "any tendency

---

[20]   Guilford, *op. cit.*,[1] 52–56.

[21]   A complete discussion of the role of factor analysis in personality assessment is beyond the scope of this text. The interested reader is referred to R. B. Cattell, *The Scientific Analysis of Personality* (Baltimore: Penguin, 1965).

[22]   Many different consumer behavior variables have been investigated. Kassarjian lists the following: purchase behavior, media choice, innovation, segmentation, fear and social influence, product choice, opinion leadership, risk taking, and attitude change (Kassarjian, *op. cit.*,[2] p. 409).

[23]   For a review of multiple correlation and regression, see M. Ezekial and K. Fox, *Methods of Correlation and Regression Analysis* (New York: Wiley, 1959).

of the person to change as a function of social pressure."[24] In his analysis of personality and influenceability, he concludes that influenceability is a weak general trait but that the relationship between influenceability and personality may vary across influence situations.[25]

In the discussion below, the literature is reviewed for the two most important marketing influence situations—conformity and persuasion. Persuasion is a relatively more important topic, and is discussed here as a preface to the greater detail of the next chapter.

Conformity Conformity implies acquiescence toward some established behavioral norm. The few marketing studies reviewed in Chapter 6 have investigated the relationship between personality variables and conforming behavior.

In one of the published attempts, the relationship between self-esteem and conformity[26] was investigated. Groups of college males were asked to evaluate the quality of three suits and publicly state their choice. Significant conformity was observed among naive subjects toward the group decision, but no relationship was found between self-esteem and conformity.[27] More research is needed in this area before any conclusions can be drawn.

Persuasion Persuasion situations are those social settings in which a source gives his position on an issue and then presents rational or emotional arguments to support this position. These conditions are often found in advertising situations and are, therefore, very important to marketers (see Chapter 13).

Self-esteem again serves as the prototypical personality variable. In the usual experiment, self-esteem is operationalized with the Janis–Field scale.[28] Subjects are dichotomized into high and low criterion groups according to their test scores, and some measure of persuasibility is taken. The amount of persuasibility is correlated with the degree of self-esteem and the appropriate generalizations are made.

Sternthal[29] has extensively reviewed the relationship between self-esteem and persuasibility in marketing and psychological studies. His data seem to indicate that this relationship is curvilinear in nature, with the highest level of persuasibility associated with intermediate levels of self-esteem. Three marketing

---

[24] W. J. McGuire, "Personality and Susceptibility to Social Influence," in E. F. Borgatta and W. W. Lambert (eds.), *Handbook of Personality Theory and Research* (Chicago: Rand McNally, 1968), pp. 1130–1187, at p. 1131.

[25] McGuire, *op. cit.*[24]

[26] M. Venkatesan, "Personality and Persuasibility in Consumer Decision-Making," *J. Advertising Research*, vol. 8, pp. 39–45 (1968).

[27] Self-esteem refers to the "value an individual attributes to various facets of his person." See A. R. Cohen, "Some Implications of Self-Esteem for Social Influence," in C. I. Hovland and I. L. Janis (eds.), *Personality and Persuasibility* (New Haven, Conn.: Yale University Press, 1959). Marketing researchers are usually more familiar with the term, self-confidence. Both terms are operationally similar.

[28] I. L. Janis and P. B. Field, "Sex Differences and Personality Factors Related to Persuasibility," in Hovland and Janis, *op. cit.*,[27] pp. 29–54.

[29] Brian Sternthal, "Persuasion and the Mass Communication Process," unpublished doctoral dissertation, (Columbus, Ohio: Ohio State University, 1972).

studies have obtained this same result.[30] Until further studies are undertaken, however, these results should only be taken as suggestive.

Implications In general, the findings on the relationship between influenceability and personality have been meager and indefinite. In fact, some researchers contend that influenceability is not a general trait at all. Carey argues, for example, that the relationship between personality and persuasability is dependent on the communication situation, and therefore is not amenable to a general parsimonious analysis.[31] McGuire offers just such a parsimonious systems model.[32] Sternthal used McGuire's model to explain the conflicting results of a large number of self-esteem personality studies.[33]

Quite obviously, the relationship between influenceability and personality requires further study. More personality variables must be tested across a wider range of communication situations. The potential role of McGuire's model in marketing personality research is an important topic and will be discussed in depth late in this chapter.

Product and Brand Choice

The rich literature on personality in psychology and other behavioral sciences has led many researchers in marketing to theorize that personality characteristics should predict brand or store preference and other types of buyer activity. Martineau, for example, postulated that there are three basic personality types underlying variations in automobile purchase behavior: (1) conservatives, (2) moderates (sociables), and (3) the attention getters.[34] In fact, he proposed that any type of buyer decision or choice is an expression of an individual's personality, and the presumption is that knowledge of personality structure has direct implications. The findings to be evaluated in this section, however, do not bear out these optimistic predictions.[35]

Personality and Automobile Purchase Evans went one step beyond Martineau and tested more rigorously the assumption that automobile buyers differ in personality structure.[36] He administered a standard personality inven-

---

[30] D. F. Cox and R. A. Bauer, "Self-Confidence and Persuasibility in Women," *Public Opinion Quart.*, vol. 28, pp. 453–466 (1964); J. A. Barach, "Self-Confidence and Reactions to Television Commercials," in D. F. Cox (ed.), *Risk-Taking and Information Handling in Consumer Behavior* (Boston: Division of Research, Graduate School of Business Administration, Harvard University, 1967); G. D. Bell, "The Automobile Buyer after Purchase," *J. Marketing*, vol. 31, pp. 12–16 (July 1967).

[31] J. W. Carey, "Some Personality Correlates of Persuasibility," in S. A. Greyser (ed.), *Toward Scientific Marketing* (Chicago: Amer. Marketing Assoc. 1963), pp. 30–43.

[32] McGuire, *op. cit.*[24]

[33] Sternthal, *op. cit.*[29]

[34] Pierre Martineau, *Motivation in Advertising* (New York: McGraw-Hill, 1959).

[35] Much of the following section is adapted from James F. Engel, David T. Kollat, and Roger D. Blackwell, "Personality Measures and Market Segmentation," *Business Horizons*, pp. 61–70 (June 1969).

[36] F. B. Evans, "Psychological Objective Factors in the Prediction of Brand Choice: Ford versus Chevrolet," *J. Business*, vol. 32, pp. 340–369 (1959).

tory, the Edwards personal preference schedule, to owners of Chevrolets and Fords. He found few statistically significant differences between the two groups. In fact, using discriminant analysis[37] he was able to predict correctly a Ford or Chevrolet owner in only 63 percent of the cases.[38] Using 12 objective variables, however (that is, age of car, income), a correct prediction was made in 70 percent of the cases. He thus concluded that personality is of relatively little value in predicting automobile brand ownership. Studies by Westfall[39] and Evans[40] support this conclusion.

Consumption of Nondurables Koponen administered the Edwards personal preference schedule to 5000 members of the J. Walter Thompson consumer panel, and purchases of various items were also recorded. Slight differences were found on certain magazines and filter and nonfilter cigarettes. Through the use of multiple regression, however, no more than 13 percent of the variance in purchase data could be explained by personality factors.[41] Massy, Frank, and Lodahl reported similar results for coffee, tea, and beer purchases.[42] The results indicate that the relationship between purchase and personality is quite low indeed.

The Advertising Research Foundation focused only on the paper products data from the above panel and extended the analysis. Information on personality was of no value in explaining the types of toilet paper purchased, brands, or quantity.[43]

On a somewhat brighter note, several studies have reported some relation between product use and personality traits.[44] Once again, however, the correlations between traits and product and brand preferences was not found to be strong.

---

[37] For a discussion of the techniques of discriminant analysis, see W. F. Massy, "On Methods: Discriminant Analysis of Audience Characteristics," *J. Advertising Research,* vol. 5, pp. 39–48 (1965).

[38] Given a dichotomous choice, a correct prediction by chance will be made 50 percent of the time.

[39] Ralph Westfall, "Psychological Factors in Predicting Product Choice," *J. Marketing,* vol. 26, pp. 34–40 (1962).

[40] F. B. Evans, "Ford versus Chevrolet: Park Forest Revisited," *J. Business,* vol. 41, pp. 445–459 (1968).

[41] A. Koponen, "Personality Characteristics of Purchasers," *J. Advertising Research,* vol. 1, pp. 6–12 (1960).

[42] W. F. Massy, Ronald Frank, and T. Lodahl, *Personal Behavior and Personal Attributes* (Philadelphia: University of Pennsylvania Press, 1968).

[43] "Are There Consumer Types?" (New York: Advertising Research Foundation, 1964).

[44] M. J. Gottlieb, "Segmentation by Personality Types," in L. H. Stockman (ed.), *Advancing Marketing Efficiency* (Chicago: Amer. Marketing Assoc. 1959), pp. 148–158; W. T. Tucker and J. J. Painter, "Personality and Product Use," *J. Applied Psychology,* vol. 45, pp. 325–329 (1961); D. M. Ruch, "Limitations of Current Approaches to Understanding Brand Buying Behavior," in J. W. Newman (ed.), *On Knowing the Consumer* (New York: Wiley, 1966), pp. 173–186.

Attitudes toward Private Brands Myers investigated the relation between personality traits and attitudes toward private brands. The data suggest some tendency for women who are enthusiastic, sensitive, and submissive to be more prone to purchase private brands than their counterparts. The predictive power of the personality variables, however, is quite low, in that less than five percent of the total variance in the purchase data is explained by personality.[45]

Recent Research Approaches Finally, two recent variations of the basic research strategy have shown slightly more positive results. Kernan used the Gorden personal profile to examine the relation between personality and several standard decision models.[46] Canonical correlation[47] was used as the associative measure, and a weak significant relationship was found between personality traits and decision behavior.

Sparks and Tucker extended this analysis into a more marketing related area. They reported significant canonical correlations between personality and product usage for a variety of convenience items.[48] The interpretation of these data, while not unequivocal, suggest the importance of trait interactions in determining the relation between personality and consumer behavior. Further research is needed to establish the validity of this technique.

Implications for Marketing

It might appear that marketing analysts would rapidly become discouraged with the effectiveness of trait-factor theory in predicting various types of buyer behavior. But negative findings do not seem to have deterred this type of research.

Two important issues militate against the future success of these research efforts. These issues include limitations on the use of standard personality tests and the pervasiveness of personality traits. These issues are discussed in greater detail in the following sections.

Limitations of Personality Tests and Measures All too frequently the standard personality measures of the psychological clinic are used in marketing without analysis of the permissibility of such an application. In the psychological clinic, various tests are used as diagnostic instruments. Seldom is one test the sole criterion of a personality disorder. In other words, the tests themselves do not

---

[45] J. G. Myers, "Determinants of Private Brand Attitude," *J. Marketing Research,* vol. 4, pp. 73–81 (Feb. 1967).

[46] J. B. Kernan, "Choice Criteria, Decision Behavior, and Personality," *J. Marketing Research,* vol. 5, pp. 155–164 (May 1968).

[47] For an explanation and description of canonical correlations, see W. W. Cooley and P. R. Lohnes, *Multivariate Procedures for the Behavioral Sciences* (New York: Wiley, 1962), chap. 3; Paul Green and Donald Tull, *Research for Marketing Decisions* (Englewood Cliffs, N.J.: Prentice-Hall, 1970), chap. 11.

[48] D. L. Sparks and W. T. Tucker, "A Multivariate Analysis of Personality and Product Use," *J. Marketing Research,* vol. 8, pp. 66–70 (1971). In this research, however, there is an unresolved issue concerning the appropriate treatment of degrees of freedom in the Wilks lambda tests.

bear the weight of explanation they have been assigned in the studies. It is not surprising that the predictive power is low.

Furthermore, the tests themselves may be unsatisfactory in terms of reliability and validity.[49] Reliability is assessed by determining whether or not a measure gives consistent results in repeated applications. If not, it certainly cannot be valid or measure what it purports to measure. In addition, validity must be assessed through comparing test results against some criterion or construct that reflect the variable under analysis.[50] It is not an overstatement to point out that this seldom is demonstrated in marketing experiments. Therefore, caution should be exercised where such measures are used as predictors of buyer behavior in a complex situation.[51]

The Problem of Personality Pervasiveness It will be recalled that a specific personality trait is postulated to elicit a consistent behavioral response across situations. The empirical results, however, have not supported the contention of stable, transsituational traits.[52] Indeed, Mischel commented, "With the possible exception of intelligence, highly generalized behavioral consistencies have not been demonstrated, and the concept of personality traits as broad response predispositions is untenable."[53]

In view of these results, there has been a growing tendency to accept the trait–situation interaction as predictive of behavior.[54] Both Yinger and Hunt have suggested techniques to measure these interactions.[55] More empirical research is needed in consumer behavior situations to determine the validity of this conceptualization. If subsequent research indicates that these interactions represent the true state of affairs, then it is unreasonable to expect a measure of personality alone to accurately predict buyer behavior.

Implications for Segmentation Strategies

Marketing managers are generally required to base strategy on an awareness that it is usually impossible to please everyone with the same thing. Total product offerings thus are adapted to the demands of relatively homogeneous groups through the process of market segmentation.

---

[49] L. J. Cronback, *Essentials of Psychological Testing*, 3rd ed. (New York: Harper & Row, 1970); M. E. Shaw and J. M. Wright, *Scales for the Measurement of Attitudes* (New York: McGraw-Hill, 1967).

[50] For a discussion of the measures of validity, see F. N. Kerlinger, *Foundations of Behavioral Research*, (New York: Holt, Rinehart and Winston, 1964).

[51] For additional discussions of the limitations of standardized personality tests, see Kassarjian, *op. cit.*;[2] Wells and Beard, *op. cit.*[3]

[52] J. M. Hunt, "Traditional Personality Theory in Light of Recent Evidence," *Amer. Scientist,* vol. 53, pp. 80–95 (1965); Mischel, *op. cit.*[18]

[53] Mischel, *op. cit.*,[18] p. 146.

[54] R. P. Abelson, "Situational Variables in Personality Research," in S. Messick and J. Ross (eds.), *Measurement in Personality and Cognition* (New York: Wiley, 1962), pp. 241–246; J. M. Yinger, "Research Implications of a Field View of Personality," *Amer. J. Sociology*, vol. 68, pp. 580–592 (1963); J. M. Yinger, *Toward a Field Theory of Behavior* (New York: McGraw-Hill, 1965); Hunt, *op. cit.*;[52] J. Block, "Some Reasons for the Apparent Inconsistency of Personality," *Psychological Bull.*, vol. 70, pp. 210–212 (1968).

[55] Yinger (1963), *op. cit.*;[54] Hunt, *op. cit.*[52]

Markets have traditionally been segmented along such demographic dimensions as age, income, occupation, and social class. Many people feel, however, that demography falls considerably short as a means of segmentation, and that markets can be analyzed to detect differences in values, motivations, and personality.[56] Negative results from the predictive studies have not deterred this speculation.

From the literature reviewed, does it seem likely that markets can be segmented meaningfully by personality variables? To date, most research attempts have ended in failure in that personality variables have not differentiated adequately between relevant groups. But even if personality traits were found to be valid predictors of buyer behavior, would they be useful as a means of market segmentation? In order for a positive answer to be given, the following circumstances must prevail:

(1) People with common personality dimensions must be homogeneous in terms of demographic factors such as age, income, and location so that they can be reached economically through the mass media. This is necessary because data are available on media audiences mostly in terms of demographic characteristics. If they show no identifiable common characteristics of this type, there is no practical means of reaching them as a unique market segment.

(2) Measures that isolate personality variables must be demonstrated to have adequate reliability and validity. The difficulties in this respect have already been pointed out.

(3) Personality differences must reflect clear-cut variations in buyer activity and preferences that, in turn, can be capitalized upon meaningfully through modifications in the marketing mix. In other words, people can show different personality profiles yet still prefer essentially the same product attributes.

(4) Market groups isolated by personality measures must be of a sufficient size to be reached economically. Knowledge that each person varies on a personality scale is interesting but impractical for a marketing firm which, of necessity, must generally work with relatively large segments.

It seems that the evidence to date falls short of these criteria, and personality has not been demonstrated convincingly as a useful means of market segmentation.[57] There is no reason to assume, for example, that individuals with a given personality profile are homogeneous in other respects; nor does it seem reasonable to expect that they have enough in common to be reached easily through the mass media without attracting a large number of nonprospects.

Therefore, it appears that future research that attempts to predict buyer behavior or identify market segments based on personality dimensions is destined

---

[56] Daniel Yankelovich, "New Criteria for Market Segmentation," *Harvard Business Rev.*, vol. 42, pp. 83–90 (1964).

[57] Segmentation along with activity, interest, and opinion dimensions have proven more useful. These techniques are reviewed at the conclusion of this chapter.

to a low practical payout. There are, however, some significant applications of personality theory not yet discussed where the outlook is much brighter. These applications are the subject matter of the next section.

PROPER UTILIZATION OF PERSONALITY THEORY IN ANALYSIS OF BUYER BEHAVIOR

The potential applications of personality theory and measures to buyer behavior may appear, until this point, discouraging. Indeed, any hope of finding a systematic theory of personality applicable to marketing (or any other applied area, for that matter) usually ends in dismay. Cofer and Appley critically evaluated the work on personality and motivation and were led to the conclusion that "a definitive psychology of motivation does not yet exist."[58]

The discussion, thus far, however, has focused only on areas that have proved to be relatively unprofitable. There are several research avenues where results have been considerably more encouraging, although the published literature is much less voluminous. In particular, four approaches appear promising: (1) market segmentation through tailor-made personality inventories, (2) market segmentation through AIO inventories, (3) use of personality as a moderator variable, and (4) use of personality as an intervening variable.

Tailor-Made Inventories

As previously discussed, the use of personality as an independent segmentation variable has usually given disappointing results. Part of the problem may lie in the fact that standard personality inventories designed for use in the psychological clinic were employed in nonclinic applications. In so doing, the value of the measure may be obscured through an improper application.

Other researchers have used personality as an independent segmentation variable measured with research instruments specially designed for this purpose. It seems obvious, of course, that better results should be expected from test items relating to the everyday processes of buying and consumption. The problem is that the construction of such instruments is difficult and tedious.

White attempted to isolate market segments that reflected traditional and modern views of housewives toward laundry detergents. Five personality dimensions were considered to be indicative of the values associated with these dichotomous orientations. These dimensions included:

(1) Flexible versus rigid. This dimension focused on the need to maintain a flexible or strict cleaning schedule and organization of time to this end.

(2) Evaluative versus nonevaluative. To what extent is cleaning central in

---

[58] C. N. Cofer and M. H. Appley, *Motivation: Theory and Research* (New York: Wiley, 1964).

a housewife's evaluation of herself and others in the role of wife and mother?

(3) Objective versus family role. This dealt with the degree to which cleaning is seen as essential to family nature as opposed to being a necessary utilitarian task. In other words, is cleaning an "act of love?"

(4) Emancipated versus limited. The emancipated housewife was defined as holding the point of view that she can participate in a larger social context outside the home.

(5) Appreciated versus unappreciated. This dimension showed the house-wife's perception of the extent of appreciation by husband and children of her efforts in their behalf.

Data were collected from a sample of 300 housewives using a battery of specially designed projective techniques.[59]

From this analysis, two basic value dimensions emerged: (1) a modern-extended segment showing a housewife who is emancipated, nonevaluative, objective, and flexible; she does not judge her worth by cleaning, and cleaning is not an expression of love, (2) a traditional-restricted segment in which the housewife feels that her worth is judged by cleaning and rigid schedules. When subsequent package and design changes were presented to these segments, clear differences in preference emerged.

Clearly, the methodology utilized in this example is more rigorous than a straightforward application of standardized personality tests. There is no reason why research of this type should not be relevant in a broad range of applications. Several authors have reported successful use of this technique.[60]

Utilization of AIO Inventories

Closely related to the topic of tailor-made personality inventories is the concept of psychographic segmentation. This technique utilizes a variety of psychological and behavioral variables[61] to describe the life styles of meaningful market segments. These descriptive segments may focus on the consumer, product benefits expected by the consumer, or clusters of consumer attitudes.[62] Research in these areas has been limited, and most available studies have concentrated on delineating psychological and behavioral portraits of consumers.

---

[59] I. S. White, "The Perception of Value in Products," in J. W. Newman, *op. cit.,*[44] pp. 90–106.

[60] J. A. Lunn, "Psychological Classification," in K. K. Cox (ed.), *Analytical View-points in Marketing Management* (Englewood Cliffs, N.J.: Prentice-Hall, 1968), pp. 47–59.

[61] Examples of these psychological and behavioral variables include activities, aspirations, beliefs, ideals, interests, opinions, perceptions, problems, tastes, values and worries.

[62] T. P. Hustad and E. A. Pessemier, *Segmenting Consumer Markets with Activity and Attitude Measures,* research paper no. 298 (Lafayette, Ind.: Institute for Research in the Behavioral, Economic, and Management Sciences, Herman C. Krannert Graduate School of Industrial Administration, Purdue University, Mar. 1971).

Most data for these studies have been collected through the use of activity, interest, and opinion (AIO) inventories.[63] In the typical research study, the completed AIO statements are correlated with a specified consumer behavior[64] (that is, product usage). Significant correlations are then identified by the researcher, and the AIO statements are factor analyzed into homogeneous categories. This analysis results in a psychographic portrait of users and nonusers of any product for which data were collected.

Wells and Tigert provide a good example of the information derived from this type of analysis. From a sample of 300 housewives, users and nonusers of eye makeup were compared in terms of their activities, interests, and opinions. Users were found to be younger, better educated, and more likely to be employed outside the home. In addition to these demographic data, users differed significantly from nonusers in degree of fashion consciousness, cosmopolitanism, and future orientation. The eye makeup user was also identified as a heavy user of other cosmetics. Eye makeup, therefore, is but a part of a consistent behavioral pattern.[65]

The marketing implications of psychographic segmentation should be obvious. Informational inputs for media selection and advertising content decisions are dramatically increased. Data can be simultaneously acquired for a large number of different products; therefore, considerable cost savings may be generated. Finally, general inventories have proven to be useful in a wide variety of applications. Future research should continue to expand the utility of the technique.[66] The limitations of AIO measures are also constantly explored in continuing research.

Personality as a Moderator Variable

Many theorists now believe that personality and the environment interact to shape behavior, as has been pointed out previously. An extension of this view leads to the prediction that a set of personality characteristics may be a better predictor of behavior in one situation than another. In other words, it may be useful

---

[63]   An AIO inventory is a larger set of statements that purportedly measure consumer activities, interests, and opinions. These inventories may also include more conventional personality statements.

[64]   Multiple measures of consumer behavior are usually taken. Examples include purchase patterns, media exposure, slogan recognition, and product usage. In addition, standard demographic information is also collected.

[65]   W. D. Wells and D. J. Tigert, "Activities, Interests, Opinions," *J. Advertising Research*, vol. 11, pp. 27–35 (Aug. 1971).

[66]   For examples of the diversity of the technique, see E. A. Pessemier and D. J. Tigert, "Personality, Activity and Attitude Predictors of Consumer Behavior," in J. S. Wright and J. C. Goldstrucker (eds.), *New Ideas for Successful Marketing* (Chicago: Amer. Marketing Assoc., 1966), pp. 332–347; C. L. Wilson, "Homemaker Living Patterns and Marketplace Behavior: A Psychometric Approach," in Wright and Goldstrucker, pp. 305–331; J. T. Plummer, "Life Style Patterns and Commercial Bank Credit Card Usage," *J. Marketing*, vol. 35, pp. 35–41 (1971); R. Ziff, "Psychographics for Market Segmentation," *J. Advertising Research*, vol. 11, pp. 3–9 (1971).

to distinguish in advance situations in which sample subgroups are differentially affected by specific personality traits. If these differentials are operative, then these personality traits are said to "moderate" the situation.[67] The resulting predictions from the use of personality inventories should then be more accurate.

Brody and Cunningham proposed a theoretical framework to predict the situational importance of consumer decision variables. In this conceptualization, the situational importance of any decision variable depends upon the choice situation.[68] Brody and Cunningham postulated personality variables will moderate the choice situation when performance risk and specific self-confidence are perceived as being high. This hypothesis was tested with a reanalysis of Koponen's data on coffee purchases. Sample subgroups were isolated on the pertinent dimensions and regression equations were recomputed. The predictions obtained increased strikingly from virtually no variance accounted for by personality to as much as 32 percent.[69]

Fry cast self-confidence as a moderator variable in cigarette brand choice. He hypothesized greater explanation of cigarette brand choice among the subset of buyers high in self-confidence. Regression equations for a combination of socioeconomic and personality variables explained between 20 percent and 30 percent of the purchase variance.[70] This increase in predictive ability is equivalent to the Brody and Cunningham result.

Both of these studies demonstrate empirical advantages in utilizing personality as a moderator variable. This usage, however, raises three pertinent issues. First, the selection procedure for useful moderator variables is not intuitively clear. Several authors have noted this problem[71] and Brody and Cunningham readily admit the deficiency of their model in this area. Second, only a fraction of explained variance is accounted for in either study. Fry indicates refinements in measurement procedures are needed. Finally, research is still needed to determine situations in which personality variables are, or are not, relevant moderators. Solutions to these questions present formidable methodological problems.

The use of personality as a moderator variable shows promise as a means

---

[67] For a more thorough discussion of the concept of moderator variables, see D. R. Saunders, "Moderator Variables in Prediction," *Educational and Psychological Measurement,* vol. 16, pp. 209–222 (1956); E. E. Ghiselli, "The Prediction of Predictability," *Educational and Psychological Measurement,* vol. 20, pp. 3–8 (1960); E. E. Ghiselli, "Moderating Effects and Differential Reliability and Validity," *J. Applied Psychology,* vol. 47, pp. 81–86 (1963).

[68] Specifically, situational importance depends on the consumer's perception of the choice situation. The perceptual filters include performance risk, specific self-confidence, and social risk.

[69] The greatest amount of explained variance was recorded for persons who were 100 percent brand loyal. Explained variance decreased directly with brand loyalty.

[70] J. N. Fry, "Personality Variables and Cigarette Brand Choice," *J. Marketing Research,* vol. 8, pp. 298–304 (Aug. 1971). Self-confidence was selected as a moderator variable because of its presumed influence on more specific personality dimensions. Fry readily admits the arbitrariness of this choice.

[71] R. P. Brody and S. M. Cunningham, "Personality Variables and the Consumer Decision Process," *J. Marketing Research,* vol. 5, pp. 50–57 (Feb. 1968); Fry, *op. cit.*[70]

of explaining conflicting results. It is, however, an area that needs considerably more experimentation before a definitive assessment can be made.

Personality as an Intervening Variable

Personality is useful in a very different way if the market is first segmented on some objective variable other than personality. Then each isolated subgroup is studied to determine any differences in psychological attributes. Any number of variables could be used for the initial market segmentation, including age, income, degree of product use, or others depending upon the nature of the problem. One approach that has proved useful is to differentiate buyers by the extent to which they use both the product and the brand. Then the inquiry focuses on why one person uses the brand while others do not.

One manufacturer followed this procedure, and it is useful to discuss briefly conclusions that resulted.[72] The Flavorfest Company (the name is fictitious) manufactures and distributes a well-known bottled condiment product. The firm has long dominated the market for this product line which includes other spices and seasoning items.

Flavorfest could base a marketing program on the assumption that all potential customers are equally valuable prospects, but such an assumption must be verified by research to be successful. It is more likely that substantial consumer differences exist. Subsequent research disclosed three distinct market segments, each of which offered very different prospects for marketing success. These research findings were as follows:

(1)   *Heavy Users* (39 percent of the market)
   (a) *Demographic attitudes:* housewives aged 20–45; well educated; higher income categories; small families with most children under 5; concentration in Northeast and Midwest regions and in suburban and farm areas.
   (b) *Motivational attributes:*
       (i)   Strong motivation not to be old fashioned and a desire to express individuality through creative action and use of exciting new things.
       (ii) The traditional role as a housewife is viewed with displeasure, and experimentation with new foods is done to express her individuality—not to please her family.
       (iii) The image of Flavorfest suggests exciting and exotic taste, and the product is reacted to favorably in terms of taste, appearance, and food value. It is highly prized in experimental cooking. Hence, there is substantial compatibility between values of the user and product image.

---

[72]   James F. Engel, Hugh G. Wales, and Martin R. Warshaw, *Promotional Strategy* (Homewood, Ill.: Irwin, 1971), pp. 160–162.

(2)   *Light to Moderate Users* (20 percent of the market)

   (a)   *Demographc attributes:* housewives aged 35–54; large families with children under 12; middle-income groups; location mostly in Southeast, Pacific states, and Southwest.

   (b)   *Motivational attributes:*

      (i)   A strong desire to express individuality through creative cookery, but this desire is constrained somewhat by a conflicting desire to maintain tradition and subvert herself to her family's desires.

      (ii)   The desire to experiment with new foods is also constrained by a lack of confidence in the results of her experimental cooking.

      (iii)   The image of Flavorfest is favorable. The product is liked in all respects, but it is confined largely to use with one type of food. It is viewed as unacceptable in other uses. Hence, her vision is limited regarding new uses for Flavorfest.

(3)   *Nonusers* (41 percent of the market)

   (a)   *Demographic attributes:* older housewives; large families; lower income brackets; location mostly in the Eastern states and some parts of the South.

   (b)   *Motivational attributes:*

      (i)   A strong motive to maintain tradition and emotional ties with the past; identification with her mother and her role in the home.

      (ii)   A conservative nonventuresome personality.

      (iii)   Her role as a mother and housewife discourages experimental cookery, and Flavorfest is thus looked upon unfavorably. The image of Flavorfest connotes exotic flavors and a degree of modernity which is unacceptable.

      (iv)   No interest is expressed in new uses and experimentation with Flavorfest, for the product does not represent the values embraced by these housewives.[73]

From this research it is clear that there are important demographic differences between users and nonusers. Therefore, it is possible through skillful use of advertising media to avoid certain segments if this is deemed desirable. Specially designed questions also isolated some important personality differences.

The heavy-user segment is relatively large, and the product is well regarded by these housewives. Because of the product's use in experimental cookery and its role in expressing individuality, the potential exists for stimulating greater use.

The nonuser segment, on the other hand, presents a different marketing situation. While this segment now tends to be large, it is made up largely of

---

[73]   Engel, *et al., op. cit.,*[72] p. 161.

people with relatively little purchasing power living in areas where population growth is stagnant. In addition, the potential for stimulating use of Flavorfest is not at all favorable. The existence of strong negative values increases the probability of selective perception of persuasive messages, and there would seem to be little market opportunity.

The light-to-moderate-user segment represents the greatest opportunity for increased sales. The desire for creative cookery is present but is constrained by a desire to maintain tradition and by a lack of confidence in results of experimental efforts. Yet the product is liked in nearly all respects. Lack of confidence, for example, might be minimized by stressing "nonfail" recipes. The interest in pleasing the family can be shown as compatible with creative cookery by stressing favorable family reaction to new tastes and recipes. Finally, Flavorfest can be featured as an ideal accompaniment to a variety of foods.

This example illustrates how yet another use can be made of personality data in designing and promoting products. Indeed, one author concludes that personality tests have no other important use for marketing planning.[74]

The Future of Personality Research

Personality research can be profitably employed to supply data that are useful in solving marketing management problems. These research approaches, however, do not explain the effect of personality variables on the model of consumer decision making. This explanation is the topic of the remainder of this chapter.

Personality and the Modeling Process The personality theories briefly outlined at the beginning of this chapter are, in essence, models of human behavior themselves. In general, however, the construction of a model is but the initial step in a more inclusive modeling process. Once constructed, logically derived predictions of the model are empirically tested. Data generated from these studies either confirm or suggest modifications in the model. It should be apparent, however, that substantial modifications are required to develop a viable personality model for marketing research.

McGuire's model, used extensively in this text, represents a more specific attempt to relate personality variables to human behavior. The influence process is utilized as the prototypical behavioral example. The analysis, however, is a potential explanation for other important consumer behavior processes.[75]

---

[74] W. D. Wells, "General Personality Tests and Consumer Behavior," in Newman, *op. cit.,*[44] pp. 187–189.

[75] One important potential application is a more complete explanation of the relationship between personality variables and the decision stages of consumer behavior. For a review of the relevant marketing literature on this topic, see John Walton, *Personality Research and Consumer Decisions,* unpublished M. A. Thesis (Columbus, Ohio: Ohio State University, 1972).

McGuire's Model of Personality
and Attitude Change[76]

McGuire defines personality as "any variable on which people differ."[77] These variables include not only traditional personality dimensions such as self-esteem, but also demographic characteristics such as age, sex, income, and social class. In terms of the model, these individual difference variables may impact on any of the influence process mediators.[78] For purposes of analysis, only the reception and yielding mediators are considered.

In simplest form, McGuire's model may be described in terms of three assumptions—multimediation, compensation, and situational weighting.

(1) The multimediation assumption postulates that personality variables may impact on reception as well as yielding. Previous research has over-emphasized the role of the yielding mediator in the influence process. This assumption points out that overemphasis on a single mediator may make interpretation of empirical results difficult.

(2) The compensation assumption asserts that in situations where individual difference variables affect multiple-influence process mediators, message transmission is enhanced through certain mediators and inhibited through others. The net effect is a nonmonotonic relationship between the personality variable and influenceability.

(3) The situational-weighting assumption specifies, at least in an ordinal sense, the influence process mediators that are likely to be operative in a particular situation. This assumption attempts to restrict the excessive explanatory power of the model.

An example should make the explanatory properties of the model more clear. Intuitively, it seems logical that education level (as a surrogate variable for intelligence) and susceptibility to influence from advertising messages should be inversely related. That is, higher educated individuals should be difficult to influence, while less educated individuals should be relatively easy to influence.

This myopic analysis, however, only considers the impact of education level on the yielding mediator. In terms of the reception mediator, higher educated people should be relatively high on advertising message reception, while less educated people should be relatively low on message reception. The net effect is that lower educated individuals (eighth-grade education or less) are difficult

---

[76]   The material from this section is drawn heavily from McGuire, *op. cit.*;[24] also W. J. McGuire, "The Nature of Attitudes and Attitude Change," in G. Lindzey and E. Aronson (eds.), *The Handbook of Social Psychology*, vol. 3 (Reading, Mass.: Addison-Wesley, 1969), pp. 136–314; W. J. McGuire, "Personality and Attitude Change: An Information-Processing Theory," in A. G. Greenwald, T. C. Brock, and T. M. Ostrom (eds.), *Psychological Foundations of Attitudes* (New York: Academic Press, 1969), pp. 171–195.

[77]   McGuire, in Lindzey and Aronson, *op. cit.*,[76] p. 175.

[78]   These mediators include exposure, attention, comprehension, yielding, retention, and action. For purposes of simplicity, McGuire combines attention and comprehension into a single reception mediator.

to influence because they do not adequately receive the message; and higher educated individuals (some college and above) are difficult to influence because, while reception is adequate, they do not yield to the advertising message. Moderately educated individuals (some high school to high-school graduate), however, are more receptive than the lower educated individual and more yielding than the higher educated individual. Therefore, maximum influence of the advertising message should occur in groups with moderate levels of education. The nonmonotonic relationship postulated by the compensation assumption is, therefore, upheld.

The exact nature of this relationship depends upon a specifiable aspect of the communication situation, namely, the complexity of the message content. If the persuasive content of the message is easily understood, the relationship between education level and the yielding mediator should bear the explanatory weight for observed attitude change.[79] If the persuasive content is not easily understood, the relationship between education level and the reception mediator should bear the explanatory weight.[80] The chapter following this one develops these ideas further.

McGuire's model represents a potentially powerful tool to understand the effect of individual difference variables on consumer behavior. Marketing analysts interested in personality research may be expected to increase their interest in such an approach.

SUMMARY

There is no agreement on a definition of personality, although it is generally linked to the concept of consistent responses to environmental stimuli. It affects evaluative criteria significantly and is an integral component of the central control unit.

Three major theories of personality are commonly accepted. *Psychoanalytic theory* focuses on the unconscious motivations of a person as a result of viewing human personality as a system consisting of the id, ego, and superego. The motivation research movement in marketing relied heavily on psychoanalytic theory. *Social-psychological theory* differs from psychoanalytic theory in its emphasis upon social variables, not biological instincts, as the important determinants in shaping behavior and in its emphasis upon motivation as a conscious process. *Trait-factor theory* is a quantitative approach viewing personality as a set of predispositional attributes called traits or the summation of individual difference variables. Most marketing research, attempting to link a set of personality variables with purchase behavior, is built upon trait-factor theory.

---

[79] In a situation where the message should be understood by everyone, the relationship between the individual difference variable and the yielding mediator should predict the findings. In this situation, an inverse relationship between education level and influenceability should be obtained.

[80] In this situation, the message is adequately received by only the highest educated. Therefore, although these people are influenced very little, it will be a greater absolute amount than individuals at lower education levels.

A number of consumer studies have been undertaken attempting to use personality variables to predict buyer behavior. These studies fall into two general classifications: (1) susceptibility to social influence and (2) product and brand choice. Numerous attempts have been made to relate personality variables to market segmentation strategies with little success.

Several alternative approaches to personality theory are emerging that appear useful to marketing strategists. These include the use of tailor-made personality inventories for market segmentation, market segmentation through AIO (attitudes, interests, opinions) inventories, the use of personality as a moderator variable, and the use of personality as an intervening variable. One promising approach is a model by McGuire which relates personality to attitude change as a part of the communication process.

REVIEW AND DISCUSSION QUESTIONS

1. What are the central components of psychoanalytic theories of personality? How have they influenced the development of marketing thought and planning?

2. Describe the trait-factor theory of personality and assess its importance in past and future marketing research.

3. Assume that researchers in a large New York advertising agency devise a measure of persuasibility that is claimed to be both reliable and valid.
   (a) What is meant by reliability and validity?
   (b) What does it mean to say that Mr. A is more persuasible than Mr. B?
   (c) Evaluate critically whether or not this measure can and will prove useful in planning the advertising campaign for a large household detergent account?
   (d) Would the account director for a line of refrigerators and freezers use this measure differently than his counterpart on the detergent account?

4. Assume that the marketing research director of a large consumer package goods firm is investigating the potential of personality variables as a basis for segmentation strategies. He is familiar with several standardized psychological tests of personality but has been advised that tailor-made inventories might also be helpful. Citing the research to date, which approach would seem to have the highest probability of being useful?

5. Critically assess the value of AIO scales for consumer analysts. Analyze the relationship of AIO scales as discussed in this chapter and the materials discussed in Chapters 4, 5, and 6.

6. The marketing management of a large automobile manufacturer has expressed interest in the relevance of the McGuire model in assessing the role of personality in communications. Prepare an outline for the automobile manufacturer that would describe the salient information.

Persuasive
Communication
and Attitude Change

The emphasis now shifts to an analysis of the effectiveness of persuasive communication, with special emphasis on attitude change. Chapter 13 has the purpose of providing essential background in the fundamentals of interpersonal and mass communication. Since mass communication attains such great significance in marketing strategy, it is discussed at greater length. Of particular importance are strategies for measurement of the ability of stimuli to attract and hold attention and lead to the desired communication result. Obviously this should be done prior to investment of funds in a persuasive campaign, so considerable emphasis is placed on pretesting of the message.

Chapter 14 reviews the vast literature on attitude change. Such variations in the message as fear appeals, distraction, one side versus two sides, and humor are evaluated. It is necessary to be somewhat meticulous in definition of terms and assessment of implications from the various avenues of research, for the areas of misunderstanding in marketing applications are many. As will become apparent, some writers in the marketing literature have been guilty of suggesting applications without careful analysis of the underlying evidence. Once greater caution is introduced, the applications of findings are sharply reduced, although the yield of fruitful avenues of inquiry is still great.

CHAPTER **13**

PERSUASIVE COMMUNICATION

It is the purpose of this chapter to explore the communication process with social emphasis on mass communication. Mass communication is of unique significance for several reasons: (1) it is a major means of consumer persuasion as is evidenced by the expenditure of more than $20 billion yearly for commercial advertising, to say nothing of persuasion by noncommercial sources, (2) it tends to draw the fire of critics more than face-to-face persuasion because of its visibility, and (3) mass communication messages can be readily screened out by the recipient, thereby presenting some real managerial difficulties.

The chapter begins with a discussion of the nature of communication. The use of mass communication then is analyzed in greater detail to clarify such important issues as design of the persuasive message and use of communication research. These considerations provide necessary background for the discussion of attitude change in Chapter 14.

THE NATURE OF COMMUNICATION

It is generally agreed that communication takes place when a message has been transmitted by a source and the intended point is grasped by the recipient.[1] The nature of this process is best understood by an analysis of communi-

---

[1] For a review of many of the definitions appearing in the literature, see D. C. Barnlund (ed.), *Interpersonal Communication: Survey and Studies* (Boston: Houghton Mifflin, 1968), pp. 4, 5.

cation between two people. Later discussion will show that mass communication does not differ greatly in fundamentals.

Interpersonal Communication

The nature of communication between two persons, Mr. *A* and Mr. *B*, is represented in Figure 13.1.[2]

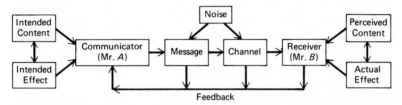

Figure 13.1 INTERPERSONAL COMMUNICATION. J. F. Engel, H. G. Wales, and M. R. Warshaw, *Promotional Strategy,* rev. ed. (Homewood, Ill.: Irwin, 1971), p. 19. Reprinted by permission of the publisher.

Mr. *A* has something he wishes to present to Mr. *B*, and he proceeds by arranging words in a pattern or sequence to be communicated. This is referred to as *encoding*. The encoded message then is transmitted through the spoken word or some other type of channel. Mr. *B* attempts to *decode* the message and arrive at its meaning. The actual meaning, however, can deviate substantially from intended meaning through selective information processing as was discussed in Chapter 8. In that case communication is hindered or even prevented altogether.

Noise also can enter into both the message and the channel in the form of conflicting signals or other forms of distraction. The fidelity of communication thereby is inhibited.

Mr. *A* receives feedback in the form of verbal or nonverbal responses from Mr. *B* and determines if he has been successful in his efforts. If not, the process will be initiated once again.

The Source Mr. *A* has both an intended content and an intended effect for the message. For this intent to be encoded into a message he must place himself in "Mr. *B*'s shoes" through the process of empathy. Empathy begins early

---

2   Figure 13.1 is a composite of many models and theories which have appeared in the vast literature on communication. Among the standard sources are L. Thayer, *Communication and Communication Systems* (Homewood, Ill.: Irwin, 1968); C. Cherry, *On Human Communication,* 2nd ed. (Cambridge, Mass.: M.I.T. Press, 1966); M. L. DeFleur, *Theories of Mass Communication* (New York: McKay, 1966); D. K. Berlo, *The Process of Communication* (New York: Holt, Rinehart and Winston, 1960); N. Wiener, *The Human Use of Human Beings* (New York: Doubleday, 1954); H. Lasswell, "The Structure and Function of Communication in Society," in L. Bryson (ed.), *The Communication of Ideas* (New York: Harper and Brothers, 1948).

in childhood through learning to take the role of another. As the child matures he is introduced to the expectations of those around him. By this means he can acquire a common set of meanings and definitions, and communication is facilitated.

The Message   Mr. *A*'s message most frequently will be in the form of oral or written language. All languages are composed of *signs* and *symbols*. A sign is an event in experience which becomes associated with another event. Dark clouds, for example, are a sign of approaching rain. A symbol, on the other hand, is a conventional sign in the form of an artificial construct deliberately employed to convey a meaning.[3] Symbols enter into language when there is general agreement that they signify a particular referent. Words, therefore, are symbols used even when the external objects of reference are absent or even nonexistent.

When a word calls forth the same responses as the external referent, it is said to have attained *denotative meaning*. It now stands for or denotes the object. Another dimension of meaning, however, comes from the selective processing within Mr. *B*'s central control unit, and that meaning, which is unique to him, is referred to as *connotative meaning*. The person who has learned to like the flavor of liver, for example, will have a different connotative meaning when he hears the term than a person with a contrary experience, even though the denotative meanings in both instances will be identical.

The symbols used by Mr. *A* should be oriented as closely as possible to Mr. *B*'s background, interest, needs, and dispositions. Otherwise the effect may be failure to capture his attention and achieve comprehension. Communication obviously is facilitated when both have a substantial overlap in the sum total of influences on their behavior. Anyone who has visited a foreign country is well aware of the communication barriers presented by language and cultural differences. The consequence is likely to be noise rather than communication.

The Channel   The medium through which an interpersonal message is sent generally will be the spoken word, although nonverbal communication also can attain significance. Such forms as body movement (kinesic behavior), paralanguage (voice qualities and nonlanguage sounds such as yawning), and such factors as use of dress and cosmetics all affect communication.[4]

The Receiver   Communication occurs when the content of the message processed by Mr. *B* closely corresponds to that which was transmitted. Because of the common phenomena of selective attention, comprehension, and retention, any attempt to communicate without regard to Mr. *B*'s motivational influences is doomed to failure unless the communicator has phenomenal luck.

---

[3]   L. Ruby, *An Introduction to Logic* (Philadelphia: Lippincott, 1950), p. 18.

[4]   S. Duncan, "Nonverbal Communication," *Psychological Bull.* vol. 62, pp. 118–137 (1969).

Feedback A smile, an affirmative reply, a frown, or some other type of response provides essential feedback as to whether or not Mr. *B* is "getting the message." If poor results are attained, Mr. *A* can modify the message immediately and try again. This instantaneous feedback makes face-to-face communication highly efficient in that both sender and receiver can keep trying until effective contact is made.

Mass Communication

In mass communication a message is transmitted to a group of individuals at roughly the same point in time as is illustrated in Figure 13.2.

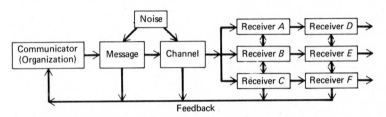

Figure 13.2 MASS COMMUNICATION.   J. F. Engel, H. G. Wales, and M. R. Warshaw, *Promotional Strategy,* rev. ed. (Homewood, Ill.: Irwin, 1971), p. 24. Reprinted by permission of the publisher.

The communicator now is designated as the output of many individuals within an organization. In addition, the recipient is an interconnected group, each of whom may interact with others and hence affect the content which is communicated.

The Communicator Most frequently the communicator through mass media is a commercial, educational, or governmental agency. Many individuals will interact to determine message content, with the result that speed of communication is drastically reduced through the necessity of collective decisions.

The Message The format of the message differs only in the sense that it usually must be more impersonal than the message transmitted through face-to-face channels. This is because the target is a group rather than an identified individual, with the result that it is difficult to orient its content to achieve optimum impact on a given person. This inflexibility of message alteration is a primary disadvantage of mass media.

Fortunately the availability of social norms partly overcomes the problem of inflexibility. As one authority points out:

> Knowledge of a social system can help us make accurate predictions about people, without the necessity of empathizing, without the necessity of interaction, without knowing anything about the people other than the roles that they have in the system. . . . For every role

there is a set of behaviors and a position. If we know what the behaviors are that go with a role, we can predict that those behaviors will be performed by people who perform that role. Second, if we can know what behaviors go with a given rank of position, we can make predictions about people who occupy that position.[5]

The Channel The channel uses such media as television, radio, magazines, and so on, all of which are published or aired at regular intervals. This factor further reduces speed and flexibility of communication. Furthermore, communication by necessity is indirect because of the fact that source and recipient are not simultaneously present in time or space. The advantage, of course, is that a large group can be reached relatively economically.

The Receivers Each member of the audience selectively responds to the message, and the probability of selective attention, comprehension, and retention is especially pronounced in that one message seldom will be on target for all recipients. This is perhaps the greatest problem faced when the mass media are used.

The effect of the message also is influenced by word-of-mouth communication between audience members. Favorable word of mouth can be a great asset, because the message is further disseminated and its effects reinforced to an extent that usually is impossible through the mass media alone. An opposite result can occur, of course, in that unfavorable word-of-mouth contact can substantially mitigate any favorable effect the message might have generated.

Feedback Effective feedback is difficult indeed, because communicator and recipient are physically separated. Feedback at best is delayed, because some type of audience survey is the usual method. The listening audience of a radio program or readership of a newspaper article usually can be determined only by asking people what they have heard or read. Some techniques which are used for this purpose are discussed later in the chapter.

Surveys of this type are expensive and time consuming. The resulting feedback is obtained too late to permit changing the message during the actual communication. This type of feedback, therefore, finds primary use in determining future message strategy.

Communication in Marketing

At one time all marketing communication was in the form of Mr. *A* communicating face to face with Mr. *B* through personal selling, and this still is a highly important type of promotion. The advantage, of course, is that the salesman can effectively determine his prospect's motivational influences and phrase his message accordingly. Direct feedback of response permits immediate modification of the message, if needed, so that the chances of successful inter-

---

5   Berlo, *op. cit.*,[2] p. 149. Reprinted by permission of the publisher.

action are increased. Both parties can engage in role taking, and the communication difficulties, while never to be minimized, are less than those presented when the mass media are used.[6]

The mass media, on the other hand, have the problems of delayed feedback, inflexibility of message, and greater probability of selective processing by audience members. It therefore becomes difficult to achieve major changes in attitudes and other dispositions. The overwhelming advantage, of course, is that a mass audience may be reached very economically from the point of view of cost per individual contacted.

Promotional strategy requires a tradeoff between two considerations: (1) communication effectiveness (flexibility and ease of feedback) and (2) cost per individual reached. These factors, in turn, usually cannot be attained simultaneously in that maximum communication effectiveness requires face-to-face contact which, of course, is most expensive on the basis of cost per individual reached.

USING THE MASS MEDIA

The remainder of this chapter focuses on consumer persuasion through mass media. The discussion thus far has covered, in a general manner, the way in which a message is transmitted from source to audience. The effects on audience members have not been analyzed in any depth. This section considers, first of all, a model of communication effects which builds on the model of consumer behavior used throughout this book. This is followed by an analysis of the market strategy implications of each of its stages.

Mass Communication Effects

It was pointed out in Chapter 8 that there are four stages in consumer information processing: (1) exposure, (2) attention, (3) comprehension, and (4) retention. No attempt has thus far been made, however, to explain the effects of this information on dispositions within the central control unit or on problem-solving behavior. Therefore, a complete model of the communication process also must include these responses. An expanded information processing model appears in Figure 13.3, and it includes three broad phases: (1) exposure, (2) reception (attention, comprehension, and retention), and (3) attitude/behavior modification.[7]

---

6 F. E. Webster, Jr., "Interpersonal Communication and Salesman Effectiveness," *J. Marketing*, vol. 32, pp. 7–13 (1968); A. L. Pennington, "Customer–Salesman Bargaining Behavior in Retail Transactions," *J. Marketing Research*, vol. 5, pp. 255–263 (1968).

7 In this form the information-processing model becomes similar to McGuire's attitude change model. See W. J. McGuire, "Personality and Susceptibility to Social Influence," in E. F. Borgatta and W. W. Cambert (eds.), *Handbook of Personality Theory and Research* (Chicago: Rand McNally, 1968).

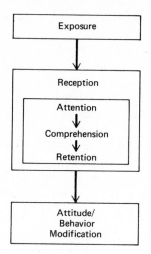

Figure 13.3   EXPANDED INFORMATION PROCESSING MODEL

Each of these stages is a necessary but not sufficient condition for its successor. A certain subtest of a given total audience will be exposed to a communication message. There is only a conditional probability, however, that the message will be received and processed. Finally, even if it is processed, there is only a conditional probability that it will have an effect on attitude and behavior.

Exposure

Achieving audience exposure is primarily a problem of selecting the right media. Audiences must be defined in precise demographic terms, and use then may be made of media audience data to permit selection of those media which most closely reach the target group. Procedures for this purpose are highly refined and need not be discussed further here.[8]

Reception

Attention   Attention occurs when there is a focus within the central control unit on an incoming stimulus. The stimulus then is processed for meaning.

The response of the individual when presented with a new stimulus is referred to as the orientation reaction.[9] As was described in Chapter 8, this response mobilizes the central nervous system in the form of arousal. Certain stimulus patterns are especially effective in stimulating the orientation response:

[8]   J. F. Engel, H. G. Wales, and M. R. Warshaw, *Promotional Strategy*, rev. ed. (Homewood, Ill.: Irwin, 1971), chap. 13–15.

[9]   R. Lynn, *Attention, Arousal and the Orientation Reaction* (Oxford: Pergamon, 1966).

(1) novelty and surprise, (2) intensity, (3) color, and (4) conditioned stimuli (those for which a previously learned pattern of response is called forth such as a turning of the head when one's name is mentioned[10]). As stimulation occurs repeatedly, however, the ability to generate the orientation reaction fades; when this occurs the stimulus is said to be habituated. Certain factors are particularly influential in bringing about habituation:[11]

(1) Stimulus intensity—the lower the intensity, the more rapidly habituation occurs.

(2) Duration of stimulus—an extremely brief stimulus is less likely to habituate.

(3) Difficulty of discrimination—the more difficult it is to grasp stimulus details, the less the likelihood of habituation.

(4) Time—habituation occurs more rapidly as time between exposures decreases.

(5) Conditioning—a stimulus which has become conditioned so that it is of personal significance to the recipient will not habituate even when it is repeated.

Habituation is a very real problem for the advertiser. Most products are highly familiar, and little can be said in a message which is truly novel or new. In addition, the "noise barrier" discussed in Chapter 8 from the glut of competing messages makes it difficult for one message to break through and capture attention. For this reason, resort is made to many of the devices mentioned above to bring about the orientation reaction, including: (1) novelty and contrast, (2) manipulation of intensity through variation of size and position of the message, and (3) use of color.

(1) **Novelty and Contrast** Very frequently contrast is effectively used in advertising messages. One well-known example is the Chiquita Brand banana advertisements which usually depict the banana in such a way that it stands out clearly in dominant fashion against its background. The appearance of the banana in such positions as standing on end is novel, with the result that attention is likely to be captured. This, of course, says nothing about the persuasive power of the message itself.

Numerous other illustrations could be given, only several of which are suggested here:

(a) A black and white advertisement featuring an unusual amount of white space with no print or illustration can stand out clearly when competitive messages are in color.

(b) A unusually shaped package captures attention when all others on a shelf are similar in design, shape, and color.

---

[10] D. E. Berlyne, *Conflict, Arousal and Curiosity* (New York: McGraw-Hill, 1960).

[11] Lynn, *op. cit.*,[9] pp. 26–32.

(c) The announcer's voice advertising a product during a break in a classical music program is likely to be noticed because of the sharp stimulus contrast.

(2) **Size and Position of the Message** There have been a number of studies on the effects of increasing the size of an advertisement on the printed page; it has been found that doubling the size does not double the impact. Readership tends to increase in proportion to the square root of the increase in space.[12]

It also is possible to generalize on the relative value of different positions on the page in print media:

(a) There is little variation in readership of advertisements appearing on the left- and right-hand pages in magazines or newspapers. The primary factor in readership is what the message says and how it says it.[13]

(b) The greatest readership in magazines is usually attracted by advertisements on the covers or in the first 10 percent of the pages, but beyond this point location is a minor factor.[14]

(c) Position within a newspaper does not appear to be crucial because of high page traffic throughout the paper.[15]

(d) Readership tends to be highest when the message is placed adjacent to compatible editorial features.

(e) Position in the gutter (the inside fold) offers little advantage in print media. In fact, position on the page itself has no effect except when competing advertisements become especially numerous, in which case the upper right-hand position offers an advantage in newspapers.[16]

Position in broadcast advertising has received less research, although it is known that commercials generally perform better when inserted as a part of the regular program rather than during the clutter of a station break.[17] It also appears that commercials at the beginning and end of a program suffer a disadvantage because of the clutter of announcements and other distracting nonprogram material.

(3) **The Use of Color** It is widely recognized that color can add significantly to the effectiveness of an advertisement for a number of reasons:

(a) The attention-attracting and holding power of the message may be sharply increased.

(b) Contemporary social trends have encouraged experimentation with color in all phases of life, ranging from the factory to the home. Thus people have become responsive to innovative color stimuli.

---

[12] R. Barton, *Advertising Media* (New York: McGraw-Hill, 1964), p. 109.

[13] "Position in Newspaper Advertising: 2," *Media/scope*, pp. 76–82 (Mar. 1963).

[14] "Position in Newspaper Advertising: 2," *op. cit.*[13]

[15] "Position in Newspaper Advertising: 1," *Media/scope*, p. 57 (Feb. 1963).

[16] "Position in Newspaper Advertising: 1," *op. cit.*[15]

[17] Barton, *op. cit.*,[12] p. 255.

(c) Most products look better in color, especially food.

(d) Color can be used to create moods, ranging from the somber appeal of dark colors to the freshness of greens and blues.

Numerous studies have demonstrated that color is a significant aid in attracting attention. For example, it appears to be the one outstanding factor in high readership of newspaper advertisements, undoubtedly because of the relative infrequency of color in that medium.[18] Moreover, data show that color commercials on the average are at least 50 percent more effective than the same television message in black and white.[19]

Comprehension and Retention The discussion in Chapter 8 demonstrated conclusively that an advertising stimulus is often interpreted in a manner consistent with the recipient's needs and predispositions, and this interpretation, in turn, may differ substantially from that intended by the source. The consumer has full powers to screen out any message which contradicts a strongly held disposition, and the only way in which this can be overcome is through control of the environment of the recipient.[20] Some mechanisms used to achieve this control might include hypnosis, psychotherapy, sensory deprivation (perhaps from solitary confinement), stimulation with drugs, stimulation of physiological stress, or brain implantation with electrodes.[21] Needless to say, such means are unavailable to the business firm. Therefore, the only strategy is to design the message in such a way that it is (1) directed toward those whose dispositions and need states are consistent with the action being suggested and (2) oriented toward reinforcing these tendencies, thereby leading to the desired action. As one authority observes,

> . . . to the social scientist, A's influence of B is not a matter of art, but of the witting or unwitting application of known or unknown scientific principles, and must be looked upon as such. The scientific analysis of human behavior is perhaps the single most potent weapon in A's arsenal. If he fails to make use of this powerful tool, he does so at his own risk.[22]

Modification of Attitude and Behavior[23] The goal of persuasive communication, of course, is modification of behavior. Earlier discussion pointed out

---

[18] "What Stirs the Newspaper Reader?" *Printers' Ink*, pp. 48–49 (June 21, 1963).

[19] *Are Color Television Commercials Worth the Extra Cost?* (New York: Assoc. of National Advertisers, 1966).

[20] J. V. McConnell, *Persuasion and Behavioral Change*, mimeograph (Ann Arbor, Mich.: University of Michigan, 1959).

[21] A. D. Biderman and H. Zimmer (eds.), *The Manipulation of Human Behavior* (New York: Wiley, 1961).

[22] McConnell, *op. cit.*,[20] p. 73.

[23] As presented here, retention precedes attitude/behavior modification. Although this is intuitively plausible, there is some evidence that retention follows rather than precedes this response. For a thorough discussion, see A. G. Greenwald, "Cognitive Learning: Cognitive Response to Persuasion and Attitude Change," in A. G. Greenwald, T. C. Brock, and T. M. Ostrom (eds.), *Psychological Foundations of Attitudes* (New York: Academic Press, 1968); C. A. Insko, *Theories of Attitude Change* (New York: Appleton, 1967); McGuire, *op. cit.*[7]

that this effect takes place through a change in attitude which, in turn, changes intention. The change in intention, all things being equal, will be reflected in behavior. Thus, attitude change is a valid goal for persuasion.

The findings of a number of recent experiments document the fact that the recipient of a communication message is actively involved in a process of acceptance or rejection of its content.[24] This appears to take the form of subvocal responses or thoughts referred to variously as rehearsal[25] or counterargumentation.[26] Thus, the message is accepted if the recipient rehearses cognitions or thoughts which are consistent with its theme and conclusions. Similarly, the communication is rejected if the recipient counterargues by rehearsing cognitions opposing the advocated position.

The most convincing evidence for this cognitive response analysis of attitude change comes from two main areas of investigation. In the first category individuals are presented with a message advocating a particular position, and recipients are asked to record their thoughts concerning the issue, judge the favorability of each thought, and classify each thought (for example, their own idea about a communication-generated thought). In a series of studies it was found that the extent of rehearsal of ideas advocated by the message and consequent attitude change were higher when the recipient's initial position was consistent with that contained in the message.[27]

In a second group of experimental studies it has been found that rejection of a persuasive communication occurs as recipients generate counterarguments or discounting responses.[28] The usual approach is to pre-expose subjects to a set of arguments useful in defending against a subsequent persuasive communication. This preexposure appears to prove useful in inoculating the individual against the message and helping him to counterargue effectively.

There is a vast literature on appeals and message variations which have proved most effective in changing attitudes. Further discussion, however, is reserved for the following two chapters.

MASS COMMUNICATION RESEARCH

One of the greatest difficulties in use of mass communication, of course, is that the message will be screened out by recipients. Since there is no way in which the message can be modified and retransmitted at that point, great care

---

[24] Greenwald, *op. cit.*[23]

[25] Greenwald, *op. cit.*[23]

[26] T. C. Brock, "Communication Discrepancy and Intent to Persuade as Determinants of Counterargument Production," *J. Experimental Social Psychology*, vol. 3, pp. 296–309 (1967).

[27] Greenwald, *op. cit.*[23]

[28] McGuire, *op. cit.*;[7] also see W. J. McGuire, "Inducing Resistance to Persuasion: Some Contemporary Approaches," in L. Berkowitz (ed.), *Advances in Experimental Social Psychology*, vol. 1 (New York: Academic Press, 1964), pp. 191–229.

must be devoted to message design. The probability of communication failure, in turn, can be reduced only through use of research undertaken before the final message is sent. This frequently is referred to as "pretesting."[29] Space will not permit discussion of all the techniques which might be used for this purpose,[30] but several of the most promising approaches are reviewed, especially those which do not rely on verbal responses.

Measurement of Attention Attraction

It generally is impossible to measure exposure on a pretest basis since that requires placement of the message in media and on-the-spot monitoring of the recipient's behavior. Therefore, the first stage of the process to be evaluated usually is attraction of attention.

The most common procedure used for this purpose is exposure of a sample of prospects to one or more messages under conditions ranging from presentation of three or four test advertisements in some type of booklet to full-scale exposure to an actual television or radio show or print publication. Respondents then are questioned sometime after exposure, and they are asked to indicate what messages they recall or recognize (upon reexposure to the same messages).

It is obvious that this approach measures *retention* rather than attention. It is to be expected that many more people attend to the message, because recall scores reflect the effects of selective information processing. Therefore, it is very difficult to assess the attention-attracting potential of one method versus another using this procedure. For that reason considerable interest has been shown in recent years in laboratory measures which focus on attention without use of verbal response.[31] Among those attracting the most interest are (1) galvanic skin response (GSR) and pupil dilation response (PDR), (2) the eye movement camera, (3) the tachistoscope, and (4) binocular rivalry.

GSR and PDR Galvanic skin response (GSR) and pupil dilation response (PDR) are discussed together, because recent research indicates that these measures reflect different aspects of attention attraction.[32] GSR measures two phenomena: (1) a decline in the electrical resistance of the skin to a passage of current and (2) a change in the potential difference between two areas of body surface.[33] When it elevates upon exposure to a stimulus, it is now felt to be an

---

[29]   Engel, *et al.*, *op. cit.*,[8] chap. 17.

[30]   For a review of the advantages and limitations of available methods, see Engel, *et al.*, *op. cit.*,[8] chap. 17.

[31]   J. S. Hensel and D. T. Kollat, "Present and Projected Uses of Laboratory Equipment for Marketing and Advertising Research," paper presented at the American Marketing Association (Sept. 1970).

[32]   J. S. Hensel, "Physiological Measures of Advertising Effectiveness: A Theoretical and Empirical Investigation," unpublished doctoral dissertation (Columbus, Ohio: Ohio State University, 1970).

[33]   R. D. Blackwell, J. S. Hensel, M. B. Phillips, and B. Sternthal, *Laboratory Equipment for Marketing Research* (Dubuque, Iowa: Kendall Hunt Publ. Co., 1970), p. 42.

accurate measure of *arousal*.[34] PDR, on the other hand, measures minute differences in pupil size as it dilates and contracts. Recent studies document that it is a sensitive measure of the amount of information or load processed within the central control unit from the incoming stimulus.[35] At one time it was felt that PDR measured affective or emotional response to a stimulus,[36] and several studies were published which purported to document that relationship in response to marketing stimuli.[37] The weight of later evidence, however, makes the load processing interpretation of PDR far more plausible.

A series of studies has been undertaken at the Ohio State University using both GSR and PDR with a variety of audio and print stimuli.[38] The most consistent finding is that when GSR and PDR are both high, the stimulus in question generates good short-term and long-term retention. In other words, the high score on attention attraction is reflected by a correspondingly high score on retention, thus indicating that the stimulus has not been screened out in information processing. In addition, there is some tentative evidence that the GSR score also correlates with attitude change, but this relationship needs further investigation under a variety of circumstances.[39]

If further replication verifies the relationships reported here, there are some significant practical implications. Different messages can be analyzed prior to the investment of funds in production to see which offers the greatest probability of attracting and holding attention. The great advantage is that reliance need not be placed on verbal recall which can be highly inaccurate. As these methods are further refined, they should see increasingly widespread use.

The Eye Movement Camera   For many years it has been possible to track eye movements through advertising copy using a camera especially designed for this purpose. This shows which parts of the message capture and hold attention and whether or not various elements are perceived in the intended order. It never has achieved especially wide use, because viewing must be done under highly unnatural conditions using awkward equipment. Nevertheless, it is a useful diagnostic tool.

The Tachistoscope   The tachistoscope is basically a slide projector with attachments which permit the presentation of stimuli under varying conditions

---

[34]   The literature on this subject is thoroughly reviewed in Hensel, *op. cit.*[32]

[35]   For an extensive literature review see R. D. Blackwell, J. S. Hensel, and B. Sternthal, "Pupil Dilation: What Does it Measure?" *J. Advertising Research*, vol. 10, pp. 15–18 (1970).

[36]   E. H. Hess and J. M. Polt, "Pupil Size as Related to Interest Value of Visual Stimuli," *Science*, vol. 132, pp. 349–350 (1960).

[37]   See, for example, H. E. Krugman, "Some Applications of Pupil Measurement," *J. Marketing Research*, vol. 1, pp. 15–18 (1964).

[38]   Most of these are reviewed in Hensel. Also see R. D. Blackwell and B. Sternthal, "Physiological Measurement of Communication Variables: Empirical Results," paper presented at the American Marketing Association, (Sept. 1970).

[39]   Two unpublished studies at the Ohio State University under the direction of J. F. Engel.

of speed and illumination. It can be used to assess the rate at which a message conveys information.[40] Response speed is recorded for various elements of the message (illustration, product, or brand name), and it has been found that high readership scores usually correlate with the speed of recognition of the elements under analysis. The writer or designer thus has a useful basis to evaluate that the message is being processed as intended.

Binocular Rivalry The binocular rivalry technique is used to measure which of two competing stimuli first attracts attention.[41] The stimuli are viewed through a stereoscopic device with an eye piece, and a different stimulus is projected to each eye. The basic underlying theory is that the stimulus exerting the greatest potential for attention attraction will dominate, and this has been verified experimentally.[42]

Comprehension and Recall

The general approach to measurement of recall was discussed at the beginning of the preceding section. The preferred method is to place the test messages within, for example, a magazine or television program and then to ask the respondent to be exposed under completely natural conditions. This, of course, closely approximates the circumstances which are present under actual field exposure. Recognition or recall then is assessed at some period after exposure, usually within 24 hours.

The procedure employed to pretest advertisements for the W. T. Grant Company illustrates this approach.[43] A test message was placed along with others in a fictitious magazine entitled *Today*. This magazine was created by Grey Advertising, Inc., to duplicate the format of a new general-interest magazine. Interviews place the magazine in homes, and women are asked to read it as they would any other magazine. Telephone interviews on the following day measure comprehension and recall as follows:

(1) *Related recall*—the percentage of actual readers who can give: (a) aided or unaided identification of the brand and (b) some playback on the message (either some specific detail or a general correct description.)

(2) *Comprehension and impact*—ability to state correctly the actual intended content of the copy.

---

[40] C. Leavitt, "Intrigue in Advertising—The Motivational Effects of Visual Organization," in *Proc. 7th Annual Conf.* (New York: Advertising Research Foundation, 1961), pp. 19–24.

[41] J. M. Caffyn, "Psychological Laboratory Techniques in Copy Research," *J. Advertising Research*, vol. 4, p. 48 (1964).

[42] Caffyn, *op. cit.*[41]

[43] "W. T. Grant Company (B): Attitude Change through Advertising," in R. D. Blackwell, J. F. Engel, and D. T. Kollat, *Cases in Consumer Behavior* (New York: Holt, Rinehart and Winston, 1969), pp. 88–94.

In this particular instance the test message scored very high on both criteria, and this was interpreted as offering a high probability of successful communication once the message was run in actual consumer magazines.

Measures of Response

Obviously it will be extremely difficult to provide a definitive measure of attitude or behavior change in the pretesting phase. This can be done only through actually running the message in one or more test markets and later evaluating the results. The investment of both costs and time required usually prove to be prohibitive. Therefore, it is necessary to employ substitute measures, none of which can provide the accuracy of the field test.

Attitude Change Attitude change usually is assessed in the same manner as comprehension and recall. In the W. T. Grant example discussed above, respondents were asked to rate W. T. Grant along with competitors using a number of evaluative criteria. Attitude scores before exposure were collected from a matched group who were not exposed to the *Today* magazine, and it was assumed that the exposed respondents would not differ significantly in initial positions. The ratings of the two groups then were compared to provide a measure of attitude shift. The Grey agency and others utilize this approach or a variation on the assumption that high retention and comprehension are not a sufficient indication of communication success.[44] It is necessary, they contend, to measure the effect on attitude, because high retention does not necessarily imply that there will be an eventual behavior change. Others disagree with this position and cease measurement at the recall stage.

It also may be possible to assess attitude change in a pretest through evaluating the effects on counterargumentation. It will be recalled that attitude change appears to take place as the recipient subvocally responds to the message. If these thoughts or cognitions are positive, attitude will change, and vice versa. Attitudes also could be changed, however, through somehow overcoming or suppressing counterarguments. McCullough designed a measure of net counterargumentation (positive thoughts minus negative thoughts) and found that the higher the net counterargumentation score, the greater the attitude change in response to a series of test advertisements.[45]

Behavioral Change Short of a full-scale field test, change in behavior can be evaluated only through some type of forced choice situation. This is the basic approach of the Schwerin Corporation. Consumers are given an initial choice of products to be given away through a lottery, exposed to advertisements

---

[44] "Ad Recall? P&G and GF Couldn't Care Less," *Marketing/Communications,* pp. 22–26 (Aug. 1971).

[45] J. L. McCullough, "The Use of a Measure of Net Counterargumentation in Differentiating the Impact of Persuasive Communications," unpublished doctoral dissertation (Columbus, Ohio: Ohio State University, 1971).

inserted in television shows viewed in a theater situation, and asked to rate products again after the show has ended.[46] There is some indication that this measurement of choice is related to short-term changes in market share,[47] but others are skeptical that the method is valid for this purpose.[48]

Concluding Comments

At the present time there is no way to provide a definitive indication that a message will be successful in generating attention, comprehension, recall, and response. Those measures relying on verbal response always will have an element of inaccuracy simply due to the fact that people often cannot or will not provide the requested information. The laboratory methodology, on the other hand, circumvents this problem, but some of the methods are only in the developmental stage. Undoubtedly they will grow in importance as methodological improvements become available. For now all that can be concluded is that the risks of sending a noneffective message can be substantially reduced, but not eliminated, through use of presently available methods. There is no excuse for failure to pretest every message.

SUMMARY

This chapter has reviewed the essentials of the process of communication, with special emphasis on mass communication. The information processing component of the model of consumer behavior used throughout the book was expanded somewhat to comprehend the following stages: (1) exposure, (2) reception (attention, comprehension, and retention), and (3) attitude/behavior modification. Each of these stages then was elaborated from two points of view: (1) the implications for design of the persuasive message and (2) pretesting consumer response. Essential background thus was provided for the analysis of attitude change in the next two chapters.

REVIEW AND DISCUSSION QUESTIONS

1. What requirements must be met if Mr. *A* is to communicate with Mr. *B*? Do these requirements change under mass communication?

2. What is meant by noise? What types of noise can enter when a salesman talks with a customer? When a commercial for beer is aired during a professional football telecast? What, if anything, can be done to reduce noise in these types of situations?

---

[46] P. J. Kelly, "The Schwerin Model: How You Can Use It to Build Your Share of Market," *Printers' Ink,* p. 31 (May 8, 1964).

[47] R. D. Buzzell, "Predicting Short-Term Changes in Market Share as a Function of Advertising Strategy," *J. Marketing Research,* vol. 1, p. 31 (1964).

[48] Engel, *et al., op. cit.,*[8] pp. 375–376.

3. What types of feedback are received by the salesman selling a vacuum cleaner to a housewife? How does feedback change when this same company uses television commercials?

4. A reader's attention is attracted by a two-page spread in *Time* advertising a new automobile. The advertisement is in four colors and features three pretty girls. What does it mean to say that attention is attracted? How does this happen?

5. The creative director of a leading New York advertising agency claims that creativity cannot be measured. He refuses to make any use of pretests of his copy and layouts and claims that his creative intuition is his best guide. If you were the director of research, what would your answer be?

6. Many critics contend that too much advertising today is "gimmicky" and "cute." The argument is that creative people are carried away by flashy attention-attracting devices and are forgetting that good advertising must sell. How would you analyze this criticism?

7. What is meant by rehearsal and counterargumentation?

8. Studies often show that recall is the most widely used measure of communication effectiveness on a pretest basis. Many refuse to measure other stages of the communication process, such as attitude change. Why does this occur? What arguments could you present in behalf of attitude and/or behavior measurement?

9. Do you agree that laboratory measures will see more use in the future? Why or why not? What is their unique advantage? Disadvantage?

CHAPTER **14**

ATTITUDE CHANGE*

It was established in preceding chapters that human beings resist a challenge to their attitudes, especially if the attitude is strongly held. Yet, attitudes are not impermeable, and much persuasive communication is undertaken to change preferences in the hope that behavior will exhibit a similar change. It is the purpose of this chapter to discuss some major ways in which mass communication can be used for this purpose, with particular emphasis on (1) discrepancy between attitude positions of members of the target audience and the position advocated by the message, (2) variations in message content, and (3) variations in message structure (that is, order of appeals and repetition). The literature on this subject is enormous; McGuire, for example, cited over 800 studies in a review of evidence through 1967.[1] Therefore, the discussion here, by necessity, is confined to those areas of inquiry which appear to have the greatest practical significance.

---

* The authors acknowledge the help of Dr. Brian Sternthal of Northwestern University in reviewing the literature and preparing this chapter.

[1] W. J. McGuire, "The Nature of Attitudes and Attitude Change," in G. Lindsey and E. Aronson (eds.), *Handbook of Social Psychology* (Reading, Mass.: Addison-Wesley, 1968), pp. 136–314.

DISCREPANCY BETWEEN MESSAGE AND RECIPIENTS' ATTITUDES

Let it be assumed that a market research survey has been completed which documents attitudes of midwestern housewives toward two brands of hair spray, brand *A* and brand *B*. Brand *A* sponsored the survey and commands 10 percent of the market. Management feels that a real opportunity exists to make inroads into the market of brand *B*.

What action should be taken if the results indicate that most users of brand *B*, which has 18 percent of the market, are loyal to their brand but will consider other alternatives? Should the advertising aimed at these housewives clearly assert the superiority of brand *A*, or should a more moderate position be taken? In other words, how far can the message deviate from an individual's own position and still induce attitude change? This question has been the focus of a considerable body of recent research, and many of the results are in direct conflict.

Basic Evidence on Effects of Message Discrepancy

A number of early investigations reported that attitude change is a monotonically increasing function of discrepancy of the message.[2] In other words, the more the message deviates from the recipient's own position, the greater the likelihood that he will change in the desired direction.

More recent studies, however, have found contradictory results.[3] While these findings vary, all agree that a point is reached after which increasing discrepancy will only serve to decrease attitude change. If this is true, then careful research must be undertaken to determine a discrepancy limit and to guarantee that the message stays within this boundary.

The Effect of Source Credibility The contradictory findings, in part, may be explained by variations in source credibility. In general it may be concluded that there is a positive linear relationship between message discrepancy and attitude change when the message is attributable to a highly credible source.[4]

---

[2] See, for example, S. Goldberg, "Three Situational Determinants of Conformity to Social Norms," *J. Abnormal and Social Psychology*, vol. 49, pp. 325–329 (1964); H. Helson, R. Blake, and J. Mouton, "An Experimental Investigation of the 'Big Lie' in Shifting Attitudes," *J. Social Psychology*, vol. 48, pp. 51–60 (1958); R. Tuddenham, "The Influence of a Distorted Group Norm Upon Influential Judgement," *J. Psychology*, vol. 46, pp. 227–241 (1956); P. Zimbardo, "Involvement and Communication Discrepancy as Determinants of Opinion Conformity," *J. Abnormal and Social Psychology*, vol. 60, pp. 86–94 (1960).

[3] See, for example, C. Insko, F. Murashima, and M. Saiyadain, "Communicator Discrepancy, Stimulus Ambiguity, and Influence," *J. Personality*, vol. 34, pp. 52–66 (1966); H. Johnson, "Some Effects of Discrepancy Level on Responses to Negative Information about One's Self," *Sociometry*, vol. 29, pp. 52–66 (1966); J. Whittaker, "Opinion Change as a Function of Communication–Attitude Discrepancy," *Psychological Reports*, vol. 13, pp. 763–772 (1963).

[4] This literature is thoroughly reviewed in Brian Sternthal, "Persuasion and the Mass Communication Process," unpublished doctoral dissertation (Columbus, Ohio: Ohio State University, 1972), chap. 4.

In other words, people seem to place greater confidence in a trustworthy source and hence are more receptive to what is said, even when there is a substantial deviation from their own position. Similarly, there is a substantially reduced tendency to accept a discrepant message when the source is of moderate or low credibility.[5]

The moderating effect of source credibility has distinct managerial significance. It is quite difficult to make an advertisement credible when it is obvious that the whole intent of the message is to persuade. The recipient generally recognizes that the source is anything but impartial and unbiased. Therefore, a message which deviates substantially from the recipient's own position is likely to be screened out as he processes the stimulus. Given this relationship it becomes necessary to predict the boundary of acceptable discrepancy, but attempts to predict this point have repeatedly failed to date.[6]

Admittedly much in this area is pure speculation not based on research undertaken under natural field conditions using commercial messages as the variable. Nevertheless, the importance of impartiality is verified. Undoubtedly the image of certain commercial spokesmen is largely attributable to this type of reputation. Arthur Godfrey, for example, is often mentioned as a credible source who would not recommend a product that does not perform as claimed. Spokesmen who capitalize upon credibility, however, are infrequent in the mass media.

It is interesting to speculate regarding the extent to which salesmen are perceived as being expert and trustworthy—the essential requirements of credibility. It would seem that most consumers feel that the salesman has a high intent to persuade and thus would show a strong reaction against what he has to say. Nevertheless, a properly trained salesman can serve as a valuable source of information, and there is no reason why credibility cannot be improved in personal selling situations. Unfortunately this point is often overlooked, especially by retailers, and salesmen are not properly trained to become a credible source.[7]

The Effect of Ego Involvement   Many of the most widely quoted studies on the effects of discrepancy have tested the theory of cognitive dissonance. The hypothesis is that a clash between an individual's own point of view and some input of voluntarily perceived information gives rise to an uncomfortable state of dissonance which can be reduced either by changing one's own position or by downgrading the credibility of the source. Presumably it is easier to change attitude than to downgrade credibility, with the result that the best strategy is to induce high dissonance by a wide discrepancy. If this proposition is true, then advertisement for brand *A* should deviate substantially from the recipient's attitudes toward this brand. It might, for example, directly assert brand *A*'s

---

[5]   Sternthal, *op. cit.*[4]

[6]   See, for example, H. Johnson and I. Steiner, "The Effects of Source on Responses to Negative Information about One's Self," *J. Social Psychology*, vol. 74, pp. 215–224 (1968).

[7]   For an interesting example of the effects of failure to capitalize upon this point, see "Columbia Furniture Company: Analysis of Retail Salesmanship," in R. D. Blackwell, J. F. Engel, and D. T. Kollat, *Cases in Consumer Behavior* (New York: Holt, Rinehart and Winston, 1969), pp. 234–241.

superiority relative to brand *B*. There are a number of studies which suggest that this strategy can be effective.[8]

Other researchers sharply challenge the findings based on the theory of cognitive dissonance. Among the leaders of this school of thought are Sherif and his colleagues who propose that sharper measurement instruments are required.[9] In brief, extremity of position on the affective dimension of an attitude (that is, agree strongly or disagree strongly) is not necessarily an indication of a person's commitment to his position. This is more adequately measured by the number of divergent positions he will accept (latitude of acceptance) versus those he rejects (latitude of rejection) or those toward which he is neutral (latitude of non-commitment). Sherif is of the opinion that dissonance researchers have utilized topics and issues where commitment is likely to be low (a broad latitude of acceptance), with the result that there can be a wide discrepancy between the recipient's own position and that of the communication without engaging selective exposure, distortion, and retention. If the message content falls into the latitude of rejection, on the other hand, *attitude change will not occur and selective perception will be engaged. Therefore, an increase in discrepancy produces attitude change only as long as the latitude of acceptance is not exceeded.*

When the position advocated in the communication is within the latitude of acceptance, there is a strong likelihood of an *assimilation effect* (the communication will appear to be nearer to the subject's own position than it actually is). This is, of course, a highly favorable result and one that most likely will induce the individual to move his own position to bring the two into consonance. On the other hand, a *contrast effect* will occur if the point of view of the communication falls into the latitude of rejection (the communication will be perceived as farther away from the person's own stand than it is in reality). There is a fair amount of research support for these conclusions.[10]

This general relationship appears to be valid regardless of commitment to the person's own position. Commitment, however, is the determinant of the level of discrepancy necessary to produce maximum attitude change. Low commitment or involvement implies a wide latitude of acceptance; thus it is difficult

---

[8] A. R. Cohen, H. I. Terry, and C. B. Jones, "Attitudinal Effects of Choice in Exposure to Counter-Propaganda," *J. Abnormal and Social Psychology*, vol. 58, pp. 388–391 (1959); A. R. Cohen, "Communication Discrepancy and Attitude Change: A Dissonance Theory Approach," *J. Personality*, vol. 27, pp. 386–396 (1959); C. I. Hovland and H. A. Pritzker, "Extent of Opinion Change as a Function of Amount of Change Advocated," *J. Social Psychology*, vol. 54, pp. 257–261 (1957); Whittaker, *op. cit.*[3]

[9] Carolyn W. Sherif, M. Sherif, and R. Nebergall, *Attitude and Attitude Change* (Philadelphia: Saunders, 1965).

[10] J. L. Freedman, "Involvement, Discrepancy and Change," *J. Abnormal and Social Psychology*, vol. 69, pp. 290–295 (1964); M. Sherif and C. I. Hovland, *Social Judgment: Assimilation and Contrast Effects in Communication and Attitude Change* (New Haven, Conn.: Yale University Press, 1961); C. I. Hovland, O. J. Harvey and M. Sherif, "Assimilation and Contrast Effects in Reaction to Communication and Attitude Change," *J. Abnormal and Social Psychology*, vol. 55, pp. 244–252 (1957); L. N. Diab, "Some Limitations of Existing Scales in the Measurement of Social Attitudes," *Psychological Reports*, vol. 17, pp. 427–430 (1965); J. Whittaker, "Attitude Change and Communication–Attitude Discrepancy," *J. Social Psychology*, vol. 65, pp. 141–147 (1965).

to fall into the latitude of rejection with a communication message. With strong commitment, however, even information that is only moderately discrepant may fall outside the latitude of acceptance. As Freedman has concluded:

> Since the point at which the latitude of rejection is reached is the point of maximum change, and since this point should be more moderate for high- than for low-involvement conditions, maximum change should occur at a more moderate level of discrepancy for high than for low involvement.[11]

If this approach is valid, then additional research is needed relative to housewives' preferences for hair spray before an advertising campaign can be planned. Notice that this section was introduced under the assumption that attitudes had been measured, but no mention was made of the various latitudes discussed here. In other words, commitment really was not measured at all, and dissonance research suffers from the key weakness that the all-important condition of high commitment generally is *assumed* rather than *measured*.[12] Therefore, Sherif's criticisms of the dissonance approach are convincing.

If commitment had been determined, however, the implications for marketing strategy become more apparent. Let it be assumed, first, that most of the women studied are strongly committed to brand *B* and usually consider no other brand to be equally acceptable. In this situation, their latitudes of acceptance are narrow and their latitudes of rejection quite large. A divergent communication most likely would fall into the latitude of rejection and therefore be screened out. The prospect of inducing these consumers to switch to brand *A* is small indeed. It is more probable that a committed consumer will notice only the advertisements for her own brand and thus have her preference further reinforced.

Other consumers may prefer brand *B* also but, in addition, consider brand *A* and others as acceptable substitutes. The commitment to brand *B* thus is much less, even though the extent of indicated preference may be equivalent to the strongly committed counterparts. In this situation, advertisements should deviate as far as possible from subjects' own position, thereby generating dissonance while, at the same time, staying within the latitude of acceptance.

This proposition has been investigated as part of the Ohio State University studies in consumer decision making.[13] Latitudes of acceptance and rejection were measured for large homogeneous groups relative to a particular brand of beer. Communications were then administered that were designed to fall at varying distances from the subjects' own positions. Maximum attitude change tended

---

[11] Freedman, *op. cit.*,[10] p. 291.

[12] J. F. Engel and M. L. Light, "The Role of Psychological Commitment in Consumer Behavior: An Evaluation of the Theory of Cognitive Dissonance," in Frank M. Bass, Charles W. King, and Edgar A. Pessimer (eds.), *Application of the Sciences in Marketing Management* (New York: Wiley, 1968), pp. 39–68.

[13] J. Shable, "The Effects of Message Discrepancy on Attitude Change," unpublished M.A. thesis (Columbus, Ohio: Ohio State University, 1968).

to be produced, as predicted, by the communication falling at the outside boundary of the latitude of acceptance.

Implications It now seems apparent that the effects of message discrepancy on attitude change are moderated by source credibility and ego involvement. Two recent studies which manipulated both of these moderating variables confirmed this conclusion.[14] In each instance highly involved subjects changed their attitude significantly less upon exposure to a discrepant message than did those who were less involved, and there was a greater tendency for this group to disparage the communication source.

Given that marketing communications usually are not perceived as highly credible, the message should deviate from the attitude position of members of the target audience only to a small extent. Attitude change is best achieved by successive exposures, each of which encompasses only small discrepancy. This generalization is especially critical when recipients' attitudes are based on ego involvement. Techniques for measuring involvement were discussed in Chapter 10.

VARIATIONS IN MESSAGE CONTENT

To what extent do variations in message content affect attitude change? It seems obvious that some approaches should be more effective than others, and the literature to be reviewed here largely supports this conclusion. The relevance of the findings for marketing, however, is less than it might seem at first for reasons discussed later.

It is necessary to point out that the great majority of the findings reported in this section come from laboratory studies as opposed to studies undertaken in natural field conditions. Generally two or more matched groups of people are asked a series of questions to determine an attitude toward a topic. Then a communication is administered to one of the groups, and the other serves as a control. Extent of change is assessed usually by change in the exposed group versus the control group.

Surprisingly, the literature encompasses only several broad categories of studies: (1) fear appeals, (2) drawing a conclusion, (3) distraction, and (4) nonovert appeals. The findings are reviewed under each of these headings, and implications then are assessed.

Fear Appeals

A study undertaken in 1953 by Janis and Feshbach indicated that a communication stressing the unfavorable consequences of not taking the suggested course of behavior (that is, fear) can have an adverse effect on attitude

---

[14] H. Johnson and J. Scileppi, "Effects of Ego-Involvment Conditions on Attitude Change to High and Low Credibility Communicators," *J. Personality and Social Psychology,* vol. 13, pp. 31–36 (1969); K. Sereno, "Ego-Involvement, High Source Credibility and Response to a Belief-Discrepant Communication, "*Speech Monographs,* vol. 35, pp. 476–481 (1968).

change if this fear appeal is too intense.[15] This negative relationship between fear arousal and persuasion was confirmed in several subsequent investigations undertaken between 1953 and 1962,[16] with the result that fear appeals are only used in such isolated instances as promotion of medical products and insurance companies.[17] Almost 100 studies have been undertaken since 1953, however, and the great majority contradict the early findings and show a positive relationship between fear and persuasion.[18] In fact, of 16 relevant experiments undertaken between 1965 and 1971, all reported a positive relationship.[19] Not surprisingly, Ray and Wilkie concluded that marketers have neglected a promising area of inquiry.[20]

Caution must be exercised in generalizing the positive fear–persuasion relationship, however, for several reasons. First, the range of topics investigated is quite narrow, encompassing only such issues as health and politics. Furthermore, most investigations employed only two levels of fear (referred to variously as "minimal," "mild," "weak," and so on), and there is no confirmation that a full range of fear arousal was consistently investigated. Therefore, it is difficult to undertake a complete comparison of results. Unfortunately, only five studies have induced more than two fear levels, and results are inconclusive.[21]

It is possible as Ray and Wilkie hypothesize that those studies reporting a positive fear–persuasion relationship induced fear levels lower than those utilized in experiments reporting a negative relationship.[22] If this is true, then the actual relationship is nonmonotonic—a positive effect is generated until a certain point is reached, at which time the effect becomes negative. Unfortunately this can only be a hypothesis at this time because of the complete absence of studies systematically varying a wide range of fear inductions.

The Effect of Source Credibility What effect does source credibility have on the fear-persuasion relationship. Only a few studies have specifically investigated the moderating effect of source, but the results have marketing significance. Hewgill and Miller hypothesized that a strong fear-arousing com-

---

[15] I. L. Janis and S. Feshbach, "Effects of Fear-Arousing Communication," *J. Abnormal and Social Psychology*, vol. 48, pp. 78–92 (1953).

[16] See, for example, I. L. Janis and R. Terwilliger, "An Experimental Study of Psychological Resistance to Fear Arousing Communications," *J. Abnormal and Social Psychology*, vol. 65, pp. 403–410 (1962).

[17] J. Stuteville, "Psychic Defenses Against High Fear Appeals: A Key Marketing Variable," *J. Marketing*, vol. 34, pp. 39–45 (1970).

[18] There have been a number of literature reviews. See K. Higbee, "Fifteen Years of Fear Arousal: Research on Threat Appeals: 1953–1968," *Psychological Bull.*, vol. 72, pp. 426–444 (1969); I. Janis, *The Contours of Fear* (New York: Wiley, 1968); H. Leventhal, "Findings and Theory in the Study of Fear Communications," in L. Berkowitz (ed.), *Advances in Experimental Social Psychology*, vol. 5 (New York: Academic Press, 1970), pp. 119–186; W. McGuire, *op. cit.*[1]

[19] Sternthal, *op. cit.*,[4] chap. 5.

[20] M. Ray and W. Wilkie, "Fear: The Potential of an Appeal Neglected by Marketing," *J. Marketing*, vol. 34, pp. 59–62 (1970).

[21] These studies are reviewed in Sternthal, *op. cit.*,[4] chap. 5.

[22] Ray and Wilkie, *op. cit.*[20]

munication will generate high cognitive dissonance and hence attitude change only when source credibility is positive.[23] On the other hand, it was anticipated that the low-credibility sources would be derogated by the recipient while attitudes remain unchanged. The hypothesis was confirmed. Similarly, Powell and Miller reported that attitude change occurred as credibility and fear increased.[24] Also, a strong fear appeal arouses greater source disparagement than a mild version when both are presented by a low-credibility source.[25]

Implications　Contrary to earlier findings it does appear that a high fear appeal can be effective in stimulating a change in attitude. It must not be overlooked, however, that this relationship appears to hold *only* when a source is highly credible. The lower perceived credibility of marketing communication was discussed earlier, with the result that one must be hesitant in recommending that greater use be made of fear appeals in marketing. Contrary to the speculation conclusion of Ray and Wilkie,[26] a high-fear advertisement probably will be screened out. Obviously the fear–persuasion relationship must be further tested with marketing stimuli under field conditions, because current evidence is inconclusive.

Drawing a Conclusion

In recent years growing use has been made of *cool commercials.*[27] Cool messages are unstructured; they tell the viewer a fragment of the story or invoke impressions so that the viewer must fill in from his own imagination. The hot commercial, on the other hand, is more structured and tells a complete story logically and sequentially, with a definite conclusion stated.

From the results of a number of communication studies, the unstructured approach of the cool commercial would appear to be ineffective. This is because experimental research has determined repeatedly that explicit conclusion drawing is more persuasive than allowing the audience to draw its own conclusions.[28]

---

[23]　M. Hewgill and G. Miller, "Source Credibility and Response to Fear-Arousing Communications," *Speech Monographs*, vol. 32, pp. 95–101 (1965).

[24]　F. Powell and G. Miller, "Social Approval and Disapproval Cues in Anxiety Arousing Communications," *Speech Monographs*, vol. 34, pp. 152–159 (1967).

[25]　G. Miller and M. Hewgill, "Some Recent Research on Fear-Arousing Message Appeals," *Speech Monographs,* vol. 33, pp. 377–391 (1966).

[26]　Ray and Wilkie, *op. cit.*[20]

[27]　K. Roman and J. Maas, unpublished manuscript (Ogilvy & Mather), chap. 4, quoting Bill Taylor's analysis of hot versus cool commercials.

[28]　E. Cooper and H. Dinerman, "Analysis of the Film 'Don't Be a Sucker': a Study of Communication," *Public Opinion Quart.*, vol. 15, pp. 243–264 (1951); B. Fine, "Conclusion-Drawing, Communicator Credibility and Anxiety as Factors in Opinion Change," *J. Abnormal and Social Psychology*, vol. 54, pp. 369–374 (1957); H. Hadley, "The Non-Directive Approach in Advertising Appeals," *J. Applied Psychology*, vol. 37, pp. 496–498 (1963); C. Hovland and W. Mandell, "An Experimental Comparison of Conclusion-Drawing by the Communicator and by the Audience," *J. Abnormal and Social Psychology*, vol. 47, pp. 581–588 (1952); N. Maier and R. Maier, "An Experimental Test of the Effects of 'Developmental' versus 'Free' Discussion on the Quality of Group Decisions," *J. Applied Psychology*, vol. 41, pp. 320–323 (1957).

Presumably the audience is not sufficiently motivated or intelligent to draw conclusions on its own.

There is contradictory evidence, however, that the message which states a conclusion only implicitly *over time* approaches the structured message in persuasive impact.[29] When the audience is highly intelligent or motivated, this approach may be particularly effective. As Brehm has pointed out, many people seem to react negatively when a conclusion is stated and feel that an attempt is being made to influence and thereby limit their freedom of choice. When this is the reaction a boomerang effect can occur in the form of solidification of initial opinion.[30]

Given that the net persuasive effect of explicit versus implicit conclusion drawing does not appear to differ, the choice between the two approaches must be resolved on the basis of other considerations.[31] The cool commercial, for example, appears to be used most appropriately to build a long-range image. Also it is effective when a product has no apparent advantage; when competitors are running hot commercials; and when the basic product appeal is primarily emotional rather than logical (as is the case with cosmetics, for example).

Distraction

It was pointed out in Chapter 13 that individuals appear to counterargue with a message that contradicts their dispositions toward a topic, with the result that attitude change is impeded. Therefore, any strategy which proves to be effective in interfering with and/or reducing counterargumentation is worthy of consideration.

There is some evidence that counterargumentation can be reduced if distraction of some type is introduced during exposure to the message.[32] This can be done through use of a variety of competing stimuli such as background music or noise.[33] Unfortunately, experiments conducted under varying conditions of

---

[29] A. Cohen, *Attitude Change and Social Influence* (New York: Basic Books, 1964), p. 10; W. McGuire, "A Syllogistic Analysis of Cognitive Relationships," in C. Hovland and M. Rosenberg, (eds.), *Attitude Organization and Change* (New Haven, Conn.: Yale University Press, 1960); E. Stotland, D. Katz, and M. Patchen, "The Reduction of Prejudice Through the Arousal of Self-Insight," *J. Personality,* vol. 27, pp. 507–553 (1959).

[30] J. W. Brehm, *A Theory of Psychological Reactance* (New York: Academic Press, 1966), chap. 6.

[31] J. F. Engel, H. G. Wales, and M. R. Warshaw, *Promotional Strategy,* rev. ed. (Homewood, Ill.: Irwin, 1971), p. 353.

[32] J. Allyn and L. Festinger, "The Effectiveness of Unanticipated Persuasive Communications," *J. Abnormal and Social Psychology,* vol. 62, pp. 35–40 (1961); L. Festinger and N. Maccoby, "On Resistance to Persuasive Communications," *J. Abnormal and Social Psychology,* vol. 68, pp. 359–366 (1964); J. L. Freedman and D. O. Sears, "Warning, Distraction, and Resistance to Influence," *J. Personality and Social Psychology,* vol. 1, pp. 262–266 (1965).

[33] In an unpublished study undertaken as part of the research program in consumer decision making at the Ohio State University in 1966 it was found that distraction in the form of varied background music enhanced attitude change.

distraction using advertising stimuli failed to show increased attitude change.[34] In fact, there is some evidence that distraction can reduce attention and comprehension and thereby overpower any positive effect on attitude.

From the studies to date distraction would appear to be a possible strategy under circumstances in which the recipient is committed to his attitude and hence resists change.[35] Counterarguing apparently can be reduced through this means, although this has not been conclusively demonstrated. Brand attitudes, however, seldom attain this degree of commitment; hence counterargumentation is less likely to occur. Therefore, distraction may only serve to inhibit attention and comprehension. The deliberate manipulation of distraction in a marketing context thus appears to be unwarranted unless attitudes to be changed are based on ego involvement (commitment).

Nonovert Appeals

Walster and Festinger reported success in producing attitude change under conditions where recipients felt they were "overhearing" a message.[36] Presumably it was felt that those who were speaking were making no conscious attempt to persuade. This may suggest that the "slice of life" commercial, ostensibly showing real-life situations with ordinary people who normally would not be commercial spokesmen, stands a better chance of success than a more overt attempt to persuade. This hypothesis, however, can only be tentative, because the Walster and Festinger study did not possess the degree of experimental control normally required for verified findings.

Marketing Implications

Certainly it is tempting to examine the potpourri of the above findings and have a field day in applying them to persuasive communication with consumers. Let it be said, however, that generalizations are fraught with peril. Many researchers have discovered that the applied use of such evidence sometimes produces unintended results in the form of selective attention, comprehension, and retention. This may seem surprising, and the key to limited generality lies in an understanding of the difference between *laboratory* versus *natural field studies* of attitude change.[37]

---

[34] M. Venkatesan and G. A. Haaland, "The Effect of Distraction on the Influence of Persuasive Marketing Communications," in J. Arndt (ed.), *Insights into Consumer Behavior* (Boston: Allyn and Bacon, 1968), pp. 55–66; D. M. Gardner, "The Distraction Hypothesis in Marketing," *J. Advertising Research*, vol. 10, pp. 25–30 (1970); S. W. Bither, "Effects of Distraction and Commitment on the Persuasiveness of Television Advertising," *J. Marketing Research*, pp. 1–5 (1972).

[35] Bither's results, *op. cit.*,[34] would suggest this conclusion, but his data are far from definitive.

[36] E. Walster and L. Festinger, "The Effectiveness of 'Overheard' Persuasive Communications," *J. Abnormal and Social Psychology*, vol. 65, pp. 395–402 (1962).

[37] C. I. Hovland, "Reconciling Conflicting Results Derived from Experimental and Survey Studies of Attitude Change," *Amer. Psychologist*, vol. 14, pp. 8–17 (1959).

In the typical laboratory study (that is, conducted under artificial conditions), it is not difficult to generate attitude change in response to persuasion, yet such a result is less frequently demonstrated convincingly in field studies, as was documented in earlier chapters. The fact is that the laboratory-type experiment often bears little resemblance to reality. In the first place, opportunity for selective exposure seldom is provided, in that all people must read or view the communication. That such is not true in a consumer's home has been shown before. Therefore, one of the individuals' natural defenses against introduction of imbalance in his attitudinal structure is thereby artificially removed.

Another limitation of many laboratory experiments is that the issues chosen for analysis are ones on which few people hold strong convictions. If centrality and the other conditions of attitude strength are not present, then attitude change should be expected. Attitudes toward United States participation in the International Monetary Fund are far different from attitudes toward civil defense or race relations. The latter are typical subjects for the field study, while the more innocuous topic all too frequently is used in the laboratory. The communications used in the laboratory, then, often appear to fall on largely unplowed psychological ground, and it is not surprising that attitude change can be demonstrated, especially when authoritative communications are utilized. Indeed, it would be surprising if selective perception were activiated under such conditions.

It now appears that substantial attitude change seldom is demonstrated by a persuasive message which is in contradiction to a person's attitudes under natural viewing and reading conditions, and when the person is committed to his point of view. The upshot seems to be that individuals avoid attitudinal imbalance by short-circuiting contrary information through selective attention, comprehension, and retention.

It becomes decidedly questionable that the findings on fear appeal and the many others examined earlier can be replicated in such unambiguous fashion under normal reading and viewing situations. Rather, all that should be concluded is that *a tentative indication has been provided of a persuasive approach that might work under certain circumstances to affect attitude change.* What is now lacking is evidence to show the effects of circumstances and variations in the psychological makeup of the individual. Until this is done, relatively little use can be made of the generalizations that seem to have emerged. Indeed, some seem all too prone to recommend applications before necessary research has been undertaken, and to do so is to render a decided disservice.

This conclusion is not new for many readers. While some advertising textbooks imply to the contrary, there are no definitive rules for designing advertising messages. Indeed, each situation is unique, and evidence is not yet available that documents the best approach under specified conditions. More research is needed on the interaction of appeal, states of motivation, and environmental circumstances. This, of course, requires sophisticated research, which to this time has not been forthcoming on any large scale.

MANIPULATION OF STRUCTURAL VARIABLES

The discussion now shifts to a third major consideration in communication strategy—manipulation of such structural factors as one-sided versus two-sided messages, order of presentation, and repetition.

One-Sided Versus Two-Sided Messages

In a variety of studies in noncommercial contexts it has been found that a two-sided message (that is, arguments favorable and unfavorable to the advocated position) induces more attitude change than a one-sided appeal. In a widely quoted study, Hovland and others reported the following findings:[38]

(1) Giving both sides produced greatest attitude change in those instances where individuals were initially opposed to the point of view which was advocated.

(2) For those convinced of the main argument, presentation of the other side was ineffective.

(3) Those with higher education were most affected when both sides were presented.

More recent evidence documents that the two-sided appeal may have a positive effect on perceived source credibility. Walster and others, for example, showed that presentation of both pro and con arguments appeared to increase audience perception of source credibility sufficiently to allow for successful utilization of a widely discrepant communication message.[39] Similar results were reported by Chu who also found that the one-sided message induced significantly more counterargumentation than a two-sided version.[40]

While it may appear that advertisers never could capitalize upon these findings, Faison suggests that such a conclusion is premature.[41] He presented both favorable and unfavorable product attributes in advertisements for automobiles, ranges, and floor waxes. The influence of the two-sided appeal was significantly greater, and this suggests a previously overlooked way to increase promotional effectiveness. It might be quite a task, however, to convince a manufacturer that his advertising campaign also should mention product flaws.

It is interesting to point out that the policy of corrective advertising instituted by the Federal Trade Commission in 1971 may have some unintended

---

[38] C. I. Hovland, A. A. Lumsdaine, and F. D. Sheffield, *Experiments on Mass Communication*, vol. 3 (Princeton, N.J.: Princeton University Press, 1948), chap. 8.

[39] E. Walster, E. Aronson, and D. Abrahams, "On Increasing the Persuasiveness of a Low Prestige Communicator," *J. Experimental Social Psychology*, vol. 2, pp. 325–342 (1966).

[40] G. Chu, "Prior Familiarity, Perceived Bias, and One-Sided Versus Two-Sided Communications," *J. Experimental Social Psychology*, vol. 3, pp. 243–254 (1967).

[41] E. W. Faison, "Effectiveness of One-Sided and Two-Sided Mass Communications in Advertising," *Public Opinion Quart.*, vol. 25, pp. 468–469 (1961).

effects. The basic premise is that manufacturers should be required to admit blame publicly in their advertisements once they have been found guilty of false and misleading appeals. This admission in a certain percentage of its future messages presumably will serve to offset past misleading efforts. The result, however, may be to enhance the credibility of the advertiser in the consumers' eyes and hence increase his promotional effectiveness. This, of course, would be contrary to the result intended by the Federal Trade Commission.

Order of Presentation

There now is a considerable body of evidence, much of it conflicting and contradictory, on the subject of the order in which appeals should be presented. This assumes, of course, that there are two or more main arguments either related to each other or pro and con. Some say that the argument presented first will prove to be most effective (*primacy*), whereas others say that the most recently presented argument will dominate (*recency*). Research investigations have focused both on the order of two-sided appeals as well as the order of major arguments in a one-sided message.

Two-Sided Appeals The available evidence of order of presentation of two-sided appeals presents an equivocal picture. Roughly equal numbers of studies report primacy, recency, or no significant order effect.[42] Attempts to explain these wide differences to date have been unfruitful, with the result that no firm generalizations can be advanced.

One-Sided Appeal Should the strongest argument in a commercial message be presented first or last? Again the empirical evidence is contradictory. Although one experimenter reports that presentation of the strong argument first is most effective,[43] the majority of published studies report no differences whatsoever.[44]

While there is no empirical resolution of the question at this point in time, there are some logical guidelines for strategy. First, initial presentation of the strongest argument may have a stronger effect on attention attraction and receptiveness to subsequent arguments. Moreover, material presented first usually is best learned.[45] On the other hand, presentation of successively weaker arguments may tend to diminish the overall persuasive effect of the message. Therefore, saving the strongest arguments for last may boost reception when it is most

---

[42]   This evidence is reviewed in Sternthal, *op. cit.*,[1] chap. 8.

[43]   H. Sponberg, "A Study of the Relative Effectiveness of Climax and Anti-Climax Order in an Argumentative Speech," *Speech Monographs*, vol. 13, pp. 35–44 (1946).

[44]   H. Gilkinson, S. Paulson, and D. Sikkink, "Effects of Order and Authority in an Argumentative Speech," *Quart. J. Speech*, vol. 40, pp. 183–192 (1954); H. Gulley and D. Berlo, "Effect of Intercellular and Intracellular Speech Structure on Attitude Change and Learning," *Speech Monographs*, vol. 23, pp. 288–297 (1956).

[45]   Sternthal, *op. cit.*,[4] chap. 8.

needed toward the end of the message. Acceptance of the overall communication also may be enhanced in this fashion.

Probably the only valid conclusion at this time is that primacy or recency depends entirely on the mediating effects of such content factors as novelty or humor, familiarity with the issue, and interpolation of activity between presentation of successive arguments. Cohen concludes that the highly confused state of findings will be clarified only when more precise theories specifying these types of interactions are evoked and tested.[46] For now, little practical use can be made of the evidence.

Repetition

It will be recalled that repetition is a fundamental tenet of learning theory. Most authorities agree that repetition of a persuasive message generally is beneficial. It is argued that preceding advertisements may have made too weak an impression to stimulate much buying interest. Later advertisements, then, can be effective in strengthening established weak impressions. Therefore, repetition can build a continuity of impression in the minds of prospects and strengthen a disposition to think and act favorably toward the advertised brand, product, or store.

In addition, markets are not static; people continually enter and leave. Therefore, a repeated message often will reach new prospects who previously have not been exposed. If this fact is overlooked, a firm can quickly experience erosion of its market share as loyal buyers decrease.

Once one goes beyond a general agreement on the benefits of repetition, however, the issues become less clear. What effect does multiple exposure have on each stage of the communication process, that is, attention, comprehension, retention, and response? Can repetition be overdone to the point that a reverse or boomerang effect occurs? In short, decision makers perceive an acute need for knowledge of the effects of repeated messages,[47] but available research evidence is fragmentary at best. Nevertheless some tentative conclusions are possible, and the literature is reviewed under the following headings: (1) message reception (awareness and comprehension), (2) retention, (3) attitude response, and (4) behavioral response.

Message Reception There is evidence that a repeated message, all things being equal, increases awareness and comprehension. The following are representative findings:

(1) The NBC Hofstra study in 1951 showed that the percentage of television set owners recalling a brand's television advertising went from 33 to 65 percent as cumulative viewing minutes increased from 2 to 20.[48]

---

[46] Cohen, *op. cit.*,[29] p. 50.

[47] M. Ray and A. Sawyer, "Repetition in Media Models: A Laboratory Technique," *J. Marketing Research*, vol. 8, pp. 20–29 (1971).

[48] "Frequency in Broadcast Advertising: 1," *Media/scope* (Feb. 1962).

(2)   Spontaneous awareness of the name Tyrex (a type of tire cord) was exhibited by 20 percent of those not exposed to spot television advertisements, by 65 percent of viewers, and by 92 percent of those viewing three or more commercials.[49]

(3)   An advertised brand was mentioned by 15.2 percent of those interviewed prior to an advertising campaign in *Post* magazine; after one exposure the brand came to mind to 18.1 percent; and the percentage of awareness increased to 20.7 percent following two exposures.[50]

(4)   A McGraw-Hill study in 1961 covered a six-year campaign period, and it was reported that recognition of the company name increased from 34 percent in 1955 to 44 percent in 1957. Then advertising was ceased, and name recognition slumped to 31 percent by 1960.[51]

(5)   In a similar study it was reported that recognition of the brand name Eversharp increased from 15 to 38 percent after only five months of advertising. Then the campaign was ceased for two months and recognition slumped to 29 percent. It was then reinstated, and it took 10 months to bring awareness up to 36 percent.[52]

In one of the most definitive investigations in the published literature, Stewart found that considerable repetition is necessary if high brand awareness is to be achieved, and the prime benefit of repeated advertising for a well-known brand is to sustain awareness.[53] In more detail:

(1)   Advertising causes a rapid initial rise in awareness and then levels off in its effects. While repeat messages sustain awareness, it tends to fall once promotion is stopped.

(2)   At least 15 consecutive exposures are needed to produce the lowest costs in terms of attracting additional prospects per dollar of advertising. Only three or four insertions proved to be inefficient.

(3)   One of the two products studied was a failure primarily because of the content of the advertising and the product itself rather than the duration of repetition.

The effects of repetition were studied by Light, and he found a significant positive relation between repetition and awareness.[54] In more detail, this relation

[49]   "Frequency in Broadcast Advertising: 1," *op. cit.*[48]

[50]   "Frequency in Print Advertising: 1" *Media/scope* (Apr. 1962).

[51]   "Recognition Increased with Advertising . . . Dropped When Advertising Stopped" (New York: McGraw-Hill Advertising Laboratory Publication, May 1961).

[52]   E. Pomerance and H. A. Zielske, "How Frequently Should You Advertise?" *Media/scope,* pp. 25–27 (Sept. 1958).

[53]   J. B. Stewart, *Repetitive Advertising in Newspapers: A Study of Two New Products* (Boston: Harvard Business School, 1964).

[54]   M. Lawrence Light, "An Experimental Study of the Effects of Repeated Persuasive Communications upon Awareness and Attitudes," unpublished dissertation (Columbus, Ohio: Ohio State University, 1967).

was found to be predicted accurately by the following mathematical model derived from Hull's studies of learning:

$$A_n = A_0 + (A_{max} - A_0)(1 - e^{-n})$$

where

A_n = level of awareness after no repetitions
A_{max} = maximum expected level of awareness
A_0 = level of awareness before first exposure
e = base of natural logarithm
n = number of repetitions.

Light's work was extended by Martin who predicted the following mathematical relationship between level of advertising spending and brand awareness:[55]

$$A_j = KA_{j-1} + (A_m - A_{j-1})(1 - e^{-\Sigma nj}),$$

where

j = time period determined by timing of data collection
A_j = level of awareness at end of time period j
e = base of natural logarithm
Σnj = cumulative average number of exposures delivered by media schedule from $j = 0$ to end of time period j
A_{j-1} = level of awareness at end of previous time period $(j-1)$
K = *fraction of* A_{j-1} remembered at end of time period j.

This model was tested empirically using market data, and it was to give an accurate prediction of actual level of awareness for a new convenience item. Assuming that all necessary input data can be collected and that a desired level of awareness has been specified, it is possible to solve this equation to determine the number of advertising exposures and consequent dollar investment needed to attain desired awareness levels. This model has been further modified in certain details and has been used successfully in many new product introductions.

Retention One of the most consistent findings of learning theory is that retention falls off rapidly in the absence of practice or repetition. Ebbinghaus found in 1885 that one third of the nonsense syllables he memorized were forgotten after 20 minutes and that nearly three quarters were forgotten after six days. This general pattern of memory decay has been found repeatedly over the years, and there is every reason to hypothesize that it is also valid with respect to retention of advertising messages. It was reported, for example, that the percentage of viewers of a duPont television program who named duPont products as

---

[55] A. J. Martin, Jr., "An Exponential Model for Predicting Trial of a New Consumer Product," unpublished doctoral dissertation (Columbus, Ohio: Ohio State University, 1969).

best for the advertised use declined from 52.1 percent one day following the show to 29.6 percent six days later.[56]

Memory decay can be greatly reduced through repetition.[57] In fact, the amount learned appears to vary directly with the frequency of repetition,[58] and the shorter the interval between presentations, the greater the effect.[59]

Utilizing these findings, of course, can present difficulties, since it is unclear where the values of repetition cease and boomerang effects enter. Perhaps the most definitive published evidence has been provided by Zielske, who experimentally altered the repetition period for an advertising product and measured the extent of recall.[60] He found that one exposure induced a retention of the message by only 14 percent of the housewives studied. Once the advertising schedule was extended to 13 weeks, however, 63 percent could recall the advertisement, and, while memory decay exhibited the Ebbinghaus pattern, there was significant recall for a number of months. Clearly the length of time the message is retained increases in rough proportion to the number of exposures.

Zielske also compared the effects of clustering the 13 messages in a consecutive period of 13 weeks as compared with spreading them throughout the year. The intensive burst of exposures increased recall by one third, thus showing the value of clustering if high impact is desired in a particular short-run period. Continuity of impact, on the other hand, is best attained by the less concentrated schedule.

In utilizing this evidence, it must be remembered that the audience is continually changing. The turnover did not take place in the Zielske study. Thus, it should be anticipated that the average number of persons remembering advertising during a year would probably be fewer under more realistic circumstances.

It is clear that content recall and repetition are related, although it is to be expected that a point of diminishing returns will be reached. Stewart found this point after 15 exposures;[61] Light found increases in awareness to stabilize after four exposures;[62] and Ray and Sawyer found that the effects differed according to product class, market position, and advertising format.[63]

It is possible that overrepetition will inhibit retention. In a recent investigation Craig and Sternthal found that seven exposures were required to learn the

---

[56]   R. Wachsler, "Notes on Frequency," unpublished memorandum (Research Department, Batten, Barton, Durstine & Osborn, Inc.).

[57]   H. Cantril and G. W. Allport, *The Psychology of Radio* (New York: Harper & Brothers, 1935).

[58]   As cited in H. Cromwell and R. Kunkel, "An Experimental Study of the Effect on Attitude of Listeners of Repeating the Same Oral Propaganda," *J. Social Psychology*, vol. 35, pp. 175–184 (May 1952).

[59]   E. K. Strong, "The Factors Affecting a Permanent Impression Developed through Repetition," *J. Experimental Psychology*, vol. 1 (1916).

[60]   H. A. Zielske, "The Remembering and Forgetting of Advertising," *J. Marketing*, vol. 23, pp. 239–243 (Jan. 1959).

[61]   Stewart, *op. cit.*[53]

[62]   Light, *op. cit.*[54]

[63]   Ray and Sawyer, *op. cit.*[47]

content of a series of twelve print advertisements.[64] Therefore, seven repetitions constituted the "hundred percent" learning condition. Fourteen and 21 repetitions of the series were defined as the "two hundred" and "three hundred" percent learning conditions, respectively. Retention of brand names was measured immediately, one day, one week, or one month after exposure. Results indicated that some overlearning (the 200-percent condition) yielded better delayed brand name retention than mere learning (100-percent condition) or extensive overlearning (300-percent condition). There were no retention differences between treatments when retention was measured immediately after stimulus presentation. Obviously these findings can only be tentative, and further research is currently underway at the Ohio State University.

It is doubtful that the evidence examined here can be generalized to all types of products and environmental situations. While repetition is desirable in many instances, the number of multiple exposures needed will vary depending on initial awareness, quality of the message, and many other factors. The only defensible conclusion is that awareness and content retention can be increased through repetition, but that the proper number and timing of exposures are unique to each situation.

Attitude Change Although repetition can increase awareness and retention, this does not necessarily mean that attitudes will change. Indeed, it may be that a change in awareness and knowledge will lead to a decrease in preference.

The evidence once again is mixed. On the favorable side Zajonc has marshalled data from a variety of published research studies, most of which are, at best, indirectly related to the subject under consideration; his conclusion is that repeated exposure is a sufficient condition for attitude modification and change.[65] Since most of the data Zajonc cited traditionally have not been considered pertinent to an understanding of repetition, this conclusion must be accepted as only tentative.

More definitive positive evidence is provided by several published studies. It is reported, for example, that positive evaluations toward a brand increased from 29.2 percent prior to advertising exposure to 38.2 percent after two exposures.[66] Similarly, the findings from the Schwerin Research Corporation indicate that repetition helps a strong campaign;[67] Gardner reports that successive repetition causes the audience to move in the direction intended by the message;[68] the Grey Advertising Agency found that frequent exposure to television shows carrying a brand's advertising is reflected in a higher attitude level and in a

---

[64] C. S. Craig and B. Sternthal, "The Effects of Overlearning on Retention," *J. General Psychology* (in press).

[65] R. Zajonc, "The Attitudinal Effects of Mere Exposure," *J. Personality and Social Psychology*, Monograph Supplement, vol. 9, pp. 1–27 (1968).

[66] "Frequency in Print Advertising: 1," *op. cit.*[51]

[67] "Frequency in Broadcast Advertising: 2," *Media/scope* (Mar. 1962).

[68] As cited in Cromwell and Kunkel, *op. cit.*[58]

greater likelihood of positive attitude change;[69] and McCullough demonstrated that exposure of individuals to print messages five times produced greater attitude change than did a single exposure.[70] Finally, it may be a general phenomenon that consumers attribute higher quality to a heavily advertised brand than to its less frequently advertised counterpart.

Repetition also can have negative effects, however. Capitman reported that a decline in preference often occurs after the fourth exposure to the same commercial.[71] This is especially likely if the claim is perceived by consumers as debatable and open to challenge. Similarly, continued acceptance of a commercial probably is associated with the level of good taste; a weak commercial seems to be especially vulnerable to a negative result.[72] Ray and Sawyer also found that attitudinal responses toward certain products were not influenced by repetition of the message.[73] A possible explanation for these results is that Ray and Sawyer reexposed subjects immediately after first exposure, and the effects of reexposure have been found to be most effective after sufficient time has elapsed to allow some decay in the impact of the original message.[74]

The factor of density (the proportion of the firm's messages to all messages received by the consumer) also is important. In his study, Light discovered a negative relation between frequency and attitude when density is high, thus showing the effects of saturation from many messages.[75]

The key also lies in the message itself, with favorable results occurring when a strong message is repeated, and vice versa. What, however, is the essential ingredient of a "good" message? While it is difficult to generalize, it appears that too frequent repetition without reward leads to loss of attention, boredom, and disregard of the communication.[76] The consumer, in other words, must perceive the appeal favorably and glean from its content some continuing positive reinforcement of his own predispositions. A commercial that stresses product improvement and continued excellence, for example, is likely to be rewarding to a prospective purchaser of color television.

It is unlikely that any message, no matter how strong, can be repeated ad infinitum without variation. The reward from the twelfth exposure to the same beer advertisement is likely to be minimal, for example, and it probably will

---

[69] "How Advertising Works: A Study of the Relationship between Advertising, Consumer Attitudes, and Purchase Behavior," unpublished study (Grey Advertising, 1968).

[70] J. L. McCullough, "The Use of a Measure of Net Counterargumentation in Differentiating the Impact of Persuasive Communications," unpublished doctoral dissertation (Columbus, Ohio: Ohio State University, 1971).

[71] "Frequency in Broadcast Advertising: 2," op. cit.[51]

[72] "Frequency in Broadcast Advertising: 2," op. cit.[51]

[73] Ray and Sawyer, op. cit.[47]

[74] T. Cook and C. Insko, "Persistance of Attitude Change as a Function of Conclusion Reexposure: A Laboratory-Field Experiment," J. Personality and Social Psychology, vol. 9, pp. 243–264 (1968).

[75] Light, op. cit.[54]

[76] C. I. Hovland, I. L. Janis, and H. H. Kelley, Communication and Persuasion (New Haven, Conn.: Yale University Press, 1953), p. 249.

be negative. Capitman's warning of wearout following approximately the fourth exposure is worthy of note. The best strategy is to *repeat the basic theme with variation* so that the reward level can remain high. Product excellence can be demonstrated in many ways, and a campaign can clearly register this theme by varying the message and thus avoiding boredom and loss of attention from over-exposure. The proper strategy, of course, is unique to each situation.

Behavior　Finally, what is the relation, if any, between repetition and buying behavior? It is logical to hypothesize that repetition of advertising and buying action are positively related, and there is confirming evidence.

The following are representative findings:

(1)　From a series of investigations at NBC, a generalization has emerged that the probability of purchasing an advertised brand increases with the frequency of exposure to television commercials.[77]

(2)　Findings from the McGraw-Hill Advertising Laboratory indicate that sustained, continuous advertising results in increased recognition of a company name, which, in turn, is positively correlated with increased sales.[78]

(3)　Before exposure to an advertising campaign in *Post* magazine, 9.1 percent of those interviewed stated that they would buy the product in question. The percentage increased to 13.8 percent, however, after two exposures.[79]

(4)　Starch reported that failure to advertise in a given year results, on the average, in a 6.0-percent decrease in sales, whereas use of 13 pages in magazines and other publications leads to a 6.8-percent increase.[80] A similar relation between advertising and sales was discovered by Mullen.[81] Four advertising insertions a year seem to be the minimum needed on the average to sustain sales, according to Starch,[82] and others agree with this generalization.[83]

(5)　In the Stewart study referred to earlier, the following results were reported:[84]

    (a)　When no advertisements were used, few tried the two new products that were studied (Lestare and Chicken Sara Lee).

    (b)　Four weekly insertions served to encourage some people to buy sooner than they otherwise would.

---

[77]　"More Exposure Means More Effectiveness," *NBC Research Bull.* (1960).

[78]　"Advertisers with Greater Continuity Achieved Greater Readership" (New York: McGraw-Hill Advertising Laboratory, 1963).

[79]　"Frequency in Print Advertising: 1," *op. cit.*[50]

[80]　D. Starch, "What Is the Best Frequency of Advertisements?" (Daniel Starch Tested Copy, 1962).

[81]　W. H. Mullen, "The Matter of Continuity," *Advertising Agency and Selling*, vol. 49 (1949).

[82]　Starch, *op. cit.*[80]

[83]　R. Barton, *Media in Advertising* (New York: McGraw-Hill, 1964).

[84]　Stewart, *op. cit.*[53]

(c)   Eight advertisements doubled the number of customers, but 15 insertions produced the best results per dollar of advertising investment.

(d)   Twenty advertisements produced the most customers, but costs of advertising exceeded the gains in sales.

(6)   In a methodologically sophisticated investigation, duPont researchers conclusively verified the negative effect of discontinued advertising on sales.[85] Purchases of Teflon cookware were significantly higher in those cities where high advertising expenditures were maintained.

It is probable that the above findings are based on the assumption that the message itself is of high quality. If this were not so, a boomerang effect could occur. Nevertheless, it is apparent that repeated communications can reinforce the behavioral dimension of a consumer's attitude and trigger buyer action either immediately or at some future point in time.

It should be recognized that it is difficult to separate experimentally the influence of advertising on behavioral predispositions versus the other dimensions of an attitude. Each dimension is, of course, related to the other, and it may be impossible to verify conclusively the exact manner in which attitude change was induced.

Implications   From this review of an extensive body of research findings it is apparent that repetition can have a positive effect on message reception, retention, attitude, and behavior. Granted these obvious advantages, the problem of persuasive wearout or boomerang looms large. At what point does the benefit of repetition reach diminishing returns and negative effects set in? Furthermore, what are the causes of wearout?

From years of experience in testing the persuasive power of television commercials, officials of the Schwerin Research Corporation have provided insights into some of these questions. The factors leading to advertising wearout appear to include:[86]

(1)   *The product*—any theme can become obsolete when products are changed or demand shifts rapidly.

(2)   *Strength of the advertisement*—an ineffectively presented message obviously cannot wear out in that it never attains a meaningful level of impact to begin with.

(3)   *Basic motivating idea*—some motivators such as mother love endure while others are fleeting.

(4)   *The presentation*—certain factors regarding the content itself are important. Humor, for example, wears out quickly under repetition.

(5)   *Frequency and pattern of exposure*—as the frequency with which the

---

[85]   J. C. Becknell and R. W. McIsaac, "Test Marketing Cookware Coated with Teflon," *J. Advertising Research,* vol. 3, pp. 2–8 (1963).

[86]   *SRC Bull.,* vol. 14 (Oct. 1966).

same people are exposed without variation becomes excessive, persuasive impact declines.

(6)   *Marketing changes*—the introduction of new brands and innovations can quickly change the environment and lead to wearout of existing campaigns.

(7)   *Competitive advertising*—in some circumstances a competitor's advertising can cancel the commercial impact of a campaign. In other situations, the efforts of a latecomer can strengthen the message of the originator and extend its life span.

Regardless of the above factors, wearout can occur for the reason that repetition often leads to a significant loss of meaning. This phenomenon is referred to as *semantic satiation*.[87] Satiation was first discovered when the meaning of a familiar monosyllabic noun repeated aloud for several seconds dropped away.[88] That is to say, repetition can lead to a decline in meaning toward a neutral point. More recently it was found that the meaning of a stimulus word as measured by an attitude scale disappears with repetition.[89] Light, however, failed to find a satiation effect with repeated advertisements.[90]

The explanation for satiation seems to be that continuous repetition calls into effect various associations with the meaning of a stimulus that sooner or later no longer are elicited. In fact, these associations (an association between pride of appearance and a brand of clothing, for example) become reduced or suppressed.[91] That this can occur in advertising was shown by Capitman, as discussed earlier.[92] As further evidence, the competitive preference scores for various commercials analyzed by the Schwerin Research Corporation generally were lower on the second test.[93] In addition Grass found that a satiation pattern emerges upon repetition in which attention is maximized at two to four exposures and is followed by a decline as the total number of exposures increases.[94] He observed a similar effect on extent of learning, but attitude formation and change do not seem to satiate in the same manner.

It seems obvious that a campaign should be monitored while it is in progress in order to detect signs of wearout. This seems easiest to do in terms of

---

[87]   Harriett Amster, "Semantic Satiation and Generation: Learning? Adaptation?" *Psychological Bull.*, vol. 62, pp. 273–286 (1964); D. E. P. Smith and A. L. Raygor, "Verbal Satiation and Personality," *J. Abnormal and Social Psychology*, vol. 52, pp. 323–326 (1956).

[88]   M. F. Basette and C. J. Warne, "On the Lapse of Verbal Meaning with Repetition," *Amer. J. Psychology*, vol. 30, pp. 415–418 (1919).

[89]   W. E. Lambert and L. A. Jakobovits, "Verbal Satiation and Changes in the Intensity of Meaning," *J. Experimental Psychology*, vol. 60, pp. 376–383 (1960).

[90]   Light, *op. cit.*[54]

[91]   L. A. Jakobovits and W. E. Lambert, "Stimulus Characteristics as Determinants of Semantic Changes with Repeated Presentation," *Amer. J. Psychology*, vol. 77, pp. 84–92 (1964).

[92]   "Frequency in Broadcast Advertising: 2," *op. cit.*[51]

[93]   Personal communication from a Schwerin user to one of the authors.

[94]   R. C. Grass, "Satiation Effects of Advertising," in *Proc. 14th Annual Conf. of the Advertising Research Foundation* (New York: Advertising Research Foundation, 1968), pp. 20–28.

awareness. Once knowledge of a brand name, product attribute, or other component of the message peaks or turns down, serious consideration should be given to change. Ongoing surveys can also be used to document changes in positive versus negative reactions for the same purpose. Finally, it is possible conceptually to document changes in behavioral tendencies in a similar manner, although less is known about this dimension of an attitude. Continuous surveys of buying intentions might provide some clues.

This type of monitoring, for the most part, is rare. One of the difficulties, of course, is that relatively little is known about wearout and its manifestations through survey measures. Nevertheless, the gains are such that growing numbers of manufacturers and advertising agencies are experimenting with information systems designed for this purpose.

SUMMARY

It was the purpose of this chapter to review a wide variety of research findings which document appropriate strategies for attitude change. Three specific questions were asked: (1) How great should the distance be between attitude position of members of the target audience and the position advocated by the message? (2) How can message content be varied to achieve a maximum effect? (3) What changes can be made in message structure (that is, the order of arguments and repetition)?

It appears that the optimum discrepancy between attitude position of recipients and that of the message should be small. This is because increasing the discrepancy appears to induce attitude change only when the message source is perceived as credible. Marketing stimuli such as advertising are viewed as having an obvious intent to persuade and usually suffer in credibility for this reason.

An extensive body of literature then was reviewed on the effects of variations in the creative message. Much is now known about the possible influence of fear appeals, distraction, nonovert appeals, and stated conclusions. Such evidence, however, is primarily of heuristic value only in that it suggests possible clues for strategy. The type of research upon which most of it is based is, by nature, artificial, and one must be cautious in generalizing to more natural circumstances.

The chapter concluded with a discussion of manipulation of structural variables. Of special importance are the effects of repetition. A substantial body of research evidence was reviewed which indicates that repetition can increase awareness, retention of content, and attitude change. The most important question then becomes, at which point does the value of repetition stabilize or decline? It has been shown, for example, that repetition can have a negative effect on attitude change. One determinant appears to be message density—that is, the proportion of the firm's messages to the total received by the individual over a period of time. The higher this proportion, the greater the probability of a declining or even negative effect from repetition. It seems obvious that continual field study is needed to monitor message effects and detect points of wearout. Removing a campaign either prior to or after the point of diminishing returns is not a profitable business practice.

REVIEW AND DISCUSSION QUESTIONS

1. Compare the various theories on placement of communication messages relative to the recipient's own position on the topic. Of what use would these approaches be to a manufacturer of toothpaste? a manufacturer of pianos and organs?

2. A large nationally known drug firm is interested in expanding market acceptance of its birth control pill. Would you recommend that a fear appeal be used? Why or why not?

3. The EXY Corporation sells aluminum cookware through door-to-door solicitation only. Although some advertising is used, the company relies primarily on its familiar company name and reputation for quality as the prime reasons for justifying a high price. How might the findings on source credibility be used by the sales manager?

4. In a laboratory study it is discovered that a foreign make of automobile is regarded more favorably when advertising messages feature positive selling points as well as the fact that problems have existed in the past with respect to brake fade, door leaks and rattles, faulty ignition, and spark-plug fouling. Would you, as the director of advertising research, recommend that this company use a two-sided campaign? What arguments might be advanced?

5. A well-known brand of refrigerator has two distinct features: (1) a mechanically excellent meat keeper and (2) a thin-wall construction which gives greatest interior capacity per foot of exterior space. Using the findings on primacy versus recency, in which order should these appeals be presented, assuming that thin-wall construction seems to be of greatest importance to consumers?

6. What can be concluded concerning the influence of repetition on knowledge and awareness?

7. What precautions should be followed in using the findings pertaining to retention and repetition?

8. "Zoomo Reduces Headache Pain." What might happen in terms of the affective dimension of attitudes if this slogan is repeated for one year on a saturation basis in newspapers, magazines, and on radio and television? What reasons can you give for your answers?

9. What might be done to reduce campaign wearout in the situation described in question 8?

10. Does advertising influence buying action? With what degree of certainty would you want to predict such an effect in the advertising of Zoomo for headache pain (question 8)? Would your answer differ if the product in question were an electric range?

11. What factors lead to campaign wearout according to the Schwerin Research Corporation? Give examples of each.

12. What is meant by semantic satiation? What are the implications for marketing management?

Decision Processes

Part V considers the processes that describe how consumers make purchasing decisions. Purchasing is viewed as a process consisting of five stages linked in a sequence: (1) problem recognition, (2) internal search and alternative evaluation, (3) external search and alternative evaluation, (4) purchasing processes, and (5) postpurchase evaluation.

Chapter 15 is concerned with the first stage in the process—problem recognition. This is the stage where consumers recognize that some decision is necessary. The nature and determinants of problem recognition are discussed, followed by an analysis of procedures and techniques for measuring purchase intentions and an appraisal of the uses of the concept for marketing strategy decisions.

After a problem is recognized, the consumer may or may not engage in internal search and alternative evaluation and/or external search and alternative evaluation in order to learn about and evaluate the characteristics and attributes of alternative solutions to the problem. Chapter 16 discusses the nature of search and alternative evaluation, those conditions and/or variables that are likely to precipitate the process, and mass media and marketer dominated sources of information. Chapter 17 analyzes the nature and marketing impact of interpersonal communications, the characteristics of opinion leaders and methods of identifying them, and alternative models of interpersonal communication and personal influence. In Chapter 18, attention is given to family role structures involved in search, the relative importance of information sources and the determinants of the importance of information sources, and, finally, the marketing implications of search processes.

With few exceptions, consumers must visit retail stores sometime during the decision-process period. Chapter 19 discusses the nature of purchasing processes and presents an extended conceptual framework for studying this type of behavior. The bulk of the chapter is devoted to an analysis of store choice processes and shopper profiles. Chapter 20 is concerned with in-store behavior. The effects of various store characteristics, including layout, displays, shelf facings and shelf height, and pricing deals are analyzed. Chapter 21 concludes the discussion of the purchasing process stage of the decision-making process. The influence of salesmen and the nature and significance of intentions—outcomes categories—specifically planned, generally planned, brand substitution, and unplanned— are discussed, and particular attention is paid to the determinants of customer susceptibility to brand substitution and unplanned purchasing.

Chapter 22 discusses the important aspects of postpurchase behavior. The types of new behavior that are likely to be triggered by a purchase are outlined and the nature and marketing implications of postdecision dissonance are presented.

CHAPTER 15

PROBLEM-RECOGNITION
PROCESSES

How do consumers recognize the need to purchase a product or service? What role do reference groups and family members play in stimulating problem recognition? Should a firm attempt to evoke problem recognition?

Since the consumer must perceive a problem before considering a purchase, it is necessary to understand the nature and significance of problem recognition—the first stage in the decision-making process. Like other stages, problem recognition is a *complex process* rather than a simple act, and, as such, it involves and occurs as the result of interactions of many variables. The nature of this complex process is discussed in the first section of this chapter. The second section analyzes procedures and techniques for measuring purchase intentions, while the final section shows how these intention measurements can be used in formulating and evaluating marketing strategies and programs.

THE NATURE OF PROBLEM-RECOGNITION PROCESSES

As was discussed in Chapter 11, attitudes give direction to purchase behavior, but they do not encompass other variables that may affect the purchase decision. Consequently, it is necessary to use purchase intentions as an intervening variable between attitude and behavior.

Referring to Figure 11.2, problem recognition—as measured by purchase intentions—incorporates some, but usually not all, of these additional variables. Even when *perfect* measures of purchase intentions are obtained, intentions are consistent with purchase behavior only when (1) intentions and behavior occur simultaneously or (2) environmental influences occurring during the remaining stages of the decision-making process have no affect on intentions. In many instances these conditions do not exist. Thus purchase intentions provide an important, but only a *partial*, linkage between attitude and behavior.

This section discusses the meaning of problem recognition and its various forms. Then various types of evironmental influences—called problem-recognition determinants—and family role structures associated with problem recognition are presented. This establishes the conceptual framework for the discussion of the measurement and uses of purchase intentions.

The Meaning of Problem Recognition

The variables and variable relations involved in problem recognition are illustrated in Figure 15.1. Problem recognition results when a consumer recognizes a difference of sufficient magnitude between what is perceived as the desired state of affairs and what is perceived as the actual state of affairs.[1]

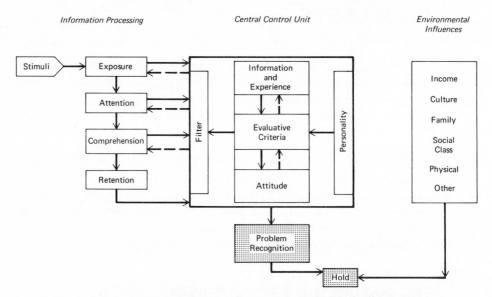

Figure 15.1 PROBLEM RECOGNITION PROCESSES

---

[1] Available research does not permit a more rigorous *conceptual* definition of problem recognition. This is not debilitating since the next section will show how problem recognition can be measured empirically.

The Desired State In a given situation the desired state may result from or involve many variables. By definition, one or more motives underlie the desired state. Since the consumer usually has several alternative ways of satisfying motives, other personality characteristics, attitudes, values, and evaluative criteria may affect the desired state. Inasmuch as culture, social class, reference group, and family influences may affect various dispositions within the central control unit, they may also influence the desired state. In some instances the condition and performance characteristics of the product or service currently being used to solve the problem as well as financial resources—including income, assets, credit availability, and expectations of future financial resources—may also exert a similar influence. Finally, exposure to such marketing efforts as advertising, point-of-purchase displays, and salesmen may affect the desired state.

The Actual State The actual state is perceived by the consumer and thus may also involve many variables interacting in complex ways. Since motives, personality characteristics, attitudes, values, evaluative criteria, and cultural, social-class, reference-group, and family influences may have influenced past purchases, they may have exerted varying degrees of influence on the actual state. The actual state may also be the result of the consumer's past financial status and past exposure to those marketing influences mentioned above. In other situations certain shopping behavior characteristics such as shopping frequency and average purchase per shopping trip may also affect the actual state.

Problem Recognition Outcomes As Figure 15.1 indicates, problem recognition results in two major types of outcomes. The first type of outcome is "hold." This can result when the consumer does not perceive a difference of sufficient magnitude between the actual and desired states. It can also occur when a desired-state–actual-state difference is perceived but the lack of financial resources, time, energy, and/or appropriate alternatives preclude further problem-solving behavior. The second type of outcome involves a perceived problem, and the decision-making process proceeds to internal search and alternative evaluation, external search and alternative evaluation, and/or purchasing processes, depending on the type of decision making that is involved.[2]

Both types of problem-recognition outcomes are stored in the information and experience component of the central control unit (Figure 15.1). Thus some problem-recognition processes are learned while others are not. In the former types of situations, for example, those involving physiological needs such as hunger or thirst, problem recognition becomes programmed or automatic.

Examples of Problem-Recognition Processes

The overview of problem-recognition processes presented above as well as the subsequent, more complicated discussion of the phenomenon will hopefully become more clear from the following examples.

---

[2] See the discussion in Chapter 3, "Variation in Decision Processes."

Case I: Simple Problems-Recognition Processes   Many, and perhaps even the majority of problems that consumers perceive result from the depletion of the product being used to satisfy the problem. Assume, for example, a housewife is in the process of preparing dinner and discovers that she is out of coffee. In her family, coffee is always served with dinner. In this case having coffee is the desired state, and out of coffee is the actual state; thus a problem is perceived. Although perhaps not arising in the same way, this general type of situation has occurred many times in the past, with the result that problem recognition is a rather simple and strongly learned type of process.

Case II: More Complicated Problem-Recognition Processes   Assume that a housewife has been purchasing brand X coffee for several months and is completely satisfied with it. She sees a commercial for brand Z coffee but does not think much about it and continues to purchase brand X. She continues to see commercials for brand Z, and a few months later she has brand Z while visiting a friend. She thoroughly enjoys it. On her next shopping trip she notices that brand Z coffee is several cents cheaper than brand X. All of these events may have no effect on the desired state. On the other hand, the desired state may have changed because of the advertisements, the consumer noticing that her friend uses brand Z, her enjoyment of brand Z, and/or the price of brand Z. In this situation, problem recognition is a much more complex process than in Case I.

Case III: Highly Complex Problem-Recognition Processes   Assume that several years ago a consumer purchased a 19-inch black and white television set. The set has worked well and the consumer is satisfied with it. He has seen advertisements for color television but feels that the quality of receptions is poor and the price is excessive. One evening he watches one of his favorite programs on his friend's new 25-inch color set. He is amazed at the quality of the picture and enjoys the program. This feeling is intensified considerably during subsequent evenings when he watches television on his small black and white set. During the next few months he spends several evenings watching color television at his friend's house. He also pays closer attention to advertisements for color television and occasionally stops at various retail outlets to watch color television and sometimes asks salesmen about prices and financing arrangements.

Finally he comments to his wife about the possibility of buying a color set. She reacts negatively, pointing out that a color set costs far too much and that she would much rather use the money for a vacation or to redecorate the den, to say nothing of the new washer and dryer that she needs.

A few weeks later the old black and white set breaks down, and it is estimated that it will cost $75 to repair it. Both husband and wife are upset, and the husband points out that after spending $75 to have it fixed they will still have the same old set; so why not go ahead and buy the color set. The wife still wants to use the money for other purposes, so nothing is done. Several weeks pass, and both husband and wife become increasingly irritable because they cannot watch their favorite programs.

At work the next day the husband learns that he has received a $50-a-month raise. During dinner he informs his wife of the raise and again brings up the color set. She agrees that something needs to be done but still thinks that the color set costs too much money. After nearly a two-hour discussion they agree to buy a smaller color television in an inexpensive cabinet and a new washer and dryer.

In this hypothetical although not unrealistic situation, it is obvious that problem recognition is a far more complex process than in cases I and II. Problem recognition has occurred over a considerable period of time as the result of the interaction of many factors, including perhaps advertisements, seeing color television at a friend's house, the breakdown of the old set and the cost of repairing it, the raise, and the discomfort of not having a set. The situation is further complicated because the spouses have different, and somewhat conflicting, attitudes and motive hierarchies.

Unique Aspects of Problem-Recognition Processes

The nature of problem recognition and the examples just cited indicate that these processes differ in many respects from the concepts discussed in previous parts of this text. An explicit discussion of the unique aspects of problem recognition is necessary for a clear understanding of the nature of the process.

First, it is apparent that problem-recognition processes may simultaneously involve many variables, including perception, learning, attitudes, personality characteristics, and various reference-group influences. The number of concepts involved vary considerably from situation to situation, as illustrated by the increasing complexity of the three examples presented above. In this sense, problem recognition may be a more comprehensive process than many concepts discussed previously.

It is also obvious that problem recognition is a more complex process than motivation. Although problem recognition involves motives, it may also involve attitudes, values, and other influences, as illustrated by cases II and III. Problem recognition is, therefore, not just another name for motivation; it embraces many other concepts and processes.

Third, problem recognition may involve complex comparisons and weighting of such things as the relative importance of various needs, attitudes about how limited financial resources should be allocated to alternative uses, and attitudes about the qualitative level at which needs should be satisfied. Moreover, these need hierarchies and attitudes may differ from one family member to another, so that conflict resolution processes may be necessary before problem recognition occurs. Case III illustrates this aspect of problem recognition.

Finally, as used here, problem recognition differs from the concepts of awareness and interest that are used in many studies of consumer behavior, particularly the diffusion of innovations.[3] Problem recognition involves an aware-

---

[3] For a discussion of much of the literature in which awareness and interest are used, see Everett M. Rogers, *Diffusion of Innovations* (New York: Free Press, 1962); Everett M. Rogers, *Bibliography on the Diffusion of Innovations,* Diffusion of Innovations Research Report no. 4 (East Lansing, Mich.: Department of Communications, Michigan State University, July 1966).

ness of a difference between an actual and a desired state. The consumer may or may not be aware of products and brands, and an awareness of, or exposure to products and/or brands may or may not precipitate problem recognition. Thus, "awareness" is a much more general term than "problem recognition" and, as such, bears no necessary relation to this phenomenon. Similarly, the concept of interest does not have any necessary relation to problem recognition. Problem recognition can occur without any interest on the part of the consumer in a product or brand. Or the consumer can be interested in a product or brand without recognizing a problem (a new car or home being among the more common examples).

Determinants of Problem Recognition

As pointed out above, problem recognition involves the interplay of many factors. The number of variables involved as well as the way they interact vary according to the type of situation. Among other things this means that the number of determinants is almost infinite. The following are among the most important variables and/or situations that elicit problem recognition through their effect on the actual state, the desired state, or both states.

Depletion of Previous Solution   Depletion of the previous solution to a problem is probably the most frequent determinant of problem recognition. The housewife runs out of laundry detergent, shampoo, milk, or a variety of other products, thereby affecting the actual state. Notice, however, that depletion of a previous solution does not automatically produce problem recognition; the underlying need must exist.

Dissatisfaction with Present Solution   The consumer may perceive a problem if the actual state is perceived as unsatisfactory. Examples include situations where a product is broken, run down, worn out, or otherwise considered unsatisfactory.[4] At other times the present solution is unsatisfactory because of its price. For example, problem recognition preceding the purchase of a home is often triggered by the high cost of renting a home or an apartment.[5]

Changing Family Characteristics   Problem recognition often occurs as the result of new needs or attitude changes brought about by changes in various characteristics of the nuclear family. The birth of children, for example, results in new needs for food, clothing, furniture, and perhaps a house instead of

---

[4] Donald H. Granbois, "A Study of the Family Decision Making Process in the Purchase of Major Durable Household Goods," unpublished doctoral dissertation, (Bloomington, Ind.: Indiana University Graduate School of Business, 1962), p. 84.

[5] Ruby T. Norris, "Processes and Objectives of House Purchasing in the New London Area," in Lincoln Clark (ed.), *The Dynamics of Consumer Reaction* (New York: New York University Press, 1955), pp. 25–29; Peter Rossi, *Why Families Move* (New York: Free Press, 1955); William T. Kelly, "How Buyers Shop for a New Home," *Appraisal*, vol. 25, pp. 209–214 (1957).

an apartment.[6] New needs and redefinitions of desired states continually occur as the size and age composition of the family changes.[7] Even a change in the husband's place of employment can affect the desirability of a family's present home, thereby evoking problem recognition.[8]

Changing Financial Status   Salary increases, tax refunds, temporary or unusual employment, cash gifts, and the retirement of other debts can all affect a consumer's perception of the desired state and hence precipitate problem recognition.[9]

Financial Expectations   Consumers' expectations of their future financial status can affect their perception of the desired state and result in problem recognition. Financial expectations are very important in the period preceding the purchase of durable goods. These expectations are a particularly important determinant of problem recognition for younger consumers.[10]

Recognition of Other Problems   Problem recognition, chiefly through perception of the desired state, is often the outgrowth of other decisions. For example, a new residence or remodeling often affects a consumer's perception of the desirability of carpeting and various pieces of furniture, even though those he has are not worn out.[11] In these situations, the consumer becomes dissatisfied with the present state because of the recognition of other problems.

Changing Reference Groups   Problem recognition sometimes occurs through a change in reference groups, which, in turn, often influences the consumer's perception of the desired state.[12] For example, reference groups sometimes influence the desired state of apparel. Many college freshmen quickly learn that there is a conspicuous difference between the types of clothing that were worn in their high schools and these worn on a college campus. The same process often occurs again when the individual enters the business world. In these situations, reference groups influence the desired state, and the consumer perceives a problem even though he has items that are useable.

Novelty   In some instances problem recognition occurs simply because the consumer wants a change. In one study about two thirds of those who changed to a new product indicated that they did so because of their dissatisfaction with their present brand while one third changed merely because they

---

6   Granbois, *op. cit.*,[4] p. 84.

7   See, for example, William D. Wells and George Gubar, "The Life Cycle Concept in Marketing Research," *J. Marketing Research*, vol. 3, pp. 355–363 (Nov. 1966).

8   Norris, *op. cit.*,[5] p. 26.

9   Granbois, *op. cit.*,[4] p. 84.

10   Eva Mueller, "The Desire for Innovations in Household Goods," in Lincoln Clark (ed.), *Consumer Behavior: Research on Consumer Reactions* (New York: Harper & Row, 1958), p. 37.

11   Granbois, *op. cit.*,[5] p. 84.

12   Granbois, *op. cit.*,[5] p. 84.

wanted a change, even though they were satisfied with their present brand.[13] A study of why people purchase new products found that 15 percent of the respondents had bought a new product because it was new.[14] Actually little is known about the role of monotony and novelty; hence research in this area would appear to be worthwhile.[15]

Marketing Efforts Various marketing efforts, including advertising, point-of-purchase displays, and, particularly, personal selling, can affect consumers' perceptions of the desired state and hence precipitate problem recognition. However, as is pointed out below, there is evidence indicating that marketing efforts, particularly advertising, are likely to be relatively ineffective for this purpose.

Stage of Market Development Whether problem recognition occurs and what types of consumers perceive a problem often depend in part on a product's stage in its life cycle. There is considerable evidence that certain types of consumers are likely to perceive the problem that ultimately results in the purchase of a new product earlier or sooner than are other consumers. Over 2400 empirical findings suggest that consumers that experience problem recognition earlier or sooner than other consumers have a tendency to possess the following characteristics:

(1) More education

(2) Higher incomes

(3) Higher standards of living

(4) More knowledge

(5) A positive attitude toward change

(6) Stronger achievement motivation

(7) Stronger aspirations for children

(8) More cosmopolitan interests

(9) Greater exposure to mass media

(10) Greater tendency to deviate from group norms

(11) Greater tendency to participate in groups

(12) Greater exposure to interpersonal communication

(13) Greater tendency to be opinion leaders

(14) Attitudes, needs, and behavior patterns that are compatible with the innovation.[16]

---

[13] Elihu Katz and Paul Lazarsfeld, *Personal Influence* (New York: Free Press, 1955).

[14] George H. Haines, "A Study of Why People Purchase New Products," in R. M. Haas (ed), *Science, Technology and Marketing* (Chicago: Amer. Marketing Assoc., 1966), pp. 685–697.

[15] For an extensive literature review, see M. Venkatesan, "Cognitive Consistency and Novelty-Seeking," unpublished working paper (June 1971).

[16] Everett M. Rogers and J. David Stanfield, "Adoption and Diffusion of New Products: Emerging Generalizations and Hypotheses," in Frank M. Bass, Charles W. King, and Edgar Pessemier (eds.), *Applications of the Sciences in Marketing Management* (New York: Wiley, 1968).

It should be pointed out that the characteristics of early problem perceivers are generalizations, and, although based on an impressive amount of research, they may not hold in every situation.

Future Research Efforts The above observations suggest two major guide lines for future research into problem-recognition processes. First, future research needs to determine how problem-recognition processes differ by product. It is obviously impossible to investigate recognition processes for every type of product. Yet, as has been pointed out, some type of control is necessary. As a compromise, types of decisions,[17] or formal decision properties,[18] might prove useful as basic problem-recognition typologies, and separate problem-recognition process models could be designed for each category comprising the typology.

Second, a specific sequence of research designs seems necessary. Initially research designs need to be sufficiently broad to take into account the many variables and conditions that may be involved in problem recognition. On the basis of the results produced by the broad exploratory studies, experimental studies can be designed to test the effects of single variables and/or variable combinations in producing problem recognition.[19] Although experimental designs are the ultimate goal, broad exploratory studies are necessary to determine what variables are involved and hence what variables should be controlled and/or experimentally manipulated.

Family Role Structures Involved in Problem-Recognition Processes

As was pointed out in Chapter 7, role structure refers to the behavior of nuclear family members at each stage in the decision-making process. At this point the emphasis is on family role structures involved in the first stage of decision making, problem recognition. Since most studies have been concerned with role structures involved in purchasing, there is little evidence that has to do with the role of family members at this stage in the decision-making process.

Table 15.1 presents part of the results of a study that investigated the roles of husbands and wives in problem recognition. Overall, the wife is involved in problem recognition to a greater extent than the husband, although if other products were included in the study this pattern might not exist. The data clearly

---

[17] For various classifications of types of decisions, see Wroe Alderson, *Marketing Behavior and Executive Action* (Homewood, Ill.: Irwin, 1957); Louis P. Bucklin, "Retail Strategy and the Classification of Consumer Goods," *J. Marketing*, vol. 28, pp. 50–55 (Jan. 1963); Walter A. Woods, "Psychological Dimensions of Consumer Decisions," *J. Marketing*, vol. 24, pp. 15–19 (Jan. 1960).

[18] Orville G. Brim, David C. Glass, David E. Lavin, and Norman Goodman, *Personality and Decision Processes* (Stanford, Calif.: Stanford University Press, 1962), pp. 14–17; Irving Roshwalb, "The Voting Studies and Consumer Decisions," in Eugene Burdick and Arthur J. Brodbeck (eds.), *American Voting Behavior* (New York: Free Press, 1959), pp. 150–162.

[19] For a discussion of experimental designs, see Seymour Banks, *Experimentation in Marketing* (New York: McGraw-Hill, 1965).

Table 15.1 *LIFE* MAGAZINE STUDY OF THE ROLES OF HUSBANDS AND WIVES IN PROBLEM RECOGNITION

| | Spouse Initially Recognizing Problem | |
| | Husband | Wife |
Product	(%)	(%)
Refrigerators	71.4	89.0
Vacuum cleaners	35.7	83.1
Automobiles	92.8	38.7
Pet foods	15.8*	33.3
Frozen orange juice	31.4	82.0
Rugs, carpets	49.3	93.5
Paint	60.0	74.2
Coffee	40.0	43.8
Toothpaste	20.9	39.3

NOTE*: Percentages are based on each spouse's self-appraisal. The percentages indicate whether the spouse in question was involved in problem recognition. Categories such as "both husband and wife" or "children" were not employed, so the percentages sometimes total more or less than 100 percent.

SOURCE: "A Pilot Study of the Roles of Husbands and Wives in Purchasing Decisions, Parts I–X, conducted for *Life* magazine by L. Jaffe Associates, Inc. (1965). Research design involved interviews with 301 middle- and upper-income households in Hartford, Cleveland, and Seattle.

indicate that the extent of husband–wife involvement varies considerably from product to product.

What determines the extent of husband–wife involvement in problem recognition? The data in Table 15.1 support the following generalizations: First, the higher the price of the item, the greater the *tendency* for the husband to be involved in problem recognition. For example, a higher percentage of husbands are involved in problem recognition culminating in the purchase of automobiles and refrigerators. Second, the extent of husband–wife involvement in problem recognition tends to vary according to cultural norms of specialization. Husbands, for example, have a greater tendency to be involved in problem recognition when the product is technically or mechanically complex, as in the case of automobiles, refrigerators, and paint.

The statistic used in Table 15.1 to measure spouse involvement is the mean percentage. As was pointed out in Chapter 7, means are likely to be deceiving in that there may be considerable interfamily variation in the degree of husband–wife involvement. Younger and higher income husbands, for example, would be expected to play a greater role in problem recognition than would older and middle- and lower-income husbands.[20] Simultaneously, working wives would be expected to be more involved in problem recognition than would wives that are not employed outside the household.[21] A marketer needs to be aware of the possibility of these variations in problem-recognition role structures when evaluating the usefulness of data expressed in mean percentages.

MEASURING PROBLEM RECOGNITION

Problem recognition is most commonly measured with various types of purchase-intention scales. The diversity reflects the search for useful techniques and the uses that are made of the data.

The accuracy of these techniques varies substantially. Whether accuracy can be improved depends on a number of factors. If purchase intentions are measured accurately but there is substantial deviation between ex-ante intentions and ex-post behavior, improving the ex-ante measure will accomplish little in terms of predictive accuracy. But, if intentions provide a poor measure of ex-ante prospects and deviations are not of great importance, predictive performance can be improved by using a better ex-ante measure.[22] This section discusses various types of research designs and scaling techniques that can be used to measure intentions.

Research Designs

The accuracy of purchase intention measures depends in part on the length of the forecasting period. As Howard and Sheth have pointed out:

> . . . To the extent . . . that the lag is greater between the measure of Intention and the Act of Purchase, greater discrepancies between Intention and Purchase would be expected because the buyer must *anticipate* environmental changes that will occur after the Intention measure and before Purchase. The longer the period of anticipation, the greater we would expect the anticipation to err.[23]

---

[20] See, for example, Elizabeth Wolgast, "Do Husbands or Wives Make Purchasing Decisions?" *J. Marketing*, vol. 23, pp. 151–158 (Oct. 1958); Mirra Komarovsky, "Class Differences in Family Decision Making on Expenditures," in Nelson Foote (ed.), *Household Decision Making* (New York: New York University Press, 1961), pp. 259–264.

[21] Robert O. Blood and Robert L. Hamblin, "The Effects of the Wife's Employment on the Family Power Structure," *Social Forces*, vol. 36, pp. 347–352 (1958); David M. Heer, "Dominance and the Working Wife," *Social Forces*, vol. 36, pp. 341–347 (1958).

[22] F. Thomas Juster, *Consumer Buying Intentions and Purchase Probability* (New York: National Bureau of Economic Research, 1966).

[23] John A. Howard and Jagdish N. Sheth, *The Theory of Buyer Behavior* (New York: Wiley, 1969), p. 133.

The most commonly used forecasting periods have been 6, 12, and 24 months.[24] Occasionally the period is three months.[25] The choice of a forecasting period is usually a compromise of many considerations, including cost. In making this compromise it should be remembered that accuracy is likely to increase as the length of the forecasting period decreases.

Longitudinal Designs   Although it is possible to obtain purchase intentions from cross-sectional surveys, a longitudinal design is preferable because. it generates information that is useful in assessing the accuracy of intentions and formulating and evaluating marketing strategies.

The General Electric Company provides an example of the use of a longitudinal design to measure purchase intentions. General Electric maintains an area probability panel of 5000 households. Interviews are conducted by an independent agency and are in no way associated with G.E. Panel members are asked many questions about household possessions other than appliances. Interviewing is conducted continuously throughout the year, with a new cohort entering the panel each month. Each panel member is interviewed a minimum of three times at six-month intervals.

During the first interview respondents are asked about their intentions to buy a large number of consumer durables, ranging from automobiles to relatively inexpensive housewares and radios. Respondents are also asked about brand intentions. When reinterviewed they are asked a number of questions that refer directly to their earlier statements of intent.[26]

The Bureau of the Census has probably had the most experience with these types of surveys, although they are concerned with product purchase intentions rather than product and brand intentions. Their estimates are based on their Quarterly Household Survey (QHS) of 11,500 households from 484 counties and 49 states. The housing units are interviewed for six quarters with one sixth of the sample retired and a new sixth introduced each quarter. Using a scaling technique as described below, respondents are asked to estimate the probability of purchasing a new car, a number of appliances, furniture, and carpeting. The accuracy of these intentions data is not affected by type of respondent (husband, wife, or other). However, this finding may not apply to the accuracy of brand intentions.[27]

---

[24] See, for example, Gertrude S. Weiss, Tynan Smith, and Theodore G. Flechsig, "Quarterly Survey of Consumer Buying Intentions," *Federal Reserve Bull.*, vol. 46, pp. 977–1003 (Sept. 1960); James C. Byrnes, "An Experiment in the Measurement of Consumer Intentions to Purchase," in *Proc. Statistical Assoc.* (Washington, D.C., 1965), pp. 265–279; Robert Ferber and R. Piskie, "Subjective Probabilities and Buying Intentions," *Rev. Economics and Statistics*, vol. 47, pp. 322–325 (Aug. 1965).

[25] C. Joseph Clawson, "How Useful Are 90-Day Purchase Probabilities?" *J. Marketing*, vol. 35, pp. 43–47 (Oct. 1971).

[26] For a more detailed description see Robert W. Pratt, Jr., "Using Research to Reduce Risk Associated with Marketing New Products," in Reed Moyer (ed.), *Changing Marketing Systems* (Chicago: Amer. Marketing Assoc., 1967), pp. 98–104.

[27] U.S. Department of Commerce, Bureau of the Census, "Consumer Buying Indicators," *Current Population Reports*, series P-65, no. 37 (Sept. 1, 1971). For additional research on the effect of type of respondent on the accuracy of intentions data, see Donald H. Granbois and Ronald P. Willett, "An Empirical Test of Probabilistic Intentions and Preference Models for Consumer Durables Purchasing," in Robert L. King (ed.), *Marketing and the New Science of Planning* (Chicago: Amer. Marketing Assoc., 1968), pp. 401–408.

Scaling Techniques

While a variety of techniques have been used to measure purchase intentions,[28] "purchase-intention scales" and "purchase-probability scales" appear to be used most widely.

Purchase-Intention Scales This type of scale was the most popular method of measuring intentions until recent years. This scale asks respondents to indicate their intentions of purchasing a product—and sometimes specific brands—according to some minor variation of the following typology:

> Definitely would buy it
> Probably would buy it
> Might or might not buy it
> Probably would not buy it
> Definitely would not buy it

Purchase-Probability Scales This type of scale requests respondents to estimate the probability that they will purchase a product or brand as follows:

> Certain, practically certain (99 in 100)
> Almost sure (9 in 10)
> Very probable (8 in 10)
> Probable (7 in 10)
> Good possibility (6 in 10)
> Fairly good possibility (5 in 10)
> Fair possibility (4 in 10)
> Some possibility (3 in 10)
> Slight possibility (2 in 10)
> Very slight possibility (1 in 10)
> No chance, almost no chance (1 in 100)

Choice of Scales The choice of a scale depends on its predictive and diagnostic value to the user. Research to date suggests that purchase-probability scales (PPS) are generally more useful than purchase-intention scales (PIS). Juster has shown that the greater predictive accuracy of PPS scales arises from the fact that those classified as nonintenders (using PIS)—but who, in fact, have some low purchase probability and who eventually reveal some incidence of purchase—are more sensitively distributed by the PPS approach.[29] Gruber has demonstrated that this also applies to low-priced convenience products.[30] Thus intentions should

---

[28] See, for example, Susan P. Douglas and Yoram Wind, "Intentions to Buy as Predicators of Buying Behavior," paper presented at the Association for Consumer Research Conf. (Sept. 1971).

[29] Juster, *op. cit.*[22]

[30] Alin Gruber, "Purchase Intent and Purchase Probability," *J. Advertising Research* vol. 10, pp. 23–27 (Feb. 1970).

be measured with purchase-probability scales unless the researcher has evidence for his specific product that indicates otherwise.[31]

APPLICATIONS OF PROBLEM-RECOGNITION PROCESS

Purchase intentions can be used in a variety of ways. This section discusses the role of intentions in formulating and evaluating marketing strategies.

Sales Forecasting

Intentions can be used—usually with other variables—to forecast product and/or brand sales. The accuracy of these forecasts varies depending on whether product or brand sales are being forecast as well as the specific product under consideration.

Douglas and Wind found considerable variation in the ability of a five-point intentions-to-buy scale to predict women's clothing purchases. Overall the authors concluded that the scale had relatively high predictive ability.[32]

Clawson used the 11-point purchase-probability scale described above to forecast purchase rates for nine products and services over a 90-day period. After fitting regression lines to correct the tendency of consumers to overestimate their probabilities, the derived equations explained from 97 to 99 percent of the variation in actual purchase rates.[33]

The Census Bureau uses the same 11-point scale to forecast quarterly purchases of new automobiles. In this product category, purchase probabilities are known to be biased downward. Using a regression equation—which includes dealer sales during the survey month, the seasonally adjusted rate of unemployment during the quarter preceding the survey month, as well as an index of buying expectations—"predicted" as a percentage of "actual" sales varied from 92 percent to 115 percent during the eight quarters of 1969 and 1970.[34]

Relationships between brand intentions and brand sales also vary across both product categories and specific brands. Banks has analyzed intentions to buy brands in seven grocery-product categories. Overall, of those who said they intended to buy some brand(s), 61.8 percent carried out their brand intention fully, 19.1 percent carried out their intention partially, and 19.6 percent switched

---

[31] For an opposing point of view, see Kerin J. Clancy and Robert Garsens, "Why Some Scales Predict Better," *J. Advertising Research*, vol. 10, pp. 33–38 (Oct. 1970). The authors maintain that purchase probability scales may reflect different response styles ("yeasay/naysay" tendencies) rather than propensity to buy.

[32] Douglas and Wind, *op. cit.*[28]

[33] Clawson, *op. cit.*[25]

[34] "Consumer Buying Indicators," *op. cit.*[27]

completely. Substantial variation was found across product categories; for example, only 39 percent of the ice cream brand intentions were fulfilled.[35]

Using General Electric Consumer Panel data, Pratt has shown that intention-fulfillment rates vary by brand as well as product category. For example, for one appliance the percentage of buyers who purchased the brand intended was 68 percent for brand *A*, 24 percent for brand *B* and 57 percent for brand *C*. In this case low fulfillment rates were clustered among well-known national brands—a tendency that will be analyzed in greater detail later.[36]

On the basis of these and other studies it is difficult to arrive at conclusions concerning the usefulness of intentions in forecasting product and brand sales. Intention measures differ from one study to another, and different techniques and procedures are used to analyze and evaluate their predictive power.

Nevertheless, several conclusions seem appropriate. In forecasting sales, purchase-probability scales are probably superior to purchase-intention scales. As indicated earlier, Juster and others have conducted a considerable amount of sophisticated research that supports this position. Many researchers have not followed this suggestion, which may explain why they have experienced disappointing results.

Second, experimentation and experience is needed to determine the relationship between intentions and sales. It may be desirable to include other variables and correct for biased estimates of purchase probabilities.

Overall, it does not appear to be legitimate to generalize about the usefulness of intentions in forecasting product and/or brand sales. Intentions may or may not be a useful forecasting tool, depending upon the specific product and brand in question.

Formulating a General Marketing Strategy

Using panel data, Pratt has shown that it is possible to estimate the average length of the planning process, that is, the time between intentions and purchase. The estimating equation used for durable goods is

$$\text{average length of the planning process} = \left[\cfrac{\text{plans at time 1 fulfilled by time 2}}{\text{total purchases} \times \text{purchases recorded at time 2}} \right] \times \left[\text{time between interviews} \right]$$

Those durables having relatively short planning periods require marketing programs characterized by relatively heavy emphasis on wide distribution,

---

[35] Seymour Banks, "The Relationship between Preference and Purchase of Brands," *J. Marketing*, vol. 15, pp. 145–157 (1950).

[36] Robert W. Pratt, Jr., "Understanding the Decision Process for Consumer Durable Goods: An Example of the Longitudinal Approach," in Peter D. Bennett (ed.), *Marketing and Economic Development* (Chicago: Amer. Marketing Assoc., 1965), pp. 244–260.

local advertising, and point-of-purchase displays. Durables with relatively long planning periods usually require a marketing strategy involving limited distribution, heavy use of national media, and less frequent advertising.[37] Thus planning periods provide a quantitative measure of buying behavior that can be used to array products in the product line and assist in the formulation of a general marketing strategy.[38]

Identifying Promotional Targets

Purchase-probability scales can be used to identify promotional targets and allocate promotional efforts. This is facilitated by grouping the brand purchase-probability scale into larger categories. One of several possible groupings is as follows:

Category	Purchase Probability Scale
I	Certain, practically certain (99 in 100) Almost sure (9 in 10)
II	Very probably (8 in 10) Probable (7 in 10)
III	Good possibility (6 in 10) Fairly good possibility (5 in 10) Fair possibility (4 in 10)
IV	Some possibility (3 in 10) Slight possibility (2 in 10)
V	Very slight possibility (1 in 10) No chance, almost no chance (1 in 100)

The first step is to determine the percentage distribution of respondents across categories I–V for the firm's brand and major competing brands. Then each category is analyzed according to the procedures spelled out in Chapters 10 and 11. Thus for each brand in each category

(1) Identify evaluative criteria and determine their relative importance
(2) Rate brands on each evaluative criterion
(3) Determine attitudes by multiplying the relative importance of the criterion times the brand's rating on the criterion
(4) Determine knowledge and centrality.

[37] Robert W. Pratt, Jr., "Consumer Buying Intentions as an Aid in Formulating Marketing Strategy," in King, *op. cit.,*[27] pp. 296–302.

[38] For a study of determinants of planning periods see Joseph W. Newman and Richard Staelin, "Multivariate Analysis of Differences in Buyer Decision Time," *J. Marketing Research*, vol. 8, pp. 192–198 (May 1971).

This detailed analysis is useful in determining the potential economic value of each category. To illustrate, if category III consumers have neutral evaluations of the firm's brand with low centrality and knowledge, category III would have a higher potential value than if the neutral evaluation had high centrality and were based on extensive knowledge. The same procedure can be used to assess the value of other categories.

Once the economic value of each category has been established, some or all of the categories—or subparts of the categories—are selected as market segments. Economic, demographic, life style, and media usage profiles can be constructed for each segment.

Promotional objectives and media plans are drawn up that focus on specific segments in order to move them up one or more categories. Copy objectives are determined by referring to differences in brand ratings on specific evaluative criteria between purchasers and consumers at each category level for the firm's brand as well as competing brands. Expenditures and reach and frequency goals are established on the potential value of moving people up one or more category levels.[39]

Murray has developed a technique for allocating promotional efforts that is less involved than the procedure outlined above. His optimal strategy index (OSI) identifies high potential geographic markets for durable goods by combining purchase probabilities with households' estimates of their future economic situation. Thus,[40]

$$OSI_{t+1} = (P_u - P_d + 100) + (BI - NI + 100)$$

where

OSI_{t+1} = optimal strategy index for next period

P_u = proportion of optimistic or up responses for household economic activity for next period

P_d = proportion of pessimistic or down responses for household economic activity for next period

BI = positive buying intentions for a selected durable good purchase

NI = negative purchasing intentions (nonintenders) for a selected durable good.

This index is used to develop a priority listing of geographic regions according to market potential during a specific time period. Promotional expenditures are allocated to regions according to their potential.

Evaluating Marketing Programs

The effectiveness of marketing programs can be evaluated by analyzing purchase intentions over time. This requires a longitudinal study and turnover tables which array the purchase probability categories along both axes. Two

---

[39] For illustrations and variations of this approach see William D. Wells, "Measuring Readiness to Buy," *Harvard Business Rev.*, vol. 39, pp. 81–87 (July–Aug. 1961); Gail Smith, "How GM Measures Ad Effectiveness," *Printers' Ink*, pp. 19–29 (May 14, 1965).

[40] J. Alex Murray, "Utilizing Exceptional Data to Allocate Promotional Efforts," *J. Marketing*, vol. 33, pp. 26–33 (Apr. 1969).

levels of analysis are useful: (1) relationships between intentions and (2) relationships between intentions and purchase behavior.

Relationships between Intentions[41] This level of analysis is concerned with the interpurchase probability category movement of consumers over time. The desirable pattern of movement depends on the firm's specific marketing and promotional objectives, that is, the categories the firm is focusing on and what it is trying to get consumers in each category to do.

Several types of analysis are possible. First, the shape of the percentage distribution across categories over time can be analyzed. Generally, the bulge in percentages should move from high categories toward lower categories; in other words, from category V toward category I. Assuming proper experimental controls, this indicates that the firm's marketing program is moving consumers toward the purchase of its brand.

More detailed analysis is also possible. For example, an increasing ratio of category I to category II means that growing numbers of consumers that are impressed with the brand intend to purchase it. Conversely, a decreasing I/II ratio means that more consumers have a favorable disposition but still need to be convinced to buy the brand.

Analyzing the cells of the turnover table also provides useful insights. For example, a movement of respondents from category III into categories IV and V instead of I and II indicates that the marketing program is failing to convince consumers that the firm's brand is worth trying. These consumers should be reinterviewed to determine the reasons for their changed probabilities and what the firm can do to correct the situation.

Relationships between Purchase Intentions and Purchase Behavior[42] This type of analysis requires some data modifications. If purchase-probability scales are used to measure product and brand intentions, then it is necessary to specify some cutoff point distinguishing intenders from nonintenders. An alternative is to ask the following questions after the purchase-probability scale has been administered:

(1) "Taking everything into consideration, will you or another member of your family purchase a *(insert product category)* during the next *(insert time period)* months?"

(2) "If 'yes,' what brand do you plan to purchase?"

Table 15.2 presents hypothetical data summarizing the purchase behavior of each person who, during a previous interview, expressed an intention to purchase one of the three brands listed.

The first level of analysis is concerned with product intention fulfillment

---

[41] Much of this section is based on Wells, *op. cit.*[39]

[42] This section is adapted from Pratt, *op. cit.*[36]

Table 15.1 RELATIONSHIPS BETWEEN PURCHASE
INTENTIONS AND PURCHASING BEHAVIOR

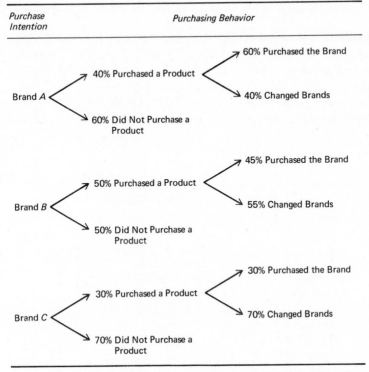

*Purchase
Intention*

Purchasing Behavior

Brand *A*

40% Purchased a Product

60% Purchased the Brand

40% Changed Brands

60% Did Not Purchase a
Product

Brand *B*

50% Purchased a Product

45% Purchased the Brand

55% Changed Brands

50% Did Not Purchase a
Product

Brand *C*

30% Purchased a Product

30% Purchased the Brand

70% Changed Brands

70% Did Not Purchase a
Product

SOURCE: Adapted from Robert W. Pratt, Jr., "Understanding the
Decision Process for Consumer Durable Goods: An Example of the Longitudinal Approach," in Peter D. Bennett
(ed.), *Marketing and Economic Development* (Chicago:
Amer. Marketing Assoc., 1965), pp. 244–260.

rates. In the example note that only 40 percent of those who stated an intention
to buy brand *A* actually purchased the generic product during the time period
involved. Thus brand *A* is doing worse than brand *B* (50 percent) but better
than brand *C* (30 percent).

These types of results must be interpreted carefully. Notice that a relatively greater percentage of respondents interviewed early in their decision
process will be found in the "unfulfilled plans" category during subsequent
interviews, because as one proceeds from intention to purchase, the *psychological
commitment* to complete the transaction increases. There are many ways of
overcoming this problem, and, since the procedures are complex, the reader is
referred to Pratt's work in this area. He has concluded that there are no percepti-
ble differences in *adjusted* product fulfillment rates and that promotional programs have little or no *direct* influence on level of fulfilled plans.[43]

---

[43]   Pratt, *op. cit.*[36]

The second level of analysis is concerned with brand intention fulfillment rates. Table 15.1 indicates that 60 percent of those who both stated an intention to purchase brand *A* and made a purchase actually did purchase the brand intended. Brand *B* trails with 45 percent and brand *C* is a distant third at 30 percent.

Table 15.1 does not reveal the entire process, because it shows the percentage of intenders who moved away from a particular brand but not the brand they switched to. The entire process can be understood through turnover table analysis.

Table 15.3 summarizes this type of analysis. Brand *A* gains 1.45 customers for each intender who changes to an alternative brand while brand *B* gains 1.25 customers. Brand *C* loses more than two intenders for every person who changes to *C*.

Table 15.3 NET GAINS AND LOSSES RESULTING FROM STATED BRAND INTENTIONS

Stated Brand Intention	*Number of Consumers Switching to the Brand (Listed at Left) for Each 100 Switchings Away from the Brand*	*Net Gain or Loss (%)*
Brand *A*	145.6	+45.6
Brand *B*	125.2	+25.2
Brand *C*	47.2	−52.8

SOURCE: Adapted from Robert W. Pratt, Jr., "Understanding the Decision Process for Consumer Durable Goods: An Example of the Longitudinal Approach," in Peter D. Bennett (ed.), *Marketing and Economic Development* (Chicago: Amer. Marketing Assoc., 1965), pp. 244–260.

Overall it appears that brand *A* has a more effective marketing program than brands *B* and *C*. Brand *A*'s superiority may reside in its distribution policy; size, location, and attractiveness of displays; shelf-space allotment; point-of-purchase advertising; salesman influence; or other programs. By interviewing respondents who changed brands and comparing the firm's marketing program with those of competitors, it is possible to identify the reasons for these differences and take action that will hopefully correct the situation.

·Problem Recognition Sets

If a consumer recently purchased an electric blanket, is it possible to predict which household durable they are likely to purchase next? It is unlikely unless there are general acquisition patterns that a significant number of consumers follow.

Researchers and strategists are beginning to investigate this phenomenon. For example, using factor analysis Wells, Banks, and Tigert have shown that homemakers who are heavy purchasers of ready-to-eat cereal also purchase peanut butter, laundry detergent, toothpaste, hair shampoo, gelatin desserts, adhesive bandages, and certain other products in large quantities.[44]

In the case of durables, there is evidence that consumers do not only seem to think in terms of characteristic sets of products in relation to their needs and values, they also tend to arrange their purchases according to acquisition priorities. Paroush, for example, derived a priority pattern for Israeli households[45] while Sargent[46] and McFall[47] have identified patterns for midwest and San Diego households. While ownership data provide clues on the development of past priorities, future purchases can be predicted only from priority patterns derived from consumers' purchase intentions. McFall has developed a procedure for making these estimates.

Marketers can use priority patterns in several ways. These patterns suggest that the market segment with the highest potential of purchasing product X are consumers that have just purchased product X-1 on the priority scale. If there is substantial line loyalty, it suggests the importance of a product line which includes products having the highest priorities and indicates what these products are. Products having high priorities may be priced lower to encourage consumers to begin with the manufacturer's brand. In the case of convenience goods, product sets and priority patterns provide guidelines for crosscouponing, joint promotions, and the location of products in retail outlets.

SUMMARY

This chapter discussed the nature and significance of the first stage in the decision-making process—problem recognition. Problem recognition refers to a difference of sufficient magnitude between what is perceived as the desired state of affairs and what is perceived as the actual state of affairs. Both the desired and actual states result from, or otherwise involve, complex interactions of motives, response traits, values, attitudes, and various reference-group influences. Several examples of problem recognition were presented to illustrate the varying complexity of the process.

Problem recognition occurs as a result of changes in variables affecting the desired state and the actual state, and the major determinants of problem recognition were presented. An analysis of past studies of problem-recognition processes generated several recommendations for future research. Finally, it was

---

[44] William D. Wells, Seymour Banks, and Douglas Tigert, "Order in the Data," in Moyer, *op. cit.*,[26] pp. 263–266.

[45] J. Paroush, "The Order of Acquisition of Consumer Durables," *Econometrica,* vol. 33, pp. 225–235 (Jan. 1965).

[46] Hugh M. Sargent, *Consumer Product Rating Publications and Buying Behavior* (Urbana, Ill.: Bureau of Business and Economic Research, University of Illinois, 1959).

[47] John McFall, "Priority Patterns and Consumer Behavior," *J. Marketing,* vol. 33, pp. 50–55 (Oct. 1969).

demonstrated how the role of family members in problem recognition varies by type of product.

The second section of the chapter discussed a research methodology for measuring product and brand purchase intentions. Longitudinal designs are most useful, and intentions should be measured with purchase-probability scales.

The final section analyzed marketing applications of problem-recognition processes. It was shown how intentions can be used to help forecast sales, identify promotional targets and allocate promotional expenditures, and evaluate the effectiveness of marketing programs. The chapter concluded with a discussion of problem-recognition sets and their uses in developing marketing strategies and programs.

REVIEW AND DISCUSSION QUESTIONS

1. What is meant by problem recognition?

2. How does problem recognition differ from the concepts of awareness and interest?

3. Discuss the problem-recognition process that occurred before you purchased your last soft drink. How does this decision process differ from the one that preceded the purchase of a suit or slacks?

4. Did problem recognition underlie your decision to attend college and/or graduate school? If so, describe the process.

5. How does problem recognition differ from a motive? Use examples to illustrate the differences.

6. Use examples from your own experiences to illustrate how some problem resulted from: (a) depletion of previous solution, (b) dissatisfaction with present solution, (c) change in some of the characteristics of your family, (d) change in your financial status and financial expectations, (e) change in your reference groups, (f) recognition of other problems, (g) marketing efforts.

7. Assume you are a consultant to a large manufacturer of refrigerators that are nationally distributed. Outline a research design that could be used to determine the problem-recognition processes that precede the purchase of refrigerators.

8. What generalizations can be drawn about the role of family members in problem-recognition processes?

9. Critically evaluate the *Life* magazine study of the roles of husbands and wives in problem recognition. (See Table 15.1 as well as text discussion of the table.)

10. As a consultant to a major household carpeting company, you find that 70 percent of the consumers interviewed preferred your brand at the point of problem recognition and 40 percent of those consumers purchasing purchased your firm's brand. On the basis of this finding, prepare an outline of your recommendations for marketing strategy.

CHAPTER **16**

SEARCH AND ALTERNATIVE EVALUATION PROCESSES: MASS MEDIA AND MARKETER DOMINATED SOURCES OF INFORMATION

After a problem is recognized, the consumer may or may not seek and/or process information concerning various characteristics of alternative solutions to the problem. What determines whether the consumer will seek information? What sources of information will be consulted?

Because this stage in the decision-making process plays a pivotal role in designing marketing strategies, and because it is one of the most researched areas of consumer behavior, three chapters are required to cover the subject adequately. The present chapter discusses the nature of search and alternative evaluation, those conditions and/or variables that are likely to precipitate the process, and some of the information sources that are used. Chapter 17 discusses the use of personal information sources, and then Chapter 18 considers the relative importance of various sources as well as the marketing implications of this stage in the decision-making process.

NATURE OF SEARCH
AND ALTERNATIVE EVALUATION

The meaning of search and alternative evaluation and the relation of this stage in the decision-making process to the variables, concepts, and processes previously discussed are depicted in Figure 16.1 and summarized below.

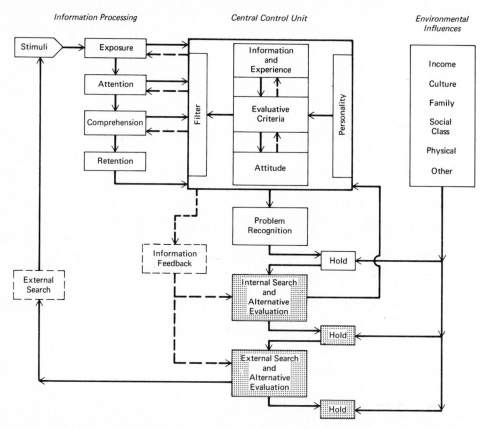

Figure 16.1   SEARCH AND ALTERNATIVE EVALUATION PROCESSES

Meaning of Search and Alternative Evaluation

In Chapter 11 it was shown that it is useful to represent attitude as follows:

$$A_b = \sum_{i=1}^{n} W_i\, B_{ib}$$

where

A_b = attitude toward a particular alternative b

W_i = weight or importance of evaluative criterion i

B_{ib} = evaluative aspect or belief with respect to utility of alternative b to satisfy evaluative criterion i

n = number of evaluative criteria important in selection of an alternative in category under consideration.

Search and alternative evaluation refers to the processes and activities the consumer uses to make judgements concerning W_i, B_{ib}, and n. Stated less formally, through search and alternative evaluation the consumer identifies the critical evaluative criteria, learns of the availability of alternative products and brands, and evaluates them relative to the evaluative criteria.

Internal Search and Alternative Evaluation

Following the recognition of a problem, the consumer engages in internal search and alternative evaluation. Relying exclusively on information from past experiences, the consumer uses existing attitudes to identify and evaluate alternative solutions to the problem. This involves the learning processes described in Chapter 9 and is shown in Figure 16.1 by the solid arrows leading to the central control unit and by the dashed information feedback arrow from the central control unit.

Internal search and alternative evaluation can produce three different types of outcomes. First, if the process produces satisfactory results, the consumer may forego external search and proceed to the purchasing process stage. Second, internal search may convince the consumer that there is no viable way of solving the problem and so the process may halt. The third and final type of outcome is that the consumer decides to engage in external search and alternative evaluation.

External Search and Alternative Evaluation

In this stage of the process the consumer uses various sources of external information, such as mass media, personal sources, and marketer-dominated sources (advertisements, dealer visits and so on), to learn about the number of alternative solutions to the perceived problem, the characteristics and attributes of these alternatives, and their relative desirability. As Figure 16.1 indicates, these types of information sources are stimuli that have varying degrees of influence on personality, evaluative criteria, attitudes, and purchase intentions—depending on their ability to affect exposure, attention, comprehension, and retention as discussed in Chapter 13.[1] These effects are depicted by the information feedback arrow in Figure 16.1.

Two types of outcomes can result from external search and alternative evaluation. First, the process can halt when the results of the search alter the

---

[1] See, for example, Paul A. Pellemans, *Relationships between Attitude and Purchase Intention toward the Brand* (Belgium: Publications Universitaires, Namur Univ. 1971), chap. 4.

difference between the desired and actual states. Or, alternatively, the consumer can move to the purchasing process stage.[2]

DETERMINANTS OF EXTERNAL SEARCH AND ALTERNATIVE EVALUATION

Although most of the items that a consumer purchases probably involved some external search at some point in time, as stated above, the consumer does not engage in this type of search before each purchase. Instead, often a past solution to the problem is remembered and implemented.[3]

Marketing strategists are interested in those instances when external search and alternative evaluation occurs. If the marketer can identify the information sources that are used, he has an opportunity to increase the probability that the consumer will at least be exposed to information about his brand and hopefully be influenced in his purchased decision. On the other hand, if only internal search occurs, the marketing task is more formidable.

In general, whether external search occurs as well as the extent to which it occurs appear to depend on the consumer's perception of the *value* of the results of search and the *costs* involved in engaging in search.[4] Learning about product characteristics, financing arrangements, and the opinions of other consumers are a few of the many benefits that may be obtained from search.[5] Costs involved in search may include time, travel, parking, psychological frustrations, time away from more pleasurable pursuits, and so on.[6] Variables that affect the consumer's perceptions of the value and cost of search are discussed below.

Perceived Value of External Search

Amount of Stored Information   The amount of stored information is a function of both the length and breadth of experience. The greater the length of time that brands comprising the generic product have been purchased, the lower

---

[2] For an example of a more elaborate model of search, see Robert F. Kelly, "The Search Component of the Consumer Decision Process—A Theoretic Examination," in Robert L. King (ed.), *Marketing and the New Science of Planning* (Chicago: Amer. Marketing Assoc., 1968), pp. 273–279.

[3] George Katona, *Psychological Analysis of Economic Behavior* (New York: McGraw-Hill, 1951), p. 47.

[4] See, for example, Louis P. Bucklin, "Retail Strategy and the Classification of Consumer Goods," *J. Marketing*, vol. 27, pp. 50–54 (January 1963); Richard H. Holton, "The Distinction between Convenience Goods, Shopping Goods, and Speciality Goods," *J. Marketing*, vol. 69, pp. 213–225 (June 1961); Louis P. Bucklin, "Testing Propensities to Shop," *J. Marketing*, vol. 30, pp. 22–27 (Jan. 1966); Donald F. Cox, "The Audience as Communicators," in Stephen Greyser (ed.), *Toward Scientific Marketing* (Chicago: Amer. Marketing Assoc., 1963), pp. 58–72; Donald H. Granbois, "The Role of Communication in the Family Decision Making Process," in Greyser, pp. 44–57; John U. Farley, " 'Brand Loyalty' and the Economics of Information," *J. Business*, vol. 37, pp. 370–381 (Oct. 1964).

[5] See, for example, Davidson W. Phillips, "On the Effects of Communication," *Public Opinion Quart.*, vol. 3, pp. 343–360 (1959).

[6] Wesley C. Bender, "Consumer Purchase Costs—Do Retailers Recognize Them?" *J. Retailing*, pp. 1–8 (Spring 1964).

the propensity to search.[7] Similarly, the greater the number of brands of the generic product that have been purchased, the lower the propensity to search.[8] Thus, whether external search will occur, as well as the extent of search, vary inversely with the length and breadth of experience.[9]

Appropriateness of Stored Information Although the consumer may have a considerable amount of stored information, it may not be considered germane. The variables that affect the relevance of stored information and their effect on external search are discussed below.

(1) *Satisfaction.* The greater the satisfaction with the results of past purchases, the lower the probability that external search will occur in the future when the same problem is recognized.[10]

(2) *Interpurchase Time.* The amount of time that elapses between purchases affects the appropriateness of stored information. The greater the interpurchase time, the higher the probability that external search will occur.[11]

(3) *Changes in the Mix of Alternatives.* The appropriateness of stored information is also affected by the rate of price and style changes as well as by the frequency of new product introductions. The greater the rate of change of these variables, the higher the probability that external search will occur.[12]

Ability to Recall Stored Information Both the amount and appropriateness of stored information are of little consequence if the consumer cannot recall the results of the experience. The variables affecting consumers' ability to recall stored information and their impact on external search are discussed below.

(1) **Problem Similarity** The ability to recall stored information depends in part on the degree to which the underlying problem is perceived to be similar to problems that have arisen in the past. The greater the degree to which the problem is perceived to be similar to one previously experienced and satisfactorily solved, the lower the probability that external search will occur.[13]

---

[7] George Katona, *The Mass Consumption Society* (New York: McGraw-Hill, 1964), pp. 289–290.

[8] Katona, *op. cit.,*[7] pp. 289–290.

[9] Paul E. Green, Michael Halbert, and J. Sayer Minas, "An Experiment in Information Buying," *J. Advertising Research,* vol. 4, pp. 17–23 (Sept. 1964); also G. David Hughes, Seha M. Tinic, and Philippe A. Naert, "Analyzing Consumer Information Processing," in Philip R. McDonald (ed.), *Marketing Involvement in Society and the Economy* (Chicago: Amer. Marketing Assoc., 1969), pp. 235–240.

[10] Katona, *op. cit.,*[7] pp. 289–290; Peter D. Bennett and Robert Mandell, "Prepurchase Information Seeking Behavior of New Car Purchasers—The Learning Hypothesis," *J. Marketing Research,* vol. 6, pp. 430–433 (Nov. 1969).

[11] Katona, *op. cit.,*[7] pp. 289–290.

[12] George Katona, *Psychological Analysis of Economic Behavior* (New York: McGraw-Hill, 1951), pp. 67–68.

[13] Katona, *op. cit.,*[7] pp. 289–290; Frederick E. May, "Adaptive Behavior in Automobile Brand Choices," *J. Marketing Research,* vol. 6, pp. 62–65 (Feb. 1969); John E. Swan, "Experimental Analysis of Predecision Information Seeking," *J. Marketing Research,* vol. 6, pp. 192–197 (May 1969). For more detailed relationships including some findings that contradict the above generalization, see Donald J. Hempel, "Search Behavior and Information Utilization in the Home Buying Process," in McDonald, *op. cit.,*[9] pp. 241–249.

(2) **Interpurchase Time**   The ability to recall stored information is also affected by the amount of time that has elapsed since the problem arose. As was previously stated, the greater the interpurchase time, the higher the probability that external search will occur.[14]

Perceived Risk   Consumers often discern some degree of financial, social, or physical risk in purchasing products or services. Obtaining information through external search is one way of reducing perceived risk to acceptable levels.[15] In general, the greater the degree of perceived risk, the greater the propensity to search.[16] The specific variables affecting perceived risk and their relations to both the occurrence and extent of external search are as follows.

(1)   **Financial Risk—Price**   The higher the price of a product or service, the greater the degree of perceived risk (financial consequences of making an incorrect decision). Therefore, the propensity to search externally increases as the price of the item increases.[17]

(2)   **Financial Risk—Length of Commitment**   The greater the length of time the consumer is committed to use the product or service, the more severe are the consequences of making an incorrect decision. Thus, the longer the length of commitment, the greater the probability that external search will occur and the greater the intensity of search.[18]

(3)   **Social Risk**   As has been pointed out in previous chapters, social influences commonly affect consumers' choices of specific products and services.

---

[14]   Katona, *op. cit.,*[7] pp. 289–290.

[15]   Raymond A. Bauer, "Consumer Behavior as Risk Taking," in Robert S. Hancock (ed.), *Dynamic Marketing for a Changing World* (Chicago: Amer. Marketing Assoc., 1960), pp. 389–398.

[16]   Paul E. Green, "Consumer Use of Information," in Joseph Newman (ed.), *On Knowing the Consumer* (New York: Wiley, 1966), pp. 67–80; Scott M. Cunningham, "Perceived Risk as a Factor in Product Oriented Word of Mouth Behavior: A First Step," in L. George Smith (ed.), *Reflections on Progress in Marketing* (Chicago: Amer. Marketing Assoc., 1964), pp. 229–238; Scott M. Cunningham, "Perceived Risk as a Factor in the Diffusion of New Product Information," in Raymond M. Haas (ed.), *Science Technology and Marketing* (Chicago: Amer. Marketing Assoc., 1966), pp. 698–721.

[17]   William P. Dommermuth, "The Shopping Matrix and Marketing Strategy," *J. Marketing Research,* vol. 2, pp. 128–132 (May 1965); George Katona and Eva Mueller, "A Study of Purchasing Decisions," in Lincoln H. Clark (ed.), *Consumer Behavior: The Dynamics of Consumer Reaction* (New York: New York University Press, 1955), pp. 30–87, at p. 46; Henry Towery, "A Study of the Buying Behavior of Mobile Home Purchasers," *Southern J. Business,* vol. 5, pp. 66–74; (July 1970). For an exception, see Ruby T. Norris, "Processes and Objectives in Home Purchasing in the New London Area," in Clark, pp. 25–29.

[18]   Katona and Mueller, *op. cit.,*[17] pp. 30–80; Donald H. Granbois, "A Study of the Family Decision Making Process in the Purchase of Major Household Durable Goods," unpublished doctoral dissertation (Bloomington, Ind.: Indiana University Graduate School of Business, 1962).

Hence, there is often some degree of social risk, and, particularly, the greater the "visibility"[19] of the product, the greater the intensity of external search.[20]

(4) **Physiological Risk** The consumption or use of some products and services may produce harmful or undesirable physiological effects. The greater the degree of physiological risk, the greater the intensity of external search.[21]

(5) **Number of Decisions Required** Some purchases require multiple decisions on such things as brand, color, size, style, and so on. The more decisions required in making a single purchase, the greater the degree of perceived risk. Therefore, the intensity of external search increases as the number of separate decisions required to make a single purchase increases.[22]

(6) **Risk Styles and Strategies** Several researchers have suggested that some consumers have risk styles and strategies that they use to reduce risk. Cox has suggested two styles: "clarifiers" and "simplifiers." The former, when confronted with ambiguity, seek additional information in order to better understand the context in which a decision must be made. Simplifiers, faced with the same degree of ambiguity, keep out or selectively reject incongruous information, thus simplifying the context within which a decision must be made.[23] Bauer has suggested several specific types of risk-reducing strategies: (1) buying only a certain brand, (2) buying only nationally advertised brands, (3) buying only the cheapest brand, (4) buying only the most expensive brand, (5) buying only a certain amount of the product, or (6) buying only products with a plain and sensible design.[24] In those purchase situations where risk-reducing strategies are used, the probability of external search occurring is greater if existing risk-reducing strategies are perceived to be inappropriate.

---

[19] "Visibility" means that (1) the product must be seen and identified by others and (2) the product must stand out and be noticed. See *Group Influence in Marketing and Public Relations* (Ann Arbor, Mich.: Foundation for Research on Human Behavior, 1956).

[20] Katona, *op. cit.,*[7] pp. 289–290.

[21] See, for example, James F. Engel, David A. Knapp, and Deanne E. Knapp, "Sources of Influence in the Acceptance of New Products for Self-Medication: Preliminary Findings," in Haas, *op. cit.,*[16] pp. 776–782. This relation can also be inferred from Sidney P. Feldman and Merlin C. Spencer, "The Effect of Personal Influence in the Selection of Consumer Services," in Peter D. Bennett (ed.), *Marketing and Economic Development* (Chicago: Amer. Marketing Assoc., 1965), pp. 440–452.

[22] Donald F. Cox and Stewart Rich, "Perceived Risk and Consumer Decision-Making—A Case of Telephone Shopping," *J. Marketing Research*, vol. 1, pp. 32–39 (Nov. 1964); Dommermuth, *op. cit.,*[17] p. 130.

[23] Donald F. Cox, "The Influence of Cognitive Needs and Styles on Information Handling in Making Product Evaluations," in D. F. Cox (ed.), *Risk Taking and Information Handling in Consumer Behavior* (Boston: Division of Research, Graduate School of Business, Harvard University, 1967), pp. 370–393. For related research, see Jeffrey A. Barach, "Advertising Effectiveness and Risk in the Consumer Decision Process," *J. Marketing Research*, vol. 6, pp. 314–320 (Aug. 1969).

[24] Bauer, *op. cit.,*[15] p. 390.

Perceived Cost of External Search

A number of different types of costs may be involved in obtaining information through external search. An awareness of these costs is necessary in order to understand fully the nature of external search.

Decision Delay Engaging in external search obviously increases the length of time that the consumer has to forego the satisfactions that may be derived from using or consuming the product or service. Several studies have demonstrated that the valuation of information depends in part on how long a decision is delayed, pending the receipt of new information.[25] The greater the perceived decision delay, the lower the intensity of external search.

Time Some forms of search, particularly visits to retail outlets, require the consumer to spend considerable amounts of time. The greater the importance of time to the consumer, the lower the intensity of external search.

Money Several types of external search involve the expenditure of money. Search involving visits to dealers, for example, requires an outlay of funds for travel and perhaps parking. The expenditure of money for travel and parking lowers the value of the information obtained. Hence, the greater the importance of money to the consumer, the lower the intensity of external search.

Psychological Costs Search involving dealer visits may also involve certain psychological costs. The consumer may experience frustration, depression, tension, and annoyance for several reasons, including fighting traffic, finding a place to park, waiting to be waited on, and dealing with incompetent sales personnel.[26] Since these costs are likely to lower the value of information-gathering efforts, the greater the psychological costs perceived to be involved, the lower the intensity of external search.

Other Determinants of External Search and Alternative Evaluation

Several additional consumer characteristics influence the cost and/or value of external search and hence affect the intensity of the behavior. These determinants include (1) motives, (2) personality characteristics, (3) family role structures, (4) social class and position, and (5) certain economic and demographic characteristics.

---

[25] John T. Lanzetta and Vera Kanareff, "Information Cost, Amount of Payoff and Level of Aspiration as Determinants of Information Seeking in Decision Making," *Behavioral Science*, vol. 7, pp. 459–473 (1962); Green, *op. cit.,*[16] p. 75, Green, *et al., op. cit.,*[9] p. 23.

[26] For a discussion of these and other costs, see Anthony Downs, "A Theory of Consumer Efficiency," *J. Retailing*, pp. 6–12 (Spring 1961); Bender, *op. cit.,*[6] pp. 1–8.

Motives   Several motives or needs affect external search. For example,[27]

(1)   The greater the urgency of the need, the lower the intensity of external search.

(2)   The greater the need for variety, the greater the intensity of external search.

Personality Characteristics   Several studies have demonstrated that certain personality characteristics are associated with external search.[28] To illustrate:

(1)   Consumers who are information sensitive tend to have a higher confidence in the degree of control that they have over their environment, while consumers who are not information sensitive tend to exhibit the characteristic of fatalism with regard to the future and lack of control over their environment.[29]

(2)   Consumers having a closed mind tend to be less information sensitive than open-minded consumers.[30]

(3)   The greater the "dependence" of the consumer, the lower his sensitivity to information.[31]

(4)   Personality traits measured by the Allport–Vernon–Lindzey study of values test and the Gordon personal profile test do not discriminate between consumers who are and are not information sensitive.[32]

Family Role Structure   Although all wives engage in a large number of activities, certain of these roles are more important to some women than they are to others. There is some evidence that when the female perceives her chief roles as relating to major physical tasks of operating the household, her external search activity will be at maximum levels. Bucklin's study of search in the context of food purchasing illustrates this type of relationship: [33]

(1)   "Liberal" women—those interested in politics and uninterested in household chores—have a lower propensity to search than other types of women.

(2)   The "traditionalist"—women who base their cooking and meal choice upon what their parents had done—has a low tendency to search.

---

27   Katona and Mueller, *op. cit.,*[17] pp. 30–87.

28   See, for example, George Fisk, "Media Influence Reconsidered," *Public Opinion Quart.,* vol. 23, pp. 83–91 (1959).

29   Green, *op. cit.,*[16] p. 76.

30   Green, *op. cit.,*[16] p. 76; Gerald D. Bell, "Developments in Behavioral Study of Consumer Action," in Smith, *op. cit.,*[16] pp. 272–282.

31   Orville Brim, David C. Glass, David E. Lavin, and Norman Goodman, *Personality and Decision Processes* (Stanford, Calif: Stanford University Press, 1962), p. 122.

32   Green, *op. cit.,*[16] p. 76.

33   Louis P. Bucklin, "Consumer Search, Role Enactment, and Market Efficiency," *J. Business,* vol. 42, pp. 416–438 (Oct. 1969).

(3) The "mother"—women strongly concerned with the welfare of their children and with being a sexual companion to their husband—has the strongest tendency to engage in external search.

There is also evidence that the type of role structure involved in purchasing affects the extent of external search. Studies indicate that the degree of external search is lower among families in which the decision-making function is performed by one partner than it is in families having joint role structures.[34]

Social Class and Position Research efforts have also found that differences in external search activity are related to social class and social position.[35] Bucklin has shown how these variables are related to food purchasing:[36]

(1) "Transient" households—those living in temporary, rented quarters, dissatisfied with their state and expecting to leave in the not-too-distant future—tend to withdraw from search activity.
(2) "Aging, bleak future" households—those who are older and perceive their current social and economic position to be worse than it has been and see the future as even more forbidding—have the strongest tendency to engage in external search.
(3) Higher social standing households have a lower tendency to search.[37]

Economic and Demographic Characteristics External search and alternative evaluation is often associated with several economic and demographic characteristics of households. For example, some studies indicate that the intensity of search is likely to be greater when[38]

(1) The consumer is under 35 years of age.
(2) The consumer is in the middle-income category rather than higher low-income categories.
(3) The consumer has more than a high-school education.

Evaluation

Several additional comments need to be made about the effect of determinants of external search and alternative evaluation. First, the effect of these

---

[34] Granbois, *op. cit.*,[18] p. 104.

[35] See, for example, Gregory P. Stone, "City Shoppers and Urban Identification: Observations on the Social Psychology of City Life," *Amer. J. Sociology*, vol. 60, pp. 38–39 (1954); Pierre Martineau, "Social Classes and Spending Behavior," *J. Marketing*, vol. 23, pp. 121–130 (Oct. 1958).

[36] Bucklin, *op. cit.*,[33] pp. 416–438.

[37] This relationship does not always hold. See, for example, Joseph N. Fry and Frederick H. Siller, "A Comparison of Housewife Decision Making in Two Social Classes," *J. Marketing Research*, vol. 7, pp. 333–337 (Aug. 1970).

[38] Katona and Mueller, *op. cit.*,[17] pp. 30–87; Hempel, *op. cit.*,[13] pp. 241–249.

variables is probable rather than certain. Studies typically find that consumers vary considerably in the extent of search behavior and that the determinants discussed above have varying degrees of influence on the propensity to search.[39]

Second, the *ceteris paribus*, or all other things being equal, assumption has of necessity been used in presenting the determinants. Unfortunately, few studies have investigated combinations of variables, even when the data permit this type of analysis.

Bucklin's investigation of search in food purchasing appears to be one of the few attempts to investigate the impact of combinations of variables on external search behavior. Using multiple correlation analysis he found that five variables—liberal woman, travel range, lack of spending money as a child, wage earner (woman), and wealth—accounted for 24 percent of the variance in a composite measure of food-store shopping. Seven variables—liberal woman, traditionalist, epicure, community activist, submissive wife, infrequent newspaper reading, and wage earner—accounted for 59 percent of the variance in advertising interest. A score designating advertising interest was derived from high factor analysis loadings on checking advertisements for food, the proportion of weeks in which the shopper scanned at least one advertisement for food, plus respondents' statements concerning the extent of their intentions to examine newspapers for price specials and to look for ads on specials at stores they normally did not patronize.[40]

It appears that future research efforts should follow Bucklin's strategy of investigating the relative importance of search determinants, including combinations of determinants. After studies have been conducted across a range of product categories, it may be possible to present reasonably defensible statements concerning the determinants of search. At the present time, the probabilistic nature of the determinants suggests that marketers cannot rely on the results of generalized research in determining the intensity of search that precedes the purchase of their product.

Finally, the analysis of the determinants of search has public policy implications. Some officials apparently feel that consumers should engage in exhaustive search before making a purchase decision. This point of view overlooks the facts that the consumer often incurs considerable costs in doing so and that the results obtained often have limited value to the consumer because of his past experience and/or the limited degree of risk that is involved in the purchase. Thus, to condemn consumers because they do not search or do not search enough (from the public officials' point of view) is to say that search is desirable per se, which is regrettably naive and a questionable basis for public policy.

---

[39] See, for example, Granbois, *op. cit.*,[4] p. 46; Katona and Mueller, *op. cit.*,[17] pp. 30–87; Engel *et al.*, *op. cit.*,[21] pp. 776–782.

[40] Bucklin, *op. cit.*,[33] pp. 416–438.

THE MASS MEDIA AS AN INFORMATION SOURCE

If external search and alternative evaluation occurs, what sources of information are consulted? This section discusses how consumers obtain information from the mass media. Additional information sources are discussed in the following two chapters.

The Mass Media

Given the near ubiquitousness of the mass media, it is not surprising that this information source is often consulted in purchasing decisions. Some mass media often serve as a type of reference group for some consumers. For example, *Better Homes and Gardens* and other magazines in the so-called shelter group are widely used sources of information about certain norms and trends in home furnishing and decorating.[41] *Mademoiselle, Charm, Esquire, Playboy,* and other magazines sometimes relay information on clothing norms and trends.

Certain mass media personnel and entertainers are often used as an information source, apparently because of their reputations for impartiality and knowledge. Arthur Godfrey, Johnny Carson, and certain newspaper and magazine columnists are examples. It should be noted, however, that the role and influence of these types of people, particularly celebrities, is considerably more complex than many people believe. Research has shown, for example, that the influence of celebrities varies considerably by product. While a male movie star's opinion may be very important in the case of liquor, it is often relatively ineffective in the case of cigarettes.[42] Similarly, a female celebrity may influence a consumer's choice of an evening dress, but she probably exerts little influence on the choice of many household cleaning products. Thus, the influence of mass media personnel and entertainers varies by product, depending, in part, on consumers' attitudes about the competence and ability of the entertainer to give advice about the product in question.

Mass Media Patterns

Recently, studies have found that television programs and magazines form clusters according to frequency of viewing and readership. Thus consumers often obtain information from certain groups of mass media. Illustrative findings are discussed below.

---

[41] *Better Homes and Gardens Impact and Action* (Des Moines, Iowa: Research Division, Meredith Publ. Co., 1964).

[42] *Building Reliability into Communications* (New York: Interpublic Group of Companies, 1966).

Daytime Television Using factor analysis, Banks found interesting patterns of viewing daytime TV by women during the month of December, 1965. Specifically, he found that certain consumers watch groups of programs. One group consists of "Search for Tomorrow," "Guiding Light," "Love of Life," "As the World Turns," "Secret Storm," and "Edge of Night." These were all daytime serial dramas that appeared in the afternoon on CBS.

Another group includes "General Hospital," "A Time for Us," "The Young Marrieds," and "The Nurses." This was the ABC afternoon lineup from 2:00 to 4:00 P.M.

Still another group consists of "Another World," "The Doctors," and "Moment of Truth." These ran from 2:00 to 3:30 P.M. on NBC. Banks found eleven additional groups of programs.[43]

Nighttime Television Using the same data and statistical technique, Swanson found that certain consumers watch groups of nighttime television programs. Twenty frequency patterns accounted for 53 percent of the variance in watching the 108 nighttime programs.

One pattern accounting for 12 percent of the total variance consists of "Donna Reed," "Patty Duke," Ozzie & Harriet," "My Three Sons," "Farmer's Daughter," "Flintstones," "Addams Family," "Shindig," "Bewitched," "Johnny Quest." Each program is a light comedy drama in a family situation.

Another group, accounting for seven percent of the total variance, includes "To Tell the Truth," "I've Got a Secret," "Password," "Perry Mason," "What's My Line," and "Andy Griffith." This pattern is dominated by panel programs. Swanson found eighteen other groups of programs.[44]

Magazines Wells, Banks, and Tigert have found that magazine readership also breaks into groups. One group consists of *House Beautiful, House and Garden, Better Homes and Gardens,* and *American Home.* Another includes *True Story, True Confessions,* and *Modern Romances. Harpers* and *Atlantic Monthly* form another group. *Life, Look,* and *Saturday Evening Post* go together as do *Newsweek* and *U.S. News and World Report.*[45]

Psychographic Profiles of Mass Media Clusters

Heavy readers or viewers of mass media groups often have interesting distinguishing characteristics. For example, Tigert has shown that readers of a set of business and news magazines—*Fortune, Time, Forbes,* and *Business Week*

[43] Seymour Banks, "Patterns of Daytime Viewing Behavior" in M. S. Moyer and R. E. Vosburgh (eds.), *Marketing for Tomorrow . . . Today* (Chicago: Amer. Marketing Assoc., 1967), pp. 139–142.

[44] Charles E. Swanson, "Patterns of Nighttime Television Viewing," in Moyer and Vosburgh, *op. cit.,*[43] pp. 143–147.

[45] William D. Wells, Seymour Banks, and Douglas Tigert, "Order in the Data," in Reed Moyer (ed.), *Changing Marketing Systems* (Chicago: Amer. Marketing Assoc., 1967), pp. 263–266.

—have a strong psychographic profile. They tend to be more liberal and self-confident than others. They are pro credit and like drinking and the arts. They are optimistic about the future and are willing to take risks. They also play an active role in the community.[46]

Tigert has also identified psychographic profiles of viewers of sets of television programs. For example, using a national sample of Canadians he found that viewers of talk shows—Johnny Carson and Merv Griffith— have the following characteristics:[47]

(1) A strong interest in new products.

(2) An inclination to transmit information and to seek out information about new products.

(3) A need for excitement in their lives; more outgoing and sociable.

(4) A strong interest in fashion and personal appearance.

(5) Pride in and care of the home; but not a fanatical concern with dirt and germs.

(6) A commitment to television and in particular to United States shows.

(7) A dissatisfaction with their life, in spite of this need for excitement.

Psychographic Profiles of Mass Media Vehicles

While factor analyzing mass media into groups produces some interesting patterns, and the groups have differing psychographic profiles, the procedure sometimes covers up useful insights. Constructing psychographic profiles of *individual* mass media vehicles often produces more vivid portraits of users of the information source.

Even vehicles that offer the same basic content and appear to be used by similar types of consumers often have dramatically different profiles. Consider the differences between *Time* only and *Newsweek* only readers.

Time only readers are younger and upscale socioeconomically from the *Newsweek* only readers. *Newsweek* readers are more conservative, more concerned about health, tend to get their main entertainment from television, yet have strong negative attitudes toward advertising. *Newsweek* only readers also complain more about the quality of merchandise and are more price conscious. They tend to use less credit and more cash and are less optimistic about the future than *Time* only readers. They like beer, camping, hunting and working outdoors. Husbands spend more time with their wives and children.

A higher proportion of *Time* only readers expect to be executives in the future. They also take more pride in their jobs and agree more than *Newsweek*

---

[46] Douglas J. Tigert, "A Psychographic Profile of Magazine Audiences: An Investigation of a Media's Climate," paper presented at the Amer. Marketing Association Consumer Workshop, Ohio State University (Aug. 22–24, 1969).

[47] Douglas J. Tigert, "Are Television Audiences Really Different?" paper presented at the American Marketing Association, San Francisco, Calif. (Apr. 12–15, 1971).

readers that they have a lot of personal ability. *Time* readers are more optimistic about their future achievements and exhibit a greater interest in travel abroad.[48]

Different *types* of vehicles often have even greater differences in their psychographic profiles. For example, *Reader's Digest* readers have radically different views of the world compared to *Playboy* readers:[49]

Psychographic Variable	Percent Who Definitely Agree Among	
	Heavy Playboy Readers	Heavy Reader's Digest Readers
My greatest achievements are still ahead of me	50	26
I go to church regularly	18	40
Movies should be censored	14	40
Most men would cheat on their wives if the right opportunity came along	27	12

Composite Portraits

Thus far we have seen that consumers have distinct patterns of media usage and that different groups of media as well as individual media vehicles have varying demographic and psychographic profiles, that is, different segments of consumers use different media as sources of information.

The choice of media is also affected by the type of consumption decision. By relating product usage, media usage, demographic variables and psychographic variables, it is possible to construct a portrait of the user of a particular product. The following example illustrates this type of analysis.

The Swinging Eye Makeup User[50]   Eye makeup users tend to be young and well educated and to live in metropolitan areas. Usage rates are much higher for working wives than for full-time homemakers, and substantially higher in the west than in other parts of the country.

The user of eye makeup is also a heavy user of other cosmetics—liquid face makeup base, lipstick, hair spray, perfume, and nail polish, for example. She is also an above-average cigarette smoker and an above-average user of gasoline and the long distance telephone.

Eye makeup users have distinct media usage patterns. On television, she likes the movies and the Tonight Show. She does not like panel programs or westerns. She reads fashion magazines, news magazines, and *Life* and *Look*. She does not read *True Confessions* or *Successful Farming*.

---

[48]   Tigert, *op. cit.*[46]

[49]   Tigert, *op. cit.*[46]

[50]   William D. Wells and Douglas J. Tigert, "Activities, Interests and Opinions," *J. Advertising Research*, vol. 4, pp. 27–35 (Aug. 1971).

Compared with the nonuser of eye makeup, the user is much more interested in fashion. Being attractive to others and especially to men is an important aspect of her self-image. She is very meticulous about her hair, face, skin, and teeth. She likes traveling, art, ballet, and parties and is not a homebody. Her reaction to her home is style conscious rather than utilitarian; she does not like grocery shopping or housework but likes to serve unusual dinners. She accepts contemporary ideas and rejects many traditional views.[51]

As illustrated in Chapter 18, this type of analysis is useful in selecting advertising media and vehicles, designing advertisements, and developing new products.

MARKETER-DOMINATED SOURCES OF INFORMATION

Consumers can obtain information from marketer-dominated sources as well as from the mass media. Advertisements and visits to retail outlets are the major marketer-dominated sources of information.

Advertisements

As a general rule, once consumers recognize a problem they become more receptive to advertising.[52] Advertisements perform the role of providing information about available brands and where they can be purchased. The consumer may use advertisements to learn about such product attributes as price and features, to compare various brands on the basis of these attributes, to visualize the product in use, to learn about possible financing arrangements, and so on.

The extent to which consumers use advertisements as a source of information unfortunately defies simple generalizations. The following are illustrative findings:

(1) Of those consumers who purchased major durable goods, 21 percent said they obtained information from reading advertisements and circulars.[53]

(2) Of those consumers purchasing small electrical appliances, 25 percent read newspaper advertisements, 15 percent read magazine advertise-

---

[51] Another example of this type of analysis can be found in F. M. Bass, E. A. Pessemier, and D. J. Tigert, "A Taxonomy of Magazine Readership Applied to Problems in Marketing Strategy and Media Selection," *J. Business,* vol. 42, pp. 337–363 (July 1969).

[52] See, for example, Robert W. Pratt, Jr., "Understanding the Decision Process for Consumer Durable Goods: An Example of the Application of Longitudinal Analysis," in Bennett, *op. cit.,*[21] pp. 244–260. Although this point of view is apparently rather widely held, there are some exceptions. One study, for example, found that the readership of newspaper advertisements is not explainable to any strong degree by the reader's disposition to purchase the advertised product. See Stewart Smith, Edwin Parker, and John Davenport, "Advertising Readership and Buying Plans," *J. Advertising Research,* vol. 3, pp. 25–29 (June 1963).

[53] Katona and Mueller, *op. cit.,*[17] p. 46.

ments, 14 percent saw television advertisements, and 7 percent heard advertisements on the radio.[54]

(3)   Of those consumers purchasing sport shirts, 4 percent said they obtained information from reading advertisements and circulars.[55]

(4)   Of those consumers purchasing food products, between 19 and 26 percent said they obtained information from advertisements.[56] (Nineteen percent was obtained by unaided recall, while aided recall produced the 26-percent figure.)

The above findings, as well as others that could be cited,[57] indicate that the use of advertisements varies considerably among products. In addition, studies typically find that the use of advertisements varies considerably among consumers.[58] Although there are probably many factors accounting for this variation, to date empirical studies have isolated only the effect of education. The relation appears uncertain because it varies from one study to another.[59] Future research efforts need to determine those factors that account for interconsumer variation in the use of advertising.

Visits to Retail Outlets

Consumers may also obtain information by shopping in retail outlets. Although this may be a relatively expensive method of search, it is often used to obtain information concerning price, quality, performance, style, appearance, other product features, and/or conditions of sale.

The intensity of this type of information seeking is rather surprising. The following are illustrative findings:

(1)   Of those consumers purchasing major durable goods, 47 percent visited only the store in which the item was purchased. About 15 percent visited two or three stores, and 26 percent visited more than three stores[60]

(2)   Of those consumers purchasing small electrical appliances, 60 percent shopped only in the store where the purchase was made, 16 percent

---

[54]   Jon G. Udell, "Prepurchase Behavior of Buyers of Small Electrical Appliances," *J. Marketing*, vol. 30, pp. 50–52, at p. 51 (Oct. 1966).

[55]   Katona and Mueller, *op. cit.*,[17] p. 46.

[56]   Fisk, *op. cit.*,[28] pp. 83–91.

[57]   See, for example, Elihu Katz and Paul F. Lazarsfeld, *Personal Influence* (New York: Free Press, 1955), chap. 5; Hugh W. Sargent, *Consumer Product Rating Publications and Buying Behavior* (Urbana, Ill.: Bureau of Economic and Business Research, University of Illinois, 1959), p. 41; K. L. Atkin, "Advertising and Store Patronage," *J. Advertising Research*, vol. 2, pp. 18–23 (Dec. 1962); Engel *et al.*, *op. cit.*,[21] p. 782; George H. Haines, Jr., "A Study of Why People Purchase New Products," in Haas, *op. cit.*,[16] pp. 665–685.

[58]   Granbois, *op. cit.*,[4] p. 46; Hempel, *op. cit.*,[13] p. 248.

[59]   Compare, for example, Katona and Mueller, *op. cit.*,[17] p. 57; and Hempel, *op. cit.*,[13] p. 248.

[60]   Katona and Mueller, *op. cit.*,[17] pp. 45–46.

shopped in the store of purchase and one additional store, and 22 percent shopped in three or more stores.[61]

(3) Another study of electrical appliances found that the percentages of purchasers shopping in only one retail outlet were as follows: for refrigerators, 42.4 percent; for television sets, 58.3 percent; for washing machines, 62.4 percent; for vacuum cleaners, 79.4 percent; for electric irons, 82.4 percent.[62]

(4) Of those consumers purchasing sport shirts, 70 percent visited only the store in which the item was purchased, 7 percent visited two or three stores, and 18 percent visited more than three stores.[63]

These and other studies[64] indicate that (1) the majority of consumers typically do not visit more than one retail outlet for purposes of obtaining information, (2) the number of stores that consumers visit varies considerably from product to product, and (3) consumers differ considerably in the number of stores that they visit. Few studies have attempted to ascertain why the extent of shopping varies by product and consumer. The studies that have been conducted generally support the cost-value hypothesis for search. For example, in general, the higher the price of a product, the greater the tendency to shop in more retail outlets.[65]

Since both length of commitment to the problem solution and interpurchase time are positively related to price, a derivative generalization is: the longer the length of commitment and/or the interpurchase time, the greater the probability that the consumer will shop in more than one retail outlet. The amount of stored information also affects the number of stores shopped. The relation is curvilinear; consumers having extensive and little stored information shop less intensively than consumers having some medium amount of stored information.[66] This finding is not inconsistent with the hypothesis since consumers having little information tended to have higher incomes; hence the opportunity cost of visiting stores may have been greater than for other consumers.[67] This fact reemphasizes the need to consider the cost as well as the value of search in attempting to explain differential patterns of information-seeking behavior.

Thus far only the number of different stores visited has been considered. Another dimension of the use of store visits as a source of information is the

---

61 Udell, *op. cit.,*[54] p. 52.

62 Dommermuth, *op. cit.,*[17] p. 130.

63 Katona and Mueller, *op. cit.,*[17] pp. 45–46.

64 See, for example, Alderson and Sessions, "Basic Research on Consumer Behavior: Report on a Study of Shopping Behavior and Methods for Its Investigation," in R. E. Frank, A. A. Kuehn, and W. F. Massey (eds.), *Quantitative Techniques in Marketing Analysis* (Homewood, Ill.: Irwin, 1962), pp. 129–145; Ross M. Cunningham, "Customer Loyalty to Store and Brand," *Harvard Business Rev.,* vol. 39, pp. 116–128 (Jan.–Feb. 1956); R. S. Tate, "The Supermarket Battle for Store Loyalty," *J. Marketing,* vol. 25, pp. 8–13 (Oct. 1961).

65 Dommermuth, *op. cit.,*[17] p. 130; Udell, *op. cit.,*[54] p. 52; Bucklin, *op. cit.,*[4] p. 25.

66 Bucklin, *op. cit.,*[4] p. 25.

67 Bucklin, *op. cit.,*[4] p. 25.

number of different times the consumer shops at the same store before making a purchase. Unfortunately the evidence on this aspect of information seeking is limited. A study of small electrical appliances found that 77 percent of the purchasers had visited the store of purchase only once, 19 percent made two visits, and 4 percent made three or more trips. Moreover, the probability of multiple trips to the same store decreased if the shopper's family income was below $5,000 or above $10,000 or if the shopper was over 50 years of age. On the other hand, the probability of multiple trips increased as the value of the item increased.[68] This differential pattern of multiple trips to the same store can also be explained by the cost-value hypothesis for search. Consumers earning under $5,000 and over 50 years of age apparently experience high explicit costs of search (transportation, parking, baby sitting) and perhaps do not fully realize the values to be gained by search. Consumers earning over $10,000 apparently feel that the opportunity cost of search when compared with the price of the item relative to their income does not justify an extended search effort.

It should be pointed out that the fact that consumers have a tendency to visit few retail outlets does not mean that retail visits are not an important source of information. Consumers can obtain much information from examining the product, perhaps observing it in use, looking at point-of-purchase displays, and, in some instances, talking with salesmen and other customers.[69] Indeed, if the store visited has a broad assortment, or if the consumer perceives other stores to have essentially similar assortments and terms of sale, visiting one retail outlet may enable the consumer to obtain almost all the information that it is possible to obtain via store visits.

SUMMARY

Search and alternative evaluation refers to the processes and activities whereby consumers use internal and external sources of information to learn about the number of alternative solutions to the perceived problem, the characteristics and attributes of these alternatives, and their relative desirability. In many purchase situations, consumers use information stored in memory in the central control unit rather than consulting external sources.

Whether external search will occur and the extent to which it occurs depend on consumers' perceptions of the cost and value involved in search. Variables and/or conditions affecting the value of search include (1) the amount of stored information, (2) the appropriateness of stored information, (3) the ability to recall stored information, and (4) the type and degree of risk perceived to be

---

68   Udell, *op. cit.*,[54] p. 52.

69   For illustrative studies of the importance of specific types of in-store sources of information the reader is referred to Risk, *op. cit.*,[28] p. 85; *Awareness, Decision, Purchase* (New York: Point-of-Purchase Advertising Institute, 1961); Ronald P. Willett and Allan L. Pennington, "Customer and Salesman: The Anatomy of Choice and Influence in a Retail Setting," in Haas, *op. cit.*,[16] pp. 598–617; David T. Kollat, "A Study of Unplanned Purchasing in Self-Service Food Supermarkets," unpublished doctoral dissertation (Bloomington, Ind.: Graduate School of Business, Indiana University, 1966), pp. 153–161.

involved in the purchase situation. Costs involved in external search include time, money, psychological discomforts involved in shopping, and the satisfaction foregone by delaying the purchase of the product. Finally, certain motives, personality characteristics, role structures, and economic and demographic characteristics influence the propensity to search.

When external search does occur, consumers use various sources to obtain the information desired about alternative products and brands. This chapter discussed the use of mass media and marketer-dominated sources—advertisements and dealer visits. The following chapter considers personal information sources while Chapter 18 shows how this stage in the decision-making process can be used to formulate marketing strategy and tactics.

REVIEW AND DISCUSSION QUESTIONS

1. Define or otherwise describe the relevance of the following concepts: (a) external search, (b) interpurchase time, (c) physiological risk, (d) psychological costs, (e) changes in the mix of alternatives.

2. A product has a long interpurchase time, a low amount of social risk, a high degree of financial risk. Will external search occur? Discuss.

3. What are the consequences of external search?

4. "The majority of purchases that a consumer makes are not preceded by external search." Why?

5. "Since consumers typically visit only one store before purchasing a product, store visits are not an important information source." Evaluate.

6. Define or otherwise describe the media pattern phenomenon.

7. Is it more useful to construct psychographic profiles of mass media clusters or individual mass media vehicles? Why?

8. Construct a media pattern of your television viewing during the past week. Compare your pattern with a typical pattern for one of your parents or friends. Prepare an essay outlining the implications of these patterns for marketing strategists.

CHAPTER 17

SEARCH AND ALTERNATIVE
EVALUATION PROCESSES:
PERSONAL SOURCES
OF INFORMATION

To what extent do consumers rely on the opinions and experiences of other individuals in making purchasing decisions? What kinds of people do consumers look to for advice? Are there generalized opinion leaders of tastemakers in America? These are the major issues that are discussed in this chapter.

INTERPERSONAL COMMUNICATIONS

Hundreds of studies have found that consumers obtain information about products and services from other people, particularly family members, friends and neighbors, and other acquaintances. This exchange of information via inter-personal channels is called *interpersonal communications*, while the effects of this behavior is termed *personal influence*. Individuals that influence the general and purchasing behavior of other people are called *opinion leaders*. This section discusses the impact and dynamics of interpersonal communication.

The Marketing Impact of
Interpersonal Communications

It is quite common for interpersonal communications to be influential in purchasing decisions. Consider the following illustrative examples:

(1) Almost 50 percent of male and female students at Florida State University discussed with their friends clothing brands, styles, retail outlets, and prices.[1]

(2) A study of the diffusion of a new food product in a married students' apartment complex revealed that exposure to favorable word of mouth was found to increase the probability of purchase, while exposure to unfavorable comments decreased the probability.[2]

(3) A large-scale study of Indianapolis housewives revealed that nearly two thirds of those interviewed told someone else about new products they had purchased or tried.[3]

(4) Another study found that the source of information most frequently consulted by durable goods buyers were friends and relatives. ". . . more than 50 percent of our buyers turned for advice to acquaintances and in most instances also looked at durable goods owned by them." Even more striking is the finding that one third of durable goods buyers bought a brand or model that they had seen at someone else's house, often the house of relatives.[4]

Other studies have found interpersonal communications to be very important in the purchase of food items, soaps, and cleansing agents, in motion picture selections, hairdo styles, makeup techniques,[5] general fashions,[6] dental products and services,[7] farming practices,[8] physicians,[9] drugs,[10] and man-made fabrics,[11] to mention just a few.

---

[1] John R. Kerr and Bruce Weale, "Collegiate Clothing Purchasing Patterns and Fashion Adoption Behavior," *Southern J. Business,* vol. 5, pp. 126–133, at p. 129 (July 1970).

[2] Johan Arndt, "Role of Product-Related Conversations in the Diffusion of a New Product," *J. Marketing Research,* vol. 4, pp. 291–295 (Aug. 1967).

[3] Charles W. King and John O. Summers, "Technology, Innovation and Consumer Decision Making," in Reed Moyer (ed.), *Consumer, Corporate and Government Interfaces* (Chicago: Amer. Marketing Assoc., 1967), pp. 63–68, at p. 66.

[4] George Katona and Eva Mueller, "A Study of Purchasing Decisions," in Lincoln H. Clark (ed.), *Consumer Behavior: The Dynamics of Consumer Reaction* (New York: New York University Press, 1955), pp. 30–87, at p. 45.

[5] Elihu Katz and Paul F. Lazarsfeld, *Personal Influence* (New York: Free Press, 1955).

[6] Charles W. King, "Fashion Adoption: A Rebuttal to the Trickle Down Theory," in Stephen A. Greyser (ed.), *Toward Scientific Marketing* (Chicago: Amer. Marketing Assoc., 1963), pp. 108–125.

[7] Alvin J. Silk, "Overlap among Self Designated Opinion Leaders: A Study of Selected Dental Products and Services," *J. Marketing Research,* vol. 3, pp. 255–259 (Aug. 1966).

[8] Elihu Katz, "The Social Itinerary of Technical Change: Two Studies in the Diffu-

A study conducted in Switzerland provides another example of the impact of personal sources of information. In February, 1965, commercial television was introduced in Switzerland. On that day a *single* 30-second television spot was aired for a new family food product (product X) which was not available in any market either at that time or previously. On each of the following four days, housewives were asked, "What new food product has been launched lately?" The percentage of housewives naming product X increased from 31.7 percent the first day to 64.6 percent the fourth day, an increase of more than 100 percent. While it should be clear that there were some unusual circumstances surrounding this experiment (the national inauguration of television), the study is probably descriptive of the outer limits of the impact of personal channels of communication.[12]

Interpersonal Communications Dyads

Although considerable research has been conducted on the importance of interpersonal communication, research on the transmitter–receiver dyad is scarce. After reviewing the literature, King and Summers concluded that although the dimensions of analyses and the methodologies used have varied between studies, the research findings are remarkably consistent:[13]

(1) *The interaction dyad appears to be relatively homogeneous across many interaction contexts.* Studies comparing the social status and age of participants in an interaction dyad indicate that people tend to exchange information with other age and social status peers.

(2) *Perceived credibility and/or expertise of the referent as an informant on a topic is an important dimension in information-seeking behavior.* Seekers search for referents "more qualified" than themselves on a topic. In contexts where expertise is not perceived available within the seekers' peer level, sources higher or lower in age and social status may be consulted.

sion of Innovation," *Human Organization*, vol. 20, pp. 70–82 (1961); E. M. Rogers and G. M. Beal, "The Importance of Personal Influence in the Adoption of Technological Changes," *Social Forces*, vol. 36, pp. 329–335 (May 1958).

⁹ Sidney P. Feldman, "Some Dyadic Relationships Associated with Consumer Choice," in Raymond M. Haas (ed.), *Science, Technology and Marketing* (Chicago: Amer. Marketing Assoc., 1966), pp. 758–776.

¹⁰ James Coleman, Elihu Katz, and Herbert Menzel, "The Diffusion of an Innovation among Physicians," *Sociometry*, pp. 253–270 (Dec. 1957); Herbert Menzel and Elihu Katz, "Social Relations and Innovation in the Medical Profession: The Epidemiology of a New Drug," *Public Opinion Quart.*, vol. 19, pp. 337–352 (Winter 1955–1956).

¹¹ George M. Beal and Everett M. Rogers, "Informational Sources in the Adoption Process of New Fabrics," *J. Home Economics*, vol. 49, pp. 630–634 (Oct. 1957).

¹² "Rare Research Opportunity in Word of Mouth Advertising" (New York: Advertising Research Foundation, 1967), p. 10.

¹³ Charles W. King and John O. Summers, "Dynamics of Interpersonal Communication: The Interaction Dyad," in Donald F. Cox (ed.), *Risk Taking and Information Handling in Consumer Behavior* (Boston: Division of Research, Graduate School of Business Administration, Harvard University, 1967), pp. 240–264, at p. 261.

(3) *The family plays an important role in interpersonal communication* in the socialization of children and in interaction within the extended family. The specific functions of family versus nonfamily interactions may be different, but this area has not been explored.

(4) *Proximity is important in facilitating interaction.* Proximity as a variable is two-dimensional, including physical proximity and social proximity. Obviously, physical proximity, for example, living in the same neighborhood, makes possible physical contact and the settings for interpersonal exchange. Physical proximity also suggests a minimum social proximity in terms of some overlap of social status, interests, life style, etc.

This brief summary of the salient characteristics of interpersonal communications dyads provides an introduction to a more detailed and rigorous discussion of the nature and dynamics of personal influence.

PERSONAL INFLUENCE

This section discusses methods of identifying opinion leaders and summarizes the major characteristics of these individuals.

Identifying Opinion Leaders

Opinion leadership refers to the degree to which an individual influences others in a given choice situation. Those who possess a disproportionately large amount of this trait are called "opinion leaders." As will soon become apparent, the term "leader" is misleading because it implies an absolute leader whom others follow. In reality, opinion leadership is a more subtle, relative phenomenon. Nevertheless, in the interests of consistency and compatability, the term "leader" will be used here.

Three basic types of techniques are used to measure opinion leadership:

(1) *The sociometric method* involves asking respondents from whom they get advice and to whom they go to seek advice or information in making a specified type of decision.[14]

(2) *The key informant method* involves the use of informed individuals in a social system to identify opinion leaders in a given situation.[15]

---

[14] For example, see Robert K. Merton, *Social Theory and Social Structure* (New York: Free Press, 1957); John G. Myers, "Patterns of Interpersonal Influence in the Adoption of New Products," in Haas, *op. cit.,*[9] pp. 750–757.

[15] See, for example, Alvaro Chaparro, "Role Expectation and Adoption of New Farm Practices," unpublished Ph.D. dissertation (University Park: Pennsylvania State University, 1955).

(3)   *The self-designating method* relies on the respondent to evaluate his own influence in a given topic area.[16]

King and Summers have studied and evaluated the advantages and disadvantages of these methods.[17] The sociometric method has face validity but it is not effective when the social system to be investigated is (1) not self-contained in terms of the flow of influence on the topic area of interest or (2) when the social system is too large to permit the interviewing of all of its members.

The key informant method is useful when the objective is to study only opinion leaders, when financial and other constraints prohibit interviewing a large number of people, and/or when the social system is small and key informants can provide accurate information on the interaction process.

Since the conditions favoring these two methods do not usually exist in marketing settings, most consumer studies use the self-designating method. This technique is a compromise between the other two methods, being simple to administer in survey research and not limited to small, self-contained social systems where a census is required.

The number of questions used in the self-designating method range from one to seven. Evidence to date indicates that longer scales have greater validity and reliability than methods involving fewer questions.[18] King and Summers have used a seven-question scale in their research. A copy of their questionnaire is reproduced in Figure 17.1.

Figure 17.1   OPINION LEADERSHIP SCALE.   Charles W. King and John O. Summers, "Generalized Opinion Leadership in Consumer Products: Some Preliminary Findings," paper no. 224, (Lafayette, Ind.: Institute for Research in the Behavioral, Economic and Management Sciences, Krannert Graduate School of Industrial Administration, Jan. 1969), p. 16.

(1)   In general, do you like to talk about _____ with your friends?

        Yes _____ — 1   No _____ — 2

(2)   Would you say *you give very little information, an average amount of information,*

———————————

[16]   For examples, see Francesco M. Nicosia, "Opinion Leaders and the Flow of Communication: Some Problems and Prospects," in L. G. Smith (ed.), *Reflections on Progress in Marketing* (Chicago: Amer. Marketing Assoc., 1965), pp. 340–359; James S. Fenton and Thomas R. Leggett, "A New Way to Find Opinion Leaders," *J. Advertising Research*, vol. 11, pp. 22–25 (Apr. 1971).

[17]   Charles W. King and John O. Summers, "Generalized Opinion Leadership in Consumer Products: Some Preliminary Findings," paper no. 224 (Lafayette, Ind.: Institute for Research in the Behavioral, Economic, and Management Sciences, Krannert Graduate School of Industrial Administration, Jan. 1969).

[18]   Everett M. Rogers and David G. Cartano, "Methods of Measuring Opinion Leadership," *Public Opinion Quart.*, vol. 26, pp. 43–45 (Fall 1962).

Figure 17.1 (*continued*)

or a great deal of information about _____ *to your friends?*

You give very little information   _____— 1
You give an average amount of information _____— 2
You give a great deal of information   _____ —3

(3) During the *past six months,* have *you told anyone* about some _____
_____ ?

Yes _____ — 1   No _____ — 2

(4) Compared with your circle of friends, are you *less likely, about as likely,* or *more likely* to be asked for advice about _____?

Less likely to be asked   _____— 1
About as likely to be asked _____— 1
More likely to be asked   _____— 3

(5) If you and your friends were to discuss _____, what part would *you* be most likely to play? Would you *mainly listen* to your friends' ideas or would *you try to convince them* of your ideas?

You mainly listen to your friends ideas _____— 1
You try to convince them of your ideas _____— 2

(6) Which of these happens more often? Do *you tell your friends* about some _____, or do *they tell you* about some _____
_____ ?

You tell them about _____— 1
They tell you about _____— 2

(7) Do you have the feeling that you are generally regarded by your friends and neighbors as a good source of advice about _____?

Yes _____ — 1   No _____ — 2

    The continuous scores from self-designating opinion leadership scales are divided into dichotomous categories of opinion leaders and nonopinion leaders. The criteria used to establish these categories include (1) comparability with previous studies, (2) comparability across product categories, and (3) reasonable categories given the distributions of the opinion leadership scores for each product category. Typically, the opinion leadership scores are arrayed, and the upper 23 to 30 percent of the respondents are classified as opinion leaders.[19]

---

[19] Katz and Lazarsfeld, *op. cit.,*[5]; King and Summers, *op. cit.*[17]

Characteristics of Opinion Leaders

From the previous discussion of interpersonal communication dyads it follows that opinion leaders are not necessarily persons of high prestige in religion, government, business, education, or other spheres of activity. Rather, they have certain distinguishing characteristics that are discussed in this section.

Scope of Influence Prior to 1968, research usually indicated that an individual was not an opinion leader in more than one or two product areas. In other words, opinion leaders were monomorphic, or product specific, rather than polymorphic.[20]

Many studies published since 1968, however, contradict the monomorphic hypothesis. King and Summers, for example, found a high degree of opinion leadership overlap across six product categories—packaged food products, women's clothing fashions, household cleansers and detergents, cosmetics and personal grooming aids, large appliances, and small appliances. About 46 percent of the respondents qualified as opinion leaders in two or more product categories, 28 percent in three or more categories, and 13 percent in four or more product categories.[21]

King and Summers also found that opinion leaders tend to overlap more across certain product combinations. Specifically, opinion leadership overlap was highest between product categories which involve similar interests. For example, the highest overlap was between large and small appliances. The second highest was between women's fashions and cosmetics and personal grooming aids. The lowest overlap was between cosmetics and personal grooming aids and large appliances.[22] Although there has been some criticism of King and Summers' methodology, it appears to be sound.[23]

In a separate study, Montgomery and Silk found overlap in opinion leadership across most but not all of the categories studied. They also found that the patterns of overlap appeared to parallel the manner in which housewives'

---

[20] See, for example, Silk, *op. cit.*,[7] p. 257; Katz and Lazarsfeld, *op. cit.*,[5] p. 334; Everett M. Rogers, *Diffusion of Innovation* (New York: Free Press, 1962), pp. 30–36; Elihu Katz, "The Two Step Flow of Communication: An Up to Date Report on an Hypothesis," *Public Opinion Quart.*, vol. 21, pp. 61–78 (Spring 1957).

[21] Charles W. King and John O. Summers, "Overlap of Opinion Leadership across Consumer Product Categories," *J. Marketing Research*, vol. 7, pp. 43–50 (Feb. 1970). For additional evidence, see Edwin J. Gross, "Support for a Generalized Marketing Leadership Theory," *J. Advertising Research*, vol. 9, pp. 49–52 (Nov. 1969).

[22] King and Summers, *op. cit.*,[21] pp. 48–49.

[23] Seymour Sudman, "Overlap of Opinion Leadership across Consumer Product Categories," *J. Marketing Research*, vol. 8, pp. 258–259 (May 1971); John O. Summers and Charles W. King, "Overlap of Opinion Leadership: A Reply," *J. Marketing Research*, vol. 8, pp. 259–261 (May 1971).

interests in these catgeories clustered together.[24] Further work by Montgomery and Silk found that patterns of association in opinion leadership for sixteen topics corresponded to the structure of interrelationships among measures of interest in the same topics.[25]

Thus research to date indicates that there are quasi-generalized opinion leaders. The nature of interest patterns seems to be one of the important factors that determine what constitutes the sphere of influence of opinion leaders.

Demographic Characteristics The demographic characteristics of opinion leaders vary depending on the product category. As noted earlier, interpersonal communications dyads *tend* to be homogeneous in terms of social status, age, and income. But, simultaneously people look to others more qualified than themselves, which sometimes means that opinion leaders differ demographically from those they influence. For example, young women seem to dominate in fashion and movie-going, while large-family wives dominate in many household cleaning and maintenance products.[26] Thus, while the tendency is toward homogeneity, there are many exceptions.

Social Characteristics Opinion leaders usually participate in more social activities and are more gregarious than nonopinion leaders.[27] In fact, of the factors used to identify opinion leaders, gregariousness is often most important.[28]

General Attitudes In the case of new products, opinion leaders tend to have more favorable attitudes toward both new products as a concept and new products within the opinion leaders' specific areas of influence. Where the norms of the population as a whole reflect positive attitudes toward new products, opinion leaders reflect even greater commitment to new products than do nonopinion leaders. Thus leaders are usually more innovative than other individuals.[29]

---

[24] David B. Montgomery and Alvin J. Silk, "Patterns of Overlap in Opinion Leadership and Interest for Selected Categories of Purchasing Activity," in Philip R. McDonald (ed.), *Marketing Involvement in Society and the Economy* (Chicago: Amer. Marketing Assoc., 1969), pp. 377–386. For supporting evidence in other areas, see Herbert F. Lionberger, *Adoption of New Ideas and Practices* (Ames, Iowa: Iowa State University Press, 1960), pp. 65–66.

[25] David B. Montgomery and Alvin J. Silk, "Clusters of Consumer Interests and Opinion Leaders' Spheres of Influence," *J. Marketing Research,* vol. 8, pp. 317–321 (Aug. 1971).

[26] See, for example, Katz, *op. cit.;*[20] Katz and Lazarsfeld, *op. cit.;*[5] Rogers, *op. cit.;*[20] W. L. Warner and P. S. Lunt, *The Social Life of a Modern Community* (New Haven, Conn.: Yale University Press, 1941).

[27] For contemporary examples, see Fred D. Reynolds and William R. Darden, "Mutually Adaptive Effects of Interpersonal Communication," *J. Marketing Research,* vol. 8, pp. 449–454 (Nov. 1971); John O. Summers, "The Identity of Women's Clothing Fashion Opinion Leaders," *J. Marketing Research,* vol. 7, pp. 178–185 (May 1970).

[28] "Who Are the Marketing Leaders?" *Tide,* vol. 32, pp. 53–57 (May 9, 1958).

[29] John O. Summers and Charles W. King, "Interpersonal Communication and New Product Attitudes," in McDonald, *op. cit.,*[24] pp. 292–299.

Personality Characteristics Robertson and Myers have studied the relationship between personality characteristics and opinion leadership. Using the California Psychological Inventory to measure personality characteristics in eighteen major areas, they concluded that none of the basic personality variables related substantially to opinion leadership for any, of the product areas studied (appliances, clothing, food).[30]

Other studies have found that opinion leaders do have some distinguishing personality characteristics. For example, Summers found that women's clothing fashion opinion leaders are more emotionally stable, assertive, likeable, less depressive/self deprecating, and tend to be leaders and more self-confident.[31] Others have also found that opinion leaders tend to be more self-confident.[32] Thus it appears that the relationship between personality characteristics and opinion leadership depends on the type of personality characteristic and the product under investigation. Tailor-made personality variables are probably more effective discriminators than are general personality characteristics.

Life-Style Characteristics Recently Tigert and Arnold constructed life-style profiles of general, self-designated opinion leaders, both in the United States and Canada. Using activity, interest, and opinion variables, they were able to construct a rich portrait of opinion leaders. Factor analysis revealed that eight factors—leadership, information exchanges, innovator, community and club involvement, independence, price consciousness, occupation, and fashion consciousness—were able to explain 27 percent in the variance of opinion leadership in Canada.[33]

Unfortunately, the Tigert and Arnold study was concerned with a composite opinion leader for a broad variety of product categories. Had they constructed profiles of opinion leaders for specific products, or products in the same interest category, they probably would have been more successful. Nevertheless, their study points up the potential value of life-style profiles of opinion leaders.

Product-Related Characteristics Opinion leaders tend to have certain additional distinguishing characteristics related to the type of decision being made. First, they perceive themselves as more interested in the topic area. For example, in women's fashions, opinion leaders are more interested in fashions than are nonopinion leaders.[34]

Second, opinion leaders are more active in receiving interpersonal communications about products within their area of influence. In other words, other

---

30 Thomas S. Robertson and James H. Myers, "Personality Correlates of Opinion Leadership and Innovative Buying Behavior," *J. Marketing Research*, vol. 6, pp. 164–168 (May 1969).

31 Summers, *op. cit.*,[27] pp. 180–181.

32 See, for example, Reynolds and Darden, *op. cit.*,[27] p. 450.

33 Douglas J. Tigert and Stephen J. Arnold, *Profiling Self-Designated Opinion Leaders and Self-designated Innovators through Life Style Research* (Toronto: School of Business, University of Toronto, June 1971).

34 Summers, *op. cit.*,[27] pp. 178–185.

consumers talk to opinion leaders more than they do to nonopinion leaders about things that are related to the leaders' alleged area of expertise.[35]

Finally, opinion leaders are usually more exposed to certain additional sources of information. They may be more exposed to the mass media in general, although not in every instance.[36] However, they are almost always more exposed to specific types of mass media that are relevant to their area of interest. Thus, for example, opinion leaders in women's fashions may not be more exposed to television in general, but they are usually more exposed to women's fashion magazines.[37]

In summary, opinion leadership is an important phenomenon. Leaders are usually—although not always—similar to those they influence and they typically differ from one sphere of interest to another. They tend to be more gregarious and innovative, are more interested in the area in question, and both receive and transmit more information about the topic.

ALTERNATIVE 'MODELS' OF INTERPERSONAL COMMUNICATION AND PERSONAL INFLUENCE

During the past twenty-five years, several attempts have been made to develop hypotheses or models of interpersonal communication and personal influence processes. This section summarizes these efforts and then attempts to construct a framework that seems consistent with the findings of recent research.

The Two-Step Flow Hypothesis

The two-step flow of communication is the traditional model of the link between the mass media and interpersonal communication. Despite some revisions and modifications, the essential elements of the hypothesis remain unchanged from its original formulation in 1948—influences and ideas "flow from (the mass media) to opinion leaders and from them to the less active sections of the population."[38] The link between the passive masses and the mass media is the opinion leader.

---

[35] Summers and King, *op. cit.*,[29] pp. 292–299.

[36] See, for example, Robert Mason, "The Use of Information Sources by Influentials in the Adoption Process," *Public Opinion Quart.*, vol. 27, pp. 455–466 (1963).

[37] See, for example, Katz and Lazarsfeld, *op. cit.*,[5] pp. 309–320; Summers, *op. cit.*,[27] pp. 178–185; Reynolds and Darden, *op. cit.*,[27] pp. 449–454.

[38] Paul F. Lazarsfeld, Bernard R. Berelson, and Hazel Gaudlet, *The Peoples Choice* (New York: Columbia University Press, 1948), p. 151. Many of the concepts and techniques utilized in this study were originated by Merton. See Robert K. Merton, "Patterns of Influence: A Study of Interpersonal Influence and of Communications Behavior in a Local Community," in P. F. Lazarsfeld and F. Stanton (eds.), *Communications Research* (New York: Harper and Brothers, 1949). An earlier exploratory study was conducted by Frank Stewart, "A Sociometric Study of Influence in Southtown," *Sociometry*, vol. 10, pp. 11–31, 273–286 (1947).

Multi-Step Interaction Models

Although the two-step flow was a historic breakthrough in understanding communications, it is no longer an accurate and complete model of the process. For one thing, it views the audience as passive receivers of information. Yet several studies have found that up to 50 percent of word-of-mouth communications are initiated by consumers seeking information from opinion leaders.[39] Moreover, at least in some instances, word-of-mouth communication is affected by selective exposure and selective response.[40]

Second, there is some evidence that there are multiple models of interpersonal communication and personal influence depending, in part, on whether consumers are earlier triers or later adopters of a product. A longitudinal study of Maxim coffee led Belk and Ross to conclude that early adopters followed communication patterns close to the two-step-flow description. Later adopters, however, engaged in a more conversational form of word of mouth that appeared to be devoid of opinion leadership.[41]

Other studies have questioned the accuracy of a *two*-step flow. For example, King and Summers found in the case of women's apparel:[42]

(1) About 39 percent of those who reported involvement in interpersonal communication mentioned participation as both a transmitter and a receiver.

(2) Nearly 53 percent of those who reported participation as a receiver *also* reported participation as a transmitter.

(3) Approximately 60 percent of those who reported participation as a transmitter *also* reported participation as a receiver.

Katz has also suggested that in some instances there may be chains of personal influence rather than simple dyads.[43] Sheth's recent study of the diffusion of stainless steel blades indicated that there may exist a three-or-more-step flow of communication.[44]

---

[39] See, for example, Donald F. Cox, "The Audience as Communicators" in Cox, *op. cit.,*[13] pp. 172–187, at p. 182; James F. Engel, Robert J. Kegerreis, and Roger D. Blackwell, "Word-of-Mouth Communication by the Innovator," *J. Marketing,* vol. 33, pp. 15–19 (July 1969).

[40] Johan Arndt, "Selective Processes in Word-of-Mouth," *J. Advertising Research,* vol. 8, pp. 19–22 (June 1968).

[41] Russell W. Belk and Ivan Ross, "An Investigation of the Nature of Word of Mouth Communication across Adoption Categories for a Food Innovation," paper presented at the Association for Consumer Research Conf., University of Maryland (Sept. 1971).

[42] Charles W. King and John O. Summers, "Dynamics of Interpersonal Communication," in Cox, *op. cit.,*[13] pp. 253–254.

[43] Katz, *op. cit.,*[20] pp. 61–78.

[44] Jagdish N. Sheth, "Word-of-Mouth in Low-Risk Innovations," *J. Advertising Research,* vol. 11, pp. 15–18. (June 1971).

These findings suggest the need for more complex multistep multisituation models that focus on consumers' needs for information, opinion leaders' motives for transmitting information, and situational determinants of the processes.

Opinion-Leader Motivation   Unfortunately, little research has been done on the forces which cause people to assume the role of opinion leaders and engage in word-of-mouth communications. The discussion that follows is based on a limited number of studies—heavily concentrated in nonmarketing areas— and should therefore be regarded as tentative until supported or refuted by further research.

In general, opinion leaders will not talk about products or services unless such a conversation produces some type of satisfaction. Motivations to talk about products or services appear to fall into one or more of the following categories: (1) product involvement, (2) self-involvement, (3) concern for others, (4) message involvement,[45] or (5) dissonance reduction. The more interested an individual is in a given topic or product or service, the more likely he is to initiate conversations about it. For example, Katz and Lazarsfeld found that public affairs and fashion leaders were more interested in their areas than were nonleaders. Similarly, marketing leadership was concentrated in wives of large families who were more interested and more experienced than were the "girls" or the small-family wives.[46] Apparently, in these and other situations, conversations serve as an outlet for the pleasure and/or excitement caused or resulting from the purchase and/or use of the product or service.

Self-involvement may also play a major role in motivating opinion leaders to comment about a product or service. Dichter's research indicated that talking about a product or service often performs such functions as (1) gaining attention, (2) showing connoisseurship, (3) suggesting status, (4) giving the impression that the opinion leader has inside information, and (5) asserting superiority.[47] Whyte found in his classic study of the diffusion of air conditioners that some respondents subscribed to *Consumer Reports* to acquire conversational material.[48]

Concern for others may also precipitate talk by opinion leaders. Some conversations are motivated by a desire to help the listener make better purchasing decisions. In other instances, talking about a product or service allows the opinion leader to share the satisfactions resulting from the use of the product or service.

---

[45]   This typology was developed by Ernest Dichter, "How Word-of-Mouth Advertising Works," *Harvard Business Rev.*, vol. 44, pp. 147–166 (Nov.–Dec. 1966).

[46]   Katz and Lazarsfeld, *op. cit.*,[5] pp. 249–252, 274–275, 239–242.

[47]   Dichter, *op. cit.*,[45] pp. 147–166.

[48]   William H. Whyte, Jr., "The Web of Word-of-Mouth," in Lincoln H. Clark (ed.), *The Life Cycle and Consumer Behavior* (New York: New York University Press, 1955), pp. 113–122.

Advertising involvement is another type of opinion-leader motivation. Some people find it entertaining to talk about certain advertisements such as those for Volkswagen and Alka Seltzer. Other people like to make jokes about advertising symbols such as the White Knight and the Jolly Green Giant.

Finally, some research suggests that under certain conditions word of mouth is used to reduce cognitive dissonance following a major purchase decision. Presumably the buyer attempts to reduce dissonance by persuading other people to buy the same product.[49] This motivation does not exist in all instances, however, as Engel, Kegerreis, and Blackwell failed to find significant amounts of this behavior following the usage of an automotive diagnostic service.[50]

Nonopinion-leader Motivation As was the case for opinion-leader motivation, few studies have been concerned with why and/or under what conditions nonopinion leaders seek information *from opinion leaders*. The general conditions that are likely to cause consumers to seek information from opinion leaders include (1) small amount of stored information, (2) stored information not appropriate, (3) high degree of perceived risk, and (4) low cost involved in using this source of information.

It should be noted that the above variables are general determinants of search. Of those mentioned, only perceived risk has been *empirically* related to the role of personal influence as a source of information. Moreover, since the interaction model of personal influence was not suggested until 1963,[51] there are very few studies that have investigated the importance of perceived risk in triggering information seeking from personal sources.

Studies investigating the relation between perceived risk and information seeking from personal sources indicate that those consumers high in perceived risk are more likely to initiate conversations, and, when they do, they are more likely to request information than those who are felt to be low in perceived risk. In other words, there appears to be a flow of information from those low in perceived risk to those high in perceived risk.[52]

Finally, there is some evidence that certain personality characteristics may influence whether or not a consumer is exposed to personal sources of information. One study found a positive and linear relation between generalized self-confidence and *exposure* to word-of-mouth communications. Interestingly enough, however, the *impact* of word-of-mouth was curvilinear, with the median

---

[49] Much of this section was based on a comprehensive literature review in Johan Arndt, "*Word-of-Mouth Advertising,*" in Cox, *op. cit.,*[13] pp. 188–239.

[50] Engel *et al., op. cit.,*[39] p. 18.

[51] Raymond A. Bauer, "The Initiative of the Audience," *J. Advertising Research,* vol. 3, pp. 2–7 (1963).

[52] Scott M. Cunningham, "Perceived Risk as a Factor in the Diffusion of New Product Information," in Haas, *op. cit.,*[9] pp. 698–721; Johan Arndt, "Perceived Risk, Sociometric Integration and Word-of-Mouth in the Adoption of a New Food Product," in Haas, *op. cit.,*[9] pp. 644–649.

self-confidence group being relatively more responsive to word-of-mouth comments.[53] Hence, self-confidence and other, as yet unexplored, personality characteristics may affect consumers' use of personal sources of information.

Situational and Conversational Determinants Belk's study of Maxim coffee points up the importance of various situational and conversational determinants of word-of-mouth communication. He found that for both senders and receivers, food-related cues (drinking coffee, general conversations concerning food, shopping for food) were present in at least three fourths of the reported incidents of word-of-mouth activity. Spontaneous word of mouth was rare. Based on the Maxim study and his previous research Belk concluded that:[54]

(1) Much informal conversation regarding a new product does not involve opinion leader/follower pairs, and often such communications are exchanges of views and information.

(2) The probabalistic occurrence of specific word-of-mouth conversations is more dependent upon the conversational and environmental context (cues) than upon the particular assemblage of persons present.

The first conclusion rejects the conventional concept of opinion leadership in favor of a more conversational form in which leader–follower role playing does not seem to occur. The second conclusion maintains that while spontaneous word of mouth may occur, a relevant context facilitates most word of mouth. An appropriate context may be created conversationally (that is, a relevant setting for discussing a certain type of product).

Evaluation

Figure 17.2 summarily compares the two-step flow hypothesis with a provisional multistep interaction model that seems to reflect the current status of research. It seems appropriate at this juncture to comment on research to date and suggest some ideas and guide lines for future efforts.

First, most research has tended to concentrate in certain areas. For the most part, interpersonal communication and personal influence findings have resulted from studies designed to deal primarily with other issues. Consequently, much of the existing literature has one or more of the following characteristics: (1) conducted in pretelevision times, (2) concerned with nonmarketing issues, (3) concerned with new products, or (4) concerned with shopping or *specialty goods*. Future efforts should correct this imbalance since it is not at all obvious that existing generalizations apply in other contexts such as heavily advertised, frequently purchased, established convenience products.

---

[53] Arndt, *op. cit.*,[52] p. 648.

[54] Russell W. Belk, "Occurrence of Word-of-Mouth Buyer Behavior as a Function of Situation and Advertising Stimuli," paper presented at the American Marketing Association Fall Conf., (Aug. 1971).

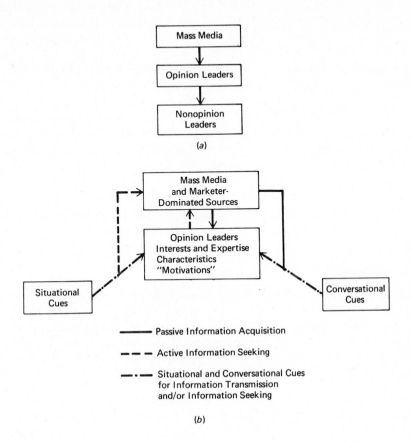

Figure 17.2 ALTERNATIVE MODELS OF INTERPERSONAL COMMUNICA-
TIONS AND PERSONAL INFLUENCE. (*A*) TWO-STEP FLOW HYPO-
THESIS. (*B*) PROVISIONAL MULTISTEP INTERACTION MODEL

Second, more attention should be given to relationships between the
volume and content of marketer-dominated advertising and the volume and
type of word-of-mouth communication. As will be discussed in the next chapter,
there is little evidence concerning whether it is possible to stimulate word of
mouth, let alone how it can be accomplished most profitably.

Third, little is known about the role of situational and conversational
cues in triggering word of mouth. Expanded investigations of this area seem
particularly worthwhile.

Fourth, more work is necessary on the relationship between interest
spheres and opinion leadership overlap. This is particularly important to manufacturers of closely related products, since if there are common leaders in many
product categories, the economics of using opinion-leader-oriented strategies
may change dramatically.

Fifth, future attempts to isolate the characteristics and motivations of opinion leaders and nonopinion leaders should utilize appropriate multivariate statistics in order to identify the relative importance of the classification variables. Moreover, if these distinguishing characteristics cannot be used to identify opinion leaders in managerial settings, attempts should be made to relate these characteristics to variables that managers can use profitably.

Sixth, more emphasis should be placed on the content of word of mouth. What product characteristics are discussed? What role do these conversations play in formulating evaluative criteria and attitudes? Do these conversations affect brand choice as well as the decision to purchase the generic product? To what extent do negative conversations discourage the purchase of a product and/or brand?

Finally, most research in this area has been concerned with aggregate effects. Future efforts might also investigate the role of interpersonal communications and personal influence for relevant market segments.

SUMMARY

This chapter has discussed the personal-sources component of the search and alternative evaluation stage in the decision-making process. The first part of the chapter documented the fact that interpersonal communications are very influential in many purchasing decisions. These conversations usually occur between consumers that have similar characteristics, providing the referent is perceived to be competent and there is sufficient proximity to facilitate the interaction.

The second part of the chapter discussed communications interactions in greater detail noting both the consistencies and inconsistencies with the generalizations advanced earlier. Techniques for isolating opinion leaders were identified and evaluated and the characteristics of opinion leaders were described.

Alternative 'models' of interpersonal communications and personal influence were presented in the last section of the chapter. It was concluded that the two-step flow hypothesis is no longer an accurate depiction of the processes involved. Consequently, an effort was made to synthesize the relevant literature into a provisional multistep interaction model and to identify some ideas and guide lines for future research projects.

REVIEW AND DISCUSSION QUESTIONS

1. Distinguish between interpersonal communication and personal influence.

2. Assume that you are a consultant for a manufacturer of men's clothing. Discuss how you would go about identifying campus opinion leaders.

3. Describe the two-step flow hypothesis. Is this hypothesis a complete model of communication flows? Why or why not?

4. Recall the last time you volunteered information to someone about a product or service. What caused you to talk about the product or service? How does this compare with the general reasons that opinion leaders pass on information?

5. How do opinion leaders differ from those they influence?

6. Why do consumers seek information from opinion leaders?

7. "Past studies of personal influence have often used oversimplified conceptualizations of the role of personal influence." Discuss the meaning of this statement and evaluate the evidence, if any, supporting it.

8. Prepare a research proposal based on one or more of the ideas and guidelines presented for future research in interpersonal communications and personal influence.

CHAPTER 18

ADDITIONAL DIMENSIONS
OF SEARCH AND ALTERNATIVE
EVALUATION PROCESSES

The discussion of search and alternative evaluation processes continues in this chapter with attention given to family role structures involved in information seeking, the relative importance of information sources, and determinants of the relative importance of these sources. The major part of the chapter is devoted to a discussion of the marketing implications of search and alternative evaluation processes.

FAMILY ROLE STRUCTURES ASSOCIATED
WITH INFORMATION SEEKING

Role structure, it will be recalled, refers to the behavior of nuclear family members at each stage in the decision-making process. Since most studies have focused exclusively on role structures involved in purchasing, there is, unfortunately, little evidence concerning the role of family members in information-seeking behavior.

Table 18.1 summarizes the results of a major study that investigated the relative involvement of husbands and wives in information seeking. Looking first at the relative importance of information sources, both husbands and wives have a greater tendency to seek information from personal sources rather than from the mass media or advertisements. Second, wives are involved in information seeking to a greater extent than husbands, except for automobiles, refrigerators, and paint. Third, although the extent of both husband and wife involvement varies across products, husband participation has a tendency to vary to a slightly greater degree than female participation.

Table 18.1   LIFE MAGAZINE STUDY OF THE ROLES OF HUSBANDS AND WIVES IN INFORMATION SEEKING

Product Category	Personal Sources		Nonpersonal Sources	
	Husband (%)	Wife (%)	Husband (%)	Wife (%)
Refrigerators	91.8	84.9	59.2	54.8
Vacuum cleaners	76.2	87.0	26.2	42.9
Automobiles	79.8	80.7	56.7	43.3
Frozen orange juice	20.0	44.1	41.4	48.6
Rugs, carpets	68.1	81.3	55.1	65.4
Paint	70.9	63.5	21.8	28.7

NOTE: Percentages are based on each spouse's self-appraisal. The percentages indicate whether the spouse in question was involved in information seeking. Categories such as "both husband and wife" or "children" were not employed, so the percentages often total more or less than 100 percent.

SOURCE: "A Pilot Study of the Roles of Husbands and Wives in Purchasing Decisions, Parts I–X," conducted for *Life* magazine by L. Jaffe Associates, Inc. (1965). Research design involved interviews with 301 middle- and upper-income households in Hartford, Cleveland, and Seattle.

What affects the extent of husband–wife involvement in information seeking? The data in Table 18.1 suggest the following generalizations. The roles of husband and wife seem to be affected by the combined influence of a product's price and mechanical complexity.[1] Husbands have a greater tendency to participate in information seeking, particularly personal sources, when the product is high priced and technically complex than they do when any other combination of price and technological complexity exists—for example, low price, high complexity; high price, low complexity; or low price, low complexity. Price and

---

[1] The reader is referred to Elizabeth Wolgast, "Do Husbands or Wives Make Purchasing Decisions?" *J. Marketing*, vol. 23, pp. 151–158 (Oct. 1958); Harry Sharp and Paul Mott, "Consumer Decisions in the Metropolitan Family," *J. Marketing*, vol. 21, pp. 149–156 (Oct. 1956).

technological complexity are important determinants of the extent of spousal involvement, because cultural norms specify that males are supposed to know about mechanical things; also as the price of an item increases, the number of alternative purchases that can be made decreases.

Finally, it should be reiterated that the extent of husband–wife involvement in information seeking is likely to vary not only across products but also across families. Younger husbands, for example, would probably play a greater role in information seeking than older males.[2] A marketer needs to be aware of the possibility of these types of variations when evaluating the usefulness of information-seeking role structure data expressed in mean percentages.

RELATIVE IMPORTANCE OF INFORMATION SOURCES

Since consumers often use several sources of information in order to learn about alternatives, the question arises as to which source is most important. Because this is a difficult question to answer, this section discusses the major problems involved in determining the relative importance of information sources before considering the relative importance of these sources.

Problems in Determining the Importance of Information Sources

The fundamental problem involved in determining the relative importance of information sources revolves around defining and expressing the term "importance." Hence it is necessary to discuss alternative criteria of importance and techniques of expressing whatever criterion is used.

Criteria of Importance One way of expressing the importance of an information source is in terms of *exposure*. For example, an information source could be judged more important than other sources in that a greater percentage of consumers report being exposed to it. This is probably the most commonly used criterion.[3]

There are, however, fundamental problems involved in using exposure in this manner. Consumers can be exposed to information sources without using them or finding them helpful in making purchasing decisions. As a consequence, there may be a significant difference between *exposure* and *effectiveness,* and an information source that is most important in terms of exposure may be of lesser importance when the criterion of effectiveness is employed.

---

[2] Wolgast, *op. cit.,*[1] pp. 151–158; Mirra Komarovsky, "Class Differences in Family Decision Making on Expenditures," in Nelson Foote (ed.), *Household Decision Making* (New York: New York University Press, 1961), pp. 259–264.

[3] Frederick C. May, "An Appraisal of Buying Behavior Research," in Peter D. Bennett (ed.), *Marketing and Economic Development* (Chicago: Amer. Marketing Assoc., 1965), pp. 393–399, at p. 397.

Moreover, consumers will often perceive information sources as having various degrees of effectiveness. For example, the following typology could be used in determining the degree of effectiveness of information sources:[4]

(1) *Decisive effectiveness*—This category could be used when an information source played a specific role and was the most important source.

(2) *Contributory effectiveness*—This category could be used when an information source played some specific role but was *not* the most important source.

(3) *Ineffective*—This category could be used to describe an information source that did not play any role in a purchase situation although the consumer was exposed to it.

Expressing Relative Importance   Regardless of whether the criterion is exposure, general effectiveness, or some typology of effectiveness, the importance of an information source should be stated in *relative* rather than absolute terms. This is necessary because information sources often vary in their degree of coverage, so that absolute measures may reflect nothing more than coverage. It is, therefore, important to use a relative measure that holds coverage constant, and this can be accomplished by employing an index such as the ratio of decisive effectiveness of a particular source to total exposure of that source.[5]

Relative Importance of Information Sources

It is difficult to determine the relative importance of information sources from the results of empirical studies because they differ in the use of a criterion of importance and whether degrees and indexes of effectiveness are used. Nevertheless, Table 18.2 summarizes rankings of the relative importance of information sources obtained from major investigations of information-seeking behavior. Studies have been classified according to whether exposure, effectiveness, or both have been used as the criterion of importance. Asterisk combinations have been used to indicate whether the study employed an effectiveness typology and/or an effectiveness index.

The results of these studies support the following generalizations:

(1) *Exposure*—If exposure is used as the criterion of importance, marketer-dominated sources of information are typically the most important. The tendency of consumers to rely to a greater degree on advertisements or

---

[4]   This typology is a slight modification of the one used by Elihu Katz and Paul Lazarsfeld, *Personal Influence* (New York: Free Press, 1955), chap. 4.

[5]   Katz and Lazarsfeld, *op. cit.;*[4] the reader is encouraged to study chapter 4 for a more comprehensive and intensive discussion of the problems involved in determining the relative importance of information sources.

Table 18.2 RANKINGS OF THE RELATIVE IMPORTANCE OF MAJOR SOURCES OF INFORMATION OBTAINED FROM MAJOR STUDIES OF INFORMATION SEEKING

Type of Choice	Exposure				Effectiveness			
	Mass Media	Information Source — Personal Sources	Marketer Dominated — Advertisements	Marketer Dominated — Dealer Visits, Salesmen	Mass Media	Information Source — Personal Sources	Marketer Dominated — Advertisements	Marketer Dominated — Dealer Visits, Salesmen
Major durables[a]		3	2	1				
Major durables and furniture[b]		2	3	1	2	1	3	
Major and small durables[c]		2	1	3		1	2	3
Small appliances[d]					3	1	2	
Fashion** items[e]			1	2		1	3	
Nylons, dacron[f]						1		2
Movies[g] **			1	2		1	2	
Food** and household products[h]			1	2		1	3	2
Food* products[i]		3	2	1		3	2	1
Food** and toiletries[j]						2	1	
Choice of supermarket[k]					2	1	*Sampling* 2	
Farmers' choice of hybrid seed[l]		1	1	*Salesman*		1		*Salesman* 2
Farmers' choice of new products[m]		3	1	*Salesman* 2				*Salesman* 2

Doctors' choice of drugs[n]	3	2	1 Salesman			1	1 If isolated from colleague and drug not risky 2
Number of first rankings	0	0	5	5	0	9	1

NOTES: [*] Study used an effectiveness index; [**] study used an effectiveness index and a typology of effectiveness.

SOURCES:
[a] George Katona and Eva Mueller, "A Study of Purchasing Decisions," in Lincoln H. Clark (ed.), *Consumer Behavior: The Dynamics of Consumer Reactions* (New York: New York University Press, 1955), pp. 30–87.
[b] Bruce Le Grand and Jon G. Udell, "Consumer Behavior in the Market Place," *J. Retailing*, pp. 32–40 (Fall 1964).
[c] Hugh W. Sargent, *Consumer Product Rating Publications and Buying Behavior* (Urbana, Ill.: University of Illinois Bureau of Economic and Business Research, 1959).
[d] Jon G. Udell, "Prepurchase Behavior of Buyers of Small Electrical Appliances," *J. Marketing*, vol. 30, pp. 50–51 (Oct. 1966).
[e] Elihu Katz and Paul Lazarsfeld, *Personal Influence* (New York: Free Press, 1955), chap. 5.
[f] George M. Beal and Everett M. Rogers, "Informational Sources in the Adoption Process of New Fabrics," *J. Home Economics*, vol. 49, pp. 630–644 (1957).
[g] Katz and Lazarsfeld, chap. 5.
[h] Katz and Lazarsfeld, chap. 5.
[i] George Fisk, "Media Influence Reconsidered," *Public Opinion Quart.*, vol. 23, pp. 83–91 (1959).
[j] George H. Haines, Jr., "A Study of Why People Purchase New Products," in Ramond M. Haas (ed.), *Science, Technology and Marketing* (Chicago: Amer. Marketing Assoc., 1966), pp. 665–685.
[k] Kenward L. Atkins, "Advertising and Store Patronage," *J. Advertising Research*, vol. 2, pp. 18–23 (Dec. 1962).
[l] B. Ryan and N. C. Gross, "The Diffusion of Hybrid Seed Corn in Two Iowa Communities," *Rural Sociology*, vol. 8, pp. 15–24 (1943).
[m] Robert G. Mason, "The Use of Information Sources in the Process of Adoption," *Rural Sociology*, vol. 29, pp. 40–52 (Mar. 1964); Everett M. Rogers and George M. Beal, "The Importance of Personal Influence in the Adoption of Technological Changes," *Social Forces*, vol. 36, pp. 329–335 (May 1958).
[n] Herbert Menzel and Elihu Katz, "Social Relations and Innovation in the Medical Profession: The Epidemiology of a New Drug," *Public Opinion Quart.*, vol. 19, pp. 337–352 (Winter 1955–1956); Raymond A. Bauer, "Risk Handling in Drug Adoption: The Role of Company Preference," *Public Opinion Quart.*, vol. 25, pp. 546–559 (Winter 1961).

salesmen than on the mass media or personal sources generally prevails regardless of the type of purchase or choice that is being made.

(2)   *Effectiveness*—In terms of effectiveness, personal sources are generally more important than the mass media or marketer-dominated sources.

Thus, while consumers generally have a greater tendency to be *exposed* to marketer-dominated sources, personal sources are usually the most *effective.*

Further analysis of these studies indicates that consumers rarely rely exclusively on one information source. Rather, information seeking tends to be a *cumulative process.* Consumers who seek information from mass media and/or marketer dominated sources also usually seek information from personal sources and vice versa. This suggests that consumers use the three types of channels as *complementary* rather than *competing* sources of information.[6]

DETERMINANTS OF THE RELATIVE IMPORTANCE OF INFORMATION SOURCES

Several studies have attempted to determine why some information sources are more important than others. Certain characteristics of the information —perceived· risk, characteristics of the decision-making unit, and the stage of market development—have been found to be the determining factors.

Characteristics of Information

The type of information desired as well as certain characteristics of information, and sources themselves, affect relative importance.

Type of Information   The information sources utilized by the consumer depend partly upon the type of information that is desired. Table 18.3 summarizes part of a study of home buying which illustrates this phenomenon. The data suggest:

(1)   Personal sources of information, particularly friends and co-workers, were most important for decisions regarding the social dimensions of the product, preferred neighborhood or location.

(2)   Personal sources as well as newspapers were also used frequently in the selection of other information sources, such as in the choice of real estate agents or builders.

---

[6]   See, for example, George Katona and Eva Mueller, "A Study of Purchase Decisions," in Lincoln H. Clark (ed.), *The Dynamics of Consumer Reactions* (New York: New York University Press, 1955), pp. 30–87, at p. 46; Bernard Berelson and Gary Steiner, *Human Behavior* (New York: Harcourt, 1964), p. 532; Donald F. Cox, "The Audience as Communicators," in Donald F. Cox (ed.), *Risk Taking and Information Handling in Consumer Behavior* (Boston: Division of Research, Graduate School of Business Administration, Harvard University, 1967), pp. 172–187.

Table 18.3 RELATIVE IMPORTANCE OF INFORMATION SOURCES FOR SELECTED DECISIONS IN THE HOME-BUYING PROCESS

Percent Exposed to Information Source and Index of Effectiveness

Decision for Which Information Was Obtained	Friends and Business Associates	Relatives	Real Estate Agents	Bankers	Builders and Contractors	Newspapers	Other	N
Preferred neighborhood or location	54%* / 0.66	19% / 0.52	35% / 0.33	8% / 0.00	8% / 0.21	30% / 0.22	7% / 0.00	244
Price range to be considered	16% / 0.41	11% / 0.48	38% / 0.43	34% / 0.52	13% / 0.42	30% / 0.34	8% / 0.33	240
Which real estate agents to contact	51% / 0.64	10% / 0.57	3% / 0.43	4% / 0.38	3% / 0.71	59% / 0.65	3% / 0.33	215
Which builders to contact	42% / 0.71	9% / 0.54	24% / 0.70	4% / 0.50	12% / 0.53	40% / 0.69	1% / 0.00	139
What characteristics of a house should be used to estimate its value	34% / 0.45	26% / 0.42	40% / 0.43	22% / 0.39	24% / 0.47	16% / 0.22	17% / 0.54	227
Fair value or price for house purchased	34% / 0.33	20% / 0.33	32% / 0.59	36% / 0.53	14% / 0.55	27% / 0.24	9% / 0.62	232
Where to apply for a mortgage loan	33% / 0.66	11% / 0.62	38% / 0.69	27% / 0.70	8% / 0.90	3% / 0.29	5% / 0.67	236
Terms and conditions for mortgage loan	25% / 0.48	12% / 0.61	26% / 0.53	52% / 0.68	5% / 0.50	4% / 0.44	15% / 0.56	236
Which firm to contact for property insurance	44% / 0.87	13% / 0.74	13% / 0.10	6% / 0.43	1% / 0.67	3% / 0.43	22% / 0.90	232

NOTE: The first number in each set indicates the proportion of respondents reporting that they referred to the information source in making the decision listed. The second number is an index measure representing the ratio of the number designating the sources as that having the "most influence" for each decision to the total number referring to that source. For example, 54 percent of the respondents mentioned friends and business associates as sources of information they referred to in decision making concerning their preferred neighborhood or location; 66 percent of those using this source also designated it as the most influential source of information for this decision. The exposure percentages do not always total 100 percent because some respondents mentioned several sources or their own personal evaluations.

SOURCE: Donald J. Hempel, "Search Behavior and Information Utilization in the Home Buying Process," in Philip R. McDonald (ed.), *Marketing Involvement in Society and the Economy* (Chicago: Amer. Marketing Assoc., 1969), pp. 241–249, at p. 247.

(3)   Commercial sources of information—agents, bankers, builders, and con-tractors—were more influential for decisions regarding technical matters such as valuation of the house and where to obtain a mortgage loan.

(4)   Real estate agents, bankers, and newspapers were most important for decisions regarding the price range considered by the home buyer.

Generally, these data indicate that friends and business associates, real estate agents, and newspapers are the most pervasive sources of information throughout the buying process, but their relative importance varies significantly with the kinds of information sought by the home buyer.[7]

The above study as well as others that could be cited[8] suggest that generally information from the mass media performs an *informing* function, whereas that from personal sources typically assumes a *legitimizing* or *evaluating* function. This is not to say that personal sources never perform an informing function or that the mass media never perform a legitimizing or evaluating function. In some cases, personal sources may perform an informing function, but whether or not this occurs depends in part on the type of information desired and social norms associated with obtaining it from this source. To cite another example, consumers may use friends and relatives for information about quality, but personal sources will seldom perform an informing function about price, particularly if the price of the product is high.[9] Generally, however, consumers will use the mass media to learn about the availability and attributes of alternatives and personal sources to evaluate the alternatives.

The interaction of information content and consumer predispositions also affects the relative importance of information sources. In a controlled experimental setting it was found that:[10]

(1)   Communications from a product-rating service did not have greater influence than similar information from salesmen. Some of the consumer-reports effects were greater than those of the salesmen only when the communications presented information inconsistent with brand preferences. When communications favored the preferred brand, the influence of the salesmen was either equal to or slightly greater than that of consumer reports.

---

[7]   Donald J. Hempel, "Search Behavior and Information Utilization in the Home Buying Process," in Philip R. McDonald (ed.), *Marketing Involvement in Society and the Economy* (Chicago: Amer. Marketing Assoc., 1969), pp. 241–249, at pp. 246–247.

[8]   Elihu Katz, "The Two Step Flow of Communication: An Up to Date Report on an Hypothesis," *Public Opinion Quart.*, vol. 20, pp. 61–78 (1957); Eugene A. Wilkining, "Joint Decision Making as a Function of Status and Role,"*Amer. Sociological Rev.*, vol. 23, pp. 187–192 (1958); Kenward L. Atkin, "Advertising and Store Patronage," *J. Advertising Research*, vol. 2, pp. 18–23 (Dec. 1962).

[9]   See, for example, Bruce Legrand and Jon Udell, "Consumer Behavior in the Market Place," *J. Retailing*, pp. 32–40, at p. 34 (Fall 1964).

[10]   Donald J. Hempel, "An Experimental Study of the Effects of Information on Consumer Product Evaluations," in R. M. Haas (ed.), *Science, Technology, and Marketing* (Chicago: Amer. Marketing Assoc., 1966), pp. 587–598.

(2) Confirming communications from either source tended to exert less influence on expressed evaluations of shirts than did disconfirming communications.

Relevant Dimensions of Information Sources Consumers use at least two dimensions in assigning value to information obtained from various sources. *Predictive value* refers to the probability that information seems associated with or predicts a specific product attribute. *Confidence value* refers to how certain the consumer is that the information obtained from a source is what he perceives it to be. Confidence values may also vary across information sources.[11]

Studies indicate that although the predictive criterion is the most important determinant of information value, confidence value is a qualifying variable. Unless the consumer is sufficiently confident of the validity of information obtained from a source, he is not likely to use the information, even if it has a high predictive value.[12] Thus, consumers' perceptions of the predictive and confidence values of information obtained from various sources apparently partially explain the configuration of importance of information sources illustrated in Table 18.3.

Acquisition costs are another relevant evaluative dimension. Time, money, and energy are examples of possible acquisition costs, and, as was true for the other dimensions, different acquisition costs may be involved in obtaining information from different sources.[13] In general, it appears that consumers prefer that source which involves the least cost and effort in order to collect the *desired* information.[14] However, the principle of least cost and effort should be viewed as tentative, pending corroborating research.

Perceived Risk

The amount and type of risk perceived by the consumer affects the specific information sources that are utilized. There is, for example, some evidence that financial risk affects the relative importance. Generally, the importance of personal sources increases as the cost of the item purchased increases.[15]

---

[11] These dimensions of information have been suggested by Donald F. Cox, "The Measurement of Information Value: A Study in Consumer Decision Making," in William S. Decker (ed.), *Emerging Concepts in Marketing* (Chicago: Amer. Marketing Assoc., 1962), pp. 413–421.

[12] Cox, *op. cit.*,[11] p. 413.

[13] Wesley C. Bender, "Consumer Purchase Costs—Do Retailers Recognize Them?" *J. Retailing*, pp. 1–8 (Spring 1964); Anthony Downs, "A Theory of Consumer Efficiency," *J. Retailing*, pp. 6–12 (Spring 1961).

[14] George Fisk, "Media Influence Reconsidered," *Public Opinion Quart.*, vol. 23, pp. 83–91, at p. 90 (1959).

[15] Donald H. Granbois, "A Study of the Family Decision Making Process in the Purchase of Major Durable Household Goods," unpublished doctoral dissertation (Bloomington, Ind.: Graduate School of Business, Indiana University, 1962), p. 106. Data in Table 18.3 also appear to support this hypothesis, although there are not enough lower priced products to really be certain.

Socioeconomic risk is also related to the relative importance of information sources. The greater the visibility and social significance of a product, the greater the importance of personal sources.[16]

There is considerable research dealing with the effect of physiological risk (or problem severity) on the relative importance of information sources. For example, certain characteristics of drugs and diseases will affect the information source consulted by physicians. Doctors are increasingly likely to consult personal professional sources of information and/or rely on the image of the pharmaceutical firm as the severity of the disease increases and the situation becomes increasingly indeterminate.[17] In consumer utilization of information sources, as the severity of the disease increases, the need for the authoritative information also increases, and the importance of marketer-dominated sources decreases.[18]

Characteristics of the Decision-Making Unit

Certain characteristics of the decision-making unit affect the types of sources used in making decisions. For example, personal sources are typically less effective than others if the consumer is socially isolated rather than integrated into primary and/or secondary groups.[19] There is also evidence that the more the husband and wife's friends constitute separate social networks, the greater will be the influence of these friends relative to other sources.[20]

Finally, in those situations where the decision-making process is performed independently by both parties, or by one spouse alone, personal sources will be more important than when other role structures exist. Apparently the

---

[16] See, for example, Michael Perry and B. Curtis Hamm, "Canonical Analysis of Relations between Socioeconomic Risk and Personal Influence in Purchase Decisions," *J. Marketing Research*, vol. 6, pp. 351–354 (Aug. 1969); Robert B. Settle, "Consumer Attributional Information Dependence," unpublished paper (Gainesville, Fla.: University of Florida, Sept. 1971).

[17] Raymond A. Bauer and Lawrence H. Wortzel, "Doctor's Choice: The Physician and His Sources of Information about Drugs," *J. Marketing Research*, vol. 3, pp. 40–47 (Feb. 1966); James Coleman, Herbert Menzel, and Elihu Katz, "Social Process in Physicians' Adoption of a New Drug," *J. Chronic Diseases*, vol. 9, pp. 1–19 (Jan. 1959); Raymond A. Bauer, "Risk Handling in Drug Adoption: Role of Company Preferences," *Public Opinion Quart.*, vol. 25, pp. 546–549 (Winter 1961).

[18] James F. Engel, David A. Knapp, and Deanne E. Knapp, "Sources of Information in the Acceptance of New Products for Self-Medication: Preliminary Findings," in Haas, *op. cit.*,[10] pp. 776–782, at p. 781. For additional studies dealing with the relationship between risk and the relative importance of information sources, see Scott M. Cunningham, "Perceived Risk as a Factor in Product-Oriented Word-of-Mouth Behavior: A First Step," in L. George Smith (ed.), *Reflections on Progress in Marketing* (Chicago: Amer. Marketing Assoc. 1964), pp. 229–238; Ted Roselius, "Consumer Rankings of Risk Reduction Methods," *J. Marketing*, vol. 35, pp. 56–61 (Jan. 1971).

[19] E. H. Schein, "Interpersonal Communication, Group Solidarity, and Social Influence," *Sociometry*, vol. 24, pp. 148–161 (June 1960); Harold L. Wilensky, "Orderly Careers and Social Participation," *Amer. Sociological Rev.*, vol. 26, pp. 521–539 (Aug. 1961); Harold L. Wilensky, "Social Structure, Popular Culture and Mass Behavior: Some Implications for Research," *Public Opinion Quart.*, vol. 24, pp. 497–499 (Fall 1960).

[20] Granbois, *op. cit.*,[15] p. 105.

desire for personal confirmation or support is at times so great that, in the absence of the spouse, it is often sought from personal sources outside the family.[21]

Stage of Market Development

The relative importance of information sources also varies depending, in part, on the length of time the product has been on the market. For example, in the case of some farm products and practices, market-dominated sources tend to decline and personal sources increase in effectiveness as the stage of market development proceeds.[22] This area will be considered in greater detail in Chapter 23, when the diffusion of innovations is discussed.

Evaluation

Several observations need to be made concerning these determinants of the importance of information sources. First, determinants have been collected from a wide variety of studies that have employed various definitions, research designs, and so on. This heterogeneity makes it difficult to compare and synthesize findings. A research tradition involving recommended definitions and methodological procedures is clearly needed.

Second, as was true for the determinants of search, the above determinants of the relative importance of specific sources are probabilistic in nature. The studies that have been reviewed typically reveal that consumers vary considerably in their use of information sources and that the determinants have varying degrees of influence.[23]

Third, whether or not the determinants do in fact affect the importance of information sources appears to depend on the extent of interaction with other variables. With few exceptions,[24] there has been little research that has investigated the influence of various combinations of determinants on the relative importance of information sources. Experimental approaches using factorial designs would seem appropriate.

Finally, all of these qualifications taken together indicate that the marketer should not rely solely on the results outlined here in determining the relative importance of information sources· utilized by consumers when purchasing the marketer's product. Rather, the marketer needs to conduct his own research to determine what affects the relative importance of information sources. More is said on this subject in the next section.

---

[21] Granbois, *op. cit.*,[15] pp. 104, 106.

[22] Everett M. Rogers and George M. Beal, "The Importance of Personal Influence in the Adoption of Technological Changes," *Social Forces*, vol. 36, pp. 329–335 (1958); Bruce Ryan and Neal Gross, "The Diffusion of Hybrid Seed Corn in Two Iowa Communities," *Rural Sociology*, vol. 8, pp. 15–24 (Mar. 1943).

[23] See, for example, Granbois, *op. cit.*,[6] p. 46; Katona and Mueller, *op. cit.*,[6] pp. 30–87; Engel, *et al.*, *op. cit.*,[18] pp. 776–782.

[24] Hempel, *op. cit.*,[10] pp. 589–598.

MARKETING IMPLICATIONS

There are many marketing implications that flow from the nature of search and alternative evaluation processes that have been discussed in this and the two preceding chapters. This section discusses the type of data needed to understand search and alternative evaluation as well as strategies for capitalizing on and adapting to this stage in the decision-making process.

Measuring Search and Alternative Evaluation Behavior

It has been pointed out several times that research concerning the nature of search, the use of information sources, and the determinants of each has several limitations. As a consequence, past research should not be substituted for the firm's own research efforts. In order to design strategies to stimulate or adapt to information-seeking behavior, the firm needs to know the following:

(1) *The percentage of the target market segment that engages in search.* If information seeking does not occur, or a profitably large enough segment of the market does not engage in search, then the firm need not be concerned with search behavior other than to conduct periodic research in order to make certain that these conditions do not change.

(2) *The percentage of the target market that uses each type of information source.* Are the same information sources used by a substantial percentage of the market segment(s) or is the variance so great that it is not practical to talk about common patterns in information seeking?

(3) *The relative importance of information sources.*

(4) *Family role structures associated with information seeking.*

Several comments concerning the most effective ways of obtaining this information are necessary.

Determining the Use of Information Sources   As is the case in other types of investigations, determining the use of information sources requires the application of sound research techniques. However, there are some unique aspects involved in determining the use of information sources that warrant special consideration. These pertain to question wording and sequence and the approach used to obtain the information.

(1) **Question Wording and Sequence**   Careful attention should be given to the type, content, and sequencing of questions used to determine the use and relative importance of information sources. The approach recommended by leading authorities in the area is a series of *specific influence* questions, followed by *assessment* questions, followed by *exposure* questions.[25]

---

[25]   Katz and Lazarsfeld, *op. cit.,*[4] chap. 4.

(a) *Influence* questions should emphasize the process of decision, and the wording should not favor one channel of information over another. Considerable experimentation is needed to develop appropriate questions for the specific product in question, and it is often advisable to ask several questions. Examples of influence questions that have been used include: (1) "How did you happen to find out about the new brand?" (2) "How did you happen to choose this particular brand?" and (3) "How did you happen to start using the new brand of food?"

(b) *Assessment* questions should be asked after specific influence questions have been administered. This increases the probability that the consumer will give some thought to the matter before answering. Relatively simple assessment questions seem appropriate, the following being examples: (1) "Summing up now, what was most important in causing you to purchase X?" or (2) "Summing up now, what do you think was the most important thing in causing you to change to this new brand?" While more sophisticated approaches to assessment are often necessary in other settings, this one appears sufficient for determining the effectiveness of information sources.

(c) *Exposure* questions should be asked after the two preceding types of questions have been administered. It is appropriate to give consumers a checklist itemizing sources of information and ask them to indicate whether they were exposed to various information sources. Representative questions are: (1) "Did you hear someone talk about it?" (2) "Did you read about it in a magazine?" and (3) "Did you see it on TV?"

(2) **Research Approach** Answers to the above questions can be obtained in a variety of ways. One common approach is to use warranty card registration forms. Although this is a relatively inexpensive way of collecting the data, it has several limitations. First, and probably most important, is the fact that the type, content, and sequencing of questions recommended above cannot be followed. Other limitations include the possibility that those consumers who return warranties may differ in important ways from those who do not, and all products do not offer warranties. For these reasons, a warranty card approach should be used only as a periodic supplement to other approaches.

Cross-sectional or longitudinal designs are probably the most appropriate way to determine how consumers use information. Cross-sectional approaches are, of course, plagued with many problems, and these have been discussed in great detail elsewhere.[26] With these limitations in mind, the use of a cross-sectional approach, involving appropriate samples of recent purchasers, should be confined to products where the decision-making period is relatively short, for example, most convenience goods. Longitudinal designs, employing appropriate samples of prospective purchasers, should be used as frequently as possible, particularly when the decision-making period is long, for example, most shopping items, particularly durable goods.

---

[26] See, for example, Donald H. Granbois and James F. Engel, "The Longitudinal Approach to Studying Marketing Behavior," in Bennett, *op. cit.*,[3] pp. 205–221.

Identifying Opinion Leaders   Techniques for identifying opinion leaders were discussed in Chapter 17. In most instances the most practical approach is to use the self-designated method. Whenever feasible, multiple questions rather than a single question should be used (see Figure 17.1).

Determining the Relative Importance of Information Sources   The problems involved in determining the relative importance of information sources were discussed in detail earlier in this chapter and therefore are only summarized here. It is desirable to distinguish between exposure and effectiveness and use a typology of effectiveness that might include such categories as "decisive effectiveness," "contributory effectiveness," and "ineffective." In order to control for variation in the coverage of various information sources, it is appropriate to use an index of effectiveness, which is the ratio of decisive exposure to a particular source to total exposure to that source. This index becomes the measure of the importance of the information source: the higher the index number, the more important the information source.

Determining Information-Seeking Role Structures   Recommended procedures for measuring role structures were spelled out in Chapter 7. Both spouses should be interviewed separately and then reinterviewed together. The information-seeking role structure for each family should be the unweighted mean of each spouse's reply. Role structures can be computed for information seeking in general and/or broken down by type of information source—mass media, personal sources, advertisements (by media if desired), and dealer visits.

Diagnosing the Impact of Search and Alternative Evaluation Behavior

After search and alternative evaluation behavior has been measured, it is useful to evaluate the impact of these activities on the performance of the firm's brand. This section introduces data presentation techniques that facilitate these evaluations.

Before–After Analysis   This procedure involves measurements of brand preference before and after information seeking. If the proper controls are used, differences between before and after brand preferences *roughly* indicate the effect of information seeking on brand preference.

Assume that the data displayed in Table 18.4 were collected using the appropriate research techniques. In this situation, information seeking is hindering brand *A*, helping brand *C*, and having no effect on brand *B*.

The relevant question—particularly to those involved in marketing brand *A*—is *why* this pattern exists. Further analysis is necessary to answer this question.

Information Utilization Analysis   This type of analysis can be used instead of, or in addition to, before–after analysis. In most instances it is a substitute for before–after analysis because before–after analysis has demanding data requirements which involve a longitudinal study sufficiently precise to measure brand preferences before and after information seeking, or reliance on recall.

Table 18.4   BEFORE–AFTER ANALYSIS OF THE IMPACT OF INFORMATION SEEKING ON BRAND PREFERENCE

Brand	Consumers Preferring Brand Before Information Seeking (%)	Consumers Preferring Brand After Information Seeking (%)
A	30	15
B	40	40
C	30	45
	100	100

The methodological requirements for information utilization analysis are less exacting. Table 18.5 illustrates the first phase of this type of analysis. Brand A is compared with the average for other brands (AOB) in terms of exposure to sources of information. Exposure is classified into three categories: decisive, contributory, and ineffective.

Brand *A* appears to be enjoying reasonable success in terms of *total exposure.* Compared to AOB, brand *A* has better total exposure in radio and television, and is about average in personal contacts and salesmen. However, purchasers of brand *A* are considerably less exposed to magazines and newspapers.

Table 18.6 carries the analysis into the second phase. Brand *A* is compared with AOB in terms of effectiveness indices (decisive exposure versus total exposure) for information sources used by purchasers. This analysis indicates that brand *A* is reasonably competitive with AOB for radio, television, magazines, and newspapers. Personal contacts and salesmen seem to be major reasons why brand *A* is being hurt by consumers' information-seeking behavior.

Table 18.7 analyzes the situation further by noting the relationship between the brand recommended through personal contacts and purchasing behavior. Compared to AOB, brand *A* suffers from a low recommendation-fulfillment rate. That is, when other consumers recommend brand *A*, consumers have a much lower tendency to actually purchase *A* compared to when other brands are recommended.

Moreover, when other brands are recommended, consumers have a below average tendency to switch to brand *A*. As Table 18.8 indicates, brand *A* loses 1.55 customers for each one who switches to *A*. Other brands net out.

In summary, information seeking adversely affects brand *A* because it is getting poor word-of-mouth advertising, it has a low recommendation-fulfillment rate, and it is doing poorly at point of sale even though it has average exposure. Several additional steps are necessary to complete the diagnosis:

Table 18.5 EXPOSURE TO SOURCES OF INFORMATION

Type of Exposure By Type of Information Source	Brand Purchased	
	Brand A (%)	Average for All Other Brands (%)
Personal contacts		
Decisive exposure	28	34
Contributory exposure	18	25
Ineffective exposure	16	6
Total	62	65
Radio		
Decisive exposure	1	1
Contributory exposure	2	2
Ineffective exposure	6	4
Total	9	7
Television		
Decisive exposure	3	2
Contributory exposure	7	7
Ineffective exposure	8	2
Total	18	11
Magazines		
Decisive exposure	15	21
Contributory exposure	22	29
Ineffective exposure	8	12
Total	45	62
Newspapers		
Decisive exposure	3	4
Contributory exposure	15	22
Ineffective exposure	11	10
Total	29	36
Salesmen		
Decisive exposure	23	33
Contributory exposure	35	54
Ineffective exposure	37	10
Total	95	97

(1) The cells in Tables 18.4 through 18.8 should be analyzed by economic, demographic, and perhaps psychographic characteristics to determine *which* types of consumers are reacting adversely to the results of these search activities.

(2) Further analysis should determine why personal contacts are more effective for other brands than they are for brand A.

Table 18.6 EFFECTIVENESS INDICES FOR
INFORMATION SOURCES

Information Source	Purchasers of Brand A	Average for Purchasers of All Other Brands
Personal contacts	45.2	52.3
Radio	11.1	14.3
Television	16.7	18.2
Magazines	33.3	33.9
Newspapers	10.3	11.1
Salesmen	24.2	34.0

NOTE: These indices are computed by calculating the ratio of decisive exposure to total exposure for each information source.

Table 18.7 RELATIONSHIP BETWEEN BRAND RECOMMENDED THROUGH PERSONAL CONTACTS AND PURCHASING BEHAVIOR

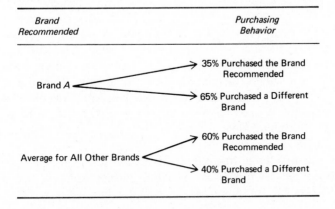

(3) The reasons for the relative ineffectiveness of salesmen should be determined. Does brand A have a lower gross margin and/or do salesmen earn lower commissions on A than on other brands? Perhaps A has service problems or maybe the delivery period is too long.

Unfortunately, the techniques do not answer every question. However, they do provide a framework for diagnosing the impact of search and alternative evaluation, and they point up areas of weakness that can be studied further with the appropriate research techniques.

Table 18.8   NET GAINS AND LOSSES RESULTING FROM
SWITCHING FROM THE BRAND
RECOMMENDED THROUGH PERSONAL
CONTACTS

Brand	Number of Customers Switching to the Brand for each 100 Switchings from the Brand	Net Gain or Loss (%)
A	45	−55
Average for all other brands	99	−01

Strategies for Capitalizing on Personal Influence Processes

In Chapter 17 it was shown that personal sources of information have a decisive impact on many purchasing decisions. This section discusses several basic strategies for adapting to and/or capitalizing on personal influence processes.

Using people who have a high degree of public exposure is another ated considerable initial interest in marketing circles, because it appeared that a key to increased promotional effectiveness was to advertise directly to opinion leaders and have them pass on the information to other consumers. However, closer analysis reveals that there are practical difficulties in implementation.

The most formidable problem lies in identifying opinion leaders. Opinion leaders, it will be recalled, exist in all stratas of society; they differ from other consumers in terms of competence, social location, the personification of certain values, and exposure to mass media; and they were thought to be monomorphic rather than polymorphic. Thus a marketer needed to conduct his own research to identify opinion leaders.[27]

There is some hope that the identification problem may be overcome in the future. If opinion leadership is specific to interest spheres, and it is possible to identify leaders for these spheres, then individualized research may not be necessary.

Even when opinion leaders are identified, it may not be profitable to direct advertising to them. For example, Tigert and Arnold found that opinion leaders could not be reached through print media any more effectively than the average consumer in the population. However, in Canada they found that it was

---

[27] Several writers have made this point. See, for example, Robert C. Brooks, Jr., "Word of Mouth Advertising in Selling New Products," *J. Marketing*, vol. 22, pp. 154–161 (Oct. 1957); Thomas Robertson, "The Process of Innovation and the Diffusion of Innovation," *J. Marketing*, vol. 31, pp. 14–19 (Jan. 1967).

possible to reach general opinion leaders through several television and print media vehicles.[28]

In situations where opinion leaders can be identified and reached effectively, several strategies are possible. First, as mentioned above, advertisements via the mass media or direct mail—if not too expensive—can be directed to them.

Second, opinion leaders can play a role in product decisions. Since opinion leaders also have a tendency to be innovators, their purchasing behavior can be monitored to obtain advance notice of consumption trends. Hollywood Vassarette has used this technique to predict fashion trends for women's intimate apparel. In addition, opinion leaders can be used to evaluate the acceptability of new products or fashions.

A third way of using opinion leaders is to give them, or loan them, a product. For example, retailers have been able to sell large quantities of merchandise that was not moving by giving it away to opinion leaders.

Finally, opinion leaders can be used as retail sales clerks. Many clothing retailers have used this approach. Manufacturers can follow this strategy in cases where they provide, or pay for sales people for retailers.

Simulating Opinion Leaders   In situations where it is not possible or practical to identify real opinion leaders, an alternative strategy is to simulate them. One technique is to use advertising to replace or reduce the need for personal influence. Advertisements can communicate the idea that the consumer's reference group buys the product and that buying it is therefore appropriate for him. A related technique is to use testimonial advertising by a famous person that is perceived as competent to give advice about the product or service.[29]

Since opinion leadership and innovativeness are often highly correlated, it is sometimes possible to use innovators as quasi-leaders, or a proxy variable for leaders. This strategy is appealing when innovators can be effectively reached through the mass media but opinion leaders can not. Tigert and Arnold found that United States innovators—like opinion leaders—could not be reached effectively through print media. However, several print and television vehicles can reach Canadian innovators effectively.[30]

Summers has studied the media exposure patterns of innovators in six product categories: (1) packaged food products, (2) household cleansers and detergents, (3) women's clothing fashions, (4) cosmetics and personal grooming aids, (5) small appliances, and (6) large appliances. He demonstrated the differential value of twelve specific types of media vehicles in *selectively* reaching the innovator for each of the product categories. For example, home magazines were effective in attracting consumer innovators in all six product cate-

---

[28]   Douglas J. Tigert and Stephen J. Arnold, *Profiling Self-Designated Opinion Leaders and Self-Designated Innovators through Life Style Research* (Toronto: University of Toronto School of Business, June 1971), pp. 28–29.

[29]   Ernest Dichter, "How Word-of-Mouth Advertising Works," *Harvard Business Rev.*, vol. 44, pp. 147–166 (Nov.–Dec. 1966).

[30]   Tigert and Arnold, *op. cit.*,[28] pp. 28–29.

gories. In comparison, television, radio, and romance magazine audiences did not contain disproportionately high concentrations of innovators for any product category. In general, different media tended to be most important for those product categories for which their editorial content was relevant. This was particularly true in the case of women's fashion magazines and women's clothing fashions.[31]

Using people who have a high degree of public exposure is another potential method of simulating opinion leadership. In the introduction of the Mustang, for example, the Ford Motor Company used several promotional approaches where college newspaper editors, disk jockeys, and airline stewardesses were loaned Mustangs.[32] Similarly, the Chrysler Corporation tried to generate conversations about the new Plymouth by offering 5,000 cab drivers in 67 cities $5 if they asked Chrysler mystery riders if they had seen the 1963 Plymouth.[33] Some restaurants and bars offer cab drivers and bell-hops meals and drinks at cost if they refer traveling executives and other "out-of-towners" to their establishments.

Creating New Opinion Leaders   An alternative or complementary strategy is to create opinion leaders. This may be an attractive approach when it is impossible to identify and/or reach real opinion leaders.

This approach has been used to transform unknown songs and unknown singing stars into hits. The initial step was to seek out social leaders among the relevant buying public—high school students. Class presidents, secretaries, sports' captains, and cheerleaders were selected from geographically diverse high schools. Later research revealed that most of these students were not opinion leaders for records.

The social leaders were contacted by mail and invited to join a select panel to help evaluate rock-and-roll records. The introductory letter stressed several major points:

(1) The recipient had been carefully selected, and the organizers felt that he, as a leader, should be better able to identify potential rock-and-roll hits than his fellow students.

(2) In return for his help, he would receive a token of appreciation for his cooperation—free records.

(3) He was encouraged to discuss his choices with friends and to weigh their opinions before submitting a final vote.

(4) He would be told something about each specific record and the singing star. In addition, *Billboard Magazine* and record stores were suggested as sources of information to verify his attitudes and eventual choices.

---

[31] John O. Summers, "Media Exposure Patterns of Consumer Innovators," *J. Marketing*, vol. 36, pp. 43–49 (Jan. 1972).

[32] Frederick D. Sturdivant *et al.*, *Managerial Analysis in Marketing* (Glenview, Ill.: Scott, Foresman, 1970), p. 233.

[33] *The Wall Street J.* (Sept. 27, 1962), p. 5.

(5) He was a member of a panel of leaders, and after the panel members had voted he would be informed of the outcome.

(6) He was under no obligation to join the panel and he could withdraw from it at any time.

(7) The experiment was essentially unstructured, but he would be informed of any expected or unexpected results.

(8) An informal two-way atmosphere was encouraged and any new ideas or suggestions would be welcomed and, if appropriate, adopted.

(9) He would be asked also to answer a few simple questions each month, and the results of the previous month's questionnaire would be made available to respondents the following month.

The total cost of the experiment was less than $5,000. The results were impressive: several records reached the top ten charts in the trial cities but did not make the top ten selections in any other cities. Thus, without contacting any radio stations or any record stores, rock-and-roll records were pulled through the channels of distribution and made into hits.[34]

Stimulating Information Seeking Another family of strategies consists of various techniques designed to stimulate information seeking. These techniques may be used instead of, or in addition to, those mentioned above.

One approach is to generate curiosity and interest in products through planned secrecy. This technique was apparently successful for the new Mustang which was "the most talked about—and least seen—auto of the year."[35]

Another technique is to use advertisements that capture the imagination of the public through various techniques, particularly slogans or phrases that become part of the everyday language. For example, Volkswagen ads are thought to stimulate conversations. Alka-Seltzer's, "try it, you'll like it" advertisements also appear to generate considerable word of mouth.

Another approach is to use advertisements that ask consumers to seek information. "Tell your friends," "ask your friends," and "ask the man who owns one" are examples of this technique.

Demonstrations, displays, and trial usage are methods that can be used to encourage consumer experience with more expensive products. For example, color television manufacturers sell their sets to hotels and motels at low prices partly because they feel it increases the chances that consumers will purchase their brands. Similarly, new types of telephones are placed in public locations because the practice is thought to accelerate adoption.

Summary and Evaluation In spite of the impressive amount of research that has been done on how consumers use personal sources of information, little attention has been given to the problems involved in practically implementing

---

[34] Joseph R. Mancuso, "Why Not Create Opinion Leaders for New Product Introductions?" *J. Marketing*, vol. 33, pp. 20–25 (July 1969).

[35] *Time* (Mar. 13, 1964), p. 91.

these processes. Specific questions about how to combine mass media and word-of-mouth advertising are rarely raised, let alone studied. Yet the potential benefits to marketers can be impressive. Consider:

(1) Advertising of a certain type for a household product was able, over a period of several months, to steadily increase word-of-mouth activity, particularly among people who might be regarded as prospective users of the product.

(2) A study of a novel consumer service found that 73 percent of consumers who had tried the service as the result of direct-mail advertising, and who had responded to a mail questionnaire, indicated that they had recommended the service to friends and relatives. Furthermore, 8 percent of these respondents claimed that they had told at least ten people about the new service.

(3) One company in a highly competitive consumer product category regularly spends only one third as much on advertising as its two major competitors, yet retains a market share roughly equal to that of the two leading competitors. . . . The apparent reason for their ability to succeed with relatively little advertising was the fact that their brand received vastly more word-of-mouth activity than did the other two brands which had about the same market shares. The other brands were moved by muscle. The word-of-mouth brand had developed an advertising program which apparently aroused curiosity which, in turn, stimulated some of the information seeking. In addition, the company had a good product which was well regarded by certain opinion leaders, and this resulted in favorable word-of-mouth activity.[36]

Research designed to discover the success requirements for the above types of strategies is necessary if the gap between research findings and operational strategies is to be bridged.

At the present stage of development it seems appropriate to conclude that whatever use is made of personal sources of information, it is necessary that advertising and distribution strategies be coordinated and consistent with personal communication. The firm needs to monitor informal channels to determine how actively they are being used, as well as the content of the communications. Additional research is necessary before it is possible to specify which of the strategies are most effective in which types of situations and the specific techniques that should be used to implement them.

Strategies for Capitalizing on Consumer Utilization of Mass Media and Marketer-Dominated Sources of Information

Chapter 16 discussed a profiling strategy that is becoming increasingly popular. To review, it was shown how heavy users of one product: (1) are heavy users of certain other products, (2) have certain economic, demographic, and

---

[36] Cox, *op. cit.*,[6] pp. 185–186.

psychographic characteristics, and (3) utilize specific types and clusters of media vehicles. The heavy eye-makeup user was cited as an example of this profiling strategy.

These profiles are very useful in making creative strategy and creative execution decisions. Data concerning other products that are consumed heavily; economic, demographic, and psychographic characteristics; and media usage patterns enable the marketer to construct a revealing portrait of the heavy user of his product. Coupled with an understanding of important evaluative criteria and attitudes, these portraits increase the probability that advertisements will be more relevant to the user and hence have greater impact.

The profiling strategy is also useful in developing advertising budgets and selecting media vehicles. Bass, Pessemier, and Tigert have developed a complex model for making these types of decisions. In their model the usual measures of media reach, frequency, duplicated audiences, and so on disappear as critical dimensions of the problem. Instead, results are expressed in terms of dollars of new sales produced per additional dollar efficiently spent on media purchases.[37]

Most studies, it will be recalled, find that a large percentage of consumers visit only one retail outlet before purchasing the product in question. If a firm does in fact face this situation, what are the strategy implications? At first blush it would appear that the firm should attempt to maximize the number of outlets handling its product. However, closer analysis would seem to suggest that limited distribution may not be undesirable if the store that the consumer shops at handles the firm's product. Basically, then, a firm has two alternatives: (1) intensive distribution or (2) limited distribution accompanied by intensive advertising designed to (a) establish brand awareness and hopefully brand preference at the point of problem recognition and (b) stimulate consumers to visit those stores handling the firm's brand. Of course, the choice between these strategies would also involve nonbehavioral considerations that affect the firm's profitability.

Strategies Based on
Information-Seeking Role Structures

Information-seeking role structures affect a firm's promotional strategies and distribution policies. For example, if both husband and wife are actively involved in information seeking, then the firm should design a media strategy that uses media that reach the greatest number of husbands and wives in the target market at the lowest cost. Similarly, a firm's creative strategy might differ from the strategy that would be used if either one of the spouses were exclusively involved in information seeking.

Finally, information-seeking role structures might influence the marketer's choice of retail outlets. For example, if both husband and wife are actively involved, the firm would be interested in having their product in outlets having

---

[37] F. M. Bass, E. A. Pessemier, and D. J. Tigert, "A Taxonomy of Magazine Readership Applied to Problems in Marketing Strategy and Media Selection," *J. Business,* vol. 42, pp. 337–363 (July 1969).

hours of operation compatible with the times most convenient for husband and wife to shop together, and having physical facilities and locations that are acceptable to both.

SUMMARY

This chapter continued the discussion of search processes. Attention was given first to the types of family role structures involved in information-seeking activity. The relative importance of information sources and many of the problems involved in determining relative importance were discussed. Marketer-dominated sources are more important in terms of exposure, but personal sources are more important in terms of effectiveness. Certain characteristics of the information and information source, perceived risk, characteristics of the decision-making unit, and the stage of market development affect consumers' choices of information sources.

Finally, some of the marketing implications of search processes were discussed. In order to design strategies based on search processes the marketer needs to know: (1) the percentage of the target market that engages in search, (2) the percentage of the target market that uses each type of information source, (3) the relative importance of information sources. After discussing how this type of information can be obtained, a case example was used to demonstrate data presentation techniques that facilitate the diagnosis of the impact of search and alternative evaluation on the success of a brand. The chapter concluded with a discussion of strategies for capitalizing on consumers' utilization of personal sources, mass media, and marketer-dominated sources of information.

REVIEW AND DISCUSSION QUESTIONS

1. What problems, if any, are involved in determining the relative importance of information sources? How should these problems be overcome?

2. How does the type of information desired affect the utilization of information sources?

3. Select a product and discuss how you would go about determining the information-seeking role structure associated with that product.

4. What is meant by predictive value and confidence value? What is the relevance of the concepts?

5. Describe the cumulative hypothesis.

6. What is the difference between effectiveness and exposure?

7. When you last bought an item of clothing, what was the relative importance of the information sources that you consulted? Why was this source most important? What type of information did you obtain from this source and how does it compare with the type of information generally obtained from the most important source?

8. Assume you are a consultant to the research director of a large manufacturer of middle-priced ($1000–$4000) boats. The research director wants to know

the relative importance of information sources and asks you to prepare a statement indicating how you would go about it.

9. Assume that your research recommendation was accepted and the research done. With the use of an index of relative effectiveness it was found that personal sources were five times more effective than advertising. Seeing this finding, the marketing vice president has asked the advertising manager to justify the amount of money being spent on advertising. You are the advertising manager. What do you say?

10. The research director for brand *C* presents you with the following data based on a rigorously controlled study:

Brand	Preferring Brand before Information Seeking (%)	Preferring Brand after Information Seeking (%)
A	30	35
B	30	35
C	40	30
	100	100

The research director is uncertain as to what the problem is and does not know how to proceed. As a consultant to Company *C*, prepare an outline indicating what procedure will allow the company to determine what the problems are.

11. Your company manufactures a full line of mobile homes in all price ranges. Several studies have indicated that personal sources of information are considerably more effective than other sources. Prepare a statement indicating (a) the alternative strategies that can be used to utilize effectively consumers' use of personal information sources, (b) the alternative that you prefer and why.

19

PURCHASING PROCESSES: STORE CHOICES AND SHOPPER PROFILES

How do consumers choose stores in which to shop? How important is a store's image in determining store patronage? What factors determine a store's image? How do consumers react when the brand they prefer is unavailable? Do private brands appeal to a distinct market segment? What types of consumers purchase private brands? Are some consumers more susceptible than others to special deals?

Each of the above questions is concerned with <u>purchasing processes, or the effects of customer interaction with various aspects of a store environment</u>. The phenomena encountered in retail outlets often exert a profound influence on the consumer's behavior, and, as is apparent from the above questions, a knowledge of purchasing processes is of vital importance in understanding consumer behavior.

Because purchasing processes have many dimensions, three chapters are required to cover the subject adequately. After discussing the meaning of purchasing processes, this chapter presents an extended conceptual framework for studying this type of behavior and then discusses store choice and shopper profiles. Chapter 20 analyzes in-store behavior, while Chapter 21 presents additional dimensions of this stage in the decision-making process.

NATURE OF PURCHASING PROCESSES

This section discusses the meaning of purchasing processes, including their relation to concepts and variables previously discussed. An extended conceptualization of purchasing processes is then advanced which specifies the variables and relations that are discussed in this and the succeeding two chapters.

Meaning of Purchasing Processes

The consumer may or may not have visited retail outlets as he passed through the previous stages in the decision-making process. However, with few exceptions, consumers visit retail stores sometime during the decision-making period. This customer–store environment interaction, called purchasing processes, is of vital importance in understanding consumer behavior.

Figure 19.1 illustrates the relation between purchasing processes and the concepts and variables previously discussed. As was true in the case of other stages in the decision-making process, purchasing processes are complex phenomena involving (1) initiating factors, (2) the processes, (3) outcomes of the processes, and (4) consequences of the processes. Each of these aspects is briefly described.

Initiators of Purchasing Processes   Purchasing-process behavior can be precipitated by two classes of variables. First, it can be problem oriented in the sense that the consumer visits a retail outlet in order to purchase a product or service that satisfies some perceived problem. In other words, problem recognition is one initiator of purchasing processes.

All purchasing-process behavior is certainly not problem oriented, however. Visiting retail stores is often precipitated by other factors, including, for example, a desire to get out of the house, a desire to get away from the spouse and children, a desire to avoid something unpleasant, or a desire to engage in fantasy. Retail visits initiated by these and many other similar factors may or may not trigger the recognition of a problem and may or may not culminate in a purchase.

Purchasing Processes   Purchasing processes may involve motives, evaluative criteria, attitudes, and the processes of selective attention, comprehension, and retention. Each of these factors may be involved in or otherwise affect the complex interactions of purchase intentions, consumer characteristics, and many other factors that comprise a store's environment.

Outcomes of Purchasing Processes   Purchasing processes produce two major types of outcomes—"purchase" or "halt." A purchase *may* occur when the

Information Processing   *Central Control Unit*   *Environmental Influences*

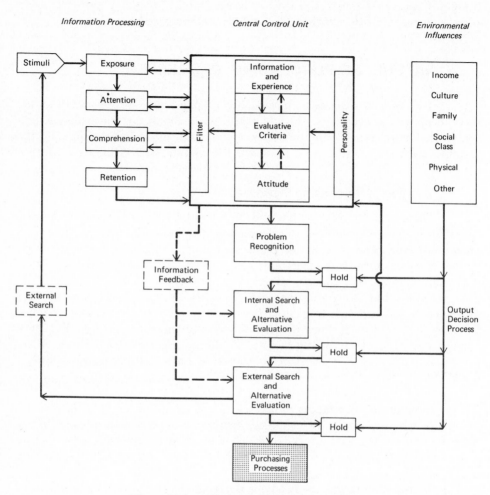

Figure 19.1 PURCHASING PROCESSES

consumer finds an alternative that satisfies his evaluative criteria. The process may halt because there are no alternatives that satisfy the evaluative criteria, or because the consumer cannot find them, or because exposure to the store environment extinguishes the underlying problem by altering the relation between the desired and actual states.

Consequences of Purchasing Processes The outcomes of purchasing-process behavior are stored in the consumer's memory. As a consequence, if the results of purchasing-process behavior are perceived as satisfactory, similar procedures may be used in the future. For example, the consumer may return to the same store, or adopt a standardized way of shopping the store, or respond to displays, deals, and/or salesmen in a way similar to past behavior.

Extended Conceptualization of Purchasing Processes

While Figure 19.1 illustrates the relations among purchasing processes and the other concepts that comprise the model of consumer behavior, it says very little about the anatomy of purchasing processes. Figure 19.2 attempts to overcome this problem by presenting an extended conceptualization of purchasing processes. Purchasing processes are viewed as consisting of four interacting categories of variables: (1) preshopping purchase intentions, (2) consumer characteristics, (3) store environment characteristics, and (4) purchase outcomes.

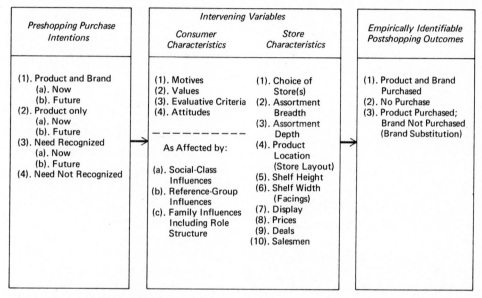

Figure 19.2   EXTENDED CONCEPTUALIZATION OF PURCHASING PROCESSES

Purchase Intentions   The preshopping purchase intentions typology consists of the *major*[1] stages or degrees of planning that exist before the customer enters the store. Stated differently, the categories comprising the typology vary in terms of the degree of *closure* that exists in the decision-making process prior to exposure to the store environment. The intentions are defined as follows:

(1)   *Product and brand*—Before entering the store the consumer knows both the product and the brand of product to be purchased.

(2)   *Product only*—Before entering the store the shopper knows which product she wants but has not decided on the brand, for example, a plan to buy color television but not a particular brand.

---

[1]   "Major" refers to the presence or absence of a product or brand decision prior to entering the store. A more sophisticated typology would be n-dimensional to accommodate preshopping decisions concerning the amount to be purchased, the kind of package or container to be purchased, and so on.

(3) *Product class only*—Before entering the store the shopper knows the class of product that she intends to purchase but has not decided on a product in that class or on a brand, for example, intention to buy meat but must decide on steak or hamburger and which brand.

(4) *Problem recognized*—Before entering the store the consumer recognizes the existence of a problem but has not decided which product class, product, or brand to purchase, for example, a need for something for the living room or for the spouse's birthday.

(5) *Problem not recognized*—Before entering the store the consumer does not recognize the existence of a problem, or the problem is latent until evoked by in-store stimuli.

Intervening Variables Both consumer and store characteristics are conceptualized as intervening between preshopping intentions and postshopping outcomes.

(1) **Consumer Characteristics** Consumer characteristics are the basic concepts comprising the model of consumer behavior used in this text (see Figure 19.1). It should be noted that these are general concepts having numerous specific applications. Attitudes toward shopping and private brands are examples of more specific attitudes that will be examined in this and the next chapter.

(2) **Store Characteristics** Provided certain other conditions exist, the store characteristics itemized in Figure 19.2 may affect decision-process behavior in several ways. First, some characteristics are constraints in the sense that they affect the number and types of alternatives perceived by consumers. Store choice, assortment breadth and depth, store layout, and shelf height and width may all perform this function. Second, some of the characteristics may increase or decrease the intensity of brand preference that existed prior to shopping.[2] Prices, deals, and salesmen may all perform this function. Finally, every store characteristic itemized in Figure 19.2 has the ability to trigger problem recognition.

Postshopping Outcomes The outcomes typology listed in Figure 19.2 consists of the major kinds of *empirically identifiable* behavior that can result from shopping. The outcomes are (1) product and brand purchased, (2) product purchased, brand not purchased, that is, brand substitution, or (3) no purchase.

Intentions–Outcomes Matrix For several reasons which will become apparent later, it is often useful to compare preshopping purchase intentions with postshopping outcomes. Conceptually, there are 15 categories that result from

---

[2] These two influences are similar to those suggested in Francesco M. Nicosia, *Consumer Decision Process* (Englewood Cliffs, N.J.: Prentice-Hall, 1966), p. 180.

the paring of intentions and outcomes. Fortunately, this categorization can be compressed, since several categories are not empirically identifiable. When the conceptual intentions–outcomes matrix is modified to reflect the operational requirements, the resulting matrix is collapsed into nine categories (see Table 19.1). The terms used to describe the cells of the matrix are:

    (1)   Specifically planned (cell 1)
    (2)   Generally planned (cells 4, 6, 8)
    (3)   Brand substitution (cell 3)
    (4)   Unplanned (cell 9)
    (5)   Abort (cells 2, 5, 7).

Table 19.1   OPERATIONAL INTENTIONS–OUTCOMES MATRIX

	Outcomes		
Intentions	*Product and Brand Purchased*	*No Purchase*	*Product Purchased; Brand Not Purchased*
Product and brand	1	2	3
Product only	4	5	
Product class only	6	7	
Problem recognized	8		
Problem not recognized	9		

Overview of Purchasing-Process Research

Table 19.2 indicates the research status of relations between the major categories of variables comprising the extended conceptualization of purchasing processes. It is instructive to note that, like many other areas of consumer behavior, research in purchasing processes has concentrated on a few relations and ignored many of the others. Most research has focused on the relations between store characteristics and outcomes, and on those between consumer characteristics and outcomes. Research has also been devoted to the following relations: (1) consumer characteristics and store characteristics, (2) consumer characteristics and outcomes, and (3) store characteristics and planning categories. The remaining relations itemized in Table 19.2 have not been researched.

The remainder of this chapter discusses relations between consumer characteristics and store characteristics, specifically store choice and shopper profiles. Both findings and marketing implications are presented.

Table 19.2 EXTENDED CONCEPTUALIZATION OF PURCHASING
PROCESSES—RELATIONS BETWEEN MAJOR CATEGORIES
OF VARIABLES

		Research Status
(1)	Purchase intentions and consumer characteristics	No research
(2)	Purchase intentions and store characteristics	No research
(3)	Purchase intentions and outcomes (purchase categories)	Limited research
(4)	Consumer characteristics and store characteristics	Limited research
(5)	Consumer characteristics and outcomes	Considerable research
(6)	Store characteristics and outcomes	Considerable research
(7)	Consumer characteristics, store characteristics, and purchase intentions	No research
(8)	Consumer characteristics and planning categories (intentions and outcomes)	Limited research
(9)	Store characteristics and planning categories (intentions and outcomes)	Limited research
(10)	Consumer characteristics, store characteristics, and outcomes	No research
(11)	Consumer characteristics, store characteristics, and planning categories	No research

STORE CHOICE

Figure 19.3 is a conceptualization of how consumers select retail outlets.
The scheme consists of four variables: (1) evaluative criteria, (2) perceived
characteristics of stores, (3) comparison processes, and (4) acceptable and
unacceptable stores. Store choice, then, is viewed as consisting of processes
whereby the consumer compares the characteristics of stores, as he perceives
them, with his evaluative criteria.

Consumers do not go through this process before each store visit. Instead,
if past experiences with a store have been satisfactory, and other conditions exist,
the store is revisited without reevaluation. The majority of store visits that consumers make are probably not preceded by deliberate store-choice processes.

The first part of this section discusses general determinants of store
choice, that is, the comparison process involving evaluative criteria and perceived
characteristics of stores. Composite determinants of store choice are discussed in
the second part followed by an analysis of store images and methods of
measuring images.

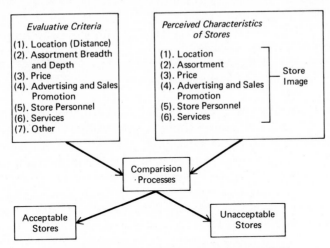

Figure 19.3   STORE-CHOICE PROCESSES

General Determinants of Store Choice

Determinants of store choice vary significantly depending on the type of product being purchased, the general type of store involved—for example, supermarket, department store, discount department store, and so on—and certain characteristics of the consumer. In general, the determinants are (1) location, (2) depth and breadth of assortment, (3) price, (4) advertising and word-of-mouth communications, (5) sales promotion, (6) store personnel, (7) services, (8) physical attributes, and (9) store clientele.

Location   The location effect on store choice is conceptually simple. Consumers farther away are less likely to purchase than are consumers who are closer to the store. The obvious reason is that as distance from a store increases so does the number of intervening alternatives. Olsson has compiled two excellent summaries of research in this area.[3]

During the last fifty years numerous attempts have been made to determine the effect of location, or distance, on patronage. These investigations have focused on cities, trading areas, shopping centers, and individual stores.

(1) Cities and Trading Areas   Many studies have investigated the impact of city, town, and trading area locations as determinants of store patronage. For example, Thompson has studied the tendency of 1543 consumers in ten small towns around Augusta, Georgia to shop in other towns. He found that over 84 percent had shopped out of town at least once during the last six months. More-

---

[3]   Gunnar Olsson, *Distance and Human Interaction: A Review and Bibliography* (Philadelphia: Regional Science Research Institute, 1965).

over, 64 percent had shopped out of town six times or more in the six months prior to the time they reported.[4]

Another study investigated the impact of out-of-town shopping patterns of the residents of State College, Pennsylvania, a unversity town of 27,000 permanent residents. Of the total sample, 301 or 71.4 percent had shopped outside a five-mile radius of the downtown area one or more times during the previous year.[5]

Several attempts have been made to explain this type of patronage behavior. In the 1920s, William J. Reilly studied patronage in Texas and then postulated that two cities attract retail trade from an intermediate town in the vicinity of the breaking point (where 50 percent of the trade is attracted to each city) in direct proportion to their population and in inverse proportion to the square of the distances from the two cities to the intermediate town.[6]

Two decades later, Converse found the following modification of "Reilly's law" useful in explaining intercity shopping patterns:[7]

$$\left(\frac{B_a}{B_b} \right) = \left(\frac{P_a}{P_b} \right) \left(\frac{D_b}{D_a} \right)$$

where

B_a = proportion of trade attracted from intermediate town by city A
B_b = proportion of trade attracted from intermediate town by city B
P_a = population of city A
P_b = population of city B
D_a = distance from intermediate town to city A
D_b = distance from intermediate town to city B

Converse found that in 1942 this formula predicted the actual flow of trade to two Illinois towns from an intermediate town with an error of 3 percent.

Although these models were useful in their day, they are too simplistic to be useful in most contemporary situations. Among other things, they ignore the relative incomes of the populations, merchandise assortments in the two cities, and consumer preferences.

For example, Herrmann and Beik found that the percentage of purchases made out of town varied from 43.8 percent for women's coats, to 8.8 percent for housewares.[8] Similarly, Thompson found wide variations across product categories. Thus, over 50 percent of respondents purchased women's coats, curtains and drapes, rugs and carpets, men's suits, and women's fancy dresses out of town.

---

[4] John R. Thompson, "Characteristics and Behavior of Out-Shopping Consumers," *J. Retailing*, vol. 47, pp. 70–80 (Spring 1971).

[5] Robert O. Herrmann and Leland L. Beik, "Shoppers' Movements Outside Their Local Retail Area," *J. Marketing*, vol. 32, pp. 45–51 (Oct. 1968).

[6] William J. Reilly, *Methods for the Study of Retail Relationships* (Austin, Tex.: Bureau of Business Research, University of Texas Press, 1929), p. 16.

[7] Paul D. Converse, "New Laws of Retail Gravitation," *J. Marketing*, vol. 13, pp. 379–388 (Oct. 1949).

[8] Herrmann and Beik, *op. cit.,*[5] p. 46.

Conversely, major appliances, automobiles, furniture, and jewelry were pur-chased out of town much less frequently.[9]

Out-of-town shopping also varies by type of consumer. For example, Thompson found that the tendency to shop out of town is higher for higher income consumers, white consumers, and young consumers.[10] Another study found out-of-town shopping to be more frequent among higher income families and families without younger children or a large number of children.[11]

It would appear that location models could be improved by incorporating these types of variables into the equations.

(2) **Shopping Centers** Several studies have investigated the impact of location, or driving time, on shopping center preference. Brunner and Mason's analysis of the Toledo, Ohio, market led them to conclude that the propensity to shop at a center is inversely associated with the driving time to reach the center, and that a time limitation of 15 minutes would be applicable for approximately three fourths of the center's patrons.[12] However, a study of the Cleveland market found wider variation, with the percentage of customers living within 15 minutes driving time ranging from 55.5 percent to 83.7 percent for the seven centers studied.[13]

The Cleveland study, like others that could be cited, found that variables in addition to distance must be considered in order to predict shopping center patronage. For example, the authors of the Cleveland study found that 98 percent of the variation in the percent of customers who drove more than 15 minutes to a shopping center was accounted for by the size of the shopping center in square feet and the limiting effect of Lake Erie on some shopping centers.[14]

Huff has developed a model that estimates the probability that con-sumers in each relatively homogeneous statistical unit (neighborhood) will go to a particular shopping center for a particular type of purchase:[15]

$$P_{ij} = \frac{\dfrac{S_j}{T_{ij}\lambda}}{\sum\limits_{j=1}^{n} \dfrac{(S_j}{T_{ij}\lambda)}}$$

---

[9] Thompson, *op. cit.*,[4] p. 79.

[10] Thompson, *op. cit.*,[4] p. 76.

[11] Hermann and Beik, *op. cit.*,[5] p. 51.

[12] James A. Brunner and John L. Mason, "The Influence of Driving Time upon Shopping Center Preference," *J. Marketing*, vol. 34, pp. 12–17 (Oct. 1970).

[13] William E. Cox, Jr. and Ernest F. Cooke, "Other Dimensions Involved in Shop-ping Center Preference," *J. Marketing*, vol. 34, pp. 12–17 (Oct. 1970).

[14] Brunner and Mason, *op. cit.*,[12] p. 16.

[15] David L. Huff, "A Probabilistic Analysis of Consumer Spatial Behavior," in William S. Decker (ed.), *Emerging Concepts in Marketing* (Chicago: Amer. Marketing Assoc., 1962), pp. 443–461.

where:

P_{ij} = probability that consumers from each of the ith statistical units will go to specific shopping center j

S_j = size of shopping center j

T_{ij} = travel time to shopping center j

λ = a parameter estimated empirically for each product category, for example, clothing, furniture.

Huff has used this equation to plot isolines which are equiprobability contours that consumers will shop in center j. The probability of patronage declines as the distance to other centers becomes less and the distance to center j becomes greater.[16]

(3) **Individual Stores** Numerous studies have investigated the effect of location, or distance, on store patronage. Figure 19.4 summarizes the findings of several studies. Caution must be exercised in drawing conclusions from these data as they were collected in different ways for different purposes. However, they do indicate a general relation between location and store patronage.[17] Of course, studies of nonfood and drug-store patronage typically yield different relations.

Depth and Breadth of Assortment In addition to location, both merchandise variety and assortment have been found to influence store preferences. Laboratory experiments and surveys indicate that stores offering either a deep assortment or a wide variety of product lines are preferred over stores having medium depth or breadth of assortment.[18]

Price The importance of price as a determinant of store patronage also varies by type of product, store, and customer. For example, studies of *department-store* shoppers have found that price is often far down the list as a reason for shopping at a particular store.[19] Some studies of *supermarket* shoppers

---

[16] For an excellent discussion of other techniques for estimating shopping center patronage, see Bernard J. LaLonde, *Differentials in Super Market Drawing Power* (East Lansing, Mich.: Bureau of Business and Economic Research, Michigan State University, 1962). For dissenting findings about these types of models, see Joseph B. Mason and Charles T. Moore, "An Empirical Reappraisal of Behavioristic Assumptions in Trading Area Studies," *J. Retailing*, pp. 31–37 (Winter 1970–1971).

[17] J. D. Forbes, "Consumer Patronage Behavior," in Robert L. King (ed.), *Marketing and the New Science of Planning* (Chicago: Amer. Marketing Assoc., 1968), pp. 381–385.

[18] Wroe Alderson and Robert Sessions, "Basic Research on Consumer Behavior: Report on a Study of Shopping Behavior and Methods for Its Investigation," in Ronald E. Frank, Alfred A. Kuehn, and William F. Massy (eds.), *Quantitative Techniques in Marketing Analysis* (Homewood, Ill.: Irwin, 1962), pp. 129–145.

[19] Stuart U. Rich and Bernard D. Portis, "The Imageries of Department Stores," *J. Marketing*, vol. 28, pp. 10–15 (Apr. 1964).

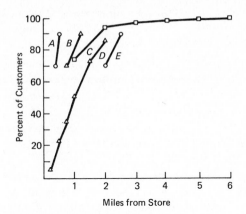

A: La Londe—Urban strip and cluster supermarkets
B: La Londe—Small town, neighborhood and community type
    center supermarkets
C: Lowry—all food and drugstores
D: Applebaum—One supermarket
E: La Londe—Supermarkets in regional shopping centers
SOURCES: W. Applebaum, "Methods for Determining Store Trade
            Areas, Market Penetration, and Potential Sales,"
            Marketing Research, vol. 3, p. 128 (May 1966),
            Bernard J. La Londe, "Differentials in Supermarket
            Drawing Power," transportation paper no. 11
            (East Lansing: Bureau of Business and Economic
            Research, Michigan State University, 1962), p. 48,
            Ira S. Lowry, "Location Parameters in the Pittsburgh
            Model," *Papers and Proc. Regional Science Assoc.*,
            vol. 11, p. 156 (1963).

Figure 19.4   DISTANCE EFFECTS ON STORE PATRONAGE IN SUPERMARKETS
AND DRUGSTORES.   J. D. Forbes, "Consumer Patronage Behavior," in
Robert L. King (ed.), *Marketing and the New Science of Planning* (Chicago:
Amer. Marketing Assoc., 1968), p. 382.

find price relatively unimportant,[20] yet others find price very important.[21] In the
case of *new car* buyers, price is the factor most frequently cited as most important
in the choice of a dealer.[22] Some surveys find that lower prices are the main
advantage seen to *discount-store* shopping,[23] while others find price is not an
important determinant.[24] In some instances, price is insignificant in deciding

---

[20]   "The Movers," *Progressive Grocer*, vol. 44, pp. K-35–K-58 (Nov. 1965).

[21]   Douglas J. Tigert and Donald J. Tigert, "Longitudinal Analysis of a Supermarket
Price War: A New Look at the Price–Quality Relationship," paper presented at the American
Marketing Association Fall Conf., Minneapolis, Minn. (Aug. 31, 1971).

[22]   Alderson Associates, Inc., *A Basic Study of Automobile Retailing* (Dearborn,
Mich.: Ford Motor Company, 1958).

[23]   "How Housewives See the Discount Store Today," *Discount Merchandiser*,
pp. 77–90 (Mar. 1970).

[24]   "Why Shoppers Chose Discount Stores vs. Downtown Stores," *Discount Merchandiser*, pp. 31–32 (Dec. 1971).

where to buy *major appliances* and *sport shirts*.[25] After reviewing the type of evidence presented above, one leading retailing authority concluded that the role of price is greatly overrated.[26] Given the diversity of findings, generalizations about the importance of price are not permissible at this time.

Advertising and Word-of-Mouth Communications   Advertising is a quasi-determinant of store patronage.[27] Advertisements are thought to inform consumers of sales, deals, new products, and so on.

Advertising's effect on store patronage is difficult to access and seems to vary depending on the type of purchase and store. For example, a study investigating information sources producing initial awareness of a new dairy products store found that advertising accounted for only 16.9 percent of awareness, compared to 50.5 percent for visual notice and 32.6 percent for word of mouth. Moreover, respondents who were asked what source of information was most influential in their decision to try the new store indicated word of mouth twice as often as advertising, and over three times more often than visual notice. Within a given neighborhood, the extent of personal influence was even more dramatic. In fact, there was a marked tendency for patrons' homes to be clustered together rather than randomly distributed (see Figure 19.5).[28]

Other studies have found that advertising can have a powerful impact on consumers' perceptions of a store. Consider:

(1)   One of the major mail-order chains talks about expanding its market upward, attracting the middle-class customer. Yet when the ads from stores of that chain were tested in three different cities where women did not know their actual identity, in every class the stores were seen as having a lower class appeal.[29]

(2)   A leading Kansas City store's copy was tested both in Kansas City and in Atlanta. The evaluations (were) by women who had no idea of the identity of the store and who were making their judgments entirely from the physical appearance of the copy . . . "I am not averse to bargains, but I wouldn't trust that store." "I imagine if you took something back, they would want to give you something in exchange and not give you the cash." . . . "The clerk standing there would be an immigrant, not enjoying

[25]   George Katona and Eva Mueller, "A Study of Purchase Decisions," in Lincoln H. Clark (ed.), *Consumer Behavior: The Dynamics of Consumer Reaction* (New York: New York University Press 1955), pp. 36–87.

[26]   William R. Davidson, "The Shake-Out in Appliance Retailing," *Home Appliance Builder,* pp. 21–29 (Mar. 1965).

[27]   See, for example, William Lazer and Eugene J. Kelly, "The Retailing Mix: Planning and Management," *J. Retailing,* vol. 37, pp. 34–41 (Spring 1961); William D. Tyler, "The Image, the Brand, and the Consumer," *J. Marketing,* vol. 22, pp. 162–165 (Oct. 1957); Pierre Martineau, *Motivation in Advertising* (New York: McGraw-Hill, 1957), chap. 15.

[28]   Robert F. Kelly, "The Role of Information in the Patronage Decision: A Diffusion Phenomenon," in M. S. Moyer and R. E. Vosburgh (eds.), *Marketing for Tomorrow . . . Today* (Chicago: Amer. Marketing Assoc., 1967), pp. 119–129.

[29]   Martineau, *op. cit.,*[27] p. 174.

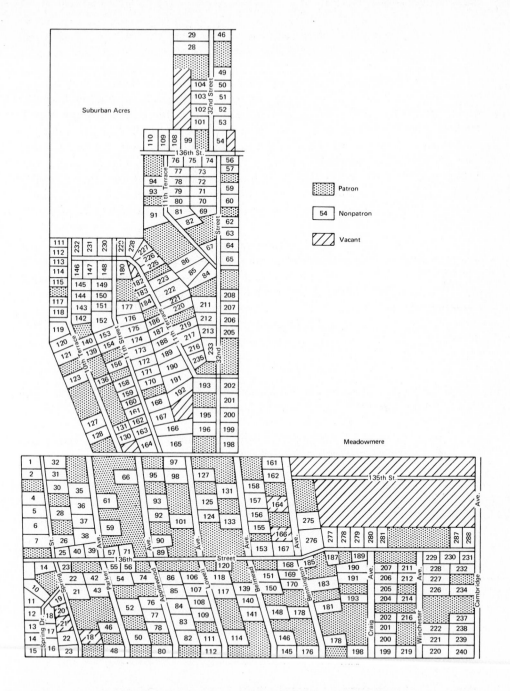

Figure 19.5 LOCATION OF NEW DAIRY-STORE CUSTOMERS' RESIDENCES IN TWO SUBDIVISIONS. Robert F. Kelly, "The Role of Information in the Patronage Decision: A Diffusion Phenomenon," in M. S. Moyer and R. E. Vosburgh (eds.), *Marketing for Tomorrow . . . Today* (Chicago: Amer. Marketing Assoc., 1967), p. 128

selling. She probably could just barely speak English." . . . "I am afraid a store like this would take advantage of my ignorance of some things."[30]

Sales Promotion   The role of sales promotion devices on store patronage also varies widely. Consider the case of trading stamps. Some studies find that while many consumers value and save these stamps, few attach enough significance to them to make them a determining factor in where they shop.[31] Similarly, another study found that consumers' perceptions of price levels and quality were the same for large supermarkets regardless of stamp status.[32] On the other hand, a longitudinal study found that a supermarket chain, in discontinuing trading stamps, suffered a significant deterioration in market share and store traffic: market share declined 12 percent and store traffic by approximately 21 percent.[33]

Store Personnel   Many studies document the importance of store personnel in the consumer's choice of a store. For example, in attempting to determine why a quality department store had been so successful in attracting Negro customers, research continually indicated that the reason was that clerks were friendlier. Similarly, neighborhood shopping centers usually rank higher than downtown stores in terms of friendliness.[34] Other studies have demonstrated that various characteristics of sales personnel, including politeness, courteousness, and product knowledge, are often used as criteria in evaluating stores.[35]

Services   The role of service also seems to vary considerably across both consumers and products. The following findings appear to be representative:

(1) A liberal return policy is very important in determining whether consumers will shop at discount houses.[36]

(2) In the purchase of new cars, expectation of good service is among the least frequently mentioned factors that buyers say caused them to select a dealer.[37]

(3) Service is one of the least frequently mentioned dealer characteristics

---

[30] Martineau, *op. cit.*,[27] pp. 175–176.

[31] T. Ellsworth, D. Benjamin, and H. Radolf, "Customer Response to Trading Stamps," *J. Retailing*, vol. 33, pp. 165–169, 206 (Winter 1957–1958); Norman Bussel "Let's Give Trading Stamps a Weigh," *Progressive Grocer*, vol. 44, pp. 154–158 (Nov. 1965).

[32] F. E. Brown and Alfred R. Oxenfeldt, "Price and Quality Comparisons between Stamp and Nonstamp Food Stores," *J. Retailing*, vol. 45, pp. 3–10, 84 (Fall 1969).

[33] Bernard J. LaLonde and Jerome Herniter, "The Effect of a Trading Stamp Discontinuance on Supermarket Performance: A Panel Approach," *J. Marketing Research*, vol. 7, pp. 205–209 (May 1970).

[34] Rich and Portis, *op. cit.*,[19] pp. 10–15.

[35] David J. Rachman and Linda J. Kemp, "Profile of the Discount House Customer," *J. Retailing*, vol. 39, pp. 1–8 (Summer 1963).

[36] Alderson Associates, *op. cit.*[22]

[37] Katona and Mueller, *op. cit.*,[25] pp. 30–87.

looked for by buyers of major appliances. Other studies present contradictory findings.[38]

Physical Attributes Physical attributes of a store affect consumers' perceptions of other store characteristics. The materials used on the exterior and interior, the kind of floors, the type of displays, and many other factors affect a store's image.

Store Clientele The type of people shopping in a store also influences store choice. One writer has stated this succinctly:

> Their personality concept is not primarily the result of physical features of the store—it is rather the result of the group of customers who have come to shop there. Customers associate themselves with a social group, shop where that group shops, and attribute to the store characteristics of the group.[39]

Composite Determinants of Store Choice

The preceding discussion demonstrated that determinants of store choice vary widely by type of product, store, and customer. Therefore, in operational situations, it is *meaningless* to talk about general determinants of store patronage. Rather, it is necessary to isolate patronage determinants for specific product categories, and then determine the relative importance of these determinants and how they vary by market segment.

Unfortunately, there are few research studies that have identified the relative importance of patronage determinants for specific product categories. The following are illustrative exceptions.

Women's Clothing Stores Perry and Norton have attempted to isolate the patronage determinants for women's clothing stores. Although their sample was limited to one hundred girls attending Oklahoma State University, and they prespecified a list of determinants rather than deriving them empirically, they did demonstrate how factor analysis can be used to isolate common determinants.

On factor I, the largest factor loadings were on the variables of courteous sales people, service, and knowledgeable sales people. On factor II, the largest loadings were on the variables of price and quality, while on factor III, the largest loadings were on atmosphere and overall impression. Further analysis led the authors to conclude that sales persons, price–quality, and congeniality were the three dimensions on which these women evaluated women's clothing stores.[40]

---

[38] John K. Ryans, Jr., "An Analysis of Appliance Retailer Perceptions of Retail Strategy and Decision Processes," in Peter D. Bennett (ed.), *Marketing and Economic Development* (Chicago: Amer. Marketing Assoc., 1965), pp. 666–671.

[39] John H. Wingate, "Developments in the Super Market Field," *New York Retailer,* p. 6 (Oct. 1958).

[40] Michael Perry and Nancy J. Norton, "Dimensions of Store Image," *Southern J. Business* vol. 5, pp. 1–7 (Apr. 1970).

These results seem consistent with the earlier findings of Fisk.[41]

Supermarkets Douglas and Donald Tigert followed a different approach by using stepwise regression to determine the relative importance of patronage determinants for two different supermarket chains in Canada. For *one* chain they found:

Evaluate Criteria or Determinants	Cumulative R^2	Beta Coefficient
Easiest to get to	0.26	0.34
Best customer service	0.38	0.19
Lowest prices	0.42	0.17
Best quality produce	0.44	0.12
Cleanest stores	0.45	0.10
Best quality meat	0.46	0.06
Total	0.46	0.98

The rank order and relative importance of determinants was different for the *second* chain:

Evaluate Criteria or Determinants	Cumulative R^2	Beta Coefficient
Lowest prices	0.33	0.29
Easiest to get to	0.46	0.32
Best customer service	0.55	0.24
Best quality meat	0.56	0.12
Best quality produce	0.57	0.07
Total	0.57	1.04

Thus location, price, and service are the dominant variables determining what supermarket an individual will patronize. The same three variables entered first in both regressions, but in different orders. For the second chain, price explained the most variance in shopping behavior, while for the first chain, location entered first with price entering third. Further analysis led the authors to conclude that while service or quality plays a role, it is subservient to price and location, and comes into play only after the latter two variables have been neutralized across chains.[42]

---

[41] George Fisk, "A Conceptual Model for Studying Customer Image," *J. Retailing,* vol. 37, pp. 1–8 (Winter 1961–1962).

[42] Douglas J. Tigert and Donald J. Tigert, *op. cit.*,[21] pp. 19–23.

Other attempts have been made to isolate composite determinants of store choice. Space limitations preclude further discussion; however, references are provided for the interested reader.[43]

Store Images

Whether a consumer patronizes a store depends not only on the evaluative criteria that he is using but also on his perceptions of store characteristics and how they compare with these criteria. This partially explains variations in the supermarket findings mentioned above, as well as the results of other similar studies.[44]

The way in which consumers perceive a store is typically referred to as a store's image. More specific definitions of store image vary from author to author. One authority, for example, defines a store's image as "the way in which the store is defined in the shopper's mind, partly by its functional qualities and partly by an aura of psychological attributes."[45] Another author defines image as "a complex of meanings and relationships serving to characterize the store for people."[46] While these definitions differ somewhat, the essential point is that the store, as perceived by the consumer, may differ from what the store "actually is" in an "objective sense."

Measuring Store Images

A number of methods are used to measure store images. Many of the techniques are rather complex and often require professionals to design, administer, and/or interpret them. The most common techniques are discussed below.

Semantic Differential   This scaling device is the most widely used method of measuring store images. It involves repeated measurements of a concept against a series of descriptive polar-adjectival scales on a seven-point equal-interval ordinal scale.[47] For example, several stores might be measured on

---

[43]   See, for example, P. Ronald Stephenson, "Identifying Determinants of Retail Patronage," *J. Marketing*, vol. 33, pp. 57–61 (July 1969); Leonard L. Berry, "The Components of Department Store Image: A Theoretical and Empirical Analysis," *J. Retailing*, vol. 45, pp. 3–20 (Spring 1969); H. Robert Dodge and Harry H. Summer, "Choosing between Retail Stores," *J. Retailing*, vol. 45, pp. 11–21 (Fall 1969); Rollie Tillman, "Semantic Differential Measurement of Consumer Images of Retail Stores," *Southern J. Business*, vol. 2, pp. 67–73 (Apr. 1967).

[44]   See, for example, R. C. Anderson and R. A. Scott, "Supermarkets: Are They Really Alike?" *J. Retailing*, vol. 46, pp. 16–24 (Fall 1970).

[45]   Pierre Martineau, "The Personality of the Retail Store," *Harvard Business Rev.*, vol. 36, pp. 47–55, at p. 47 (Jan.–Feb. 1958).

[46]   Leon Arons, "Does Television Viewing Influence Store Image and Shopping Frequency?" *J. Retailing*, vol. 37, pp. 1–13, at p. 1 (Fall 1961).

[47]   William Mindak, "Fitting the Semantic Differential to the Marketing Problem," *J. Marketing*, vol. 25, pp. 28–33(Apr. 1961). The basic reference work on the semantic differential is C. E. Osgood, C. J. Suci, and P. H. Tannebaum, *The Measurement of Meaning*, (Urbana, Ill.: University of Illinois Press, 1957).

such characteristics as convenience, services, prices, merchandise assortments, and so on. An example of semantic differential scales for patronage research is shown in Figure 19.6.

This technique has the advantages of being relatively simple, easy to replicate (so that trends in consumers' reactions can be detected), and amenable to uncomplicated interpretation. However, care must be taken to make certain that *actual* determinants of patronage are included as bipolar adjectives. Another problem is that some consumers are reluctant to score a store unusually good or bad even though they may feel that way (mediocrity bias).

Staple Scale   The staple scale is a ten-point nonverbal rating scale that can simultaneously measure both the direction and intensity of an attitude. This technique has proved to be economical, easy to administer, and capable of indicating changes in image over time.[48]

Guttman Scale   The Guttman scaling device measures the content and intensity of an attitude. After a regular pattern of responses is observed and 90 percent of the individual answers fit into this particular set of response patterns, an attitude is said to exist toward the store and a Guttman scale may be constructed to analyze its nature.[49]

Customer Prototypes   This procedure involves the selection of social stereotypes or customer prototypes whose social strata are obvious enough in the minds of respondents to enable them to project a personal image of each prototype. Respondents are asked to state where each of the prototypes would be most likely and least likely to shop. This method is useful in discovering the difference in the image of stores held by different social strata.[50]

Q-Sort   The Q-sort requires consumers to specify the extent to which they agree or disagree with a series of statements. This approach permits the determination of the relative importance of specific image determinants. The approach is also quite flexible and capable of yielding quantifiable information. Its complexity and cost of administration are its major disadvantages.[51]

Projective Techniques   The thematic apperception, pictorial, and word-association tests are examples of projective techniques that can be used to measure a store's image. These nondirective approaches are sometimes used because customers are unable or unwilling to specify what image they have, or

---

[48]   Irving Crespi, "Use of a Scaling Technique in Surveys," *J. Marketing*, vol. 25, pp. 69–72 (July 1961).

[49]   For an illustrative example, see Elizabeth A. Richards, "A Commercial Application of Guttman Attitude Scaling Techniques," *J. Marketing*, vol. 22, pp. 166–173 (Oct. 1957).

[50]   W. B. Weale, "Measuring the Customer's Image of a Department Store," *J. Retailing*, vol. 37, pp. 40–48 (Spring 1961).

[51]   See, for example, William Stephenson, "Public Images of Public Utilities," *J. Advertising Research*, vol. 3, pp. 34–39 (Dec. 1963).

GENERAL CHARACTERISTICS OF THE COMPANY

	Extremely	Quite	Slightly	Neither One Nor The Other	Slightly	Quite	Extremely	
well known generally	___:	___:	___:	___:	___:	___:	___:	unknown generally
small number of stores operated by company	___:	___:	___:	___:	___:	___:	___:	large number of stores operated by company
long time in community	___:	___:	___:	___:	___:	___:	___:	short time in community

PHYSICAL CHARACTERISTICS OF THE STORE

dirty	___:	___:	___:	___:	___:	___:	___:	clean
unattractive decor	___:	___:	___:	___:	___:	___:	___:	attractive decor
easy to find items you want	___:	___:	___:	___:	___:	___:	___:	difficult to find items you want
easy to move through store	___:	___:	___:	___:	___:	___:	___:	difficult to move through store
fast checkout	___:	___:	___:	___:	___:	___:	___:	slow checkout

CONVENIENCE OF REACHING THE STORE FROM YOUR LOCATION

near by	___:	___:	___:	___:	___:	___:	___:	distant
short time required to reach store	___:	___:	___:	___:	___:	___:	___:	long time required to reach store
difficult drive	___:	___:	___:	___:	___:	___:	___:	easy drive
difficult to find parking place	___:	___:	___:	___:	___:	___:	___:	easy to find parking place
convenient to other stores I shop	___:	___:	___:	___:	___:	___:	___:	inconvenient to other stores I shop

PRODUCTS OFFERED

wide selection of different kinds of products	___:	___:	___:	___:	___:	___:	___:	limited selection of different kinds of products
fully stocked	___:	___:	___:	___:	___:	___:	___:	understocked
undependable products	___:	___:	___:	___:	___:	___:	___:	dependable products
high quality	___:	___:	___:	___:	___:	___:	___:	low quality
numerous brands	___:	___:	___:	___:	___:	___:	___:	few brands
unknown brands	___:	___:	___:	___:	___:	___:	___:	well known brands

PRICES CHANGED BY THE STORE

low compared to other stores	___:	___:	___:	___:	___:	___:	___:	high compared to other stores
low values for money spent	___:	___:	___:	___:	___:	___:	___:	high values for money spent
large number of items specially priced	___:	___:	___:	___:	___:	___:	___:	small number of items specially priced

STORE PERSONNEL

courteous	___:	___:	___:	___:	___:	___:	___:	discourteous
cold	___:	___:	___:	___:	___:	___:	___:	friendly
unhelpful	___:	___:	___:	___:	___:	___:	___:	helpful
adequate number	___:	___:	___:	___:	___:	___:	___:	inadequate number

ADVERTISING BY THE STORE

uninformative	___:	___:	___:	___:	___:	___:	___:	informative
unhelpful in planning purchases	___:	___:	___:	___:	___:	___:	___:	helpful in planning purchases
appealing	___:	___:	___:	___:	___:	___:	___:	unappealing
believable	___:	___:	___:	___:	___:	___:	___:	misleading
frequently seen by you	___:	___:	___:	___:	___:	___:	___:	infrequently seen by you

YOUR FRIENDS AND THE STORE

unknown to your friends	___:	___:	___:	___:	___:	___:	___:	well known to your friends
well liked by your friends	___:	___:	___:	___:	___:	___:	___:	disliked by your friends
poorly recommended by your friends	___:	___:	___:	___:	___:	___:	___:	well recommended by your friends
numerous friends shop there	___:	___:	___:	___:	___:	___:	___:	few friends shop there

Figure 19.6 SEMANTIC DIFFERENTIAL FOR PATRONAGE RESEARCH; GENERAL CHARACTERISTICS OF THE COMPANY. Robert F. Kelly and Ronald Stephenson, "The Semantic Differential: An Information Source for Designing Retail Patronage Appeals," *J. Marketing*, vol. 31, p. 45 (Oct. 1967). Reprinted by permission of the publisher.

how or why that image was formed. The major problems with these techniques are that they typically are time consuming, costly, difficult to administer and interpret, difficult to replicate, and sometimes of questionable validity.[52]

SHOPPER PROFILES

As noted above, evidence to date indicates that there are important differences in the criteria that different consumers use to evaluate stores, as well as their images of stores. This section discusses how store images and patronage vary by consumer characteristics and then analyzes consumers according to their shopping orientations and strategies.

Store Image Profiles

Consumers often differ in the images they have of stores. To illustrate, consider department-store images. Some illustrative findings are:

(1) Consumers in different social classes[53] and consumers in different life cycle stages hold different images of department stores.[54]

(2) Department-store images held by members of groups at different stages in the family life cycle vary in some situations but not in others.[55]

Other studies have also found that store images do not always vary across consumer types. For example, Anderson and Scott analyzed ratings of supermarkets by various income, age, education, and occupational groups. They found that the rating of an individual supermarket, while differing from other supermarkets, was fairly consistent across each socioeconomic segment.[56]

Thus research to date is inconclusive. Sometimes there are important

---

[52]   See, for example, H. H. Anderson and G. L. Anderson (eds.), *An Introduction to Projective Techniques* (Englewood Cliffs, N.J.: Prentice-Hall, 1951); I. R. Weschler, "Problems in the Use of Indirect Methods of Attitude Measurements," *Public Opinion Quart.*, vol. 15, pp. 133–138 (Spring 1951).

[53]   See, for example, Robert G. Wyckham, "Aggregate Department Store Images: Social and Experimental Factors," in Reed Moyer (ed.), *Changing Marketing Systems* (Chicago: Amer. Marketing Assoc., 1967), pp. 333–337; Charles J. Collazzo, *Consumer Attitudes and Frustrations in Shopping* (New York: National Retail Merchants Association, 1963); Pierre Martineau, "Sharper Focus for the Corporate Image," *Harvard Business Rev.* vol. 36, p. 53 (Nov.–Dec. 1958).

[54]   William Lazer and Robert G. Wyckham, "Perceptual Segmentation of Department Store Markets," *J. Retailing*, vol. 45, pp. 3–14 (Summer 1969); M. S. Heidingsfield, "Building the Image—An Essential Marketing Stratagem," in Fred E. Webster (ed.), *New Directions in Marketing* (Chicago: Amer. Marketing Assoc., 1965), p. 138.

[55]   Wyckham, *op. cit.*,[53] pp. 333–337; Collazzo, *op. cit.*[53]

[56]   Anderson and Scott, *op. cit.*,[44] pp. 16–24.

differences in consumers' perceptions of stores, other times there are more similarities than differences.[57]

Patronage Profiles

Most consumers have shopped in every type of store at one time or another. However, different types of consumers shop at some kinds of stores more than others, depending, in part, on the type of product being purchased. This section summarizes socioeconomic and psychographic profiles of patrons of different retail establishments.

Socioeconomic Profiles Studies investigating socioeconomic characteristics of store patrons typically have numerous methodological shortcomings.[58] Nevertheless, these studies usually yield remarkably similar conclusions:[59]

(1) Department and specialty stores tend to attract a disproportionately large share of consumers over 40 to 45 years of age. Department-store chains, discount stores, and variety stores tend to attract a larger proportion of younger consumers.

(2) Department and specialty stores tend to attract upper-income consumers while department-store chains, discount stores, and variety stores attract more middle- and lower-income consumers.

(3) Families with children have a greater tendency to shop in discount stores, while families without children tend to shop more in department and specialty stores.

It should be reemphasized that most consumers shop in all of the types of stores mentioned above. However, the stores identified tend to attract a disproportionately large percentage of certain types of consumers.

Psychographic Profiles Tigert, Lathrope, and Bleeg have shown how

---

[57] For discussions of difficulties in measuring consumer variations in store images, see Joseph B. Mason and Morris L. Mayer," The Problem of the Self-Concept in Store Image Studies," *J. Marketing*, vol. 34, pp. 67–69 (Apr. 1970); Ira J. Dolich and Ned Shilling, "A Critical Evaluation of the Problem of Self-Concept in Store Image Studies," *J. Marketing*, vol. 34, pp. 71–73 (Apr. 1970).

[58] See, for example, Ben M. Enis and Keith K. Cox, "Demographic Analysis of Store Patronage Patterns: Uses and Pitfalls," in King, *op. cit.,*[17] pp. 366–370.

[59] These conclusions were based on the results of the following studies: Stuart U. Rich, *Shopping Behavior of Department Store Shoppers* (Boston: Division of Research, Graduate School of Business Administration, Harvard University, 1963); Robert H. Myers, "The Discount Store Shopper in Cincinnati," *J. Retailing*, vol. 39, pp. 36–43 (Winter 1963–1964); David J. Rachman and Linda J. Kemp, "Profile of the Boston Discount House Customer," *J. Retailing*, vol. 39, pp. 1–8 (Summer 1963); Rachel Dardis and Marie Sandler, "Shopping Behavior of Discount Store Customers in a Small City," *J. Retailing*, vol. 47, pp. 60–72, 91 (Summer 1971); *Consumer Attitudes and Shopping Habits in Conventional Retail Stores and Discount Stores* (New York: Bureau of Advertising, American Newspaper Publ. Assoc., 1963); *The Retail Customer* (New York: Bureau of Advertising, American Newspaper Publ. Assoc., 1965), and numerous studies conducted by *Discount Merchandiser*.

psychographic variables can be combined with product usage and socioeconomic characteristics to construct a richer portrait of patrons of retail outlets.[60] They analyzed female users of chicken drive-in restaurants providing ready-to-eat carry-out fried chicken (RECFC).

The heavy user of RECFC has a well defined demographic profile. She is more likely to be working full time, young, and in a family with an above average number of children. Despite the larger income, the heavy user's family is not upscale in terms of either educational or occupational status of the husband or wife.

The heavy user of RECFC is also a heavy user of eye makeup, nail polish, perfume, cologne and toilet water, regular soft drinks, chewing gum, and candy. In addition, she does an above average amount of in-town driving, and she buys a lot of gasoline and new shoes. She is also a heavy user of a wide range of convenience foods.

The heavy user of RECFC has a revealing psychographic profile (see Table 19.3). She is optimistic about her personal and financial future, fashion and appearance conscious, pro credit, active, influential, and ready to take risks. She is not afraid to borrow or invest money, and likes to go to exciting parties.

Although she is above average in income, she is not at the top of the social ladder. She shops in casual clothes at places like Sears and Wards and uses TV dinners and canned foods.

The heavy user seems to have liberal attitudes. For example, she disagrees more than nonusers that "most people do not have enough discipline today," and that "there is too much emphasis on sex today."

The heavy user also spends some of her time in a dream world. Not only does she agree more that she likes to do things that are bright, gay, and exciting; but she also agrees more, compared to the nonuser, that she likes science fiction, and she disagrees more that television should have more serious programs.

Shopper Typologies

Several studies have attempted to classify consumers according to their attitudes toward shopping and their shopping behavior. These studies are summarized below.

The Stone Typology   The most widely quoted study is Gregory Stone's investigation of 150 female residents of Chicago's northwest side.[61] Respondents were asked whether they would rather do business with local merchants or large chain stores and why. Analysis of the responses to these questions revealed disparate definitions of shopping situations and different orientations to stores in

------

[60] Douglas J. Tigert, Richard Lathrope, and Michael Bleeg, "The Fast Food Franchise: Psychographic and Demographic Segmentation Analysis," *J. Retailing*, vol. 47, pp. 81–90 (Spring 1971).

[61] Gregory P. Stone, "City Shoppers and Urban Identification: Observations on the Social Psychology of City Life," *Amer. J. Sociology*, vol. 60, pp. 36–45 (1954).

Table 19.3   CARRY-OUT FRIED CHICKEN USER PROFILE: PERCENTAGE OF NONUSERS AND HEAVY USERS WHO GENERALLY OR DEFINITELY AGREE WITH EACH AIO QUESTION

Life Style (AIO) Questions	Never Use (N=201) (%)	Use Once a Month or More (N=138) (%)
The Swinging Party-Goer		
I like parties where there is lots of music and talk	31	49
I like to think I am a bit of a swinger	17	37
I do more things socially than do most of my friends	16	31
I like to do things that are bright, gay, and exciting	38	48
Not a Homebody in a Rut		
I am a homebody	66	50
Our days seem to follow a definite routine such as eating meals at a regular time, and so on	72	55
I would like to have a maid to do the housework	25	42
Optimistic Mobiles		
My greatest achievements are still ahead of me	34	55
Five years from now, the family income will probably be a lot higher than it is now	37	69
I will probably have more money to spend next year than I have now	38	62
We will probably move once in the next five years	22	40
Fashion and Personal Appearance Conscious		
I often try the latest hairdo styles when they change	10	27
I would like to be a fashion model	15	30†
Women wear too much makeup these days	53	39
I like to feel attractive to men	36	55
I like the natural color of my hair	67	41
Credit, Borrowing, and Investment		
I buy many things with a credit card or charge card	30	45
In the past year, we have borrowed money from a bank or finance company	28	41†
I like to pay cash for everything I buy	65	48
Investing in the stock market is too risky for most families	56	44
I find myself checking the prices in the grocery store even for small items	75	57
Influential, New Brand Buyer, Information Seeker		
I often try new brands before my friends and neighbors do	46	70
I sometimes influence what my friends buy	23	33

Table 19.3 CARRY-OUT FRIED CHICKEN USER PROFILE: PERCENTAGE OF NONUSERS AND HEAVY USERS WHO GENERALLY OR DEFINITELY AGREE WITH EACH AIO QUESTION (*Continued*)

Life Style (AIO) Questions	Never Use (N=201) (%)	Use Once a Month or More (N=138) (%)
My neighbors usually give me pretty good advice on what brands to buy in the grocery store	41	65
I like to be considered a leader	17	31
Convenience Foods, Casual Shopping		
I *never* go shopping in shorts or slacks	48	25‡
A good mother will not serve her family TV dinners	31	21
I depend on canned food at least one meal a day	41	58
I use Metrecal or other diet foods at least one meal a day	23	35
Signs of Middle-Class America		
I buy many things at Sears Roebuck or Montgomery Ward	47	67†
Every family should have a dog	39	57
I thoroughly enjoy conversations about sports	16	26
I like bowling	29	45
I would rather live in or near a big city than in or near a small town	31	52

NOTES: *31 percent of those respondents who never purchase at carry-out fried chicken restaurants generally or definitely agreed they like parties where there is lots of music and talk.
  †Percent who moderately, generally, and definitely agreed rather than just generally or definitely agreed.
  ‡Definitely agreed only.

SOURCE: Douglas Tigert, Richard Lathrope and Michael Bleeg, "The Fast Food Franchise: Psychographic and Demographic Segmentation Analysis," *J. Retailing*, vol. 47, pp. 86–87 (Spring 1971).

general. Based on orientations toward stores and the purchasing process, Stone identified four types of shoppers.[62]

(1) **The Economic Shopper**   This type of shopper was extremely sensitive to price, quality, and assortment of merchandise, all of which were considered when purchasing a product. Clerical personnel and the store were, for her, the instruments of her purchase of goods. The efficiency of sales personnel, as well as relative prices, quality, or the selection of merchandise, were decisive in

---

[62]   Stone, *op. cit.*,[61] pp. 36–45.

affecting her evaluation of the store. (Thirty-three percent of all respondents were in this category.)

(2) **The Personalizing Shopper**   The personalizing shopper formed strong personal relations with store personnel, and these relations were crucial to store patronage. Her conception of a good clerk was one who treated her in a personal, relatively intimate manner. (Twenty-eight percent of all respondents were in this category.)

(3) **The Ethical Shopper**   This type of shopper was willing to sacrifice lower prices, or a wider selection of goods, "to help the little guy out," or because "the chain store has no heart or soul." She shopped where she thought she "ought to," and strong attachments were sometimes formed with personnel and store owners, or with "stores" in the abstract. (Eighteen percent of all respondents were in this category.)

(4) **The Apathetic Shopper**   For this type of consumer, shopping was an onerous task. Experiences in stores were not important enough to leave any impression on her. Convenience of location was crucial to her selection of a store rather than price, quality of goods, relations with store personnel, or ethics. The costs of shopping far exceeded the value, and every attempt was made to minimize her expenditure of effort in purchasing goods. (Seventeen percent of all shoppers were in this category.)

In addition, each of the four types of shoppers was characterized by a distinctive patterning of social position and community identification. Economic and personalizing orientations were more often adopted by housewives who had recently moved into the area, and ethical and apathetic orientations by those who had lived in the area for relatively long periods of time. Moreover, the findings indicated that:[63]

(1)   The higher the level of aspiration among newcomers to a residential community, the greater the probability that they will adopt economic orientations to shopping.

(2)   The lower the level of aspiration the greater the marginality of new-comers (degree of social isolation), the greater the probability that they will adopt personalizing orientations.

(3)   The greater the success that long-time residents of a residential area have enjoyed, the greater the probability that they will adopt ethical orientations.

(4)   The less the success that long-time residents have enjoyed, the greater the probability that they will adopt apathetic orientations to shopping.

Recently, Darden and Reynolds tested and extended Stone's typology in a study of 167 households in six middle to upper-middle-class suburban areas of

---

[63]   Stone, *op. cit.*,[61] pp. 36–45.

Athens, Georgia. Their data, concerned with health and personal care items, support Stone's shopping types.[64]

The Stephenson–Willett Typology In the late 1960s, Stephenson and Willett developed a shopper typology based on purchasing processes for six product categories: children's apparel, ladies' shoes, gloves, and dresses, mens' hosiery, and toys.[65] The shopper taxonomy was constructed by combining indices of patronage concentration and the extent of search for patronage alternatives. Shopper types, their frequency of occurrence, and the researchers' inferences about their identity are summarized in Figure 19.7.

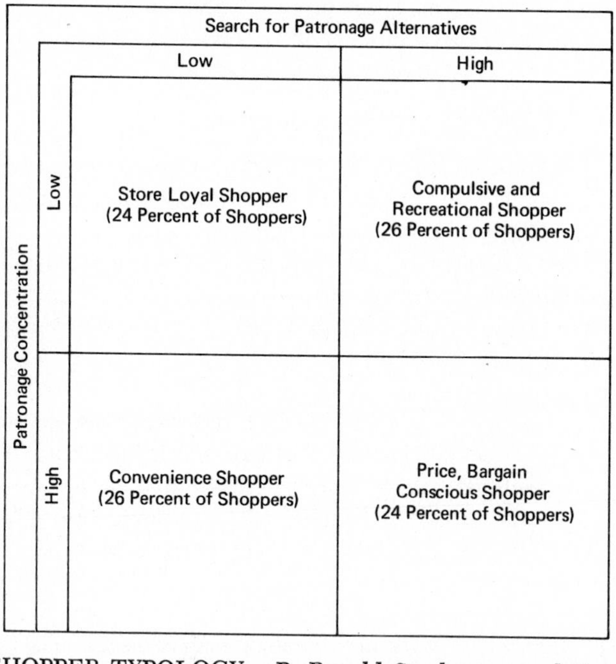

Figure 19.7   SHOPPER TYPOLOGY.   P. Ronald Stephenson and Ronald P. Willett, "Analysis of Consumers' Retail Patronage Strategies," in Philip R. McDonald (ed.), *Marketing Involvement in Society and the Economy* (Chicago: Amer. Marketing Assoc., 1969), p. 322

MARKETING IMPLICATIONS

This section discusses the marketing implications of store choice processes and shopper profiles for manufacturers and retailers.

---

[64]   William R. Darden and Fred D. Reynolds, "Shopping Orientations and Product Usage Rates," *J. Marketing Research*, vol. 8, pp. 505–508 (Nov. 1971).

[65]   P. Ronald Stephenson and Ronald P. Willett, "Analysis of Consumers' Retail Patronage Strategies," in Philip R. McDonald (ed.), *Marketing Involvement in Society and the Economy* (Chicago: Amer. Marketing Assoc., 1969), pp. 316–322.

Implications for Manufacturers

Store choice processes and shopper profiles have several important implications for manufacturers' distribution strategies. Basically a manufacturer is interested in a distribution strategy that has the necessary coverage of the target market(s) to achieve the firm's marketing objectives. In order to achieve these results, the manufacturer needs to know:

(1) The percentage distribution of industry sales by type of retail outlet (currently and future projections).

(2) The percentage distribution of the manufacturer's sales by type of retail outlet.

(3) The percentage of each relevant market segment that purchases the industry's product in each type of retail outlet.

(4) The percentage of each relevant market segment that purchases the manufacturer's brand in each type of retail outlet.

If the manufacturer is following a mass-marketing or nonsegmentation strategy, then the percentage distributions in (1) and (2) should be approximately equal. That is, the percentage distribution of the manufacturer's sales by type of outlet should be the same as the percentage distribution of total industry sales.

On the other hand, if the manufacturer is following a market segmentation strategy, then the percentage distributions in (3) and (4) should be approximately equal. In other words, the percentage of each target market segment that purchases the manufacturer's brand in each type of retail outlet should be about the same as the percentage of each target market that purchases the sum of all industry sales in each type of retail outlet.

Deviations from these guidelines should be remedied through corrective distribution programming. This may involve a number of marketing activities—including product, pricing, promotion, and sales force programs—designed to improve penetration in those retail outlets where the manufacturer is weak.

If there are significant differences in consumers' shopping patterns, and/or if these consumers have important variations in shopping orientations, the manufacturer should consider multiplex distribution programs. These may include derivative models, programmed merchandising, associate brands, modular merchandising programs, family brands, multiple franchise programs, and private labels.[66]

Implications for Retailers

Using one or more of the methods of measuring store image discussed above, and/or newer approaches such as the Fishbein model and nonmetric multidimensional scaling,[67] the retailer needs to determine:

---

[66] These multiplex distribution strategies have been advanced by Dr. Bert C. McCammon, Jr., Executive Vice President, Management Horizons, Inc., Columbus, Ohio.

[67] See Chapter 11, "Attitude Measurement."

(1) The specific evaluative criteria that consumers use in selecting the retailer's general *type* of store (for example, drug stores or department stores) and competing types of stores (for example, intertype competition).

(2) The relative importance of these evaluative criteria.

(3) How the retailer's store is evaluated on each of these criteria.

(4) How the ratings of the retailer's store compare with consumer's ratings of their "ideal" store.

(5) For consumers that do not patronize or are infrequent patrons of the retailer's store, how the ratings of the retailer's store compare with ratings of the store the consumer patronizes regularly.

The above information can be used to design new types of retailing establishments, evaluate a newly opened store, and evaluate an established store.[68]

In designing new types of retailing establishments, it is necessary to isolate the relative importance of evaluative criteria, obtain ratings on each criterion for each competitive store in the trading area, and obtain ratings on each criterion for the respondent's ideal store. This information can be used to determine how well stores in the trading area are serving the needs of consumers, including areas where competitors are doing a particularly poor job. It may also be possible to identify major groups of consumers who are unique in their product or service expectations, thus providing the basis for market segmentation. A retailing strategy—combining location, physical facilities, store decor and layout, hours of operation, merchandise assortments, price, advertising and sales promotion, store personnel, and store services—can be designed to provide an optimum match between what the new store has to offer and what consumers are seeking and other stores are providing.

A newly opened store can also use the five types of information itemized above. First, the retailer may learn whether the new store is appealing successfully to the target market segment. Second, the retailer may determine whether the attitudes consumers are forming about the new store are consistent with the development and maintenance of a profitably large group of loyal patrons. If appropriate attitudes are developing, additional reinforcement is probably appropriate. Conversely, if the desired attitudes are not developing, store ratings on each criterion can be used to identify changes that are necessary in the retailing strategy.

An established store can compare ratings of the store with those for an ideal store. The divergences identify the changes in retailing strategy necessary to match more closely store offerings with consumer expectations. Ratings of the established store can also be compared with ratings of competing stores, thus providing the information for retailing strategies that may allow the established store to capture some of the patrons of competing establishments.

---

[68] Much of this section is based on Robert F. Kelly and Ronald Stephenson, "The Semantic Differential: An Information Source for Designing Retail Patronage Appeals," *J. Marketing*, vol. 31, pp. 43–47 (Oct. 1967).

SUMMARY

A basic understanding of the nature of purchasing processes is necessary in order to comprehend consumer decision processes and, ultimately, consumer behavior. Purchasing processes refer to all aspects of customer–store environment interaction. This chapter is concerned with store choice and shopper profiles. Other purchasing-process dimensions are presented in the following two chapters.

Store choice is a complex process involving comparisons of perceived store characteristics with evaluative criteria to produce acceptable and unacceptable stores. General and composite determinants of store choice were discussed, and methods of measuring store image were identified.

Shopper profiles are important because consumers differ in their perceptions of stores as well as in their patronage patterns. Store image profiles, patronage profiles, and shopper typologies were examined.

Store choice processes and shopper profiles have important implications for both manufacturers and retailers. The chapter concluded with a discussion of these implications.

REVIEW AND DISCUSSION QUESTIONS

1. Describe or otherwise define the following: (a) semantic differential, (b) evaluative criteria, (c) store image, and (d) personalizing shopper.

2. Discuss why it is necessary to understand purchasing processes in order to understand decision processes and consumer behavior.

3. The last time you bought a product, how did you decide which store to patronize? How does your behavior compare with the conceptualization presented in Figure 19.3?

4. What is the image of the two largest stores in your area? How do your perceptions of these stores compare with your friends' images? Your parents'? Why do these differences exist?

5. Assume you are a consultant to the largest store in your area. The owner of the store is interested in understanding why people shop in a particular store. Prepare a research proposal specifying how you would go about determining: (a) what evaluative criteria are operative, (b) the images of the store in question and its major competitors.

6. What is meant by purchase intentions? Are purchase intentions a necessary variable in a purchasing-process model? Why or why not?

7. Assume you are a consultant for a major department store. Describe how you would go about determining whether the types of shoppers found in the Stone study exist for your store. Of what value are shopper categories identical or similar to those used in the Stone study?

CHAPTER 20

PURCHASING PROCESSES: IN-STORE BEHAVIOR

What effect do store layout, point-of-purchase displays, end-aisle displays, and shelf height of merchandise have on consumer behavior? How do consumers react to multiple-unit pricing? Is there an identifiable market segment for private brands and "deals"?

Discussion of the extended conceptualization of purchasing processes, originally presented in Figure 19.2, continues in this chapter. Attention is focused on the above questions as well as other dimensions of in-store behavior.

PURCHASING ROLE STRUCTURES

This section discusses the role of family members in purchasing and the implications of these role structures for marketing strategists.

Illustrative Studies

Table 20.1 summarizes the results of one of the recent studies that have investigated which family members actually perform the physical act of purchasing products. As was true for other stages of the decision-making process, it is evident that the extent of husband–wife involvement varies considerably from product to product.

Table 20.1   *LIFE* MAGAZINE STUDY OF THE
ROLES OF HUSBANDS AND WIVES
IN PURCHASING

| | Spouse Purchasing | |
| | Husband | Wife |
Product	(%)	(%)
Refrigerators	71.4	79.4
Vacuum cleaners	54.8	81.8
Automobiles	93.8	52.0
Pet foods	39.5	93.0
Frozen orange juice	38.6	93.7
Rugs, carpets	58.0	91.6
Paint	70.0	47.2
Coffee	28.6	89.0
Toothpaste	34.9	89.3

NOTE: Percentages are based on each spouse's self-appraisal. The percentages indicate whether or not the spouse in question was involved in purchasing. Categories such as "both husband and wife" or "children" were not employed, so the percentages sometimes total more or less than 100 percent.

SOURCE: "A Pilot Study of the Roles of Husbands and Wives in Purchasing Decisions, Parts I-X," conducted for *Life* magazine by L. Jaffe Associates, Inc. (1965). Research design involved interviews with 301 middle- and upper-income households in Hartford, Cleveland, and Seattle.

Overall, wives are involved in purchasing to a greater extent than husbands, as is evidenced by the fact that in seven of nine product categories women are more likely to be involved in purchasing. However, it is instructive to note that a significant number of husbands *are* involved in purchasing, and this is true for all products. Husbands have a greater *tendency* to be involved in purchasing if the product is high priced and technically complex. For example, a higher percentage of husbands are involved in purchasing automobiles, refrigerators, and paint.

The figures presented in Table 20.1 are averages, and there is likely to be substantial interfamily variation in the degree of husband–wife participation in purchasing. For example, younger and higher income husbands would be expected to be more involved in purchasing processes than would older, and middle- and lower-income husbands.[1] These and other types of variations encourage the marketer to analyze purchasing role structures by economic, demographic, and behavioral characteristics.

Marketing Implications

The marketing implications of purchasing role structures depend, to a considerable extent, on the customer's preshopping purchase intentions. Stated differently, the significance of purchasing role structures depends on what decisions, if any, are being made by the shopper in the store. From the viewpoint of both a manufacturer and a retailer, it makes a considerable amount of difference for policy purposes whether the customer is purchasing what he or she was told to purchase, or whether decisions about a brand, or both a product and a brand, are being made in the store.

What if the marketer does not know the types of decisions being made by those family members purchasing the product? If this information is lacking, it appears reasonable to assume that an individual involved in purchasing is more likely to be influential in making purchasing decisions than not. Until the appropriate studies can be made, there is some justification for considering purchase role structures and influence role structures to be the same, provided the marketer does not formulate strategies based on the purchase role structure by reducing other marketing efforts.

Provided those individuals purchasing the product have some influence on such decisions as where to buy, what product to buy, or what brand to buy, purchasing role structures have several implications for marketing strategy for both retailers and manufacturers.

Retailing Implications Purchasing role structures affect almost every element of the retailing mix. Physical facilities, particularly store interiors, should be designed and color schemes chosen with an eye to who will frequent the outlet. Decisions concerning hours of operation should be affected by whether the husband or wife shop alone or together. Services offered, particularly delivery, should be based partially on who does the shopping. The choice of advertising media, and location within a medium, especially newspapers, should be based, at least in part, on purchasing role structures. Other elements in the retailing mix—merchandise variety and assortment, point-of-purchase display strategies, and pricing decisions—might also be affected by purchasing role structures.

Implication for Manufacturers Purchasing role structures also affect almost every variable in a manufacturer's marketing mix. The functional, esthetic,

---

[1] See, for example, Elizabeth Wolgast, "Do Husbands or Wives Make Purchasing Decisions?," *J. Marketing*, vol. 23, pp. 151–158 (Oct. 1958); Mirra Komarovsky, "Class Differences in Family Decision-Making on Expenditures," in Nelson Foote (ed.), *Household Decision Making* (New York: New York University Press, 1961), pp. 259–264. Other major studies include Harry Sharp and Paul Mott, "Consumer Decisions in the Metropolitan Family," *J. Marketing*, vol. 21, pp. 149–156 (Oct. 1954); "Customer Traffic Patterns: Key to Selling Efficiency," *Progressive Grocer*, pp. K-75–K-106 (Jan. 1967).

and perhaps symbolic aspects of product design and strategy might be influenced by who makes the purchasing decision. Media selection and creative strategy might also be affected by a purchasing role structure. Finally, the role of husband and wife in purchasing would affect the manufacturer's channel strategy, particularly the selection of the types of retail outlets that should handle a product.

THE EFFECTS OF STORE LAYOUT AND DISPLAYS ON CONSUMER BEHAVIOR

A substantial percentage, perhaps even a majority, of purchasing process research has concentrated on the effects of various store and merchandising characteristics on consumer behavior. This section discusses the effects of store layout and displays on in-store behavior.

Store Layout

Store-layout research is concerned with the effect of store layout on customer behavior, particularly sales. This section presents some illustrative studies and discusses the marketing implications.

Illustrative Studies   Traffic pattern studies seem to be the most common way to determine the effect of store layout on sales. Although these studies are conducted in many types of retail outlets, they are probably used most often in supermarkets. In these studies, interviewers plot the paths of a sample of customers on a small replica of the store layout. The paths are summed to obtain the density of customer traffic in different parts of the store (see Figure 20.1) and then converted into the number of customers who pass and buy from major product groups (Table 20.2).[2]

In supermarkets these studies typically find considerable variation among shoppers in overall store coverage.[3] A positive, or direct relation usually exists between locations passed and purchases, that is, the greater the number of locations passed, the greater the number of purchases.[4] A positive relation also typically exists between time spent in the store and money spent.[5]

---

[2]   See, for example, "Colonial Study," *Progressive Grocer*, pp. C-81–C-96 (Jan. 1964); N. Havas and H. M. Smith, *Customers' Shopping Patterns in Retail Food Stores* (AMS 400) (Washington, D.C.: U.S. Department of Agriculture, Agriculture Marketing Services, Aug. 1960).

[3]   Havas and Smith, *op cit.;*[2] "Customer Traffic Patterns," *op. cit.,*[1]; Lawrence W. Patterson, *In-Store Traffic Flow* (New York: Point-of-Purchase Advertising Institute, 1963).

[4]   See, for example, "Colonial Study," *op. cit.,*[2] p. C-91; Bert C. McCammon and Donald H. Granbois, *The Super Drugstore Customer* (New York: Point-of-Purchase Advertising Institute, 1962).

[5]   "Colonial Study," *op. cit.,*[2] p. C-85; "Customer Traffic Patterns," *op. cit.,*[1] p. K-83.

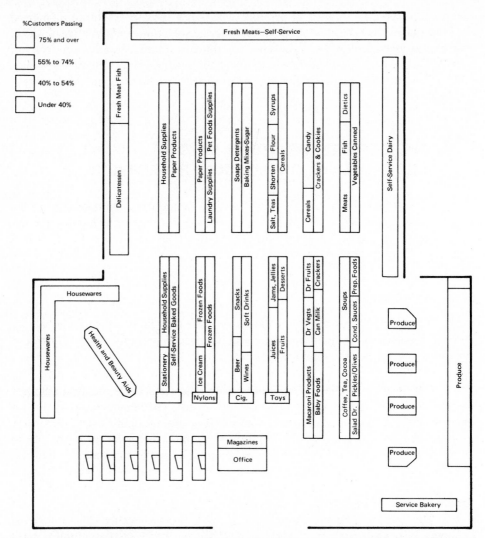

Figure 20.1 DENSITY OF CUSTOMER TRAFFIC IN DIFFERENT PARTS OF A SUPERMARKET. "Colonial Study," *Progressive Grocer*, p. C-90 (Jan. 1964). Reprinted by permission of the publisher.

Table 20.2 NUMBER OF CUSTOMERS WHO PASS AND BUY FROM MAJOR PRODUCT GROUPS IN AN AVERAGE SUPERMARKET

Out of 100 customers 94 pass and 80 buy fresh meats
Out of 100 customers 90 pass and 56 buy produce
Out of 100 customers 93 pass and 78 buy dairy products
Out of 100 customers 63 pass and 28 buy frozen foods
Out of 100 customers 61 pass and 14 buy ice cream

Table 20.2   NUMBER OF CUSTOMERS WHO PASS AND BUY FROM MAJOR PRODUCT GROUPS IN AN AVERAGE SUPERMARKET (*Continued*)

Out of 100 customers 70 pass and 41 buy self-service baked foods
Out of 100 customers 64 pass and 15 buy service baked foods
Out of 100 customers 57 pass and 18 buy service deli products
Out of 100 customers 45 pass and 12 buy baby foods
Out of 100 customers 53 pass and 24 buy baking mixes, needs, flour
Out of 100 customers 57 pass and 13 buy beer
Out of 100 customers 49 pass and 11 buy candy
Out of 100 customers 63 pass and 25 buy cereal
Out of 100 customers 65 pass and 13 buy cigarettes, tobacco
Out of 100 customers 61 pass and 21 buy coffee, tea, cocoa
Out of 100 customers 75 pass and 17 buy condiments, sauces
Out of 100 customers 68 pass and 35 buy crackers, cookies
Out of 100 customers 59 pass and 16 buy desserts
Out of 100 customers 55 pass and 7 buy dietetic foods
Out of 100 customers 63 pass and 13 buy fish, canned
Out of 100 customers 53 pass and 20 buy fruit, canned
Out of 100 customers 55 pass and 9 buy fruit, dried
Out of 100 customers 61 pass and 14 buy household supplies
Out of 100 customers 72 pass and 19 buy jams, jellies, spreads
Out of 100 customers 55 pass and 13 buy juices, canned
Out of 100 customers 53 pass and 10 buy macaroni products
Out of 100 customers 64 pass and 19 buy meat, canned
Out of 100 customers 49 pass and 12 buy milk, canned
Out of 100 customers 64 pass and 37 buy paper products
Out of 100 customers 48 pass and 15 buy pet food supplies
Out of 100 customers 66 pass and 15 buy pickles, olives, relishes
Out of 100 customers 56 pass and 10 buy prepared foods
Out of 100 customers 59 pass and 19 buy salad dressing, mayonnaise
Out of 100 customers 57 pass and 13 buy salt, seasoning, spices
Out of 100 customers 49 pass and 12 buy snacks
Out of 100 customers 61 pass and 24 buy soaps, detergents, laundry supplies
Out of 100 customers 55 pass and 22 buy soft drinks
Out of 100 customers 62 pass and 24 buy soups
Out of 100 customers 60 pass and 29 buy vegetables, canned
Out of 100 customers 55 pass and 12 buy vegetables, dried
Out of 100 customers 46 pass and 18 buy health and beauty aids
Out of 100 customers 30 pass and 6 buy housewares
Out of 100 customers 38 pass and 13 buy magazines and books
Out of 100 customers 36 pass and 2 buy stationery
Out of 100 customers 35 pass and 4 buy toys
Out of 100 customers 39 pass and 1 buys records

SOURCE: "Colonial Study," *Progressive Grocer*, p. c-91 (Jan. 1964). Reprinted by permission of the publisher.

Marketing Implications

The findings of traffic pattern studies apparently serve as the basis for several types of retailing strategies. Studies have recommended that passing–buying ratios be used to make store layout decisions. Those products having high passing–buying ratios should be scattered throughout the store in order to maximize customer exposure to product assortments.[6] Because a positive relation usually exists between time and money spent, retailers have been advised to devise ways and provide facilities that will result in shoppers spending more time in the store.[7]

Traffic pattern studies have certain limitations that are apparently not widely recognized. These limitations are: (1) traffic pattern studies do not measure preshopping purchase intentions, and (2) they measure association rather than causation.

Passing, buying, and passing–buying ratios are of limited value in determining the effect of location on product sales and hence in making store-layout decisions. Buying ratios, in and of themselves, are meaningless because there are too many explanations for them. Products may have certain buying ratios because they are located near other products that are frequently purchased, or because they are located in areas having heavy consumer traffic because of the function performed in these locations. Still other products may have buying ratios that are totally independent of their location in the store, that is, shoppers intend to purchase the products and will search the store until they find them.

Passing ratios are even less meaningful. Products can have certain passing ratios for any one combination of the following reasons: (1) customers intended to purchase the product and they did, (2) customers intended to purchase the product, passed it, but did not purchase it, (3) customers did not intend to purchase the product but did purchase it, and (4) customers did not intend to purchase the product, passed it, but did not purchase it. Like buying ratios, then, passing ratios have multiple meanings.

The real meaning of a positive relation between passing and buying is also elusive. The conventional explanation for the relation is that customers buy an item because exposure to in-store stimuli creates a need, or reminds them of a previously recognized need that is temporarily latent. However, an equally plausible explanation is completely overlooked; if shoppers intend to purchase an item and carry out this purchase plan, then they obviously must pass the item! Actually, then, there are three possible explanations for a relation between passing and buying: (1) customers buy an item because they pass it, (2) customers pass an item because they intend to buy it, or (3) both (1) and (2).

For the above reasons, contrary to the beliefs of many retailing practitioners and researchers, these ratios do not yield clearcut implications for store-

---

[6] Patterson, *op. cit.,*[3] p. 2; "Customer Traffic's Effect on Super's Sales Studied," *Food Topics,* pp. 6–12 (June 1960); "Colonial Study," *op. cit.,*[2] p. C-84.

[7] "Colonial Study," *op. cit.,*[2] p. C-95.

layout decisions. The proper use of these ratios depends on what they mean, and this cannot be determined until traffic pattern studies are designed in such a manner as to be able to account for the effects of the variables itemized in Figure 19.2, particularly purchase intentions.

Strategy recommendations based on a positive relation between time spent and money spent should also be viewed with caution. This relation does not necessarily mean that sales can be increased by increasing the amount of time that shoppers are in the store. Rather, the relation can exist simply because shoppers are carrying out their preshopping purchase intentions; the greater the number of items that they intend to purchase, the greater the amount of time spent in the store. In short, does increased time in the store increase purchases, or do a greater number of purchases increase the time spent in the store? Thus, a relation between the time spent and money spent may be a misleading basis for formulating retailing strategies.[8]

Point-of-Purchase Displays[9]

Studies of the effect of point-of-purchase displays vary in purpose and sophistication. One study attempted to determine consumers' *awareness* of point-of-purchase materials and their effect on sales. Interviews were conducted with 5215 shoppers in randomly selected supermarkets, variety stores, drugstores, hardware stores, liquor stores, and service stations. Nearly 82 percent of the respondents indicated that they recalled seeing at least two of the test displays during their shopping trip, 44 percent said that they used displays to guide purchase decisions, and 33 percent purchased one or more of the displayed items.[10]

The degree to which point-of-purchase display *induces brand switching* has also been investigated. Interviews were conducted with 2803 consumers in 16 drugstores located in nine major metropolitan areas geographically scattered from Boston to Los Angeles. Approximately 18 percent of the consumers interviewed said that they decided to try a new brand after entering the store, and 30 percent of these brand switches were allegedly made because the selected item was given point-of-purchase display treatment.[11]

Another study interviewed 2055 customers shopping in 36 package liquor stores across the country. Point-of-purchase displays were reputed to be responsible for 39 percent of the brand switches.[12]

---

[8] For studies of the effects of store layout on shopper behavior in drugstores, see *Super Drug X-Ray* (New York: Point-of-Purchase Advertising Institute, 1962).

[9] The term "point-of-purchase display" refers to such devices as counter cards, banners, window streamers, shelf extenders, wire racks, merchandise displayers, easel back displays, and others.

[10] *Awareness, Decision, Purchase* (New York: Point-of-Purchase Advertising Institute, 1961), p. 14.

[11] *Drugstore Brand Switching and Impulse Buying* (New York: Point-of-Purchase Advertising Institute, 1961), p. 14.

[12] *Package Store Brand Switching and Impulse Buying* (New York: Point-of-Purchase Advertising Institute, 1963), p. 11.

The above are illustrative of studies that have relied on customers' assessments of the influence of point-of-purchase displays on postpurchase outcomes. Other studies have used experimental designs and other more sophisticated techniques in an attempt to determine the effect of point-of-purchase materials. The following studies appear to be illustrative:

(1) Using a before–after with control group design, tests were conducted in supermarkets on juice, beer, and cigarettes; in grocery stores, on beer; in package stores, on blended whiskey and bourbon; in drugstores, on personal care items; in stationery stores, on pens; and in camera stores, on cameras. Displays without motion averaged a gain of 37 percent above normal shelf sales, while a display with motion increased sales by 83 percent above the no-display treatment.[13]

(2) Another study utilized five supermarkets in Wilmington, Delaware, to test five different types of point-of-purchase materials over a five-week period. Using a before–after with control group design, a latin square was used to rotate the point-of-purchase materials across supermarkets and weeks. The results indicated that point-of-purchase materials influenced the sales of spices. The percentage increase varied considerably depending on the type of point-of-purchase material used—shelf extenders and floor bins were more effective than spotters and recipes.[14]

(3) Using a randomized block design, tests were conducted in four drugstores and four stationery stores in Boston. The purpose was to determine the effect of a new counter-top wire carrousel display on the sales of dacron felt tip marker pens. The new display had a positive influence on sales.[15]

A series of display merchandising tests were conducted by *Progressive Grocer* magazine using a panel of test supermarkets over a five-month period during mid 1970. All test stores were matched in terms of volume, layout, size, and demographics. Display experiments were conducted in pairs of stores with comparison control stores retaining normal operating procedures during the length of each specific test. These tests also demonstrate the power of displays in generating sales:[16]

(1) Displays of new health and beauty-aid items increased sales from 100 percent to 400 percent more than normal shelf movement.

(2) One of the most effective sales producers among displays was the related item presentation. Individual items sold as much as 418 percent more

---

[13] *Motion Moves More Merchandise* (New York: Point-of-Purchase Advertising Institute, undated), p. 3.

[14] *Increasing Spice Sales with Point-of-Purchase Advertising* (New York: Point-of-Purchase Advertising Institute, undated), p. 9.

[15] Peter J. McClure and E. James West, "Sales Effects of a New Counter Display," *J. Advertising Research*, vol. 9, pp. 29–34 (Mar. 1969).

[16] "How In-Store Merchandising Can Boost Sales," *Progressive Grocer*, pp. 94–97 (Oct. 1971); "How the Basics of Special Display Affect Sales and Profits," *Progressive Grocer*, pp. 34–45 (Jan. 1971); "How to Make Displays More Sales Productive," *Progressive Grocer*, pp. 34–45 (Feb. 1971).

in combination arrangements than when presented by themselves elsewhere in the store.

(3)   Added sales also resulted from relating mid-aisle displays to neighboring products rather than competing with them. For example, a salad dressing display was related via crepe paper streamers to an adjacent section of salad greens. Sales of individual items increased from 29 percent to 250 percent more than regular shelf movement.

(4)   Displays featuring interdepartmental tie-ins also increased sales. For example, stores using a display combining fresh lemons and instant tea sold $23.24 more product than stores not using this display technique.

(5)   "As advertised" signs, "cents-off" signs, and "product identification" signs increased sales by 124, 23, and 18 percent, respectively.

(6)   The average display tended to decrease in sales after the first week, but items constantly promoted or seasonally related and kept well stocked were productive for much longer periods.

End-Aisle Displays

End-aisle displays differ from point-of-purchase displays in that they are located in one specific position—at the end of a selling counter. These displays are used almost exclusively in self-service outlets, particularly supermarkets and drugstores.

The following are illustrative of some of the more sophisticated attempts to determine the effect of end-aisle displays on in-store behavior:

(1)   Using 10 experimental and 10 control stores, a before–after with control group design was used to measure the sales effectiveness of 36-inch three-dimensional displays in supermarkets. The displays increased sales for three of the four products tested. The test brand of coffee experienced a gain in share of market of 125 percent in the test stores as compared with 10 percent in the control stores. The sales of competing brands declined. The test brand of gelatin gained 177 percent in the test stores, 15 percent in the control stores, and the sales of competing brands declined. The test brand of bathroom tissue gained 8 percent in the test stores and 3 percent in the control stores while competitive brands declined. Sales of the test brand of beer declined less in the test stores than in the control stores.[17]

(2)   A before–after with control group design was used to test the effect of end-aisle displays on the sales of the following products: pancake mixes, flour, shortening, coffee, condiments, canned fruits, luncheon meat, cereals, tuna fish, foil wrap, paper napkins, snacks, peanut butter, syrup, and canned corn. End-aisle displays increased the sales of all products included in the study. Sales of substitute items generally decreased during the display week. The week after the display, total sales of displayed

---

[17]   Mary L. McKenna, "The Influence of In-Store Advertising," in Joseph Newman (ed.), *On Knowing the Consumer* (New York: Wiley, 1966), pp. 114–115.

items decreased relative to their normal weekly sales. Finally, even if the price of a displayed item was increased, unit sales still increased.[18]

(3) Another study audited 734 displays of 360 grocery items in five supermarkets. Unit sales of items on special display increased significantly over normal shelf position.[91]

(4) A before–after with control group design was used to test the effectiveness of end-aisle displays in 12 super drugstores. Displays increased the number of units sold by from 142 percent to 217 percent. Moreover, displays with signs produced better results than displays without signs, and fluorescent and larger signs were more effective than regular and smaller signs.[20]

(5) Using a three-by-three latin square design, tests were conducted in six Vancouver, Canada, supermarkets over a four-week period to determine how displays affected sales of carton cigarettes. End-aisle displays produced greater sales increases than displays in an island shelving unit located in front of one of the store checkouts, or regular shelving.[21]

Marketing Implications of Displays

On the basis of these and other studies,[22] it appears legitimate to conclude:

(1) Displays typically increase the sales of items displayed.

(2) The sales of some products increase to a greater extent than others. Reasons for interproduct variation to displaying are largely unexplored.[23]

(3) Displays often cause the sales of substitute, nondisplayed items to decrease.

(4) The effectiveness of displays is often overstated.

There are two basic reasons why the effectiveness of displays is exaggerated. First, most studies do not determine the extent to which consumers respond by accumulating inventory rather than increasing the rate of consumption.

---

[18] George J. Kress, *The Effect of End Displays on Selected Food Product Sales* (New York: Point-of-Purchase Advertising Institute, undated).

[19] George E. Kline, "How to Build More Profit into Your Display Programs," *Progressive Grocer,* pp. 48–72 (Jan. 1960).

[20] McCammon and Granbois, *op. cit.,*[4] pp. 12–18.

[21] John R. Kennedy, "The Effect of Display Location on the Sales and Pilferage of Cigarettes," *J. Marketing Research,* vol. 7, pp. 210–215 (May 1970).

[22] For other studies, see B. A. Dominick, Jr., *Research in Retail Merchandising of Farm Products* (Washington, D.C.: U.S. Department of Agriculture, Agricultural Marketing Service, 1960); "Display Ideas for Supermarkets," *Progressive Grocer* (1958); *Triggering Plus Sales and Profits* (New York: Point-of-Purchase Advertising Institute, undated); *The Tavern Study: Parts I, II* (New York: Point-of-Purchase Advertising Institute, undated).

[23] Some studies have investigated some of the reasons why end-aisle displays increase the sales of some products more than others. See, for example, "Displays Add Sales, Profit, and Personality to Kroger of Bay Village," *Progressive Grocer,* pp. 63–70, (Jan. 1967); Kress, *op. cit.,*[18] pp. 18–22; Robert Kelley, "An Evaluation of Selected Variables of End Display Effectiveness," unpublished doctoral dissertation (Cambridge, Mass.: Harvard University, 1965).

Second, many studies do not determine the extent to which customers purchase from the display instead of purchasing the product in its regular location (location substitution). Of the two sources of bias, the first is probably the most pervasive. The results of studies that do not use "pretest periods," "during-test periods," and "posttest periods" that are at least as long as a multiple of the average period of time that normally elapses between purchases, should be viewed with caution.

Despite the inflation, in most instances displays appear to increase sales. There are two basic explanations for this behavior: (1) the exposure hypothesis and (2) the comparison-process hypothesis.

The *exposure hypothesis* maintains that end-aisle displays and/or point-of-purchase material increase the percentage of customers who are exposed to the product(s) in question. Exposure either creates a new need, or reminds the consumer of a latent need, which in turn triggers the purchase.

It was previously pointed out (Chapters 10 and 11) that consumers compare, either directly or indirectly, perceived product attributes with evaluative criteria, or what they are looking for in a problem solution. It is well known that a majority of customers, particularly supermarket shoppers, do not know the prices of products. The *comparison-process hypothesis* maintains that a substantial proportion of customers think that prices have been reduced on displayed items. For many consumers, buying items on display is a response trait or a performance strategy that is used indirectly to evaluate alternatives. The tendency for the sales of display items to increase even when the price is increased lends support to this hypothesis. Sufficient research has not been conducted to determine the relative importance of these two explanations for the effectiveness of end-aisle displays and point-of-purchase materials.

Regardless of the above limitations, a sufficient number of sophisticated studies have been conducted to conclude that displays have important marketing implications for both manufacturers and retailers.

Implications for Manufacturers Unless unusually high premiums must be paid, it is usually desirable for a manufacturer to attempt to obtain special display treatment for his items. In fact, even if high premiums must be paid, in view of the effectiveness of displaying, careful consideration should be given to the strategy, even if it requires a reduction in other promotional expenditures.

In many instances, the problem is being able to obtain special display treatment, rather than whether to follow the strategy. The probability of obtaining special treatment increases: (1) when the manufacturer's brand has a higher profit contribution or gross margin than other brands in the product category, (2) when the manufacturer provides the displays, and (3) when the manufacturer installs the displays or provides displays that the retailer can install cheaply. Conditions (1) and (3) are particularly important since many studies find that retailers use less than 50 percent of the displays provided by manufacturers.[24]

---

[24] Bert C. McCammon, Jr., "The Role of Point-of-Purchase Display in the Manufacturer's Marketing Mix," in Taylor Meloan and Charles Whitto (eds.), *Competition in Marketing* (Los Angeles: Graduate School of Business, University of Southern California, 1964), pp. 75–91, at p. 78.

Implications for Retailers   Retailers view display materials from a different perspective. They are interested in displays that increase *product category* sales and profits in relation to the display space required, that is, they want to increase product category profits per square or linear foot of selling space.[25] As a consequence, they look favorably on displays that can be installed cheaply and produce additional sales rather than cause brand switching.[26]

Displays help increase retailer profits in several ways:[27]

(1) *Help shape store image*—Continuous scheduling of special-priced displays can convey a low-price store image.

(2) *Pull traffic through the store*—Using displays for advertised sale-priced items in areas of the store which have lower traffic levels, but good shopper visibility, can help draw customers to those areas of the store.

(3) *Stimulate related-item sales*—Displays are often more productive when they are used to showcase related items such as picnic products or drinking mugs and coffee.

(4) *Launching new products*—Displays are ideal for launching new items. New products are very important because they are major contributors to sales and profits and give consumers the impression they can find the newest items in the store.

(5) *Make loss-leader items profitable*—Loss leaders, or near-cost items, are used extensively to attract consumers into a store. Joint displays of these items, together with profit-making related items, can help reduce the loss on one with profit on the other.

THE EFFECTS OF PRODUCT SHELVING ON CONSUMER BEHAVIOR

The way products are shelved also influences the behavior of consumers, particularly in self-service retail outlets. This section discusses the effects of shelf facings (the number of rows of a product that are displayed) and shelf height on consumer behavior.

Shelf Facings

Several studies have attempted to determine the relationship between shelf facings and sales. For example:

---

[25] For a more comprehensive discussion, see James P. Cairns, "Suppliers, Retailers, and Shelf Space," *J. Marketing*, vol. 26, pp. 34–36 (July 1962).

[26] Some retailers have banned brand-switching displays. See "With Showmanship on the Shelf, Flair on the Floor," *Printers Ink*, p. 386 (June 14, 1963). Brand switching is a legitimate display objective when there are variations between brands in gross margins. For example, retailers use displays extensively for their private labels, partly because they usually have higher gross margins than on national brands.

[27] "How the Basics of Special Display Affect Sales and Profits," *op. cit.*,[16] pp. 36–37.

(1) Three self-service supermarkets were selected in such a manner as to obtain variation in the income levels of consumers. Using two soap powder products, three shelf display situations were used in each of the three stores, with the number of facings of each soap being varied. The results indicated that an increase in the number of facings did not increase sales of the product.[28]

(2) An experiment utilized a 6 × 6 latin square design (six supermarkets over a six-week period) to determine the effect of shelf width on the sale of baking soda, hominy, Tang, and powdered coffee cream. Displays, prices, shelf locations, and promotions were controlled during the study. The results indicated that there was some increase in the sales of all four product classes as the number of facings was increased. However, only one of the products—hominy—responded with consistently large increases in sales.[29]

(3) A study by the U.S. Department of Agriculture measured sales response to various display widths of 17 canned vegetable and fruit product classes. All other variables were controlled. Weekly sales varied consistently with the number of facings used. Sales for six facings were 41 percent higher than sales for two facings. Increasing the number of facings from two to four resulted in a 13 percent increase in sales.[30]

(4) A latin square design was used to test the effect of shelf facings on sales of Crest toothpaste, Preparation H Suppositories, Hook's Red Mouth Wash, and Johnson and Johnson Band Aids in eight Hook Drug Stores. Increased shelf facings increased sales of all products except the suppositories. Band Aids displayed a relatively uniform increase in sales for each additional shelf facing of the product. However, for Crest, the marginal sales increment between a two- and three-facing situation only amounted to three units. Mouth wash sales were greater with six shelf facings than with the maximum of seven.[31]

(5) A 5 × 5 latin square experiment was conducted in retail supermarket dairy departments and replicated in the far west, midwest, New England, and middle Atlantic regions. In general, sales of items in the dairy department were not affected by the number of shelf facings. In those situations where consumer response was statistically significant, the increase in unit sales was too low to justify economically the continued use of more linear space.[32]

Thus, studies investigating the relationship between shelf facings and

---

[28] Douglas H. Harris, "The Effect of Display Width in Merchandising Soap," *J. Applied Psychology*, pp. 283–284 (1958).

[29] Keith R. Cox, "The Responsiveness of Food Sales to Shelf Space Changes in Supermarkets," *J. Marketing Research*, vol. 1, pp. 63–67 (May 1964).

[30] *Better Utilization of Selling Space in Food Stores*, Marketing Research Report no. 30 (Washington, D.C.: U.S. Department of Agriculture, 1952).

[31] Jeffry A. Kotzan and Robert V. Evanson, "Responsiveness of Drug Store Sales to Shelf Space Allocations," *J. Marketing Research*, vol. 6, pp. 465–469 (Nov. 1969).

[32] Harry F. Krueckeberg, "The Significance of Consumer Response to Display Space Reallocation," in Philip R. McDonald (ed.), *Marketing Involvement in Society and the Economy* (Chicago: Amer. Marketing Assoc., 1969), pp. 336–339.

unit sales are inconclusive. Increasing the number of shelf facings increases the sales of some products but not others. Moreover, when sales increase, they do not necessarily increase uniformly for each additional shelf facing.

Unfortunately, little attention has been given to interproduct variation in response to shelf facings. One study found that in supermarkets there was no relationship between the amount of shelf space and sales of: (1) a staple product brand (Morton and Food Club Salt); (2) an impulse product brand that has high consumer acceptance (Coffeemate); and (3) an impulse product brand that has low consumer acceptance (Creamora).[33] However, additional research is necessary to support even these limited insights.

Shelf Height

In order to determine the effect of shelf height on sales, products of varying size, variety, and popularity are changed from their normal shelf position to an alternate location for a test period, normally two weeks. The sales in the test positions are compared with normal shelf position movement to determine the effect of change.

In general, studies indicate that the following order of shelf locations is most effective in increasing sales: (1) eye level, (2) waist level, and (3) knee or ankle level.[34] However, this generalization does not apply to all products. For example, in some instances, shelf height has only a modest effect, if any, on sales.[35] The *Progressive Grocer* study cited above found that shelf height–sales relationships depend on the product's package size, its normal movement, whether it is being advertised, and the market for the product.[36]

The importance of product size and weight is illustrated by the movement of a 54-ounce juice item from a lower shelf to a top shelf. Instead of the expected increase in sales, unit movement dropped 15 percent, apparently because of the difficulty of lifting such a heavy item from that height.[37]

The bottom shelf is actually very effective for certain types of products. For example, as noted above, consumers prefer to purchase many heavier products and larger sized containers when they are located on the bottom shelf. Specialed or promoted items with normal heavy customer demand attract consumer attention, and shelf height plays a minor role. Lower shelves are also effective for products appealing to children. To illustrate, in candy, sales increases in ranges of 14 to 39 percent have resulted from the placement of multipacks of penny candies, suckers, and TV-advertised products on the bottom shelf.[38]

---

[33] Keith R. Cox, "The Effect of Shelf Space upon Sales of Branded Products," *J. Marketing Research,* vol. 7, pp. 55–58 (Feb. 1970).

[34] "Shelf Merchandising Strategy: A Key to Increased Sales," *Progressive Grocer,* pp. C-121–C-125 (Mar. 1964); "Shelf Attitudes Affect Buying Attitudes," *Progressive Grocer,* p. C-126 (Mar. 1964).

[35] Ronald E. Frank and William F. Massy, "Shelf Position and Space Effects on Sales," *J. Marketing Research,* vol. 7, pp. 59–66 (Feb. 1970).

[36] "Merchandising, Part III," *Progressive Grocer,* pp. 41–49 (Mar. 1971).

[37] "Merchandising," *op. cit.,*[36] p. 43.

[38] "Merchandising," *op. cit.,*[36] p. 44.

Marketing Implications of Shelving

Shelf management is important to both the retailer and the manufacturer. These implications are discussed below.

Implications for Retailers In 1963 General Foods Corporation funded a McKinsey Company study of the economics of food distribution. Part of this study measured differences in costs and profits among items and then calculated direct product profit (DPP) for various items. The study concluded that DPP information reflects more accurately the worth of a product than do such conventional measures as gross margin, gross profit, and gross profit per unit of space. The major reason for the superior accuracy of DPP is that it includes variations in the handling costs of individual products.[39]

In 1965 Pet Milk funded a study at the Harvard Graduate School to investigate relationships between DPP and shelf space. Based on a series of experiments in sixteen food stores, the researchers concluded that retailers can increase total profit for a product family by shifting space from less profitable to more profitable items and by eliminating items with low profitability.[40]

In 1970 a study was conducted in four Australian supermarkets over a sixteen-week period. The results showed that whenever space was allocated to the products in the canned pet foods section in proportion to their relative profits (1) the total sales of the canned pet foods section increased, and (2) the total profits of the canned pet foods section increased. Further, these improvements occurred in any supermarket allocating space in this manner, and statistically there was a high level of confidence in the results.[41]

A study by Fladmark and Bennett yielded results inconsistent with the above studies. They experimentally manipulated shelf space for brands of cooking oil, mayonnaise, and peanut butter in independent supermarkets affiliated with an IGA wholesaler. For none of the three product classes was it possible to accept the decision rule that an item should get the same proportion of total space given a particular family as the item contributes to the total profit contribution of that product family. However, as the authors point out, their findings may be due to certain artifacts of their design.[42]

To date, the bulk of the evidence indicates that in most instances retailers can increase total profit for a product family by allocating the same proportion

---

[39] *McKinsey–General Foods Study: The Economics of Food Distribution* (New York: General Foods Corp., 1963), p. 28.

[40] Robert D. Buzzell, Walter J. Salmon, and Richard F. Vancil, *Profitability Measurement and Merchandising Decisions* (Boston: Division of Research, Graduate School of Business Administration, Harvard University, 1965), p. 38.

[41] *Managing Shelf Space for Profit* (North Sydney, Australia: P. A. Management Consultants Pty. Ltd., 1970).

[42] Kenneth O. Fladmark and Peter D. Bennett, "An Experiment Testing the Value of Item Profitability Data in Allocating Shelf Space in Supermarkets," in McDonald, *op. cit.,*[32] pp. 330–335.

of space to an item as it contributes to the total profit contribution of its product family. This decision rule may, however, not hold in every instance.

With regard to shelf height, items having the highest DPP per square or linear foot should be given maximum exposure at eye level unless:

(1) Consumer preference is sufficiently strong that they will search for and purchase the item regardless of its height on the shelf.

(2) The item is bulky or heavy.

(3) Young children are important purchasers.

Implications for Manufacturers The manufacturer's objective is to increase the profitable sales of his items rather than the retailer's entire product category. Thus the manufacturer should strive to obtain the maximum number of facings for each item and try to get eye level placement unless the item is bulky or heavy or is purchased by young children.

THE EFFECTS OF PRICING TECHNIQUES ON CONSUMER BEHAVIOR

Chapter 10 discussed the role and significance of price as an evaluative criterion. It was shown that not all consumers are concerned with price,[43] and that the importance of price varies from product to product.[44]

Given these findings, it is not surprising that the relation between price and sales is difficult to predict. Contrary to microeconomic theory, sales do not always increase following a decrease in price. In fact, a price increase sometimes precipitates an increase in sales.[45] Thus, in a given situation, the price–sales relation needs to be empirically determined rather than relying on the "inverse-relation" generalization.

This section discusses dimensions of price not covered in previous chapters. Attention is given to price perceptions, dual pricing, and multiple-unit pricing.

Price Perceptions

Many studies find that most consumers do not have accurate perceptions of the prices of items. This is even true for frequently purchased convenience items found in supermarkets and drugstores.

---

[43] See, for example, George Haines, "A Study of Why People Purchase New Products," in Raymond M. Haas (ed.), *Science, Technology and Marketing* (Chicago: Amer. Marketing Assoc., 1966), pp. 665–685; Gregory P. Stone, "City Shoppers and Urban Identification: Observations on the Social Psychology of City Life," *Amer. J. Sociology*, vol. 60, pp. 36–45 (July 1954).

[44] William D. Wells and Leonard A. LoSciuto, "Direct Observation of Purchasing Behavior," *J. Marketing Research*, vol. 3, pp. 227–233 (Aug. 1966); A. Gabor and C. W. J. Granger, "Price Sensitivity of the Consumer," *J. Advertising Research*, vol. 4, pp. 40–44 (Dec. 1964).

[45] See, for example, Kress, *op. cit.*,[18] pp. 18–22.

Illustrative Studies   A *Progressive Grocer* study selected 59 items that industry executives considered to be frequently advertised and highly price competitive. These items were broken up into groups of six. Tables were set up in Colonial test stores, and on each table a different group of items was placed. Several thousand customers were shown these items and asked to state the price of each. As Table 20.3 indicates, less than 50 percent of the respondents estimated price within ± 5 percent of the actual price for 57 of the 59 items.[56]

Table 20.3 COMPARISON OF CUSTOMERS' ESTIMATES OF PRICES WITH ACTUAL RETAIL PRICES ON HIGHLY ADVERTISED ITEMS

Product	Rank in Exact Price Recognition	Customers Naming Exact Price (%)	Customers Within 5% Higher or 5% Lower (%)
Coca-Cola (6-pack)	1	86	91
Camel cigarettes	2	39	54
Kleenex 400's	3	34	44
Texize cleaner	4	31	38
Colonial apple sauce	5	30	57
Campbell tomato soup	6	30	49
Cut-Rite wax paper	7	28	41
6-pack Colonial frozen orange juice	8	27	38
Carnation milk	9	25	33
Clorox, ½ gallon	10	25	31
Tide, large	11	24	52
Pet milk	12	23	49
Pillsbury pancake mix	13	23	25
Colonial fruit cocktail	14	22	30
Duke's mayonnaise	15	21	38
Ballard biscuits	16	20	53
Colonial canned milk	17	20	45
Domino sugar, 5 lb	18	20	67
Morton cream pie	19	19	25
Kellogg's corn flakes	20	19	31
Breck shampoo	21	19	21
SOS soap pads	22	18	22
Kraft mayonnaise	23	18	32
Colonial mayonnaise	24	18	20
3-D detergent (colonial)	25	18	23
Del Monte fruit cocktail	26	18	25
Red Band flour, 5 lb	27	18	42
Land-o-Lakes butter	28	17	43
Ivory bar, large	29	17	32

---

[56] "Colonial Study," *op. cit.*[2]

Table 20.3 COMPARISON OF CUSTOMERS' ESTIMATES OF PRICES WITH ACTUAL RETAIL PRICES ON HIGHLY ADVERTISED ITEMS (*Continued*)

Product	Rank in Exact Price Recognition	Customers Naming Exact Price (%)	Customers Within 5% Higher or 5% Lower (%)
Scott towels, large	30	16	24
Parkay margarine	31	16	18
Crest toothpaste, large	32	15	19
B & M baked beans	33	15	27
Waldorf tissue	34	14	20
Pillsbury flour, 5 lb	35	13	51
Heinz catsup	36	13	27
Maxwell House instant coffee	37	12	29
Fab, large	38	12	20
3-D bleach, ½ gallon (Colonial)	39	12	15
Colonial orange juice (46 oz)	40	12	20
Saran wrap (25 ft)	41	11	15
Silver Label coffee, 1 lb (Colonial)	42	11	13
Tide, giant	43	10	35
Staflo liquid starch	44	10	18
Dole sliced pineapple	45	9	22
Nestle Quick, 1 lb	46	9	12
Crisco, 3 lb	47	9	29
Black peas, 1 lb	48	8	19
Peter Pan peanut butter	49	8	25
Mazola oil	50	6	27
Pillsbury angel mix	51	6	13
Maxwell House coffee, 1-lb bag	52	5	29
Dixie crystal sugar, 10 lb	53	5	42
Span, 12 oz	54	5	20
Comet cleanser, 14 oz	55	4	24
Pillsbury flour, 10 lb	56	4	15
Minute rice	57	3	13
Maxwell House coffee, 2 lb	58	3	27
Colonial shortening, 3 lb	59	2	34

SOURCE: "Colonial Study," *Progressive Grocer* (1964).

Similar patterns exist for other types of products and stores. For example, the authors have unpublished data which indicate that consumers have inaccurate perceptions of prices of drugstore items and major appliances.

Brown has attempted to determine what types of consumers perceive supermarket prices most validly. He interviewed over 1000 shoppers in 27 different supermarkets in five communities. Perceptual validity for individual shoppers was computed by comparing their ordinal ranking of stores' price levels with the stores' market basket indices.

Three types of independent variables were tested as discriminators of perceptual validity: shopping behavior, shopping attitudes, and socioeconomic variables. These variables exhibited weak relationships with perceptual ability, leaving over 85 percent of the variance among shoppers unexplained. Shopping variables were more potent explanatory variables than demographics, but they led to less valid perceptions in some communities. Demographics showed more consistent relationships across communities, but their effects were much smaller.[47]

Marketing Implications   Although there are some methodological problems with the types of price perception studies discussed above, several provisional conclusions are possible. Confronted with thousands of items, consumers find it difficult to know specific prices. Since the items tested are purchased frequently, it seems logical to assume that consumers have even less knowledge of actual prices of the vast majority of supermarket items. If a store wants to create a low-price impression, regular price along with special price should be used in advertising and point-of-purchase materials.

Dual Pricing[48]

Dual pricing refers to the recent practice in supermarkets of maintaining conventional pricing practices as well as unit pricing—for example, price stated per ounce, per serving, etc. More than 30 supermarket chains have launched dual price programs.

Illustrative Studies   In October 1970, Jewel Tea supermarkets released a study of the effects of their Compar-A-Buy (CAB) program, then seven months old. About 45 percent of the respondents had used the system one or more times, 41 percent considered it worthwhile, but only 30 percent said they used it on a regular basis. Most importantly, only 5 percent said they had changed a shopping decision on the basis of CAB. Finally, while the device was originally intended as an aid for lower income shoppers, use appeared to increase with income and education.

Another study, conducted under the auspices of the Consumer Research Institute, took place in six Kroger stores over a 16-week period. The percentage of those polled who had actually used the unit pricing system in shopping was about 31 percent, close to Jewel's 30 percent. As with the Jewel tests, the Kroger study also found higher use among the more educated and affluent, and negligible changes in buying patterns, that is, product movement analysis showed that most product categories displayed no tendencies to shift toward lower or higher price points.

---

[47]   F. E. Brown, "Who Perceives Supermarket Prices Most Validly?" *J. Marketing Research*, vol. 8, pp. 110–113 (Feb. 1971).

[48]   This section was adapted from "Dual Pricing," *Progressive Grocer*, pp. 46–50 (Feb. 1971).

Another study was co-sponsored by the National Association of Food Chains and Safeway supermarkets. The study found that 31 percent of respondents used dual pricing—exactly the same as in Kroger stores. The study also concluded:

> ". . . that shoppers are not able to make many price comparisons of supermarket packages effectively without the aid of dual-price labels . . . indeed our figures indicate that label usage may increase the number of correctly made cost comparisons involving such packages by factors ranging from 2.5 to 7."

Marketing Implications The above studies as well as other information suggest that some of the worst fears about dual pricing—that it would benefit private label to the detriment of brand name sales, and that it would cause a mass movement to size—appear to be overstated. Buying decisions involve more than cost considerations.

Costs of establishing and maintaining dual pricing programs are not excessive. Estimates range from over $2000 a year per store down to negligible costs offset partly by system benefits, such as lower costs for stocking, reordering, and inventory control.

Finally, by demonstrating an interest in consumer information techniques and a willingness to experiment, the industry may avoid restrictive legislation. Hopefully the future will witness increased use by those who need it most, but appear to be least aware of it—the poor.

Multiple-Unit Pricing

As the name implies, multiple-unit pricing refers to the practice of pricing items in multiple-unit quantities, such as 5/89¢ or 3/69¢. The impact of this pricing technique is discussed in this section.

Illustrative Studies The effect of multiple-unit pricing was investigated in *Progressive Grocer's* panel of matched supermarkets during a six-month period of 1970.[49] Controlled experiments were made with various forms of multi-unit and single-unit pricing. Normal sales were measured during control periods, and careful audits of commodity movement were made during test periods when experimental prices were being analyzed.

Some of the results of the study are summarized in Table 20.4. In general, at least in the supermarket industry, multiple-unit pricing is effective in increasing immediate sales. However, whether this pricing technique increases the rate of product consumption, or merely encourages the consumer to store up for future use, has apparently not been determined.

---

[49] "How Multiple-Unit Pricing Helps . . . and Hurts," *Progressive Grocer*, pp. 52–58 (June 1971).

Table 20.4 EFFECTS OF MULTIPLE-UNIT PRICING IN SUPERMARKETS

(a) *Switching from Single-Unit to Multiple-Unit*

Item	Single-Unit Price (¢)	Single-Unit Product Movement	Multiple-Unit Price (¢)	Multiple-Unit Product Movement	% Change
Catsup, 14 oz	24	11	2/47	15	+36
Aluminum foil, 25 feet	25	34	2/49	47	+38
Macaroni and cheese, 7¼ oz	15	8	3/44	14	+75
Mustard, 9 oz	17	34	2/33	39	+15
Onion sauce, 6 oz	27	10	2/53	11	+10

(b) *Switching from Multiple-Unit to Single-Unit*

Item	Multiple-Unit Price (¢)	Multiple-Unit Product Movement	Single-Unit Price (¢)	Single-Unit Product Movement	% Change
Mustard, 9 oz	2/37	69	19	50	−28
Macaroni and cheese, 7¼ oz	2/43	75	22	54	−28
Catsup, 14 oz	2/49	28	25	18	−36
Frozen peas, 10 oz	2/43	32	22	29	− 9
Salt, 26 oz	2/25	32	13	23	−28

(c) *Switching Multiples*

Item	Multiple-Unit Price Before (¢)	Unit Movement Before	Multiple-Unit Price After (¢)	Unit Movement After	% Change
Frozen corn, 10 oz	2/43	19	3/65	15	−21
Dog food, 15½ oz	2/29	24	7/$1	60	+150
Catsup, 14 oz	2/47	15	3/72	11	−27
Macaroni and cheese, 7¼ oz	2/43	6	3/64	7	+17

SOURCE: "How Multiple-Unit Pricing Helps . . . and Hurts," *Progressive Grocer*, p. 55 (June 1971).

Marketing Implications Several factors need to be considered in the use of multiple-unit pricing. First, the price has to be easy to understand; complicated multiple prices—6 for 59 cents, 8 for 79 cents—are usually less effective than simple multiples—2 for 18 cents. Second, the bargain concept of multiple pricing appears to reach its peak within the one-dollar limit. Multiples in excess of one dollar are usually relatively ineffective. Third, even with the additional thrust of multiple-unit pricing, the sales of a product are influenced by neighboring brands and various sizes which compete for the shoppers' attention. Finally, the check-out operator must be able to calculate prices accurately when less than the full number of units is purchased. In one test of 80 transactions of an item, 14 percent were rung incorrectly. These mistakes have a strong impact on profits since supermarkets' after-tax profit margins range from 0.5 to 1.5 percent of sales.[50]

These limitations should not deter retailers from evaluating the desirability of multiple unit pricing in their respective establishments. Customers accept many forms of this type of pricing, apparently because they perceive quantity buying as involving greater savings. Pricing strategies that recognize the limitations, as well as the advantages, of multiple-unit pricing are frequently an effective way of increasing volume.[51]

THE EFFECTS OF OUT-OF-STOCKS, BRANDS, DEALS, AND PACKAGING ON CONSUMER BEHAVIOR

Product availability, private brands, deals, and packaging all have an important impact on consumers' in-store behavior. This section summarizes findings in these areas and notes their implications for marketing strategists.

Out-of-Stock Conditions

Consumer reactions to out-of-stock conditions are an important consideration in planning merchandise assortments. Unfortunately, published research is limited to consumers' reactions to supermarket merchandise assortments. The results reported below are based on studies conducted by the A. C. Nielsen Company[52]

Nonavailability of Preferred Brand   Nielsen research indicates that 42 percent of supermarket shoppers refused to buy a substitute brand when their favorite brand is out of stock. However, this type of behavior varies widely by product category. For example, 62 percent refused to buy a substitute brand of toothpaste compared to only 23 percent for toilet tissue.

---

[50] "How Multiple Unit Pricing Helps . . . and Hurts," *op. cit.,*[49] p. 38.

[51] For additional research, see "Multiple-Pricing Makes the Most of the Moment of Purchase," *Progressive Grocer,* pp. C-128–C-132 (Mar. 1964).

[52] This section is adapted from research reported in "Out-of-Stocks Disappoint Shoppers, Force Store Switching," *Progressive Grocer,* pp. S-26–S-23 (Nov. 1968).

Nonavailability of Brand or Size An average of one out of five customers would not substitute either a brand or size when faced by a stock-out. Of the product categories studied, instant coffee led the list; nearly 25 percent of customers would not substitute. In comparison, only 13 percent of respondents refused to purchase another brand or size of toilet soap.

Nonavailability of Colors An important percentage of consumers were also uncompromising when it came to desired product colors. For example, one out of ten shoppers refused to buy any substitute for the desired color in toilet soap and toilet tissues. Although strong brand loyalty apparently exists in these product categories, about 28 percent of toilet tissue purchasers and 17 percent of toilet soap purchasers say they switch brands in order to obtain the desired color.

Nonavailability of New Items Customers also react when new items are not available. Nearly 50 percent say they go elsewhere to get a desired new item.[53]

Marketing Implications The above research should be viewed as *suggestive* of the kinds of studies that can focus on consumer reactions to various merchandise assortment dimensions. Although very few of these types of studies have been conducted, they are useful in making merchandise assortment decisions.

In planning a merchandise assortment in supermarkets as well as other types of retail establishments, the retailer is interested in optimizing the relationship between dollar inventory and lost sales due to out-of-stock conditions. Inventory investment is important since it is a critical determinant of asset turnover and hence return on investment. Lost sales also are significant, since the operating expense configurations of most retailers mean that a lost sale tends to reduce net profit by the amount of the gross margin on the item.

The missing link in making the type of decision described above is information concerning the types of assortment factors that consumers will accept substitutes for. What is the relative importance of brand, size, color, fabric, style, and so on in gaining and maintaining customer loyalty? Armed with this information, retailers can build assortments on the dimensions that consumers are unwilling to substitute and hence increase their return on investment.

Private-Brand Proneness

Several studies have documented the fact that consumers have different attitudes toward, and are differentially attracted by, private and national brands.[54] However, attempts to explain this type of behavior have been relatively unsuccess-

---

[53] For additional research see James D. Peckham, "The Consumer Speaks," *J. Marketing*, vol. 27, pp. 21–26 (Oct. 1963).

[54] See, for example, John G. Myers, "Determinants of Private Brand Attitude," *J. Marketing Research*, vol. 4, pp. 73–81 (Feb. 1967); Ronald E. Frank and Harper W. Boyd, "Are Private-Brand-Prone Grocery Consumers Really Different?" *J. Advertising Research*, vol. 5, pp. 27–35 ((Dec. 1965); Harold Demsetz, "The Effect of Consumer Experience on Brand Loyalty and the Structure of Market Demand," *Econometrica*, vol. 30, pp. 22–33 (Jan. 1962).

ful. One study found that women who are enthusiastic, sensitive, and submissive had a higher probability of purchasing private brands than their counterparts; however, these personality variables were weak, accounting for less than 5 percent of the total variance.[55] There are some relatively small associations between private-brand proneness and household socioeconomic and consumption patterns:

(1) *Family size*—Large families are more private-brand prone than small families.[56]

(2) *Employment status of wife*—Housewives have a greater acceptance of private brands than working women.[57]

(3) *Education*—The greater the educational level of the household head, the higher the household's private-brand proneness.[58]

(4) *Rate of consumption*—The higher the rate of consumption of a product, the greater the probability that the household will be private-brand prone.[59]

(5) *Store loyalty*—The higher a housewife's store loyalty, the greater the chance of her purchasing private brands.[60]

The total impact of socioeconomic and personality variables is weak, indicating that if differences do exist between private- and manufacturer-brand-prone customers, they are relatively slight. There are several reasons why there do not appear to be strong determinants. First, a variety of factors might account for private-brand proneness but not be strongly associated with other consumer characteristics.[61] Second, many potential determinants of private-brand proneness, such as price activity, price level, extensiveness of private-brand availability, and other structural variables[62] have not been analyzed. Finally, measures of private-brand attitude and proneness may not be valid or reliable.

At the present time, then, it does not appear feasible to segment markets for *grocery* products on the basis of attitudes toward, or propensity to purchase, private brands. Whether or not purchasers of private brands of other types of

---

[55] Myers, *op. cit.*,[54] p. 77. A form of Cattell's sixteen-personality-factor inventory was used to measure personality in Raymond B. Cattell and Glen P. Stice, *Handbook for the Sixteen Personality Factor Questionnaire, the 16 P.F. Test, Forms A, B, and C* (Champaign, Ill.: Institute for Personality and Ability Testing, 1957).

[56] Frank and Boyd, *op. cit.*,[54] p. 34.

[57] Myers, *op. cit.*,[54] p. 79.

[58] Frank and Boyd, *op. cit.*,[54] p. 34.

[59] Frank and Boyd, *op. cit.*,[54] p. 34; "Colonial Study: A Report on Supermarket Operations and Consumer Habits," *Progressive Grocer* (1963).

[60] Tanniru R. Rao, "Are Some Consumers More Prone to Purchase Private Brands?" *J. Marketing Research*, vol. 6, pp. 447–450 (Nov. 1969).

[61] Howard Trier, Henry Clay Smith, and James Shaffer, "Differences in Food Buying Attitudes of Housewives," *J. Marketing*, vol. 25, pp. 66–69 (July 1960).

[62] These structural variables are sometimes more important than the characteristics of consumers. See, for example, John U. Farley, "Why Does Brand Loyalty Vary over Products?" *J. Marketing Research*, vol. 1, pp. 9–14 (Nov. 1964).

products differ from other consumers is, at this point, unknown, and future research in this area would be useful.

Deal Proneness

Each year manufacturers spend millions of dollars promoting the sale of their products by various kinds of coupons, price-off labels, and other types of deals. Is there a deal-prone consumer? Are there demographic, socioeconomic, or purchasing characteristics that differentiate a deal-prone consumer from other consumers?

Webster has attempted to answer these questions by analyzing the three-year purchase records of a food item by 366 families located in a major metropolitan area. Deal proneness was defined as the difference between actual dealing behavior and the opportunity to deal. After examining more than 200 regression models, Webster found only 4 of 45 socioeconomic and consumption pattern variables that were consistent predictors of consumer deal proneness:[63]

(1) *Age of housewife*—Deal proneness tends to increase as the age of the housewife increases.

(2) *Number of brands purchased*—Deal proneness tends to increase as the number of different brands purchased increases.

(3) *Number of units purchased*—Deal proneness tends to decrease as the total number of units purchased increases.

(4) *Brand loyalty*—Deal proneness tends to decrease as brand loyalty increases.

Thus, the deal-prone consumer is likely to be an older housewife who purchases fewer units but buys more brands and is not brand loyal. However, these four variables, taken together, explain only 15 percent of the variability in deal proneness.

Massy and Frank studied the relationships between price and dealing variables on the market share of a brand. They also found that brand-loyal consumers were less responsive to dealing than were nonloyal consumers.[64]

Montgomery has studied the relationship between consumer characteristics and deal purchasing of dentrifice products before and after August 1, 1960, the date on which the American Dental Association (ADA) announced its endorsement of Crest toothpaste. The results for dealing activity prior to the ADA endorsement were:[65]

---

[63] Frederick E. Webster, Jr., "The Deal-Prone Consumer," *J. Marketing Research*, vol. 2, pp. 186–189 (May 1965).

[64] William F. Massy and Ronald E. Frank, "Short-Term Price and Dealing Effects in Selected Market Segments," *J. Marketing Research*, vol. 2, pp. 171–185 (May 1965).

[65] David B. Montgomery, "Consumer Characteristics and 'Deal' Purchasing," (Cambridge, Mass.: Marketing Science Institute, 1970).

(1) Brand loyalty is inversely related to dealing activity.

(2) Venturesomeness is directly related to dealing activity.

(3) Media exposure is directly related to dealing activity.

(4) Gregariousness is directly related to dealing activity.

(5) Opinion leadership, interest, and the presence of children do not seem to relate to dealing activity.

Brand loyalty was by far the most important factor, followed by venturesomeness, media exposure, and gregariousness. However, the adjusted R^2 for these variables was only 8.6 percent.

After the ADA endorsement, the directions of effects of brand loyalty, venturesomeness, media exposure, and gregariousness were all the same as during the earlier period. However, the magnitude of all these effects diminished, with only brand loyalty remaining statistically significant. The adjusted R^2 fell to only 3.2 percent.

Since information on deal proneness is limited to a few studies, generalizations are risky. At the present time, however, it does not appear that grocery-product deal-prone consumers are likely to constitute an identifiable market segment. Hopefully, future research will be more successful in isolating differentiating characteristics, since this information would be useful in determining what type of deal would be most effective, in predicting the response to a given consumer deal, and in estimating the extent of market coverage—"the reach"—achieved by dealing.

Packaging

Packaging plays an important role in the purchase of many products, particularly those distributed through self-service retail outlets. Packaging is often an important evaluative criterion, particularly for products purchased on impulse.[66] This section presents illustrative studies of the role of packaging in in-store purchasing decisions.

The Role of Packaging in In-Store Decisions   During 1970, *Sales Management* magazine sponsored a major study of the role of packaging on consumer decisions in drugstores.[67] The study involved mail interviews with 1578 United States families conducted by National Family Opinion, Inc. The NFO sample is matched with the universe of United States families in terms of geographic division, population density, age of home maker, and annual family income. The survey consisted primarily of female members of families and, as such, did not include nonfamily consumers such as bachelors and career girls.

About one half of the respondents named "past experience with a product" as the most important factor in their choice of drugs, and about 60 percent said experience was also most important in buying cosmetics and toiletries (Table 20.5).

---

[66] Impulse purchasing will be discussed in Chapter 21.

[67] "Drugstore Packages," *Sales Management*, pp. 41–52 (Sept. 15, 1970).

Packaging was also important, as responses to statements 1 and 3 in Table 20.5 indicate. More than 38 percent of the respondents said that the package container had a "great influence" on their choice of brands when they first purchased a cosmetic or toiletry product, and 30 percent said they switched brands for a better package.

Over 50 percent said they would pay more for a more convenient or efficient drugstore package (statement 9), and 42 percent said they would pay extra for an attractive cosmetic or toiletries package (statement 11).

At the same time, packages do not rescue mediocre products. Only 9 percent assumed that the best looking packages contain quality products, and 90 percent made no such assumption (statement 5). Respondents were interested in style, complaining about packages that look "medicinal" or "gimmicky" and complimenting packages for neat designs and clear graphics.

Although there were differences in attitudes by age and income, most variations do not appear to be statistically significant. One exception was that the over-60s were most emphatic about buying "the brands I like" than were younger consumers. About 89 percent of the older group insisted that they buy their favorite brands regardless of the package, compared to only 65 percent for the under-30s.

Of course, consumer reactions to packaging depend on the type of product involved. Table 20.6 shows 43 container and closure types and the percentage of respondents who liked them, or did not care one way or another. A good dispenser or a sturdy box are key package attributes.

The ten best liked packages were handbag-sized dispensers for breath fresheners and other toiletries, metal boxes for adhesive bandages, aerosol dispensers as well as other types of spray-top dispensers for toiletries, individually foil-wrapped tablets, and five different plastic containers. In contrast, glass was rated poorly, with six of the ten most disliked containers.

The study has numerous methodological weaknesses. For example, it is hazardous to ask consumers what they will and will not do. It is better to ascertain what they do in fact do using appropriate experimental designs.[68] Nevertheless, the study does suggest some interesting hypotheses for future research.

Package-Size Proneness Frank, Douglas, and Polli studied the package-size proneness of 491 households belonging to the *Chicago Tribune* 1961 consumer panel.[69] Based on a multiple regression analysis with a separate analysis for each of 31 products, they found that four variables were positively correlated with package-size proneness:

---

[68] For other methods of measuring reactions to packages, see David T. Kollat, Roger D. Blackwell, and James F. Robeson, *Strategic Marketing* (New York: Holt, Rinehart and Winston, 1972) chap. 11.

[69] Ronald E. Frank, Susan P. Douglas, and Rolando E. Polli, "Household Correlates of Package-Size Proneness for Grocery Products," *J. Marketing Research*, vol. 4, pp. 381–384 (Nov. 1967).

Table 20.5 CONSUMERS' ATTITUDES TOWARD PACKAGES

	Total (%)	Age of Homemaker					Annual Family Income				
		Under 30	30-39	40-49	50-59	60 & over	Under $3999	$3999-$6999	$7000-$8999	$9000-$11,999	$12,000 & over
(1) When I buy a cosmetics or toiletries product for the first time, the package or container has a great influence on my choice of brands	Agree 38 / Disagree 60	41 / 59	39 / 60	40 / 59	41 / 57	31 / 64	31 / 65	39 / 59	33 / 65	39 / 59	43 / 57
(2) When buying headache remedies and other nonprescription drugs, I pay careful attention to the information given on the label	Agree 89 / Disagree 11	84 / 16	86 / 13	87 / 13	93 / 6	93 / 6	95 / 3	92 / 7	89 / 11	87 / 11	84 / 16
(3) When buying cosmetics and toiletries products, I pay careful attention to the information given on the label	Agree 71 / Disagree 29	63 / 37	64 / 35	66 / 34	78 / 22	82 / 16	84 / 14	73 / 27	73 / 27	66 / 33	65 / 34
(4) I sometimes change brands if a competing company comes out with a package I like better	Agree 30 / Disagree 70	33 / 67	32 / 67	30 / 70	28 / 72	27 / 71	27 / 71	32 / 68	29 / 71	28 / 71	31 / 69
(5) When it comes to products like bath powder and hand lotion, I assume that the best looking packages contain quality products	Agree 9 / Disagree 90	11 / 89	10 / 89	10 / 89	5 / 95	10 / 89	14 / 86	7 / 92	8 / 92	9 / 91	9 / 90
(6) I think manufacturers pay too much attention to making their packages pretty, and not enough to making them safe and practical	Agree 64 / Disagree 35	67 / 33	63 / 36	61 / 37	66 / 33	63 / 35	71 / 28	63 / 36	66 / 32	67 / 31	58 / 41
(7) I am more likely to purchase a brand new drugstore product if I am offered a free sample of it in the store	Agree 74 / Disagree 26	82 / 17	79 / 20	74 / 25	68 / 31	67 / 33	73 / 26	73 / 27	73 / 26	77 / 23	73 / 26

Statement											
(8) I often buy the drugstore's own brand of a product if the nationally advertised brands of that same product cost more	Agree 60	59	64	(65)	(53)	59	(65)	58	58	61	60
	Disagree 38	39	35	(33)	(46)	40	(33)	41	40	38	39
(9) Given the choice between similar products, I'd be willing to pay more for the product in the more convenient or efficient package	Agree 57	55	54	58	58	58	54	53	55	56	(62)
	Disagree 42	44	44	41	40	40	44	45	43	43	(36)
(10) I wish druggists would list the ingredients on the labels of drugs I buy with a doctor's prescription	Agree 87	85	85	85	87	91	89	87	85	88	85
	Disagree 12	15	14	13	12	8	10	12	13	11	14
(11) I am willing to spend a few cents more for a cosmetics or toiletries package that looks nice on my shelf at home	Agree 42	44	41	40	43	44	44	39	38	39	(48)
	Disagree 57	56	58	60	56	55	55	60	(63)	60	(51)
(12) On the whole, I think the labels on packages of nonprescription drug products give the shopper enough information to buy wisely	Agree 69	(65)	69	72	65	72	71	(74)	(74)	(59)	68
	Disagree 30	(35)	29	28	33	27	26	(25)	(25)	(40)	31
(13) On the whole, I think the labels on packages of toiletries and cosmetics give the shopper enough information to buy wisely	Agree 69	68	70	68	68	73	(75)	72	67	69	66
	Disagree 29	32	29	32	30	25	(24)	27	32	30	32
(14) I know the brands I like and will continue to buy them regardless of the way they are packaged	Agree 77	(65)	74	(72)	81	(89)	(88)	80	75	(72)	73
	Disagree 22	(34)	24	(27)	19	(10)	(12)	20	25	26	24

SOURCE: "Drugstore Packages," reprinted by permission from *Sales Management*, *The Marketing Magazine*, p. 44 (Sept. 15, 1970).

NOTE: Results, categorized by age and income, are circled when percentages vary five or more points from average.

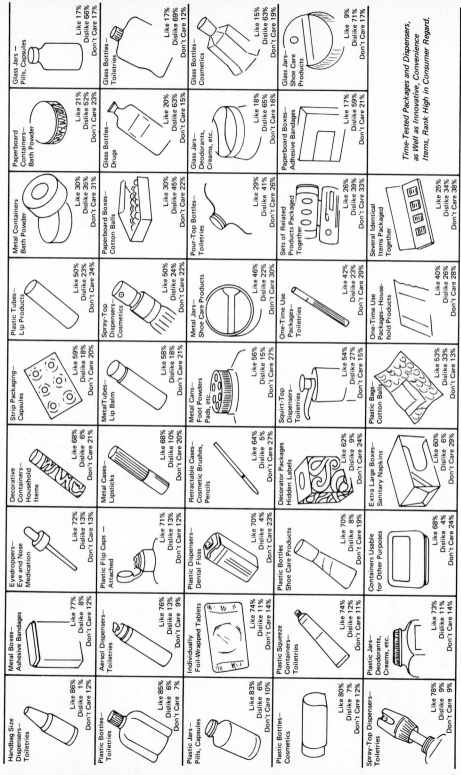

Table 20.6 CONSUMERS' EVALUATIONS OF VARIOUS CONTAINERS AND CLOSURES. "Drugstore Packages," reprinted by permission from *Sales Management, The Marketing Magazine.* pp. 50–51 (Sept. 15, 1970)

(1) *Number of adults in family*—The more adults, the higher the proportion of purchases made in small package sizes.

(2) *Building size*—Households in high-rise apartments had a higher proportion of purchases in small package sizes.

(3) *Housewife status*—Single male household heads tended to purchase a higher proportion of small package sizes.

(4) *Average price paid*—The higher the average price paid per unit purchased, the higher the proportion of small package sizes purchased.

Seven of the variables were negatively correlated with package-size proneness:

(1) *Number of persons in family*—The greater the number of children, the greater the tendency to purchase large package sizes.

(2) *Income*—The higher the income of the household, the greater the tendency to purchase large package sizes.

(3) *Occupation*—Households with low income relative to their occupational status tended to buy a higher proportion of small package sizes.

(4) *Education*—Better educated shoppers tended to purchase larger package sizes.

(5) *National brands*—The greater the proportion of purchases of national brands, the greater the tendency to purchase large package sizes.

(6) *Consumption*—The greater the total food consumption of the household, the greater the tendency to purchase large package sizes.

(7) *Brand loyalty*—The tendency to purchase large package sizes increased as brand loyalty increased.

While these findings were statistically significant, the magnitude of the effects were modest. The highest average absolute value of the partial correlation coefficient for a given variable, based on all 31 products, was 0.36 for average price paid per unit purchased. The next highest was 0.11 for total consumption, followed by brand loyalty with 0.05.

Although the correlation between the percentage of purchases by a household on small package sizes and socioeconomic and purchase characteristics was relatively modest, the direction of the effects for a number of variables was reasonably consistent across product categories. Thus, to some extent, package size may be a useful basis for market segmentation. However, the variables that are most useful in segmenting this market appear to be purchase attributes, such as light usage and absence of brand loyalty, rather than household socioeconomic characteristics.

SUMMARY

This chapter continued the discussion of the purchasing-process stage in the decision-making process by focusing on various dimensions of in-store behavior. Attention was given first to the types of family role structures involved in purchasing and their implications for both retailers and manufacturers.

Several relations between store characteristics and postshopping outcomes were presented. Although there are several types of outcomes, most studies have been concerned with the effect of various store characteristics on sales. It was demonstrated how consumers' in-store behavior, and hence sales, are affected by such store characteristics as store layout, point-of-purchase displays, end-aisle displays, number of shelf facings, shelf height, and various pricing techniques, including dual pricing and multiple-unit pricing.

Merchandise assortments and presentations also affect customers' in—store behavior. The chapter concluded with a discussion of the effects of out-of-stocks, branding, deals, and packaging on consumer behavior.

REVIEW AND DISCUSSION QUESTIONS

1. What is the relation between the number of shelf facings and sales? What are the implications for retailers? For manufacturers?

2. Does it matter to a retailer whether a shopper is a purchasing agent for other family members or a decision maker? Why? How?

3. "A positive relation exists between passing and buying. Therefore, the way to increase sales is to increase the percentage of product locations that consumers pass." Critically evaluate.

4. When you shop in a supermarket, how do you react to the nonavailability of your preferred brands? What do you do? How does your behavior compare with the results summarized in the text?

5. When multiple-unit pricing is used, why do sales often increase even when the single unit price is higher than normal?

6. Why should a retailer be interested in the effect of point-of-purchase materials, end-aisle displays, and so on, on brand substitution as well as sales?

7. To what extent do your parents (their friends) purchase private brands and "deals?" How do their characteristics compare with those summarized in the chapter?

CHAPTER 21

ADDITIONAL DIMENSIONS
OF PURCHASING PROCESSES

To what extent do salesmen influence consumers' in-store behavior? How important is brand substitution and impulse purchasing? Are certain types of consumers high-impulse purchasers? Are there identifiable market segments that shop over the telephone or by mail?

This chapter concludes the discussion of the purchasing-process stage of the decision-making process. Attention is focused on the above issues and their implications for marketing strategists.

THE EFFECTS OF CUSTOMER-SALESMAN
INTERACTION ON CONSUMER BEHAVIOR

Despite the fact that salesmen are among the most extensively studied phenomenon in the business world,[1] little is known about the role and impact of the salesman in the ultimate sale of consumer goods.[2] During the last few years,

---

[1] J. B. Miner, "Personality and Ability Factors in Sales Performance," *J. Applied Psychology,* vol. 46, p. 6 (Feb. 1962).

[2] James G. Hauk, "Research in Personal Selling," in George Schwartz (ed.), *Science in Marketing* (New York: Wiley, 1965), pp. 213–249, at p. 217.

however, attempts have been made to overcome these problems by viewing selling as one form of dyadic interaction.

Selling as Dyadic Interaction

Traditionally, studies of personal selling have focused on predicting some measure of salesman performance based on the salesman's background characteristics, and a broad spectrum of personality, interest, and ability factors measured by various psychological testing instruments.[3] The purpose of these studies has usually been to discover predictor variables that are useful in selecting and recruiting salesmen.

The results of these studies have been mixed. High correlations between predictor variables and salesman performance have been found in some instances. In other sales occupations, however, useful relationships have not been found.[4]

Even in those situations where strong associations exist, this research strategy contributes very little to our understanding of why or how a salesman becomes effective. Davis and Silk have summarized the problems:

> In attempting to predict sales performance, this research has concentrated almost entirely on the characteristics of salesmen and has failed to take explicit account of who the salesman interacts with in attempting to make a sale. The assumption tacitly made is that differences among salesmen with respect to the types of prospects they contact are minimal, and hence variations in performance must be due to differences among the salesmen themselves . . . such an assumption seems tenuous for many if not most types of selling.[5]

Evans summarizes some of the results of his research as follows:

> . . . the sale (or no sale) is the result of the particular interaction situation, the face-to-face contact of the given salesman and his prospect. The result of the contact depends not on the characteristics of either party alone but how the two parties view and react to each other.[6]

Figure 21.1 is an interpretation of what appears to be an emerging con-

---

[3] For an excellent review of this literature, see James C. Cotham, III "Selecting Salesmen: Approaches and Problems," *MSU Business Topics,* vol. 18, pp. 64–72 (Winter 1970).

[4] See, for example, James C. Cotham, III, "Predicting Salesmen's Performance by Multiple Discriminant Analysis," *Southern J. Business,* vol. 4, pp. 25–34 (Jan. 1969); James C. Cotham, III, "Job Attitudes and Sales Performance of Major Appliance Salesmen," *J. Marketing Research,* vol. 5, pp. 370–375 (Nov. 1968).

[5] Harry L. Davis and Alvin J. Silk, "Behavioral Research on Personal Selling: A Review of Some Recent Studies of Interaction and Influence Processes in Sales Situations" (Cambridge, Mass.: Marketing Science Institute, 1971), p. 4.

[6] Franklin B. Evans, *Dyadic Interaction in Selling: A New Approach* (Chicago: Graduate School of Business, University of Chicago, 1964), p. 25.

ceptualization of customer–salesman interaction.[7] Relative to approaches used in the past, this one has several unique aspects. First, it is recognized that outcomes (including sales) are the result of the particular dyadic interaction of a salesman and customer rather than a result of the individual qualities of either alone.[8] Second, in addition to those relations explored by past approaches, the extended approach focuses on the nature and characteristics of the interaction—the transaction—as well as the roles played by each party to the interaction. Finally, a greater number of more sophisticated variables and relations are used in an attempt to isolate the determinants of successful transactions. For example, the

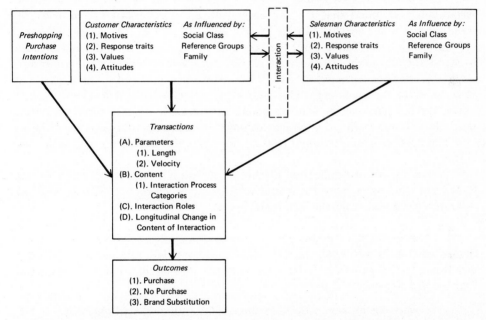

Figure 21.1 EXTENDED CONCEPTUALIZATION OF CUSTOMER–SALESMAN INTERACTION. The figure is based almost entirely on the Willett–Pennington mode. Ronald P. Willett and Allan L. Pennington, "Customer and Salesman: The Anatomy of Choice and Influence in a Retail Setting," in Raymond M. Haas (ed.), *Science, Technology and Marketing* (Chicago: Amer. Marketing Assoc., 1966), pp. 598–616. Used by permission of the authors and the publisher.

---

[7] This conceptualization is based on Ronald P. Willett and Allan L. Pennington, "Customer and Salesman: The Anatomy of Choice and Influence in a Retail Setting," in R. M. Haas (ed.), *Science, Technology and Marketing* (Chicago: Amer. Marketing Assoc., 1966), pp. 598–616. For an alternative conceptualization, see James H. Bearden, "Decision Processes in Personal Selling," *Southern J. Business,* vol. 4, pp. 189–199 (Apr. 1969).

[8] Franklin B. Evans, "Selling as a Dyadic Relationship—A New Approach," *Amer. Behavioral Scientist,* vol. 6, pp. 76–79, at p. 76 (May 1963).

nature and content[9] of the interaction, the interaction roles played by each of the participants,[10] and the change in each of these variables during the transaction can be used to explain how and why sales occur. The remainder of this section discusses the major variables comprising this conceptualization.

Customer–Salesman Interaction

This section summarizes the results of major studies that have investigated customer–salesman relationships.

The Waitress–Customer Dyad Whyte's study of human relations in restaurants concluded that the customer–waitress relationship varied with the standing of the restaurant.[11] In lower standard restaurants, the relationship was very informal. The waitress "put the customer in his place" if he did not conform to standards acceptable to the waitress. By contrast, in higher standard restaurants, the relations were more formal. Waitresses had to suppress their desire to "talk back" to the customers. The higher the perceived social level of the customer, the less personal the waitress acted. A waitress in a lower standard restaurant who set and maintained street customer behavior standards received larger tips than another who attempted to treat the customers according to middle-class norms.

An important implication of the Whyte study is that conformity to customer expectations of behavior is more rewarding, even though it may be a less desirable treatment from the waitresses' point of view.

The Salesgirl–Customer Dyad Lombard's study of retail salesgirls found that interaction is a function of the values that both the customer and the salesgirl bring to the situation.[12] Behavior patterns developed from the interaction that seemed to persist. Thus:

> Once one of these patterns became established, a salesgirl's behavior tended to produce a feeling on the part of the customer that in turn resulted in the customer's behaving in ways that proved to the salesgirl that her evaluations of this customer were correct. Thus the salesgirl

---

[9] "Content" refers to the categories used in Bales' interaction-process analysis. The observation categories are (1) shows solidarity, (2) shows tension release, (3) agrees, (4) gives suggestion, (5) gives opinion, (6) gives orientation, (7) asks for orientation, (8) asks for opinion, (9) asks for suggestion, (10) disagrees, (11) shows tension, (12) shows antagonism. These observational categories are usually collapsed into four interaction-process categories. The Bales system is by far the most highly developed and widely used method of describing interaction. See Robert F. Bales, *Interaction Process Analysis: A Method for the Study of Small Groups* (Reading, Mass.: Addison-Wesley, 1950).

[10] In this case, roles are measured as ratios of customer to salesman acts for each of the interaction-process categories.

[11] William F. Whyte, *Human Relations in the Restaurant Industry* (New York: McGraw-Hill, 1948).

[12] George F. Lombard, *Behavior in a Selling Group* (Boston: Harvard University, 1955).

felt and perceived no need to correct or change her behavior. Her
evaluations of customer and herself came true.[13]

The customers who got along with the salesgirls were the ones who received the
best service in the store. This may have occurred because this type of relationship facilitated interaction.

Customer–Salesman Similarity

Why do the above types of interaction patterns occur? There is a considerable body of evidence that suggests that at least part of the answer lies in
how "similar" the two individuals are. Most of the evidence comes from theoretical and empirical efforts in nonmarketing areas.[14] Nevertheless, some marketing studies have been conducted.

Insurance Salesman–Customer Similarity Evans selected a random
sample of 168 sold and 183 unsold insurance prospects.[15] He demonstrated that
whether a prospect would buy insurance from a particular agent could *not* be
predicted solely on the basis of knowledge of the prospect's attitudinal, personality, or demographic characteristics. As groups, the sold and unsold consumers were essentially similar in all respects.

However, the salesmen appeared to be more like the sold customers than
the unsold. The similarity was true for age and height as well as a broad spectrum
of variables, including economic and demographic characteristics, and variables
that may be related to response traits (politics, smoking). Moreover, the sold
consumers tended to perceive the salesmen as more like themselves than the
unsold ones did.

Sold and unsold prospects had different reactions to the salesman:

> The successful salesman was seen by sold prospects as (1) an expert
> in insurance, (2) similar to themselves in outlook and situation, (3) a
> person they would like to know better, and (4) interested in them
> personally, not just as a source of revenue.[16]

Gadel also conducted a study of life insurance selling.[17] After analyzing
22,000 policies, he concluded that agents' sales tended to be concentrated among
consumers who were in the same age group as themselves. However, this concentration tended to decrease as the agents' experience increased.

---

[13] Lombard, *op. cit.,*[12] p. 24.

[14] See, for example, Dana Bramel, "Interpersonal Attraction, Hostility and Perception," in Judson Mills (eds.), *Experimental Social Psychology* (New York: Macmillan, 1969),
pp. 1–120; Fritz Heider, *The Psychology of Interpersonal Relations* (New York: Wiley, 1961);
George C. Homans, *Social Behavior: Its Elementary Forms* (New York: Harcourt, 1961).

[15] Evans, *op. cit.*[8]

[16] Evans, *op. cit.*[8]

[17] M. S. Gadel, "Concentration by Salesman on Congenial Prospects," *J. Marketing*,
vol. 28, pp. 64–66 (Apr. 1964).

Drug Salesman–Retail Pharmacist Similarity Tosi investigated customer-salesman similarity for a group of 40 wholesale drug salesmen and 103 retail pharmacists.[18] Agreement between the customer and salesman about how the salesman ought to behave did not appear to have any impact on the salesman's effectiveness. However, the closer the salesman came to meeting the customer's expectations about how he should function, the fewer other wholesalers the pharmacist tended to deal with.

Paint Salesman–Customer Similarity Brock conducted a field experiment to determine the relative importance of salesman expertise and customer-salesman similarity in influencing sales.[19] Over a five-month period, two part-time salesmen in the paint department of a retail store attempted to influence customers to purchase paint at a different price level than they initially preferred.

After a consumer indicated he wanted to buy a certain amount of some paint at a particular price, the salesman tried to change his selection by presenting one of two predetermined appeals. Half the time the salesman represented himself as being similar to customers by emphasizing that his own recent paint consumption was the same as the amount being purchased by the customer. In the remaining 50 percent of the cases, the salesman played the expert role by stating that he had just used twenty times the quantity of paint the consumer planned to buy. The salesmen attempted to influence some customers to buy at higher prices and others at lower prices than they originally intended.

Brock found that similarity was more important than expertise. Although the expert salesman was presumably perceived as more knowledgeable about paint, he was less effective than the salesman who identified his own paint consumption as similar to that of his customers. This difference in effectiveness held for attempts to persuade patrons to buy higher as well as lower priced paints.

Other Studies A few studies have investigated the impact of response trait similarity in salesman and customer. According to one study, a highly dependent person is suggestible and prefers assistance in his decision making, while a highly independent person prefers a minimum of suggestion and assistance. This seems to suggest that the degree to which a customer is dependent or independent will affect the type of retail salesman he prefers.[20]

Stafford and Greer attempted to determine the relation between the customer's independence–dependence and his responsiveness toward sales aggressiveness. Some 263 college undergraduates filled out the Edwards personal preference schedule and a semantic differential on one of three types of salesmen —shoe, book, or home appliance. As predicted, the results indicate that dependent

---

[18] Henry L. Tosi, "The Effects of Expectation Levels and Role Consensus on the Buyer–Seller Dyad," *J. Business,* vol. 39, pp. 516–529 (Oct. 1966).

[19] Timothy C. Brock, "Communicator–Recipient Similarity and Decision Change," *J. Personality and Social Psychology,* vol. 1, pp. 650–654 (June 1965).

[20] M. Zuckerman and H. J. Grosz, "Suggestibility and Dependency," *J. Consulting Psychology,* vol. 26, pp. 32–38 (Oct. 1958).

persons prefer more aggressive salesmen, although the degree of preference is not very strong. Contrary to the hypothesis, independent persons had neutral preferences toward salesmen.[21]

Finally, studies have indicated that preference for aggressive salesmen varies by sex. The Stafford and Greer study found that males were slightly favorable toward aggressive salesmen while females were slightly unfavorable.[22] Another study found that women intensely dislike a salesman who is aggressive in any way.[23]

Transaction Characteristics

One published study has investigated transaction characteristics in a marketing situation. As Figure 21.1 shows, transactions can be analyzed in terms of their length, velocity, content, interaction roles, and longitudinal change in the content of interactions. The major findings of this study of appliance shoppers are summarized below.[24]

Length The average retail transaction observed lasted 23 minutes. Length of time varied from one minute to over two hours, with 75 percent of the transactions lasting less than 30 minutes.

Velocity Customer–salesman interactions per minute were found to exhibit a rather stable pattern. Over 50 percent of all transactions generated rates of between 6 and 11 acts per minute, and the mean interaction rates for all transactions was approximately 10 acts per minute.

Content of Interaction[25] The most frequent type of interaction was the giving of orientation (information, clarification, and so on), followed by the giving of opinion. On the average, these two categories accounted for over 75 percent of the interaction.

Customer and Salesman Interaction Roles Interaction roles refer to the relative contribution of interaction acts[26] by customer and salesman. In general, the customer performed half as many interaction acts as the salesman. Attempted answers were primarily the domain of the salesman, while in the question categories, customer acts outnumbered salesman acts by a multiple of four.

---

[21] James E. Stafford and Thomas V. Greer, "Consumer Preference for Types of Salesmen: A Study of Independence–Dependence Characteristics," *J. Retailing*, pp. 27–33 (Summer 1965).

[22] Stafford and Greer, *op. cit.*,[21] p. 32.

[23] Gilbert Burck, "What Makes Women Buy?" *Fortune*, pp. 93–94, 174–194 (Aug. 1956).

[24] Willett and Pennington, *op. cit.*,[7] pp. 598–616.

[25] For an itemization of interaction categories, see footnote 9.

[26] For an itemization of types of interaction acts, see footnote 9.

Interestingly, customers were more frequently responsible for positive reactions (categories 1–3 above), while salesmen were nearly solely responsible for disagreement, tension, and antagonism. In general, by the proper patterning of interaction and response to customer interaction, the salesman controlled the interaction.

Interaction Determinants of Transaction Outcomes

There are, of course, many factors in addition to the structure and characteristics of interaction that determine whether consumers will purchase a product. There is some evidence, however, that a sale differs from a nonsale in terms of the pattern of interaction.

Table 21.1 presents additional findings from the Willett–Pennington study of appliance shoppers.[27] Using the values of each of the 11 variables (see

Table 21.1 RELATIONSHIPS BETWEEN KEY SHOPPING AND BARGAINING VARIABLES AND PURCHASE AT TIME OBSERVED

Shopping or Bargaining Variable	Correlation of Variable with Purchase at Time Observed (Point-Biserial r)
(1) Number of stores shopped by customer	−0.27[c]
(2) Frequency of direct offers	+0.18[b]
(3) Relative frequency of attempts to change concession limits	−0.25[c]
(4) Frequency of commitment to concession limits	+0.33[c]
(5) Frequency of attempts to change concession limits by devaluating other's product	−0.17[a]
(6) Frequency of reference to product quality	−0.17[a]
(7) Frequency of reference to delivery	+0.25[c]
(8) Frequency of reference to styling	+0.21[b]
(9) Relative frequency of reference to price	−0.24[c]
(10) Relative frequency of reference to warranty	+0.18[b]
(11) Relative frequency of reference to brand	−0.16[a]

NOTES:
[a] Significant at 0.05 level.
[b] Significant at 0.01 level.
[c] Significant at 0.001 level.

SOURCE: Allan L. Pennington, "Customer–Salesman Bargaining Behavior in Retail Transactions," *J. Marketing Research*, vol. 5, pp. 255–262, at p. 261 (Chicago: Amer. Marketing Assoc., Aug. 1968).

---

[27] Allan L. Pennington, "Customer–Salesman Bargaining Behavior in Retail Transactions," *J. Marketing Research*, vol. 5, pp. 255–262 (Aug. 1968).

Table 21.1) for a given transaction, multiple discriminant analysis was employed to predict whether a transaction should have been completed at the time observed, or whether it was not likely to be completed then. The predictions, based on the values of the explanatory variables for each transaction, were then compared with the true outcomes of the transactions.

The composite behavior of the 11 variables accurately predicted purchase outcomes in 80.3 percent of the cases. Deleting the shopping variable from the analysis and considering only the ten bargaining variables, the percentage of accurate predictions remained the same, although the level of significance was less impressive. Thus, transaction characteristics were considerably more reliable than chance in their ability to identify the consumer most likely to purchase when the transaction was observed.

Marketing Implications

The customer–salesman interaction model has emerged only recently and has not as yet been extensively researched. Consequently, at this juncture, generalizations about marketing strategy are premature. However, there is reason to believe that interaction models will, in the future, generate useful insights for marketing management purposes. Indeed, interaction models may become an exciting and useful approach to consumer behavior during the next decade.

If further research verifies the characteristic-similarity hypothesis, or if the firm finds that this hypothesis holds for its personal selling efforts, then measurements of customer characteristics of the target market segment might permit a firm to hire more effective salesmen. Notice that this approach differs from conventional attempts to identify successful salesmen, in that the latter approach considers only the characteristics of the salesman, while the former considers the interaction of customer–salesman characteristics.

The transaction characteristics component of the interaction model provides retailers and manufacturers with a conceptual approach for analyzing and thinking about the importance of the personal sales effort in the marketing mix. The marketer may desire to isolate the determinants of successful transactions and use this information in designing sales presentations and in training and selecting salesmen. Similarly, understanding the nature of interaction roles and the change in these roles throughout the transaction may be useful in selecting and training salesmen.

RELATIONSHIPS BETWEEN PURCHASE INTENTIONS AND PURCHASE BEHAVIOR

In Chapter 19 it was pointed out that intentions–outcomes categories result from the pairing of preshopping purchase intentions with postshopping outcomes.[28] These categories are useful in understanding purchase-process

---

[28] Before proceeding, the reader is urged to review the section in Chapter 19, "Extended Conceptualization of Purchasing Processes."

behavior, because they explicitly include the customer's intentions as a potentially relevant variable. It has been demonstrated how both the results and implications of many purchasing-process studies, particularly traffic-pattern investigations, are ambiguous because they have focused only on outcomes and have ignored purchase intentions. Intentions–outcomes categories hopefully obviate these kinds of problems.

This section presents a profile of the relative occurrence of intentions–outcomes categories in various types of retail outlets as well as the store attributes and customer characteristics that account for the frequency of occurrence of each category.

Nature of Intentions–Outcomes

While intentions–outcomes categories can occur in any retail setting, empirical studies have unfortunately been confined to a limited variety of retail outlets. Table 21.2 compares the occurrence of intentions–outcomes categories in the three types of outlets in which studies of this type have been conducted. The occurrence of each of the categories varies considerably by type of retail outlet. In both drugstores and package liquor stores, *specifically planned* is the most common type of purchase. Supermarkets differ in that *unplanned purchasing* is the most frequent type of purchase. There have been no empirical attempts to determine why the relative importance of the categories varies across stores.

Table 21.2 COMPARISON OF STUDIES OF BUYING DECISIONS IN VARIOUS TYPES OF RETAIL OUTLETS

| | Intentions–Outcomes Categories | | | |
Type of Retail Outlet	Specifically Planned (%)	Generally Planned (%)	Brand Substitution (%)	Unplanned (%)
Drugstores[a]	56.0	15.0	7.0	22.0
Package liquor stores[b]	62.5	19.5	9.8	8.2
Supermarkets[c]	31.1	17.2	1.8	49.9

SOURCES: [a] *Drugstore Brand Switching and Impulse Buying* (New York: Point-of-Purchase Advertising Institute, 1963), p. 29.

[b] *Package Store Brand Switching and Impulse Buying* (New York: Point-of-Purchase Advertising Institute, 1963), p. 7. Categories have been adjusted to correspond to those used in this text.

[c] *Consumer Buying Habits Studies* (E. I. duPont de Nemours and Co., 1965).

Table 21.3 presents illustrative data showing how the occurrence of intentions–outcomes categories varies across products in supermarkets. Data on a limited number of categories are available for other types of retail outlets, and

Table 21.3 FREQUENCY OF INTENTIONS–OUTCOMES CATEGORIES IN
SUPERMARKETS BY MAJOR PRODUCT CATEGORY,
1959 AND 1965

| | *Intentions-Outcomes Categories* | | | | | | | |
| | *Specifically Planned* (%) | | *Generally Planned* (%) | | *Brand Substitution* (%) | | *Unplanned* (%) | |
Major Product Category	1959	1965	1959	1965	1959	1965	1959	1965
Baked goods	22.0	19.6	18.1	19.3	4.7	2.6	55.2	58.5
Beverages	36.9	36.0	10.1	10.4	1.9	1.9	51.1	51.7
Dairy products	30.1	32.7	24.0	16.9	2.6	1.9	43.3	48.5
Drugs, toiletries	27.2		8.0		1.1		63.7	
Frozen foods	17.3	19.0	17.6	16.9	6.1	2.7	59.0	61.4
Groceries	26.0	25.3	16.0	17.5	2.4	1.5	55.6	55.7
Household needs	30.3	30.2	9.7	11.2	2.3	2.1	57.7	56.5
Meats, poultry, fish	35.3	34.3	14.4	13.9	3.5	2.7	44.0	49.1
Produce	44.2	41.1	9.5	13.3	.8	.4	45.5	45.2
Miscellaneous	19.4	24.7	2.4	7.7	.1	.7	78.1	66.9
Average	30.5	31.1	15.9	17.2	2.7	1.8	50.9	49.9

SOURCE: *Consumer Buying Habits Studies* (Film Department, E. I. duPont de Nemours and
Co. (Inc.), Wilmington, Del., 1959, 1965). Figures are *approximate* percentages
as calculated by the authors.

these will be presented later in this chapter.[29] Considerable interproduct variation
in the relative importance of intentions–outcomes categories also exists in other
retail settings.

Finally, the data in Table 21.4 indicate trends in the relative importance
of intentions–outcomes categories in supermarkets for the years 1949, 1954, 1959,
and 1965.[30] The most significant changes are the reduction in *specifically planned*
and *generally planned* purchases, and the increase in *unplanned* purchases that
occurred during the 1949–1954 period. The period since 1954 has been characterized by overall stability, with the reduction in *generally planned* purchasing
being offset by nearly equal increases in *specifically planned* and *unplanned*
purchasing. Unfortunately, supermarkets are the only type of retail institution
for which trend data are available.

---

[29] See, for example, "Consumer Buying Patterns in Self-Service General Merchandise
Stores," *Hardlines Wholesaling*, pp. 27–33 (Summer 1971); Gerald O. Cavallo and M. Lewis
Temares, "Brand Switching at the Point of Purchase," *J. Retailing*, vol. 45, pp. 27–36 (Fall
1969); Martin Simmons, "Point of Sale Advertising," *J. Market Research Society*, vol. 10,
pp. 102–110 (Apr. 1968).

[30] Latest data available.

Table 21.4 BUYING DECISIONS IN SUPERMARKETS, 1949–1965

Year	Specifically Planned (%)	Intentions–Outcomes Categories Generally Planned (%)	Brand Substitution (%)	Unplanned (%)
1949	33.4	26.7	1.5	38.4
1954	29.2	21.0	1.8	48.0
1959	30.5	15.9	2.7	50.9
1965	31.1	17.2	1.8	49.9

SOURCE: *Consumer Buying Habits Studies* (Film Department, E. I. duPont de Nemours and Co. (Inc.), Wilmington, Del., 1949, 1954, 1959, 1965).

Why do specifically planned, generally planned, brand substitution, and unplanned purchases occur? Why does the occurrence of these categories vary across stores and products? Are some consumers more likely to plan specifically or substitute brands than others? Do consumers differ in their susceptibility to unplanned purchasing? What effect do such store characteristics as point-of-purchase and end-aisle displays have on brand substitution and unplanned purchasing? Research in this area has concentrated on brand substitution and unplanned purchasing, so the remainder of this section focuses only on these categories.

Brand Substitution

Brand substitution, as used here, differs from brand loyalty. Brand substitutions occurs when the consumer buys a brand that differs from the one that he or she intended to purchase before entering a retail outlet. Brand substitution bears no necessary relation to brand loyalty, the latter being an important type of behavior that will be discussed in Chapter 23.

As Table 21.2 demonstrated, brand substitution is the least important intentions–outcomes category in terms of frequency of occurrence. It accounts for less than 10 percent of purchases in liquor stores and drugstores, and less than 2 percent of supermarket purchases. Table 21.3 demonstrated that brand substitution is relatively unimportant in terms of frequency of occurrence for all major product categories found in supermarkets.

Few studies have been concerned with the correlates of brand substitution. Rigorous attempts to relate store characteristics and/or customer characteristics to product rates of brand substitution, or attempts to determine whether certain types of consumers are more brand-substitution prone than others, have not been conducted. Instead, studies have relied on customers' assessments of the reason(s) why they substituted brands.

Table 21.5 summaries reasons for brand substitution in supermarkets and drugstores. According to these studies, exposure to merchandise, either in its regular location or in a display, and sales or price reductions are the most important determinants of brand substitution.

Table 21.5 REASONS FOR BRAND SUBSTITUTION AS DETERMINED BY RESPONDENTS' SELF-ASSESSMENTS

Reason(s) Stated by Respondent	Type of Retail Outlet	
	Drugstore[a] (%)	Supermarket[b] (%)
Saw merchandise	48	Not Used
Display	30	25
Less expensive, on sale	9	21
Wanted a change	Not used	19
Usual brand out of stock	2	7
Recommended by family or friends	2	9
All other	9	19

SOURCES: [a] *Drugstore Brand Switching and Impulse Buying* (New York: Point-of-Purchase Advertising Institute, 1963), pp 22–23.
[b] "Colonial Study," *Progressive Grocer,* p. C-118 (1964).

Evaluation and Marketing Implications

The reasons for brand substitution should be viewed as suggestive rather than definitive. The self-assessment approach has many problems emanating from the customer's inability and/or unwillingness to specify why brand substitution occurred. Carefully controlled experimental designs need to be employed before much confidence can be placed in the results of studies purporting to identify the determinants of brand substitution.

Although a basic understanding of brand substitution does not now exist, it is important that such knowledge be obtained. Progressive retailers are interested in increasing profit per square foot and are, therefore, more interested in product category sales rather than brand sales, unless competing brands have widely varying profit contributions. Expenditures of time, money, and space that result in brand substitution rather than increased sales are wasteful. Hence it is advantageous for the retailer to understand the nature and determinants of brand substitution.

In contrast, the manufacturer is interested in maximizing substitutions to his brand and minimizing substitution to other brands. A thorough understanding of why brand substitution occurs, who substitutes away from his brand, and who substitutes to his brand is a prerequisite to designing successful marketing programs.

Unplanned Purchasing

"Unplanned" or "impulse"[31] purchasing is the most frequently studied intentions–outcomes category. As Table 21.2 demonstrated, this type of behavior is very important in drugstores and supermarkets. Other studies have found that unplanned purchases represent over 33 percent of all purchases in variety stores and drugstores.[32] While the occurrence of unplanned purchasing is not confined to any retail institution, it seems to occur most frequently in supermarkets, and most of what is known about it has used the supermarket as the setting.

Table 21.3 demonstrated how unplanned purchasing varies by product. Unplanned purchasing rates can be computed for customers as well as for products. One study found that the average customer purchased 50.5 percent of the products on an unplanned basis. Equally if not more interesting is the fact that customers differed widely in their susceptibility to unplanned purchasing.[33]

After discussing the meaning of unplanned purchasing, the store characteristics and customer attributes that account for product and/or customer variation are examined. A presentation of competing explanations and marketing implications completes the discussion of the subject.

Meaning of Unplanned Purchasing

Despite the fact that unplanned purchasing is a widely recognized and frequently talked about type of behavior, there is little consensus about the meaning of the phenomenon. The following are illustrative of the variety of definitions:

(1) An impulse purchase is an unplanned, spur-of-the-moment decision to purchase a product[34]

(2) An impulse purchase is a logical and efficient way of making purchase decisions since by waiting until one is in the store to finalize purchase intentions, a more comprehensive and realistic evaluation of purchase alternatives can often be made.[35]

(3) There is no such thing as *an* impulse purchase. Rather, there are four types of unplanned purchases: (a) *pure impulse* is a novelty or escape

---

[31] As used here, the terms "unplanned" and "impulse" are synonymous.

[32] Vernon T. Clover, "Relative Importance of Impulse Buying in Retail Stores," *J. Marketing*, vol. 15, pp. 66–70 (July 1950).

[33] David T. Kollat and Ronald P. Willett, "Customer Impulse Purchasing Behavior," *J. Marketing Research*, vol. 4, pp. 21–31, at p. 23 (Feb. 1967).

[34] William R. Davidson and Alton Doody, *Retailing Management* (New York: Ronald, 1966), p. 180.

[35] Saul Nesbitt, "Today's Housewives Plan Menus as They Shop" (Nesbit Associates Release, 1959), pp. 2–3.

type purchase which breaks a normal buying pattern, (b) *reminder impulse* occurs when a shopper sees an item or recalls an advertisement or other information and remembers that the stock at home is low or exhausted, (c) *suggestion impulse* purchasing occurs when a shopper sees a product for the first time and visualizes a need for it, and (d) *planned impulse* purchasing takes place when the shopper makes specific purchase decisions on the basis of price specials, coupon offers, and the like.[36]

(4) Shoppers are questioned upon entering the store as to what they plan to purchase and records are made of what they do in fact purchase. Those items purchased but not mentioned during the first interview are impulse purchases.[37]

(5) Impulse purchasing is the difference in purchases between a sample of customers reporting actual purchases (exposed to in-store stimuli) and another sample of customers reporting what they anticipated buying while sitting in their living rooms (not exposed to in-store stimuli).[38]

(6) Impulse purchasing is the difference in a store's sales volume during weeks in which a holiday occurred with the week immediately following during which a holiday did not occur.[39]

There are, then, considerable differences of opinion about what unplanned purchasing is and what it involves.[40] This makes it difficult to compare findings and accumulate information about the nature of the behavior. As used in this text, unplanned purchasing in defined as category 9 in Table 19.1.

Store Characteristics Product characteristics, point-of-purchase materials, end-aisle displays, and product location have been related to unplanned purchasing in an attempt to understand the phenomenon better.

(1) **Product Characteristics** Stern has suggested that several product characteristics are likely to affect a product's unplanned purchase rate. These factors include low price, amount of advertising, ease of storage, and short product life.[41] The only study attempting to investigate this hypothesis found that

---

[36] Hawkins Stern, "The Significance of Impulse Buying Today," *J. Marketing*, vol. 26, pp. 59–62 (Apr. 1962).

[37] *Consumer Buying Habits Studies* (E. I. duPont de Nemours and Co., 1949, 1954, 1959, 1965).

[38] James D. Schaffer, "The Influence of Impulse Buying or In-The-Store Decisions on Consumers' Food Purchases," journal paper no. 2591 (Michigan Agricultural Experimental Station), p. 317.

[39] Clover, *op. cit.,*[32] p. 68.

[40] For other definitions of impulse buying, see *How People Shop for Food* (Market Research Corporation of America, undated manuscript); *Impulse Buying* (Philadelphia: Curtis Publ. Co., Research Department, Feb. 1952).

[41] Stern, *op. cit.,*[36] p. 61.

price, ease of storage, and amount of advertising do not affect the proportion of purchases of a product that are transacted on an unplanned basis in supermarkets. A product's purchase frequency was used as a proxy variable for product life, and an inverse relation was found between it and the unplanned purchase rate, that is, the more frequently a product is purchased, the lower its unplanned purchase rate.[42]

(2) **Point-of-Purchase Materials** Few studies have attempted to determine the influence of point-of-purchase materials on unplanned purchase rates. The only available study found that point-of-purchase materials were more effective than price cuts in precipitating unplanned purchasing, while, for other products, price cuts increased unplanned rates to a greater extent than point-of-purchase materials.[43]

(3) **End-Aisle Displays** The only study investigating the effect of end-aisle displays on unplanned purchasing involved six controlled experiments in 14 supermarkets using latin square and test versus control designs. The results indicated that products with a relatively high probability of being purchased on an unplanned basis (pie crust mix and apple pie filling) did not, when merchandised in end-aisle displays, produce greater direct profit benefits than products with a relatively low probability of being purchased on an unplanned basis (spaghetti, spaghetti sauce).[44]

(4) **Product Location** A product's unplanned purchase rate is also affected by its location in the store. For example, it has been demonstrated that the store location of such products as milk, bread, and dairy products is instrumental in precipitating unplanned purchases of surrounding products.[45]

Customer Characteristics Customers have been found to differ widely in their susceptibility to unplanned purchasing. The nature of unplanned purchasing decision making and variables associated with differential rates of unplanned purchasing shed light on the nature of the behavior.

(1) **Unplanned Purchasing Decision Making** One way that unplanned purchasing can be studied is to identify the nature of decision making involved in unplanned purchasing and how it varies from the decision making associated with other intentions–outcomes categories. One study consisted of a sample of

[42] David T. Kollat, "A Study of Unplanned Purchasing in Self Service Food Supermarkets," unpublished doctoral dissertation (Bloomington, Ind.: Indiana University Graduate School of Business, 1966), pp. 194–197.

[43] *Triggering Plus Sales and Profits* (New York: Point-of-Purchase Advertising Institute, undated).

[44] Robert Kelly, "An Evaluation of Selected Variables of End Display Effectiveness," unpublished doctoral dissertation (Cambridge, Mass.: Harvard University, 1965).

[45] Lawrence W. Patterson, *In-Store Traffic Flow* (New York: Point-of-Purchase Advertising Institute, 1963).

200 housewives who were asked, via aided recall, to reconstruct the decision processes involved in purchasing several grocery products. The results were crossclassified by intentions–outcomes category, and it was discovered that none of the dimensions of decision making itemized in Table 21.6 differentiated an

Table 21.6 DIMENSIONS OF DECISION MAKING THAT DO NOT DIFFERENTIATE AN UNPLANNED PURCHASE FROM OTHER INTENTIONS–OUTCOMES CATEGORIES

(1) Whether the product has been purchased before.
(2) Whether the brand has been purchased before.
(3) Length of time the brand has been purchased.
(4) The frequency with which the product has been purchased.
(5) Number of brands that have regularly been purchased.
(6) Family members who use the product.
(7) Whether any family member insists that a particular brand be purchased.
(8) Family members who insist the brand be purchased.
(9) What happened in the store that caused the brand to be first noticed.
(10) Family member that first noticed the brand.
(11) Whether advertisements featuring the brand or other brands had recently been seen.
(12) What useful information, if any, was obtained from these advertisements.
(13) Whether the product or brand had been recently mentioned during conversation with other people. Who are these people?
(14) What useful information, if any, was obtained from these conversations.
(15) Whether the shopper saw any displays for the brand purchased and/or other brands.
(16) Whether product packages or containers were read or examined.
(17) What useful information, if any, was obtained from product packages or containers.
(18) Whether the shopper talked with anyone in the store about the brand purchased or other brands of the product.
(19) Whether while in the store the shopper remembered any information she had recently seen or heard about the brand purchased and/or other brands.
(20) What happened that caused the shopper to remember this information.
(21) Number of brands considered before the purchase decision.
(22) Length of time that the purchase could have been postponed.

SOURCE: David T. Kollat, "A Decision-Process Approach to Impulse Purchasing," in Raymond M. Haas (ed.), *Science, Technology and Marketing* (Chicago: Amer. Marketing Assoc., 1966), p. 632.

unplanned purchase from any other type of purchase. In terms of decision processes, then, there does not appear to be anything unique about unplanned purchasing.[46]

---

[46] David T. Kollat, "A Decision-Process Approach to Impulse Purchasing," in Raymond M. Haas (ed.), *Science, Technology and Marketing* (Chicago: Amer. Marketing Assoc., 1966), pp. 626–639.

(2) **Correlates of Unplanned Purchasing** The only study that attempted to isolate the determinants of customer susceptibility to unplanned purchasing found that economic, demographic, and personality characteristics did not affect a shopper's rate of unplanned purchasing. General food-shopping behavior characteristics, such as the use of a food budget, use of trading stamps, and use of newspaper advertising, also did not affect the percentage of purchases that a shopper transacts on an unplanned basis. The only variables that affected customer rates of unplanned purchasing were:"—the results were a relationship (probably a correlation) and therefore it is difficult to say that these variables affected unplanned purchases.

(a) *Grocery bill*—The percentage of unplanned purchases increased as the shopper's grocery bill increased.

(b) *Number of products purchased*—The percentage of unplanned purchases increased as the number of products that the shopper purchased increased. Moreover, as the number of products purchased increased, the probability that additional purchases would be unplanned approached certainty.

(c) *Type of shopping trip*—The percentage of unplanned purchases was higher during major shopping trips than during fill-in shopping trips.

(d) *Product purchase frequencies*—The more frequently the product was purchased, the lower the probability that the product would be purchased on an unplanned basis.

(e) *Shopping list*—The presence of a shopping list affected the percentage of unplanned purchases when a large number of products (15 or more) were purchased—shoppers with a list purchased a smaller percentage of products on an unplanned basis. When a small number of products was purchased (less than 15), the presence of a shopping list did not affect the percentage of unplanned purchases.

(f) *Number of years married*—The percentage of unplanned purchases increased as the number of years that the shopping party had been married increased.

Explanations for Unplanned Purchasing

There are two competing explanations for unplanned purchasing: (1) the exposure to in-store stimuli hypothesis and (2) the customer-commitment hypothesis. In many ways the hypotheses are the antithesis of one another, and, as will become apparent below, they lead to different conclusions concerning the nature and significance of the phenomenon.

(1) **Exposure to In-Store Stimuli Hypothesis** The exposure hypothesis is the traditional explanation for unplanned purchasing, and it can account for the findings that have been presented. This hypothesis maintains that differences between purchase intentions and actual purchases are due to the effects of in-store stimuli. Customer exposure to in-store stimuli produces unplanned purchases

---

[47] Kollat, *op. cit.,*[46] p. 632.

because (1) the shopper uses in-store stimuli to remind her of her shopping needs, that is, she makes purchase decisions in the store rather than relying on a shopping list, and/or (2) in-store promotional techniques create previously unrecognized needs.

(2) **Customer-Commitment Hypothesis** This hypothesis emerged from a recent study of customer unplanned purchasing behavior.[48] While the exposure hypothesis maintains that unplanned purchasing, or differences between purchase intentions and actual purchases, are attributable to in-store stimuli, the customer-commitment hypothesis asserts that these differences are due to incomplete measures of purchase intentions. In other words, the customer-commitment hypothesis argues that the customer is *unwilling* and/or *unable* to commit the time and cognitive resources necessary to make "measured purchase intentions" equal to "actual purchase intentions."

The shopper may be *unwilling* to itemize her purchase intentions because she does not want to invest the amount of time and thought necessary to give the interviewer a complete roster of her purchase plans. Instead, she articulates only an incomplete itemization of what she plans to purchase, thereby satisfying the requirements of the interview without spending too much time or having to think too much.

The shopper may be *unable* to itemize her purchase plans for a variety of reasons. First, she may know what she will purchase but may be unable to articulate these purchase intentions because of the characteristics of the interview. The methodology used in most studies of unplanned purchasing forces the shopper, in the absence of a shopping list, to rely on memory for purchase intentions. In other words, unaided and nearly spontaneous recall is usually used to measure purchase plans. This methodology alone makes it highly probable that measured purchase plans will deviate to some degree from actual purchase plans.

Second, the shopper may know what she plans to purchase but may be unable, in the absence of a shopping list, to relate these intentions regardless of the amount of assistance given by the interviewer. That is to say, without exposure to in-store stimuli, the customer may be unable cognitively to construct and relate to the interviewer what she will purchase.

The findings to date do not permit a firm conclusion as to the relative roles of these two explanations. In the interim it seems reasonable to assume that both hypotheses actually account for unplanned purchasing. Some unplanned purchases are probably really triggered by customer exposure to product assortments and/or in-store promotional devices. However, some purchases that are presently termed unplanned are not unplanned at all but rather are an artifact of the way in which the behavior is usually measured. These purchases are classified as unplanned because "measured purchase intentions" deviate from

---

[48] Kollat, *op. cit.*,[46] pp. 626–639; Kollat and Willett, *op. cit.*,[33] pp. 21–31. The basic problem generating this hypothesis was pointed out several years ago. See William Applebaum, "Studying Customer Behavior in Retail Stores," *J. Marketing*, vol. 16, pp. 172–178, at p. 178 (Oct. 1951).

"actual purchase intentions" due to the customer's inability and/or unwillingness to commit the amount of time and thought necessary to tell the interviewer what she will purchase.

Marketing Implications

Several types of retailers, particularly supermarket managers, allegedly use unplanned purchasing as a criterion for several types of decisions. Certain store layouts, product locations, shelf locations, and types of displays are apparently thought to be more conducive to and consistent with unplanned purchasing than are others.

Unplanned purchasing is also of interest to some manufacturers. Some packaging and point-of-purchase decisions,[49] for example, are based, at least in part, on a product's present, or potential, rate of unplanned purchasing.

There are three basic problems with unplanned purchasing that are apparently not widely recognized. These problems need to be given serious consideration in evaluating the usefulness of the concept or a basis for marketing strategy. The problems are:

(1) *Not an operational objective*—It has been pointed out that unplanned purchasing has a variety of meanings. The marketing implications sometimes vary according to what definition is accepted. For example, if definition (1) is accepted, it may be desirable to increase customer exposure to products having high unplanned rates. If, however, definition (2) is accepted, this strategy may not be desirable, particularly if the location is inconsistent with where shoppers typically look for the product. It is questionable whether intelligent marketing decisions can be made concerning how to influence unplanned purchasing when there is so little agreement about what the phenomenon is or what it involves.

(2) *May exaggerate the potential for increasing sales*—To the extent that unplanned purchasing is attributable to the customer-commitment hypothesis, unplanned purchasing is not unplanned at all but rather an artifact of the way in which the behavior is measured. Consequently, *true* unplanned rates may be considerably lower than those currently accepted.[50] In other words, preshopping decisions about products and brands to be purchased are considerably more common than past studies have indicated. This may encourage an excessive investment of promotional expenditures designed to increase the rate of unplanned purchasing.

(3) *May be a misleading criterion for selecting products for special promotional efforts*—Retailers sometimes use product unplanned purchasing rates to select products for special promotional efforts. Such decisions as store location, shelf height, number of shelf facings, and end-aisle treatment are often based, in part, on product unplanned purchase rates.

---

[49] Bert C. McCammon, Jr., "The Role of Point-of-Purchase Display in the Manufacturer's Marketing Mix," in Taylor Meloan and Charles Whitto (eds.), *Competition in Marketing* (Los Angeles: Graduate School of Business, University of Southern California, 1964), pp. 75–91, at p. 78.

[50] See, for example, *Consumer Buying Habits Studies, op. cit.,*[37] pp. 3–4.

Since some unplanned purchasing is not unplanned at all but rather an artifact of the way in which the behavior is measured, true unplanned purchasing rates are considerably lower than those that are currently accepted. It seems risky to assume that all product unplanned purchasing rates are inflated to the same degree. Rather, some product unplanned purchasing rates are probably more overstated than are others.

Assume, for example, that product A's unplanned purchase rate is 65 percent and that product B has an unplanned purchase rate of 55 percent. Product A's unplanned purchase rate may be inflated by 40 percentage points and B's by 20 percentage points. The true unplanned purchase rates for A and B would be 25 percent and 35 percent, respectively. While the *gross* unplanned purchasing rates indicate that A should be given special promotional treatment, *true* rates indicate that B should receive the emphasis.

Increasing the Usefulness of Unplanned Purchasing

From the discussion above it is apparent that several problems must be overcome before unplanned purchasing can become a useful concept for marketing decisions. First, the concept must be precisely defined. Since the value of the concept hinges in large part on empirical studies of the extent and nature of the behavior, it seems desirable to adopt or adapt a definition used in empirical studies. Second, field studies must be designed so that the measured rate and characteristics of unplanned purchasing correspond to the empirical definition rather than being an artifact of the design itself.

Overcoming these problems will involve a substantial commitment of time and resources. However, the potential value of *true* rates of unplanned purchasing may exceed the costs of obtaining them.

When *true* rates of unplanned purchasing are determined, other categories of planning—specifically planned, generally planned, and brand substitution—would probably differ, both in magnitude and in relative occurrence, from those that are currently accepted. These refined measures of various types of in-store decisions would provide more sensitive indices of the amount and type of promotional effort that should be allocated to products.

In addition, refined measures of unplanned purchasing would permit a partial functional analysis of the strengths and weaknesses of a firm's promotional program. For example, if unplanned purchasing were defined and measured in such a way as to be equivalent to in-store purchase decisions, a manufacturer could use brand rates of unplanned purchasing as a criterion for evaluating the effectiveness of his in-store promotional strategy.

Finally, *pure* measures of unplanned purchasing and other categories of planning would constitute one of the most potentially meaningful indices of the real effects of specific in-store product promotions. For example, the difference in a product's unplanned purchase rate before and after a special in-store promotional strategy could be used as a measure of the effectiveness of that strategy. Other planning categories could also be used in this manner. These measures of effectiveness seem particularly useful, since they indicate both the *type* and *extent* of behavioral change precipitated by an in-store promotional strategy. These more sophisticated measures of effectiveness would be useful to retailers as well as manufacturers.[51]

ATTRACTION–CONVERSION ANALYSIS

Some consumers shop retail outlets because they believe the store carries the brand they are looking for. Other consumers do not have brand preferences prior to shopping. The sequence of these decisions—brand choice followed by store choice; or store choice followed by brand choice—has important implications for manufacturers and retailers.

Attraction–conversion analysis is based on two basic concepts:

(1) *Attraction power*—The number of consumers who visit a retail outlet because they want to purchase a specific brand.

(2) *Conversion power*—The percentage of consumers shopping a retail outlet for a brand that actually purchase the brand.

Table 21.7 illustrates how attraction and conversion indices can be constructed for hypothetical brands in various stores. In constructing the indices, 100 equals the average for all brands and all stores. Thus in store 1, brand *A* is 20 percent above average in terms of attraction power, but 20 percent below average in conversion power.

Implications for Retailers

Retailers can use attraction and conversion indices in several ways. However, in all instances, these measures must be interpreted within the context of the retailer's merchandising strategy. Attraction power is useful because it allows retailers to evaluate the relative effectiveness of brands in generating store traffic. In store 1, for example, brand *A* is drawing a greater number of customers than are brands *B* or *C*. In evaluating relative effectiveness, the retailer must make certain that differences in attraction power are not due to *his* advertising and sales promotion emphasis.

Conversion power must also be interpreted cautiously. If the retailer is giving equal sales and merchandising emphasis to each brand, then conversion power is a true measure of the ability of a brand to convert shoppers into purchasers. On the other hand, if the retailer is emphasizing a brand, then variations in conversion power may simply reflect his merchandising strategy for the product category.

---

[51] For examples of these uses of impulse purchasing see Simmons, *op. cit.*,[29] pp. 102–110.

Table 21.7 ATTRACTION AND CONVERSION
INDICES FOR HYPOTHETICAL
BRANDS AND STORES

	Brands		
Stores	*A*	*B*	*C*
Store 1			
Attraction power	120	102	98
Conversion power	80	98	105
Store 2			
Attraction power	100	107	94
Conversion power	100	102	102
·			
·			
·			
Store *N*			
Attraction power	90	95	93
Conversion power	120	97	94

NOTE: For attraction and conversion, 100 is the average for
all brands and all stores. For example, for brand *A*,
Store 1's attraction power is 20 percent above average
while store *N*'s is 10 percent below average.

Retailers can also compute other measures that might be termed *sales
power* indices. For a given brand, sales power could be (1) the percentage of
shoppers that purchase any brand in the product category, or (2) the gross
margin, or direct product profits, resulting from the fact that consumers are
attracted to the store by the brand. The latter measure incorporates the profit
resulting from all purchases made by the customer during the shopping trip.

Implications for Manufacturers

Manufacturers can use attraction, conversion, and sales power measures
to demonstrate the importance of their brands to retailers. Again, however, these
measures can be used for this purpose only if retailers' sales and merchandising
emphasis do not vary across brands in a product category.

Manufacturers can also use variations of this type of analysis. First, the
percentage of purchasers who decide on a brand prior to shopping is a rough
measure of the effectiveness of the manufacturer's promotion program, as well
as an indication of the relative importance of retail support.

Second, conversion power provides the manufacturer with a gross
measure of how effectively his distribution strategy is converting preferences into
purchases. Moreover, he can assess his strengths and weaknesses further by

determining how his conversion power varies by type of retail outlet, as well as by individual retailers.

Third, the manufacturer can perform the type of gain–loss analysis previously described in Chapters 15 and 17. Using brand preference before shopping as the base statistic, the manufacturer can determine the number of consumers switching to his brand as the result of shopping for each one that switches away from his brand. This allows the manufacturer to identify the brands he is gaining from and those he is losing to.

The next step is to obtain ratings of brands on the relevant evaluative criteria by following the procedures spelled out in Chapter 11. Economic, demographic, psychographic, and media-usage profiles can be constructed for consumers who switch away from and switch to the manufacturer's brand. Armed with this information the manufacturer can determine whether it is possible to improve his conversion ratio and, if so, the target market, the product benefits that should be emphasized, and the media vehicles that should be used.

PURCHASING PROCESSES WITHOUT CUSTOMER–STORE ENVIRONMENT INTERACTION

Thus far in this and the preceding two chapters it has been assumed that the consumer visits a retail outlet before purchasing. Store visits are, of course, not necessary, since the consumer can order by mail, by telephone, and from a door-to-door salesman. In fact, for a variety of reasons,[52] consumers are purchasing an increasing percentage of some types of products from these sources.[53] This section reviews studies that profile the characteristics of consumers who purchase various products from nonstore sources.

Telephone Shopping

Unfortunately, there is very little published evidence on telephone shopping. The problem is complicated by the fact that many stores that sell by telephone do not categorize their sales according to whether the merchandise was purchased in the store or via the telephone. Moreover, most of the empirical studies that have been conducted group telephone shoppers with catalog purchases and/or consumers who purchase from door-to-door salesmen,[54] Studies investigating consumers purchasing from combinations of nonstore sources are reviewed in the last part of this section.

---

[52] See, for example, George M. Naimark, "A Shift in the Point of Purchase," *J. Marketing*, vol. 29, pp. 14–17 (Jan. 1955).

[53] Unpublished estimates of Management Horizons, Inc., Columbus, Ohio

[54] See, for example, Peter L. Gillett, "A Profile of Urban In-Home Shoppers," *J. Marketing*, vol. 34, pp. 40–45 (July 1970); Laurence P. Feldman and Alvin D. Star, "Racial Factors in Shopping Behavior," in Keith Cox and Ben Enis (eds), *A New Measure of Responsibility for Marketing* (Chicago: Amer. Marketing Assoc., 1968), pp. 216–226.

One study has attempted to determine why some consumers are more likely to shop by phone than are others.[55] The study was part of a larger study of department-store shopping behavior.[56] The first stage involved interviews with 2092 New York housewives and 853 Cleveland housewives. The second stage involved telephone interviews with 723 New York housewives and 461 in Cleveland who had recently ordered something by telephone.

Three general customer characteristics were most commonly associated with telephone shopping:[57]

(1) *Need for convenience*—Telephone shoppers tended to have a greater need for convenience in shopping. They placed a high value on shopping quickly, were more likely to have young children, and were more likely to be residing in the suburbs.

(2) *Means to shop by telephone*—Possession of the means to shop easily by phone was also an important determinant of telephone shopping. Volume of phone ordering increased with income and the possession of a charge account.

(3) *Risk perceived in phone shopping*—When shopping in person, a customer has the opportunity to reduce uncertainty by personally evaluating the merchandise, by comparing brands, by comparing prices, colors, sizes, and so on. In contrast, the telephone shopper is limited to two methods of uncertainty reduction: reliance on past experience with the store, brand, or product, or reliance on a newspaper advertisement that may or may not picture the product.

Nonphone shoppers perceived intolerable amounts of risk in telephone shopping and were unwilling and/or unable to use newspaper advertising as a useful means of obtaining information and reducing uncertainty.

Mail-Order Shopping

Mail-order shopping is another form of nonstore purchasing. As used here, mail-order shopping differs from catalog purchasing in that the consumer does not receive a catalog.

One study attempted to determine whether consumers perceive greater risk in the act of buying by mail than in buying from a store or a salesman.[58] The primary product investigated was a supplementary hospitalization insurance plan marketed through the mail. Using in-home interviews, a quasi-experimental study was conducted with three groups of 100 respondents each. Group A was a

---

[55] Donald F. Cox and Stuart U. Rich, "Perceived Risk and Consumer Decision Making–The Case of Telephone Shopping," *J. Marketing Research*, vol. 1, pp. 32–39 (Nov. 1964).

[56] Stuart U. Rich, *Shopping Behavior of Department Store Customers* (Cambridge, Mass.: Division of Research, Harvard Business School, 1963).

[57] Cox and Rich, *op. cit.*,[55] p. 34.

[58] Homer E. Spence, James F. Engel, and Roger D. Blackwell, "Perceived Risk in Mail-Order and Retail Store Buying," *J. Marketing Research*, vol. 7, pp. 364–369 (Aug. 1970).

random sample of policy holders living in the Columbus, Ohio, area. Group *B* was selected randomly from the prospect list of the company that had received a promotional mailing from that company one week before the study but had not yet purchased. Group *C*, the control group, consisted of respondents selected randomly from geographical areas matched to those of Group *B*, but they received no promotional mailings.

The study found in general that people perceived more risk in the act of buying by mail than in buying from a store or a salesman. However, mail-order buyers of hospitalization insurance did *not* perceive significantly less risk in mail-order buying other products. Moreover, mail-order buyers of hospitalization insurance did not perceive significantly less risk in the mail-order purchase of such insurance than nonbuyers. Thus, although there was a general tendency for people to perceive more risk in buying by mail than in buying from a store or a salesman, there was an apparent inconsistency between this finding and the finding that mail-order buyers could not be distinguished from nonbuyers in terms of risk perception.[59]

In another study, Feldman and Star[60] analyzed the purchasing behavior of 760 white and 240 nonwhite participants in the 1963 *Chicago Tribune* study, "Chicago Shops."[61] Grouping phone with mail-order shopping, they found on an overall basis that the proportion of whites shopping via phone *or* mail order (30 percent) was more than twice that of the 13 percent proportion of nonwhites. However, when further classified by income, there was a general similarity in the pattern of phone or mail-order usage by both racial groups. Specifically, as income increased, the proportion of *each* racial group shopping via phone or mail order increased.[62]

Catalog Shopping

Catalog sales are also growing at a much faster rate than total retail sales. Sales during 1971 were estimated in the tens of billions, with Sears accounting for $2.3 billion; Montgomery Ward, $600 million; Spiegel's, $300 million; Penney's $300 million; and others capturing the remainder.[63]

Despite the importance of this market, little is known about the types of consumers that purchase merchandise via catalogs. In fact, the Feldman–Star study apparently is the only published investigation.

Feldman and Star found that about 40 percent of whites and 18 percent of nonwhites purchased merchandise from catalogues. For both races, catalog buying tended to increase as income increased up to the $5000–$6900 level. The only statistically significant difference between the two racial groups was found at the lowest income level. According to the authors, the explanation for this

---

[59] Spence, *et al., op. cit.,*[58] pp. 364–369, at pp. 367–368.

[60] Feldman and Star, *op. cit.,*[54] pp. 216–226.

[61] "Chicago Shops," *Chicago Tribune* (1963).

[62] Feldman and Star, *op. cit.,*[54] p. 218.

[63] "Pretty Penney," *Forbes,* p. 46 (Mar. 15, 1972).

difference may have been the lack of credit by nonwhites at this income level, in combination with a lower level of literacy.[64]

Door-to-Door Purchasers

Door-to-door sales are important for some products, particularly cosmetics and some household cleaning products. Peters and Ford conducted a study of heavy in-home buyers and heavy in-store buyers of cosmetics.[65] "Heavy" was defined as consumers purchasing more than one half of their cosmetics from one or the other source. The judgment sample consisted of 690 housewives from the Madison, Wisconsin, area. Heavy in-home buyers numbered 136, and 113 were classified as heavy in-store customers.

Compared to the woman who buys over half of her cosmetics in a retail store, the heavy in-home buyer:[66]

(1)   Had less access to a car for daytime shopping.

(2)   Tended to be less educated.

(3)   Was more likely to have children living at home.

(4)   Was more likely to have a family income under $15,000 annually.

(5)   Had a greater chance that the head of household would be a blue-collar worker, clerical employee, or a salesman rather than a professional.

Composite In-Home Shoppers

Gillett conducted a study of in-home shopping, which he defined as placing a mail or telephone order from the home, or ordering in person from a catalog office or a catalog counter of a retail store.[67] Using a stratified quota sample, interviews were conducted with 210 female shoppers in Grand Rapids, Michigan.

In-home shopping was widespread; 70 percent of the women had shopped at home at least once during the 11-month period of the study. About 43 percent had shopped by direct mail, 38 percent by phone, and 29 percent from catalogs. However, only a small fraction of total family expenditures for general merchandise was purchased in the home.

In-home shoppers were not a "captive" market, either by retail store default in providing convenient and enjoyable shopping, or from necessity due to shopper difficulty in getting to the store. Rather, in-home shopping was most often discretionary; avoiding an extra trip to pick up a needed item and buying in response to an advertisement were typical examples of purchase motivations.

---

[64]   Feldman and Star, *op. cit.,*[54] p. 218.

[65]   William H. Peters and Neil M. Ford, "A Profile of Urban In-Home Shoppers: The Other Half," *J. Marketing,* vol. 36, pp. 62–64 (Jan. 1972).

[66]   Peters and Ford, *op. cit.,*[65] p. 64.

[67]   Gillett, *op. cit.,*[54] pp. 40–45.

Women buying at home were also active store shoppers who were no less inclined to consider store shopping as difficult or unpleasant than were other shoppers. In-home shoppers were flexible in their choice of shopping alternatives; they were not bound by shopping traditions and perceived less than average risk in buying by mail or phone. They were more affluent and better educated than other shoppers, but differed little in terms of other major demographic characteristics.[68]

Marketing Implications

In view of the dollar volume importance of in-home buying, it is frustrating to find so little consumer research in the area. Several provisional statements can be made, however, on the basis of the limited available evidence. Historically retailing executives have been reluctant to promote nonstore sales. They are usually thought of as more expensive to process and as substitutes for store sales rather than additional business. Now, however, it appears that much, if not most, in-home buying represents incremental volume.

Many factors must, of course, be considered in deciding whether to attempt to develop volume via telephone, mail, or catalog.[69] If such a decision is made, it is important to design a strategy that reduces perceived risk. Advertisements and catalogues should be informative and written to facilitate ordering by brand, size, or color. Liberal return privileges are also important.

The evidence to date also indicates that in-home buyers constitute a unique market segment rather than being distributed uniformly throughout society. The characteristics and behavioral attributes of consumers comprising this segment can be used to design more effective promotional strategies for stimulating in-home buying in those cases when it is profitable to the retailer.

In the future it would appear useful to focus more effort on the types of products that are purchased in the home and the kinds of consumers that purchase them.

A GENERAL EVALUATION OF PURCHASING–PROCESS RESEARCH

Since the research presented has been evaluated as it has been discussed, this section is both general and brief. In the authors' opinions, the research presented above has several salient characteristics that need to be discussed.

In comparing the studies reviewed in this and the preceding two chapters with the information presented in Figure 19.2 and Table 19.2, certain conclusions

---

[68] Gillett, *op. cit.*,[54] pp. 44–45.

[69] See, for example, Cyrus C. Wilson, "Telephone Order Promotion Strategy as an Aspect of Merchandising Strategy for Full Service Retail Stores in the Central Business District" (Columbus, Ohio: Department of Business Organization, Ohio State University, 1964).

seem inescapable. First, it is apparent that research has tended to concentrate on certain relations and has ignored others. A comprehensive, balanced understanding of purchasing processes requires that these unexplored areas be investigated.

Second, purchasing-process research has typically used reduced-form conceptualizations of purchasing processes. Few, if any, studies have rigorously controlled, or otherwise accounted for, the variables itemized in Figure 19.2. Since variable interactions can produce different effects on dependent variables than single variables, this is an important problem.

Third, most purchasing-process research has not been consumer oriented. Studies typically fail to consider the shopper's purchase intentions. As a consequence, the findings are often meaningless and the implications fallacious. Despite the fact that consumers react to displays, make unplanned purchases, and select stores, the customer and his attributes are typically not included in these studies.

Finally, purchasing processes are a relatively underresearched area of consumer behavior. Most of the studies that have been made have been sponsored, if not conducted, by private organizations that could conceivably have something to gain depending on the type of findings that are reported. While accusations are not being made here, it appears that research conducted by independent organizations might be desirable.[70]

SUMMARY

This chapter completed the discussion of purchasing processes begun in Chapter 19. Attention was given first to the effects of customer–salesman interaction on consumer behavior. The similarity of customers and salesmen and certain transaction characteristics were identified as key determinants of sales.

The nature and correlates of intentions–outcomes categories were then discussed. These categories are more useful than postshopping outcomes as an effectiveness criterion since consumer intentions are explicitly taken into consideration. Unfortunately, most studies have used postshopping outcomes, and, as a result, they are less useful than if intentions–outcomes categories had been used. Greater use of these categories in the future is desirable.

Most studies using intention–outcomes categories have been conducted in drugstores and/or supermarkets and have been concerned with brand substitution and/or unplanned purchasing. Further studies need to be conducted in other types of retail outlets, and the nature, significance, and correlates of the other categories—specifically planned and generally planned—need to be studied.

Attraction, conversion, and sales power measures were examined. It was shown how both retailers and manufacturers can use these variables to increase the effectiveness of their marketing programs.

Finally, purchasing processes not involving customer–store environment interaction were discussed. Research to date indicates that in-home shoppers

---

[70] For other perspectives, see Donald H. Granbois, "Improving the Study of Customer In-Store Behavior," *J. Marketing,* vol. 32, pp. 28–33 (Oct. 1968).

may constitute a unique and identifiable market segment, and that certain strategies seem necessary in order to increase this source of sales volume. Additional investigations of in-home buying would be useful.

REVIEW AND DISCUSSION QUESTIONS

1. Compare and contrast the explanations for unplanned purchasing. Do the alternative explanations produce different marketing implications? Explain.

2. Prepare an outline indicating an appropriate method of determining whether or not customers who order by mail differ from those who do not.

3. Suppose that customers who order by mail differ from other customers in the following ways: (a) higher income (over $15,000), (b) greater tendency to have charge accounts, and (c) greater tendency to live in the suburbs. How can this information be used in designing specific marketing strategies? (Optional: Design a marketing program based on this information.)

4. "Most purchasing-process studies have used reduced-form models." What does this mean? What are the consequences of using reduced-form models of purchasing processes?

5. "Most studies of purchasing processes have omitted the consumer." What does this mean?

6. Using Figure 19.2 and Table 19.2, prepare a list of five or more aspects of purchasing processes that have not been researched. (Optional: Choose one of these aspects and prepare a research design.)

7. How can a firm use the customer–salesman similarity hypothesis?

8. How can a manufacturer use attraction and conversion indices? How can a retailer use these indices?

9. Prepare a research outline indicating how you would go about measuring customer–salesman interaction in a retail setting.

22

POSTPURCHASE PROCESSES

The discussion of decision processes continues in this chapter, with the emphasis now on the consequences of a decision and the various forms of resulting behavior. Referring once again to the model of consumer motivation and behavior (Figure 22.1), notice that two outcomes are specified: (1) triggering of new behavior and (2) postpurchase evaluation. The latter category includes three possible consequences: (1) reward and satisfaction, (2) postpurchase attitude change, and (3) postdecision dissonance. Some interesting implications emerge, many of which have not previously been explored in the marketing literature.

TRIGGERING NEW BEHAVIOR

Once a decision is made to buy, there is a limitless variety of additional actions that can result. Because these are unique to each situation, no attempt is made here to explore a great many possibilities. Rather, the purpose is to look at several and to evaluate the significance for marketing planning.

Possible Types of New Behavior

Of particular importance are these three outcomes: (1) the need to make financial outlays, (2) product installation and use, and (3) generated interest in related products and services. Many others could, of course, be mentioned.

529

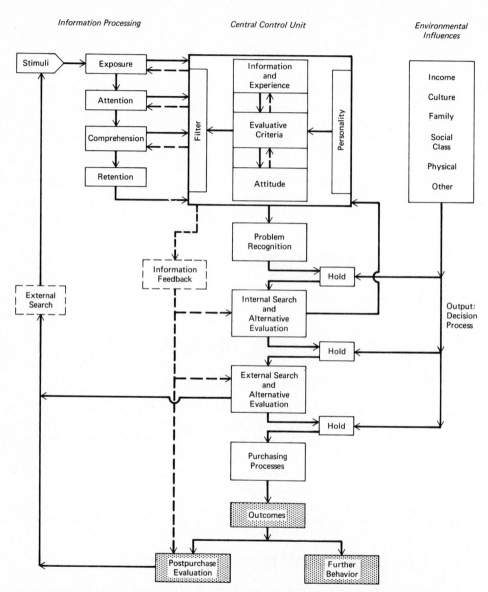

Figure 22.1 MODEL OF CONSUMER MOTIVATION AND BEHAVIOR SHOW-
ING OUTCOMES OF A BUYING DECISION

Once a product is purchased, a financial outlay of some type generally is
required at the time of purchase. This frequently can present genuine problems,
and the need often arises for a renewal of extended problem solving. Should
installment credit be used? Should a loan be taken from a bank? Will the family

budget support complete payment at this point in time without jeopardizing other needed expenditures? This decision obviously is among the most important to be faced in many buying situations.

Once the purchase is consummated, the product then presumably is placed in use. This, however, is not necessarily an automatic action, for additional problems can be generated. As most fathers can attest, one major difficulty often is assembly of the product following "simple directions." Another is the period of learning necessary for proper use. Each of these circumstances can occupy considerable time and thought, to say nothing of the consternation that can result if inadequate directions are provided.

Then, too, the purchase of one item may generate interest in others. The presence of a new sofa in the living room, for example, can trigger an awareness that other items of furniture appear shabby by comparison. As a result, the purchase of the sofa may, in effect, open a Pandora's box in that total redecorating may be the final outcome.

Marketing Implications

All too frequently manufacturers view their responsibilities to the consumer as ending once the purchase is made. The problems of installation and use, for example, often are totally neglected. This practice, however, is a shortsighted one, because a dissatisfied user is likely to be a poor future prospect. Moreover, considerable damage can be done by negative word-of-mouth communication to friends and relatives. Marketing planning should be based on an awareness of how the product fits into the consumer's total style of life.[1] On this basis suggestions can be made that will help the consumer to maximize the satisfactions gained from product use.

In addition, many opportunities are lost by manufacturers and retailers who are unaware of the extent to which one purchase can lead to others. Much can be gained by preparing accompanying literature that points out possible accessories, companion products, and so on.

Finally, as has been mentioned previously, concern over financing and credit arrangements can be a barrier that delays or even prevents a purchase. Retailers have long been aware of this fact, and many offer such a variety of convenient credit arrangements that the need for extended problem solving by the purchasing family relative to this issue is virtually eliminated.

Manufacturers and resellers are well advised to undertake research that leads to a greater understanding of the *total purchase act*. Failure to do so may lead to a dissatisfied customer and engage the danger of missing additional profit opportunities resulting from the sale of companion items.

---

[1] H. W. Boyd, Jr., and S. J. Levy, "New Dimensions in Consumer Analysis," *Harvard Business Rev.*, pp. 129–140 (Nov.–Dec. 1963).

POSTPURCHASE EVALUATION

As was mentioned earlier, there are two outcomes of postpurchase evaluation: (1) reward and satisfaction and (2) postdecision dissonance. These are not mutually exclusive categories, but there are differences in resulting practical implications.

Reward and Satisfaction

Learning processes were discussed in Chapter 9, and it will be recalled that a given response is reinforced either positively or negatively to the extent that it is followed by reward. In the present context, satisfaction may be defined as ". . . the buyer's cognitive state of being adequately or inadequately rewarded in a buying situation for the sacrifice he has undergone."[2]

The Effects of Reward Although the relationship between reward and behavior has not been studied in complex choice situations involving many alternatives,[3] thousands of studies in the learning of literature affirm that a response is reinforced to the extent that it serves to reduce the motivating drive state. Therefore, the probability of making a similar buying act will be increased if there are positive consequences in the act or purchase and use, and vice versa. This fundamental proposition underlies many of the mathematical theories of brand loyalty discussed in the next chapter.

It may be concluded that brand loyalty will develop and be strengthened as long as there is positive reinforcement, *all other things being equal.* This conclusion must be qualified for the reason that the relationship between response tendencies and behavior is not monotonic. Other factors intervene to affect action, and it must not be overlooked that the consumer will, on occasion, seek novelty and deliberately act contrary to established patterns.

Finally, the other variables in the central control unit (CCU) also are reinforced by outcomes. Evaluative criteria, for example, are learned and hence are strengthened or weakened in importance by experience. Similarly, there is growing interest in the field of psychology in the manner by which attitudes are learned and reinforced. Many feel that learning theories are directly applicable here as well.[4] Thus, the degree of reward and satisfaction can have profound future effects not only on behavior but on information processing—the other major function of the CCU.

The Problem of Unconfirmed Expectancies An expectancy is a type of hypothesis formed by the consumer regarding the consequences of an act, and

---

[2] John A. Howard and Jagdish N. Sheth, *The Theory of Buyer Behavior* (New York: Wiley, 1969), p. 145.

[3] Howard and Sheth, *op. cit.,*[2] p. 146.

[4] For an excellent review of many viewpoints, see H. E. Greenwald, T. C. Brock, and T. M. Ostrom (eds.), *Psychological Foundations of Attitude* (New York: Academic Press, 1968).

input of information after purchase will serve either to confirm or to reject it. If it is confirmed, there are probably no further psychological consequences other than reinforcement of the expectation. An unconfirmed expectancy, on the other hand, generates a state of cognitive inconsistency. Knowledge of what took place contradicts the expectancy, and the individual is motivated to overcome the resulting imbalance.

A study by Carlsmith and Aronson alerted researchers to the promise of this area of inquiry.[5] Individuals were required to taste bitter or sweet solutions under conditions in which expectations regarding the taste were experimentally manipulated. If the expectancy was not confirmed by the actual taste, findings showed that the bitter solution was reported to taste *more bitter* and the sweet solution *less sweet*. In other words, disappointed people were found to magnify the differences between expectations and reality. There has been mixed success in replicating these findings,[6] but it does appear that a product which fails to confirm a consumer's expectations may be evaluated negatively, regardless of whether it exceeds or falls short of the expectancy.

Part of the explanation for inconsistent findings may be that there seldom is just one simplistic expectancy for an action, especially when choices are complex.[7] In addition, the downgrading of behavioral outcomes seems to take place only when the decision is made on the basis of reasonably complete information.[8] Nevertheless, it is widely accepted that the hypothesized events are produced under a wide variety of circumstances.[9]

In one published application to marketing, Cardozo showed that a negative disconfirmation of an expectancy (results were poorer than anticipated) produced an unfavorable product evaluation.[10] This effect was substantially less, however, as the effort expended to procure the product increased. Cardozo did not test whether or not a positive disconfirmation (results exceed expectations) also produces disappointment. One possible conclusion is that a disparity between a purchase outcome and expectations regarding that outcome can generate dissonance which, in turn, can be reduced by evaluating the outcome less favorably than it would have been had the disconfirmation not taken place. This hypothesis, however, was not supported in a more recent study by Olshavsky

---

[5] J. M. Carlsmith and E. Aronson, "Some Hedonic Consequences of the Confirmation and Disconfirmation of Expectancies," *J. Abnormal and Social Psychology*, vol. 66, pp. 151–156 (1963).

[6] For a review of the evidence, see W. A. Watts, "Predictability and Pleasure: Reactions to the Disconfirmation of Expectancies," in R. P. Abelson *et al.* (eds.), *Theories of Cognitive Consistency: A Sourcebook* (Chicago: Rand McNally, 1968), pp. 469–478.

[7] Watts, *op. cit.*[6]

[8] J. M. Carlsmith and J. L. Freedman, "Bad Decisions and Dissonance: Nobody's Perfect," in Abelson *et al.*, *op. cit.*,[6] pp. 485–490.

[9] R. B. Zajonc, "Cognitive Theories in Social Psychology," in G. Lindzey and E. Aronson (eds.), *The Handbook of Social Psychology*, 2nd ed., vol. I (Reading, Mass.: Addison-Wesley, 1968), pp. 320–411.

[10] R. A. Cardozo, "An Experimental Study of Consumer Effort, Expectation, and Satisfaction," *J. Marketing Research*, vol. 2, pp. 244–249 (1965).

and Miller.[11] This investigation analyzed the effects on product ratings of both overstatement and understatement of product quality. The results showed that overstatement resulted in more favorable ratings and understatement had an opposite effect. This, of course, is contrary to the prediction of dissonance theory.

While the issues are unclear at this point in time, advertisers should be cautious in assuming that a "little exaggeration is the name of the game." The need to create realistic expectations in promotional messages was noted by one of the authors who was induced through advertising to investigate a particular make of compact automobile. Advertisements stressed quality, maneuverability, and general excellence of performance. The model on the showroom floor, however, performed poorly in a trial run, and no amount of persuasion could dispel the conclusion that the product was totally unsatisfactory. Whether the advertising message was false or the demonstrator was poorly maintained never was determined. The point is that a discomfirmed expectancy created a nonprospect in short order.

Although the evidence reviewed here is admittedly incomplete and tentative, it sounds a needed warning for marketing management. A case can be made for realistic research that documents consumer desires as well as product capabilities. Advertisement and selling messages, then, should be designed to create expectancies that will be fulfilled by the product insofar as is possible. The extent to which this seemingly common-sense precaution is violated through use of "cute" exaggerations and other forms of creative "gimmickery" in advertisements is, at times, appalling.

Similarly, product designers should be keenly aware of the way in which a product fits into the consumer's style of life. What does it mean to the consumer? How is it used? The product should be designed and promoted so that performance will be satisfactory under conditions actually experienced in the home. Many housewives, for example, use electric toasters for English muffins, rolls, and other forms of baked goods besides bread. If the toaster will not handle these items satisfactorily, disconfirmed expectancies and buyer dissatisfaction are the probable result.

Many consumers, in turn, become quite vocal when they are dissatisfied and do not hesitate to spread unfavorable word-of-mouth communication. One low-priced brand of automobile seems to have been particularly damaged in this fashion by product performance that violated its advertising claims. This, in turn, becomes compounded in that those who become aware of this fact will tend to "screen out" advertisements for this make. Little opportunity thus exists to turn these people into prospects.

Finally, it is worth commenting on Cardozo's somewhat unexpected findings. It will be recalled that product satisfaction was greater when high effort was expended to purchase the product.[12] This would imply that a rigorous shopping expedition would result in greater satisfaction than purchase at the

---

[11] R. W. Olshavsky and J. A. Miller, "Consumer Expectations, Product Performance, and Perceived Product Quality," *J. Marketing Research*, vol. 9, pp. 19–21 (1972).

[12] Cardozo, *op. cit.*[10]

corner store. Yet, today's retailing is oriented, by and large, toward generating great convenience and ease of shopping. Should this long-standing retailing practice be modified? Further research may shed light on this question.

Postpurchase Attitude Change

It generally is assumed that a change in attitude must *precede* a corresponding change in behavior. This has repeatedly been shown to be a fallacious conclusion, however.[13] When knowledge enters memory that a particular action has been taken, it can be seen as contradicting an existing attitude, with the result that dissonance is aroused. Dissonance, of course, is an uncomfortable state, and the individual is motivated to restore consonance or balance.

In this circumstance, the buying action itself usually cannot be changed; and the average person is reluctant to admit that he has made a mistake once funds have been committed to an alternative. Therefore, it is probable that attitudes will change instead. Mills discovered, for example, that those who engaged in cheating later changed their attitude toward this type of behavior.[14] Similarly, Atkin reports that attitudes toward various stores changed after consumers shopped there.[15]

It thus would appear to be a valid marketing goal to induce people to engage in attitude-discrepant behavior. Perhaps the offer of a free coupon, for example, might induce a housewife to try a previously avoided brand of coffee. If she were strongly committed to her brand *and* if she actually purchased and used the other brand voluntarily, then dissonance most likely would occur. Brand preferences thus could change as a result of this product trial.

This change probably would not occur, however, if the behavior advocated were perceived as nonacceptable. Under that circumstance it most likely would fall into her latitude of rejection. She might feel, for example, that the brand of coffee in question will never be served in her home. In such a situation, it is most likely that she would resist dissonance and avoid the advocated behavior. This has largely been overlooked by the dissonance researchers, who usually claim that greatest attitude change results when the discrepancy between attitude and behavior is maximum.

Is it reasonable to expect a free sample to induce a strongly committed consumer to switch brands? Quite an opposite result might occur in that she would use the sample but never really give the product a fair trial. In other words, she does not waste the sample, but, at the same time, she does not fully expose herself to the information the sample can give and thereby let her preferences be challenged. One cannot help wondering whether or not many of

---

[13] B. Lipstein, "Anxiety, Risk and Uncertainty in Advertising Effectiveness Measurements," in L. Adler and I. Crespi (eds.), *Attitude Research on the Rocks* (Chicago: Amer. Marketing Assoc., 1968), pp. 11–27.

[14] J. Mills, "Changes in Moral Attitudes Following Temptation," *J. Personality*, vol. 26, pp. 517–531 (1958).

[15] K. Atkin, "Advertising and Store Patronage," *J. Advertising Research*, vol. 2, pp. 18–23 (1962).

the coupons, samples, and other "giveaways" are falling on unfertile ground for these reasons.

Postdecision Dissonance

Charlie Johnson, an insurance salesman in a midwestern community, suddenly became aware that his three-year-old automobile will need major repairs. After extensive family discussion, a decision was made to purchase a new four-door hardtop with "four on the floor," even though family financial status was limited at the time. During the decision-making process there was disagreement on which of three popular makes was preferable. Each had its desirable features, and none clearly stood out as superior. The choice finally was made, although there never was a complete meeting of minds.

This situation contains all of the prerequisites for postdecision dissonance. Dissonance arises when two relevant cognitions or beliefs do not fit together, hence generating a state of psychological discomfort. Charlie is now aware that he has purchased the car, but this is dissonant with the fact that there are desirable unchosen alternatives. He can reduce dissonance by (1) reevaluating the desirability of each alternative to favor his choice, (2) searching for information to buttress his decision, or (3) changing his attitude structure. Since attitude change following behavioral change has already been discussed, this section concentrates on the first two alternatives.

Antecedent Conditions When are postdecision doubts most likely to occur? From an extensive body of research findings, it is known that dissonance is most probable when:

(1) A certain minimum level of dissonance tolerance is surpassed. Individuals can live with inconsistency in many areas of their lives until this point is reached.[16]

(2) The action is irrevocable[17]

(3) Unchosen alternatives have desirable features.[18]

(4) A number of desirable alternatives are available.[19]

(5) The individual is committed to his decision because of its psychological significance to him.[20]

(6) Available alternatives are qualitatively dissimilar—that is, each has some

---

[16] M. T. O'Keefe, "The Anti-Smoking Commercials: A Study of Television's Impact on Behavior," *Public Opinion Quart.*, vol. 35, pp. 242–248 (1971).

[17] H. B. Gerard, "Basic Features of Commitment," in Abelson *et al, op. cit.*,[6] pp. 456–463.

[18] See, for example, H. J. Greenwald, "Dissonance and Relative vs. Absolute Attractiveness of Decision Alternatives," *J. Personality and Social Psychology*, vol. 11, pp. 328–333 (1969).

[19] J. W. Brehm and A. R. Cohen, "Re-evaluation of Choice Alternatives as a Function of Their Number and Qualitative Similarity," *J. Abnormal and Social Psychology*, vol. 58, pp. 373–378 (1959).

[20] C. A. Kiesler, "Commitment," in Abelson *et al., op. cit.*,[6] pp. 448–455; Gerard, *op. cit.*;[17] J. W. Brehm and A. R. Cohen, *Explorations in Cognitive Dissonance* (New York: Wiley, 1962), p. 300.

desirable unique features (referred to in the terminology of dissonance theory as low "cognitive overlap").[21]

(7) Perception and thought about unchosen alternatives is undertaken as a result of free will (volition) with little or no outside applied pressure.[22] If pressure is applied, the individual will do what he is forced to do without letting his own point of view or preference really be challenged.

The automobile purchase decision described above fully meets these criteria: presumably a dissonance tolerance threshold has been passed, the decision is irrevocable, there are other unchosen desirable alternatives which apparently are dissimilar, there is commitment to the decision, and no pressure was applied to make the decision. Obviously postdecision dissonance is largely confined to extended problem-solving situations. Indeed, avoidance of such doubts can be an incentive for establishment of purchasing routines.

Reevaluation of Alternatives When dissonance occurs it can be reduced by increasing the perceived attractiveness of the unchosen alternative and/or downgrading the desirability of those that were not chosen.[23] In addition, it is possible to accomplish the same result by concluding that all alternatives are essentially identical, even though this was not felt to be true during prepurchase deliberations.[24] By so doing, of course, none would stand out over others, and doubts would be removed.

There have been a number of recent studies in the marketing literature which confirm that consumers do spread apart alternatives in order to reduce dissonance. LoSciuto and Perloff, for example, found that a chosen record album was reranked as more desirable than the unchosen alternative which was then downgraded in desirability.[25] In addition, this tendency was found one week after the first postdecision rating. Similar findings are reported by Anderson[26] et al., Cohen and Goldberg,[27] Holloway,[28] and Sheth.[29]

---

[21] Brehm and Cohen, op. cit.[19]

[22] A. R. Cohen, H. I. Terry, and C. B. Jones, "Attitudinal Effects of Choice in Exposure to Counter-Propaganda," J. Abnormal and Social Psychology, vol. 58, pp. 388–391 (1959); L. Festinger and J. M. Carlsmith, "Cognitive Consequences of Forced Compliance," J. Abnormal and Social Psychology, vol. 58, pp. 203–210 (1959); A. R. Cohen, J. W. Brehm, and W. H. Fleming, "Attitude Change and Justification for Compliance," J. Abnormal and Social Psychology, vol. 56, pp. 276–278 (1958); T. C. Brock, "Cognitive Restructuring and Attitude Change," J. Abnormal and Social Psychology, vol. 64, pp. 264–271 (1962).

[23] L. Festinger, A Theory of Cognitive Dissonance (Evanston, Ill.: Row, Peterson, 1957).

[24] Festinger, op. cit.[23]

[25] L. A. LoSciuto and R. Perloff, "Influence of Product Preference on Dissonance Reduction," J. Marketing Research, vol. 4, pp. 286–290 (1967).

[26] L. K. Anderson, J. R. Taylor, and R. J. Holloway, "The Consumer and His Alternatives: An Experimental Approach," J. Marketing Research, vol. 3, pp. 62–67 (1966).

[27] J. Cohen and M. E. Goldberg, "The Dissonance Model in Post-Decision Product Evaluation," J. Marketing Research, vol. 7, pp. 315–321 (1970).

[28] R. J. Holloway, "An Experiment on Consumer Dissonance," J. Marketing, vol. 31, pp. 39–43 (1967).

[29] J. N. Sheth, "Cognitive Dissonance, Brand Preference and Product Familiarity," in J. Arndt (ed.), Insights into Consumer Behavior (Boston: Allyn and Bacon, 1968), pp. 41–54.

One interesting possibility is that this state of postdecision regret is only a temporary phenomenon.[30] It may well be that reestablishment of the original state of equilibrium through bolstering one's choice will make selection of that alternative more probable in the future. Mittelstaedt verified this hypothesis and showed that the probability of purchasing the same brand again is increased in proportion to the magnitude of postdecision dissonance surrounding the initial purchase.[31] This may shed useful light on the psychological mechanisms of brand loyalty.

The findings reported here are perhaps of greatest interest to those with a scholarly interest in understanding consumer behavior. Those with a more applied interest, however, are more likely to question their relevance. In reality there is little the marketer can do to affect or capitalize upon postdecision reevaluation of alternatives. The marketer, of course, desires to differentiate his firm's offerings as much as possible from competitors and to induce the consumer to make a purchase. All things being equal, dissonance will be generated in the presence of qualitatively dissimilar alternatives, and it often is resolved to the company's benefit by reinforcing the decision. This process takes place as a result of what has happened *before* purchase, so there are no significant implications for marketing planning.

Postdecision Information Search   Doubts following purchase also can be reduced by searching for additional information that serves to confirm the wisdom of the choice. This is shown by the search arrow in Figure 22.1. In the purchase of an automobile, for example, dissonance cannot be reduced by changing the behavior and admitting a mistake because of great financial loss if the car is returned to the dealer. Also, most people are reluctant to admit that a wrong decision was made and to live with that knowledge. Although both of these acts would reduce dissonance and restore consonance, it is more likely that a person experiencing dissonance will buttress his choice through procuring additional information. This information-seeking tendency has been widely documented,[32] although much of the evidence must be regarded as tentative for methodological reasons to be discussed later.

(1) **Preference for Consonant versus Discrepant Information**   It seems reasonable to hypothesize that "a person experiencing dissonance will avoid further inconsistent information and seek out consistent information in order to reduce his dissonance."[33] Consonant information is that which confirms his choice

---

[30]   E. Walster and E. Berscheid, "The Effects of Time on Cognitive Consistency," in Abelson *et al., op. cit.,*[6] pp. 599–608.

[31]   R. Mittelstaedt, "A Dissonance Approach to Repeat Purchasing Behavior," *J. Marketing Research,* vol. 6, pp. 444–447 (1969).

[32]   See, for example, J. S. Adams, "Reduction of Cognitive Dissonance by Seeking Consonant Information," *J. Abnormal and Social Psychology,* vol. 62, pp. 74–78 (1961); J. Mills, E. Aronson, and H. Robinson, "Selectivity in Exposure to Information," *J. Abnormal and Social Psychology,* vol. 59, pp. 250–253 (1959).

[33]   A. R. Cohen, J. W. Brehm, and B. Latané, "Choice of Strategy and Voluntary Exposure to Information under Public and Private Conditions," *J. Personality,* vol. 27, p. 63 (1959).

and vice versa. There is some evidence supporting this hypothesis,[34] but the overwhelming consensus now is that there is no tendency one way or another.[35] In some instances people deliberately seek out discrepant facts in order to refute them and thereby reduce dissonance.[36] In other instances, people seek *useful* information, *regardless* of its content;[37] this factor now is felt by many authorities to be a major determinant.[38]

The type of information utilized also appears to be a function of several additional factors. First, the consumer should feel more free to seek out discrepant as well as consonant information if he perceives a strong probability that a wise selection was made. In other words, he perceives himself to be capable of evaluating any type of *relevant* information.[39] Second, supportive as well as discrepant information will be used if a substantial body of evidence had been gathered during the decision process which bolstered the final choice.[40]

(2) **Use of Marketing Literature to Reduce Dissonance** It is a reasonable extension of the discussion thus far to predict that a consumer who is not especially confident in his choice would be receptive to advertisements and other literature provided by the manufacturer. The selling arguments and points of alternative superiority stressed there could prove useful in bolstering his perception that the decision was wise and proper.

This hypothesis was given preliminary verification by Ehrlich and others, who found that purchasers of new automobiles showed greater readership of advertisements for the make purchased than for other makes.[41] The Ehrlich study was replicated by Engel, and quite different findings were produced.[42] Interviews were conducted with two matched samples of consumers in Ann Arbor, Michigan, one of which had purchased a new Chevrolet within a period of one day to four weeks prior to the interview. Data were collected on readership of automobile

---

[34] See, for example, Adams, *op. cit.*[32]

[35] See, for example, R. H. Lowe and Ivan D. Steiner, "Some Effects of the Reversibility and Consequences of Decisions on Postdecision Information Preferences," *J. Personality and Social Psychology*, vol. 8, pp. 172–179 (1968).

[36] J. L. Freedman, "Preference for Dissonant Information," *J. Personality and Social Psychology*, vol. 2, pp. 287–289 (1965).

[37] J. Mills, "Effect of Certainty about a Decision upon Postdecision Exposure to Consonant and Dissonant Information," *J. Personality and Social Psychology*, vol. 2, pp. 749–752 (1965); also J. L. Freedman, "Confidence, Utility, and Selective Exposure," *J. Personality and Social Psychology*, vol. 2, pp. 778–780 (1965).

[38] T. C. Brock, S. M. Albert, and L. E. Becker, "Familiarity, Utility, and Supportiveness as Determinants of Information Receptivity," *J. Personality and Social Psychology*, vol. 14, pp. 292–301 (1970); also L. Festinger, *Conflict, Decision, and Dissonance* (Stanford, Calif.: Stanford University Press, 1964).

[39] Festinger, *op. cit.*;[38] Mills, Freedman, *op. cit.*[37]

[40] T. C. Brock, "Commitment to Exposure as a Determinant of Information Receptivity," *J. Personality and Social Psychology*, vol. 2, pp. 10–19 (1965).

[41] D. Ehrlich, I. Guttman, P. "Schönbach, and J. Mills, "Post Decision Exposure to Relevant Information," *J. Abnormal and Social Psychology*, vol. 54, pp. 98–102 (1957).

[42] J. F. Engel, "The Psychological Consequences of a Major Purchase Decision," in W. S. Decker (ed), *Marketing in Transition* (Chicago: Amer. Marketing Assoc., 1963), pp. 462–475; J. F. Engel, "Are Automobile Purchasers Dissonant Consumers?" *J. Marketing*, vol. 27, pp. 55–58 (1963).

advertisements in the local newspaper, as well as ratings of agreement or disagreement with statements that alternately challenged and asserted the superiority of Chevrolet over another popular make. In addition, recall of these statements was tested after the lapse of at least 15 minutes during the interview.

If Chevrolet purchasers were experiencing dissonance, the theory of cognitive dissonance would predict the following differences between the two groups: (1) the new owners should show significantly greater awareness and recall of advertisements asserting Chevrolet superiority as well as dealer advertisements stressing low prices, (2) there should be significant differences in the percentages of agreement and disagreement with statements alleging Chevrolet superiority, and (3) owners should show significantly greater recall of favorable statements and greater underrecall of those with opposite content.

None of these predictions was supported, with the exception of a finding that new owners showed higher recall of the dealer advertisement. While there was no apparent dissonance over the choice of Chevrolet over other makes, there were substantial doubts that the price paid was as low as it might have been had more bargaining been undertaken. Widespread concern was voiced over this point.

This study is open to the criticism that dissonance should not be expected in the purchase of a popular make of automobile. The argument is that most people should feel that they cannot really go wrong with any of the low-priced three. The decision to buy a lesser known make (perhaps an import) should, accordingly, be quite different. Many people in the automobile industry, however, are of the conviction that dissonance can occur *regardless* of the make; in fact, Brown has reported that the Ford Motor Company designates certain advertisements for new purchasers for this reason.[43] In addition, the above study was replicated with new purchasers of Volkswagens, and no evidence of dissonance was found.[44]

There have been two recent studies which have shed some additional light. Both were undertaken to assess the effects of postpurchase messages sent by retailers. In one it was found that those who received positive reinforcing information showed lower instances of backout or cancellations.[45] In the other it was felt that the posttransaction letter helped to reduce dissonance.[46] It should be noted, however, that the information was not sought by consumers in either study, and it is difficult to state whether or not it was used for dissonance reduction.

These findings do not provide a definitive explanation for the common

---

[43] George H. Brown, "The Automobile Buying Decision within the Family," in N. N. Foote (ed.), *Household Decision-Making* (New York: New York University Press, 1961), pp. 193–199.

[44] J. F. Engel, " 'Further Pursuit of the Dissonant Consumer': A Comment," *J. Marketing*, vol. 20, p. 17 (1965).

[45] J. H. Donnelly, Jr., and J. M. Ivancevich, "Post-Purchase Reinforcement and Back-Out Behavior," *J. Marketing Research*, vol. 7, pp. 399–400 (1970).

[46] S. B. Hunt, "Post-Transaction Communications and Dissonance Reduction," *J. Marketing*, vol. 34, pp. 46–51 (1970).

observation that new purchasers do attend to marketing literature. Caution should be exercised in assuming that dissonance reduction is the reason. It is more probable that the owner will be "set" to notice advertisements, for example, more than he otherwise would be, simply because of the fact that an important new product has entered his life. This is a common phenomenon that probably is unrelated to dissonance.

(3) **Marketing Implications**   It is obvious that the evidence to date has raised more questions than it has answered. While readership of advertisements after purchase to reduce dissonance has not been demonstrated convincingly, this possibility still remains. Moreover, the dissonant purchaser could turn to many other information sources, including dealer literature of all types. Manufacturers should be cognizant of this possibility, and there may be justification for preparing special communication materials for this purpose. The danger in not doing so, of course, is that the individual may otherwise become dissatisfied with his purchase and not make a repeat purchase in the future.

Yet, one should be cautious about assuming that special communications materials are needed for those engaging in postdecision search. These consumers, in effect, are searching for the main selling points which probably appear in most advertisements and other forms of selling material. Given this fact there is no need for special communications in most instances. Perhaps the only major exception is a stress on product superiority in instruction manuals and other material enclosed in the package to be read by the new owners. In addition, some manufacturers follow the practice of sending a letter to consumers shortly after purchase to assert once again the wisdom of their choice.

The Methodological Problems of Dissonance Research   The theory of cognitive dissonance has generated more research in social psychology than any other recent theoretical contribution. This explains, in part, why there have been so many published applications in marketing. Indeed, it has almost become a fad. Over 15 years of experience with this theory, however, have given rise to methodological insights that have largely been ignored in recent applications of this theory to marketing. Some serious methodological critiques have been published, and the major conclusions are worthy of review.[47]

To illustrate some of the problems it is useful to evaluate one experiment which was designed to test four main hypotheses through use of a complex factorial design:[48]

(1)   Individuals with low inducement to buy will experience greater dissonance than those with high inducement.

---

[47]   E. Aronson, "Dissonance Theory: Progress and Problems," in Abelson *et al., op. cit.,*[6] pp. 5–27; N. Chapanis and A. Chapanis, "Cognitive Dissonance: Five Years Later," *Psychological Bull.,* vol. 61, pp. 1–22 (1964); S. T. Margulis and E. Songer, "Cognitive Dissonance: A Bibliography of Its First Decade," *Psychological Reports,* vol. 24, pp. 923–935 (1969).

[48]   Holloway, *op. cit.*[28]

(2) Individuals exposed to a condition of high anticipated dissonance will reflect greater dissonance than their counterparts.

(3) Individuals to whom additional positive information is provided during the process of decision making will experience less dissonance than others.

(4) A condition of high cognitive overlap will create more dissonance than low cognitive overlap (that is, greater dissonance was anticipated when alternatives were essentially similar).

With the exception of the fourth hypothesis, these are straightforward applications of the findings discussed earlier.

The research design encompassed a situation in which individuals were told that a battery was dead and could not be recharged; thus they must buy a new one if they expected to operate their automobile. Then various manipulations were performed regarding the alternatives and their features. Price and warranties were varied, for example. Dissonance presumably was measured by changes in ratings of preferred and nonpreferred brands.

While this design is ingenious, it raises some serious questions. It will be recalled that dissonance should occur only when (1) the individual is committed to a choice, (2) the action is psychologically important, (3) the individual is under complete volition, that is, he retains freedom of choice and action, and (4) there are several alternatives, each of which has distinct features. It is doubtful that these criteria were demonstrated in this experiment.

In the first place, are consumers committed to a brand of automobile battery? In other words, is this product sufficiently important that they would experience dissonance if forced to purchase some other brand? It is questionable that commitment to a brand of automobile battery should have been anticipated, and there is no evidence cited whatsoever.

Second, the choice situation hardly can be construed as voluntary. If an individual were on a trip and wanted to continue, he would purchase whatever battery he could get. If his preferred brand were not available, this would not deter the purchase. Moreover, his brand preference, if indeed one existed, probably would not be challenged because of the fact that he did not have complete freedom of choice to consider other alternatives. His preferences never were put to the test.

Finally, a condition of high cognitive overlap should lead to *less*, not *more*, dissonance as was predicted. The researcher's prediction at this point deviated from the theory being tested.

One additional comment should be made. Dissonance presumably was demonstrated if attitudes toward the various brands changed. Yet, it is now known that dissonance can be reduced in many ways, and attitude change is only one possibility.[49] Alternative modes of dissonance reduction should have been permitted.

---

[49] I. D. Steiner and H. H. Johnson, "Relationships among Dissonance Reducing Responses," *J. Abnormal and Social Psychology*, vol. 68, pp. 38–44 (1964).

The purpose here is not to criticize one study, because most of the published experiments suffer from similar limitations. Rather, it is to call attention to the rigorous requirements of experimental research if this theory is to be tested. The requirements are so demanding, in fact, that many researchers discount most of the evidence.

One final point must be made, and it pertains to the requirement of demonstrating commitment. If there is no commitment, there will be no dissonance.[50] Commitment, in turn, cannot be *assumed*; it must be *measured*. Often this is totally overlooked. The Sherif method was suggested in Chapter 11 as one promising method for this purpose,[51] and other approaches can be used as well.

SUMMARY

Several primary consequences of a purchase decision have been investigated in this chapter: (1) triggering of new behavior and (2) postpurchase evaluation (reward and satisfaction and postdecision dissonance).

Because of unusually heavy emphasis in the published literature on postdecision dissonance, this outcome of purchase was evaluated at length. There are some marketing implications, especially in the area of postdecision information search. It was necessary to put forth in some detail the requirements and assumptions of the theory of cognitive dissonance. This theory more than any other pertains to the outcomes of an act, so it is uniquely applicable to the phenomena discussed here. It is apparent, however, that research is hampered by real difficulties, and future efforts must be based on important recent methodological and theoretical insights.

REVIEW AND DISCUSSION QUESTIONS

1. What types of behavior can be triggered by a purchase other than those mentioned in the chapter? What implications can you suggest for marketing management?

2. What is meant by the statement, "Manufacturers and resellers are well advised to undertake research that leads to a greater understanding of the *total purchase act*?"

3. The brand manager for a laundry detergent sees an article on cognitive dissonance and goes to his advertising agency with the question of whether or not consumers of this product should experience dissonance. What would your answer be? How would you arrive at this conclusion?

4. Would dissonance be likely if the product in question 3 were a new stereophonic sound system featuring speakers no larger than a book? Why or why not?

---

[50] Brehm and Cohen, *op. cit.*,[20] p. 300.

[51] C. W. Sherif, M. Sherif, and R. E. Nebergall, *Attitude and Attitude Change* (Philadelphia: Saunders, 1965).

5. Assuming that dissonance is experienced by a purchaser of the stereo set mentioned in question 4, what would be the possible outcomes? Would the purchaser search for consonant or discrepant information? What would determine his course of action in information search?

6. Assume that a research report indicates a pronounced tendency for purchasers of power lawn mowers to notice advertisements for their brand. What explanations could you offer? What are the implications, if any, for advertising management?

7. What is an expectancy? How are expectancies formed regarding products and services?

8. Research documents the fact that consumers were surprised to discover the excellent sound output of the small speakers in the stereophonic system mentioned in question 4. Is this finding necessarily favorable? Explain.

9. Some tentative findings indicate that satisfaction with a product increases to the extent that the consumer has expended considerable shopping effort. What would you recommend if you were research director for a large retail department store chain?

10. What is meant by commitment? Why is it so important if cognitive dissonance is to be demonstrated?

11. What are the requirements of research in cognitive dissonance? What difficulties are presented when this theory is applied to marketing?

Additional Dimensions
of
Consumer Behavior

Throughout this book, attention has been primarily directed at
discovering how an individual consumer decides to purchase one
product and brand from the range of choices available to him. For
analytical purposes the focus has usually been on the individual,
although the importance of environmental influences and market
segments has also been emphasized.

In Chapters 23 and 24 the emphasis shifts. Specifically, greater
attention is given to aggregates of consumers and the time
dimension of decision making.

Chapter 23 presents an overview of brand loyalty. The chapter
describes various attempts at defining brand loyalty and summarizes
the variables that have been employed in an attempt to understand
the variation in loyalty between customers and across products.
Various stochastic models relating some of these correlates to
measures of brand loyalty are also discussed, along with the
implications of loyalty for marketing strategy.

Chapter 24 analyzes the diffusion of innovations, or how adoption
of a new product spreads through the population. The chapter

demonstrates that the process is a learning process that is influenced by the nature of interaction with the social system through which the innovation is being diffused. Fortunately, there has been considerable research in a variety of disciplines which have studied this phenomenon. This chapter describes these findings and indicates how they are applied by marketing organizations to the introduction of new products.

CHAPTER **23**

BRAND LOYALTY*

Brand loyalty—the tendency of some consumers to purchase a particular brand consistently—has intrigued marketers for decades. How important is brand loyalty? Why does it occur? Are certain consumers more "loyal prone" than others? If so, do they constitute an identifiable market segment? The present chapter attempts to answer these and other related questions.

The discussion begins with a consideration of the meaning of brand loyalty and research results supporting the existence of the phenomenon. The second section analyzes the structural and behavioral correlates of brand loyalty. Various stochastic models relating some of these correlates to various measures of brand loyalty are presented in the third section. The chapter closes with a brief discussion of marketing strategy implications.

NATURE OF BRAND LOYALTY

Whether brand loyalty exists, and, of course, the extent to which it exists, depend partly on how it is defined. Definitions that have been used include (1) brand-choice sequences, (2) proportion of purchases, (3) repeat-purchase probabilities, (4) brand preferences over time, and other definitions. This section dis-

---

* The authors gratefully acknowledge the contributions of Professor B. Venkatesh of the University of Wisconsin in revising and extending this chapter.

cusses these approaches, notes their strengths and limitations, and presents a new approach that may obviate some of the weaknesses of past definitions.

Brand-Choice Sequences

The first major study of brand loyalty was published by Brown in 1952 and 1953 in a series of articles in *Advertising Age*.[1] His results were based on purchase records of 100 households from the *Chicago Tribune* panel, reporting on such frequently purchased items as coffee, orange juice, soap, and margarine. For each product category, each household making five or more purchases was placed in one of four brand-loyalty categories depending on the sequence of brands purchased. Thus, if *A,B,C,D,E,F,* . . . are various brands in a particular product category, then[2]

(1) *Undivided loyalty* is the sequence AAAAA.
(2) *Divided loyalty* is the sequence ABABAB.
(3) *Unstable loyalty* is the sequence AAABBB.
(4) *No loyalty* is the sequence ABCDEF.

Using this definition of brand loyalty, Brown observed that the percentage of households demonstrating some degree of loyalty varied from 54 to 95 percent, depending on the product involved. In fact, the percentage of households that were undividedly loyal varied from 12 percent to 73 percent across products.

More recently, other variants of the brand-choice sequence approach were reported by Tucker[3] and Stafford.[4] They defined brand loyalty as three successive choices of the same brand and were able to document the existence of loyalty defined in this manner.

Proportion of Purchases

Cunningham used the proportion of total purchases within a given product category devoted to the most frequently purchased brand (or set of brands) as a definition, as well as a measure, of brand loyalty.[5] Thus, in addition to providing a more quantifiable measure of brand loyalty than the one proposed

---

[1] George Brown, "Brand Loyalty—Fact or Fiction?" *Advertising Age*, vol. 23, pp. 53–55 (June 19, 1952); pp. 45–47 (June 30, 1952); pp. 54–56 (July 14, 1952); pp. 46–48 (July 28, 1952); pp. 56–58 (Aug. 11, 1952); pp. 80–82 (Sept. 1, 1952); pp. 82–86 (Oct. 6, 1952); pp. 76–79 (Dec. 1, 1952); pp. 75–76 (Jan. 26, 1953).

[2] Brown, *op. cit.*,[1] p. 75 (Jan. 26, 1953).

[3] W. T. Tucker, "The Development of Brand Loyalty," *J. Marketing Research*, vol. 1, pp. 32–35 (Aug. 1964).

[4] James E. Stafford, "Effect of Group Influences on Consumer Brand Preferences," *J. Marketing Research*, vol. 3, pp. 68–75 (Feb. 1966).

[5] Ross M. Cunningham, "Brand Loyalty—What, Where, How Much? *Harvard Business Rev.*, vol. 34, pp. 116–128 (Jan.–Feb. 1956); Ross Cunningham, "Customer Loyalty to Store and Brand," *Harvard Business Rev.*, vol. 39, pp. 127–137 (Nov.–Dec. 1961).

by Brown, Cunningham was able to introduce the concept of multibrand loyalty. *Dual*-brand loyalty, according to his definition, would be the percent of total purchases devoted to the two most favorite brands; *triple*-brand loyalty refers to the three most favorite brands; and so on. Using *Chicago Tribune* panel data and product categories similar to those studied by Brown, Cunningham observed a considerable degree of brand loyalty among panel members. He used a similar approach in a later study to investigate "store loyalty."[6] Other researchers, using different panels and products, have also documented the existence of brand loyalty, when defined this way.[7]

Farley has used variations of the proportions of purchases approach.[8] He used two summary measures of brand loyalty, one a cross-sectional measure based on "the average number of brands bought by families of a given product during the period of study," and another, a time-series measure based on "the percent of families in a given market whose favorite brand is different in the first half of the period studied from in the second half." Small values of each measure indciate brand loyalty, whereas large values indicate frequent brand switching.

Others have employed measures similar to the ones used by Farley. For example, Tate has used a parallel definition to investigate store loyalty.[9] Similarly, Massy, Montgomery, and Morrison report the use of a definition wherein a consumer is considered brand loyal if his preferred brand during the first half of the period under study is the same as the one during the second half, preferred brand being defined as the one which is purchased most often in a given period.[10]

Brand Preference

In contrast to the previously mentioned approaches that employed actual purchase data in defining brand loyalty, Guest used preference statements over time as the criterion.[11] In 1941 he obtained data on brand awareness and preferences from 813 public-school students. Follow-up studies were conducted twelve and twenty years later, and responses were obtained from approximately 160 respondents from the original group. Although the percentage of respondents whose present and past preferences agreed varied widely across products, Guest

---

[6] Ross M. Cunningham, "Customer Loyalty to Store and Brand," *Harvard Business Rev.*, vol. 39, pp. 127–137 (Nov.–Dec. 1961).

[7] Ronald E. Frank, "Is Brand Loyalty a Useful Basis for Market Segmentation?" *J. Advertising Research*, vol. 7, pp. 27–33, at p. 29 (June 1967); William F. Massy, Ronald E. Frank, and Thomas Lodahl, *Purchasing Behavior and Personal Attributes* (Philadelphia: University of Pennsylvania Press, 1968).

[8] John U. Farley, "Why Does Brand Loyalty Vary over Products?" *J. Marketing Research*, vol. 1, pp. 9–14 (Nov. 1964); John U. Farley, "Brand Loyalty and the Economics of Information," *J. Business*, vol. 37, pp. 370–381 (Oct. 1964).

[9] R. S. Tate, "The Supermarket Battle for Store Loyalty," *J. Marketing*, vol. 25, pp. 8–13 (Oct. 1961).

[10] William F. Massy, David B. Montgomery, and Donald G. Morrison, *Stochastic Models of Buying Behavior* (Cambridge, Mass.: M.I.T. Press, 1970), p. 119.

[11] Lester Guest, "A Study of Brand Loyalty," *J. Applied Psychology*, vol. 28, pp. 16–27 (1944); Lester Guest, "Brand Loyalty—Twelve Years Later," *J. Applied Psychology*, vol. 39, pp. 405–408 (1955).

found suggestive evidence of a high degree of loyalty toward brand names.[12] This was especially true when factors such as unavailability, price considerations, and respondent not being the buyer, did not play a major part in brand selection. Jacoby reports at least 15 other studies employing similar definitions of brand loyalty based on brand preference over time.[13]

Other Measures of Loyalty

Several researchers have employed a combination of two or more of the above criteria in defining brand loyalty. Thus, the factor analytic approach employed by Sheth uses a definition of brand loyalty based on both the frequency of purchase of a brand and the pattern of these purchases.[14] Pessemier used an entirely different approach based on the price increase in the most preferred brand relative to the price of the other brands necessary to induce brand switching.[15] Cunningham, on the other hand, attempted to evaluate probable behavior when confronted with the absence of one's favorite brand as an indicator of brand loyalty.[16]

Limitations of Traditional Definitions of Brand Loyalty

The definitions discussed above have one common characteristic: they provide an operational measure of brand loyalty. Unfortunately, however, the large number of approaches causes several problems.

First, it is difficult to compare and synthesize findings. Assume, for example, that two consumers exhibit the following pattern of purchases during a given period:

$$\text{Consumer } 1 = ABCABC$$
$$\text{Consumer } 2 = ABCCCC.$$

The definition—"number of brands purchased during the time period"—would treat both consumers alike. However, the "purchase sequence" definition would treat them differently.

---

[12]   Lester Guest, "Brand Loyalty Revisited: A Twenty Year Report," *J. Applied Psychology,* vol. 48, pp. 93–97 (1964).

[13]   Jacob Jacoby, "Brand Loyalty—A Conceptual Definition," in *Proc. 79th Annual Conv. American Psychological Association* (1971), pp. 655–656.

[14]   John A. Howard and Jagdish N. Sheth, *The Theory of Buyer Behavior* (New York: Wiley, 1969) p. 249; also Jagdish N. Sheth, "A Factor Analytic Model of Brand Loyalty," *J. Marketing Research,* vol. 5, pp. 395–404 (Nov. 1968); Jagdish N. Sheth, "Measurement of Multidimensional Brand Loyalty of a Consumer," *J. Marketing Research,* vol. 7, pp. 348–354 (Aug. 1970).

[15]   Edgar A. Pessemier, "A New Way to Determine Buying Decisions," *J. Marketing,* vol. 24, pp. 41–46 (Oct. 1959).

[16]   Scott M. Cunningham, "Perceived Risk and Brand Loyalty," in Donald F. Cox (ed.), *Risk Taking and Information Handling in Consumer Behavior* (Boston: Harvard University Press, 1967), pp. 507–523.

Why did the second consumer buy brand *C* on each of the last four purchase occasions? Is it because he really prefers brand *C* and has developed a sort of loyalty toward that brand, or is it because the store he patronizes has stopped carrying the other brands? Maybe brand *C* is being promoted with a long series of promotional deals, or the store has rearranged the merchandise, providing a better shelf display for *C*. This illustrates the importance of distinguishing between "intentional loyalty" and "spurious loyalty." As Day points out:

> . . . the spuriously loyal buyers lack any attachment to brand attributes, and they can be immediately captured by another brand that offers a better deal, a coupon, or enhanced point-of-purchase visibility through displays and other devices.[17]

Another basic problem is that most traditional definitions do not deal with multiple-brand loyalty. Although Brown, Cunningham, and a few other pioneers conceived the possibility of loyalty to more than one brand, it has been dealt with seriously only in recent years.[18]

Finally, it seems risky to define and measure loyalty to accommodate empirical data. Instead, once a conceptual framework has been developed, a comprehensive set of relevant variables could be identified and studied.

Extended Definitions of Brand Loyalty

The distinction between intentional and spurious loyalty suggests that repeat purchase behavior is a necessary, but not a sufficient, condition for true or intentional brand loyalty. Day contends that to be truly brand loyal, the consumer must hold a favorable attitude toward the brand in addition to purchasing it repeatedly.[19] Jacoby concurs, suggesting that brand loyalty has at least two primary dimensions—brand loyal behavior and brand loyal attitude:

> Brand loyal behavior is defined as the overt act of selective repeat purchasing based on evaluative psychological decision processes, while brand-loyal attitudes are the underlying predispositions to behave in such a selective fashion. . . . to exhibit brand loyalty implies repeat purchasing behavior based on cognitive, affective, evaluative and predispositional factors. . . .[20]

Following this line of analysis, an extended definition of brand loyalty would be: Brand loyalty is the preferential attitudinal and behavioral response

---

[17]   George S. Day, "A Two-Dimensional Concept of Brand Loyalty," *J. Advertising Research*, vol. 9, pp. 29–35 (Sept. 1969).

[18]   See, for example, Massy *et al., op. cit.;*[7] Sheth, "Measurement of Multidimensional Brand Loyalty of a Consumer," *op. cit.;*[7] A.S.C. Ehrenberg and G. J. Goodhardt, "A Model of Multi-Brand Buying," *J. Marketing Research*, vol. 7, pp. 77–84 (Feb. 1970).

[19]   Day, *op. cit.*[17]

[20]   Jacob Jacoby, "A Model of Multi-Brand Loyalty," *J. Advertising Research*, vol. 11, pp. 25–31 (June 1971).

toward one or more brands in a product category expressed over a period of time by a consumer (or buyer).

This definition has many implications. Foremost is the fact that any measure of brand loyalty should incorporate behavioral as well as attitudinal components. An example is a measure proposed by Day:[21]

$$L_i = \frac{P(B_i)}{KA_i^n} = f(X_a, X_b, \cdots, X_j)$$

where

L_i = brand-loyalty score for *ith* buyer of brand *m*

$P(B)_i$ = proportion of total purchases of product that buyers devoted to brand *m* over period of study

A_i = attitude toward brand *m* at beginning of study, scaled so that a low value represents a favorable attitude

$X_a, \cdots, X_j$ = descriptive variables to be fitted to L_i by least squares

k, n = constants whose values are varied by trial and error to maximize fit between L_i and $X_a, \cdots, X_j$.

Day provides empirical evidence to demonstrate the superiority of such a measure over the traditional approaches that use only purchase data. His measure isolates spurious loyalty and achieves a better statistical fit with a set of descriptive variables.[22]

The extended conceptualization has several other attractive features. First, it explicitly recognizes the existence of multibrand loyalty. Second, brand loyalty is viewed as a *product-specific* phenomenon rather than a general attribute. Thus a consumer may be highly brand loyal in product category X, but not in categories Y or Z.

Third, the definition recognizes that brand loyalty is a temporal phenomenon. Model builders can specify the time span over which the behavior is to be studied. Fourth, the definition focuses on the responses of the decision maker. Since the final consumer need not always be the buyer, it would be difficult otherwise to study the correlates of brand loyalty using data on buyers who are not consumers.

Fifth, the definition proposes a continuum of brand loyalty as opposed to the artificial "loyal–disloyal" dichotomy. Finally, the approach points out the need to incorporate variables affecting brand–loyal attitudes as well as purchase behavior.

---

[21] Day, *op. cit.*[17]

[22] Day, *op. cit.*[17] The student may find it interesting to contrast Day's measure of brand loyalty with the entropy measure proposed by Carman and Stromberg (footnote 29). The latter is based strictly on purchase data and makes no provisions for the attitudinal component.

BRAND LOYALTY CORRELATES

Numerous attempts have been made to determine why brand loyalty varies across consumers and products. This section summarizes the consumer, shopping pattern and market structure characteristics that are, or are not, associated with differential degrees of brand loyalty. Because of the wide variety of definitions of brand loyalty, the following correlates and noncorrelates should be viewed as provisional rather than definitive.

Consumer Characteristics

In one of the earlier studies attempting to identify characteristics of brand–loyal consumers, the Advertising Research Foundation reported results based on toilet-tissue purchasing behavior for 3206 members of the J. Walter Thompson panel.[23] They found virtually no association between personality (as measured by the Edwards personal preference schedule), socioeconomic variables, and household brand loyalty.

Employing the same data source, but analyzing beer, coffee, and tea purchasing behavior, Frank, Massy, and Lodahl observed only a modest association between socioeconomic, demographic, and personality variables and brand loyalty. Using a brand–loyalty score based on a large number of measures of household purchasing behavior, such as number of brands purchased, percent spent on most frequently purchased brands, and so on, they observed some relationships between brand loyalty and certain personality measures from the Edwards test. Thus husbands' and wives' endurance, deference, and succorance scores, wives' need for autonomy and change, and husbands' need for affiliation seem to have been somewhat related to brand loyalty. The overall conclusions of the study, however, were that high brand loyal households apparently have a profile of personality and socioeconomic characteristics that is virtually identical to that of households exhibiting a lower degree of loyalty.[24]

Frank and Boyd, in their investigation of household brand loyalty to private brands, also concluded that socioeconomic variables could not differentiate between private and manufacturer brand–loyal consumers.[25] Similarly, Coulson found that knowledge of the brand preferences of other family members did not significantly affect whether respondents had a regular brand that was purchased more than others. He also observed that housewives who tended to have a

---

[23] *Are There Consumer Types?* (New York: Advertising Research Foundation, 1964).

[24] Ronald E. Frank, William F. Massy, and Thomas M. Lodahl, "Purchasing Behavior and Personal Attributes," *J. Advertising Research,* vol. 9, pp. 15–24 (Dec. 1969); Ronald E. Frank, "Correlates of Buying Behavior for Grocery Products," *J. Marketing,* vol. 31, pp. 48–53 (Oct. 1967).

[25] Ronald Frank and Harper Boyd, Jr., "Are Private-Brand-Prone Grocery Customers Really Different?" *J. Advertising Research,* vol. 5; pp. 27–35 (Dec. 1965).

regular brand that was purchased more than others, did not differ from other housewives in terms of age or social class.[26] Guest, in his his 20-year study of brand preferences through time, also found that sex, intelligence, or marital status were unrelated to brand loyalty.[27]

In a study attempting to relate the influence of reference groups on brand–loyal behavior, Stafford found no significant relation between level of group cohesiveness and member brand loyalty. However, in the more cohesive groups, the extent and degree of brand loyalty of members was closely related to brand choice behavior of the informal leader.[28]

In a more recent study, Carman used an entropy measure of loyalty based on purchase data alone[29] and the Morgan–Sonquist automatic interaction detector scheme (AID) to analyze the results.[30] On the one hand, he was unable to relate most personality characteristics and consumer mobility—geographic, intergenerational, and social—to brand loyalty. However, he did find some relationships and concluded:

(1) Personal characteristics of consumers will explain differences in store loyalty which in turn is the single most important predictor of brand loyalty.

(2) Loyalty is positively correlated with the extent to which the housewife socializes with her neighbors.

(3) The characteristics of consumers which are associated with brand loyalty differ between products. Thus, a loyal coffee buyer possesses the characteristics representative of high self-confidence. Furthermore, in the case of coffee, reference-group influence is most obvious, with consumers most interested in status being the most loyal. For canned fruits and frozen orange juice, reference-group influence is insignificant.

As a result of the richness of the data bank and the versatility of the AID technique in handling a large number of predictor variables, Carman was able to identify relations that would normally go undetected. For example, he describes the characteristics of the brand loyal coffee buyer as follows:

She respects the food-shopping opinion of her neighbors but, in general, trusts technical sources of food information more than personal sources. . . . (she indicates) stronger home or career orientation. She

---

[26] John S. Coulson, "Buying Decisions within the Family," in Joseph Newman (ed.), *On Knowing the Consumer* (New York: Wiley, 1966), p. 66.

[27] Guest, *op. cit.*[12]

[28] Stafford, *op. cit.*[4]

[29] Their measure θ, based on purchase data alone, is defined as

$$\theta = \sum_{i=1}^{K} P_i \log P_i$$

where P_i is the true proportion of purchases going to brand i and K the number of brands available on the market.

[30] James M. Carman, "Correlates of Brand Loyalty: Some Positive Results," *J. Marketing Research*, vol. 7, pp. 67–76 (Feb. 1970). It should be noted that some Monte Carlo studies with AID raise several questions regarding its unfortunate propensity for capitalizing on specific sample variation.

lives in the better neighborhoods of the shopping area, and she does not cook the kind of meals served in her parent's home. However, she considers herself a permanent part of the neighborhood. Loyal coffee buyers have a higher income consistent with the neighborhood than the nonloyal group. . . . (they have) high self-confidence. These results appear to be in agreement with the hypothesis of Brody and Cunningham[31] that brand loyal coffee consumers should have high self-confidence.[32]

Using the extended attitudinal/behavior measure of brand loyalty described earlier in the chapter, Day also detected significant associations between loyalty and certain consumer characteristics.[33] He found the brand-loyal consumer to be very conscious of the need to economize when buying, confident of her judgments, and older in a smaller than average household (who needs to satisfy the preferences of fewer family members).

Shopping-Pattern Characteristics

Studies have also investigated the relationships between brand loyalty and various shopping-pattern characteristics, including store loyalty, shopping proneness, amount purchased, brand last purchased, and interpurchase time. The results of these studies are summarized below.

As was pointed out above, Carman found that store loyalty was the most important correlate of brand loyalty.[34] Other researchers have also demonstrated the importance of store loyalty in determining brand loyalty.[35] This relationship is due, in part, to the fact that store loyalty tends to restrict the number of brand alternatives available to the consumer. However, Carman maintains that the brand–store loyalty relationship is more complex than the simple reduction in available choices.[36]

Shopping proneness is another characteristic that has been related to brand loyalty.[37] Consumers who are not shopping prone shop in relatively few stores. Within these stores, they tend to remain loyal to a small number of brands rather than make careful choices between the values being offered by these stores.

Studies investigating the relationship between the amount purchased and brand loyalty yield contradictory findings. Based on the purchase habits of 66 households in seven product categories including soap, cleansers, coffee, peas,

---

[31] Robert P. Brody and Scott M. Cunningham, "Personality Variables and the Consumer Decision Process," *J. Marketing Research*, vol. 5, pp. 50–57 (Feb. 1968).

[32] Carman, *op. cit.*,[30] pp. 73–74.

[33] Day, *op. cit.*[17]

[34] Carman, *op. cit.*,[30] pp. 69–71.

[35] Tanniru R. Rao, "Consumer's Purchase Decision Process: Stochastic Models," *J. Marketing Research*, vol. 6, pp. 321–329 (Aug. 1969).

[36] Carman, *op. cit.*[30]

[37] Carman, *op. cit.*[30]

margarine, orange juice, and head-ache remedies, Cunningham found very little relationship between purchasing activity and brand loyalty.[38] Massy, Frank, and Lodahl report similar findings for coffee and beer, although they found some association between activity and brand loyalty for tea.[39] In contrast, Kuehn, using frozen orange juice purchases from a *Chicago Tribune* panel of 650 households, found that brand loyalty was higher for heavy purchasers than for light purchasers.[40] Day, in a more recent study using certain convenience foods, also found that true brand-loyal buyers were also heavy users of the products.[41]

Several studies have investigated the relationship between interpurchase time and brand loyalty. Based on purchases of frozen orange juice, Kuehn observed that the probability of a consumer's buying the same brand on two consecutive purchases (a measure of brand loyalty) decreased exponentially with an increase in time between these purchases.[42] Morrison[43] and Carman,[44] on the other hand, observed no significant change in brand loyalty as the time between purchases varied. These contradictory findings may very well be due to the use of different product categories by these researchers.

Finally, attempts have been made to relate factors such as perceived risk and cognitive dissonance to brand loyalty. Thus, Sheth and Venkatesan, based on a laboratory study, suggest that "perceived risk is a necessary condition for the development of brand loyalty. The sufficient condition is the existence of well-known market brands on which the consumer can rely."[45] Using a different laboratory experiment, Mittelstaedt suggests that brand loyalty may be a function of the dissonance experienced at the time of purchase, and that the experience coupled with its subsequent reduction may lead one to repeat a choice.[46]

Market-Structure Characteristics

Several studies have investigated the relationship between brand loyalty and certain market-structure characteristics, such as the availability of brands, price fluctuations, and dealing activity. The importance of these types of variables was demonstrated by Farley's study of the purchases of 199 families in 17 diverse product categories.[47] He found that:

---

[38] Cunningham, *op. cit.*[5]

[39] Massy *et al., op. cit.*[7]

[40] Alfred A. Kuehn, "Consumer Brand Choice as a Learning Process," *J. Advertising Research*, vol. 2, pp. 10–17 (Dec. 1962).

[41] Day, *op. cit.*[17]

[42] Kuehn, *op. cit.*[40]

[43] Donald G. Morrison, "Interpurchase Time and Brand Loyalty," *J. Marketing Research*, vol. 3, pp. 289–291 (Aug. 1966).

[44] James M. Carman, "Brand Switching and Linear Learning Models," *J. Advertising Research*, vol. 6, pp. 23–31 (June 1966).

[45] Jagdish N. Sheth and M. Venkatesan, "Risk Reduction Process in Repetitive Consumer Behavior," *J. Marketing Research*, vol. 5, pp. 307–310 (Aug. 1968); Cunningham, *op. cit.*[16]

[46] Robert Mittelstaedt, "A Dissonance Approach to Repeat Purchasing Behavior," *J. Marketing Research*, vol. 6, pp. 444–446 (Nov. 1969).

[47] Farley, "Why Does Brand Loyalty Vary Over Products?" *op. cit.*[8]

(1) Consumers tended to be less loyal toward products with many available brands, where number of purchases and dollar expenditures per buyer are high, where prices are relatively active, and where consumers might be expected to simultaneously use a number of brands of the product.

(2) Consumers tend to be loyal in markets where brands tend to be widely distributed, and where market share is concentrated heavily in the leading brand.

Based on these findings Farley concluded that:

> Much of the apparent difference over products in some important aspects of brand choice can apparently be explained on the basis of structural variables describing the markets in which the products are sold, and does not depend on specific characteristics of the products or on attitudes of consumers towards products.

Other researchers have also found relationships between market characteristics and brand loyalty. For example, Day found that the true brand-loyal buyer was less influenced by day-to-day price fluctuations and special deals than were others.[48]

Not all researchers, however, are convinced of the influence of market structure variables on brand loyalty. Thus, if brand loyalty were successful in building up the resistance of buyers to switch to other brands in the face of changes in market conditions, one would expect that the elasticities for loyal buyers with respect to some of the major market structure variables would be less than those for the nonloyal group. Massy and Frank, however, found no statistically significant difference between the price, dealing, and retail advertising elasticities for families who were brand loyal and those who were not.[49]

Moreover, another study casts doubts on Farley's conclusions concerning the relationship between brand loyalty and the number of brands available in the market. Specifically, a laboratory experiment conducted by Anderson, Taylor, and Holloway found that the greater the number of alternatives available, the greater the concentration on the most frequently chosen alternative.[50]

Brand Loyalty Correlates: Summary and Critical Appraisal

The major conclusions that can be drawn concerning the correlates of brand loyalty are:

(1) Socioeconomic, demographic, and psychological variables generally do not distinguish brand-loyal consumers from other consumers when traditional definitions of brand loyalty are used.

---

[48] Day, *op. cit.*[17]

[49] William F. Massy and Ronald E. Frank, "Short Term Price and Dealing Effects in Selected Market Segments," *J. Marketing Research,* vol. 2, pp. 171–185 (May 1965).

[50] Lee K. Anderson, James R. Taylor, and Robert J. Holloway, "The Consumer and His Alternatives: An Experimental Approach," *J. Marketing Research,* vol. 3, pp. 62–67 (Feb. 1966).

(2) When extended definitions of brand loyalty are used, some socio-economic, demographic, and psychological variables are related to loyalty. However, these relationships tend to be product specific rather than ubiquitous across product categories.

(3) There is limited evidence that the loyalty behavior of an informal group leader affects the behavior of other group members.

(4) Store loyalty is commonly associated with brand loyalty. Moreover, store loyalty appears to be an intervening variable between certain consumer characteristics and brand loyalty. In other words, certain consumer characteristics are related to store loyalty which in turn is related to brand loyalty.

(5) There is some evidence that brand loyalty is inversely related to the number of stores shopped.

(6) The relationship between amount purchased and brand loyalty is uncertain because of contradictory findings.

(7) The relationship between interpurchase time and brand loyalty is also uncertain due to contradictory findings.

(8) There is limited evidence that perceived risk is positively related to brand loyalty.

(9) Market structure variables, including the extensiveness of distribution and the market share of the leading brand, exert a positive influence on brand loyalty.

(10) The effects of the number of alternative brands, special deals, and price activity are uncertain due to contradictory findings.

The fact that many of the findings concerning brand-loyalty correlates are inconclusive and/or contradictory is due, in part, to the infancy of this type of research and, hence, the absence of a widely accepted research tradition. Future research efforts might be more productive if certain guidelines were adopted.

First, the absence of a standardized definition is probably responsible for some of the contradictions. Each measure quantifies varying aspects of brand loyalty, and, as such, studies employing different measures do not necessarily provide compatible results. Does the absence of statistically significant differences between brand-loyal and disloyal consumers reflect the actual lack of differences or the inability of the definitions and measures to produce realistic distinctions between groups of buyers? In a group of consumers with high brand-loyalty scores as traditionally measured, a substantial proportion of the subjects may be *spuriously loyal*. As a group these consumers may differ from *truly loyal* consumers. However, when both groups are treated together as a homogeneous segment, attempts to identify the characteristics of this segment may be unsuccessful. Therefore, the extended conceptualization of brand loyalty encompassing both brand-loyal behavior and brand-loyal attitude appears to be the most promising way to define the phenomenon.

Second, in attempting to isolate correlates, the evidence suggests that brand loyalty should be treated as a product-specific rather than a general attribute. Many studies have demonstrated that correlates vary across products. Thus, attempts to determine characteristics of consumers who are brand loyal across all product categories are confounded by inherent product differences. As such, a study based on product X showing a relationship between brand loyalty and certain characteristics is not necessarily contradicting another study based on product Y that concludes that the same characteristics are unrelated to brand loyalty.

Third, studies based on correlations generally do not permit the researcher to impute cause and effect relationships. The latter require carefully controlled laboratory and field experiments. Greater use of panels specifically designed for a longitudinal analysis of brand loyalty (as contrasted with existing commercial panels) would probably accelerate progress.

Finally, progress may be improved by the use of more powerful statistical techniques. Simplistic analysis based on proportions and rank correlations should at least be supplemented with factor analysis, regression analysis, AID analysis, discriminant analysis, and various clustering approaches.[51]

BRAND LOYALTY MODELS

Since 1958 a wide variety of mathematical models have been designed in an attempt to understand brand–loyalty behavior over time. The primary emphasis has been on stochastic models, that is, models with built-in probability components.[52] Pioneering attempts were made in this area by Lipstein and Kuehn.[53] Since then other sophisticated models have been developed.

Following a brief overview of the basic logic and terminology of models, this section examines the most widely used ones, describing them and pointing out their strengths and limitations.[54] The section closes with a discussion of potentially useful areas for future research.[55]

Overview of Brand-Loyalty Models

The models that follow describe a functional relationship between the probability of choosing a brand during a purchase occasion and the factors that

---

[51] The above problems plague many other areas of consumer research in addition to brand loyalty. Consequently, they will be discussed in greater detail in the concluding chapter.

[52] Stochastic models treat the response in the marketplace as the outcome of some probabilistic process. These may be contrasted with deterministic models, wherein an attempt is made to predict behavior in exact, or nonprobabilistic, terms.

[53] Benjamin Lipstein, "The Dynamics of Brand Loyalty and Brand Switching," in *Proc. 5th Annual Conf. Advertising Research Foundation* (New York: The Foundation, 1959); Alfred A. Kuehn, "An Analysis of the Dynamics of Consumer Behavior and Its Implications for Marketing Management," unpublished doctoral dissertation (Pittsburgh: Carnegie Institute of Technology, 1958).

[54] For an excellent summary of these models, see Massy *et al., op. cit.*[10]

[55] Although many brand-loyalty models involve sophisticated mathematical techniques, this section assumes only a modest understanding of quantitative techniques. The reader with an advanced background is referred to the sources cited for each model.

have an effect on this probability.[56] Some of these factors include feedback from past purchases, influence of exogenous market forces, and factors indigenous to various households.

Purchase-event feedback is normally expressed in terms of the number of previous purchases that are allowed to have an effect on the present purchase. The effect of market forces is normally incorporated in the form of a time trend term in the model. Finally, population heterogeneity is treated by allowing the parameters of a given model to have a distribution over the entire population, by a priori dividing the population into more homogeneous groups and developing model parameters separately for each group, or by explicitly including in the model some of the factors causing heterogeneity. The models presented below cover a wide range of complexity, from the very simple Bernoulli model that treats the population as being homogeneous, with no purchase event feedback and no effect of external factors, to the more complex probability diffusion models that permit inclusion of effects due to most of these factors.

Bernoulli Models

The original investigators of brand loyalty[57] assumed, at least implicitly, that the behavior could be described as a Bernoulli process where the consumer is assumed to have a constant probability p of purchasing the brand under study. The probability p is determined from aggregate brand choice data and is assumed to be independent of all external influences, prior purchases, or consumer characteristics. These early models offered limited insight into the dynamics of brand loyalty and, although they fit some data well, generally they have been abandoned in favor of more complex and realistic models.

Modifications to the Bernoulli Model Several variations of the basic Bernoulli model have been developed by explicitly considering the heterogeneity in the population. One variation is called the compound Bernoulli model, where the probability p, while being constant for each particular individual, varies over the entire population according to some prespecified probability distribution. In other words, different individuals in the population are permitted to have different fixed values of p.[58]

In another variation—termed the dynamic Bernoulli model—the purchase

---

[56] In *Stochastic Models of Buying Behavior*, Massy, Montgomery, and Morrison provide a clear distinction between "brand choice models" and "purchase incidence models." Whereas the former deal with the probability of choosing a brand on a given purchase occasion, the latter are concerned with purchase timing and amount of purchase. Although brand choice models may be modified to include purchase timing, specialized purchase incidence models are often more useful when describing specific sales prediction during a given period. Because of the greater relevance of brand choice models to our discussion, the presentation is limited to models in this category. For a thorough analysis of some of the purchase incidence models, including the negative binomial, Poisson, logistic, exponential and others, the student is referred to Chapters 8 through 11.

[57] Brown, *op. cit.;*[1] Cunningham, *op. cit.*[5]

[58] Massy *et al., op. cit.,*[10] p. 59.

probability p is not only allowed to vary between individuals, but is also allowed to change from one purchase situation to another for the same individual.[59]

The basic model as well as its variations all assume a "zero-order process," that is, they assume that past history has no effect on the present or future purchase probability. As will soon become apparent, this assumption limits the usefulness of the model in most situations.

Markov Models

In contrast with Bernoulli models, Markov models consider the influence of past purchases on the probability of current purchases. The number of previous purchases that are assumed to affect the current purchase is designated by the *order* of the model. For example, first order means the last purchase, second order means the last two purchases, and so on.

The First-Order Stationary Markov Model To illustrate the characteristics of a first-order Markov model, consider a product category with three brands: *A, B,* and *C*. Based on past purchase data for a sample of consumers, the researcher estimates the conditional (or transitional) probabilities of moving from one state to another in *any two* consecutive time periods. These transitional probabilities are shown in Table 23.1.

Table 23.1 HYPOTHETICAL MARKOV
TRANSITIONAL PROBABILITIES

	Next Purchase			
Last Purchase	*A*	*B*	*C*	*Total*
A	0.7	0.1	0.2	1.0
B	0.3	0.6	0.1	1.0
C	0.4	0.1	0.5	1.0

Table 23.1 is interpreted as follows. If a consumer purchased brand *A* during a certain period, then during the next period there is a 70-percent chance that he will buy *A* again, a 10-percent chance of buying *B*, and a 20-percent chance of buying *C*. Similarly, a buyer of brand *B* during the last period would have a 30-percent probability of buying *A* during the next period, a 60-percent chance of buying *B*, and a 10-percent chance of buying *C*.

Table 23.1 is called a transitional matrix. It is essentially a measure of brand-switching (or conversely, brand-loyal) behavior. Most Markov models assume that the matrix is stationary, that is, the transition probabilities remain unchanged through time.

---

[59] Ronald A. Howard, "Dynamic Inference," *J. Operations Research Society of America*, vol. 13, pp. 712–733 (Sept. 1965).

To illustrate the mechanics of the Markov process, it is useful to compute the probabilities of a consumer's purchasing brands A, B, or C during future purchase periods, given the actual purchase during the present period. Thus, if the consumer's purchased brand A during period I, the probability of buying the dffierent brands during periods II, III, IV, and V would be as follows:[60]

| Period | Brand | | |
	A	B	C
II	0.70	0.10	0.20
III	0.60	0.15	0.25
IV	0.57	0.17	0.26
V	0.55	0.19	0.26

On the other hand, if brand B was purchased during period I, the corresponding probabilities for future periods would be as follows:

| Period | Brand | | |
	A	B	C
II	0.30	0.60	0.10
III	0.43	0.40	0.17
IV	0.49	0.30	0.21
V	0.52	0.25	0.23

Similar computations could be made for brand C by following the procedures outlined in footnote 60.

If this process were continued indefinitely, the probabilities of the consumer being in states A, B, and C during future periods will approach a set of equilibrium, or "steady-state" values. These steady-state probabilities are inde-

---

[60] These probabilities can be computed by methods of matrix algebra or by simply tracing behavior by means of a tree diagram. Only sample computations are shown below.

For a consumer buying A during period I, the probabilties during period II are obvious. The probability of his buying A during period III would be .7 × .7 + .1 × .3 + .2 × .4 = .60; for B it would be 0.7 × 0.1 + 0.1 × 0.6 + 0.2 × 0.1 = 0.15; and for C it would be 0.7 × 0.2 + 0.1 × 0.1 + 0.2 × 0.5 = 0.25. For the student familiar with matrix algebra, all nine probabilities for period III (three each for different purchases during period I) can be obtained by multiplying the transition matrix by itself. The new matrix can be postmultiplied by the original transition matrix to obtain probabilities for period IV.

The probabilities that we have computed here should not be confused with the transition matrix probabilities. The latter simply refer to the effect of the *immediately preceding* purchase expressed in the form of the probability of purchase during the next period. The probabilities that we have computed (using the transition probabilities) correspond to many future periods *given* the actual purchase during the first period and *assuming a stationary transition matrix* between each pair of consecutive periods.

pendent of past history; that is, regardless of the actual purchases during period I, the probability of the consumer's buying *A, B,* or *C* after a theoretically infinite number of transitions would approach a predetermined set of values dependent only on the transition matrix. For the transition matrix in the example, these steady state probabilities would be 0.54, 0.20, and 0.26.[61]

For a more detailed discussion of Markov models and their characteristics, the reader is referred to the work of Herniter and Magee,[62] Maffei,[63] Lipstein,[64] Harary and Lipstein,[65] and others noted below.[66]

Criticisms of the First-Order Stationary Markov Model The model described above is plagued with numerous problems. First, since there is evidence that brand choice is influenced by many past purchases, the first-order assumption has been challenged by many as being too restrictive.[67]

Second, the stationarity assumption underlying the transition matrix has been criticized. Thus, although Maffei,[68] and Styan and Smith[69] report the acceptability of the assumption in their research, they have been strongly challenged by Ehrenberg[70] and Massy,[71] the latter concluding that stationarity is the exception rather than the rule.

The homogeneity assumption is another problem. The model assumes that all buyers have the same transition probabilities. Several researchers have demonstrated that homogeneity is inconsistent with empirical evidence.[72]

The aggregation problem is a fourth criticism. This problem occurs

---

[61] The steady-state probabilities p_1, p_2, and p_3 can be derived by solving the following set of simultaneous equations (stated in matrix notation):

$$(p_1 \ p_2 \ p_3) \begin{matrix} 0.7 & 0.1 & 0.2 \\ 0.3 & 0.6 & 0.1 \\ 0.14 & 0.1 & 0.5 \end{matrix} = (p_1 \ p_2 \ p_3)$$

and $p_1 + p_2 + p_3 = 1$.

[62] Jerome D. Herniter and John F. Magee, "Customer Behavior as a Markov Process," *Operations Research,* vol. 9, pp. 105–122 (Jan.–Feb. 1961).

[63] Richard B. Maffei, "Brand Preferences and Simple Markov Processes," *Operations Research,* vol. 8, pp. 210–218 (Mar.–Apr. 1960).

[64] Lipstein, *op. cit.*[53]

[65] F. Harary and B. Lipstein, "The Dynamics of Brand Loyalty: A Markovian Approach," *Operations Research,* vol. 10, pp. 19–40 (Jan.-Feb. 1962).

[66] George P. H. Styan and H. Smith, Jr., "Markov Chains Applied to Marketing," *J. Marketing Research,* vol. 1, pp. 50–55 (Feb. 1964); J. E. Draper and L. H. Nolin, "A Markov Chain Analysis of Brand Preference," *J. Advertising Research,* vol. 4, pp. 33–39 (Sept. 1964); J. S. Stock, "Paired Market Choice Model—A Simplified Approach to Markov Chains," in Henry Gomez (ed.), *Innovation—Key to Marketing Progress* (Chicago: Amer. Marketing Assoc., 1963), pp. 99–105.

[67] See, for example, Howard and Sheth, *op. cit.,*[14] pp. 237–238.

[68] Maffei, *op. cit.*[63]

[69] Styan and Smith, *op. cit.*[66]

[70] A. S. C. Ehrenberg, "An Appraisal of Markov Brand Switching Models," *J. Marketing Research,* vol. 2, pp. 347–362, at p. 353 (Nov. 1965).

[71] William F. Massy, "Order and Homogeneity of Family Specific Brand Switching Processes," *J. Marketing,* vol. 3, pp. 48–54, at p. 53 (Feb. 1966).

[72] See, for example, Ronald E. Frank, "Brand Choice as a Probability Process," *J. Business,* vol. 35, pp. 43–56 (Jan. 1962).

because the probability of a particular consumer's buying a brand is actually inferred from the relative frequency of purchasing that brand in the aggregate sample. In other words, if 60 consumers in a group of 100 buy brand *A*, each of the 100 customers is said to have a 60-percent probability of buying that brand. Howard[73] has suggested a vector Markov model which, while resolving the aggregation problem, necessitates making other unacceptable assumptions.[74]

A fifth problem inherent in Markov models deals with interpurchase time. All consumers cannot be expected to purchase on a precise cycle with a prespecified interpurchase time. Approaches that attempt to overcome this objection include the introduction of a dummy "no purchase" brand to take the place of an actual purchase. However, a purchase versus no purchase decision is different from a brand-choice decision. As a result, Howard[75] has suggested a time-dependent semi-Markov model which explicitly treats time as a random variable. Kuehn and Rohloff[76] and Morrison[77] offer other approaches to incorporate different interpurchase times.

Other criticisms of the first-order Markov model revolve around the problem of inferring transition probabilities for the entire population based on sample estimates. Updating these probabilities, based on other relevant information, also presents problems. Under these conditions, Herniter and Howard recommend use of a Bayesian framework for revising a priori probabilities.[78]

A seventh problem lies in determining how issues such as multiple-brand purchases or multiple purchases of the same brand should be handled. Unfortunately, most of the recommended approaches necessitate forcing actual data into an artificial format suitable for Markov analysis.[79]

Finally, it is difficult to obtain valid purchase data unless expensive longitudinal designs are used.[80] This may limit the profitable use of the model.

Proposed Modifications to the First-Order Markov Model　A variety of attempts have been made to overcome the limitations of the first-order stationary Markov model. The most popular variations are discussed below.

---

[73]　Ronald A. Howard, "Stochastic Process Models of Consumer Behavior," *J. Advertising Research*, vol. 3, pp. 35–40 (Sept. 1963).

[74]　Howard and Sheth, *op. cit.*,[14] pp. 236–237.

[75]　Howard, *op. cit.*,[73] p. 40.

[76]　Alfred A. Kuehn and A. C. Rohloff, "New Dimensions in Analysis of Brand Switching," in Fred E. Webster (ed.), *New Directions in Marketing* (Chicago: Amer. Marketing Assoc., 1965), pp. 297–308.

[77]　Donald G. Morrison, "Interpurchase Time and Brand Loyalty," *J. Marketing Research*, vol. 3, pp. 289–292 (Aug. 1966).

[78]　Jerome D. Herniter and Ronald Howard, "Stochastic Marketing Models," in D. B. Hertz and R. T. Eddison (eds.), *Progress in Operations Research*, vol. 2 (New York: Wiley, 1964).

[79]　See, for example, Draper and Nolin, *op. cit.*,[66] pp. 33–39; Styan and Smith, *op. cit.*,[66] pp. 50–55.

[80]　See, for example, Donald H. Granbois and James F. Engel, "The Longitudinal Approach to Studying Marketing Behavior," in Peter D. Bennett (ed.), *Marketing and Economic Development* (Chicago: Amer. Marketing Assoc., 1965), pp. 205–221.

(1) **Models Overcoming the Stationarity Assumption** Lipstein has attempted to deal with objections to the stationarity assumption by developing a Markov model of brand loyalty that has a nonstationary transition matrix.[81]

(2) **Models Overcoming the Homogeneity Assumption** Morrison has suggested a variety of ways of overcoming the unrealistic homogeneity assumption.[82] One approach is to divide consumers into two groups—hard-core loyal buyers and potential switchers. This dichotomous classification can be extended into a continuum of loyalty, yielding what are generally termed compound Markov models.[83] However, these models require a dichotomous treatment of the brands available, for example, the favorite brand versus all other brands. Examples of transition matrices under these conditions are discussed below.[84]

(a) *The symetric first-order markov model*—In this model the transition matrix appears as follows and p varies over the entire population according to some prespecified probability distribution.[85]

		Brand Purchased at Time $t+1$	
		A	B
Brand Purchased at Time t	A	p	$1-p$
	B	$1-p$	p

where A=brand being studied
   B=all other brands

(b) *The brand-loyal model*—In this model p is distributed as before, but another parameter, $k(0 < k < 1)$, which is the same for all individuals, is also introduced. The reasoning, as seen in the matrix below, is that an individual with a high probability of remaining with his brand A will also have a higher probability of leaving brand B (other brands) to buy A, than another individual with a lower p.

		Time $t+1$	
		A	B
Time t	A	p	$1-p$
	B	kp	$1-kp$

[81] B. Lipstein, "A Mathematical Model of Consumer Behavior," *J. Marketing Research*, vol. 2, p. 259–265 (Aug. 1965); B. Lipstein, "Test Marketing: A Perturbation in the Market Place," *Management Science*, vol. 14, pp. 3437–3448 (1968).

[82] Massy *et al.*, *op. cit.*,[10] pp. 92–93.

[83] Donald G. Morrison, "Testing Brand-Switching Models," *J. Marketing Research*, vol. 3, pp. 401–409 (Nov. 1966).

[84] Massy, *op. cit.*,[10] pp. 118–136.

[85] The β distribution has often been employed for this purpose. For details, see Massey *et al.*, *op. cit.*,[10] pp. 60–61.

(c) *The last purchase loyal model*—This model uses somewhat different logic. It argues that a consumer with a high p is more loyal to the brand he purchased last—regardless of which brand it was—than a consumer with a lower p. (Both k and p are defined as before.)

		Time $t+1$	
		A	B
Time t	A	p	$1-p$
	B	$1-kp$	kp

(d) *The general first-order compound model*—In this model the parameters p and q are jointly distributed according to some prespecified distribution.

		Time $t+1$	
		A	B
Time t	A	p	$1-p$
	B	$1-q$	q

Using the coffee purchases of 531 members of the *Chicago Tribune* panel, Massy, Montgomery, and Morrison obtained a very good fit between the data and "the brand loyal model" described in (b). They concluded that if strong loyalty exists, it is generated toward a particular brand and not toward the most recently purchased brand.[86] In addition, they concluded that loyal consumers are more "Bernoulli" than nonloyals, meaning that recent purchase decisions have a smaller effect on the current purchase decisions of loyals than they do on nonloyals.[87]

(3) **Models Overcoming the First-Order Assumption** Another objection to the basic Markov model is that it is first-order, that is, it considers only the previous purchase when modeling the current purchase situation. One way of overcoming this objection is to use higher order Markov formulations. For example, a second-order Markov model considers the effect of two previous purchases. The transition matrix is as follows:

		Purchases During Times $t-1$ and t			
		AA	BA	AB	BB
Purchases	AA	p_1	—	$1-p_1$	—
During Times	BA	p_2	—	$1-p_2$	—
$t-2$ and $t-1$	AB	—	$1-q_2$	—	q_2
	BB	—	$1-q_1$	—	q_1

---

[86] Massy *et al., op. cit.,*[10] pp. 118–136.

[87] Note that when $k=1$, the brand-loyal model is the same as the Bernoulli model. In other words, the higher the k $(0<k<1)$, the more "Bernoulli" the group of consumers.

Some of the entries in the matrix are blank because the corresponding combinations of states are not possible. For example, a consumer who purchased A in t-2 and B in t-1 could not purchase A in t-1 and either A or B in time t.[88]

Second-order models are unquestionably more realistic than first-order models. However, the data requirements of the higher order models are usually so large that they are unmanageable.

Linear Learning Models

Models in this category are an outgrowth of the work done by Kuehn[89] based on the learning theory constructs of Bush and Mosteller.[90] The primary concept underlying the development of these models is that past brand choices affect future behavior, and that there is a linear relationship between pre- and postpurchase probabilities. More specifically, let the purchasing process be represented in the form of a dichotomous choice A representing the brand under study and B all other brands. Also let p_t be the probability of buying A during trial t. Using subscripts to represent trials, the model specifies two relationships termed the purchase operator and the rejection operator:

purchase operator: $p_{t+1} = \alpha + \beta + \lambda p_t$, if brand A is purchased at t

or

rejection operator: $p_{t+1} = \alpha + \lambda p_t$, if brand B is purchased at t.

These two operators are graphically illustrated in Figure 23.1. The parameters α and β representing the intercepts ($\alpha + \beta$ for the purchase operator and α for the rejection operator) and λ, the common slope, are assumed to be the same for all consumers and are estimated from panel data.

Suppose at trial $t=0$ there is a certain probability p_0 that a particular respondent would buy brand A. If he actually buys brand A during that trial, the probability of his buying A on the next trial is determined by referring to the purchase operator. A perpendicular drawn from p_0 to intersect the purchase operator will yield the probability at t_1 on the Y axis. This can be transferred to the X axis with the help of the 45° line. Now at t_1, suppose the consumer buys a brand other than A (that is, B), the probability of his buying A at trial t_2 can now be obtained by referring to the rejection operator. The purchase probabilities can thus be revised after each purchase by referring to the appropriate operator.

An interesting characteristic of the model is that the purchase probability approaches, but never exceeds, the maximum value p_u (obtained at the intersection of the purchase operator and the 45° line). Similarly it never falls below p_L (obtained at the intersection of the rejection operator and the 45° line). This

---

[88]   The model does not allow the consumer to buy both brands during any one time period.

[89]   Alfred A. Kuehn, *op. cit.*[53]

[90]   Robert Bush and Frederick Mosteller, *Stochastic Models for Learning* (New York: Wiley, 1955).

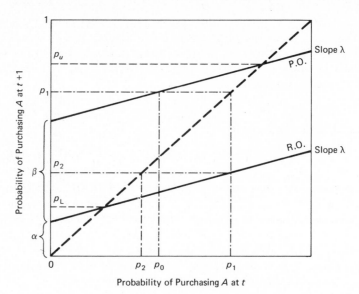

Figure 23.1 GRAPHICAL REPRESENTATION OF LINEAR LEARNING MODEL

is equivalent to saying that consumers generally will not develop such a strong brand loyalty as to ensure either complete acceptance or rejection of a given brand. Another characteristic of the model is that consecutive purchases of brand *A* increase the probability of buying *A* on the next purchase, but only at a decreasing rate.

The model has been tested extensively using many branded nondurable consumer grocery and drug items and was found very useful in analyzing brand-switching data.[91] Practical applications of the model, in the form of analyzing effects of advertising and other merchandising influences, have also been suggested.[92] However, in general, learning models have been less popular than their Markov counterparts, especially among practitioners. This may be due to the fact that it is more difficult to estimate the parameters of the learning model, as well as the limitations imposed by the need to treat brand choice in a dichotomous fashion.

Modifications to the Learning Model Modifications to the basic model include treatment of population heterogeneity, resulting in what is called a compound learning model. Another modification involves recasting the learning

[91] Alfred A. Kuehn and Ralph L. Day, "A Probabilistic Approach to Consumer Behavior," in Revis Cox, Wroe Alderson, and Stanley Shapiro (eds.), *Theory in Marketing* (Homewood: Ill.: Irwin, 1964), pp. 380–390.

[92] See, for example, Alfred A. Kuehn and Ralph L. Day, "Probabilistic Models of Consumer Buying Behavior," *J. Marketing,* vol. 29, pp. 27–31 (Oct. 1964); Alfred A. Kuehn, "How Advertising Performance Depends on Other Marketing Factors," *J. Advertising Research,* vol. 2, pp. 2–10 (Mar. 1962).

model into a special type of first-order Markov formulation.[93] The learning Markov model, so derived, treats the transition probabilities as a function of two effects—a retention effect and a merchandising activity effect. The former represents the fraction of purchases retained by a brand through habit, whereas the latter represents the effect of the brand's merchandising strategy. Finally, under special conditions the linear learning model would degenerate into a Bernoulli or Markov model. Thus if $\lambda = 0$ (the slope of the purchase or rejection operator), the relationships specifying the purchase and rejection operators are equivalent to the transmission matrix:

	time t+1	
	A	B
time t A	$\alpha + \beta$	$1 - \alpha - \beta$
B	α	$1 - \alpha$

Similarly if $\alpha = \beta = 0$ and $\lambda = 1$, $p_{t+1} = p_t$, and we have the simple zero-order Bernoulli model.

Probability Diffusion Model

The probability diffusion model[94] is another recent addition to the list of stochastic models of brand-choice behavior. The model is zero order in that it does not consider purchase-event feedback. It can be described by outlining the major underlying assumptions:

(1) Let the brand-choice behavior be described as a dichotomous selection (as in the case of learning models).

(2) Assume that each respondent possesses a number N of hypothetical elements, some of which are at any given response occasion associated with response A, and the remainder with response B.[95]

(3) If at a particular response occasion t, the respondent has i of his N elements associated with response A, his probability p_t of making response A on that occasion is i/N.

---

[93] Alfred E. Kuehn, "A Model for Budgeting Advertising," in Frank M. Bass *et al.*, (eds.), *Mathematical Models and Methods in Marketing* (Homewood, Ill.: Irwin, 1961), pp. 315–348; A. C. Rohloff, "New Ways to Analyze Brand-to-Brand Competition," in Stephen Greyser (ed.), *Toward Scientific Marketing* (Chicago: Amer. Marketing Assoc., 1963), pp. 224–232.

[94] Massy *et al., op. cit.*,[10] chap. 6.

[95] Although these elements may have behavioral significance, they are proposed strictly as hypothetical constructs for modeling purposes.

(4) The response elements change allegiance between A and B according to a mechanism that can be described as follows:

$$\lambda_i = (\alpha + \sqrt{i}) \, (N-i)$$
$$\mu_i = (\beta + (N-i)\nu)i$$

where:

α = the probability of an element associated with response B to change to A

β = the propensity of change from A to B

ν = a proportionality factor whereby the propensity of each element to change allegiance is increased by an amount for each element associated with the opposite response.

The first expression above is a product of the single-element propensity to change from response B to A and the number of response elements in B. The second expression is interpreted similarly.

The above assumptions, together with the assumption of no purchase feedback and independence of responses of various consumers, lead Montgomery to describe the behavior of the average probability of purchase over time. Thus he shows that the expected value of p_t can be described by the following functional relationship:

$$m(t) = E\left[p(t)\right] = p_j(t_0)e^{-(\alpha+\beta)(t-t_0)} + \frac{\alpha}{\alpha+\beta}\left[1-e^{-(\alpha+\beta)(t-t_0)}\right].$$

In the function, t_0 is the time at which the model was first applied and $p_j(t_0)$ is the initial probability of purchase for individual j. The equation is represented by the curve in Figure 23.2.

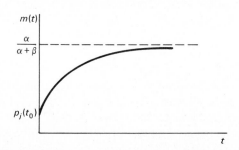

Figure 23.2 BEHAVIOR OF EXPECTED VALUE OF p_t FOR THE PROBABILITY DIFFUSION MODEL OF BRAND LOYALTY

The model represents a change over time in the expected probability of purchase, independent of any purchase feedback effect. The change is therefore assumed to be the result of external environmental factors including promotion.

Modifications to the Probability Diffusion Model The inability of the probability diffusion model to consider purchase event feedback led Jones to develop what he terms a dual-effects model.[96] In essence, Jones proposes a modification to the propensities of change of the response elements as follows:

$$\lambda_i = (\alpha_n + \sqrt{i})\,(N-i)$$
$$\mu_i = [\beta_n + \sqrt{(N-i)}]\,i$$

where subscript n denotes the nth purchase, and α_n and β_n are allowed to change from one purchase to another according to a certain mechanism.[97] Thus a simple mechanism would be

$$\alpha_n = \begin{cases} \alpha_{n-1} + \lambda, & \text{if } A \text{ was purchased at } n \\ \alpha_{n-1}, & \text{if } B \text{ was purchased at } n \end{cases}$$

$$\beta_n = \begin{cases} \beta_{n-1}, & \text{if } A \text{ was purchased at } n \\ \beta_{n-1} + \phi & \text{if } B \text{ was purchased at } n. \end{cases}$$

Using this model, the change in average purchase probability through time can be expressed by the curve in Figure 23.3.

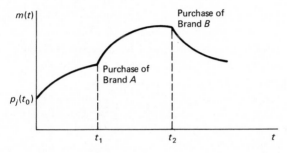

Figure 23.3   BEHAVIOR OF EXPECTED VALUE OF p_i FOR DUAL-EFFECTS MODEL OF BRAND LOYALTY.   J. Morgan Jones, "A Dual-Effects Model of Brand Choice," *J. Marketing Research,* vol. 7, pp. 458–464, at p. 461 (Nov. 1970). Reprinted by permission of the author and the publisher.

Evaluation of Brand-Loyalty Models

From the above discussion it is apparent that a wide variety of models have been employed in an attempt to understand and predict brand–loyalty behavior. Numerous statistical tests have been utilized to demonstrate the goodness of fit of each of the models to empirical data.[98]

It appears that the complexity of brand choice behavior precludes the development of a model that is applicable across a wide variety of product categories and buying situations. Numerous assumptions, discussed in conjunction with each of the models, make the models manageable, but introduce various

---

[96]   J. Morgan Jones, "A Dual-Effects Model of Brand Choice," *J. Marketing Research,* vol. 7, pp. 458–464 (Nov. 1970); also J. M. Jones, "A Comparison of Three Models of Brand Choice," *J. Marketing Research,* vol. 7, pp. 466–473 (Nov. 1970).

[97]   Jones, "A Comparison of Three Models of Brand Choice," *op. cit.*[96]

[98]   For details of these tests, see Massy *et al., op. cit.*[10]

artificialities. The zero-order assumption, suppression of population heterogeneity, and inability to incorporate the influence of external factors are some of the problems associated with many models.

It is also clear that most avoid the issue of multibrand loyalty. Yet many researchers have empirically documented the common-sense notion that some consumers exhibit varying degrees of loyalty to several brands in a product category. For example, using a factor analytic approach, Sheth has demonstrated multibrand loyalty and developed a multidimensional measure of brand loyalty.[99] His approach consists of factor analyzing a consumer X trial data matrix and using the factor scores as measures of brand loyalty. A consumer, regularly buying more than one brand, can yield more than one nonzero factor score, each representing his loyalty score for a brand. Jacoby, on the other hand, uses Sherif's assimilation-contrast model to describe multibrand loyalty.[100] Accordingly, a consumer tends to organize the various brands in a product category into regions of acceptance, rejection, and neutrality, with the acceptance region including the most preferred brand as well as those that are acceptable. Jacoby proposes a relationship between brand loyalty and the distance between the various regions as well as the number of brands in each region. Other recent attempts at treating multibrand loyalty include the works of Ehrenberg and Goodhardt[101] and Massy, Frank, and Lodahl.[102] This trend is refreshing and promises to provide greater understanding of the true nature of brand loyalty.

Finally, the models discussed above do not consider the attitude component of brand loyalty. Only purchase data representing the behavioral component are employed in model construction. This may be one of the factors introducing a degree of artificiality in the models.

In summary, models, while providing a statistically significant fit to data in certain product categories, suffer from oversimplification. Explicit treatment of the influence of marketing variables as well as the differences between individual consumers needs to be emphasized. Also needed is a model (or set of models) that starts out with the determinants of brand loyalty and then attempts to relate these determinants to a valid measure of brand loyalty.

In the future it would seem useful to develop a typology of brand loyalty and focus some attention on explaining the "why" of loyalty as against simply providing correlates of the observed behavior. A plausible typology has been proposed by Engel, distinguishing brand loyalty resulting from inertia, psychological commitment, and marketer strategies.[103] Brand loyalty through inertia may represent an effort to reduce perceived risk and/or certain costs—time, energy, psychological frustration, and so on—incurred in a buying situation. In contrast, brand loyalty through psychological commitment may be the result of

---

[99]   Sheth, "Measurement of Multidimensional Brand Loyalty of a Consumer," *op. cit.*[14]

[100]   Jacoby, *op. cit.*,[20] pp. 25–31.

[101]   A. S. C. Ehrenberg and G. J. Goodhardt, "A Model of Multi-Brand Buying," *J. Marketing Research*, vol. 7, pp. 77–84 (Feb. 1970).

[102]   See Massy *et al.*, *op. cit.*[7]

[103]   James F. Engel, "The Influence of Needs and Attitudes on the Perception of Persuasion," in Greyser, *op. cit.*,[93] pp. 18–29.

factors such as ego involvement, reference-group influence, or a dissonance-reducing strategy. Finally, brand loyalty from marketing strategy may be due to the availability of brands, advertising, or even certain contractual arrangements. More research needs to be done to substantiate or refute these suggested typologies and develop others that may be more relevant.

Finally, an area of research that may benefit from current developments multidimensional scaling is the study of the relationship between brand loyalty and the perceptual and preference structures of consumers. Thus, questions such as the following may be raised and investigated: In a given product category, does the perceptual configuration of brand-loyal consumers differ from disloyal consumers? More specifically, do brand-loyal consumers perceive the various brands in a product category as being substantially dissimilar, whereas disloyal consumers perceive all the brands as being very similar? On the other hand, one may argue, in view of the concept of brand loyalty through inertia, that a brand-loyal consumer may indeed perceive all brands as being very similar and become loyal to one in order to reduce the effort necessary to choose between the many similar brands. A related question may be: Is the object of loyalty perceived as being very different from the other brands? Also, in the case of multiple-brand loyalty, is the consumer loyal to a group of brands that are perceived as being similar, or does he pick a few dissimilar brands and become loyal to them?

MARKETING IMPLICATIONS

Some marketing implications have been discussed throughout the chapter. To avoid being redundant, the discussion that follows is confined to the general implications of brand loyalty to marketing strategists.

Brand loyalty is one way of segmenting a market. For example, some of the ways a manufacturer of brand A could attempt to increase his sales are:

(1) Increase the number of consumers who are loyal to brand A.
(2) Decrease the number of consumers who are loyal to competing brands.
(3) Increase the number of nonloyal consumers who purchase the product to purchase brand A.
(4) Increase the amount purchased among consumers who are loyal to brand A.
(5) Convince those who do not purchase the product to purchase brand A.

Marketing programming to any of these segments is practical only if the consumers comprising these segments are identifiable. In some instances, brand loyalty is not a useful basis for segmenting markets. For example, in the case of grocery products, brand-loyal customers do not seem to differ from other customers in terms of attitudes, personality and socioeconomic characteristics, amount purchased, or sensitivity to pricing, dealing, retail advertising, or the introduction of new brands.[104] However, this finding may not be applicable to other product categories, and may not even hold for individual grocery products if the suggestions articulated in this chapter are implemented.

A previous section of the chapter identified typologies of consumer loyalty. Although the classification is only tentative, it is possible to indicate how marketing strategy would differ between types of loyalties. Thus, if loyalty is attributable to inertia, then significant product improvements, price reductions, effective advertisements pointing out unperceived product benefits, and several other strategies could all trigger a change in buying behavior. In other words, meaningful changes in marketing variables might not be screened out through selective perception, so that it might be possible to change brand loyalty through appropriate promotion, product, and pricing strategies.

These types of strategies, however, are less likely to be effective if loyalty is caused by psychological commitment to a brand. In these situations, the probability that selective attention, comprehension, and recall will weaken the effects of marketing strategies is probably much higher.

To illustrate a somewhat different approach, consider a market where a significant segment of consumers is loyal to a particular brand. Assume that research indicated that these consumers consider certain other brands as falling in their region of acceptance, and the rest of the brands distributed over the regions of neutrality and rejection.

What is the most effective marketing strategy for brands in the various regions? The most preferred ("loyal") brand could emphasize the importance of the product attribute(s) that has led consumers to become loyal to that brand. Marketers of other brands in the region of acceptance could emphasize the comparability between themselves and the "loyal" brand on this attribute(s), and minimize any perceived or real differences. Marketers of brands in the regions of neutrality and rejection, on the other hand, would probably be better advised to focus their efforts on a different product attribute(s), and make that attribute(s) salient.[105]

Finally, consider the relevance of brand loyalty models—the Markov models as a specific example—to the marketing strategist. The transition matrix in the model represents brand switching behavior. In addition to the long run steady-state probabilities, which approximate eventual market shares, a marketer may be particularly interested in the changes that take place in the transition matrix as the result of promotional efforts. Conceptually, the optimum level of promotional effort can be determined by relating changes in transition probabilities to the investment required to bring about the changes.

The transition probabilities also suggest certain general types of marketing strategies. For example, if all the diagonal entries of the matrix are of high magnitude (0.9), the implication is that the marketer should direct his efforts at inducing consumers to try his brand. If a reasonable degree of success is achieved,

[104] Ronald E. Frank, "Is Brand Loyalty a Useful Basis for Market Segmentation?" *J. Advertising Research*, vol. 7, pp. 27–33, at p. 33 (June 1967).

[105] For more details, see Jacoby, *op. cit.*,[20] pp. 30–31.

there is a high probability that these consumers will stay with the brand and become loyal consumers.[106]

SUMMARY

This chapter was concerned with a temporal aspect of consumer behavior —brand loyalty. Researchers define loyalty in a wide variety of ways. Consequently, it is difficult to compare and synthesize findings. Therefore, the need for a new and extended definition of brand loyalty was articulated and a definition incorporating both behavioral and attitudinal components was presented.

Regardless of the precise definition, researchers have found conclusive evidence of the existence of brand loyalty. Attempts to determine the reasons for the variation in loyalty across products and consumers have, however, produced contradictory results. The chapter discussed at length numerous characteristics of consumers, their shopping patterns, and the market structure, that have been investigated by researchers in attempts to identify correlates of brand loyalty. Studies concentrating primarily on the economic, demographic, and social-psychological characteristics of consumers have yielded the most discouraging results.

In recent years, many attempts have been made to develop and/or use stochastic models to relate probabilities of brand choice to factors such as purchase feedback, influence of external marketing activities, and characteristics of consumers. The most popular models were presented and evaluated. Unfortunately, the models usually begin with a mathematical formulation and manipulate empirical data to fit them. Future research in this area needs to concentrate on more valid measures of brand loyalty and an explicit treatment of marketing influences as well as consumer heterogeneity.

Finally, the marketing implications of brand loyalty were discussed. Brand loyalty is a useful way of segmenting markets provided that consumers exhibiting various kinds and degrees of loyalty can be identified and reached profitably. The approach used may vary depending on whether loyalty is due to inertia, psychological commitment, or marketer influence. Finally, it was shown how a Markov model transition matrix can be used to help formulate promotional strategy.

REVIEW AND DISCUSSION QUESTIONS

1. Define or otherwise describe the following: (a) state, (b) brand loyalty, (c) transition probability, (d) stationarity, (e) homogeneity, and (f) psychological commitment.

2. How does the learning model differ from a first-order Markov model?

3. What are the various definitions of brand loyalty? How should brand loyalty be defined?

---

[106] For further discussion, see John U. Farley and Alfred E. Kuehn, "Stochastic Models of Brand Switching," in George Schwartz (ed.), *Science in Marketing* (New York: Wiley 1965), pp. 446–464.

4. Is brand loyalty a useful basis for market segmentation? Discuss.

5. What conclusions can be drawn concerning the correlates of brand loyalty?

6. What are the uses and limitations of first-order Markov models?

7. Give an example of a multidimensional definition of brand loyalty.

8. Discuss the limitations of the learning model.

9. How does brand loyalty through inertia differ from brand loyalty due to psychological commitment?

10. How would marketing strategy differ depending on whether brand loyalty is due to commitment or inertia?

11. Are Bernoulli models adequate representations of brand loyalty? Why or why not?

12. Formulate a hypothetical model postulating a relationship between brand loyalty and all the factors that have an influence on brand loyalty. Propose a quantifiable measure for each of the variables. What problems do you anticipate in operationalizing your model?

CHAPTER **24**

DIFFUSION OF INNOVATIONS

Almost everyone has watched a stone fall into a pool of water. From the initial splash concentric circles move out through the rest of the pool. At first the small waves reach only the area immediately surrounding the splash, but with time the widening waves reach across the expanse of water into nearly every area of the pool.

The acceptance of a new product by large numbers of people is in some ways analogous to the waves caused by a stone dropped into the pool. A few people purchase a product. Those around the initial purchasers then try the product, and eventually the acceptance of the product may diffuse throughout the entire population. Unfortunately, this neat pattern of acceptance does not always occur.

From this sample illustration, however, there are a number of questions that can be asked about the diffusion of new products:

(1) How is the initial "splash" accomplished? Are certain types of people more likely than others to accept new products?

(2) How rapidly do the "waves" of acceptance of new products move from the initial innovators to other members of the population?

(3) What is the pattern of the "waves" of acceptance that move through the population?

(4)   How can the diffusion process be influenced by marketing activity?

These questions form the basis of the discussion in this chapter.

CONSUMER DECISION MAKING
FOR NEW PRODUCTS

This chapter differs from preceding chapters in at least three respects. First, it deals with a special type of decision—the decision to buy an innovation. The decision model developed throughout this book is designed to present the structural variables and relations that apply to buying behavior in general. The variables involved in the adoption of new products, however, are approached with different perspectives. The adoption of a new product in the market, for example, is more of a *learning process* involving new inputs to the social system. This is in contrast to decisions concerning existing brands of a product, which tend to be more of a *choice process*.

A second characteristic of diffusion studies is the emphasis on aggregate behavior. That is, diffusion models identify stages of acceptance by segments of the population. The individual buying a product is still central, but the focus tends to shift to segments of the population responding to an innovation with similar behavior at a point in time.

A third characteristic of the study of the adoption of innovations is the emphasis that is placed on *time*. There is a tendency in the preceding chapters to focus upon the identification of the consumer's decision making at a *point* in time. In diffusion research, however, the adoption decision is considered an *ongoing* process and one that cannot be properly understood except in terms of what precedes and follows a specific stage of adoption.

Research Strategies

The research strategies used to investigate consumer behavior in general can also be used to study the adoption of new products. In diffusion research, the *distributive* approach is frequently found. With such an approach, effort is directed at dividing the market into adopters (or early adopters) and nonadopters or triers and nontriers. When such classification is achieved, the research usually focuses upon determining *correlates* of these various outcomes.

The *analytical/morphological* approach is also found in diffusion research. With this strategy of research, the market is viewed as consisting of individuals going through various stages in a decision-making process leading to adoption or nonadoption of an innovation. Both approaches are described in this chapter.

It should be pointed out that there is much similarity between the stages of adoption discussed in the diffusion literature and the general stages of decision making in the model presented throughout this book. The different names for diffusion stages are purposely used throughout this chapter, however, in order to avoid terminological confusion.

THE DIFFUSION RESEARCH TRADITION

The topic of diffusion has spawned considerable research in the past few decades. This research has been prompted by a variety of macro and micro societal problems. Three specific problems have caused sociologists, economists, and marketing researchers to consider legitimate the concern about how consumers react to new ideas and products.

The first problem is the economic waste caused by investing resources in the introduction of new products that are rejected by cónsumers. Estimates vary concerning the proportion of new products that are successful, but nearly all report that the majority fail. A study of leading companies by Booz-Allen & Hamilton reported that only one new product is successful out of each 58 ideas.[1] In the food-processing areas, Buzzell and Nourse found that only about 2 out of each 58 ideas are successful new products.[2] These failures are expensive; a single product failure can cost from $75,000 to $20,000,000.[3] Furthermore, firms often make serious errors in their prediction of sales levels of products which do succeed. Tull found in a study of 63 new products a mean relative error of sales forecasts of 65 percent and a mean relative error for profit forecasts for 53 new products of 128 percent.[4]

The second reason for concern with diffusion research might be termed the desire to manipulate human behavior into accepting socially desirable ideas and products. Rural sociologists have been particularly interested and helpful in obtaining acceptance of new ideas that contributed to increased efficiency in farming practices or the health of a community. The motivation for such studies stems from the notion that people should be changed so that they more closely conform to some norm of what is good for society. This had led to research (with the goal of changing behavior) on improved sanitation techniques, birth control methods, and increased use of political information.

A third reason for interest in diffusion research lies in the criticality of new product acceptance in the survival and growth of contemporary business firms. Historically, growth industries in the American economy have had new products as a major propellant. Additionally, profits are heavily influenced by new products. Profit margins peak during the latter stage of the growth phase in the product life cycle and then continuously decline during subsequent stages. This means that a company must systematically introduce new products—and/or modified products—that can command better margins. As the life cycle of products continues to shorten, profits can be sustained in the long run only by a

---

[1] *Management of New Products* (New York: Booz-Allen & Hamilton, 1965).

[2] Robert D. Buzzell and Robert E. M. Nourse, *Product Innovation in Food Processing 1954–1964* (Boston: Division of Research, Harvard Business School, 1967).

[3] Theodore L. Angelus, "Why Do Most New Products Fail?" *Advertising Age,* pp. 85–86 (Mar. 24, 1969).

[4] Donald S. Tull, "The Relationship of Actual and Predicted Sales and Profits in New-Product Introductions," *J. Business,* vol. 40, pp. 233–250 (July 1967).

continuing flow of successful new products, not only to replace sales volume, but also to sustain and increase profit margins.[5]

At least 13 identifiable disciplines have studied the diffusion of innovations. These include anthropology, early sociology, rural sociology, education, medical sociology, communication, marketing, general sociology, agricultural economics, psychology, general economics, geography, and industrial engineering. Results of research from these disciplines have been collected in a central depository at Michigan State University called the Diffusion Documents Center. In mid-1968, this depository contained 1084 publications, and it increases every year.[6]

Many diffusion studies are completed outside the marketing discipline but are of interest to consumer analysts because the studies involve consumer products. Some of the products studied in well-known diffusion studies include health-care practices, child-rearing practices, health insurance, leisure and recreational activities, new synthetic fabrics, fluoridation, self-medication, new food products, durable goods, auto insurance, women's apparel, the selection of a physician, new drug products, new retail stores, automobiles and automobile services, vacations, furniture, movies (such as "In Cold Blood"), and new types of telephones.[7]

The importance of diffusion research for consumer analysts is not derived solely from the fact that these studies dealt with products of specific interest. Rather, the importance derives from the conclusion that throughout the diffusion studies of many disciplines, generalizations can be made that demonstrate a consistency of pattern independent of the disciplinary affiliation, the specific type of respondents studied, or the nature of the innovation. Although marketing strategists must use care in applying detailed findings of the diffusion traditions to marketing problems,[8] the general consistency among disciplines is one of the basic reasons for the importance diffusion research has attained.

ELEMENTS OF THE DIFFUSION PROCESS

The diffusion process is conceptualized to have four basic elements, or analytical units. These elements or structural variables have been identified as

---

[5] For amplification of these ideas, see David T. Kollat, Roger D. Blackwell, and James Robeson, *Strategic Marketing* (New York: Holt, Rinehart and Winston, 1972), chap. 11.

[6] Everett M. Rogers and F. Floyd Shoemaker, *Communication of Innovations* (New York: Free Press, 1971), pp. 50–51.

[7] For a review of diffusion research by marketing researchers as well as studies in other disciplines of interest to marketing analysts, see Charles W. King, "Adoption and Diffusion Research in Marketing: An Overview," in Raymond M. Haas (ed.), *Science, Technology and Marketing* (Chicago: Amer. Marketing Assoc., 1966), pp. 665–684.

[8] Some researchers have produced evidence to demonstrate, for example, that significant differences exist in the communication of information concerning new products from what has been found to be true in rural sociology. See William Lazer and William E. Bell, "The Communications Process and Innovation," *J. Advertising Research*, vol. 6, pp. 2–7 (Sept. 1966).

(1) the *innovation*, (2) the *communication of the innovation* among individuals, (3) the *social system,* and (4) *time.*[9]

The Innovation

An innovation can be defined in a variety of ways. In a search of the literature, one researcher found 51 different concepts of innovation, defined either explicitly or by implication.[10] The most commonly accepted definition of an innovation, however, appears to be *any idea or product perceived by the potential innovator to be new.*[11] This may be called a subjective definition of innovation, since it is derived from the *thought structure* of a particular individual.[12]

Innovations can also be defined objectively on the basis of criteria external to the potential adopter. The anthropologist Barnett described innovations in such a way, defining them as "any thought, behavior, or thing that is new because it is qualitatively different from existing forms."[13] In consumer behavior, classifying an innovation using this definition focuses upon *product characteristics* to determine if differences occur between new products and previously existing ones. The question that arises is how "different" a new product must be to be considered "qualitatively different." References are sometimes found in the marketing literature which emphasize that substantial technological change must be present in a product for it to be considered an innovation. One marketing scholar, for example, denies that the new products brought out by a food company in a given year are innovations and limits the term to products with such a magnitude of change that they produce a significant effect upon the economy.[14]

The operational definition of innovation that appears to have been most used by consumer researchers is *any form of a product that has recently become available in a market.* According to this definition, an example of an innovation is a brand of coffee that was not previously available in a given geographical

---

[9]   Everett Rogers, *Diffusion of Innovations* (New York: Free Press, 1962), pp. 12–20. This conceptualization is retained in the later edition by Rogers and Shoemaker, *op. cit.*[6]

[10]   Douglass K. Hawes, "An Inspection of Innovation," unpublished paper submitted for a graduate course in consumer behavior (Columbus, Ohio: Ohio State University, 1968).

[11]   This definition is used by Rogers, *op. cit.,*[9] p. 13; King, *op. cit.,*[7] p. 666.

[12]   There are many examples of how products are perceived to be "new" even though they may reflect no new physical characteristic or process. See Chester R. Wasson, "What Is 'New' about New Products," *J. Marketing,* vol. 24, pp. 52–56 (1960).

[13]   H. G. Barnett, *Innovation: The Basis of Cultural Change* (New York: McGraw-Hill 1953), p. 7.

[14]   Paul D. Converse, "Marketing Innovations: Inventions, Techniques, Institutions," in Frederick E. Webster, Jr. (ed.), *New Directions in Marketing* (Chicago: Amer. Marketing Assoc., 1965), pp. 35–41. This view of innovation has its roots in the economic theory of innovations contained in Joseph A. Schumpeter, *Business Cycles,* vol. 1 (New York: McGraw-Hill, 1939).

area.[15] Other examples are modifications of existing products, such as new features in the annual model change on automobiles[16] or a new package for a food. An innovation can also be, of course, a totally new product such as television, the electric toothbrush, or automobile diagnostic centers. It can also be the opening of a new retail store.[17] Additionally, an innovation in some marketing studies has been defined as any product that has achieved less than x percentage of market penetration.[18]

The variety of definitions of innovations dictate an important *caveat: diffusion findings developed in varied research traditions do not necessarily apply to all types of new-product purchase decisions.* Most of the research in the diffusion tradition was conducted on major technological innovations. It is reasonable to expect that the details of the diffusion process may differ considerably when the innovation is a product of less consequence than a major technological change, although this area needs further investigation.

There is thus a need for a classification system to handle widely differing types of product innovations. One such classification system is based on the impact of the innovation on the social structure accepting the innovation. In this taxonomic system, innovations may be classified as (1) continuous, (2) dynamically continuous, and (3) discontinuous.

(1)   A *continuous* innovation has the least disrupting influence on established patterns. Alteration of a product is involved rather than the establishment of a new product. Examples: fluoride toothpaste, new-model automobile changeovers, menthol cigarettes.

(2)   A *dynamically continuous* innovation has more disrupting effects than a continuous innovation, although it still does not generally alter established patterns. It may involve the creation of a new product or the alteration of an existing product. Examples: electric toothbrushes, the Mustang automobile, Touch-Tone telephones.

(3)   A *discontinuous* innovation involves the establishment of a new product

---

[15]   An example is the introduction of Folgers coffee to the Chicago market reported in Ronald E. Frank, William F. Massy, and Donald G. Morrison, "The Determinants of Innovative Behavior with Respect to a Branded, Frequently Purchased Food Product," in L. George Smith (ed.), *Reflections on Progress in Marketing* (Chicago: Amer. Marketing Assoc., 1964), pp. 312–323. See also a study of new brands of tooth-paste and deodorants by George H. Haines, Jr., "A Study of Why People Purchase New Products," in Haas, *op. cit.,*[7] pp. 685–697.

[16]   John B. Stewart, "Functional Features in Product Strategy," *Harvard Business Rev.*, pp. 65–78 (Mar.–Apr. 1959).

[17]   Robert F. Kelly, "The Diffusion Model as a Predictor of Ultimate Patronage Levels in New Retail Outlets," in Haas, *op. cit.;*[7] also Robert F. Kelly, "The Role of Information in the Patronage Decision: A Diffusion Phenomenon," in M. S. Moyer and R. E. Vosburgh (eds.), *Marketing for Tomorrow . . . Today* (Chicago: Amer. Marketing Assoc., 1967), pp. 119–129. This work is based upon Fred C. Allvine, The Patronage Decision,[11] unpublished doctoral dissertation (Bloomington, Ind.: Indiana University, 1966).

[18]   An example is found in Lazer and Bell, *op. cit.,*[8] p. 4, where they use the operational definition, "A product is an innovation if less than 10 per cent market penetration exists in a given geographic location." This definition is common in marketing studies.

and the establishment of new behavior patterns. Examples: television, computers.[19]

Many of the conflicting findings that exist in the diffusion literature stem from the fact that diffusion models developed for dynamically continuous or discontinuous innovations are being applied to research on continuous innovations. This may be appropriate in developing a broad conceptual framework for analyzing innovations, but when applied to such details as the amount of decision making involved in a purchase, the sources of information, or other important details, the assumption that the same generalizations are applicable to each type of innovation is tenuous. Unfortunately, research on the marketing of new products often has not clarified these issues.

Communication

The nature of communications involved in effective diffusion is a central issue for consumer analysts in the study of diffusion. Communications affecting the diffusion of innovation may be of two types, informal and formal. Informal communications are largely outside the influence of the marketer and consist of reference-group and family influences. There is a temptation to assume that the people who first adopt a product are the ones who influence others to purchase the product and that their communications are therefore instrumental in the diffusion process. However, the interpersonal influence relations appear to be much more complex.

Formal communications can often be influenced by marketers. They include advertising, various forms of reseller support, and personal salesmen. When control of communications is possible, questions arise such as: What types of media are most likely to transmit messages to those persons who are most likely to be the first adopters of an innovation? What media are most likely to be considered authoritative? What messages are most likely to influence new product acceptance?

Understanding the role of communications in the diffusion process is sufficiently important to justify a special section later in the chapter describing what is known about this topic.

The Social System

The diffusion of innovations is an aggregative phenomenon. The word "diffusion" has little meaning, except as it relates to a group of people. Acceptance or rejection of a product can apply to an individual person, but diffusion is a concentration gradient and refers to some aggregate of individuals. The individual's acceptance of a product and his relation to the rest of the group are both so important that one cannot be appropriately analyzed without considering the

---

[19]   Thomas S. Robertson, "The Process of Innovation and the Diffusion of Innovation," *J. Marketing*, vol. 31, pp. 14–19, at p. 15 (Jan. 1967).

other. Consequently, diffusion research focuses not only on characteristics of a decision-making unit (individual or family) but also on the environment of diffusion provided by the social system.

The social system is defined as a population of individuals who are functionally differentiated and engaged in collective problem-solving behavior.[20] Even though a decision-making unit operates within a system bound together by common problems, that system may permit a wide latitude of individual choice. The consumer may choose a solution to his consumption problem completely at deviance with the rest of the group, or he may be contractually bound to a group decision, such as the fluoridation of a city's water supply. Most consumption decisions fall somewhere between these extreme positions, but, in any case, the adoption decision is influenced to some extent by the norms of the group, the status of the decision-making unit relative to other units of the social system, and other aspects of the individual's orientation to the social system.

Time

Adoption of new products is a temporal phenomenon and needs to be analyzed as such. The decision to adopt a new product, like all other consumption decisions described by the model in this book, is a *process* rather than an event. People recognize problems, search for alternatives, evaluate new products as potential alternatives, decide to purchase the new product, and perhaps eventually purchase it. The adoption process is not considered complete, however, until postpurchase evaluation and perhaps a further behavior sequence is generated, because adoption is defined to be the *decision to continue full use of an innovation.*[21] To study the rate of diffusion in a social structure, it is necessary to evaluate the exact position of individual consumers in the *process that leads to adoption.*

There is a striking incongruity between the theoretical concept of adoption as a process and the way it is ordinarily measured by consumer analysts. The theoretical concept of adopter should be measured by determining the intention of the consumer to incorporate the new product into his habitual pattern of consumption. In actual practice, the measurement of adoption is usually a "yes–no" measure. If a consumer is observed to have purchased a new product or patronized a new store, he is considered to be an adopter. This may cause misleading results when the product has been purchased because of some variable unrelated to the consumer's long-run intention to adopt the product (such as an out-of-stock situation for the consumer's true preference) or when the consumer has begun the process that leads to adoption (such as deciding in his mind to try the product at the next purchase occasion) but has not yet purchased the new product.

---

[20] Rogers, *op. cit.,*[9] p. 14.
[21] Rogers, *op. cit.,*[9] p. 17.

THE INNOVATION-DECISION PROCESS

The process individuals move through in adopting a new product has been conceptualized as a stage process. These stages have been discussed thoroughly in Rogers and are described in Figure 24.1 along with the variables that influence each stage [22] The stages described below are knowledge, persuasion, decision (which may lead to adoption or rejection), and confirmation.

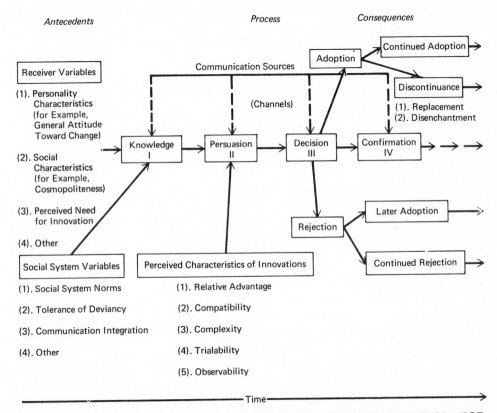

Figure 24.1 PARADIGM OF THE INNOVATION-DECISION PROCESS. FOR SIMPLICITY, ONLY CONSEQUENCES OF PROCESS ARE SHOWN, NOT OF INNOVATION. Everett M. Rogers and F. Floyd Shoemaker, *Communication of Innovations* (New York: Free Press, 1971), p. 102

[22] The process was described earlier in George F. Beal and Joe M. Bohlen, "The Diffusion Process," Special Report 18 (Ames, Iowa: Iowa Agricultural Extension Service, 1957). Other publications by Beal and Bohlen contain much of the empirical work verifying the stage concepts of diffusion, but Rogers' *Diffusion of Innovations* has had the most profound effect on marketing thinking. This section is a condensation of Rogers and Shoemaker, *op cit.,*[6] pp. 100–133.

Knowledge

The knowledge stage begins when a consumer receives physical or social stimuli that give him exposure to the innovation's existence and some understanding of how it functions. The consumer is aware of the product but has made no judgment concerning the relevance of the product to a problem or need that exists for him. His information is incomplete and the knowledge or awareness that exists is stored in the central control unit for potential future use.

Knowledge is a result of selective perception, but beyond this many questions remain unanswered. The marketing analyst needs to know more about the antecedents of knowledge. Do some consumers have more knowledge of new products in general than other consumers? Of all the stimulus sets that are constantly being sampled by a consumer, what makes one set have an impact and be remembered while another set appears to have no impact and be lost to consciousness? Is increased knowledge of new products necessarily associated with early adoption of that product? These are provocative questions in need of additional research.

Persuasion

Persuasion, in the Rogers–Shoemaker paradigm, refers to the formation of favorable or unfavorable attitudes toward the innovation. The individual may mentally apply the new idea to his present or anticipated future situation before deciding whether to try, which might be called vicarious trial. All of the influences on consumer decision making described in previous chapters of this book are brought to bear in the evaluation of the innovation which leads to the rejection or acceptance (the evaluation) of the idea of the innovation.

The persuasiveness of a *new* idea may be related to the perception of risk in the new product, with uncertainty reduction as a determinant of evaluation.[23] The theorem may be stated in the following manner: When an individual considers a new product, he must weigh the potential gains from adopting the product with the potential losses from switching from his present product strategy. The consumer recognizes that if he adopts the new product, it may be inferior to his present product, or the cost may be greater than the increased value. Thus, adopting the new product has a risk involved that he can avoid by postponing acceptance until the value has been clearly established. If, however, the product is designed to solve a problem that is of significant concern to the consumer, there is also the risk that he may lose value from delaying adoption of a product that is truly superior to his present product.

---

[23] The concept of risk perception in consumer behavior first received widespread attention in Raymond A. Bauer, "Consumer Behavior as Risk Taking," in Robert S. Hancock (ed.), *Dynamic Marketing for a Changing World* (Chicago: Amer. Marketing Assoc., 1960), pp. 389–398. A description of research that has followed the Bauer work is found in Scott M. Cunningham, "Perceived Risk as a Factor in the Diffusion of New Product Information," in Haas, *op. cit.*,[7] pp. 698–721.

The consumer can reduce the risk of adopting the new product—and therefore his uncertainty about the buying situation—by acquiring additional information about the new product. He may seek out news stories, pay particular attention to advertising for the product, subscribe to product-rating services, talk with individuals who have already tried the product-rating services, talk with individuals who have already tried the product, talk with experts on the subject, or try the product on a limited basis (where possible). Each of these strategies, however, has an economic and/or psychological cost. Moreover, they are unlikely to yield information with certainty.

A number of laboratory experiments have been conducted at the University of Pennsylvania that, for the most part, support the risk-reduction information theory of new product adoption.[24] In these experiments, housewives and graduate students were asked to make decisions on the basis of incomplete information. Their decisions could be altered through use of information that they could acquire at a cost. The following generalizations have emerged from this set of experiments:

(1) In general, consumers seek more information about options as their uncertainty about the options increases.

(2) The more ambiguous their perceptions of a situation, the more likely consumers are to accept new information.

(3) When new information conflicts with previous beliefs and attitudes, previous information will tend to prevail.

(4) Large interpersonal differences exist in the amount of information sought and used in evaluating decisions.

(5) A large proportion of consumers—at least in the laboratory situation—do not differentiate between relevant and irrelevant information.

(6) The valuation of information appears to be higher early in the decision process than late in the process.

(7) There appear to be some personality variables that differentiate information seekers and information avoiders. Respondents who were information sensitive tended to have open mindedness and adaptable attitudes, while those who were not information sensitive tended to be rigid in their attitudes and exhibit fatalism with regard to the future and control over one's destiny.[25]

It should be emphasized that these findings deal with an abstract laboratory situation. They suggest conclusions that may apply to the evaluation stage of new product acceptance. There is some support in other portions of the diffusion literature, but, to date, general applicability is unproved.

---

[24] Paul E. Green, "Consumer Use of Information," in Joseph W. Newman (ed.), *On Knowing the Consumer* (New York: Wiley, 1966), pp. 67–80.

[25] Green, *op. cit.,*[24] pp. 73–77. For details of these experiments and the qualifications that refer to them, see the sources cited in the footnotes to this article.

Decision

The decision stage involves activities which lead to a choice between adopting or rejecting the innovation. The immediate consideration is whether or not to try the innovation, which is often influenced by the ability to try the innovation on a small scale (including vicarious trial by observing the trials of others). Innovations which can be divided are generally adopted more readily. Trial can sometimes be stimulated by the use of free samples or other small units with low risk.

Figure 24.1 shows that the output of decision can just as well be rejection as adoption. Rejection can be continuous or may be reversed for later adoption. Conversely, adoption may be continuous or may lead to later discontinuance.

Confirmation

Confirmation refers to the process postulated by Rogers and Shoemaker of consumers seeking reinforcement for the innovation decision that has been made and of the situation in which consumers sometimes reverse previous decisions when exposed to conflicting messages about the innovation. This stage involves the issue of cognitive dissonance, discussed earlier in Chapter 22.

Discontinuance is, of course, as serious a question as the original process of adoption. The rate of discontinuance may be just as important as the rate of adoption, with the corresponding need for marketing strategists to devote attention to preventing discontinuance of innovations. Rogers and Shoemaker report that later adopters are more likely to discontinue innovations than are earlier adopters[26] and are generally likely to have the opposite characteristics (in education, social status, change agency contact, and the like) to those of the innovators. Discontinuance is most likely to occur when the innovation is not integrated into the practices and way of life of the receivers, suggesting the need for after-the-purchase activity by marketing strategists designed to ensure integration.

Marketing and the Rogers Paradigm

The early Rogers paradigm and the revised Rogers–Shoemaker paradigm serve as theoretical models for diffusion research by consumer analysts. The original Rogers model underlies much of the consumer research in this area and must be considered a landmark conceptualization and stimulant to research.

The Rogers approach, in spite of its emphasis on the *process* approach, has generated limited amounts of process research in the consumer behavior field. Instead, diffusion research typically has treated adoption as dichotomous (that is, adopt or reject).

A more serious problem with the Rogers paradigm for marketing strat-

---

[26] Rogers and Shoemaker, *op. cit.*,[6] p. 116.

egists is that it deals mostly with discontinuous innovations, whereas most marketing decisions involve continuous or dynamically continuous innovations. Conceptually, it is probably helpful to use a general model of consumer behavior which permits analysis of all types of products. The determination of when a product is sufficiently different to be an innovation fitting the conditions of the Rogers paradigm and when it is merely a modification of an existing product appears to be an arbitrary decision.

Another problem in applying the diffusion paradigm is how to handle the situation when a consumer *moves into* a social structure that has already widely adopted a product. For example, when a consumer moves to a new city, stores and products are perceived to be *new to him*. Using the traditional definition of innovations, the new products would have to be fitted into the paradigm. The most useful approach appears to be to use the findings that have been generated with the Rogers paradigm, but to consider adoption of new products as one form of the generalized consumer decision process.

PREDICTING DIFFUSION
AND ADOPTION SUCCESS

Marketing strategists are interested in predicting the behavior of aggregates of consumers rather than individual behavior. There are a number of models developed in recent years which, with varying degrees of success, have been used to predict market acceptance of new products. The output of these models usually involves predictions of the number of consumers who will accept a new product and the timing of acceptance.

New product models can be placed into two categories.[27] The first category can be called *diffusion* models which are based upon fitting a mathematical curve to new product sales, based upon a parsimonious set of parameters. The parameters may or may not have definite behavioral content. The mathematical curves are determined from historical situations or theoretical propositions and applied to current problems. The variables in diffusion models are such things as time the product has been introduced and number of persons in the market (with assumptions about interaction between consumers). Numerous types of diffusion models are possible. In the following paragraphs basic penetration models and epidemiological models are described.

The second category of models are *adoption* models. These focus upon variables that describe consumer decision making concerning the new product. Some of them also include variables which describe marketer activity. Several of these models are included in the following discussion.

---

[27] This categorization is from Philip Kotler, *Marketing Decision Making: A Model Building Approach* (New York: Holt, Rinehart and Winston, 1971). See Chapter 17 of this source for an excellent overview of new product models.

Penetration Models

The most basic models of new product acceptance permit predictions of the level of penetration by a new product in a given time period based upon early sales results. These models require data with which the analyst can separate the initial purchasers in early time periods from repeat purchasers. Thus these models separate the "triers" from the "adopters."

Penetration models assume some "ceiling" penetration—a percentage of households that represents the maximum proportion that can be expected for a product of this type. The ratio of repeat purchasers in a period to triers can be represented by r, and the ceiling proportion can be represented by x. The penetration in the first period would be rx. The penetration in the second period would be equal to rx less those first-period triers who did not repeat their purchase. The penetration in period two, therefore, would be $rx\,(1-r)$. In period three, penetration would be $rx\,(1-r)^2$, and similarly for other periods until the ceiling is reached. Frequently, the effects of some external force (such as advertising) are added to the model as K. If this model were realistic, the marketer could project the total number of adopters at any point of time. Figure 24.2 shows how the penetration curve is calculated. In Figure 24.3 an application of this model is presented. Kelly found that the model was useful in predicting the penetration of the market area for a new dairy store.[28]

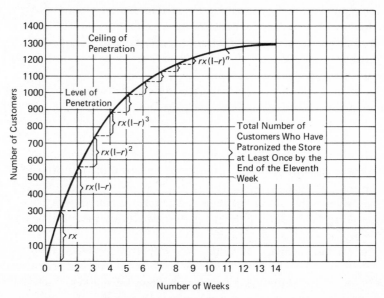

Figure 24.2 EXPLICIT CHARACTER OF THE PENETRATION MODEL   Robert F. Kelly, "Estimating Ultimate Performance Levels of New Retail Outlets," *J. Marketing Research*, vol. 4, pp. 13–19, at p. 18. (Feb. 1967). Reprinted by permission of the author and the publisher.

---

[28] Robert F. Kelly, "Estimating Ultimate Performance Levels of New Retail Outlets," *J. Marketing Research*, vol. 4, pp. 3–19 (Feb. 1967).

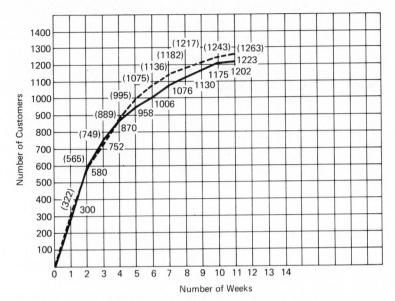

Figure 24.3 COMPARISON OF ESTIMATED AND ACTUAL PENETRATION CURVES FOR A RETAIL STORE (BASED ON THE FIRST THREE WEEKS' DATA). Solid curve—actual penetration; dotted curve—estimated penetration. Robert F. Kelly, "Estimating Ultimate Performance Levels of New Retail Outlets," *J. Marketing Research*, vol. 4, pp. 13–19, at p. 17 (Feb. 1967). Reprinted by permission of the author and the publisher.

The penetration model was introduced by Fourt and Woodlock.[29] It depends upon adequate data (usually from a consumer panel) to ascertain early penetration ratios and stability of these ratios over time. In spite of the impracticality of many of its assumptions for most innovations, it is one of the general group of brand share models[30] that has influenced diffusion thought and research.

Epidemiological Models

A number of models have been developed which view new product diffusion as a process of social interaction about the product in which innovators and early adopters "infect" the rest of the population. Thus, these models based upon social-interaction assumptions have been compared to epidemics with the social structure. Predictions are usually based upon acceptance–rejection criteria

---

[29] L. A. Fourt and J. W. Woodlock, "Early Prediction of Market Success for New Grocery Products," *J. Marketing*, vol. 25, pp. 31–38 (Oct. 1962); also William D. Barclay, "Probability Model for Early Prediction of New Product Market Success," *J. Marketing*, vol. 27, pp. 63–68 (Jan. 1963).

[30] For a description of the fundamentals underlying these early brand-switching models, see David W. Miller and Martin K. Starr, *Executive Decision and Operations Research* (Englewood Cliffs, N.J.:Prentice-Hall, 1960), pp. 173–182.

in a time setting. The assumptions of these models and the number of variables are usually simple, although the mathematics involved may be sophisticated. The new product models of this type that are useful to marketing strategists have precedent in other areas of social science.[31]

Interaction models often involve the assumption that the number of persons adopting an innovation will be proportional to the number of contacts between persons within the social system. Some models assume complete intermixing, that is, every user has contact with every nonuser, and, thus, diffusion spreads through the population according to a logistic curve. Recent attempts have been made to relax these assumptions and compute the probability of diffusion with incomplete mixing between groups. The work of Coleman has stimulated much work in this type of model which has led to more directly applicable models for marketing strategists.[32]

One model which has yielded good predictions of actual data was developed by Bass.[33] The assumptions underlying this model are that initial purchases of a new product will be made *both* by innovators and imitators, the distinction between the two being buying influence. Innovators are influenced in their initial purchase by marketing-controlled communications, but imitators are influenced by the number of previous buyers; imitators "learn" from the experiences of those who have already bought. Bass defines p as the coefficient of innovation and r as the coefficient of imitation. The importance of innovators is greater at first and diminishes monotonically with time.

The model of Bass is described in the following manner:[34]

$$S(T) = mf(T) = P(T)[m - Y(T)] = [p + q \int_0^T S(t) \, dt/m][m - \int_0^T S(t) \, dt]$$

where

$$q/m = \text{initial purchase rate (a constant)}$$
$$p = \text{probability of initial purchase (a constant)}$$
$$f(T) = \text{likelihood of purchase at } T$$
$$Y(T) = \text{total number purchasing in the } (0,T) \text{ interval}$$
$$S(T) = \text{sales at } T.$$

Using standard maximization techniques, it is possible to predict the peak and timing of peak sales for the product. Bass has applied this model to sales of eleven durable goods with the result of generally excellent predictions. Using regression

[31] Representative models include Stuart C. Dodd, "Diffusion Is Predictable: Testing Probability Models for Laws of Interaction," *Amer. Sociological Rev.*, vol. 20, p. 392 (Dec. 1955); A Rapoport, "Spread of Information through a Population with Socio-Structural Bias: I. Assumption of Transivity," and "II. Various Models with Partial Transivity," *Bull. Mathematical Biophysics*, vol. 15, pp. 523–533, 534–544 (1953); Melvin H. DeFleur and Otto N. Larsen, *The Flow of Information* (New York: Harper & Row, 1958).

[32] James S. Coleman, "Diffusion in Incomplete Social Structures," in Fred Massarik and Philburn Ratoosh (eds.), *Mathematical Explorations in Behavioral Science* (Homewood, Ill.: Irwin, 1965), pp. 214–232.

[33] Frank M. Bass, "A New Product Growth Model for Consumer Durables," *Management Science*, vol. 15, pp. 215–227 (Jan. 1969).

[34] Bass, *op. cit.*,[33] p. 217.

analysis with data for three years, Bass was able to predict sales of room air-conditioners that coincided with actual sales with a coefficient of determination of $R^2 = 0.92$. For color television, the predictions of sales through 1970 using the Bass model apparently were more accurate than the forecasts made by the manufacturers of color television. An example of the closeness of fit between actual and predicted sales is shown in Figure 24.4 for power lawnmowers.

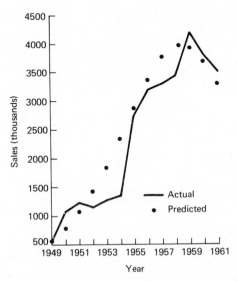

Figure 24.4 ACTUAL SALES AND SALES PREDICTED BY BASS MODEL OF NEW PRODUCT DIFFUSION (POWER LAWN MOWERS). Frank M. Bass, "A New Product Growth Model for Consumer Durables," *Management Science*, vol. 15, p. 223 (Jan. 1969)

Other stochastic models have been used successfully to predict new product diffusion. Some of these (STEAM, for example, by Massy) are based upon time intervals between purchase and repurchase. These models use panel data and simulate market performance using a Weibull distribution with the assumption of marketing information transmitted to households on the basis of gamma probability distribution. Massy simulated actual sales data with enough accuracy to be helpful in managerial decisions for an unidentified product,[35] and Burger, Bass, and Pessemier have produced estimates of sales for a new laundry detergent using this type of model.[36]

[35] William F. Massy, "Forecasting the Demand for New Convenience Products," *J. Marketing Research*, vol. 6, pp. 405–412 (Nov. 1969). For a related but somewhat different approach, see David H. Ahl, "New Product Forecasting Using Consumer Panels," *J. Marketing Research*, vol. 7, pp. 160–167 (May 1970).

[36] Philip C. Burger, Frank M. Bass, and Edgar A. Pessemier, "Forecasting New Product Sales," working paper (Evanston, Ill.: Northwestern University, Graduate School of Management, 1968).

Alderson Time-Value Model

A model by Alderson serves to make the transition from diffusion models to adoption models. In the latter, variables are included which explicitly relate adoption of internal-to-the-consumer variables. That is, decision making by the consumer is included as a determinant of the dependent variable in the model. This usually causes the model to be more complex than diffusion models and often increases the difficulty of data collection.

Alderson, shortly before his death, proposed a model to estimate the probability that an innovation would be accepted in a market. The model was based upon the value of the innovation to consumers and one of the primary variables was the amount of time involved and saved by the innovation. The model was the form:[37]

$$V = V_{t_0} - P_{t_0}(I_{t_0} - I_{t_1}) + K(C_{t_1} - C_{t_0})$$

where

V = value of an innovation to a market

P = population affected by innovation in time period t

I_t = amount of time spent using innovation in time period t

C_t = amount of "congenial" behavior spent in time period t (that is, enjoyable activity before innovation)

K = adjustment factor to represent amount of satisfaction associated with "congenial" behavior.

The expression $(I_{t_0} - I_{t_1})$ represents an index of the time saved by the innovation, thus recognizing a variable that appears to be of increasing value in understanding many innovations.[38] (See Chapter 4.) Alderson recognized that "in this crude form the formula has no significance except to show that, in principle, the importance of an innovation can be measured."[39]

Market Classification Models

Some models predict the success of a new product based upon data from similar markets for the same or similar products. If all variables are continuously measured, multiple regression would be an appropriate technique to evaluate the probability of success in similar situations. If it is possible only to group markets into "good" or "bad" categories with reference to adoption, the appropriate multivariate technique may be discriminant analysis.

---

[37] Wroe Alderson, *Dynamic Marketing Behavior* (Homewood, Ill.: Irwin, 1965), chap. 7.

[38] Empirical support for the importance of time is suggested in Nelson N. Foote, "The Time Dimension and Consumer Behavior," in Newman, *op. cit.*,[24] pp. 38–46; also Philip B. Schary, "Consumption and the Problem of Time," *J. Marketing,* vol. 35, pp. 50–55 (Apr. 1971).

[39] Alderson, *op. cit.*,[37] p. 117.

The multiple-discriminant technique has been demonstrated using only early performance data for independent variables.[40] For example, assume the following has been calculated:

$$D_{tN} = 0.31x_{1t} + 0.42x_{2t} + 0.19x_{3t} + 0.23x_{4t} - 0.011x_{5t} - 0.012$$

where

D_{tN} = discrimination function of adoption success for time period t for group N
x_{1t} = market share of total market in period t
x_{2t} = product-type market share in period t
x_{3t} = per capita sales in period t
x_{4t} = advertising expenditure per unit sold in period t
x_{5t} = advertising share in period t.

(Note: if we use gasoline as an analogy, all gasoline sales would be what is termed "product-type market.")

This functional relationship can then be used to evaluate the probability of obtaining an acceptable market position in time periods $t = 2, 3, \cdots, 12$. With this information, a decision can be made concerning the feasibility of introducing a new product.[41]

DEMON Model

The DEMON model is an example of multistage models in which an assumption is made that consumers pass through stages of decision making leading to purchase of a new product. As each stage is reached, it is assumed that a higher probability of purchase results than in the preceding stage.[42]

DEMON was developed at the advertising agency of Batten, Barton, Durstine, and Osborne to predict acceptance of new products and to improve management decisions concerning marketing strategy for new products. DEMON is represented in Figure 24.5. The figure shows the stages involved in acceptance of a product new to a consumer. In the model, awareness is an important variable. Awareness is predicted by measuring the advertising dollars spent to the number of delivered gross impressions and the ratio of impressions to level of attained reach and frequency.[43]

In the DEMON model, each variable is first dependent, then independent.[44] Thus, trial *depends* on awareness, but once activated, trial becomes the

---

[40] William R. King, "Early Prediction of New Product Success," *J. Advertising Research*, vol. 6, pp. 8–13 (June 1966).

[41] Modified from King, *op. cit.*,[40] p. 13.

[42] David B. Learner, "Profit Maximization through New-Product Marketing Planning and Control," in Frank Bass (ed.), *Application of the Sciences in Marketing Management* (New York: Wiley, 1968), pp. 151–167.

[43] "Reach" and "frequency" are commonly used terms in advertising. Reach is the percentage of the population contacted at least once by an advertisement. Frequency is the average number of times each person is reached, or gross impressions divided by reach.

[44] James K. DeVoe, "Plans, Profits, and the Marketing Program," in Webster, *op. cit.*,[14] pp. 473–488.

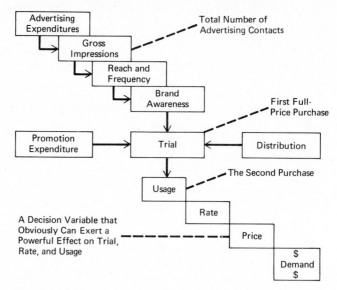

Figure 24.5 DEMON MODEL OF NEW PRODUCT ACCEPTANCE. James K. DeVoe, "Plans, Profits, and the Marketing Program," in Frederick E. Webster, Jr. (ed.), *New Directions in Marketing* (Chicago: Amer. Marketing Assoc., 1965)

independent variable for prediction of *usage*. Each of these variables is influenced in turn by variables such as advertising, which are controllable by the marketing organization. It should be noted that Figure 24.5 does not show the nature of the relations among variables, although the computer program for DEMON does contain explicit equations. This model has been refined by Light and Pringle using a recursive regression approach called NEWS (new product early warning system).[45]

Ayer New Product Model

Another multistage model of new product acceptance has been developed at the advertising agency of N. W. Ayer and Son. This model is presented graphically in Figure 24.6 and shows initial purchase and repeat purchase to be a function of specified variables, some controlled by marketers and some not controlled. Claycamp and Liddy have reported results to indicate that the model produces highly accurate predictions of the level of initial purchases.[46] Their use of the model indicates that "correct recall of advertising claims" is an important determinant of new product acceptance.

---

[45] Lawrence Light and Lewis Pringle, "New Product Forecasting Using Recursive Regression," in David Kollat, Roger Blackwell, and James Engel, *Research in Consumer Behavior* (New York: Holt, Rinehart and Winston, 1970), pp. 702–709.

[46] Henry J. Claycamp and Lucien E. Liddy, "Prediction of New Product Performance: An Analytical Approach," *J. Marketing Research*, vol. 6, pp. 414–420 (Nov. 1969).

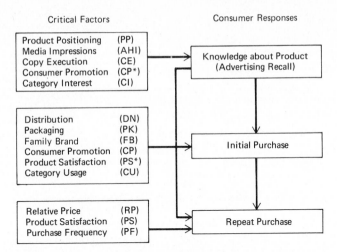

Figure 24.6 AYER NEW PRODUCT MODEL. Henry J. Claycamp and Lucien E. Liddy, "Prediction of New Product Performance: An Analytical Approach," *J. Marketing Research,* vol. 6, pp. 414–420 (Nov. 1969)

Other Models

Prediction of new product acceptance has been the concern of a number of other models. Most of these are multistage, microbehavioral in nature, assuming a hierarchy of effects in decision making that is compatible with the decision-process approach to consumer behavior. Hamburg and Atkins present a computer model that identifies the importance of awareness and attitude as adoption variables.[47] A much more ambitious model has been developed by Amstutz and takes into consideration not only consumer variables but detailed information concerning marketing activities.[48] It is very difficult to obtain all the data needed for Amstutz's model, but Claycamp and Amstutz report that good results were obtained in one simulation of the prescribing behavior of physicians for drug products.[49] A microbehavioral model that includes many of the more traditional variables associated with the literature on diffusion of innovation was developed by Alba using data from a study of new telephone products.[50] A model called

---

[47]   Morris Hamburg and Robert J. Atkins, "Computer Model for New Product Demand," *Harvard Business Rev.,* vol. 45, pp. 107–115 (Mar.–Apr. 1967). For an approach emphasizing the importance of attitude shifts in new product adoption, see George S. Day, "Using Attitude Change Measures to Evaluate New Product Introductions," *J. Marketing Research,* vol. 7, pp. 474–482 (Nov. 1970).

[48]   Arnold Amstutz, *Computer Simulation of Competitive Market Response* (Cambridge, Mass.: M.I.T. Press, 1967).

[49]   Henry J. Claycamp and Arnold E. Amstutz, "Simulation Techniques in the Analysis of Marketing Strategy," in Frank M. Bass, Charles W. King, and Edgar Pessemier (eds.), *Applications of the Sciences in Marketing Management* (New York: Wiley, 1968), pp. 113–150.

[50]   Manuel S. Alba, "Microanalysis of the Socio-Dynamics of Diffusion of Innovation," unpublished doctoral dissertation (Evanston, Ill.: Northwestern University, 1967).

NOMMAD assumes the importance of an individual's characteristics but measures these based upon past purchase behavior.[51]

One other model which has received considerable testing with actual data and which has influenced the literature on new produce adoption is SPRINTER developed by Urban.[52] Urban assumes five stages of buyer activity leading to trial: (1) awareness, (2) intent, (3) search, (4) selection, and (5) postpurchase behavior. Like other models, passing from one stage to another increases the probability of purchase. SPRINTER has received favorable acceptance and appears to be strong in its application to managerial decision making about new product introduction.

Evaluation of Models of Diffusion and Adoption

There has been a rapid expansion of knowledge in recent years concerning the development of models for new product acceptance. In many cases, extensive data have been presented to show the efficacy of respective models. To date there has been little application of a model developed by one individual or group to data or problems faced by other individuals or groups. That is the ultimate test of a model's generality. This type of testing is occurring (with NEWS and the Ayer model, for example), but the situations involved do not lend themselves to widespread publication of the results.

It must be concluded, however, that new product models appear to be one of the most successful applications of mathematics to consumer behavior problems. The Bass model has been shown to be more useful than conventional methods of forecasting (for color television, for example), and other models have been demonstrated to be very useful. It is clear that the adoption models have more behavioral assumptions made explicit and presumably should have more general applicability to many types of new product introductions. The diffusion models, however, are generally more parsimonious. Data collection is generally more feasible with the diffusion models. The more simplistic, curve-fitting types of models appear to have been more feasible and economical to date than the complex models.

CORRELATES OF INNOVATIVENESS

Marketers are strongly motivated to determine what variables are associated with innovativeness. This is based upon a persistent belief that innovators are different in important ways from later adopters.[53] With knowledge of such

---

[51] Jerome D. Herniter, Victor J. Cook, and Bernard Norek, "Microsimulation of Purchase Behavior for New and Established Products," paper presented at the University of Chicago Conf. on Behavioral and Management Science in Marketing (June 1969).

[52] Glen L. Urban, "A New Product Analysis and Decision Model," *Management Science,* vol. 14, pp. 490–517 (Apr. 1968); also David B. Montgomery and Glen L. Urban, *Management Science in Marketing* (Englewood Cliffs, N.J.: Prentice-Hall, 1969).

[53] William E. Bell, "Consumer Innovators: A Unique Market for Newness," in Stephen A. Greyser (ed.), *Toward Scientific Marketing* (Chicago: Amer. Marketing Assoc., 1963), pp. 85–95.

differences, it may be possible to design new products that are compatible with variables leading to innovativeness or to direct other marketing efforts toward potential innovators. There are three primary groups of variables that are examined in connection with innovativeness. These are consumer characteristics, product characteristics, and social relations within the potential market.

The Diffusion Documents Center at Michigan State University has compiled findings based upon an exhaustive search of the diffusion literature. Each empirical study is placed on punch cards so that cross tabulations can be accomplished readily. In a compilation of 4197 empirical findings, it was found that 2486 related to the problem of determining independent variables associated with innovativeness. The following section of this chapter relies heavily on findings from this compilation.[54] In these studies, innovativeness is operationally defined as (1) the adoption or nonadoption of one new idea or a set of ideas or (2) the degree to which the unit of adoption is relatively earlier in adopting new ideas than other members of his social system.

Consumer Characteristics Associated with Innovativeness

Sociodemographic Variables. A few variables emerge fairly consistently as associated with early adoption of innovations. Table 24.1 summarizes the results of studies relating to these consumer characteristics. The table indicates that sociodemographic variables most often associated with innovativeness are education, literacy, income, and level of living. These findings, it should be noted, and those that follow are primarily based upon *correlational* studies. Thus they indicate only associations between the variables and innovativeness. They should not be construed as *causation*. In many cases they only indicate to the marketer that these variables *facilitate* understanding and buying new products when other reasons exist for buying them.

Attitudinal Variables Some attitudinal variables emerge as consistently associated with innovativeness, as indicated in Table 24.1. Many parents apparently want to provide the latest and best products to enable their children to compete with others. This is manifested in the consistent findings that the variable *"aspirations for children"* is associated with innovativeness. Related to this is *achievement motivation.* Both of these indicate the individual's desire to better the life of his family, especially in his children's education and occupation. *Knowledge ability* refers to the awareness that an individual has of the external world and events in general that occur about him. Also associated with innovativeness is *attitude toward change. Mental rigidity* or *satisfaction with life*, conversely, lead to rejection of innovations.

---

54 Everett M. Rogers and J. David Stanfield, "Adoption and Diffusion of New Products: Emerging Generalizations and Hypotheses," paper presented at the Conf. on the Application of Sciences to Marketing Management, Purdue University (July 12–15, 1966); also in Bass *et al., op. cit.*[49]

Table 24.1 CONSUMER CHARACTERISTICS RELATED TO INNOVATIVENESS

	Number of Empirical Findings Indicating Relation to Innovativeness (%)					
	Positive	*None*	*Negative*	*Conditional*	*Total*	*Total Number of Published Findings*
Sociodemographic						
(1) Education	74.6	16.1	5.2	4.1	100	193
(2) Literacy	70.4	22.2	3.7	3.7	100	27
(3) Income	80.3	10.7	6.3	2.7	100	112
(4) Level of living	82.5	10.0	2.5	5.0	100	40
(5) Age	32.3	40.5	17.7	9.5	100	158
Attitudinal						
(6) Knowledgeability	78.8	16.7	1.5	3.0	100	66
(7) Attitude toward change	73.6	14.5	8.2	3.8	100	159
(8) Achievement motivation	64.7	23.5	0.0	11.8	100	17
(9) Aspirations for children	82.6	8.7	4.3	4.3	100	23
(10) Business orientation	60.0	20.0	20.0	0.0	100	5
(11) Satisfaction with life	28.6	28.6	42.8	0.0	100	7
(12) Empathy	75.0	0.0	25.0	0.0	100	4
(13) Mental rigidity	20.8	25.0	50.0	4.2	100	24

SOURCE: Modified with special permission from Everett M. Rogers and J. David Stanfield, "Adoption and Diffusion of New Products: Emerging Generalizations and Hypotheses," paper presented at the Conf. on the Application of Sciences to Marketing Management, Purdue University (July 12–15, 1966), tables 4 and 5.

Marketing Applications A great deal of research in recent years has been directed toward the profiling of innovators in a manner helpful to marketing strategists.[55] Like more general innovation studies, the marketing studies have almost always indicated the importance of *income* in profiling the innovator. Robertson found that out of thirteen studies where this variable was examined,

---

[55] An excellent summary and synthesis of this literature is available in Thomas S. Robertson, *Innovative Behavior and Communication* (New York: Holt, Rinehart and Winston, 1971). The authors express their gratitude for Professor Robertson's contribution through his book in the revision of the present chapter.

nine show higher income level to be associated with higher innovativeness, while four show a lack of relationship.[56] It may be more useful to use the concept of "privilegedness" than income. This refers to the amount of income an individual has relative to the other individuals with which he normally associates.[57] When the product is a frequently purchased low-priced product, however, income (and education and occupation) may have little relation to early adoption.[58] In one study, a curvilinear relationship was found between income and innovativeness, with the middle-income group containing less innovators because of unwillingness to take risks.[59]

Marketing strategists probably should assume that income will be important in profiling the innovator but that it should be weighted in direct proportion to the price of innovation. Also, the ability to try or sample the new product with little risk may mitigate the importance of income in innovation.

Social status appears also to be positively related to consumer innovation. Using the Reiss index of occupational status, one study revealed that among the earliest adopters of a new automobile service, one in three had an occupational index higher than 75. This is compared to a ratio of only one in seven for the population at large (of noninnovators). The 75-point level of the socioeconomic index consists only of the highest status professions such as architects, scientists, lawyers, doctors, engineers, auditors, and top management positions.[60]

Highly mobile people also appear to be more likely to be early adopters of new products. Shaw found that people who traveled extensively, had advanced in their jobs and income, and moved around were more likely to accept new products than stay-at-homes, even with income held constant.[61] Heavy users of the product were found by King[62] to be more likely to accept a new style of millinery, although this was not found to be true for heavy coffee users when faced with a new brand of coffee.[63] There is a need for a great deal more research relating consumer characteristics and product categories.

Of various personality or attitudinal variables that explain early adoption by consumers, one of the most explanatory appears to be *venturesomeness*. Robertson and Kennedy found that the trait of venturesomeness was able to explain about 35 percent of the difference between innovators and noninnovators

[56] Robertson, *op. cit.*,[55] p. 104.

[57] Richard P. Coleman, "The Significance of Social Stratification in Selling," in Martin L. Bell (ed.), *Marketing: A Maturing Discipline* (Chicago: Amer. Marketing Assoc., 1960), pp. 171–184.

[58] Frank *et al.*, *op. cit.*,[15] p. 318.

[59] Frank Cancian, "Stratification and Risk-Taking: A Theory Tested on Agricultural Innovation," *Amer. Sociological Rev.*, vol. 32, pp. 912–927 (Dec. 1967).

[60] Robert J. Kegerreis, James F. Engel, and Roger D. Blackwell, "Innovativeness and Diffusiveness: A Marketing View of the Characteristics of Earliest Adopters," in Kollat *et al.*, *op. cit.*,[45] pp. 671–689, at p. 678.

[61] Stephen J. Shaw, "Behavioral Science Offers Fresh Insights on New Product Acceptance," *J. Marketing*, vol. 29, pp. 9–14, at p. 10 (Jan. 1965).

[62] Charles W. King, "The Innovator in the Fashion Adoption Process," in Smith, *op. cit.*,[15] pp. 324–339, at p. 335.

[63] Frank *et al.*, *op. cit.*,[15] pp. 318–320.

for a new telephone product.[64] Jacoby found in a study of 15 product categories that "openmindedness" was significantly related to innovative responses.[65] Scores on "dogmatism" have also been investigated as a variable in innovativeness but with inconclusive results.[66]

Innovation Proneness   Early in diffusion research, an assumption was sometimes made that some individuals were "innovation prone" and that consequently the person who was an innovator for one product would also be the innovator of other products. Robertson and Myers found that appliance, clothing, and food innovators were statistically related but at such a low level (of correlation) as to dispute the notion that innovativeness is a general trait possessed by consumers.[67] Arndt concluded that a general receptiveness to innovation exists, but his investigation was in closely related product lines related to food consumption.[68]

The earliest adopters of a new automobile service, compared to the population as a whole, were found to be

(1)   Much *more willing to experiment* with new ideas
(2)   *More likely to buy new products* (in general) earlier
(3)   *Less likely to switch brands* because of a small price change
(4)   *Less interested in low prices* per se
(5)   *Less likely to try new convenience items* if the innovation represented only minor changes.[69]

In this study, it was concluded that innovators were the best informed sector of the population and that they engaged in considerable planning before purchasing innovations. It is not surprising (because of better information and planning) that innovators are more willing to experiment with new ideas and that they are *not* willing to be classified as hasty purchasers just because a product is new. The superior education, occupational status, and purchasing planning are likely to contribute to innovativeness for other types of products, but the desire for "newness" per se does not seem to be a reason for innovation proneness.

After a rigorous assessment of the literature in this area, Robertson concluded that "the consistency of innovativeness cannot be expected across product

---

[64]   Thomas S. Robertson and James N. Kennedy, "Prediction of Consumer Innovators: Application of Multiple Discriminant Analysis," *J. Marketing Research*, vol. 5, pp. 64–69 (Feb. 1968).

[65]   Jacob Jacoby, "A Multiple-Indicant Approach for Studying Innovators," Purdue Papers in Consumer Psychology, no. 108 (Lafayette, Ind.: Purdue Unversity, 1970).

[66]   Brian Blake, Robert Perloff, and Richard Heslin, "Dogmatism and Acceptance of New Products," *J. Marketing Research*, vol. 7 pp. 483–486 (Nov. 1970).

[67]   Thomas S. Robertson and James H. Myers, "Personality Correlates of Opinion Leadership and Innovative Buying Behavior," *J. Marketing Research*, vol. 6, pp. 164–168 (May 1969).

[68]   Johan Arndt, "Profiling Consumer Innovators," in Johan Arndt (ed.), *Insights into Consumer Behavior* (Boston: Allyn and Bacon, 1968), pp. 71–83.

[69]   Kegerreis *et al., op. cit.*,[60] p. 687.

categories, but can be expected within product categories and, sometimes, between related product categories."[70]

Product Characteristics Associated with Innovativeness

The acceptance of a new product by innovators is determined to a large degree by characteristics of the product itself. It is more correct to say that the product's acceptance is determined by what consumers *perceive* the product to be. Diffusion research indicates a number of product characteristics associated with the early adoption of the product. Those that have been investigated in multiple studies are presented in Table 24.2 and are described briefly below.[71]

Table 24.2 PRODUCT CHARACTERISTICS RELATED TO INNOVATIVENESS

	Number of Empirical Findings Indicating Relation to Innovativeness (%)					*Total Number of Published Findings*
	Positive	*None*	*Negative*	*Conditional*	*Total*	
(1) Relative advantage	78.8	15.2	3.0	3.0	100	66
(2) Compatibility	86.0	14.0	0.0	0.0	100	50
(3) Fulfillment of felt needs	92.6	3.7	3.7	0.0	100	27
(4) Complexity	18.8	37.5	43.7	0.0	100	16
(5) Trialability	42.9	42.9	14.3	0.0	100	14
(6) Observability	75.0	25.0	0.0	0.0	100	8
(7) Availability	55.6	22.2	16.7	5.6	100	18
(8) Immediacy of benefit	57.1	28.6	14.3	0.0	100	7

SOURCE: Modified with special permission from Everett M. Rogers and J. David Stanfield, "Adoption and Diffusion of New Products: Emerging Generalizations and Hypotheses," paper presented at the Conf. on the Application of Sciences to Marketing Management, Purdue University (July 12–15, 1966), table 7.

Relative advantage of the new product is an important determinant of a product's success. The product must be perceived by consumers to be superior to the product it supersedes or to offer a "benefit" recognized as more attractive

---

[70] Robertson, *op. cit.*,[55] p. 111.
[71] The following section is based upon Rogers and Shoemaker, *op. cit.*,[6] pp. 137–157.

than present products. Similarly, research indicates the stronger the *fulfillment of felt needs* is perceived by the consumer, the more readily he seeks information about a new product, maintains interest, and undertakes trial and adoption. Some evidence indicates that the more *immediate the benefit,* the more likely the consumer is to try the product.

The *compatibility* of a new product refers to the degree to which the product is consistent with existing values and past experiences of the adopter. The norms of the relevant reference group will retard acceptance of products that are not compatible with the social system. If the consumer perceives the product to be similar to previously tried and rejected products, acceptance of the new product will also be retarded. The color and design of the package, product, and promotional material accompanying the product act as a symbol to the consumer, communicating to him the compatibility of the new product with his existing value and cognitive structure. A marketer attempting to evaluate the compatibility of a new product needs to investigate the total *consumption system* into which the new product must fit.[72]

The *observability* (or communicability) of an innovation influences its rate of acceptance. Products that are visible in social situations or that have significant impact upon the social system appear to be those that are most communicable.

Some product characteristics have been identified that appear to inhibit the rate of adoption. One such characteristic is *complexity,* or the degree to which a new product is difficult to understand and use. Products that require detailed personal explanation, for example, are unlikely to diffuse rapidly. Although the research is far from conclusive, it appears that the *trialability* (or divisibility) of a product affects the rate of acceptance. This is due to the desire of consumers to try the product in a small quantity before deciding to adopt it. When the consumer is forced to buy a large unit at one time, he is likely to perceive more risk in the purchase than if he were able to purchase a little at a time.

There is a serious lack of consumer research attempting to validate diffusion findings concerning product characteristics. It is difficult to conduct such research because of the necessity of evaluating a number of different products simultaneously. Normally, diffusion studies in marketing have dealt with only one type of product at a time. At some point in the future, enough studies of this type may be accumulated that comparisons among products will be possible. In the interim, the marketer probably will rely upon the basic conceptualization or general diffusion studies as useful hypotheses in evaluating the probable success of a new product.

Social and Communication Variables Associated with Innovativeness

The relations between a consumer and other members and objects of the social system influence the rate of adoption of new products. The relations that affect new product acceptance are of two basic types: marketing dominated and

---

[72] Harper W. Boyd, Jr., and Sidney J. Levy, "New Dimensions in Consumer Analysis," *Harvard Business Rev.,* pp. 129–140 (Nov.–Dec. 1963).

nonmarketing dominated. The effectiveness of one is often influenced by the other.

Marketing-Dominated Influences   Intensive contact with the mass media and commercial change agents tends to produce individuals who accept innovations more readily than others. This fact is indicated in items (2) and (3) of Table 24.3. The majority of research on diffusions indicates that communications from the mass media affect the adoption process most strongly at the awareness stage, the most important function being to inform the public of new products or ideas.[73] This research indicates that at later stages in the adoption process—

Table 24.3   SOCIAL AND COMMUNICATIONS VARIABLES RELATED TO INNOVATIVENESS

	Number of Empirical Findings Indicating Relation to Innovativeness (%)					
	Positive	*None*	*Negative*	*Conditional*	*Total*	*Total Number of Published Findings*
(1) Cosmopolitaness	80.8	11.0	2.7	5.5	100	73
(2) Mass media exposure	85.7	12.2	0.0	2.0	100	49
(3) Contact with change agencies	91.9	6.6	0.0	1.5	100	136
(4) Deviancy from norms	53.6	14.3	28.6	3.6	100	28
(5) Group participation	78.8	10.3	6.4	4.5	100	156
(6) Interpersonal communication exposure	70.0	15.0	15.0	0.0	100	40
(7) Opinion leadership	64.3	21.4	7.1	7.1	100	14

SOURCE: Modified with special permission from Everett M. Rogers and J. David Stanfield, "Adoption and Diffusion of New Products: Emerging Generalizations and Hypotheses," paper presented at the Conf. on the Application of Sciences to Marketing Management, Purdue University (July 12–15, 1966), table 6.

interest and evaluation—personal influences become more important. These conclusions have been challenged by Lazer and Bell, however, who present some contradictory findings. They found that only 13.8 percent of consumers in one study of appliances used mass media in the awareness stage and that 96 percent of those seeking information at the interest and evaluation stages turned to the mass media.[74] Engel, Knapp, and Knapp, however, found that advertising is an effec-

---

[73]   Rogers, *op. cit.*,[9] p. 99.

[74]   Lazer and Bell, *op. cit.*,[8] pp. 4–5.

tive communication in creating awareness of new drug products when coupled with other sources,[75] and King found that mass media sources were the most important sources of information to early adopters of millinery.[76]

Other activities under the control of the marketing organizations have a significant impact on adoption. Sampling has been shown to be one of the most effective techniques for informing consumers of a new product.[77] Also, the research of Willett and Pennington on the nature of the salesman–customer problem-solving process is consonant with the view that the personal salesmen play a very important role in providing information to the consumer.[78] Stefflre and Barnett have advanced a technique called cognitive mapping to determine how consumers view a product category with the objective of determining how effective advertising should be developed for new products.[79]

Word-of-Mouth Communications

Word-of-mouth, or personal, communications play a critical role in the adoption of new products. Numerous studies have indicated such a finding, as indicated in item (6) of Table 24.3. Traditionally, it has been postulated that as an individual moves through early stages and toward adoption, the individual increasingly turns to other individuals for confirming information. The individual seeking information turns either to someone who has already purchased the new product or to an "expert"—someone who by reason of training or experience has superior ability to judge the product. For example, a consumer interested in buying a new model of a camera may ask a photographer or a serious camera hobbyist to help evaluate the new model.

Individuals apparently turn to personal sources of influence as the amount of perceived risk in the new product increases.[80] Generally it has also

---

[75] James F. Engel, David A. Knapp, and Deanne E. Knapp, "Sources of Influence in the Acceptance of New Products for Self-Medication: Preliminary Findings," in Haas, *op. cit.*,[7] pp. 776–782, at p. 778.

[76] Charles W. King, "Communicating with the Innovator in the Fashion Adoption Process," in Peter D. Bennett (ed.), *Marketing and Economic Development* (Chicago: Amer. Marketing Assoc., 1965), pp. 425–439, at p. 435.

[77] Haines, *op. cit.*,[15] p. 689.

[78] Ronald P. Willett and Allan L. Pennington, "Customer and Salesman: The Anatomy of Choice and Influence in a Retail Setting," in Haas, *op. cit.*,[7] pp. 598–616. The influence of salesmen in distributing information about new drugs to physicians is also well documented. See Theodore Caplow, "Market Attitudes: A Research Report from the Medical Field," *Harvard Business Rev.*, vol. 30, pp. 105–112 (Nov.–Dec. 1952).

[79] Volney Stefflre, "Market Structure Studies: New Products for Old Markets and New Markets (Foreign) for Old Products," in Bass *et al.*, *op. cit.*,[49] pp. 251–268; Norman L. Barnett, "Developing Effective Advertising for New Products," *J. Advertising Research*, vol. 8, pp. 13–18 (Dec. 1968).

[80] Herbert Menzel and Elihu Katz, "Social Relations and Innovation in the Medical Profession: The Epidemiology of a New Drug," *Public Opinion Quart.*, pp. 337–352 (Winter 1955–1956). For an overview of the physician studies, see Raymond A. Bauer and Lawrence H. Wortzel, "Doctor's Choice: The Physician and His Sources of Information about Drugs," *J. Marketing Research*, vol. 3, pp. 40–47 (Feb. 1966). For additional research concerning the

been found that individuals turn to personal sources of information when the choice between products is ambiguous.[81]

Word-of-mouth influence about new products is a two-way information flow. A study of adoption of a new automobile service demonstrated that word of mouth was the most important influence in the *trial* stage leading to adoption (as differentiated from *awareness* and *interest*), and that the innovators actively *sought* opinion from a variety of personal sources.[82] Myers and Robertson in a study of household products found that opinion leadership for these products was a two-way phenomenon. They concluded that the opinion leader is moderately more innovative than nonopinion leaders and is only relatively more influential than the average person. The housewife who is an opinion leader and innovator is also a "recipient of influence, not a dominant leader influencing a passive set of followers."[83]

Marketing strategists should also be concerned about the potential of *unfavorable* as well as favorable word-of-mouth communications. Arndt found that consumers who received unfavorable word-of-mouth comments were 24 percentage points *less* likely to purchase a new product than other consumers, while persons who received favorable word-of-mouth comments were only 12 percentage points more likely to buy.[84]

Social Integration There is a considerable body of research attempting to determine the role that social integration of an individual plays in his decision to adopt a new product. In general, persons who are well integrated into the social system and who are respected by a group appear to adopt new products more rapidly than those who are less integrated.[85] An example of empirical research in this area is shown in Figure 24.7. A new food product was introduced

---

role of perceived risk in innovative behavior, see Johan Arndt, "Perceived Risk, Sociometric Integration, and Word of Mouth in the Adoption of a New Food Product," in Donald F. Cox (ed.), *Risk Taking and Information Handling in Consumer Behavior* (Boston: Division of Research, Graduate School of Business Administration, Harvard University, 1967), pp. 289–316; also Donald T. Popielarz, "An Exploration of Perceived Risk and Willingness to Try New Products," *J. Marketing Research*, vol. 4, pp. 368–372 (Nov. 1967).

[81] James Coleman, Herbert Menzel, and Elihu Katz, "Social Processes in Physicians' Adoption of a New Drug," *J. Chronic Diseases*, vol. 9, pp. 1–19 (Jan. 1959).

[82] James F. Engel, Roger D. Blackwell, and Robert J. Kegerreis, "How Information Is Used to Adopt an Innovation," *J. Advertising Research*, vol. 9, pp. 3–10 (Dec. 1969).

[83] James H. Myers and Thomas S. Robertson, "Dimensions of Opinion Leadership," *J. Marketing Research*, vol. 9, pp. 41–46 (Feb. 1972).

[84] Johan Arndt, "Role of Product Related Conversations in the Diffusion of a New Product," *J. Marketing Research*, vol. 4, pp. 291–295, at p. 242 (Aug. 1967). Arndt has conducted numerous other studies of personal influence upon innovativeness. Among his conclusions is the finding that some overlap occurs in opinion leadership, especially for closely related product categories. See Johan Arndt, "New Product Diffusion: The Interplay of Innovativeness, Opinion Leadership, Learning, Perceived Risk and Product Characteristics," *Markedskommunikasion*, vol. 5, pp. 1–9 (1968); Johan Arndt, "Exploring Consumer Willingness to Buy New Products," *Markedskommunikasion*, vol. 8, pp. 1–12 (1971).

[85] For a review of the literature supporting this statement, see Rogers, *op. cit.*,[9] pp. 237–247.

into a social system; the figure shows that housewives who were named most often as "a relatively good friend" were also among the earliest adopters of the product.[86] Coleman and co-workers, in their studies of physicians, have demonstrated that the reliance upon highly respected members of the group increases markedly with the amount of risk perceived to be associated with adopting a new product.[87]

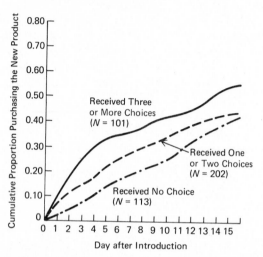

Figure 24.7 RELATION BETWEEN TIME OF FIRST PURCHASE OF NEW FOOD PRODUCT AND NUMBER OF CHOICES RECEIVED BY HOUSE-WIVES AS "RELATIVELY CLOSE FRIEND." Johan Arndt, "Role of Product-Related Conversations in the Diffusion of a New Product," *J. Marketing Research*, vol. 4, pp. 291–295, at p. 293 (Aug. 1967). Reprinted by permission of the author and the publisher.

Gregariousness is a trait usually associated with innovativeness, both on the part of the opinion leader and the individual being influenced.[88] King found that the fashion innovator is characterized by an active life style in which innovators were likely to visit or entertain friends frequently, attend church or synagogue frequently, attend spectator sports, eat at restaurants frequently, and attend teas, concerts, plays, and club meetings.[89] An additional observation is that individuals who adhere fairly closely to the norms of their group in other forms of social

[86] Johan Arndt, "Role of Product Related Conversations in the Diffusion of a New Product," *op. cit.*,[84] pp. 291–295, at p. 293.

[87] James Coleman, Elihu Katz, and Herbert Menzel, "The Diffusion of an Innovation among Physicians," *Sociometry*, vol. 20, pp. 253–269 (Dec. 1957).

[88] The classic documentation of this finding is Elihu Katz and Paul F. Lazarsfeld, *Personal Influence* (New York: Free Press, 1955), esp. chaps. 10 and 11; also W. Erbe, "Gregariousness, Group Membership and the Flow of Information," *Amer. J. Sociology*, vol. 67, pp. 502– 516 (Mar. 1962).

[89] King, *op. cit.*,[62] p. 335.

behavior will perform similarly with regard to innovations.[90] Exceptions may be those who have achieved very high status in their reference group and are freer to deviate from the norms of behavior and those so low in status that they no longer observe the group norms. Presumably, it might be reasoned, these exceptions may be expected to deviate from norms more readily than others when considering the acceptance of a new product.

SUMMARY

The marketing organization plays the role of a "professional change agent" in the adoption of new products. Therefore, it is the task of the consumer analyst to determine how the marketing organization can most effectively influence consumer acceptance of new products and services.

Perhaps the most valuable function of diffusion studies described in this chapter is to indicate that acceptance of a new idea does not come all at once in a social system. The idea is transmitted to a few innovators who must pass through various stages leading to adoption. After some innovators have adopted the product, others may follow, depending on the value of the innovation and the process of influence. In general, the process has great stability and has been shown to apply in many areas of social research. A number of studies have shown the process to follow the logistic curve, represented in Figure 24.8. The logistic curve produces a distribution of innovator types shown in Figure 24.9. This distribution has been widely disseminated through the work of Rogers. In more recent years, the logistic curve has been challenged as representing the acceptance of new products, and the exponential curve (also shown in Figure 24.8) or other mathematical functions have been investigated. Much additional research is needed to clarify the conditions under which such models are appropriate for predicting new product acceptance.

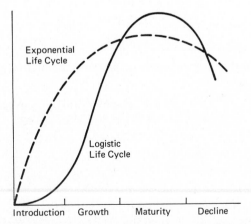

Figure 24.8 LOGISTIC AND EXPONENTIAL LIFE CYCLE PATTERNS

---

[90] George C. Homans, *Social Behavior: Its Elementary Forms* (New York: Harcourt, 1961), chap. 5.

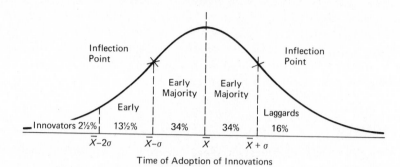

Figure 24.9 MARKET SEGMENTS IDENTIFIED BY TIME OF ADOPTION OF NEW PRODUCT (AS PROPORTION OF TOTAL WHO EVENTUALLY ADOPT PRODUCT). X—MEAN TIME FOR ADOPTION Everett M. Rogers, *Diffusion of Innovations* (New York: Free Press, 1962), p. 162. Reprinted by permission of the publisher.

It should be concluded that the acceptance of new products does not occur for "one" reason or because of a "single" influence. A variety of forces are necessary to stimulate adoption. Some of these influences are marketer dominated such as advertising, sampling, and the sales force. Effective utilization of these marketing forces depends upon knowledge of the diffusion characteristics of the product category. At the same time, other variables influence the adoption process which are beyond the control of the marketing strategist. In the latter instance, the consumer analyst provides information helpful in adapting to consumer realities rather than trying to change them.

REVIEW AND DISCUSSION QUESTIONS

1. It is easy to understand the interest of a marketing manager in the topic of diffusion of innovation. Explain why a macroeconomist might be interested in the subject.

2. Several definitions of innovation are presented in the chapter. Which would you use to conduct research in your field? Defend your choice.

3. Explain as precisely as possible the differences among continuous, dynamically continuous, and discontinuous innovations.

4. A manufacturer of automotive parts has invented a new product that he hopes to sell to consumers on a wide-scale basis. This product is used to start automobiles in cold weather without requiring the consumer to leave his home. It has an electrical device attached to the ignition system of the car which starts the car by remote control from inside the house. This permits the driver to have the heater on and the car warm when he is ready to use the car. The car must be parked in such a way that the clutch can be left out of gear. As a consultant to this firm, you are asked to predict the diffusion process for this

product, and your task is to help him accomplish the diffusion, not evaluate whether or not to introduce it. Outline your analysis.

5. A new bakery product is being introduced by a large firm. The company believes that it should obtain about 20 percent penetration in a market of 20 million people. In a test market, it was found that 3 percent of the people tried the product within the first week of introduction and that of those who tried it about half purchased the product again. However, of those who repurchased, usage was only one unit every two weeks. The bakery has asked you to help estimate the amount of production that will be needed each week until the product reaches a stable market position. Prepare a method to use.

6. The manufacturer of a new product is attempting to determine who the innovators for his product might be. His product is a game that requires players to answer each other with phrases from various foreign languages. Who would you identify for him as the most likely innovators? What appeals would you suggest he use in promoting the product?

7. A large manufacturer of drug and personal grooming products wants to introduce a new toothpaste brand in addition to the three he already markets. Evaluate for the firm what information he might use from innovation studies to guide him in introducing the product.

8. A large pharmaceutical firm has successfully marketed an infant formula for several years. This product has good acceptance among pediatricians, who recommend the product for babies up to six months. In an attempt to expand their market, the firm has developed a new liquid food for babies between the ages of 6 and 18 months. The new food is flavored with vegetables, fruits, or cereal, yet is fed through a bottle. It will compete directly with regular strained baby food, and the firm knows that competition will be keen. However, the firm is prepared to release an authoritative report by a well-known medical school to show that morbidity rates among liquid-fed babies are significantly lower than among strained-food-fed babies. This report indicates that it takes 100 spoonfuls of strained food each day to give a baby a nutritionally sound diet. Since babies tend to throw the food on the floor they often receive a deficient diet and the liquid food will remedy this. The firm is convinced it must receive the endorsement of the liquid food by pediatricians to be successful. Your job is to outline a program to gain adoption of liquid food as the food recommended by pediatricians.

Epilogue

PART

The conclusion of this book deals mostly with the beginning of some new directions in the study of consumer behavior. Two final chapters deal with consumerism from a consumer research standpoint and with the current status of consumer behavior research.

Chapter 25 is an analysis of consumerism using the tools for analyzing consumer behavior presented throughout this book. A brief treatment of the meaning and evolution of consumerism is presented but the focus of this chapter is upon the criticality of a research approach, especially one using decision process models and important concepts such as market segmentation. In this context the chapter describes some of the research potentials in understanding control of consumer choice, environmental responsibility, marketing of social products, product safety and quality, consumer information, and the responsibilities of marketing to the minority poor.

Chapter 26 is a summary statement on the prospects and problems of consumer research. This chapter assesses current progress in consumer research and outlines the major obstacles to be overcome or at least recognized if future progress in understanding of consumer decisions is to proceed at an accelerated rate.

25

CONSUMERISM

President John F. Kennedy, in his 1962 declaration of rights for the consumer, stated that consumers have:

(1)   The right to safety.
(2)   The right to be informed.
(3)   The right to choose.
(4)   The right to be heard.[1]

These rights have been reaffirmed by every United States president since Kennedy. Yet, the following conditions exist:

(1)   An Opinion Research poll reports that one out of every five Americans polled said he had been cheated or deceived in regard to at least one product or service purchased during 1969.[2]
(2)   The Federal Food and Drug Administration estimates that about $1

---

[1]   Quoted in E. B. Weiss, "Marketers Fiddle while Consumers Burn," *Harvard Business Rev.*, p. 45 (July–Aug. 1968).
[2]   Quoted by Virginia Knauer, Special Assistant for Consumer Affairs to the President of the United States, in Remarks before National Appliance and Radio–TV Dealers Association, Chicago, Ill. (Apr. 21, 1971), p. 3.

billion is spent annually on worthless or extravagantly misrepresented quack devices, drugs, foods, and cosmetics.[3]

(3)   From 3000 to 5000 deaths and 250,000 injuries resulted in 1970 from accidents with flammable fabrics and approximately 700,000 unsuspecting children were the victims of hazardous toy injuries.[4]

(4)   Bumpers on United States produced automobiles are able to withstand impacts only to the point that collision speed is less than 2.8 miles per hour.[5]

(5)   Over 20,000,000 persons in the United States live in housing below the level of decent human occupancy.[6]

The situations described above illustrate why the topic of consumerism has become of major significance in contemporary society. The solutions to the above problems extend far beyond the discipline of consumer behavior, of course. This chapter does not provide solutions to the above (and other) problems. It does attempt an assessment of how the discipline of consumer behavior can contribute to progress in developing solutions.

NATURE OF CONSUMERISM

If this book is placed aside and an attempt is made to find a definition of consumerism in a dictionary, the search probably will be unsuccessful. The concept is too new. The following pages describe emerging definitions of consumerism, the historical antecedents of consumerism, and its social–ethical basis.

Definitions of Consumerism

Consumerism, like most "isms," has many meanings. Ferber has described these meanings as ranging from nothing more than people's search for getting better values for their money to challenging that goal of a society that calls for an ever-increasing amount of material goods through time. Consumerists of the first type believe that prices are too high, quality and safety of goods are not adequate, and that service facilities need to be improved. The latter group of consumerists question whether the emphasis should be on increasing material wealth or whether it might be better to focus more resources on public welfare, health, and education programs and better leisure facilities and programs.[7]

---

[3]   Quoted by Doris Sasser, Associate Director, President's Committee on Consumer Interests, in Remarks before Council of Chief State School Officers, Atlantic City, N.J. (Feb. 19, 1971), p. 3.

[4]   Sasser, *op. cit.*[3]

[5]   Virginia Knauer, "The Consumer and the Conglomerate," paper presented at the Federal Bar Association, Washington, D.C. (Sept. 17, 1970), p. 9.

[6]   Daniel Bell, "Social Trends of the 70's," *Conference Board Record*, pp. 6–9, (June 1970).

[7]   Robert Ferber, "Rising Consumerism Primary Concern to Market Managers," paper presented at the American Marketing Association, Hawaii Chapter (May 7, 1970); reprinted in *Marketing News*, pp. 4ff (Mid–June 1970).

Some analysts have defined consumerism as:

> . . . the organized efforts of consumers seeking redress, restitution, and remedy for dissatisfaction they have accumulated in the acquisition of their standard of living.[8]

This definition can be broadened usefully by dropping the requirement that consumerism be limited to "organized efforts." Cravens and Hills achieve this in their view that consumerism is a "social force:"

> . . . Consumerism is a social force within the environment designed to aid and protect the consumer by exerting legal, moral, and economic pressure on business.[9]

Even this definition may be too limiting in that pressure is focused only on *business*. The concept of consumerism might correctly focus pressure on *schools* to educate consumers adequately. Thus, the definition used in this text will be a wide concept of what is meant by consumerism (including individual activity), similar to that of Day and Aaker:

> The most common understanding of consumerism is in reference to the widening range of activities of government, business and independent organizations that are designed to protect individuals from practices that infringe upon their rights as consumers. . . . Because it is an evolving concept, there is no accepted list of the various facets. . . . The following is representative: (1) Protection against clear-cut abuses . . . (2) Provision for adequate information . . . (3) The protection of consumers against themselves and other consumers.[10]

A broad definition of consumerism is necessary for consumer researchers because of the variety of functions which they may perform concerning consumerism. Some consumer researchers may be primarily involved in the investigation of consumerism in order to assist business firms develop marketing strategy; other researchers may investigate consumerism in order to assist nonbusiness organizations to develop marketing strategy; and still other researchers may assist government, other organizations, or individuals to *counteract* marketing strategies. Some consumer researchers may even determine an integrative function which encompasses diverse interests.

Historical Antecedents of Consumerism

Consumerism has numerous historical antecedents even though the term may be new. The genesis of consumerism may have been in Upton Sinclair's *The Jungle* or other books at the turn of the century which exposed consumer

---

[8] Richard H. Buskirk and James T. Rothe, "Consumerism—An Interpretation," *J. Marketing*, vol. 34, pp. 61–65 (Oct. 1970).

[9] David W. Cravens and Gerald E. Hills, "Consumerism: A Perspective for Business," *Business Horizons*, vol. 13, pp. 21–28 (Aug. 1970).

[10] George S. Day and David A. Aaker, "A Guide to Consumerism," *J. Marketing*, vol. 17, pp. 12–19 (July 1970).

and worker exploitation, resulting in consumer protection regulation such as the Meat Inspection Acts.[11] Other observers see consumerism arising during the last quarter of the 19th century but attribute it to concern over the economic environment and large-scale business power and concentration.[12]

Three eras of consumerism are identified in a history of consumerism by Herrmann.[13] The first era was the early 1900s, mentioned above. The second era was the mid-1930s resulting in the Pure Food and Drug Act in 1938 after more than 100 people died from *Elixir Sulfanilamide*, a new sulfa wonder drug which proved lethal when misused. The third era was the 1960s, perhaps beginning with President Kennedy's "Consumer Message" in March, 1962.

The value for consumer analysts in studying the history of consumerism is in the attempt to learn why consumerism activism occurs. Herrmann postulates that each era occurred after several decades of rapidly rising incomes followed by rising prices which caused decreases in the rise of real purchasing power.[14] A Gallup poll in 1940 indicated that it was the highly educated and high-income individuals who contributed to leadership as consumerists in the 1930s, and a study of Consumers Union members recently indicated that they had a median income of $14,000 with 58 percent having college degrees.[15] This supports a view that consumerism also arises in periods of marked increases in literacy and income.[16]

The causes of consumerism were investigated by Gaedeke in a study of businessmen, consumer spokesmen, and government officials. In the survey, 38 possible causes of consumerism were investigated, but there was a consensus on only seven as related to the underlying causes of consumerism. They were

(1)   The political appeal of consumer protection legislation

(2)   The mechanical and impersonal nature of the marketplace

(3)   The language of advertising

(4)   A bandwagon effect

(5)   Greater public concern for social problems

(6)   A feeling that business should assume greater "social responsibilities"

(7)   A change in national attitude.[17]

---

[11]   This is described in Carolyn Shaw Bell, "Consumer Economic Power," *J. Consumer Affairs,* vol. 2, pp. 155–156 (Winter 1968).

[12]   Arthur M. Schlesinger, Jr., *A Crisis in Confidence* (New York: Bantam, 1969), pp. 55–56.

[13]   Robert O. Herrmann, "Consumerism: Its Goals, Organizations and Future," *J. Marketing,* vol. 34, pp. 55–60 (Oct. 1970).

[14]   Herrmann, *op. cit.*[13]

[15]   Herrmann, *op. cit.*[13]

[16]   E. B. Weiss, *A Critique of Consumerism* (New York: Doyle Dane Bernbach, 1967).

[17]   Ralph M. Gaedeke, "What Business, Government and Consumer Spokesmen Think about Consumerism," *J. Consumer Affairs,* vol. 4, pp. 7–18, at p. 16 (Summer 1970).

Social–Ethical Issues in Consumerism

Outcries for corporate sensitivity to human and social needs are becoming a major input into the planning of many firms and other organizations. Executives of firms are increasingly plunged into the search for decency and responsibility in the midst of a confusing and sometimes overwhelming environment. Marketing, because it is the primary interface of business with society, is often more directly confronted by the quest for social and ethical responsibility than other functions of business.

Two types of responsibility impinge upon the planning of marketing strategy. The first is *social responsibility*, defined simply as accepting an obligation for the proper functioning of the society in which the firm operates. It involves accountability for the activities through which the firm can reasonably contribute to the society. *Ethical responsibility*, the second type, is more fundamental than social responsibility. Ethical responsibility is concerned with the determination of *how* things should be, human pursuit of the right course of action, and the individual's doing what is morally right.[18]

Actions alone determine social responsibility, and a firm can be socially responsible even when doing so under coercion. For example, the government may pass laws that *force* firms to be socially responsible in matters of pollution or inflammability of products, and consumers may *force* marketers to provide nutritional information on packages. To be ethically responsible, on the other hand, it is not sufficient to act correctly; ethical intent is also necessary.

Consumer behavior research often focuses on social responsibility. Consumer research has the potential of investigating the social norms of responsibility that might be desirable among consumers, given the prevailing ethical makeup of the population and then measuring the results of business strategy to determine if results and expectations coincide.

The rationale for consumerism stems from the humanistic or Judaic–Christian belief that people who live on earth ought to take care of the environment and ought to treat each other as they expect to be treated themselves.[19] Beyond that, there is great dispute about the extent of marketing's responsibility for society and proper activities involved in such responsibility. This debate and the literature which surrounds it are important but beyond space requirements of the present text.[20] The need for marketing education and use of research in analyzing these responsibilities is described by Gelb and Brien.[21]

---

[18] For amplification of these concepts, see David Kollat, Roger Blackwell, and James Robeson, *Strategic Marketing* (New York: Holt, Rinehart and Winston, 1972), chap. 22.

[19] An exposition and extension of these ideas in business is found in Harold L. Johnson, "Can the Businessman Apply Christianity?" *Harvard Business Rev.*, p. 68 (Sept.–Oct. 1957).

[20] A highly selected sample of this literature includes the following: James M. Patterson, "What Are the Social and Ethical Responsibilities of Marketing Executives?" *J. Marketing*, vol. 30, pp. 12–15 (July 1966); George Champion, "Creative Competition," *Harvard Business Rev.*, pp. 61–67 (May–June 1967); Arthur W. Lorig, "Where Do Corporate Responsibilities Really Lie?" *Business Horizons*, vol. 10, pp. 51–54 (Spring 1967); Leland Hazard, "Business Must Put Up," *Harvard Business Rev.*, pp. 2–13ff (Feb. 1968); Hazel Henderson,

CONSUMER BEHAVIOR AND CONSUMERISM

Consumer behavior, as a discipline of study, has a critical role to occupy in the analysis of consumerism. The criticality of this role lies in the potential of the consumer behavior discipline to provide an analytical framework with which to resolve some of the conflict that arises between business, government, and consumer groups.

Criticality of a Research Approach

The discipline of consumer behavior has the potential to be a powerful boundary spanning agent by providing a rigorous research framework for the investigation of issues in consumerism. Resolution of the disparate views of diverse groups seeking to respond to consumerism needs the objectivity of information that is the output of well-designed research on consumer behavior.

A research approach to consumerism emphasizes the collection of information about consumer attitudes and behavior rather than policies that should evolve from the research. Throughout this chapter, with a few exceptions, literature is emphasized which is based upon empirical studies rather than normative thinking. The approach is not to attempt a determination of what business "ought to do," not to specify what protective policies "ought" to be enacted by the government, or not even to provide a rationale for a particular type of consumer choice in the economic system. It is too early for consumer researchers to provide these answers which can only emerge by social concensus.

A research approach to consumerism provides an alternative to normative authoritarianism. There is a consistent ideological conflict reflected in the literature of consumerism concerning the issue of what consumers *want* versus what they *ought* to want and what they know about products versus what they need to know about products. Moran has investigated the opinions of both

---

"Should Business Tackle Society's Problems?" *Harvard Business Rev.*, pp. 77–85 (July–Aug. 1968); William Lazer, "Marketing's Changing Social Relationships," *J. Marketing*, vol. 33, pp. 3–9 (Jan. 1969); Irwin Miller, "Business Has a War to Win," *Harvard Business Rev.*, pp. 4–6ff (Mar.–Apr. 1969); Leslie M. Dawson, "The Human Concept: New Philosophy for Business, Marketing Concept Outmoded Today," *Business Horizons*, vol. 12, pp. 29–38 (Dec. 1969); Robert J. Lavidge, "The Growing Responsibilities of Marketing," *J. Marketing*, vol. 34, pp. 25–28 (Jan. 1970); "The Place of Business in Society," *Financial Executive*, pp. 34–46 (Oct. 1970); Rodman C. Rockefeller, "Turn Public Problems to Private Account," *Harvard Business Rev.*, pp. 131–138 (Jan.–Feb. 1971); Burton G. Malkiel and Richard E. Quandt, "Moral Issues in Investment Policy," *Harvard Business Rev.*, pp. 37–47 (Mar.–Apr. 1971). Also see the entire July, 1971, issue of *J. Marketing*. These topics are also discussed in the trade press including *Business Week, Fortune, Dun's Rev., Sales Management, Saturday Rev.* and many other magazines.

[21] Betsy D. Gelb and Richard H. Brien, "Survival and Social Responsibility: Themes for Marketing Education and Management," *J. Marketing*, vol. 35, pp. 3–9 (Apr. 1971); also J. Irwin Miller, "A New Partnership: Business, Education, Society," *Business Horizons*, vol. 10, pp. 21–30 (Spring 1967).

marketing executives and consumerists on this subject and observes persistent differences between the two groups:

> This difference appeared almost without exception when I asked marketers and critics a question of the sort, "What do consumers *need* to know when deciding among the competing brands and models of product?" The critic was never fazed by the question and could easily speak at this normative level. The marketer in most cases would respond not to the question that had been asked but rather to the quite different question, "What do consumers *want* to know . . . ?" Only with prodding and a subsequent feeling of uneasiness and meaninglessness of reply would marketers get out into what they considered to be a "big-brother" way of looking at the consumer.[22]

The research approach emphasizes investigation of how consumers actually feel and behave. Research is more difficult in situations where new alternatives are proposed for consumers than in situations relating only to existing alternatives. Moran has described methods, however, for "test marketing" proposed new consumerism regulation and policies in much the same way that business firms have successfully test marketed new product offerings.[23]

In a society where normative authoritarianism prevails, the groups that will specify the rules for consumers are the groups that have the most power. The holders of power vary through time and between consumption choices depending on personal charisma, economic control, and so forth. The countervailing force that provides a more democratic alternative is rigorous research into the actual behavior of consumers rather than reliance on normative statements of how the consumer *should* behave.

Criticality of Consumer Behavior Analytical Models

Analytical models of consumer behavior are equally important in understanding consumerism programs as they are in understanding the marketing of products generally. A decision process model such as the one used throughout this text is an important need in understanding what kinds of information are needed by consumers, why some products and programs introduced or endorsed by consumerists fail, and how to introduce products deemed to be in consumers' interest in such a way that they will be accepted into consumers' behavioral patterns. Consumer behavior models, in other words, help analyze what goes wrong with consumerism policies and how to prevent such problems before they occur.

An empirical example of the failure of a socially responsive marketing act is provided by low-lead gasoline. One of the most consistent pressures among consumerists has been for products which contribute to environmental quality instead of add to pollution. In a 1970 survey of American adults more than half

---

[22] Robert Moran, "Formulating Public Policy on Consumer Issues: Some Preliminary Findings," working paper P-57-A (Boston: Marketing Science Institute, Sept. 1971), p. 31.

[23] Moran, *op. cit.*[22]

rated reducing air pollution a matter of major importance. This was up from 17 percent in 1965 and in 1970 was rated second only to crime control as a major national priority.[24] In response to such concern, Senator Edmund Muskie sponsored pollution control legislation that required "that the auto industry reduce air pollution at least 90 percent from current levels (1970 standards) in cars produced after January 1, 1975."[25]

In response to legislation, the auto industry began developing a catalytic emission control device. However, this catalytic muffler will not function properly unless unleaded fuels are used. Thus, the auto industry urged the petroleum refiners to cooperate by developing nonleaded gasolines. The oil refiners developed such gasolines and began marketing them. It should be mentioned that the regulatory, or forced, assumption of social responsibility could have been delayed until 1975. But the oil industry voluntarily assumed this responsibility nearly four years in advance of this date.

Initially low-leaded and nonleaded gasolines were not purchased by consumers in significant magnitude. In spite of aggressive marketing by the refiners, the no-lead/low-lead gasolines received less than half of the 10-percent volume expected of them.[26]

Research is needed to determine why the failure occurred. Analysis of consumer decision making suggests several hypotheses. First, it may be that gasoline purchases represent habitual decision making, and the adoption of a new type of gas represents extended decision making. The marketing programs that are successful for one may have failed for the other because of the existence of radically greater search behavior and alternative evaluation than in habitual decision making. Second, problem recognition may have been of a much different nature than suspected. In habitual decision making, problem recognition occurs when the fuel gauge indicates need for gas, and, normally, decision making is shunted directly to purchase. It would be fallacious to assume that the generalized concern with pollution necessarily results in a preferred alternative of low-lead gasoline. Possibly consumers are concerned about pollution generally but do not perceive their own consumption of gasoline to be serious enough to result in a problem that would generate extended problem solving.[27]

Even if problem recognition were generated, it appears that the consumer would have little basis for internal search about the new alternative nor would the consumer have found much information from either marketing or nonmarketing dominated sources to satisfy the need for external search. If

---

[24] From a national poll conducted by the American Institute of Public Opinion, Princeton, New Jersey, May 14, 1970, cited in William J. Gaskill, "What's Ahead for Corporations in Social Responsibility," *Financial Executive*, pp. 10–18 (July 1971).

[25] Quoted in K. A. Kaufman, "Pollution Bill Packs KO Wallop," *Iron Age* pp. 38–39 (Oct. 1, 1970).

[26] Low-Lead Gas Sales Take Off at a Crawl," *Business Week*, p. 44 (Aug. 21, 1971); also "Does Ecology Sell?" *Sales Management*, pp. 32–34 (Nov. 15, 1970).

[27] In geographic areas where air pollution is very acute, the results may have been different. See Harold H. Kassarjian, "Incorporating Ecology into Marketing Strategy: The Case of Air Pollution," *J. Marketing*, vol. 35, pp. 61–65 (July 1971).

alternative evaluation did occur, it is possible that a great deal of risk was perceived in the new low-lead gasoline. First, there is the risk of damaging the car's engine. For years before, advertisements and personal sources of information had stressed the need for lead to reduce engine wear and to produce smooth valve operation. For people who have suffered "engine knock" in the past, the effect of stored information probably was to produce strongly held attitudes against the new product. A second risk would be the performance risk of lower fuel economies and slower acceleration (because of lower compression ratios). The third type of risk may be that an individual consumer will buy the low-lead gasoline but others will not. Thus, an individual consumer risks paying for societal benefits while other consumers can get away without paying.

There also may have been factors at the purchasing stage which prevented sales. Initially, low-leaded gasolines ranged from one to six cents higher than traditional gasolines. Some stations did not have pumps to accommodate the gasoline, and sales clerks in service stations were not trained to answer questions (and in some instances may have actually discouraged sales of the antipollution product). Finally, postpurchase evaluation may have been negative.

A decision-process model of consumer behavior points out the complexity of evaluating consumerism issues. It also shows why attitudes toward pollution control may not result in the purchase of an antipollution product. Supporting this, Yankelovich reported that in one study 70 percent of the public expressed grave concern about air pollution, but buried in the detailed findings were a number of items suggesting that much smaller numbers, perhaps ranging from 10 to 30 percent, were willing to pay higher prices, suffer inconvenience, or accept reduced performance to do anything about air pollution.[28]

It is critical that consumerism pressures ranging from rights of minorities to environmental quality control be subjected to the rigorous analysis that is possible with a multistage consumer behavior analytical model.

Criticality of Segmentation Approach

It is fallacious to assume an aggregative market response to pressures for consumerism. In many cases, the abuses which lead to outcries for consumerism only affect a small portion of the market. In other cases, a majority of a market is concerned about some aspect of consumerism but will vary greatly in response or acceptance of a solution to the problem (as the low-lead example above indicates). A review of the literature of consumerism reveals that most of the time, little empirical support is presented to answer the question of what portion of the aggregate market is affected by a particular problem or abuse.[29] It is apparent that a critical need exists for a *market segmentation approach to the problems of consumerism.*

The variety of responses to consumerism is illustrated in a large survey

---

[28] Daniel Yankelovich, "How Opinion Polls Differ from Social Indicators," paper presented at the 1st Annual Social Indicators Conf., American Marketing Association, Washington, D.C. (Feb. 17–18, 1972).

[29] A number of studies revealing this problem are cited in Bernard A. Morin, "Consumerism Revisited," *MSU Business Topics,* pp. 47–51 (Summer 1971).

conducted by *Better Homes and Gardens* magazine. Of the respondents, 53 percent felt package sizes are deliberately confusing, and similarly, 50 percent felt strongly that fractional quantities listed on packages are purposely done to make price–quantity comparisons difficult. An indication of the difficulty in developing consumerism policies is the finding in this survey that 43 percent felt it very desirable for the federal government to test and grade a wider variety of products, but only 26 percent felt that government is qualified to perform the testing. Additionally, 75 percent of the respondents felt that voluntary codes of ethics established by businesses themselves have been successful in regulating their actions.[30] Such findings as these emphasize the need for a segmentation approach to consumerism policies.

The statistic cited at the beginning of this chapter that one in five Americans feels he was cheated or deceived during the past year argues for a segmentation approach to consumerism. It is necessary to consider carefully the effects on the other 80 percent who feel they were not cheated when protecting the 20 percent who feel they were cheated. If prices must increase to pay for the protection, are the rises justified? If consumer choice must be decreased to achieve protection of the 20 percent, is the decrease justified? Many other questions such as these require careful and comprehensive research. The importance of a segmentation approach is further emphasized by the results that the consumers who most often feel they are cheated or deceived are higher income, college-educated women.[31]

ISSUES IN CONSUMERISM

Issues in consumerism can be analyzed using the research-oriented model-based segmentation approach described above. A selected group of issues in consumerism is discussed in such a context in the following pages. A more complete collection of issues is available in other sources.[32] Various groupings of the issues are possible, and many of the issues discussed below are related to each other.

Control of Consumer Choice

The control of consumer choice is a basic issue in consumerism and one that permeates the discussion of nearly all other issues. Who has the right to determine what is *offered* to consumers? Who has the right to *control* what the

---

[30] "Better Homes and Gardens Consumer Questionnaire," Meredith Corp., Des Moines, Iowa (Mar. 1968).

[31] Knauer, *op. cit.*[2]

[32] David A. Aaker and George S. Day, *Consumerism: Search for the Consumer Interest* (New York: Free Press, 1971). A vivid and fascinating description of marketing abuses is found in Gerald Leinwand (ed.), *The Consumer* (New York: Washington Square Press, 1970). A "business view" of consumerism is provided in *The Challenge of Consumerism* (New York: Conference Board, 1971). A collection of related readings is available in Lee E. Preston, *Social Issues in Marketing* (Glenview, Ill.: Scott, Foresman, 1968).

consumer chooses from among the offerings? In traditional laissez-faire economics, the answer to the first question would be business firms freely competing with each other, and the second answer would have been individual consumers, constrained only by their economic and physical resources.

The thrust of consumerism is toward control of what a firm offers, justified on the basis that contemporary corporations possess unequal power with consumers. Through merger and growth corporations have become so powerful, according to the assertion, that they can act without regard to the consumers' interests, thus justifying control by government or other institutions over their offering. Furthermore, rapid increases in innovation bring social change which historically has stimulated government intervention in attempts to mitigate social problems created by change.[33] A sociological analsyis of the United States lead Bell to predict the rise of nonmarket public decision making. He concludes, ". . . more and more of the problems confronting us cannot be settled by the market, cannot be settled by the private sector, but involve community decisions."[34]

There is an implicit assumption in many consumerist policies that consumers ought to be forced to do what is "best" for them. Thus consumerism has resulted in laws which force consumers to purchase seat belts rather than allow the consumer to make the choice himself. Laws have been passed in some states that require motorcyclists to purchase and wear helmets for their own protection.

At a more basic level, consumerists raise the issue of whether the consumers are spending their resources on the "right" products. In Moran's study of consumerism and public policy, he quotes a consumerist view on this subject:

> What does a contemporary consumer do, faced with the bewildering array of new products, new materials, new processes, compounded by the brand explosion? How does he choose? He is influenced by the sweet purrings of an attractive salesman (or woman) often less informed about product differences than the customer and also biased by push money, spiffs, and other manufacturer bribes. He is beguiled by style at the expense of safety and stamina, by gleam instead of guts, by features and gimmicks in place of performance and economy.[35]

This view is also related to earlier opinions of Galbraith, Packard, and others that the consumer should be prevented from spending his money on luxuries and should instead spend them on better schools, highways, health care, and basic needs.

Adaptionists believe that the control of consumer choice can be achieved by *educating* consumers to make "better" decisions. More radical positions indicate the need for government *intervention* and regulation to ensure that choices are made for products that are good for the consumer and the society.

Consumer research cannot solve these basic policy and philosophical

---

[33] Evidence for this view is presented in Robert W. Austin, "Who Has the Responsibility for Social Change—Business or Government?" *Harvard Business Rev.*, pp. 45–52 (July–Aug. 1965).

[34] Bell, *op. cit.*,[6] pp. 6–9.

[35] Moran, *op. cit.*,[22] p. 35.

issues, but it can contribute information helpful in their resolution. At least three contributions of a research approach can be described.

Studies of Consumer Values and Lifestyles Consumer research can be conducted which determines which values and life styles are important to the members of society. It would not be unreasonable to design measures of satisfaction and contentment and administer them to groups of consumers with varying allocations of their income to consumer goods of varying types. Studies should be made which measure changing values, preferences concerning the use of time, attitudes toward external control, and other related topics. (See Chapter 4.)

Studies of Consumer Decision and Usage Studies are needed which analyze how consumer decisions are made concerning the products in question. The results of these studies would be helpful in deciding policy issues. For example, an in-depth study of seat-belt nonusage might produce one of several results. One result might be that certain design features could be built into seat belts that would increase usage dramatically. Another might be that improved education and promotion could achieve similar results. Still another possible outcome of the study would be that there was no feasible way to induce consumers voluntarily to wear seat belts. A final possible outcome might be that behavior patterns of consumers are so strong that if a strong law was passed requiring usage of seat belts, consumers still would refuse, resulting in nonusage with the added problem of wide-scale evasion of the community's laws. In this example, the consumer research would not yield the answer to how much control is justified, but it would provide information helpful in arriving at an answer.

Studies of Cost–Benefit Relationships Consumerism activities are usually stated in terms of benefits. They usually also have costs. Recycling, automobile safety (with seat belts and other devices), unit pricing, and class actions for redress of product defects all have obvious costs. In one trade association recently the members were told that they should add one half to one percent to the price of products in order to cover the cost of additional claims and redress likely to result from extension of liability past sale of the product. It is reasonable to expect consumer researchers to develop mathematical models which relate probability of usage of benefits from consumerism to their costs.

Consumer research can also aid in deciding *who* should control consumers' behavior. A poll by the Opinion Research Corporation in 1969, for example, showed several shifts in fears about control. The poll found that in 1965, about 15 percent of adult Americans thought Big Labor posed the greatest threat to personal freedom, with 14 percent fearing Big Business and 35 percent fearing Big Government. By the end of the decade, fears of Big Labor were expressed by 17 percent of adult Americans, fears of Big Business by 12 percent, and fears of Big Government had increased to 44 percent.[36]

---

[36] Public Opinion Index, Opinion Research Corp., Princeton, N.J., (Oct. 15, 1969), quoted in Gaskill, *op. cit.*,[24] p. 13.

Consumer behavior as a discipline cannot decide between the polarities of control represented by a competitive market economy or by an economy controlled by bureaucracy. It can reasonably be expected to provide objective, research-based information to aid in the discussion of these issues.[37]

Environmental Responsibility

Large numbers of people with large amounts of money in a technologically advanced society produce large amounts of pollution and other stress on the society. This condition requires radically increased information about the feasibility of institutional responses to the problem and consumer priorities for those responses. An increased need for research and analytical thinking about consumption is also the result of the increased interdependency of consumer decisions. Feldman describes how a system based upon individual choice but with societal effects must be analyzed differently (with a systems approach) from a system with only individual implications:

> One reason . . . is that marketing decisions have been made which expanded the range of consumer product choice but disregarded their environmental impact. There has been a failure to recognize that these products, which are marketing outputs designed for individual satisfaction, are simultaneously inputs to a large environmental system and as such may affect the well-being of society.[38]

The first task of consumer research is to aid in the definition of what might be acceptable environmental goals. Assuming that perfection is impossible, consumer research should aid in determining what levels of pollution (air, water, and so forth) are really required to coincide with consumers' desired use of time for leisure, physical products, food preferences, location preferences, and so forth. One of the few researchers to analytically approach the issue of environmental goals is Feinberg. He observes that:

> Given the wide variety of environments existing in the world, each inhabited by people who are reasonably content with it, I have the impression that a person's idea of a good environment is usually the one he grew up in, and that not much thought has really been given to the general question of what makes an environment good.
>
> It is conceivable that most people would prefer the whole world to be like Polynesia with respect to climate and easy availability of food, and that we could actually engineer the world into such a form. If so, it would be good to know this preference so that we could set about working to satisfy it.[39]

---

[37] For a discussion of these issues and the case why voluntary self-regulation is not likely to be effective, see Louis L. Stern, "Consumer Protection via Self-Regulation," *J. Marketing,* vol. 35, pp. 47–53 (July 1971); also Laurence P. Feldman, "Societal Adaptation: A New Challenge for Marketing," *J. Marketing,* vol. 35, pp. 54–60 (July 1971).

[38] Feldman, *op. cit.,*[37] p. 55.

[39] Gerald Feinberg, "Long-Range Goals and the Environment," *The Futurist,* pp. 241–247, at p. 244 (Dec. 1971).

Feinberg continues by pointing out that from the point of view of basic science, no aspect of the natural environment is really essential to human life. Rather, protection or creation of any specified type of environment must be viewed in terms of offsetting aspects of the environment that must be forfeited:

> I believe that eventually we will be forced into making many choices of this type, where doing one thing precludes doing something else which otherwise might be desirable. We must ask ourselves whether preserving the environment is to be the controlling factor in making all such choices, or if not, what other principles can be brought to bear. To me, the answer is clearly that preserving the environment is only one of several factors in making any decision, and that we would do well to clarify these other factors.[40]

The other factors that must be given up to attain certain types of environments include many things besides money. The monetary costs of simply maintaining a basic stability in the existing environment, however, have been estimated by the Harvard Center for Population Studies to be about $5.1 billion for capital costs and $8.4 billion of operating costs on an annual basis.[41] These costs include air pollution, water pollution, and solid waste disposal. One of the functions of consumer research could be to establish priorities among these if all are not accepted by voters.

The study of consumer behavior should also disclose the degree to which consumers will voluntarily purchase ecologically beneficial products in preference to polluting products. Henion found that consumers voluntarily purchased low-phosphate detergents in sufficient numbers to produce a shift in market share to the ecologically preferred brands.[42] There is a considerable amount of information found in the business press to indicate that for some products and under some circumstances, consumers do respond favorably to firms which offer ecological products for sale and follow business practices designed to protect the environment.[43] The problem in assessing this literature is that generally only "success stories" are reported. Also, these products have often been marketed with massive advertising campaigns, special in-store promotions, favorable press reports, and increased personnel enthusiasm. The effects of these other marketing variables are very difficult to separate from the

---

[40]   Feinberg, *op. cit.,*[39] p. 245.

[41]   "Who Will Foot the Cleanup Bill," *Business Week,* pp. 63–64 (Jan. 3, 1970); also William W. Sihler and Charles O. Meiburg, "The War on Pollution: Economic and Financial Impacts," *Business Horizons,* vol. 14, pp. 19–30 (Aug. 1971).

[42]   Karl E. Henion, "The Effect of Ecologically Relevant Information on Detergent Sales," *J. Marketing Research,* vol. 9, pp. 15–18 (Feb. 1972).

[43]   For numerous examples of efforts to market ecological products, see the following: "Business Fights Pollution—and the Nation Profits," *Nation's Business,* pp. 29–30 (Feb. 1970); "Turning Junk and Trash into a Resource," *Business Week,* pp. 66–75 (Oct. 10, 1970); "Waste Control," *Chain Store Age,* pp. 23–34 (Nov. 1970); "Does Ecology Sell?" *Sales Management,* pp. 32–34 (Nov. 15, 1970); "Can Pollution Pay Off?" *Business Week,* pp. 46–47 (Jan. 16, 1971); "Pollution: Its New Dimensions for Business," *Can. Business,* pp. 32–36 (Mar. 1971); "More Stores Will Switch to 'Home Ecology' in '71," *Chain Store Age,* pp. 66–67ff (July 1971); "An Operator Who Sells Ecology," *Progressive Grocer,* pp. 78–82 (Oct. 1971).

basic issue of ecological information and products. Thus it is apparent that a great opportunity and need exists for experimental and other rigorous consumer research in this area.

Pollution is one consumer problem that is receiving a great deal of activity. Some of this is being undertaken voluntarily.[44] Other activities are coerced by regulatory agencies.[45] The United States Administrator of the Environmental Protection Agency has stated that such efforts will cost in excess of $100 billion, will cause unemployment as firms are forced to close down polluting plants, and will dampen the growth in gross national product.[46] It would seem an absolute prerequisite that much more knowledge of consumer priorities and responses to ecological activities be obtained to assist development of such important policies.

Marketing of Social Products

Another problem affecting consumers is the one created when they *fail* to buy products which are beneficial to themselves or to the human community of which they are a part. This is the converse of the problem discussed above. One solution that has been proposed to this problem is to apply the tools of marketing practitioners to "social products." The possibility of broadening the concept of marketing to products, services, ideas, and people (such as politicians) of nonbusinesses was analyzed in a classic article by Kotler and Levy.[47]

Kotler and Levy, writing from a background of considerable personal research, describe the importance of understanding consumer behavior for organizations such as fund raisers:

> Fund raising illustrates how an industry has benefited by replacing stereotypes of donors with studies of why people contribute to causes. Fund raisers have learned that people give because they are getting something. Many give to community chests to relieve a sense of guilt because of their elevated state compared to the needy. Many give to medical charities to relieve a sense of fear that they may be struck by a disease whose cure has not yet been found. Some give to feel pride. Fund raisers have stressed the importance of identifying the motives operating in the marketplace of givers as a basis for planning drives.[48]

---

[44]   James J. Hanks and Harold D. Kube, "Industry Action to Combat Pollution," *Harvard Business Rev.*, pp. 49–62 (Sept.–Oct. 1966); "Practical Answers to Pollution," *Nation's Business,* pp. 18–21 (Jan. 1971); "Mapping a Battle against Pollution," *Commerce Today,* pp. 4–9 (Feb. 22, 1971).

[45]   "The Environment Dilemma," *Nation's Business,* pp. 50–57 (Nov. 1970); "A Corporate Polluter Learns the Hard Way," *Business Week,* pp. 52–56 (Feb. 6, 1971); "Commerce Moves on Oil Pollution," *Commerce Today,* pp. 8–12 (Feb. 8, 1971); "Pittsburgh Goes after the Big Polluters," *Business Week,* pp. 124–130 (Mar. 13, 1971).

[46]   William D. Ruckelshaus, Administrator, U.S. Environmental Protection Agency, News Conference (Mar. 1972).

[47]   Philip Kotler and Sidney J. Levy, "Broadening the Concept of Marketing," *J. Marketing,* vol. 33, pp. 10–15 (Jan. 1969).

[48]   Kotler and Levy, *op. cit.,*[47] p. 14; also William A. Mindak and H. Malcolm Bybee, "Marketing's Application to Fund Raising," *J. Marketing,* vol. 35, pp. 13–18 (July 1971).

There are several areas of social marketing that have received considerable research. Kotler and Zaltman review these areas.[49] The marketing of birth control devices and the concept of planned parenthood is perhaps one of the best researched social products.[50] In analyzing pricing of hospital services, Feldstein included several consumer demographic variables and a proxy variable for consumer attitudes toward medical services.[51] Considerable consumer research was conducted in a study of consumer decision making for physician services.[52] In another social product area the importance of marketing strategy for religious organizations was described but no research was reported.[53] Finally, it appears that there is considerable consumer research of a sophisticated and comprehensive nature used in the development of marketing strategy for political candidates. While most of the research is not published, one publication of such research received widespread circulation.[54]

The kind of research required for the development of marketing strategies for social products does not differ greatly from traditional marketing problems. A decision-process market-segmentation approach is needed for better understanding of important areas of social marketing.

Product Safety and Quality

Advertising and communications have stressed the quality of American business products to the extent, apparently, that consumers have become convinced it should be true. When it is not, they react strongly enough to provide considerable consumerism pressure. This is manifested in complaints, litigation (including class actions), and regulation requiring specified levels of safety and performance. There are two major contributions of consumer research toward solving problems of product safety and quality in determining levels of safety and determining usage patterns.

---

[49] Philip Kotler and Gerald Zaltman, "Social Marketing: An Approach to Planned Social Change," *J. Marketing*, vol. 35, pp. 3–12 (July 1971).

[50] Julian L. Simon, "A Huge Marketing Research Task—Birth Control," *J. Marketing Research*, vol. 5, pp. 21–27 (Feb. 1968). This article reviews prior research on the subject.

[51] Martin S. Feldstein, "Hospital Cost Inflation: A Study of Nonprofit Price Dynamics," *Amer. Economic Rev.*, pp. 853–869 (1971); also Gerald Zaltman and Ilan Vertinsky, "Health Service Marketing: A Suggested Model," *J. Marketing*, vol. 35, pp. 19–27 (July 1971).

[52] "The Ohio Association of Osteopathic Physicians and Surgeons," in James F. Engel, W. Wayne Talarzyk, and Carl M. Larson (eds.), *Cases in Promotional Strategy* (Homewood, Ill.: Irwin, 1971), pp. 28–50.

[53] James F. Engel and Roger D. Blackwell, "Communicating Religious Truth," paper presented at the American Marketing Association, Boston (Sept. 1, 1970); also "Campus Crusade for Christ International," in Engel *et al., op. cit.*,[52] pp. 148–158.

[54] Joe McGinnis, *The Selling of the President, 1968* (New York: Trident Press, 1969).

Levels of Safety   Consumer research can help in the development of specifications of safety and performance levels. Given the assumption that perfect safety is as impossible as zero defects in most other processes, some definition must be made of acceptable levels of safety or nonsafety. While this is partly a question of technical research, it is also a question of consumer research. For example, assume that a manufacturer of automobiles could install as standard equipment an improved braking system that would decrease injuries, but that the cost of the improved system would be $1000. Or suppose that a manufacturer now averages 1 defect in the steering mechanism per 800,000 cars. Improved inspection systems and employee incentive compensation, it might be shown, could cut these defects to 1 in 1,000,000 cars, but at an additional cost per car of $40. Consumer research should be able to provide inputs helpful in making such decisions. For example, a safer computerized braking system is standard equipment on one line of automobiles that costs approximately $10,000. If *all* automobiles were required to have this system, would society be better off or not? This is a segmentation question, and consumer research should be able to supply the number of low-income customers who would be denied the ability to purchase a car because of the increased safety standards. Are consumers better or worse served by laws which require high levels of safety and performance but at the same time reduce the possibility of purchasing the product by low-income consumers? Similar questions could be raised in many other industries.

Consumer Usage Patterns   Consumer research can make a substantial contribution to improvements of product safety and performance by in-depth studies of consumer usage patterns of products. The reason many products perform poorly or unsafely is because they are used incorrectly by some segments of the market. Laundry equipment frequently provides poor performance because consumers overload the machine with clothes, soap, or both. Usage studies should be able to determine segments of the consumer population most likely to cause such problems and thereby provide an input to tactics that may prevent some of the occurrences.

Consumer research can aid manufacturers in the problems they face due to the "doctrine of forseeability." This is a legal doctrine which holds that manufacturers are best able to evaluate the risks inherent in their products and figure out ways to avoid them. This implies not only technical knowledge of the product but in-depth knowledge of how the product is likely to be used by varying segments of the market. A noted consumerist lawyer notes that the courts "should protect not just the unwitting consumer from the consequences of a manufacturer's error, but also the 'witless boobs' who misuse a product in ways that can be anticipated."[55] A Kentucky Court of Appeals held, for example, that a manufacturer was liable for damages that occurred when one of its vacuum cleaners was plugged into a 220-volt circuit and blew up. The label on the product

---

[55]   "Business Responds to Consumerism," *Business Week*, p. 108 (Sept. 6, 1969).

stated that it was to be used in 115-volt outlets but did not warn about the serious consequences that would occur with improper usage.[56]

Another example of the contribution of consumer research on usage patterns is in the area of defining what types of safety features a product should have. Controversy surrounds the usage of seat belts and air bags on automobiles, for example. The problems due to consumer usage patterns of seat belts may cause the government to require producers to supply (and, therefore, consumers to buy) a very expensive air bag (which may have its own defects). After describing the air bag it was pointed out that, "although lap and shoulder harnesses give similar protection, officials brandish the inescapable facts that not even 40 percent of all car occupants wear lap belts and fewer than 5 percent bother with shoulder belts."[57]

Warranties and Consumer Redress   It is likely that consumers are going to be involved in increasingly active methods of redress for the inadequate performance and unsafe products that have been put on the market. The extent of dissatisfaction is reported by Louis Harris, President of a major research organization continually polling American consumers. He reports:

> . . . consumers feel cheated on a mass basis. Majorities of the public express real worry, in health terms, about their soft drinks and the food they eat, the safety of their automobiles (even though a majority still will not wear seat belts), the dangers of birth control pills, the dangers of taking tranquilizers, sleeping pills, pep-up pills, and a plethora of other instant curatives.[58]

The specific types of problems for which consumers are seeking redress through better warranties, better product design, and individual and class action suits are vividly described by Bishop and Hubbard:

(1)   A 16-month-old boy took the legs off a doll, exposing three-inch spikes, described by his mother as a "lethal weapon."

(2)   A 13-month-old boy hanged himself in his crib with the string of a musical toy designed to entertain babies.

(3)   A woman in New York City wrote, "The plastic lid of my gift coffee-maker caught fire . . . the flame reached almost to the ceiling."

(4)   "For the third time this year my son has had a severe fall from his swing set," wrote a woman from Garland, Texas, "all because the hooks attached to the swing sets last only five days and chains last only about six months."

---

[56]   "Business Responds to Consumerism," *op. cit.*[55]

[57]   "The Air Bag Faces a Showdown Fight," *Business Week*, pp. 74–75 (Aug. 14, 1971).

[58]   Louis Harris, quoted in Holly MacNamee, "The Socially Conscious Consumer," *Conference Board Record*, pp. 11–13, at p. 12 (May 1970).

(5)   A 62-year-old woman in California was standing in a puddle when her electric edger clipped its cord. She was electrocuted.[59]

Consumer research will be employed in a variety of ways to aid consumer redress. First, it is probable that consumer research results will increasingly be used in class actions and other litigation to secure redress. Second, it is probable that government will increasingly seek the results of consumer research in establishing standards of reasonableness of performance and safety. Third, it is probable that marketers will increasingly turn to consumer research on usage patterns in developing safe, reliable products, inhibiting consumer redress by preventing the problem. An example of such a program is provided by Whirlpool Corporation with its "cool line" to provide instant information on proper care and solution of minor difficulties (before they grow to major problems), with simplified and extended warranties, and with changed distribution policies that permit increased service by service centers when problems do occur.[60]

Berens observes that even the best of warranties usually only compensate consumers for direct money costs associated with product failure. He describes the *indirect* costs of redress:

> Indirect money costs . . . are the net dollars a consumer must spend in his efforts to receive service on a product (such as phone calls, taxi fares when an automobile needs service, and so forth) or those which are incurred because the product is no longer performing its normal function (such as food spoilage due to a defective refrigerator or eating out when a cooking range is not operable). Other indirect money costs are incurred when one product's failure causes economic loss in other products, for example, when a defective phonograph needle ruins a record.[61]

The ultimate consumer redress for poor quality and safety is not in warranties or in contingent liability; it is in the design of products so they will not produce the problems. Berens quotes a consumer who summarizes this concept pointedly, "I don't want a paint that's *guaranteed* to cover in one coat; I want a paint that *will cover* in one coat."[62]

Consumer Information

The right to be informed, enunciated by President Kennedy, was described as the right of the consumer "to be protected against fraudulent, deceitful, or grossly misleading information, advertising, labeling, or other practices,

[59]   James W. Bishop, Jr., and Henry W. Hubbard, *Let the Seller Beware* (Washington: Washington National Press, 1969).

[60]   Stephen E. Upton, "The Use of Product Warranties and Guarantees as a Marketing Tool," address given to American Marketing Association, Cleveland, Ohio (Dec. 11, 1969); also reprinted in Aaker and Day, *op. cit.*,[32] pp. 277–282.

[61]   John S. Berens, "Consumer Costs in Product Failure," *MSU Business Topics,* vol. 19, pp. 27–30, at p. 28 (Spring 1971).

[62]   Behrens, *op. cit.*,[61] p. 30.

and to be given the facts he needs to make an informed choice." The contributions of consumer research to an understanding of these rights can be described under the issues of *consumer deception* and *informed choices.*

Consumer Deception   The issue of consumer deception has two major thrusts. The most basic is that advertising deceives consumers by causing them to want products that are not good for them or that yield less satisfaction for themselves or society than other types of products. This serious issue is analyzed in a research framework by Howard and Tinkham.[63] A more objective issue is the question of whether or not consumers are *fraudulently persuaded* by advertising, personal selling, or other marketing activities. *Prima facie* evidence for the existence of massive amounts of deception is provided by the development of massive amounts of regulation by the Federal Trade Commission and other agencies in the past few decades.[64] The question of what is deceptive, however, is a constantly changing interpretation of the law, current creativity in promotion strategy, and capability of the consumer to defend himself.[65] There have been massive amounts of behavioral research accumulated by marketing strategists to communicate persuasively (responsibly and irresponsibly) with consumers, but to date there has been relatively little use of the same behavioral data to assist consumers in their task of choosing with competence from the communication messages offered to them.

A nationwide survey of consumers revealed that about 60 percent of the respondents feel that recent criticism of advertising is totally justified.[66] Less than half of advertising was rated honest and informative. The greatest complaint was that advertising is misrepresentative and exaggerated, followed by complaints against hardsell and insults against the public's intelligence. The survey also revealed that consumers were hostile toward government regulation of advertising, preferring instead more self-regulation by the industry. In spite of the negative feelings, 96 percent of the respondents said they would not like to see advertising eliminated.

Informed Choices   Consumer research has a major function in defining the information required and its method of presentation to guarantee that consumers have the opportunity to make informed choices. The specific information that should be disseminated varies greatly by the type of product involved and

---

[63]   John A. Howard and Spencer F. Tinkham, "A Framework for Understanding Social Criticism of Advertising," *J. Marketing,* vol. 35, pp. 2–7 (Oct. 1971).

[64]   A review of these practices and the laws that have evolved to regulate them is available in basic advertising texts. For example, see James F. Engel, Hugh G. Wales, and Martin R. Warshaw, *Promotional Strategy* (Homewood, Ill.: Irwin, 1971), chap. 8.

[65]   Perhaps the best summary of the current interpretation is gained from reading "Legal Developments in Marketing," which appears in each issue of *J. Marketing.* An excellent summary is provided by Earl W. Kintner, *A Primer on the Law of Deceptive Practices: A Guide for the Businessman* (New York: Macmillan, 1971).

[66]   Study by Warwick and Legler, Inc., quoted in "The Public Is Wary of Ads, too," *Business Week,* p. 69 (Jan. 29, 1972).

the nature of the choice process. The research needs include knowledge about the importance and complexity of the product in the mind of the consumer, the features that are significant to him, the accessibility of information, and the processability of information. The difficulty of attaining adequate standards of information is that the answers to these questions vary among consumer segments.[67]

A major thrust in the issue of improved information is the need for *standardization* to aid consumers in their choices. This issue and the feasibility of solutions such as grade labeling have been thoroughly analyzed in other sources.[68] The major problem with standards, and the one that must be established through consumer research, is in determining the type of evaluative criteria that are relevant to consumers. Standards which are defined only in terms of some normative criteria are unlikely to be very satisfying or helpful to consumers who make decisions on different criteria. Buzzell has observed widely different definitions between business leaders and consumerist leaders of key terms, in what he calls, "the dialogue that never happens" (see Table 25.1). If leaders are

Table 25.1 DEFINITIONS OF BUSINESS LEADERS AND CONSUMERIST LEADERS IN "THE DIALOGUE THAT NEVER HAPPENS"

| | *Concept Definitions and Meaning* | |
Concepts	*Business Leaders*	*Consumerism Leaders*
Competition	Product differentiation	Price
Product	Multiple features, Multiple uses	Primary function only
Needs	Multiple and shifting	Efficiency in primary function only
Information	Anything that makes product attractive	"Specifications"

SOURCE: Robert Buzzell, "Consumerism: Challenge and Opportunity for Marketing in the 1970's," paper presented to the American Marketing Association Doctoral Consortium (Aug. 1971).

using different assumptions about the consumers' criteria for decisions, it would appear that consumer research could be a boundary-spanning agent.

Many solutions have been proposed and enacted to provide consumers

---

[67] These information needs were suggested by Professor Robert Buzzell, Harvard University Graduate School of Business.

[68] Theodore N. Beckman, William R. Davidson, and James F. Engel, *Marketing* (New York: Ronald, 1967), chap. 25; also Richard L. D. Morse, "Are Consumer Grades Needed?" *J. Marketing*, vol. 30, pp. 52–53 (July 1966); Walker Sandbach, "The Costs of Inadequate Standards to the Consumer," in John S. Wright and Jac L. Goldstucker (eds.), *New Ideas for Successful Marketing* (Chicago: Amer. Marketing Assoc., 1966), pp. 169–177.

with more information. These include truth-in-lending bills, cooling-off laws,[69] and unit pricing. The latter is an example that was widely heralded as an important step to giving consumers better information with which to improve their choices. Yet there are persistent reports that although it has been an effective public relations tool, it has little effect on consumer choices. After interviewing numerous firms that installed unit pricing in supermarkets, Mueller asserts:

> It is unfortunate, to hear from unit pricing retailers that, while a majority of customers say they are aware of this new feature in their stores, only a very small minority report that they actually use unit pricing as a guide while shopping.
>
> Even more depressing is the attrition in consumer reference to unit price data, which seems to increase with each succeeding shopping trip. The novelty wears off relatively soon and many operators indicated that after a month or two, the tags tend to be ignored as shoppers revert to their normal selection processes. Furthermore, those who might theoretically benefit from price comparison information, say some retailers, appear to use it the least![70]

If this assertion is correct, it indicates a great many research needs concerning consumer decision processes and possible consumerism policies.[71]

Responsibility to Minorities and the Poor

The United States is a nation that in 1970 had 25.5 million consumers living in poverty. Nearly a third of these were black consumers, the largest racial minority group.[72] Among the consumerism thrusts is a recognition of a special responsibility for the problems of minorities and of the poor.[73]

Consumer research appears to have three major contributions to relieving the problems of minorities and of the poor. The first is research directed toward the question of how to "stretch" or *allocate more efficiently the limited resources* of the poor and of those who have been subject to discrimination. These studies require two outputs. First, they need to compare consumption problems of the minorities with consumption problems of the majorities to determine if the basis exists for separate strategies. Are there a unique set of problems among minorities and the poor to which special efforts in regulation, marketing information, or education should be directed? Second, studies directed toward stretching the resources of the poor need to determine the feasibility of possible changes in marketing activities. Table 25.2 presents the results of a dialogue at Temple Uni-

---

[69]   Orville C. Walker, Jr., and Neil M. Ford, "Can 'Cooling-Off Laws' Really Protect the Consumer?" *J. Marketing*, vol. 34, pp. 53–58 (Apr. 1970).

[70]   R. W. Mueller, "An Appraisal of Unit Pricing," *Progressive Grocer*, p. 6 (Oct. 1971).

[71]   For additional discussion of this issue, see Louis L. Stern, "Consumer Protection via Increased Information," *J. Marketing*, vol. 31, pp. 48–52 (Apr. 1967).

[72]   These and other relevant statistics are presented in Eli P. Cox, "What Is Poverty? Who Are the Poor?" *MSU Business Topics*, pp. 5–10 (Summer 1971).

[73]   See Chapter 6; also Donald E. Sexton, Jr., "Do Blacks Pay More?" *J. Marketing Research*, vol. 8, pp. 420–426 (Nov. 1971).

Table 25.2 TEMPLE DIALOGUE ON INNER-CITY CONSUMER PROBLEMS.

Major Problem	Nature of Problem	Suggestions for Action
(1) *Fraud*	Misrepresentation of used merchandise as new Misleading advertising of products as bait to switch consumers to higher priced models without their knowledge or their consent Filling in terms of credit contract by seller after agreement secured in writing from buyer Misrepresentation of terms of sale to ignorant buyer by failure to explain what is being sold, at what price, under what credit terms, and with what guarantee or warranty	Organize district consumer committees through church groups, community and neighborhood associations, and Consumer Education and Protective Association to spread word of mouth information about fraudulent practices which are documented by investigation Publicize local emergency numbers of community groups able to give: (a) buying advice, (b) legal advice, (c) channel complaints to City Solicitors' office Organize student volunteers from law and social work schools to handle investigations of fraud, advice, and complaints Organize inner-city residents to elect their own constables Picket and publicize practices in local neighborhoods
(2) *Enforcing Laws Protecting Consumer*	Consumers ashamed to complain to city authorities about swindles Consumers ignorant of sources of aid in enforcing laws Consumers too poor to prosecute fraudulent vendors Lawyers unwilling to take cases in constable and sheriff sales District Attorney and City Solicitor offices undermanned and underfinanced to handle complaints Violations too numerous for Department of Licenses	Meet with city and state legislators to explain the need for money to secure enforcement against: (a) deceptive and misleading advertising, (b) insurance frauds, (c) credit contract frauds, (d) use of false weights, measures, packages, and labels, (e) mislabeling, misrepresenting, and misbranding merchandise in personal sales, solicitations by peddlers Complain immediately to City Solicitor's office, Department of Licenses and Inspections and other

agencies empowered to administer present laws

Encourage victims of constable and sheriff brutality to complain to the City Solicitor's office

Inform Better Business Bureau, Consumers Education and Protective Association, and neighborhood businessmen's associations when violations are known to occur, explaining to them what law is being violated and what the law requires; not all violations are intentional

Lobby in state legislature for repeal of outdated laws that give sellers massive power over consumer; "holder in due course", "confession of judgment", constable and sheriff liens

Lobby with congressmen to repeal outdated laws favoring the sellers

Hold hearings with victims of fraud and sheriff sales in local neighborhoods to find out what kind of consumer protection should be recommended to the President's Committee on the Consumer Interest

Organize car pools for weekly grocery shopping outside of inner city

Encourage chain stores to increase assortment on an experimental trial basis after survey of local residents' wants

Organize consumer committees to notify local merchants of inner city consumer wants and secure buying pledges for selective patronage of mer-

and Inspections, Bureau of Weights and Measures, and Sanitation and Health to cope with

(3) *Laws Protecting Seller at Expense of Buyer*

"Confession of judgment" renders buyer legally defenseless and guilty without evidence of guilt

"Holder in due course" protects financial agency collecting payment from customer who has been defrauded by a seller without any responsibility to consumer by bank or credit agency that has purchased time-payment contract from merchant

Sheriff lein and sale permits sheriff to seize property of consumer and sell it to satisfy outstanding judgment against buyer, regardless of size of unpaid debt relative to the value of the property seized for resale

(4) *Limited Choice Available to Inner City Consumers*

Stores in inner city are small and have limited merchandise selections

Merchandise assortment available in inner city is more limited than in suburbs

Cash not available to take advantage of bona-fide special offers at reduced prices

Car fare to and from center city raises price of shopping

Table 25.2 TEMPLE DIALOGUE ON INNER-CITY CONSUMER PROBLEMS
(Continued)

	Nature of Problem	Suggestions for Action
	Shabby appearance keeps some inner-city residents from attempting to shop outside the area	chants complying with recommended credit and service policies
	Level of service in chain stores lower in inner city than in suburbs	Support entry into business by local inner city residents who can secure financial backing from government and corporate sources
	Credit terms often available for off brands and at higher prices than from center city stores	Organize consumer credit unions for emergency purchases
	Insurance, health, credit services may be severely limited or unavailable	
(5) *Consumer Ignorance*	Inner city consumers sometimes are unaware of contract terms of sale, seller's bait, and switch tactics	Organize shoppers' day-care centers
		Organize community-leader training programs
	Inner city residents often unfamiliar with terms of sale available to them outside of inner city	Handbill and leafleting of good values in food, and so on
	Some consumers lacking budget skills	TV shows on how to buy the best of the week's offerings, comparisons of prices and quality, and so on
	Product information not made available by merchants	
	Legal aid information not widely distributed	Organize consumer conferences in inner city neighborhoods through church groups, political action groups, consumer groups, unions
	Availability of buying advice not known or used before purchase	Organize comprehensive investigation of consumer problems of the poor with results of buying experience survey to be distributed on a periodic basis

SOURCE: "Dialogue on Inner City Consumer Problems," Temple University (Chicago: Amer. Marketing Assoc., Apr. 22, 1968).

versity which delineated five major problems of inner-city consumers, the manifestations of the problems, and possible actions for improvement. An outline such as this is in need of the further step of consumer research to determine the probability of success of the suggested actions as well as an ordering of priorities.

A second basic contribution of consumer research in this area is in the *improvement of marketing efficiency* among firms and organizations which serve minorities and the poor. For example, in a study of black store managers it was found that one of the major problems deterring success was the reluctance on the part of the black community to buy in black-run stores.[74] Sturdivant has conducted considerable research on ghetto retailers and has concluded that investment guarantees and enlarged investment tax credits are needed in order to stimulate adequate retail facilities to serve the consumers of the ghetto.[75]

A third contribution of consumer research is through *studies of the majority segments* to determine the degree to which they contribute to the consumer problems of the minority. Housing is a major problem among black consumers, for example, and a thorough study by Sanoff *et al.* discloses many relationships between nonwhite housing availability and white movements.[76] This study shows that whites often move out when blacks move in, partially because of fear of declining property values. Yet Sanoff's research shows that the fear that whites have of property values declining is unfounded. Similar research by Rapkin indicates that if the black population in a neighborhood rises above 40 percent, the demand for housing in that area by whites will tend to be zero, thereby causing the neighborhood to turn completely black in about five years.[77] Research such as these studies can provide important inputs into the development of policies by government, business firms, and other organizations that will aid consumers, both of minority groups and of majority groups.

The responsibility to minorities and the poor is connected to broader issues about urban areas as a whole. It is clear that business in general and consumer behavior specifically will want and probably be required to play a vital role in the determination of the kind of urban environment that should be built for consumers of the future and the ways that acceptance will be achieved.[78] It would be difficult to expect, for example, that new towns would be successful

[74]   Dan H. Fenn, Jr., "NAFC Probes Three Major Issues of the 70's: Economy, Technology, Consumerism," *Chain Store Age*, pp. 31–34 (Dec. 1970).

[75]   Frederick D. Sturdivant, "Better Deal for Ghetto Shoppers," *Harvard Business Rev.*, pp. 130–139 (Mar.–Apr. 1968). For additional solutions to these problems, see Allan T. Demaree, "Business Picks up the Urban Challenge," Fortune, vol. 79, pp. 102–104ff (Apr. 1969); Richard F. America, Jr., "What Do You People Want," *Harvard Business Rev.*, pp. 103–112 (Mar.–Apr. 1969).

[76]   Henry Sanoff, Man Mohan Sawhney, Henry K. Burgwyn, and George Ellinwood, "Changing Residential Racial Patterns," *Urban and Social Change Rev.*, vol. 4, pp. 68–71 (Spring 1971).

[77]   Chester Rapkin, *The Demand for Housing in Racially Mixed Areas* (Berkeley: University of California Press, 1960), p. 68.

[78]   Myron Lieberman, "New Communities: Business on the Urban Frontier," *Saturday Rev.*, pp. 20–31ff (May 15, 1971).

without a great deal of research into all aspects of consumer decision making about and in them.[79]

THE FUTURE OF VOLUNTARISM

There is, in the literature of consumerism, a persistent belief expressed that consumers ought to voluntarily act in a way that is beneficial to the society they live in. At the same time, there is persistent evidence that they will act in a way that is beneficial to themselves as individuals. Other actions are only undertaken when the problem becomes so severe that it personally impinges upon their desired behavior.

There are few studies that attempt experimentally or with other rigorous methodologies to determine the degree to which people will voluntarily do what is socially responsible. The empirical experience derived from case studies of innovations that have occurred in the past few years leads to the conclusion that consumers are not willing personally to sacrifice money or convenience for products in the public benefit. They do show willingness to pass laws (or, more accurately, support legislators who pass laws) which regulate the responsibility of others. That is, consumers do not voluntarily purchase catalytic emission control devices for their automobiles (which are available) but are willing to support laws which require manufacturers to install them. Perhaps consumers realize that these indirect decisions are passed on to themselves as added costs or perhaps not. Research is needed to clarify this question.

The process of decision making concerning social responsibility was described in a research report by Yankelovich, who found:

> . . . that people typically move through five stages of concern on those social issues which have cost consequences. In the first stage there is growing awareness that a problem exists. In the second stage the problem moves closer to the top of the hierarchy of the public's major concerns. Third, there is willingness to support various solutions if they do not involve personal sacrifices. Fourth, there is a willingness to make a personal sacrifice provided that others make the same sacrifice. And fifth, there is a demand for government legislation to guarantee that everyone *will* make the necessary sacrifice to solve the problem.[80]

Similar limits on voluntarism probably exist in the efforts of business firms to respond to consumerism. This will lead to increased government intervention, in the opinion of the President of International Business Machines Corporation:

---

[79] John B. Lansing, Robert W. Marans, and Robert B. Zehner, *Planned Residential Environments* (Ann Arbor, Mich.: Braun-Frumfield, 1970); Gurney Breckenfeld, *Columbia and the New Cities* (New York: Washburn, 1971).

[80] Yankelovich, *op. cit.*[28]

Voluntarism has its limits. It burdens the responsible corporation with extra costs and lets the other fellow get away with murder. The marketplace is not a pollution discriminator. To clean up pollution, we are necessarily going to have to look to government to establish more stringent standards, provide in many cases tax incentives to those companies that meet them, or exact penalties from those which do not. And ultimately the cost will *have* to be borne by the consumer in higher prices.[81]

SUMMARY

The consumer has the right to safety, the right to be informed, the right to choose from an adequate selection of products, and the right to be heard. These rights have been reaffirmed by every United States president since John F. Kennedy. Yet, there is ample evidence to show that the rights are violated constantly.

Historical antecedents of consumerism resulted in legislation such as the Pure Food and Drug Act, just as the outcries of consumers have resulted in contemporary protective legislation. Increased pressures for social and ethical responsibility are also an impetus for protection of consumers' rights.

A research approach to consumerism is provided by the discipline of consumer behavior. A research approach can be expected to yield more realistic inputs for protective activities. The use of consumer behavior models should help to understand the failure of some efforts to protect the consumer and to provide a better environment.

Specific issues in consumerism are examined in the context of suggesting research that is needed to supplement the limited amount of research already completed. The issues discussed include control of consumer choice, environmental responsibility, marketing of "social" products, product safety and quality, consumer information, and responsibility of minorities and the poor. The chapter also describes the problems of depending on voluntarism for solutions to these problems.

REVIEW AND DISCUSSION QUESTIONS

1. Is the consumerism of the 1970s fundamentally similar or different compared to historical movements to provide protection for consumers?

2. Provide a definition of consumerism that will be adequate for research purposes in consumer behavior.

3. Why does marketing and consumer behavior have a central role in exercising the social responsibility of a business firm? Discuss.

---

[81] T. V. Learson, "The Greening of American Business," *Conference Board Record*, pp. 21–24 (July 1971). For additional discussions of the topic of business–government responsibility in response to issues of this chapter, see John T. Dunlop, "New Forces in the Economy," *Harvard Business Rev.*, pp. 121–129 (Mar.–Apr. 1968); John McDonnel, "How Social Responsibility Fits the Game of Business," *Fortune*, pp. 104–133 (Dec. 1970); Holly MacNamee, "Business Leadership in Social Change," *Conference Board Record*, pp. 25–32 (July 1971).

4. Prepare a list of the most pressing problems of consumers in the United States. Prepare a research proposal which would establish priorities for solutions.

5. Prepare a list of the most pressing problems of consumers in selected countries other than the United States. Analyze the underlying factors which explain differences, if they exist, in the list of consumer problems.

6. Justify the position that the use of analytical decision-process models of consumer behavior is critical in the analysis of consumerism.

7. Describe the issue of consumer information and analyze the role of market segmentation in understanding this issue.

8. What is "social marketing?" What should be the role of consumer research in social marketing?

9. Analyze the issues raised in this chapter concerning responsibility to minorities and the poor. Develop a proposal for consumer research that might be helpful in solving some of these problems.

CHAPTER **26**

THE CURRENT STATUS OF
CONSUMER BEHAVIOR RESEARCH:
PROBLEMS AND PROSPECTS

This book has attempted to identify most of what is known about consumer behavior today.[1] From thousands of references, hundreds of propositions have been collected and synthesized in the preceding pages. Hopefully, most are valid statements about consumer behavior. Some, unfortunately, are wrong. Almost all are subject to qualification. Many will change in the future.

This chapter attempts to assess this vast catalog of theories, models, and research findings. The first section of the chapter presents some basic generalizations about the nature of consumer behavior. The second section tries to evaluate the current status of consumer research in terms of the insights that it has generated for explaining and predicting consumer behavior. Recommendations for improving consumer research constitute the subject matter of the concluding section.

---

[1] While we have endeavored to be comprehensive, in many areas we have been selective due to space and ability limitations. Moreover, we have been able to present only a small fraction of unpublished research.

SOME PROVISIONAL GENERALIZATIONS
ABOUT CONSUMER BEHAVIOR

A summary of this volume is impractical because even the most adroit effort would require an unacceptably large number of pages. An alternative is to identify some basic provisional generalizations about the nature of consumer behavior.

The Adaptive Problem Solver

Man is good at adaptive behavior—at doing or learning to do things that increase his chances of satisfactorily interacting with his environment. He is often influenced, but he also influences. Underlying capacities and processes—perceiving, learning, thinking, choosing, communicating—are integrated by the consumer in reacting to new problems, new influences, and new products. His behavior is purposeful and potentially understandable.

The marketing strategist recognizes the adaptive character of the problem-solving consumer and integrates this fact into marketing strategy. He does not view the consumer as an inert individual capable of being manipulated. Instead, the consumer is recognized as an information seeker who evaluates communications and product choices in terms of his drives and aspirations. When products are consonant with his problem-solving strategies, the consumer chooses those products. When products are unsatisfactory, he chooses others. Thus, to say that consumers are controlled by marketers is naive, unless one means that marketers induce consumers to buy their products by producing what they want and telling them about it. In reality, it is the marketer who is controlled by the adaptive, satisfaction-seeking behavior of the consumer.

In an affluent economy, the ever-changing adaptive behavior of consumers can be released in continuously updated product choices. This breeds disaster for a rigid marketing organization but breathes dynamism into the firm that plies with the consumer.

The Selective Information Processor

Every consumer has his own image of reality. He receives and interprets the stimuli that bombard him so that they conform to his own image. Berelson and Steiner have vividly described this process:

> Thus, he adjusts his social perception to fit not only the objective reality but also what suits his wishes and his needs; he tends to remember what fits his needs and expectations, or what he thinks others will want to hear; he not only works for what he wants but wants what he has to work for; his need for psychological protection is so great that he has become expert in the "defense mechanisms;" in the mass media he tends to hear and see not simply what is there but what he prefers to be told, and he will misinterpret rather than face up to an opposing set of facts or point of view. . . .[2]

---

[2] Bernard Berelson and Gary A. Steiner, *Human Behavior: An Inventory of Scientific Findings* (New York: Harcourt, 1964), p. 664.

A company or any other organization does not offer a physical product or service; it markets an image of that product or service. The image may conform closely to the objective characteristics of the product or service, or there may be disparities. The ultimate success, however, depends on what the consumer *perceives* to be true and whether that satisfies his evaluative criteria.

The Social Organism

The statement, "No man is an island" has empirical support. No man exists who does not reflect interaction with other people. Values, learning patterns, and symbolism are some of the results of the society in which a consumer develops. Sometimes social influences are negative rather than positive influences, but always they are influences. Man evaluates his self against the behavior of others and the values he has learned from others on previous occasions. He depends on others as a source of new information about product decisions and as a reference for evaluating the information.

Organizations seeking to influence consumer behavior should realize that they must communicate not only with an individual but also with a social system.

The Unique Individual

Every consumer differs from every other consumer. Each is an individual, understandable only as a unique person in the human race. This is the chief deterrent to predictive statements that have complete generality. Man is such a complex bundle of past influences that the generalization which applies to one consumer frequently is overruled by a higher generalization for another consumer. Each man is the result of millions of influences over a lifetime. The sheer impossibility of any two consumers receiving the same set of influences precludes making a definitive statement about what the purchasing behavior of a single consumer will be.

Individuals may be aggregated, however. This is possible because individual deviations are usually randomly distributed and tend to cancel each other out, yielding valid market models. The individuality of each consumer is also one of the problems associated with *research* on purchasing decisions. The presence of important individual differences is one reason why studies based upon a small group of consumers are often suspect.

It is easier to measure a few basic characteristics about large groups of consumers than to conduct intensive measurement on them. Yet, if a rich, comprehensive understanding of consumer behavior is to be attained, it must include individual differences among consumers. That is accomplished in the decision-process approach used in this book.

The Decision Processor

The decision-process approach to understanding consumer behavior is an abstraction of the myriad decisions made by consumers. The decision-process model is comprehensible without reference to any particular occasion of purchase experience, a basic requirement of abstraction in the social sciences.[3] Although the model can be analyzed on a theoretic basis, this does not mean that abstraction of decision processes can be disconnected from actual product decisions.

The decision-process model presented in this book does not explain the details of consumer action in every specific situation. Rather, the model delineates (1) the *variables* associated with consumer decision processes, (2) the general *relations* that exist among model variables, and (3) the general *principles* that express the model's ingression in particular purchase occasions.

The value of an abstract model to guide research in consumer behavior cannot be overemphasized. Without a model specifying the range of variables to be measured, the researcher may be lured into looking at a problem from a narrow perspective. A famous story by Sir Arthur Eddington illustrates this danger.[4] It seems that an ichthyologist wished to draw some generalizations concerning the size of fish. He took into the sea a fishnet of two-inch mesh. It was dropped into the water and he collected a large number of fish. After meticulous measurement, the scientist announced the generalization, "All fish are two inches long or more." This, unfortunately, is what often happens in consumer research. In spite of rigor in the research design, the facts collected are only partially accurate because only a partial theory has guided the collection.

Inadequate data collection can occur in other ways. The story of Procrustes, the giant who obliged weary travelers to spend the night with him, further illustrates the problem.[5] Procrustes required travelers to sleep in his bed and always trimmed them to fit, stretching the shorter ones on the rack and lopping pieces of the longer ones until their corpses were exactly the right length. With or without a theory, the consumer analyst is often a Procrustes and empirical data are the travelers. Making data fit a model often involves about the same process as that used by Procrustes.

One of the goals of this book is to develop among consumer analysts a sensitivity to the presence of such a process in consumer research findings. The decision-process model should be an aid to collecting facts in an organized and unbiased way. The model points to important gaps in knowledge about consumer decisions that might go unnoticed with a less comprehensive method of analysis.

THE CURRENT STATUS OF CONSUMER BEHAVIOR RESEARCH

During the last few decades, particularly the last five years, there have been remarkable efforts made toward the advancement of knowledge in consumer behavior. This section attempts to evaluate the literature of consumer research

---

[3] This section is heavily influenced by Whitehead's chapter on "Abstraction," in Alfred North Whitehead, *Science and the Modern World* (New York: Macmillan, 1925), chap. 10.

[4] Quoted in Stephen Toulmin, *The Philosophy of Science* (New York: Harper & Row, 1953), pp. 124–129.

[5] Toulmin, *op. cit.,*[4] pp. 124–129.

in terms of its usefulness for explaining and predicting consumer behavior.[6] The observations are of a general nature, and, hence, their rectitude varies considerably among disciplines and specialties within the field.

Explaining Consumer Behavior

In general, scientific explanations must meet two requirements: (1) explanatory relevance, meaning that the account of some type of consumer behavior constitutes acceptable grounds for expecting that the behavior will occur under the specified circumstances, and (2) testability, meaning that scientific explanations must be capable of empirical tests. Explanations satisfying the first requirement automatically satisfy the second, but the converse does not always hold.[7]

In general, most consumer behavior insights have been derived from empirical studies and, hence, usually satisfy the second requirement. Unfortunately, however, as the following discussion points out, efforts to date do not fare well in terms of explanatory relevance.

Levels of Explanation There are at least four levels of explanation in the behavioral sciences that are applicable to consumer behavior:[8]

Level of Explanation	Explanation
I	A certain phenomenon has an empirical existence
II	The phenomenon is of the nature Q and is produced by factors $X_1, X_2, \cdots, X_n$
III	Factors $X_1, X_2, \cdots, X_n$ are interactive or have interacted in manner $Y_1, Y_2, \cdots, Y_n$ to produce in some past or present time a phenomenon of the nature Q
IV	Factors $X_1, X_2, \cdots, X_n$ interact in a manner $Y_1, Y_2, \cdots, Y_n$ for reasons $W_1, W_2, \cdots, W_n$, thus producing a phenomenon of the nature Q

The higher the level, the more scientific the explanation.

Various specialties or disciplines within consumer behavior are at different levels of explanation. However, in general, it is rare to reach level three. For

---

[6] The structure and some of the content of this section are adapted from Gerald Zaltman, Reinhard Angelmar, and Christian Pinson, "Metatheory in Consumer Behavior Research," in David M. Gardner (ed.), *Proc. 2nd Annual Conf. of the Association for Consumer Research* (College Park, Md.: University of Maryland, 1971), pp. 476–497.

[7] C. G. Hempel, *Philosophy of Natural Science* (Englewood Cliffs, N.J.: Prentice-Hall, 1966), p. 49.

[8] J. T. Doby, "Logic and Levels of Scientific Explanation," in E. F. Borgatta (ed.), *Sociological Methodology* (San Francisco: Jossey-Gass, 1969).

example, consider problem recognition and search processes. In both cases, a list of determinants has been discovered through research. However, it is not known whether this list is complete, let alone how the determinants interact, or their relative importance. The same is true for brand loyalty, store choice, and a number of other phenomena. Thus, at the present time, explanations of consumer behavior are largely confined to lower levels.

Evaluating Explanations There are four basic criteria for evaluating explanations:[9]

(1) *Scope*—The range of events to which an explanation can be applied.
(2) *Precision*—The exactness with which the concepts used in explanation are related to empirical indicators, and the precision with which the rules of interaction of the variables in the system are stated[10]
(3) *Power*—The degree of control over the environment an explanation provides. Power depends on the precision of the description and explanation and upon the completeness of the variables.
(4) *Reliability*—The frequency with which factors not included in the explanation interrupt the situation the explanation concerns.

In using these criteria to evaluate explanations of consumer behavior, conclusions depend on the level of abstraction. For example, selective perception, attitude change, and the decision-making process are applicable in a wide number of choice situations. However, the specific importance of selective perception, the specific determinants of attitude change, or the specific nature of the decision-making process vary due to the substantial variations that occur across consumers and choice situations.

Thus, at the more abstract level, the concepts and processes involved in consumer behavior appear to be acceptable in terms of scope and, perhaps, power and reliability. Precision is low because the rules of variable interaction have not been articulated completely. At less abstract levels, current explanations of consumer behavior appear, for the most part, to have limited scope, precision, power, and reliability.

Predicting Consumer Behavior

In consumer behavior, prediction can be used in two ways.[11] First, it can be used to make deductions from known to unknown events within a conceptually static system. For example, discrimination function analysis is used to predict successful sales transactions on the basis of customer–salesman bargaining variables. Second, prediction is used to make assertions about future behavioral outcomes, for example, forecasting. The logical structure of scientific prediction

---

[9] Zaltman *et al., op. cit.,*[6] pp. 481–482.

[10] E. J. Meehan, *Explanation in Social Science: A System Paradigm* (Homewood, Ill.: Dorsey Press, 1968), p. 117.

[11] Zaltman *et al., op. cit.,*[6] pp. 482–483.

is the same as that of explanation, although we may have the paradox of being able to predict without explaining, and explaining without being able to predict.

Levels of Prediction   As in the case of explanation, there are different levels of prediction. These levels are identical to the ones mentioned above except that they are future oriented.

In general, most consumer research seems to have focused on attempting to describe and explain current or past behavior rather than predicting future behavior. There are, of course, some exceptions, such as brand loyalty models, diffusion models, store patronage models, attitude change theories, and new brand penetration models, such as NEWS.[12]

Prediction attempts rarely go beyond the second level of prediction. Brand loyalty models, for example, attempt to predict future market shares Q, based on a limited number of factors, $X_1, X_2, \cdots X_n$. Generally they do not specify how these factors will interact, or why they will interact in that manner. The same is true of models of store patronage and new brand penetration, and theories of attitude change. Diffusion models appear to be an exception as they use all four levels of prediction.[13]

Evaluating Predictions   Like explanations, predictions can be evaluated using our basic criteria. While the criteria have the same titles, they are defined differently. Thus:[14]

(1)   *Scope*—The longitudinal and latitudinal range of events covered by a prediction.

(2)   *Precision*—The degree of mathematical isomorphism between the concepts involved in the prediction and their empirical indicators.

(3)   *Power*—The precision of the predictive statement and its completeness.

(4)   *Reliability*—The frequency with which factors not included in the predictive explanation cause it not to happen exactly as the explanation predicted.

It appears that most attempts to predict consumer behavior, or some aspect of it, have wide to limited scope, and low precision, power, and reliability. As discussed earlier, evaluations of scope depend on the level of abstraction—the more abstract the concept, the wider the scope, and vice versa. Precision, power, and reliability are low because consumer behavior differs widely in a given purchase situation, and the same consumer often behaves differently from one type of purchase situation to another. As has been observed in previous chapters, it is difficult to construct probabilistic or stochastic models. Deterministic models do not appear to be feasible, at least in the near future.

---

12   Lawrence Light and Lewis Pringle, "New Product Forecasting Using Recursive Regression," in David T. Kollat, Roger D. Blackwell, and James F. Engel (eds.), *Research in Consumer Behavior* (New York: Holt, Rinehart and Winston, 1970), pp. 702–709.

13   Zaltman *et al., op. cit.*,[6] pp. 483–484.

14   Zaltman *et al., op. cit.*,[6] pp. 484–485.

A Concluding Note

The reader may disagree with some of the conclusions expressed in the preceding paragraphs. They represent the authors' judgments, and their applicability varies among the specialties comprising the field of consumer behavior.

Even allowing for a few differences of opinion, it seems that what looks like a well-researched and developed discipline of consumer behavior does not fare well when evaluated against the criteria of explanation and prediction. Others share this view.[15]

Recently, the National Science Council evaluated the state of knowledge in the behavioral sciences. They concluded that actual accomplishment has not been consistent with the magnitude of effort.[16] It does not appear that consumer behavior as an interdisciplinary area of research is exempt from this statement. The following section presents the authors' recommendations for correcting the results–effort imbalance in the future.

RECOMMENDATIONS FOR IMPROVING CONSUMER BEHAVIOR RESEARCH[17]

There are at least two reasons for the results–effort imbalance and the lack of more progress in terms of explanation and prediction. First, consumer behavior is a relatively new discipline, dating back less than fifty years, with the majority of research conducted during the last decade.[18] Second, there is no overall research strategy or plan; rather, a large number of academicians and industry and government personnel have conducted individual projects consistent with their interests, problems, perspectives, and skills. Given these two conditions, the current status of consumer research is inevitable.

Relative to many other disciplines, there have been few attempts to evaluate the overall status of consumer research. Past efforts have concentrated primarily on summarizing and synthesizing findings into proposition inventories.[19]

---

[15] See, for example, Jagdish N. Sheth, "A Review of Buyer Behavior," *Management Science*, vol. 13, pp. B-718–B-756 (Aug. 1967).

[16] National Science Council, *The Behavioral and Social Sciences* (Englewood Cliffs, N.J.: Prentice-Hall, 1969).

[17] Part of the structure and content of this section are adapted from David T. Kollat, James F. Engel, and Roger D. Blackwell, "Current Problems in Consumer Behavior Research," *J. Marketing Research*, vol. 7, pp. 327–332 (Aug. 1970).

[18] For a discussion of the evolution of consumer research, see Francesco M. Nicosia, "Consumer Research: Problems and Perspectives," *J. Consumer Affairs*, vol. 3, pp. 9–25 (Summer 1969).

[19] Robert Ferber, "Research on Household Behavior," *Amer. Economic Rev.*, vol. 52, pp. 19–63 (Mar. 1962); Frederick E. May, "Buying Behavior: Some Research Findings," *J. Business*, pp. 379–396 (Oct. 1965); James N. Morgan, "A Review of Recent Research on Consumer Behavior," in Lincoln Clark (ed.), *Consumer Behavior*, vol. 3 (New York: Harper & Row, 1958), pp. 93–108; Dik Warren Twedt, "Consumer Psychology," *Annual Rev. of Psychology*, vol. 16, pp. 265–293 (1965); Sheth, *op. cit.*[15]

With noteable exceptions,[20] these critical evaluations have been confined to particular aspects of consumer behavior, such as cognitive dissonance,[21] brand loyalty,[22] the diffusion of innovations,[23] and personality.[24] These summaries and evaluations have been useful, but many important issues have not been explored.

This section is intended to supplement other critical evaluations, not attempting to compare and synthesize findings, or develop propositional inventories, but to deal with complementary and equally important issues involved in a research tradition or strategy of inquiry. Discussion and resolution of these problems could contribute greatly to the development of a growing body of knowledge.

Greater Utilization of Theories and Models

As we have observed throughout this volume, the majority of consumer research has utilized, explicitly or implicitly, hypothetical constructs, theories, and what Nicosia has called "reduced-form" models.[25] Examples include motivation,[26] perception,[27] learning,[28] personality,[29] attitudes and attitude

---

[20]   W. T. Tucker, "Consumer Research: Status and Prospects," in Reed Moyer (ed.), *Changing Marketing Systems* (Chicago: Amer. Marketing Assoc., 1967), pp. 267–269; Sheth, *op. cit.*[15]

[21]   James F. Engel, "The Dissonance Dilemma," *Bull. Business Research* (Columbus, Ohio: Bureau of Business Research, Ohio State University, July 1968), p. 1 ff.

[22]   A. S. C. Ehrenberg, "An Appraisal of Markov Brand Switching Models," *J. Marketing Research*, vol. 2, pp. 347–363 (Nov. 1965); John U. Farley and Alfred E. Kuehn, "Stochastic Models of Brand Switching," in George Schwartz (ed.), *Science in Marketing* (New York: Wiley, 1965), pp. 446–464.

[23]   Elihu Katz, Martin L. Levin, and Herbert Hamilton, "Traditions of Research on the Diffusion of Innovations," *Amer. Sociological Rev.*, vol. 28, pp. 237–252 (1963); Charles W. King, "Adoption and Diffusion Research in Marketing: An Overview," in Raymond M. Haas (ed.), *Science, Technology and Marketing* (Chicago: Amer. Marketing Assoc., 1966), pp. 665–685.

[24]   Harold H. Kassarjian, "Personality and Consumer Behavior: A Review," *J. Marketing Research*, vol. 8, pp. 409–418 (Nov. 1971); James F. Engel, David T. Kollat, and Roger D. Blackwell, "Personality Measures and Market Segmentation," *Business Horizons*, vol. 12, pp. 61–70 (June 1969).

[25]   Francesco M. Nicosia, *Consumer Decision Processes* (Englewood Cliffs, N.J.: Prentice-Hall, 1966).

[26]   Ernest Dichter, *The Strategy of Desire* (New York: Doubleday, 1960); Ernest Dichter, "Toward an Understanding of Human Behavior," in Robert Ferber and Hugh G. Wales (eds.), *Motivation and Market Behavior* (Homewood, Ill.: Irwin, 1958), pp. 21–30.

[27]   G. V. Haigh and D. W. Fiske, "Corroboration of Personal Values as Selective Factors in Perception," *J. Abnormal and Social Psychology*, vol. 47, pp. 394–398 (1952); N. Pastore, "Need as a Determinant of Perception," *J. Psychology*, vol. 28, pp. 457–475 (1949).

[28]   Herbert E. Krugman, "The Learning of Consumer Preference," *J. Marketing*, vol. 26, pp. 31–33 (1962); Alfred E. Kuehn, "Consumer Brand Choice as a Learning Process," *J. Advertising Research*, vol. 2, pp. 10–17 (Dec. 1962).

[29]   Robert P. Brody and Scott M. Cunningham, "Personality Variables and the Consumer Decision Process," *J. Marketing Research*, vol. 5, pp. 50–57 (Feb. 1968); Franklin B. Evans, "Psychological and Objective Factors in the Prediction of Brand Choice: Ford versus Chevrolet," *J. Business*, vol. 32, pp. 340–369 (1959); W. T. Tucker and J. J. Painter, "Personality and Product Use," *J. Applied Psychology*, vol. 45, pp. 325–329 (1961).

change,[30] social class,[31] reference groups,[32] dissonance,[33] and risk taking.[34] These constructs have been employed in a variety of ways in an attempt to explain and /or predict some aspect of consumer behavior.

There is no doubt that these and other constructs are often significant and useful. However, several problems are apparent.

First, there have been several instances where constructs and theories have not been used properly. This problem is evident in many studies investigating the relationship between personality and consumer behavior. Jacoby has summarized the status of much of this type of research:

> Investigators usually take a general, broad coverage personality inventory and a list of brands, products, or product categories, and attempt to correlate subjects' responses on the inventory with statements of product use or preference. Careful examination reveals that, in most cases, the investigators have operated without the benefit of theory and with no a priori thought directed to *how*, or especially *why*, personality should or should not be related to that aspect of consumer behavior being studied. Statistical techniques, usually simple correlation or variants thereof, are applied and anything that turns up looking half-way interesting furnishes the basis for the Discussion section. Skill at post-diction and post hoc interpretation has been demonstrated, but little real understanding has resulted.[35]

Jacoby illustrates his points by reanalyzing Evans' classic study of the personality differences between Ford and Chevrolet owners. Evans employed the Edwards personal preference schedule and found only one difference significant at better than the 0.05 level.[36] From this Evans concluded that personality had little, if any, relationship to consumer behavior.

Jacoby shows that an entirely different picture emerges when the data

---

[30] Kenward Atkin, "Advertising and Store Patronage," *J. Advertising Research*, vol. 2, pp. 18–23 (1962); J. T. Klapper, *The Effects of Mass Communication* (New York: Free Press, 1960).

[31] Sidney Levy, "Social Class and Consumer Behavior," in Joseph W. Newman (ed.), *On Knowing the Consumer* (New York: Wiley, 1966), pp. 146–160; Pierre Martineau, "Social Classes and Spending Behavior," *J. Marketing*, vol. 23, pp. 131–130 (Oct. 1958).

[32] Foundation for Research on Human Behavior, *Group Influence in Marketing and Public Relations* (Ann Arbor, Mich.: The Foundation, 1956); James E. Stafford, "Effects of Group Influences on Consumer Brand Preferences," *J. Marketing Research*, vol. 3, pp. 68–75 (Feb. 1966).

[33] James F. Engel, "Are Automobile Purchasers Dissonant Consumers?" *J. Marketing*, vol. 27, pp. 55–58 (1963).

[34] Raymond A. Bauer, "Consumer Behavior as Risk Taking," in Robert S. Hancock (ed.), *Dynamic Marketing for a Changing World* (Chicago: Amer. Marketing Assoc., 1960), pp. 389–398; Donald F. Cox and Stuart U. Rich, "Perceived Risk and Consumer Decision Making —the Case of Telephone Shopping," *J. Marketing Research*, vol. 1, pp. 32–39 (Nov. 1964); Scott M. Cunningham, "Perceived Risk as a Factor in the Diffusion of New Product Information," in Haas *op. cit.*,[23] pp. 698–721.

[35] Jacob Jacoby, "Towards Defining Consumer Psychology: One Psychologist's Views," paper presented at the American Psychological Association 77th Annual Convention, Washington, D.C. (Sept. 4, 1969).

[36] Evans, *op. cit.*[29]

are reexamined using specific hypotheses derived from a conceptual–psychological orientation. Specifically, Jacoby's analysis of Evans' data yielded 8 out of 11 correct predictions. If Jacoby's procedure is correct, Evans' results do not preclude the possibility of a relationship between personality and consumer behavior.

The Jacoby argument is not an isolated situation. For example, Brody and Cunningham[37] and others[38] have demonstrated the value of personality and personality-oriented variables when used properly. Similarly, Bass, Sheth, and Talaryzk have shown the importance of attitude in predicting consumer behavior when the theoretical basis for the concept is understood and used properly.[39]

As will become apparent later, this discussion should not be interpreted as suggesting that all research should be confirmed to testing theories. Rather, the simple point is that when an aspect of consumer behavior is studied, theoretical aspects should be examined in *detail* and the theory should be used *correctly*.

The second problem in using hypothetical constructs, theories, and reduced-form models is that each plays a limited role in that consumer behavior is influenced by a variety of phenomena interacting in complex ways. According to Nicosia,[40] Morgan[41] was probably the first to realize that the exponential growth in the number of determinants of consumer behavior was causing increasing perplexity. The situation has certainly become more acute since Morgan's observation.

As was discussed in Chapters 2 and 3, several attempts have been made to design comprehensive models that specify the interrelationships of various constructs, theories, and reduced-form models. Nicosia,[42] Engel, Kollat, and Blackwell,[43] Howard and Sheth,[44] and others[45] have proposed models of varying degrees of comprehensiveness and sophistication.

---

[37] Brody and Cunningham, *op. cit.*[29]

[38] See, for example, William D. Wells and Douglas J. Tigert, "Activities, Interests and Opinions," *J. Advertising Research*, vol. 11, pp. 27–35 (Aug. 1971).

[39] Jagdish N. Sheth and W. Wayne Talaryzk, "Perceived Instrumentality and Value Importance as Determinants of Attitudes," *J. Marketing Research*, vol. 9, pp. 6–9 (Feb. 1972); Frank M. Bass and W. Wayne Talaryzk, "An Attitude Model for the Study of Brand Preference," *J. Marketing Research*, vol. 9, pp. 93–96 (Feb. 1972).

[40] Francesco M. Nicosia, "Brand Choice: Toward Behavioral–Behavioristic Models," paper presented at the Symposium on Behavioral Sciences and Management Sciences in Marketing, sponsored by the College of Marketing of the Institute of Management Science and by the Graduate School of Business, University of Chicago (June 29–July 1, 1969).

[41] Morgan, *op. cit.*[19]

[42] Nicosia, *op. cit.*[25]

[43] James F. Engel, David T. Kollat, and Roger D. Blackwell, *Consumer Behavior* (New York: Holt, Rinehart and Winston, 1973).

[44] John A. Howard and Jagdish N. Sheth, *The Theory of Buyer Behavior* (New York: Wiley, 1969).

[45] See, for example, Alan R. Andreason, "Attitudes and Consumer Behavior: A Decision Model," in Lee R. Preston (ed.), *New Research in Marketing* (Berkeley: Institute of Business and Economic Research, University of California, 1965), pp. 1–16; A. S. C. Ehrenberg, "Towards an Integrated Theory of Consumer Behavior," *J. Marketing Research Society*, vol. 11, pp. 305–337 (Oct. 1969); Gordon Wills, Frederick Lumb, and Richard M. S. Wilson, "Vector Analysis of Buyer Behavior," *J. Marketing Research Society*, vol. 11, pp. 214–233 (July 1969); Tanniru R. Rao, "Computer Simulation of a Model of Market Behavior," paper presented at the American Marketing Association Fall Conf., Minneapolis, Minn. (Aug. 1971).

Unfortunately, a very small percentage of consumer research has utilized, or been based on, any type of comprehensive, integrative model.[46] This generates some disturbing questions.

Regarding past research, how many findings (or lack of findings) are artifacts of the conceptualizations that have been used? Stated differently, if the research had been based on comprehensive models rather than relatively insular constructs, how many of the "significant" and "nonsignificant" findings would change because of the effects of variables that have not been included in the study or otherwise controlled? This problem will continue to plague future consumer research efforts because, lacking an integrative model, how does the researcher know what variables should be included and controlled?

The severity of what might be called the "conceptualization artifact" problem suggests the need to devote more resources to the development, testing, and revision of comprehensive models. Are the models identified above adequate, or are they too simplistic? Is is possible to have *a* model of consumer behavior, or are several necessary? If several are required, then what are the relevant underlying assumptions and the conditions under which each is appropriate?

The final problem is the modeling–testing sequence. Most comprehensive models attempt to do at least two things. First, they record which variables are known to interact with which other variables. Second, they reveal which interactions need to be and have not yet been studied (theoretically and empirically). Most of the research used to construct these models proceeds from theoretical statements—"Y is caused by X, Z, and V"—to direct empirical tests.

As Nicosia has pointed out, one of the shortcomings of this procedure is that the statistics obtained may actually be produced by different causal networks of interactions among the variables. As long as the interpretation of statistical results is ambiguous, it is not clear which theory is actually being tested; thus, the empirical results cannot be used to refine the original idea of how the phenomenon works. Rather, the result is an endless cascade of qualifications and an unmanageable number of empirically tested and nonrejected hypotheses.[47]

To overcome these problems Nicosia recommends the insertion of a methodological operation between the set of theoretical statements and the empirical test. The operation is a formal mathematical specification of the network of interactions the researcher has in mind. This is done by translating the hypothesized network (flow charts) into formal models.[48]

Unfortunately, there has been little work done in building, analyzing, and testing sophisticated *mathematical* models of theories that predict and explain brand choice on the basis of interactions among a variety of variables

---

[46] For exceptions, see Paul A. Pellemans, *Relationships between Attitude and Purchase Intention toward the Brand* (Namur, Belgium: Publications Universitaries, Namur University, 1971); Louis V. Dominquez and Philip C. Burger, "An Empirical Analysis of the Process of Consumer Behavior," (paper presented at the American Marketing Association Fall Conf., Minneapolis, Minn. (Aug. 1971).

[47] Nicosia, *op. cit.*,[40] pp. 11–12.

[48] Nicosia, *op. cit.*,[40] p. 18.

over time. For the most part, those knowledgeable in substantive areas lack supersophisticated mathematical skills. On the other hand, those possessing modeling expertise often do not understand the substantive dimensions of the behavior being modeled. A merger of these two types of skills would probably accelerate progress in the future.

Establishing Research Priorities

The research priorities issue is another problem area, and it has at least two dimensions: (1) what "aspects" of consumer behavior are of the greatest importance, that is, what are the "key areas?" and (2) what phenomena need to be investigated and in what order, so that these key areas can be understood?

An analysis of the consumer research literature yields the conclusion that a substantial percentage of research has occurred because of the availability of data, the convenience of research and mathematical techniques, and/or the attractiveness and appeal of certain behavioral constructs.[49] In other words, most research has been "data-technique-construct" motivated and oriented. While the infancy of consumer research makes this orientation understandable and perhaps justifiable in the short run, it is no longer an efficacious strategy. An alternative approach would be to become more problem oriented. Yet problem orientation as a focus for future research wavers somewhat under closer examination in spite of its obvious appeal from a conceptual point of view. The difficulty lies in defining what constitutes key problem areas, primarily because of fundamental differences of opinion as to the key areas which should be of concern to the researcher. For example, some could be defined as:

(1)   Those behavioral constructs and relationships that, if understood, would permit the understanding of the greatest number of other constructs and relationships.

(2)   Those behavioral constructs and relationships that, if understood, would make the greatest contribution to business firms' rate of return on investment and/or the appropriate measures of performance and efficiency for other organizations.

(3)   Some combination of (1') and (2).

It would be presumptuous for the authors to suggest how key areas ought to be defined. The germane point is that research priority issues of this variety have never been publicly raised, let alone resolved. For example, if the second strategy above is followed, should research efforts focus on those problems having the greatest immediate payout, or should they concentrate on longer range problems having fewer immediate applications but a potentially greater number of longer range uses? What are the long-range high-payout issues? Discussion and, hopefully, resolution of these issues should accelerate progress.

---

49   For an exception, see Nicosia, *op. cit.*, [25] chap. 7.

Attaining Critical Mass

The literature of consumer research is dominated by small-scale "one-shot" studies. Samples are typically small, out of date (*Chicago Tribune* 1961 panel), or objectionable on other grounds (college students, women's club members, and so on). The one-shot characteristic limits the researcher's ability to investigate the phenomenon in a rigorous and comprehensive manner.

In contrast, research efforts that seem to have had a decisive impact on the discipline during the last five years are major research *programs*. These programs are longer term efforts that systematically investigate many dimensions of a phenomenon and usually, but not always, involve larger and better quality samples. Examples include the King–Summers thrust in opinion leadership and diffusion,[50] the Pessemier–Tigert–Wells investigations of psyographics and other profiling and clustering techniques,[51] the Bass–Sheth–Talaryzk studies of the Fishbein approach to attitude measurement,[52] the Green *et al.* stream in multidimensional scaling,[53] and the Howard–Sheth *et al.* empirical tests of their theory of buyer behavior.[54]

These and other researchers have attained critical mass in studying some aspect of consumer behavior. If the research program approach were used in other areas—social class, reference groups, purchase intentions, store choice, and shopper profiles, to mention just a few—progress would probably accelerate.

Utilizing Longitudinal and Experimental Designs

As has been observed throughout this volume, consumer behavior researchers typically utilize three types of research designs—cross-sectional surveys, longitudinal, and experimental or quasi-experimental. Cross-sectional surveys are the most common.

The appropriateness of each method depends, of course, on the type of problem, the reasons for the study, the research budget, and the researcher's conceptualization of the problem. In general, however, there are serious problems involved in using the cross-sectional method. Of greatest significance is the fact that consumer behavior is inherently a dynamic on-going phenomenon, a process that occurs over time rather than at a given point in time. Others[55] share the view

---

[50]   See, for example, Charles W. King and John O. Summers," Overlap of Opinion Leadership across Consumer Product Categories," *J. Marketing Research*, vol. 7, pp. 43–50 (Feb. 1970).

[51]   Wells and Tigert, *op. cit.*[38]

[52]   Sheth and Talaryzk, *op. cit.*;[39] Bass and Talaryzk, *op. cit.*[39]

[53]   Paul E. Green and Vithala R. Rao, *Applied Multidimensional Scaling: Comparison of Approaches and Algorithms* (New York: Holt, Rinehart and Winston, 1972).

[54]   See, for example, John A. Howard, "New Directions in Buyer Behavior Research," paper presented at the American Marketing Association Fall Conf., Minneapolis, Minn. (Aug. 1971).

[55]   All flow charts and comprehensive models of consumer behavior treat it as a process. See, for example, Howard and Sheth, *op. cit.*;[44] Nicosia, *op. cit.*;[25] A. R. Andreason, *op. cit.*[45] For the logic behind the decision process approach, see James M. Patterson, "Buying as a Process," *Business Horizons*, pp. 59–60 (Spring 1965).

of this volume that there are compelling reasons for conceptualizing and studying consumer behavior as a process rather than an act. Cross-sectional designs are the least appropriate method for studying consumer behavior over time, because of the serious biases resulting from inaccurate memory, interaction, and response style.[56] Moreover, a cross-sectional survey also suffers from weakness in isolating cause and effect relationships.

The longitudinal design is the ideal method of studying many, if not most, dimensions of consumer behavior. But these studies are very expensive to conduct. A great deal of imagination and persistence—including, perhaps, multi-university and/or multisource funding—will be required to overcome the cost problem.

Laboratory experiments make it easier to measure variables and their relationships, including cause and effect. But only a limited number of relationships can be measured in each experiment, and generalizing findings to real situations is often difficult because the conditions controlled in the laboratory may be active in the normal life of consumers.[57]

Despite these problems, longitudinal and experimental designs are generally superior to cross-sectional studies. Although longitudinal studies are still relatively rare,[58] the growing use of experimental designs is encouraging.[59] More widespread use of these two designs should increase the quality of future consumer research.

Standardized Definitions

Throughout this text there have been numerous examples of widely varying definitions of what are presumably the same variables and constructs. Brand loyalty, for example, has been defined in terms of brand choice sequences,[60]

---

[56]   Donald H. Granbois and James F. Engel, "The Longitudinal Approach to Studying Marketing Behavior," in Peter D. Bennett (ed.), *Marketing and Economic Development* (Chicago: Amer. Marketing Assoc., 1965), pp. 205–221.

[57]   Nicosia, *op. cit.*,[18] p. 12.

[58]   For examples of longitudinal studies, see James F. Engel, David A. Knapp, and Deanne E. Knapp, "Sources of Influence in the Acceptance of New Products for Self-Medication—Preliminary Findings," in Haas, *op. cit.*,[23] pp. 776–782; Allan L. Pennington, "Customer–Salesmen Bargaining Behavior in Retail Transactions," *J. Marketing Research*, vol. 5, pp. 255–262 (Aug. 1968); Robert W. Pratt, Jr., "Understanding the Decision Process for Consumer Durable Goods: An Example of the Application of Longitudinal Analysis," in Bennett, *op. cit.*,[56] pp. 244–260.

[59]   Examples of experimental studies include Lee K. Anderson, James R. Taylor, and Robert J. Holloway, "The Consumer and His Alternatives: An Experimental Approach," *J. Marketing Research*, vol. 3, pp. 62–67 (Feb. 1966); Robert Holloway, "An Experiment on Consumer Dissonance," *J. Marketing*, vol. 31, pp. 39–43 (Jan. 1967); Donald J. Hempel, "An Experimental Study of Information on Consumer Product Evaluations," in Haas, *op cit.*,[23] pp. 589–597; J. Douglas McConnell, "The Price–Quality Relationship in an Experimental Setting," *J. Marketing Research*, vol. 5, pp. 300–303 (Aug. 1968).

[60]   George Brown, "Brand Loyalty—Fact or Fiction?" *Advertising Age*, vol. 23, pp. 53–55 (June 19, 1952); pp. 45–47 (June 30, 1952); pp. 54–56; (July 14, 1952); pp. 46–48 (July 28, 1952); pp. 56–58 (Aug. 11, 1952); pp. 80–82 (Sept. 1, 1952); pp. 82–86 (Oct. 6, 1952); pp. 76–79 (Dec. 1, 1952); pp. 75–76 (Jan. 26, 1953); W. T. Tucker, "The Development of Brand Loyalty," *J. Marketing Research*, vol. 1, pp. 32–35 (Aug. 1964).

proportion of purchases,[61] repeat purchase probabilities,[62] and brand preference over time.[63] Definitions of impulse purchasing[64] and opinion leader[65] vary from study to study. The importance of information sources is sometimes defined in terms of exposure, other times in terms of effectiveness.[66] There are at least 45 definitions of innovation and 164 definitions of culture.[67] Examples in other areas could be cited.[68]

Definitions, of course, are relative to purposes—they are means or tools rather than ends. Even so, it is difficult to visualize how there can be this many different purposes. Some of this confusion is inevitable given the infancy of consumer behavior research. But with a few exceptions, such as attitude measurement,[69] very little progress has been made, even in the last four years, in dealing with this problem. In fact, in general it has become more intolerable.

This situation is not an insignificant problem. Definitional heterogeneity makes it extraordinarily difficult and hazardous to compare, synthesize, and accumulate findings. Definition and classification of terms and variables is, of

---

[61] Ross Cunningham, "Brand Loyalty—What, Where, How Much," *Harvard Business Rev.*, vol. 34, pp. 116–128 (Jan.–Feb. 1956); Ross Cunningham, "Customer Loyalty to Store and Brand," *Harvard Business Rev.*, vol. 39, pp. 127–137 (Nov.–Dec. 1961).

[62] Ronald E. Frank, "Brand Choice as a Probability Process," *J. Business*, vol. 35, pp. 43–56 (Jan. 1962).

[63] Lester Guest, "Brand Loyalty—Twelve Years Later," *J. Applied Psychology*, vol. 39, pp. 405–408 (1955).

[64] Vernon T. Clover, "Relative Importance of Impulse Buying in Retail Stores," *J. Marketing*, vol. 15, pp. 66–70 (July 1950); *Consumer Buying Habits Studies* (Wilmington, Del.: E. I. DuPont de Nemours and Co., 1949, 1954, 1959, 1965); James D. Schaffer, "The Influence of Impulse Buying or in-the-Store Decisions on Consumers' Food Purchases," journal paper no. 2591 (Michigan Agricultural Experimental Station).

[65] Francesco M. Nicosia, "Opinion Leadership and the Flow of Communication: Some Problems and Prospects," in L. George Smith (ed.), *Reflections on Progress in Marketing* (Chicago: Amer. Marketing Assoc., 1964), pp. 340–358; Charles W. King and John O. Summers, "Generalized Opinion Leadership in Consumer Products," paper no. 224 (Lafayette, Ind: Institute for Research in the Behavioral, Economic, and Management Sciences, Krannert Graduate School of Industrial Administration, Jan. 1969).

[66] Robert G. Mason, "The Use of Information Sources in the Process of Adoption," *Rural Sociology*, vol. 29, pp. 40–52 (Mar. 1964); George Fisk, "Media Influence Reconsidered," *Public Opinion Quart.*, vol. 23, pp. 83–91 (1959).

[67] Alfred L. Kroeber and Clyde Kluckhohn, "Culture: A Critical Review of Concepts and Definitions," *Papers of the Peabody Museum*, vol. 27 (1952).

[68] For example, compare the following approaches to motivation: Muzafer Sherif and Carolyn W. Sherif, *An Outline of Social Psychology*, rev. ed. (New York: Harper & Row, 1956); Bernard Berelson and Gary Steiner, *Human Behavior* (New York: Harcourt, 1964), p. 532; David Krech, Richard S. Crutchfield, and Egerton L. Ballachey, *Individual in Society* (New York: McGraw-Hill, 1962), chap. 5.

[69] See, for example, J. B. Cohen and O. T. Ahtola, "An Expectancy X Value Analysis of the Relationship between Consumer Attitudes and Behavior," paper presented at the Association for Consumer Research (Sept. 1971); R. Moinpour and D. L. MacLachlan, "The Relations among Attribute and Importance Components of the Rosenberg–Fishbein Type Attitude Models: An Empirical Investigation," paper presented at the Association for Consumer Research (Sept. 1971); J. E. Scott and P. D. Bennett, "Cognitive Models of Attitude Structure: 'Value Importance' is Important," paper presented at the American Marketing Association Fall Conf., Minneapolis, Minn. (Aug. 1971).

course, an essential step in any area of inquiry that purports to use the scientific method. It may not be possible to develop a single definition of each construct and variable that can be used in all situations, but, at the very least, there must be an agreed-upon point of departure.

Standardized Variable Categories

There is also considerable heterogeneity in the categories used to measure many variables and constructs. For example, a comprehensive review of the family life-cycle literature by Wells and Gubar pointed up the wide variation in life-cycle categories in published research.[70] Similarly, there are significant variations in the categories used to measure the influence of family members in purchasing decisions[71] and nearly every social-class researcher uses a different typology.[72]

This lack of standardized variable categories also makes it difficult to compare and integrate research findings. Instead of improving, this problem has also intensified during the last five years. The development of standard, or recommended categories would increase the value of future empirical efforts.

Richer Dependent Variables

In recent years there has been a growing use of multivariate techniques by consumer researchers. In many instances, these studies have demonstrated that single independent variables are not statistically related—or only weakly related—to whatever dependent variable is being investigated. On the other hand, combinations of independent variables often prove to be statistically significant and/or much more strongly related to the dependent variable.[73]

This same approach is rarely applied to dependent variables. Regardless of the complexity of the dependent variable, researchers typically measure it unidimensionally.

There are some interesting exceptions. For example, studies of brand

---

[70] William D. Wells and George Gubar, "Life Cycle Concept in Marketing Research," *J. Marketing Research*, vol. 3, pp. 355–363 (Nov. 1966).

[71] See, for example, Harry Sharp and Paul Mott, "Consumer Decisions in the Metropolitan Family," *J. Marketing*, vol. 21, pp. 149–156 (Oct. 1956); Elizabeth H. Wolgast, "Do Husbands or Wives Make Purchasing Decisions?" *J. Marketing*, vol. 23, pp. 151–158 (Oct. 1958); "A Pilot Study of the Roles of Husbands and Wives in Purchasing Decisions, Parts I–X," conducted for *Life Magazine* by L. Jaffe Associates, Inc. (1965).

[72] Charles B. McCann, *Women and Department Store Newspaper Advertising* (Chicago: Social Research, 1957); James M. Carman, *The Application of Social Class in Market Segmentation* (Berkeley: University of California Graduate School of Business Administration, Institute of Business and Economic Research, 1965).

[73] John U. Farley, "Dimensions of Supermarket Choice Patterns," *J. Marketing Research*, vol. 5, pp. 206–208 (May 1968); Jerome B. Kernan, "Choice Behavior, Decision Behavior and Personality," *J. Marketing Research*, vol. 5, pp. 155–164 (May 1968); John G. Myers, "Determinants of Private Brand Attitude," *J. Marketing Research*, vol. 4, pp. 73–81 (Feb. 1967).

loyalty (measured unidimensionally) have been characterized by the absence of significant relationships with consumer characteristics. Yet, when loyalty is measured multidimensionally, significant relationships have surfaced.[74]

In most consumer research studies, if the relationship between the dependent variable and the independent variable(s) is not statistically significant, it is concluded that the independent variable(s) is not important in understanding and predicting the dependent variable. The above discussion suggests that in some instances the "dimensionality artifact" may provide an alternative explanation. In other words, if dependent variables were measured multidimensionally, the independent variables that are significant and nonsignificant might change. Hence wider use of multidimensional measures of dependent variables would appear useful.

Use of Group Differences

Studies investigating various aspects of consumer behavior often make conclusions about the relevance of variables in "accounting for" behavior, or identifying market segments, on the basis of statistical tests measuring the variance in the behavior of individuals. Product-moment correlations of 0.2, and seldom higher than 0.3 or 0.4, are typical. Hence it is concluded that the variables do not "explain the variance" very well, even when combined into a prediction equation.

Interestingly, when the unit of analysis is changed from individuals to groups or market segments, findings that were not significant sometimes become significant. Wells and Tigert have found this to be true in constructing psychographic profiles of heavy users of various convenience products.[75] Similarly, Bass, Tigert, and Lonsdale have found that the inability of socioeconomic variables to explain a substantial part of the variance in usage rates of persons does not necessarily imply that there are not substantial differences in the mean usage rates for different socioeconomic market segments.[76] Greater use of "group-differences" analysis would appear worthwhile.

Generalizing across Types of Decisions

The unresolved issue here is the extent to which findings derived from an analysis of a specific type of consumer decision are applicable to other types of decisions. There is considerable evidence that many consumer behavior findings

---

[74] James M. Carman, "Correlates of Brand Loyalty: Some Positive Results," *J. Marketing Research*, vol. 7, pp. 67–76 (Feb. 1970); George S. Day, "A Two-Dimensional Concept of Brand Loyalty," *J. Advertising Research*, vol. 9, pp. 29–35 (Sept. 1969).

[75] Wells and Tigert, *op. cit.*[38]

[76] Frank M. Bass, Douglas J. Tigert, and Ronald T. Lonsdale, "Market Segmentation: Group versus Individual Behavior," *J. Marketing Research*, vol. 5, pp. 264–270 (Aug. 1968).

are applicable only to the type of decision or choice being studied, and this can create another dilemma.

For example, many studies reveal that the role of family members in purchasing decisions varies widely across products.[77] The extent of information seeking and the importance of information sources vary from one type of decision to another.[78] Unplanned purchasing,[79] the effectiveness of point-of-purchase displays,[80] end-aisle displays,[81] number of shelf facings,[82] and shelf height[83] also vary widely across products.

These, as well as other examples that could be cited, indicate that in many cases it is not proper to generalize findings across products or decision situations. On the other hand, it is obviously desirable to generalize as far as possible in order to avoid researching consumer behavior in unduly minute detail. This points up the growing need for classification systems for types of decisions and choices which, if properly designed, would permit a legitimate degree of generalization. Research to date indicates that the traditional convenience, specialty, and shopping goods typology is inappropriate because of wide intercategory variation in behavior.[84] Future efforts using alternative conceptual schemas[85] or empirically derived classifications[86] should increase the progress of consumer research.

---

[77] "Customer Traffic Patterns: Key to Selling Efficiency," *Progressive Grocer,* pp. k-75–k-106 (Jan. 1967).

[78] Louis P. Bucklin, "The Informative Role of Advertising," *J. Advertising Research,* vol. 5, pp. 11–15 (Sept. 1965); George Katona and Eva Mueller, "A Study of Purchase Decisions," in Lincoln H. Clark (ed.), *The Dynamics of Consumer Reactions* (New York: New York University Press, 1955), pp. 30–87; Bruce LeGrand and Jon G. Udel, "Consumer Behavior in the Market Place," *J. Retailing,* pp. 32–40 (Fall 1964).

[79] *Consumer Buying Habits Studies, op. cit.;*[64] James D. Schaffer, *op. cit.*[64]

[80] *Awareness, Decision, Purchase* (New York: Point-of-Purchase Advertising Institute, 1961); B. A. Dominick, Jr., *Research in Retail Merchandising of Farm Products* (Washington, D.C.: U.S. Department of Agriculture, Agricultural Marketing Service, 1960); *Drugstore Brand Switching and Impulse Buying* (New York: Point-of-Purchase Advertising Institute, 1963).

[81] George E. Kline, "How to Build More Profit into Your Display Program," *Progressive Grocer,* pp. 48–72 (Jan. 1960); George J. Kress, *The Effect of End Displays on Selected Food Product Sales* (New York: Point-of-Purchase Advertising Institute, undated); Bert C. McCammon and Donald H. Granbois, *The Super Drugstore Customer* (New York: Point-of-Purchase Advertising Institute, 1962).

[82] Keith Cox, "The Responsivesness of Food Sales to Shelf Space Changes in Supermarkets," *J. Marketing Research,* vol. 1, pp. 63–67 (May 1964); Douglas H. Harris, "The Effect of Display Width in Merchandising Soap," *J. Applied Psychology,* pp. 283–284 (1958).

[83] "Shelf Attitudes Affect Buying Attitudes," *Progressive Grocer,* p. C-126 (Mar. 1964); "Shelf Merchandising Strategy: A Key to Increased Sales," *Progressive Grocer,* pp. C-121–C-125 (Mar. 1964).

[84] Richard H. Holton, "The Distinction between Convenience Goods, Shopping Goods, and Specialty Goods," *J. Marketing,* pp. 53–56 (July 1958).

[85] Orville Brim *et al., Personality and Decision Processes* (Stanford, Calif.: Stanford University Press, 1962).

[86] John G. Myers and Francesco M. Nicosia, "On the Study of Consumer Typologies," *J. Marketing Research,* vol. 5, pp. 182–193 (May 1966).

Developing a Replication Tradition

In many disciplines, replication is accepted and rigorously practiced. In the physical sciences, sociology, and psychology, for example, findings are generally not accepted until they have been replicated a number of times in separate studies.

Replication is rarely practiced in consumer research. Many findings and propositions are based upon single studies by a single researcher. This, of course, is dangerous because it invites invalid conclusions due to unusual characteristics of the sample, distortion in experimental control, and other methodological artifacts. All too frequently, findings are used uncritically in marketing literature, especially general textbooks, and the dangers of misleading conclusions increase as the body of consumer behavior findings increases. A replication tradition would make an invaluable contribution to the scientific advancement of consumer research. Such a tradition would allow researchers to determine the conditions under which an effect may exist, establish hierarchies of effects, and test the validity of previously reported findings.

Developing Information Summary and Retrieval Systems

The amount of consumer research is increasing at an accelerating rate. For example, the first edition of this book was published in 1968. Between 1968 and 1972 there has been more published research than during all years prior to 1968. In revising one of the chapters in this text, the authors reviewed 125 studies and 10 monographs, all published since 1968. It is becoming increasingly difficult, and soon may become impossible, for both researchers and practitioners to have an awareness and working knowledge of published research relevant to their problems.

There are at least two steps that can be taken to accommodate the research explosion. First, it would appear useful to initiate a program of yearly literature reviews which would critically evaluate and summarize evidence that has been published, or otherwise become publicly available, during the year. This technique is widely used in other areas including, for example, *The Annual Review of Psychology.*

The second step would be to establish a consumer behavior research retrieval system. Although this type of system presents numerous complex problems, other disciplines such as law, medicine, and chemistry have advanced in this direction. An example is the American Chemical Society, which through its subsidiary, Chemical Abstracts, operates a service which makes possible computer research across the full range of the world's current chemical literature. The service consists of machine-searchable tapes containing the title, authors' names, complete bibliographic citation, and key descriptive indexing terms for each journal article and patent abstracted in current issues of *Chemical Abstracts.*

Furthermore, within consumer research itself, the Diffusion Documents Center at Michigan State University has devised procedures for cataloging and summarizing studies.[87] Although serious problems must be solved before such a system could be made operational, it would appear strategic to begin work immediately rather than waiting until the research explosion has become even more formidable.

Developing New Business–Government– University Relationships

For the most part, consumer research has been conducted independently by personnel in business, government, and universities. With some notable exceptions, relatively few businesses have supported university-based research. Moreover, government agencies and congressional committees have typically not supported consumer research projects, or used the expertise of consumer analysts in congressional hearings and legal deliberations. If this independence can be dissolved in favor of cooperation and new alliances, the future and horizons of consumer research will be extended considerably.

Business–University Relationships   The situations and events that have precluded any widespread business–university alliance are many and varied. Some university personnel have traditionally assumed a condescending attitude toward business firms and their personnel. In turn, some businessmen have stereotyped university researchers as "ivory towerish" and unwilling and/or unable to deal with practical, operational problems. It is undeniable that some university faculty members have accentuated this latter problem by spending disproportionate amounts of resources on what business perceives as marginally relevant, or totally irrelevant, concepts and problems. All too often the consequence has been a state of intensified mutual aggravation.

Fortunately, it is becoming increasingly clear that these conditions and perceptions are dissolving. Armed with sizeable research budgets and facilities, consumer researchers in business are often among the most prolific, and the issues investigated often have great general relevance. Simultaneously, many university researchers have become increasingly dedicated to areas of inquiry that have more substantial and immediate payouts for business firms.

It would seem, then, that in many cases the ingredients for a new coalition exist. First, university-based researchers should reevaluate their differential advantage. They typically do not have the data-generating capability possessed by industry. Business, on the other hand, often does not have the time and, in some cases, the skills necessary to analyze research data fully. This frequently is where a university researcher's greatest capability lies, because most leading universities now have excellent computer hardware, software, and manpower to permit data analysis that would have been impossible several years ago, for example, cluster analysis and factor analysis.

---

[87]   Everett M. Rogers and J. David Stanfield, "Adoption and Diffusion of New Products: Emerging Generalizations and Hypotheses," in Frank M. Bass, Charles W. King, and Edgar Pessemier (eds.), *Applications of the Sciences in Marketing Management* (New York: Wiley, 1968).

One avenue toward a more meaningful business–university relationship might be to allow university researchers to be involved in the design of some industry research with opportunity to add appropriate questions which might illuminate some of the broader questions that are of concern to all. Once the data have been put to proprietary use, they could be turned over to the university for additional analysis. If such an approach were to become widespread, progress would seem to be inevitable.

Government–University Relationships The reasons for the absence of government–university cooperation in consumer research are unclear, although several explanations can be hypothesized. It could be that government officials preceive university researchers to be identified with business interests so that research grants could contribute to further exploitation of consumers. Another explanation may be that government officials are unaware of the growing scope and magnitude of consumer research.

Whatever the explanation, consumer researchers should become more actively involved in consumer-related legislation and in representing consumer as well as business interests. Significant progress has been made in these areas during the last few years, but much remains to be done. Why should consumer researchers not have as much influence on consumer affairs as the American Bar Association or the American Medical Association?

Greater Emphasis on Macro
Consumer Behavior Research

As we have observed, there are many approaches to the study of consumer behavior. However, one connecting thread is that all approaches focus on individual consumers or market segments.

Although this emphasis is understandable and healthy, very little attention is being given to what might be called macro consumer behavior research. As Nicosia and Glock have pointed out, a large number of economic and social problems cannot be solved unless we gain an understanding of the relationships between changing patterns of consumption and changes in social and cultural values.[88] Consider these issues:

(1) What effect would smaller families have on consumption patterns?

(2) Will the new values and life styles of some youth change as they grow older? If not, how will they affect consumption levels?

(3) Will the women's liberation movement become more important? If so, how will it affect purchasing and consumption patterns?

(4) How will the cost of clean air and water change consumption patterns?

(5) How will the four-day work week affect family expenditures?

---

[88] F. M. Nicosia and C. Y. Glock, "Marketing and Affluence: A Research Prospectus," in Robert L. King (ed.), *Marketing and the New Science of Planning* (Chicago: Amer. Marketing Assoc., 1968), pp. 510–527.

These are not idle issues. Some observers have estimated that variations in these behavioral patterns could make a difference of $500 billion in 1980 gross national product.[89] These types of questions deserve serious attention.[90]

A Concluding Note

The problems discussed in this section are due primarily to the infancy of consumer research. An enormous amount of research has been conducted in a relatively short period of time, and significant strides have been made toward the development of a mature science. If the problems raised here, and others that have undoubtedly been overlooked, are resolved, another significant step will be taken toward understanding consumers.[91]

SUMMARY

This, the concluding chapter of this volume, attempted to assess the current status of consumer research in terms of problems and prospects. The chapter began with some provisional generalizations about consumer behavior. Consumers use decision processes to adapt to and solve their consumption problems. They perceive phenomena selectively in solving these problems. They are also unique: they differ in terms of how they solve problems, and the same consumer solves different problems in different ways. Yet consumers are also social organisms, and, as such, there is more homogeneity in their behavior than might otherwise be expected.

The second section tried to evaluate the explanatory and predictive power of the current body of consumer research. What looks like a well researched and developed discipline does not fare well when evaluated against the criteria of explanation and prediction. Moreover, actual accomplishment has not been consistent with the magnitude of the effort.

The final section presented recommendations for improving consumer behavior research. It was suggested that theories and models be used more extensively and intensively, that research priorities be identified, that more research be conducted on a "program" basis so that the benefits of critical mass can be attained, that longitudinal and experimental designs be used more widely, that standardized definitions and variable categories be developed, that richer dependent variables be employed, that results be analyzed in terms of group as well as individual differences, that typologies be developed that allow us to generalize across types of decisions, that information summary and retrieval systems be developed, that business–government–university research relationships be strengthened, and that greater attention be given to macro types of consumer behavior research.

---

[89] Charles E. Silberman, "The U.S. Economy in an Age of Uncertainty," *Fortune,* pp. 72ff (Jan. 1971).

[90] For approaches used in other areas, see David T. Kollat, "Environmental Forecasting and Strategic Planning: Perspectives on the Methodology of Futurology," paper presented at the American Marketing Association Fall Conf., Minneapolis, Minn. (Aug. 1971).

[91] For additional recommendations, see Nicosia, *op. cit.*[40]

This book has attempted to present the current body of knowledge about consumer behavior that is available to the public. Many studies have been omitted, not because they are unimportant, but because of space limitations. This volume exists not because of the authors but, rather, because of the researchers who make it possible to put something of substance in a text. An incredible amount of progress has been made, but even more remains to be done. Hopefully, the new generation will help supply the competence necessary for consumer behavior to attain the status of a mature science.

REVIEW AND DISCUSSION QUESTIONS

1. Evaluate the bases of consumer behavior presented in the early part of this chapter. Are they valid generalizations? What additional summary generalizations could be added to these?

2. "Consumers are manipulated by marketing organizations." Evaluate this comment.

3. What are the purposes of a model such as the consumer decision-process model?

4. A national chain of department stores has been faced with a persistent decline in its share of the market. Management believes it is because changes are occurring among consumers that are not being evaluated or met adequately by the firm. The marketing organization has suggested that a major research effort be implemented to study consumer behavior. Describe how the decision-process model might be used to guide the firm's research.

5. Select one of the topics described in the section "Recommendations for Improving Consumer Behavior Research." Justify this as an important need in consumer research. Cite studies to illustrate and substantiate your position.

6. Prepare a paper identifying, analyzing, documenting, and justifying what you believe to be the most pressing issue in consumer research at the present time.

NAME INDEX

Aaker, David A., 616
Adams, Bert N., 157
Adler, Alfred, 32
Ahtola, O. T., 277–278
Alba, Manuel S., 597
Albaum, Gerald, 78
Alderson, Wroe, 6, 14, 594
Amstutz, Arnold, 597
Anderson, Lee K., 537, 557
Anderson, R. C., 456
Angell, R. C., 81
Appley, M. H., 297
Arndt, Johan, 602–603, 607
Arnold, Stephen J., 401, 409
Asch, S. E., 168
Atkin, K., 535
Atkins, Robert J., 597

Baker, Raymond W., 78
Banks, Seymour, 371, 385
Barber, Bernard, 120
Barnett, Normal L., 606
Barth, Ernest A. T., 124–125
Bartlett, F. C., 220
Bass, Frank M., 433, 592–593, 653, 656, 660
Bauer, E. J., 220
Bauer, Raymond A., 178, 184, 379
Becker, Howard S., 77
Beik, Leland L., 444
Belk, Russell W., 403, 406
Bell, William E., 605, 624
Bennett, Peter D., 277, 481
Bensman, Joseph, 134
Berelson, Bernard R., 218–219, 644
Berens, John S., 632
Berger, Bennett, 132
Birdwell, Al E., 171
Bishop, Doyle W., 153, 154
Bishop, James W., Jr., 631–632
Blackwell, Roger D., 405, 653
Bleeg, Michael, 457–458
Bogart, Leo, 216–217
Bourne, 174–175
Bower, George H., 229–230
Boyd, Harper, Jr., 553
Brehm, J. W., 333
Brien, Richard H., 618
Brock, Timothy C., 504
Brody, R. P., 300

Brogden, W. J., 239
Brown, F. E., 484–485
Brown, George H., 540, 548, 549, 551
Brunner, James A., 445
Bryan, J. H., 164–165
Bucklin, Louis P., 381–382, 383
Burger, Philip C., 593
Bush, Robert, 567
Butler, James E., 157
Buzzell, Robert D., 92, 579, 634

Capitman, 344, 346
Cardoza, R. A., 533
Carlsmith, J. M., 533
Carman, James M., 128, 554–555, 556
Carroll, J. D., 278
Carson, Johnny, 384, 386
Chang, J., 278
Chapin, F. Stuart, 125–126
Chu, G., 336
Clawson, C. Joseph, 364
Claycamp, Henry J., 596, 597
Cofer, C. N., 297
Cohen, A., 338
Cohen, J. B., 277–278, 289, 537
Coleman, James S., 592, 608
Coleman, Richard P., 128, 135, 139, 149, 150, 153
Combs, Arthur W., 29
Converse, Paul D., 444
Cook, Victor J., 175–176
Cooley, Charles Horton, 170
Coombs, C. H., 278
Cooper, Eunice, 219
Cooper, Joseph, 171
Cox, Harvey, 104
Craig, C. S., 341–342
Cunningham, Ross, 548–549
Cunningham, Scott M., 184, 300, 550, 551, 556, 653
Cuzzort, R. P., 73

Darden, William R., 461–462
Davis, Harry L., 500
Day, George S., 273, 551, 557, 616
DeCharms, R., 81
Deutscher, L., 270

Dewey, John, 46
Dichter, Ernest, 404
Dill, F., 167
Dolich, Ira J., 171, 172
Domhoff, G. W., 133
Douglas, Susan P., 273–274, 364
DuBois, C., 271
Duijker, H. C. J., 79
Duncan, Beverly, 182
Duncan, Otis D., 182
Dunn, S. Watson, 94

Ebbinghaus, 340, 341
Eddington, Sir Arthur, 646
Edwards, Alba M., 125
Ehrenberg, A. S. C., 94, 563, 572
Ehrlich, D., 539
Ehrlich, H. J., 272
Elinder, Erik, 92
Ellis, Robert A., 128
Engel, James F., 405, 539, 572, 605–606, 653
Estes, William K., 236
Evans, Franklin B., 293, 500, 503, 652–653

Faison, E. W., 336
Farley, John U., 549, 556–557
Farley, Reynolds, 182
Fatt, Arthur C., 92
Feinberg, Gerald, 626–627
Feldman, Laurence P., 10, 524–525, 626
Feldstein, Martin S., 629
Ferber, Robert, 615
Feshback, S., 330–331
Festinger, L., 270, 334
Fishbein, M., 270–271, 279, 656
Fisk, George, 452
Fladmark, Kenneth O., 481
Foner, Anne, 106
Frank, Ronald E., 149, 293, 491, 553, 556, 557, 572
Freedman, J. L., 329
Freud, Sigmund, 31–32
Frijda, N. H., 79
Fry, J. N., 300

Gabel, M. S., 503